501

DAYS OUT FOR KIDS IN THE UK & IRELAND

501

DAYS OUT FOR KIDS IN THE UK & IRELAND

Bounty
Books

Publisher: Polly Manguel

Project Editor: Emma Hill

Designer: Ron Callow/Design 23

Production Manager: Neil Randles

First published in Great Britain in 2010 by
Bounty Books, a division of Octopus Publishing Group Limited
2-4 Heron Quays, London E14 4JP
www.octopusbooks.co.uk

An Hachette UK Company
www.hachette.co.uk

A CIP catalogue record is available from the British Library

ISBN: 978-0-753718-87-2

Printed and bound in China

Please note: Given the possibility of e-coli outbreaks on farms, all care must be taken when
petting animals. Please bear this in mind and make sure your children wash their hands afterwards.

The guidance sometimes given for people with mobility problems is intended only as a very rough
guide and those concerned about this issue should make their own appropriate investigations
before setting off on their day out.

The advice given on costs, which is based on a day out for a family of two adults and two children,
is a rough indication only and excludes the cost of travel, food and drink. **Low**: £20 or less,
Reasonable: £20 - £50 and **Expensive**: over £50*. Admission charges often change and discounts
for families and for online bookings are frequently available, so always check before you set out.

* or the Euro equivalents in Ireland

Contents

Introduction

Packed with ideas to suit all ages and all budgets, here is the book that provides the answers to the inevitable 'What are we going to do today?' question.

Every parent knows how hard it is to keep children happily occupied during the school holidays, and how sometimes the weeks of free time that stretch ahead can seem almost daunting. Children are easily bored, and when they are, they let their parents know, loud and clear. Past generations of parents were able to tell their kids just to 'go out and play', but life in the 21st century is a different ballgame altogether. Physical freedom, independence and outdoor fun have largely lost out to the virtual world and indoor life. Thus the day out with the family has become a crucial bonding experience.

All families are different: sometimes both parents work, and the children are cared for during the day or collected from school by grandparents or other relatives. Some families only have one adult. Sometimes there is only one child to think about, other families, of course, have several children, ranging from teenagers to little ones. In today's world, free time can be something of a headache. Children are just as diverse as the families they are from – some will be sporty and keen to be out of doors as much as possible, others will be bookworms or glued to their computer screens – so choosing a day out that suits everyone can be tricky. *501 Days Out for Kids* helps you find the best and most appropriate places to go wherever you are, whatever the composition of your family and whatever your kids are interested in.

Sometimes the best days out, the days that remain in your memory, are when the whole family goes on a trip somewhere. However, as kids reach their teens, some prefer to be with their own peer group, away from their parents. Equally, parents may need a day to themselves, for umpteen reasons, and included in this book are a number of attractions where you can drop your child off in the morning and pick them up at the end of the day, safe in the knowledge that they are having a fabulous time in a secure environment.

There are so many things here that you can do – peaceful days out at the seaside, cycling, canoeing, kayaking, messing around on the river, exploring woodlands, visiting museums and farms and, of course, theme parks. You'll find things here to do in cities and towns, as well as in the wilds of the countryside. There are visits to famous football and rugby clubs and days out for kids who are obsessed with cars, or steam railways or even submarines. Most children love wildlife and within these pages, as well as zoos, nature reserves, safari parks and marine centres you'll find a monkey sanctuary, butterfly farms and a hedgehog hospital, not to mention lots of places where you can observe deer or dolphins, swans or seals, otters or ostriches.

There are days out which include several different excursions, in order to keep everyone happy, so you might visit a farm park in the morning and go cycling in the afternoon, or go to a museum in the morning and an adventure centre in the afternoon. You could visit an attraction that has different areas of interest, so while the younger children are happily occupied in a soft play area, their older siblings can do something much more daring.

Many of the places suggested will be of interest to adults too. You will find ideas here suitable for sunny summer days, and for cold winter ones, for days that have to be spent indoors, and for days that can be spent in the fresh air. There are days that are most suitable for boys and their Dads, and others for girls and their Mums, as well as unusual days that might be given as a birthday present or for another special occasion. Whatever your children are interested in, you'll surely be able to find a place where they are happy, engaged, learning new skills or honing existing ones, being creative or active. It's not just useful for the traditional parents either – it should come in very handy for weekend Mums and Dads, and for grandparents faced with deciding where to take the kids for the day. When you're away on holiday in the UK or Ireland it's often difficult to know what there is to do in the area – with this book you'll no longer have an excuse for not venturing out!

So look through this book every time you are going somewhere new, or use it to find something out of the ordinary to do within striking distance of home – you'll find you're all in for a treat.

 SUNNY: Best enjoyed on a fine day although some elements of this day out could easily be undertaken when the weather is less clement.

 RAINY: Most elements of this day out take place indoors and can therefore be enjoyed whatever the weather.

 PICNIC: This denotes there's a great spot for a picnic or that picnic areas are provided.

 365: These days out can be enjoyed at any time of year. However, please check before leaving home as many may be closed over Christmas and New Year and on some other public holidays.

 FREE: Costs are either non-existent or minimal.

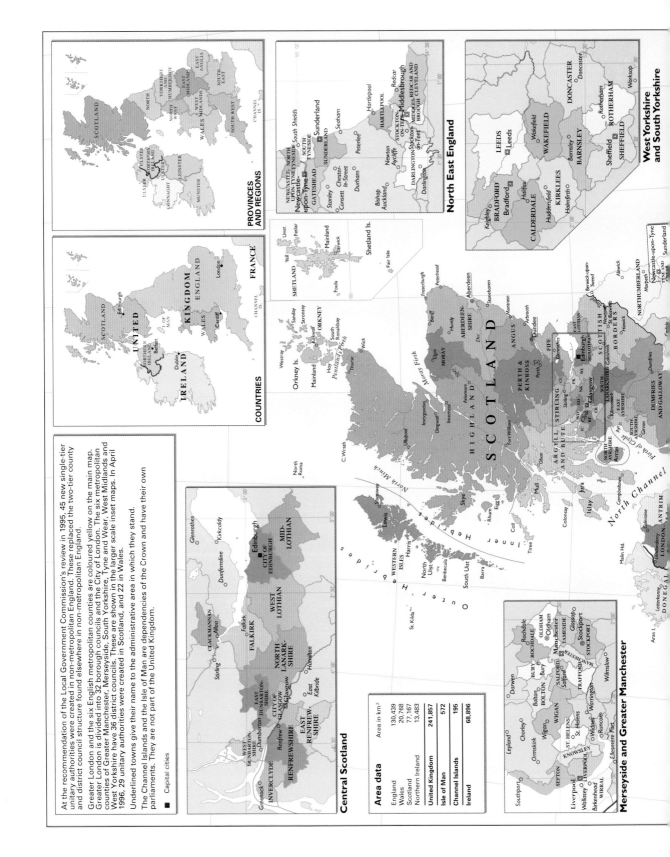

At the recommendation of the Local Government Commission's review in 1995, 45 new single-tier unitary authorities were created in non-metropolitan England. These replaced the two-tier county and district council structure found elsewhere in non-metropolitan England.

Greater London and the six English metropolitan counties are coloured yellow on the main map. Greater London is divided into 32 borough councils and the City of London. The six metropolitan counties of Greater Manchester, Merseyside, South Yorkshire, Tyne and Wear, West Midlands and West Yorkshire have 36 district councils. These are shown in the larger scale inset maps. In April 1996, 29 unitary authorities were created in Scotland, and 22 in Wales.

Underlined towns give their name to the administrative area in which they stand.

The Channel Islands and the Isle of Man are dependencies of the Crown and have their own parliaments. They are not part of the United Kingdom.

■ Capital cities

COUNTRIES

PROVINCES AND REGIONS

North East England

West Yorkshire and South Yorkshire

Central Scotland

Area data

	Area in km²
England	130,439
Wales	20,768
Scotland	77,167
Northern Ireland	13,483
United Kingdom	**241,857**
Isle of Man	572
Channel Islands	195
Ireland	68,896

Merseyside and Greater Manchester

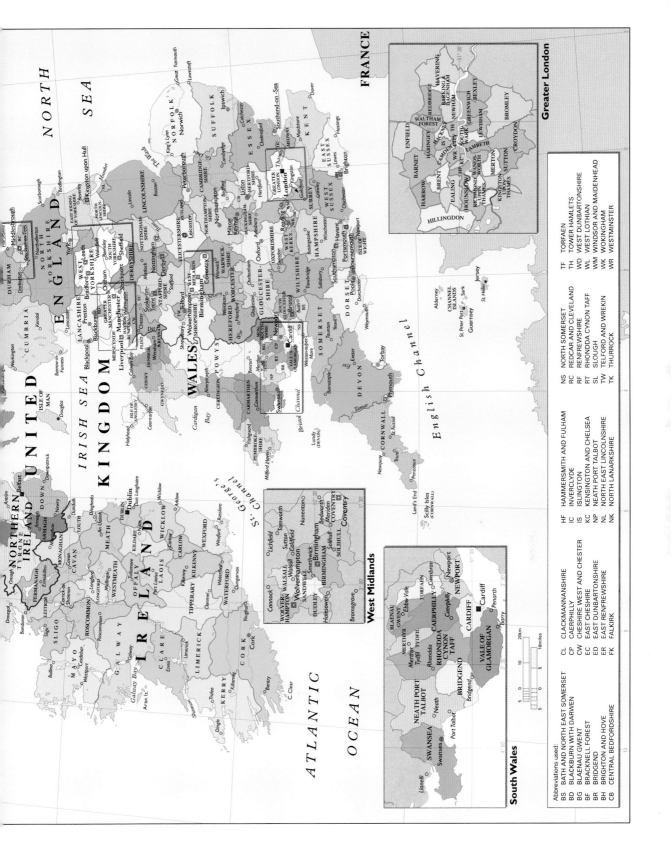

OY MUSEUM

ENGLAND

A day on the Docklands Light Railway

A llama's view of Canary Wharf

Combine the Docklands Light Railway with London's regenerated East End and you have the recipe for a great family outing. The DLR is thrillingly high tech: computer-operated driverless trains swoosh along an elevated track through Docklands' futuristic cityscape. And within minutes of leaving the DLR terminus at Bank, the kids can be frolicking on a farm in the Isle of Dogs or exploring the World Heritage Site of Maritime Greenwich, historic playground of Henry VIII.

But first, get off the train at West India Quay for the ultra child-friendly Museum of London Docklands, housed in five floors of a Georgian warehouse. There's far too much to absorb in a single visit, so be selective: go inside a replica World War II air-raid shelter, see the terrific detailed scale model of old London Bridge and visit Sailortown, an enthralling re-creation of the sinful streets of Victorian Wapping; and let the kids loose in Mudlarks, a gallery devoted entirely to children's activities with an educational soft-play area for the under fives.

Hop back onto the DLR and head for Mudchute, Europe's largest urban farm, set in a glorious stretch of 13 ha (32 acres) of meadowland. While the children are occupied petting calves and getting up close to rare breeds, you can scoff home-made cake in the excellent Mudchute Kitchen. Or cross the river to Maritime Greenwich where the kids can steam down the hill in Greenwich Park, travel to the stars at the Royal Observatory's state-of-the-art Planetarium, straddle the eastern and western hemispheres on the Prime Meridian and fritter their pocket money in the vibrant street market.

The train glides back to Central London in under half an hour, and on the journey home you'll already be planning your next DLR day.

Sightseeing round the Circle Line

All kids love the Tube; given half a chance, they'll treat it like a fairground ride. Why not join in the game? Get them to escort you on a whistle-stop tour of the Circle Line, letting them operate the ticket machine and barrier gates, find the platform, read the 'yellow line' stations on the famous tube map and calculate how many stops *en route*. You can get enormous satisfaction introducing them to the great civic sights, history and geography of the capital city while enabling them to practise their cognitive skills and boosting their self-confidence.

Whichever sights you decide to explore – and there are numerous options: Kensington High Street for Kensington Palace and 'Millionaires' Row', Baker Street for Regents Park, St James Park for Buckingham Palace – do surface at Westminster to see the iconic landmark of Big Ben, the Houses of Parliament and Westminster Abbey; and a two-minute walk takes you to Horseguards Parade, where you may see mounted soldiers changing guard.

The other 'must' stop is Tower Hill to gawp at the Tower of London. You can get so close to the walls with such good views of the medieval ramparts and towers that you may think twice about taking the rather long-winded official tour inside. But do go onto Tower Bridge for a spectacular juxtaposition of ancient and modern: William the Conqueror's White Tower and the Mayor of London's City Hall confronting each other across the Thames with World War II cruiser *HMS Belfast* moored between.

Finally, head for Embankment. The London Transport Museum at Covent Garden is five minutes from the station. The kids will get a huge buzz out of connecting their new-found knowledge of the Tube to the museum displays, and be delighted to discover that they've been on the world's longest underground train system.

A family group admires the cannons surrounding the Tower of London with Tower Bridge in the background.

WHERE:
Central London
BEST TIME TO GO:
October/November or February/March. Steer clear of the tourist season and Christmas sales and avoid travelling in hot weather and during 'rush hour'.
DON'T MISS:
Walking up Whitehall to peer through the Downing Street railings and see where the Prime Minister lives; Cleopatra's Needle, on the riverside by Embankment station; the street entertainers in Covent Garden.
AMOUNT OF WALKING:
Moderate
COST:
Low – unless your family insists on going on the guided tour inside the Tower of London, which is expensive. The Tower Bridge Exhibition is much better value, and you can get a joint ticket that also entitles you to climb to the top of Monument, the tallest freestanding stone column in the world. Both *HMS Belfast* and the London Transport Museum are free for children accompanied by an adult.
YOU SHOULD KNOW:
Changing of the Guard takes place at Horseguards Parade weekdays at 11.00. Tower Bridge lifts irregularly – check website for times. A Day Travelcard is the cheapest way to travel and a non-stop round trip covering all 27 stations on the Circle Line would take about an hour.

London RIB voyage, London Eye and London Aquarium

For a really memorable action thrill, take the kids along the Thames in a high-powered RIB (Rigid Inflatable Boat). They'll see far more of London's heritage on the voyage from Waterloo Pier to Canary Wharf (or all the way to the Thames Barrier) than on any of the ubiquitous open-top bus tours, while a surprisingly entertaining and well-informed guide supplies plenty of laughs together with the low-down on all the famous sights along the river, including Lambeth Palace, the Houses of Parliament, Tate Modern, St Paul's Cathedral, Tower Bridge and the Millennium Dome. Then the action starts – the RIB revs up to 30 knots for a white-knuckle rollercoaster ride. The kids won't be disappointed – and nor will you.

The RIB lands you at the London Eye. No trip to London is complete without a ride on this iconic landmark. Devised by husband-and-wife team Marks & Barfield as a Millennial symbol for the turning of time, the giant wheel has 32 observation pods, representing the 32 London boroughs. Standing 135 m (443 ft) high, the Eye rotates at 0.9 km (0.6 mi) per hour, slowly enough for passengers to get on and off while it's on the move. Needless to say, the views over London and beyond are staggering.

From mid-air to ocean depths: cross Jubilee Square to the London Aquarium, in the basement of London's imposing old County Hall building. One of Europe's largest collections of marine life, the aquarium has 14 marine zones ranging from a pond habitat to the Pacific Ocean, with more than 35,000 specimens. Kids will especially enjoy handling starfish, crabs and molluscs in the Touch Pool and watching divers feeding giant rays in the Atlantic zone. And if they misbehave, you can threaten to fling them to the sharks.

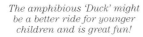

The amphibious 'Duck' might be a better ride for younger children and is great fun!

WHERE:
Central London
BEST TIME TO GO:
May to October
DON'T MISS:
Strolling beside the river from Jubilee Gardens to the South Bank Centre and seeing the street entertainers.
AMOUNT OF WALKING:
Little
COST:
Expensive
YOU SHOULD KNOW:
It is best to buy tickets online for all attractions to avoid queuing. RIBs depart from Waterloo Millennium Pier every hour seven days a week. Each boat holds 12 passengers and life jackets are provided to fit all sizes from toddler to adult. If you think a child might be too young to enjoy the RIB, opt for a London Duck instead: an exciting tour in a bright-yellow amphibious vehicle that goes round the sights of Westminster by road before sliding into the Thames and cruising back to base.

Regent's Park and London Zoo

Minutes away from the mad rush of London's West End, Regent's Park is a beautifully landscaped public space where you can easily lose all sense of time and direction in 166 ha (410 acres) of meadows, trees, shrubberies, formal gardens, sports fields and playgrounds.

The highlight has to be the wildfowl lake that snakes its way through the park. Winding paths lead to footbridges across sheltered sidewaters where countless species of exotic wildfowl breed. You can hire rowing boats at the Boathouse Café, near the Hanover Gate entrance. Strike out for the opposite shore and play Swallows and Amazons round the central islands. Wander along the lakeside and spot the herons standing like statues among the weeping willows. Cross the York Gate bridge and you will stumble upon the magical wildlife garden where at every step there is something to capture the kids' attention: a potting shed, miniature bog, artistically arranged woodstack, fungus-sprouting tree stumps . . . all designed to encourage creepy crawlies and fascinate youngsters through the 'yuck' factor.

The world-famous London Zoo is situated at the northern end of the Broadwalk bordering the Regent's Canal. First opened to the public in 1848, the zoo is one of London's oldest tourist attractions with its wacky Victorian animal houses, penguin pool and huge aviary. In recent years, mindful of the ethical issues involved in caging wild animals, the zoo has transferred most of its big game animals to a more natural habitat at Whipsnade. But it still holds 750 species and the kids will enjoy the much-vaunted Gorilla Kingdom and the Rainforest Lookout. The children's section has recently been revamped as Animal Adventure, an educational playground in which kids can climb, splash around in water, enter a tunnel to observe burrowing animals and be introduced to the zoo's resident porcupines.

WHERE:
North London
BEST TIME TO GO:
May to September
(boat hire is seasonal)
DON'T MISS:
Chocolate milkshakes and ice cream at the Cow & Coffeebean Café on the Broadwalk; tropical birds in London Zoo's Blackburn Pavilion.
AMOUNT OF WALKING:
Lots
COST:
Boat hire is reasonable; entry to London Zoo is expensive.
YOU SHOULD KNOW:
London Zoo is open every day of the year except Christmas Day. Children under 16 must be accompanied by an adult. There is a pedalo pond next to the Boathouse Café for under fives, and a spacious sandpit in the very pleasant nearby playground.

Meerkats viewed from the underground 'bubble'.

Battersea Park

WHERE:
Southwest London
BEST TIME TO GO:
April to September. Boat hire is seasonal – every day July and August, weekends only April to June and September.
DON'T MISS:
The Peace Pagoda – a startlingly incongruous but beautiful Buddhist shrine overlooking the Thames; seeing the fountains spring into action once an hour; spotting the herons, cormorants and grebes among the waterfowl on the lake; walking across the Rustic Bridge.
AMOUNT OF WALKING:
Potentially lots
COST:
Low if you are happy simply walking by the Thames, hanging out in a lovely environment and going boating; reasonable if you stick either to boating plus the children's zoo or the recumbent bikes; expensive if you want to do everything, but well worth every penny.
YOU SHOULD KNOW:
If you don't feel like spending all day outdoors or if the weather threatens to change, the Latchmere Leisure Centre is only two minutes from Battersea Park. It has an excellent leisure pool with wave machine and a soft-play area for toddlers; extra activities are laid on during school holidays.

Many parents rate Battersea as the best of the main London parks. For a start, it's the only one in central London that overlooks the Thames. Then there's its size – 83 ha (200 acres) of attractive parkland, gardens, trees and wildlife. And finally, there's so much to do that keeping the kids amused is no problem at all.

Battersea Park hasn't always been quite such a desirable public amenity. It was once a desolate marshland known as Battersea Fields, notorious as a criminal haunt and duelling spot, until the marshes were drained and turned into a park as part of a mid-Victorian drive to clean up London and improve the health of its sickly inhabitants. More recently, after years of neglect, National Lottery funds have been poured into transforming Battersea into one of London's best-kept public spaces.

The kids' amenities are really well arranged: the adventure playground is right next to the toddlers' play area so you can relax about leaving older kids to play alone while you supervise the little ones, and there is a lovely Italian café next to the boating lake where you can sit under the trees while the kids fool around on a pedalo. The children's zoo is unusually good, with a motley collection of exceptionally well-tended animals: a lemur, meerkat, otters and giant rabbits among more conventional species like Shetland ponies and pygmy goats; and a beautiful barn owl.

But the high point has to be the laid-back thrill of feet-up pedalling on a recumbent bike. You can cycle completely safely along miles of bike-friendly carriageways and paths; and London Recumbents, the park bike centre, also hires out conventional bikes, trikes and family tandems (with toddler trailers) for anyone who prefers to view the world from an upright perspective.

Cooling down in the water jets at Battersea Park.

BBC Television Centre Tour and Holland Park

BBC Television Centre

Budding TV directors will find a visit to the BBC's Wood Lane Centre a fascinating experience. Older children (aged nine to 15) can go on an award-winning, in-depth tour of Television Centre where they will see what a working day is like inside studios and dressing rooms, visit the newsroom and tinker with the gadgetry in the interactive studio. Younger children (seven to 12s) are given a similar tour of the CBBC Studio where they can see the Blue Peter Garden and participate in making a TV programme either in front of or behind the camera. The helpful and well-informed guides take the trouble to answer even the most searching questions and anyone interested in the medium of TV will learn a lot. There are 12 tours a day, except on Sundays, so you can easily book a time to suit you.

One stop on the Central Line tube gets you to Holland Park. A small but particularly charming London park, it was once the grounds of Holland House. Although most the house was flattened by bombs in World War II, the Orangery and East Wing are both still standing. The park has a wonderfully romantic, timeless atmosphere with woodland paths, an enchanting Japanese Garden, peacocks strutting around in the flowerbeds, and rabbits and squirrels scampering through the undergrowth. The children's amenities are excellent and the park patrols ensure that it's safe for kids to play freely so you can relax outside the very pleasant café under the canopy of huge old trees while the kids work off any excess energy exploring the woods, kicking a ball around in the huge grass meadow or clambering about in an adventure playground that must be among the best in London.

WHERE:
West London
BEST TIME TO GO:
April, to catch the bluebells and rhododendrons in flower, and to watch courting frogs in the woodland pond.
DON'T MISS:
Treating yourselves to the expensive but out-of-this-world cakes from the patisserie near the tube station in Holland Park Avenue.
AMOUNT OF WALKING:
Lots. Television Centre is a vast building and the TV tour involves walking quite long distances to see round it. There is disabled access and a wheelchair can be provided if requested in advance. And to get the most out of Holland Park, you should be prepared for quite a bit of strolling around.
COST:
Reasonable
YOU SHOULD KNOW:
BBC tours last for one-and-a-half to two hours. They must be pre-booked and children under 15 must be accompanied by an adult. If the weather isn't good enough for Holland Park, you can find good places to eat at Westfield Shopping Mall, conveniently near Television Centre and purpose-built for families, with regular kids' events and activities, a play area for under fives, babies' changing rooms, a cinema and car park.

Platform 9¾ at King's Cross Station in London

Harry Potter at King's Cross Station and the Foundling Museum at Coram's Fields

As every Harry Potter fan knows, the *Hogwarts Express* departs from a secret platform between Platforms 9 and 10 at Kings Cross Station. Take the kids to the station annexe to see the 'Platform 9¾' sign, and the luggage trolley that looks as though it's going through the wall. Fun though this is, sharp-eyed kids are bound to notice that neither the station entrance nor the platforms look anything like they did on film. You can put it down to Muggle incompetence as you herd them to Platforms 4 and 5 in the main station to see the site of the actual filming and then down the road to the magnificent neo-Gothic edifice of St Pancras Station that stood in for King's Cross.

Plunge your kids back into reality at the Foundling Museum, an engaging collection with lots of period atmosphere and child appeal. Returning from his sea travels, 18th-century philanthropist Thomas Coram was so appalled by the plight of London's destitute children that he devoted the rest of his life to the Foundling Hospital, the first children's charity. It's touching to see how involved your kids become in the stories and exhibits – and you'll find they suddenly start being exceptionally nice to you.

Any excess energy can be burnt off in Coram's Fields next to the Museum. This atmospheric 3-ha (7-acre) children's park is on the site of the original Foundling Hospital, demolished in the 1920s. There are excellent amenities: paddling pool, sandpits, slides and sports pitches, a pets' corner for fondling sheep, goats and rabbits, a sensory play area for children with disabilities, a nursery for under fives, and a very decent vegetarian café. It will not escape the kids' notice that adults (i.e. you) are not allowed in unless accompanied by someone under 16.

WHERE:
Central London
BEST TIME TO GO:
May to September
DON'T MISS:
The poignant display of keepsakes (sometimes only a button) that mothers left with their babies when they handed them over to the care of the Hospital.
AMOUNT OF WALKING:
Moderate. The Foundling Museum is a ten-minute walk from King's Cross Station. It has wheelchair access.
COST:
Low. The Foundling Museum is free for children under 16.
YOU SHOULD KNOW:
Coram had to campaign for 17 years before he got a Royal Charter from King George II in 1739 'to establish a hospital for the maintenance and education of exposed and deserted young children'.
The Foundling Hospital was not only Britain's first children's charity but also its first public art gallery – painters like William Hogarth donated works in the hope that they would attract potential benefactors to visit.

Battlebridge Basin, London Canal Museum and Kings Place

For the better part of the 20th century the London canal network was more or less synonymous with urban decay, but British Waterways has done a magnificent job of transforming it into a recreational resource; so if you want to take the kids out for some fresh air but can't face the prospect of another day hanging around the park, why not explore a London backwater for a change?

Battlebridge is one of the largest basins on Regent's Canal, named after the eponymous village on the River Fleet where Boudicca is said to have crossed swords with the Roman army in AD 61. The area round the village became known as King's Cross after 1830 when a monument to George IV was erected at the local crossroads, only to be demolished a few years later. The canal towpath and basin have recently been regenerated and rows of colourfully painted narrow boats with their canal-side flower beds make a picturesque contrast to the glitzy new buildings round about.

You will find the London Canal Museum in a 19th-century ice house overlooking the canal. This is where Carlo Gatti, manufacturer of the first commercial ice cream, stored his ice. Kids will love looking round this small independent museum where they can learn everything there is to know about ice cream, climb inside the cabin of a narrowboat and see down an ice well.

On the opposite side of the Basin stands Kings Place, a trendy arts centre and home to the *Guardian* newspaper. It's worth popping in to see what's going on here. There are regular exhibitions, community events and family workshops and there's a great café in the central atrium where you can fill hungry young mouths with nutritious soup and delicious pastries after you've explored the canal towpath.

WHERE:
Central London
BEST TIME TO GO:
Sundays, May to September, when the Museum runs narrowboat trips along the canal through Islington Tunnel. (There are only 12 places so you must pre-book. See London Canal Museum website for details).
DON'T MISS:
Spotting the different 'castles and roses' designs on the canal boats.
AMOUNT OF WALKING:
Moderate
COST:
Low
YOU SHOULD KNOW:
Regent's Canal is the extension of the Grand Union Canal. It was opened in 1816 and cuts right across London. Large sections of the towpath are open to the public for walking and cycling.

Colourful canal boats at Battlebridge Basin

Chelsea Football Club Tour and Bishops Park

WHERE:
West London
BEST TIME TO GO:
April to October
DON'T MISS:
The Bishops' Tree – an ancient cedar tree turned into an extraordinary environmental sculpture with various bishops carved out of cedar going all the way up the trunk.
AMOUNT OF WALKING:
Lots
COST:
Reasonable, unless your kids succeed in pestering you into buying stuff for them from the Chelsea 'megastore' club shop, in which case it will soar astronomically. Entry to Fulham Palace is free.
YOU SHOULD KNOW:
Chelsea Stadium tours are daily on the hour from 11.00 to 15.00, except on home game days.

An aerial view of Chelsea Football Club in London, also known as Stamford Bridge Stadium.

Naturally all Blues supporters will find a tour of Chelsea's Stamford Bridge ground riveting, whatever their age. But what about the rest of the family? Believe it or not, the Chelsea Stadium Tour is surprisingly good fun even for hopelessly half-hearted soccer fans. This is largely due to the enthusiasm of the guides, who really bother to engage everyone's interest with all sorts of gossipy snippets as they take you behind the scenes. You will see the changing rooms, go into the TV and Press rooms and – the highlight for any young dreamer – through the players' tunnel to the pitch side, and even sit in the manager's dugout. Then you can look round the Centenary Museum, full of memorabilia from Chelsea's first hundred years at Stamford Bridge, and everyone can be photographed with their favourite player's shirt as a souvenir. The stadium tour is bound to make the kids hanker after some 'footie' practice. No problem. Hop on a bus to Bishops Park, off Fulham Palace Road. In this lovely local park, with its playgrounds, boating lake, café and beautiful riverside walk along the Thames, there's loads of space for practising kick-ups and penalty shots. And Bishops Park just happens to be right next to Craven Cottage, home of Fulham FC – London's oldest league club and home of former England captain Johnny 'The Maestro' Haynes, who played for Fulham FC from 1952 to 1970 and was the first professional

footballer to earn £100 per week!– so there are nearly always some other soccer-mad kids up for a kick around.

Inside Bishops Park you'll find the entrance to Fulham Palace. Once the main residence of the Bishop of London, this intriguing building is well worth exploring properly. The kids will like the scale replica of the palace, have a laugh guessing the smells of herbs from the knot garden and find all sorts of surprises along the Moat Trail, following the line of what was once the largest medieval moat in Britain.

Freightliners City Farm and The Little Angel Children's Puppet Theatre

One of the oldest of London's urban farms, Freightliners was set up as a community project in 1973 with little funding but a lot of idealism – based on nothing but a few disused railway goods vans as animal shelters on a scrap of wasteland behind King's Cross Station. It's hard to believe that the working farm you see today could have emerged from such humble origins. In 1978, the farm moved to its present half hectare (1.2-acre) Islington site, where it has thrived as a self-supporting community enterprise and is now set on further expansion. It's a great place for inner-city kids to experience a miniature version of rural life. They can see how fruit and vegetables are grown and interact with all sorts of farm animals – pigs, cows, goats, ducks, bantams and rabbits, and often a newborn lamb, a baby calf or chicks to coo over. You can relax in the tranquil haven of the ornamental garden while the kids play with the animals, and you'll almost certainly leave with bagfuls of home-grown goodies from the farm shop.

Not far away, hidden down an Islington backstreet, is The Little Angel Theatre. This internationally acclaimed company runs a 100-seat puppet theatre, adjoining a workshop where new productions are designed and all the puppets are constructed. For nearly 50 years the company has been enchanting both children and adults with shows that draw on a wide range of cultural influences, using all sorts of different kinds of puppets and techniques. Bringing your kids to a performance here is a brilliant way of initiating them to the experience of theatre. They are invariably so mesmerized by the staging and mechanics of the puppets that you don't have to worry about them getting bored or fidgety. A really novel treat.

WHERE:
North London
BEST TIME TO GO:
Anytime. Freightliners is open all year round except Christmas week. It's closed on Mondays, apart from Bank Holidays.
DON'T MISS:
Seeing the bees at work making honey in Freightliners apiary.
AMOUNT OF WALKING:
Moderate
COST:
Reasonable; entrance to Freightliners is free.
YOU SHOULD KNOW:
Freightliners has a gardening club and a Saturday market selling homemade food, arts and crafts and clothes. The Little Angel has a varied programme; check times and book tickets in advance. As well as staged productions, there are kids' fun days, a Puppet Club for five to 11 year olds and a Puppet Academy for 12 to 16s. (There are also very popular adult evening courses in puppetry skills and puppet making.)

A young visitor examines the skeleton of a sabre-toothed tiger.

Natural History and Science Museums

Of all London's world-class museums and galleries, the Natural History and Science Museums stand out as being exceptionally accessible to kids. They are part of London's Victorian heritage but have continually evolved to stay one step ahead of the times and remain as popular today as they were when they first opened.

Housed side by side in impressive buildings, the museums hold such vast collections that you can't possibly explore them both in a single day. Rather, they are places that you find yourself returning to time and time again. You'll find the kids become touchingly attached to their favourite exhibits, taking an almost proprietorial pride when they revisit them.

Few people forget their first childhood visit to the Natural History Museum – the *diplodocus* skeleton in the main hall stays etched in the memory forever, as does the giant life-size model of a blue whale. The museum is arranged in four zones and provides (downloadable) floor maps to help you plan where to go. There are loads of interactive exhibits: kids can experience an earthquake and a volcanic eruption, and walk through an amazing rotating globe; and the dinosaur gallery is a perennial favourite.

The Science Museum exhibits everything from steam engines to computers and there is something to engage children's interest in almost every gallery as well as the attractions specifically designed for them. Little ones will love The Garden, an interactive sensory gallery where they can learn about water, light and sound, while older children can problem-solve at the push of a button in the Launch Pad. There is also a constantly changing programme of entertaining one-off shows and events. So, whenever you're at a loose end in London with kids in tow, make a beeline for one or other of the great museums.

WHERE:
Central London
BEST TIME TO GO:
A rainy day when you want to tear the kids away from computer gaming.
DON'T MISS:
The amazing painted ceiling and carved animals in the central hall of the Natural History Museum.
AMOUNT OF WALKING:
Lots – both museums are huge.
COST:
Low. Museum entry is free, although there is a reasonable admission fee for the special temporary exhibitions.
YOU SHOULD KNOW:
The new Darwin Centre (aka The Cocoon) at the Natural History Museum has some 20 million plant and animal specimens on public display and you can see research scientists at work.

Primrose Hill and Camden Lock

Primrose Hill is a small but idyllic green space within spitting distance of Regent's Park, and once part of the same Royal hunting grounds. Today it is more memorably associated both with the numerous celebrities who live in the immediate vicinity and, of course, with the classic story *101 Dalmations* (it is from the top of Primrose Hill that Pongo joins in the 'twilight barking' to call for dogdom's aid in finding his stolen pups).

Whatever the time of year, this is a brilliant contained space in which to let children loose. The top of the hill commands a sensational panoramic view to the outer edges of London and beyond, and after a marathon climb you can park yourself on a well-earned bench while the kids identify London's landmarks then race through the long grass to the bottom of the hill, or roll down, or (if it's snowy) toboggan, or skateboard round the paths. There's a tiptop old-fashioned playground with swings and roundabouts and a spacious meadow for playing Frisbee or football. And you're more than likely to spot a fading rock star or famous actor nonchalantly walking their dog.

There are several small backstreet cafés in Regents Park Road where you can stop for refreshment before crossing the railway bridge to Chalk Farm and heading for Camden Lock. The cheap and cheerful street market, which started in 1975, has grown to be one of the biggest tourist draws in London. Its vibrant atmosphere is redolent of a fair with jugglers, fortune-tellers and street musicians among myriad *bric-a-brac* stalls and home-cooked food stands. And you can escape the throng by going onto the towpath to watch the boats negotiating the lock, or even taking a canal cruise in the *Jenny Wren*, a traditional narrowboat.

WHERE:
North London
BEST TIME TO GO:
Any time
DON'T MISS:
Marine Ices at the junction of Haverstock Hill and Chalk Farm Road, a family-run business that has been selling its famous ice creams and sorbets here since 1931.
AMOUNT OF WALKING:
Lots; not recommended with a pushchair.
COST:
Low unless you go on a spending spree at Camden Lock Market or decide to take a (seasonal) canal cruise, which is quite a reasonable price.
YOU SHOULD KNOW:
Camden Lock Market is closed on Mondays and is at its busiest and liveliest at weekends. A pleasant alternative to the street route from Primrose Hill is via the Regent's Canal towpath, which can be accessed beside the entrance to London Zoo. This day out is recommended for ages seven up, but especially for ten to 14s.

Crowds enjoy the views from Primrose Hill.

Queensway and Kensington Gardens

WHERE:
Central London
BEST TIME TO GO:
Any time
DON'T MISS:
The Elfin Oak outside the Princess Diana Playground – the remains of an oak tree with picturesque painted carvings of pixies, elves, mice and birds that have been preserved intact for nearly 100 years.
AMOUNT OF WALKING:
Moderate
COST:
Likely to end up expensive but you can reduce costs by checking out special offers and family reductions.
YOU SHOULD KNOW:
On Sundays there is a free art show along the railings of Kensington Gardens in Bayswater Road where London's artists and crafts people exhibit their work. Queens Ice Bowl is open 365 days a year and you can book single skating lessons. Whiteleys Odeon Kids Club shows cut-price reruns of popular children's films at weekends, and on weekdays in school holidays. Children aged 12 and under are admitted to the Princess Diana Playground.

If your kids have reached that awkward age when they're striking out for independence while you still don't dare let them out of your sight, Queensway is a perfect compromise. Thanks to its distinctive long-time Eastern Mediterranean cultural influence, the area has a cosmopolitan yet relaxed ambience, quite unlike the edgy no man's land of the West End.

Britain's first ice rink opened in Queensway in 1930 and many a champion has practised here. The original Queens Skating Rink has been transformed into Queens Ice Bowl, London's only combined ice skating and ten-pin bowling centre, with the added attractions of video gaming and karaoke. Pre-teens will happily hang out here for hours.

Along the road is Whiteleys, London's first department store. Long since converted into a shopping mall, the huge art deco building retains its original façade, marble-floored atrium, and sweeping balustraded staircase, making it feel rather more soulful than the average mall. It houses a cinema and bowling alley as well as shops, cafés and restaurants – a great place to let kids off the parental lead.

Kensington Gardens is a stone's throw away, with the Princess Diana Memorial Playground right by the park entrance. Fringed by dense shrubs and shaded by trees, the playground is a veritable 'Neverland' with immaculate white sand, palm trees, paddling stream and wigwams, and a wondrous pirate ship complete with rigging to climb and a crow's nest to sit in. Even older kids will find it hard to appear nonchalant.

At the far end of Queensway stands the old Porchester Baths, opened in 1925. This lovely listed building has been revamped but still has its wonderful old-fashioned pools. Once the kids have organized their entertainment, you can retreat here and relax in the splendidly atmospheric Turkish Baths.

Children enjoying the Princess Diana Memorial Playground in Kensington Gardens.

The Serpentine and Wellington Arch

London's successful bid for the 2012 Olympics has had the knock-on effect of ensuring a facelift for Hyde Park's Serpentine lake, the designated site for the Triathlon swimming event. The Serpentine has always been a popular place to bring children, but nowadays it's more family-friendly than ever.

Boating on the Serpentine in Hyde Park.

At the recently built boathouse you can hire a rowing boat or pedalo to take out on the lake, dodging the resident Canada geese. On the far side is the Lido, where people have revelled in open-air swimming for the past 100 years and which has been extended to incorporate a lovely paddling pool and play area for little ones, all enclosed by dense shrubbery to give a wonderful sense of seclusion. The main drag round the Serpentine is great for cycling or rollerblading, or you can go for a family horse-ride down Rotten Row and along 8 km (5 mi) of bridle paths. A pleasant lakeside stroll leads under the Serpentine Bridge to the Long Water in Kensington Gardens where you can see the famous statue of Peter Pan. Bring a picnic to eat under the trees and sit beside the Princess Diana Memorial Fountain while the kids paddle in the flume (strictly against park regulations but, needless to say, everybody does it).

Follow the Serpentine Road to the Queen Elizabeth Gate to reach Wellington Arch at Hyde Park Corner. The Arch commemorates Britain's victory in the Napoleonic Wars and once housed the smallest police station in Britain. Inside there are three floors of exhibits but the really fun part is standing on the terrace just underneath the immense bronze statue on top of the arch, from where you get sensational views of the Royal Parks and the Houses of Parliament, and can even peer into the Queen's garden at Buckingham Palace.

WHERE:
Central London
BEST TIME TO GO:
June to September when the Lido is open for swimming, or end of November to beginning of January when a Winter Wonderland with funfair, outdoor skating rink and market is set up alongside Serpentine Road.
DON'T MISS:
Hyde Park's famous weeping beech or 'upside down tree' at the Hyde Park Corner end of the Serpentine, a bizarre natural wonder; cruising majestically across the Serpentine from the Lido to the Boathouse in the solar-powered ferry shuttle
AMOUNT OF WALKING:
Lots
COST:
Reasonable
YOU SHOULD KNOW:
Kids aged 12+ may be allowed to hire a boat without adult supervision at the management's discretion. You can find out about rollerblade and inline skating lessons at Skatefresh in the boathouse; they also operate a kids' holiday skate club for six to ten year olds. Hyde Park Stables by Lancaster Gate caters for riders of all abilities from age five upwards. The Lido Café has baby changing facilities.

Dressing up at the Wallace Collection.

The West End: Oxford Street and Piccadilly Circus

Taking kids sightseeing in London's crowded West End doesn't have to be unbearably stressful. You can make it fun . . . and educational too. Start off gently in Hyde Park at the Reformers' Tree – a pebble mosaic marking the spot where the right to public assembly was first established; then stroll through Speaker's Corner, where since 1872 soapbox orators have had the right to hold forth on Sundays. At Marble Arch the kids can find the plaque marking the site of the infamous Tyburn gallows, where until 1783 huge crowds turned out for ghoulish Hanging Day entertainment while street urchins sang *Oranges and Lemons*.

WHERE:
Central London
BEST TIME TO GO:
Any time
DON'T MISS:
Selfridges Food Hall – the best place to grab something to eat, with a mouth-watering selection. Kids usually get attracted to the revolving sushi bar.
AMOUNT OF WALKING:
Moderate
COST:
Reasonable. The Wallace Collection is free.
YOU SHOULD KNOW:
The mosaic monument in Hyde Park known as the Reformers' Tree marks the spot where a tree burnt down during the 1866 Reform League riots in the struggle for political franchise. The Shaftesbury Memorial Fountain at Piccadilly Circus was erected in 1892 to commemorate the Earl of Shaftesbury's philanthropic work on behalf of the London poor.

Battle your way through the Oxford Street crowds to Manchester Square for a peek at the Wallace Collection, an idiosyncratic 18th- and 19th-century family art collection displayed in Hertford House, bequeathed to the nation by Lady Wallace in 1897. The star attraction for kids is the armoury – the best collection in Britain with amazing oriental daggers, chain mail, early firearms and even knuckledusters.

Back in Europe's biggest high street, you must go into Selfridges if only so the kids can say they've been. The second largest shop in the UK – only Harrods is larger – it was founded by entrepreneur Harry Selfridge in 1909. He introduced the notion of shopping as entertainment and supposedly coined the phrase 'the customer is always right'. The kids will be wide-eyed at the window displays, renowned for being the most imaginative in London.

Take an obligatory top-deck London bus ride by hopping on a No.15 and trundling along Oxford Street, down Regent Street to the bright lights of Piccadilly Circus. Here the kids can stand under the famous statue of Eros, one of the best-known symbols of London, and end the day with some entertainment West End style in the Trocadero arcades.

The West End: Pollock's Toy Museum, Chinatown and Leicester Square

The Victorian craze for toy theatres was the equivalent of the fixation on video gaming today, and Benjamin Pollock (1856–1937) was a toy theatre bigwig. He was the last of the Victorian toy theatre makers, an eccentric character who became a society legend. The museum named after him is a fascinating backstreet curiosity housed in a quirky building behind Tottenham Court Road. Two period houses have been knocked together to create a labyrinthine interior and the kids will love exploring the warren of rooms, each stuffed with a mind-boggling collection of weird and wonderful toys from all over the world. One room is devoted entirely to the original puppets and stages from Pollock's collection with a reconstruction of his workshop showing how toy theatres were made.

Make your way to London's theatre-land, stopping off for a dim sum (fast food) in the exotic world of Chinatown. In recent years the Chinese community has turned the surrounding area from being one of the seedier parts of central London into a major tourist attraction, a vibrant pedestrianized precinct with pagodas, oriental food shops and Chinese herbalists. There are restaurants galore and the staff are exceptionally tolerant of children.

Leicester Square has been the centre of West End entertainment for over 200 years. Take the kids to a film in the Odeon or Empire, where all the major films are premiered, but first let them look for the names of their favourite stars among the pavement plaques and take them into the park to see the statue of Shakespeare. Even in the age of video on demand, there's nothing quite like the thrill of being caught up in the buzz of the milling crowds to the accompaniment of the buskers' street music as you make your way towards a West End movie.

WHERE:
Central London
BEST TIME TO GO:
If you enjoy a lively atmosphere, plan your visit around any of the Chinese festivals – there are several throughout the year, the largest being the New Year celebrations in late January or early February (date varies).
DON'T MISS:
The huge Swiss Glockenspiel clock at Leicester Square
AMOUNT OF WALKING:
Lots
COST:
Expensive
YOU SHOULD KNOW:
There is also a Benjamin Pollock's Toyshop in Covent Garden that is famous for its wonderful hand-crafted toys. It is a friendly family-owned business connected with, but run separately from, the museum.

Pollock's Toy Museum in Scala Street, Covent Garden

The Arch Climbing Wall and Millennium Bridge

WHERE:
Central London
BEST TIME TO GO:
Any time
DON'T MISS:
Checking out the cool graphics and graffiti on the walls of The Arch.
AMOUNT OF WALKING:
Moderate
COST:
Reasonable
YOU SHOULD KNOW:
The French were the first to formalize bouldering as a sport in its own right on the huge stones in the forest of Fontainebleau; the first competition circuits were devised there in 1947.
The Millennium Bridge is an impressive feat of engineering – a virtually horizontal steel suspension bridge spanning 325 m (1,066 ft) with a 4-m (12-ft) wide deck designed to hold up to 5,000 pedestrians at any one time.

The Millennium Bridge takes you over the Thames from Southwark to St Paul's Cathedral in the City of London.

The Arch is a purpose-built cliff-face hidden away in an old warehouse under the railway arches of London Bridge – the perfect place for kids to release their pent-up instinct to scramble around like monkeys. The sport of bouldering (clambering on rocks without ropes or harness) evolved from alpine climbers' training exercises; and while your kids think they're just having a lot of fun doing what comes naturally, they are at the same time improving their coordination, developing problem-solving skills and gaining self-confidence.

Bouldering is a sport for the whole family – The Arch provides induction lessons for all ages – but if you prefer to sit it out there's a comfortable spectator area with an organic café, where you can loll on a sofa while the kids unleash their inner Spiderman. The Arch has 400 sq m (4,300 sq ft) of plywood bouldering with 100 circuits to climb, graded at various levels of difficulty and reaching a maximum height of 4.8 m (16 ft); and, in case you're worried, there are thick mats to fall onto.

Nearby is the famous 'wobbly' Millennium Bridge, the first pedestrian crossing of the Thames to be built since Tower Bridge in 1894, designed by architect Sir Norman Foster and abstract sculptor Sir Anthony Caro to represent (perhaps a little over-ambitiously) a millennial blade of light beaming across the river. The bridge was opened to a massive fanfare – and was immediately closed again.

For whenever people tried to walk on it, the 'blade of light' started to sway in a most alarming manner; an engineering glitch that took two years to fix – long enough for the 'wobbly bridge' moniker to stick fast. As you cross the bridge, admiring the picture-postcard view of St Paul's dome, you can't help experiencing just the tiniest tremor of trepidation.

Bankside – The *Golden Hind* and Globe Theatre

The south side of the Thames between Blackfriars and London Bridge is one of the most vibrant districts of London with so many attractions that it's hard to choose between them. But if you want to take the kids somewhere educational as well as fun, introduce them to the Tudors at Bankside.

Berthed in St Mary Overie Dock is a truly magnificent replica of Sir Francis Drake's galleon *Golden Hind*, the boat in which he set off on his epic voyage of exploration in 1577. For three years he swashbuckled his way around the world, returning in 1880 to fame and fortune: the *Golden Hind* was so weighed down with plundered Spanish treasure that Drake had discarded the ship's ballast to make room for it. The replica, built in 1973, is no model – it, too, has proved its seaworthiness by circumnavigating the globe, sailing more than 225,000 km (140,000 mi). Guides in Tudor costume give a lively account of life aboard, taking you round the five decks, explaining the exhibits and demonstrating how the weaponry worked. The kids should be suitably awed by the cramped conditions and poor diet that 16th-century pirates had to endure.

The impossibly picturesque reconstruction of Shakespeare's Globe Theatre on Bankside has been built using entirely authentic materials and is the only thatched building to have been permitted in London since the Great Fire of 1666. The Globe exhibition and tour is a fascinating insight into Elizabethan theatre, guaranteed to awaken the children's interest in the bard. And when they've seen round the theatre and open-air yard, inspected the costume collection and discovered how special effects and musical sounds were produced in Shakespeare's day, you can be pretty certain they'll be open to the idea of coming to watch a play here.

The Golden Hind, *a full size replica of Sir Francis Drake's 16th-century galleon, docked near Southwark Cathedral.*

WHERE:
Central London
BEST TIME TO GO:
July or August for a guided pirate tour of the *Golden Hind* (check with box office for times and dates).
DON'T MISS:
Trying on the costume armour at The Globe Theatre
AMOUNT OF WALKING:
Moderate. The Globe is wheelchair and pushchair friendly.
COST:
Expensive
YOU SHOULD KNOW:
Advance tickets for the *Golden Hind* can be obtained over the internet or from the office in Clink Street. The ship is open for viewing throughout the year and there are regular pirate fun days and family events during the summer months. The Globe Theatre has aids for the visually or hearing impaired. Children under 12 must be accompanied by an adult.

The Unicorn Theatre

WHERE:
Central London
BEST TIME TO GO:
Any time
DON'T MISS:
Seeing Tower Bridge, the Tower of London and City Hall from the pedestrian precinct outside the theatre.
AMOUNT OF WALKING:
Little
COST:
Reasonable
YOU SHOULD KNOW:
Unicorn Youth Theatre workshops are open to young people (aged ten to 16) who live or go to school in Southwark or Tower Hamlets. Children under 12 must be accompanied to performances by an adult; children under 18 months are allowed in free.

The Unicorn is England's longest-established children's theatre, dating back to 1947 when the country was in the post-war doldrums. Using a decommissioned civil defence van, Caryl Jenner and her troupe started to tour the southeast, performing plays for both adults and children. Caryl Jenner's Mobile Theatre was such a huge hit that the company soon had three vans on tour, and by the late 1950s the English Children's Theatre was firmly established. In 1962, shortly after the company had found a permanent home in the Arts Theatre, Jenner changed her company's name to Unicorn Theatre Club.

The Arts Theatre served as a tolerable base, but Jenner had a long-term ambition to build a theatre specifically for children. After her death in 1973, her successors kept the idea alive. It took years of persistent fund-raising and repeated applications to local authorities but Jenner's vision was eventually realized in 2005 when the company moved into its present newly built purpose-designed Tooley Street premises.

The Unicorn is a superb space with two separate stages, an education centre and a café, all with excellent facilities for the disabled including performance aids for the visually and hearing impaired. Unusually, seating is unreserved so you can sit wherever you like. As well as staging its own highly rated productions throughout the year, the Unicorn hosts young people's theatre companies from other countries and runs youth theatre groups.

Best of all are the 'family days': the morning drama workshop is a stimulating shared experience where you and your kids will end up surprising yourselves and each other; then you watch an afternoon performance and have tea with the cast after the show. If you have aspiring thespians among your offspring, a Unicorn family day is a terrific way of introducing them to the world of theatre.

Brick Lane and the Museum Of Childhood

WHERE:
East London
BEST TIME TO GO:
Sunday morning for Brick Lane, Spitalfields and Petticoat Lane markets, when the area is at peak activity – any other day if you want to avoid the crowds.

For a generation of children who have grown up in the blandly uniform world of mass marketing, a trip to Brick Lane is a mind-expanding experience. London's multi-ethnic cultural roots are nowhere more apparent than in this famous East End street. For hundreds of years different migrant communities have settled here and integrated themselves into the capital's fabric as traders, artisans and restaurateurs; and in recent years hordes of artists and designers have gravitated to the area, attracted by the eclectic local culture and vibrant atmosphere. In particular, the Sunday market stalls, selling everything from bicycle parts to vintage clothes, will bowl over young teenage kids as they make their first tentative forays into the world of style.

The Museum of Childhood in Bethnal Green has perhaps the best collection of children's paraphernalia to be found anywhere in the world, containing the entirety of the V&A's collections of toys, costumes and childhood artefacts. For many years the museum was a little-known East End curiosity, neglected and under-used, but a substantial National Lottery grant in 2003 has effected a transformation. The permanent displays have been imaginatively reorganized in three galleries that are a joy to explore. There is also a full programme of temporary exhibitions, events, workshops and courses so there's always something new going on.

The museum has forged strong community ties and gone to great lengths to ensure that activities are inclusive and not at all intimidating: kids get drawn into story-telling sessions, dressing up, drawing and painting, and can even ride on a rocking horse as they compare their experience of growing up with the lives of children throughout the ages. For you, the Museum of Childhood is a marvellous opportunity to travel down memory lane and for your kids, to broaden their minds through a wealth of exhibits.

DON'T MISS:
Beigel Bake – the iconic 24/7 bagel bakery in Brick Lane.
The mosaic panels on the upper north and south façades of the Museum of Childhood.

AMOUNT OF WALKING:
Moderate. All parts of the Museum of Childhood have pushchair/wheelchair access.

COST:
Low. The Museum of Childhood has free entry with minimal charges for temporary special exhibitions and events.

YOU SHOULD KNOW:
The first immigrants to settle in Brick Lane were 17th-century French Huguenots, fleeing from religious persecution. Famous for their weaving skills, they established the area as the centre of London's rag trade. An early 18th-century Huguenot house still stands in Princelet Street round the corner from Brick Lane.

Interior of the Museum of Childhood, Bethnal Green

Hackney City Farm and London Fields Lido

Once a rather depressing, run-down borough, Hackney has become the trendiest part of town with amenities to match.

Hackney City Farm is a breath of country air in an area more usually associated with urban grime. Established in 1984, the farm is hidden in a corner of Haggerston Park and, although it is one of London's smaller city farms, what it lacks in size it makes up for in atmosphere. It is a secluded little paradise with a charming outdoor café and plenty of activities to keep the kids occupied. After the children have had their fill of the farm animals, do explore the rest of Haggerston Park. Created in the 1950s on the site of a former gas works, the park succeeds in looking as though it's been here for ever, with a lovely woodland walk, romantic walled garden, and a pond in a wild flower meadow that feels just like being in the country.

From Haggerston Park it is only a short walk through Broadway Market – the hippest shopping street in Hackney – to London Fields. Overlooked by Georgian terraces, this beautiful expanse of green meadow with lines of tall plane trees has a calm, timeless feel about it. As it should; for it is an incredibly ancient patch of common grazing land, used for centuries by shepherds as they drove their flocks from Essex to sell them in the City.

The great attraction at London Fields is its lido – the pool is heated! Originally built in 1932, the lido was earmarked for demolition in 1988. It took 18 years of constant community activism to get the Olympic-sized pool refurbished instead and the lido was finally reopened in 2006. Despite stiff competition, London Fields Lido is the most highly rated of all London's outdoor pools.

Feeding the goats at Hackney City Farm.

Ragged School Museum and Mile End Park

If you're fed up with listening to your kids moan about their homework, take them to the Ragged School. This fascinating museum is a salutary reminder of what life could be like for children in the days before education was a universal human right.

The museum is in an old warehouse beside Regents Canal, the original site of Copperfield Road Ragged School, which was started by Dr Barnado in 1877 and became the largest free school in London. Thousands of street children passed through this building to be provided with meals, basic education, and help in finding a job. Your kids will be shocked when they find out about Victorian living conditions and discover how and why the 'ragged' or free schools were set up by the philanthropists of the day. The museum runs a regular programme of activities and events: children will be intrigued by the archaic cooking implements in a replica of a typical Victorian kitchen, and more than grateful for their own school life when they experience a lesson seated at old desks with slates and dunce's caps.

After wallowing in the misery of a deprived Victorian childhood, hurl your kids into the 21st century at the new Mile End Park – a strip of abandoned industrial land alongside the Regents Canal cleverly converted into a huge leisure amenity stretching all the way from Limehouse to Victoria Park. The park is an innovative design containing an Ecology Park, an Arts Park, a tranquil Terrace Garden, a Children's Park where kids under eight can wallow in a massive sandpit with bridges and boats, fountains and a castle, and an Adventure Park with extreme sporting activities for 11 to 17 year olds. The electric go-kart track is an incredibly popular attraction and there is also perhaps the best indoor climbing centre in London.

The Copperfield Road School in Hackney, formerly the largest ragged school in London but now a museum of Victorian schooling.

WHERE:
East London
BEST TIME TO GO:
The first Sunday of each month to participate in re-enactments of Victorian school lessons. The museum is also open on Wednesdays and Thursdays.
DON'T MISS:
The award-winning Green Bridge in Mile End Park, with trees and grass growing on it.
AMOUNT OF WALKING:
Moderate or lots if you want
COST:
Low to expensive – the Ragged School Museum and Mile End Park are free, but go-karting is pretty costly.
YOU SHOULD KNOW:
Ragged School Museum – children under eight must be accompanied by an adult; there is play space for children under six. Mile End Park – you should organize wall climbing or go-karting in advance (full details can be found on the internet). Under 18s must be at least 1.5 m (5 ft) tall for the go-karting.

Parliament Hill Lido, Hampstead Ponds and Hampstead Village

Children enjoying the Parliament Hill Lido.

Open-air swimming was once all the rage and throughout the 1920s and '30s lidos were built all over London. But the outdoor pool came to an untimely end with the advent of multiplex leisure centres, and Parliament Hill is one of the few original lidos to have survived the axe.

Opened in 1938, the lido in Parliament Hill Fields on the edge of Hampstead Heath is a charming anachronism with delightfully retro changing rooms and art deco terrace café. You'll feel as if you've been transported back to a simpler less frenetic time, and the kids will love the sensation of being open to the elements – a completely different experience from the chlorinated fug of torpid air that greets you in most indoor pools. The pool itself is brilliant: although unheated, it is a full 60 m (200 ft) long (more than Olympic size) with the shallow end roped off for safety. There's a broad surround for the kids to run around and you to sunbathe. And, amazingly, even at the height of summer it rarely feels overcrowded.

Don't leave without climbing to the top of Parliament Hill. From here you can see for miles across London and watch the kite fliers competing with each other (or fly kites yourselves). Then wander down towards South End Green so that the kids can play in the woods along the banks of the ponds, sploshing around in the mud and feeding the ducks.

The vague sense of having stepped back in time continues if you explore the picturesque winding back streets of Hampstead Village on your way to the High Street. Head for the pancake stand outside the King William IV pub. There's invariably a long queue but it really is worth the wait. A perfect end to a perfect day.

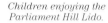

WHERE:
North London
BEST TIME TO GO:
On a warm day May to August
DON'T MISS:
The quaint shops in Flask Walk, Hampstead
AMOUNT OF WALKING:
Moderate or lots if you want
COST:
Low
YOU SHOULD KNOW:
Parliament Hill got its name during the English Civil War when it was seized by pro-parliament, anti-royalist troops on the side of Oliver Cromwell. The term 'lido' is derived from the famous Venice Lido (pronounced in Italian as lee-doh, but in London parlance usually as lie-doh).

Hampstead West Heath Woods, Hill Garden and Golders Hill Park

Known as the lungs of north London, Hampstead Heath is a stretch of ancient common land between the then rural villages of Hampstead and Highgate – some 320 ha (almost 800 acres) of rolling meadows, woods and heathland, with 25 ponds fed by London's underground rivers.

West Heath is relatively unfrequented with some magical hidden corners. The woody bogland behind Leg of Mutton Pond is nature's version of an adventure playground – the kids can let rip chasing each other through the trees, jumping over ditches and clambering along logs. Look for the side gate in the dauntingly high brick wall alongside the main path, where some steps spiral up to a Georgian colonnade. You'll suddenly find yourselves in a fairy tale: overhead, a pergola cascades wisteria, honeysuckle and clematis, and the colonnade leads mysteriously round corner after corner, until eventually you reach a stone stairway that descends into an amazing secret garden – with an ornamental fish pond the size of a swimming pool and a view over the trees to Golders Hill and beyond.

From the Hill Garden, plunge back into the woods and follow the path to Golders Hill, a gem of a park backing onto West Heath. No city in the world does parks quite as well as London, and Golders Hill is a classic of its kind. You will appreciate the beautiful formal flower beds and rolling lawns; the kids will love running down the hill, befriending the deer in the animal enclosure and pretending to be Amazon explorers in the water garden – a jungle of tropical plants around ponds alive with dragonflies. On a summer's day it feels pretty much as good as it gets picnicking on the grass while you listen to live music wafting from the bandstand and watch the children play.

WHERE:
North London
BEST TIME TO GO:
May or June to catch the Hill Garden and colonnade in full flower, or on a sunny October day for the autumn foliage.
DON'T MISS:
The historic 16th-century Spaniard's Inn pub, legendary birthplace of highwayman Dick Turpin; the delicious home-made ice cream in the Italian café at Golders Hill Park.
AMOUNT OF WALKING:
Lots
COST:
Low
YOU SHOULD KNOW:
The bad traffic congestion and lack of parking space round Hampstead Heath can prove frustrating, so take public transport if possible. The tube station is only a short (and interesting) walk from West Heath.

Children playing in autumn snow on Hampstead Heath.

Abney Park Cemetery and Clissold Park

WHERE:
Northeast London
BEST TIME TO GO:
A sunny day between April and September
DON'T MISS:
The grave of William Booth, founder of the Salvation Army and the white marble lion dedicated to Frank C. Bostock, animal trainer at the turn of the 20th century.
AMOUNT OF WALKING:
Lots
COST:
Low
YOU SHOULD KNOW:
Abney Park Cemetery is one of several London cemeteries established between 1832 and 1842 to cater for London's rapid increase in population. Highgate, Brompton and Kensal Green cemeteries are of the same period.

Abney Park Cemetery

A cemetery may seem an odd sort of place to take the children but Abney Park is a really extraordinary adventure; and not in the least bit grim. It would be hard to find a more magical spot anywhere, let alone in the middle of London. Slip through the gateway at the junction of Stoke Newington High Street and Church Street to enter a wild woodland world of birdsong and butterflies. Winding paths lead through the undergrowth past tumbledown memorials until eventually you stumble upon the mysterious semi-intact ruin of Abney Park Chapel.

Abney Park was once London's main burial ground for dissenters and non-conformists. At its height, the cemetery had a larger arboretum than Kew Gardens, with more than 2,500 species of trees and shrubs. After years of neglect, the cemetery has been taken over by a charitable trust as a community nature reserve and outdoor learning centre. Every year the programme of activities and events for youngsters gets bigger, so it's best to go soon before Abney Park loses its amazing atmosphere of other-world wildness.

After your magical mystery tour, stroll down Stoke Newington Church Street, a road more reminiscent of a Victorian English market town than inner London with picturesque little shops and cosy street cafés geared for families. At the end of Church Street is the 22-ha (54-acre) Clissold Park. In 1889 the local mansion, Clissold House, and its landscaped grounds were annexed to Stoke Newington Common to create an idyllic family park where the kids can go pond-dipping, see terrapins and deer, creep through the butterfly tunnel and nature garden, and splash around in what seems like the biggest paddling pool ever. And if you've got toddlers in tow, the one o'clock club is a brilliant place for fraught mums to recover their wits.

Horniman Museum and Crystal Palace Park Dinosaur Walk

Dinosaur models at Crystal Palace Park

Forest Hill may not be the easiest place in the world to get to but it's definitely worth making the effort in order to take the kids to the Horniman, a museum that deserves any number of repeat visits. Inside is a treasure trove of weird and wonderful cultural and natural objects – from an over-stuffed walrus to a Spanish Inquisition torture chair – and a marvellous aquarium with a mangrove swamp and Fijian coral reef. Outdoors, there are 6.5 ha (16 acres) of award-winning grounds to explore, with a nature trail, medicinal garden, Victorian conservatory and panoramic views over the South Downs.

The museum was founded by Frederick Horniman, a 19th-century world traveller and obsessive collector whose avowed intent was to 'bring the world to Forest Hill'. When the family home ran out of space for his ever-expanding hoard of cultural artefacts, natural history specimens and musical instruments, he solved the problem quite simply – by having a museum purpose-built. The Horniman's trustees have continued adding to the collection, maintaining the same eclectic principles as its founder and zealously pursuing a child-centred policy with masses of imaginative activities for kids of all ages.

Prehistoric monsters are among the few natural wonders you won't find at the Horniman – so take the kids to walk among the dinosaurs in Crystal Palace Park. Originally modelled in 1854 and beautifully renovated, the park's concrete dinosaurs were copied from fossil evidence under the guidance of Professor Sir Richard Owen, founder of the Natural History Museum. Wandering through the gardens along a pretty path, you are caught off guard by the giant reptiles and early mammals lurking in the shrubbery and rising up out of the lake. The monsters are scary-looking enough to be exciting; and little ones may have to be persuaded that they aren't real!

A young visitor at the Horniman Museum looking at skeletons of primates.

WHERE:
South London
BEST TIME TO GO:
Any time
DON'T MISS:
The Horniman sundial trail – an open-air collection of some of the world's most inventive timepieces. The CUE (Centre for Understanding the Environment) building – constructed from sustainable materials with a grass roof and water recycling system – designed to promote awareness of conservation and ecology, and housing the Horniman library.
AMOUNT OF WALKING:
Moderate. Wheelchair and pushchair access throughout the museum.
COST:
Low. Museum entrance is free.
YOU SHOULD KNOW:
Frederick Horniman was the son of the founder of Horniman's Tea Company. Professor Sir Richard Owen coined the word 'dinosaur'.

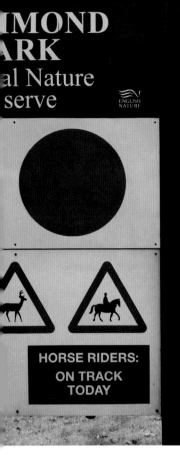

**HORSE RIDERS:
ON TRACK
TODAY**

Horse Riding in Richmond Park

Horse riding is a wonderful all-weather exercise and even if you can't afford to take the kids very often, it's worth investing in a couple of lessons for the lasting pleasure and confidence that youngsters gain from learning the basics of handling a horse.

Richmond is probably the best place to go riding in the London area. Stretching from Roehampton to Kingston, it is by far the

Trot-on! Off they go through Richmond park.

WHERE:
Southwest London
BEST TIME TO GO:
October for the autumn colour or a crisp day in January for some exhilarating outdoor exercise
DON'T MISS:
King Henry VIII's Mound, the highest point in Richmond Park, from where there is an uninterrupted view of St Paul's 16 km (10 mi) away and a panoramic view over the Thames Valley.
AMOUNT OF WALKING:
Little if you ride, but lots if you decide to explore the park on foot.
COST:
Expensive
YOU SHOULD KNOW:
Richmond Park is a National Nature Reserve and Site of Special Scientific Interest.

largest of London's royal parks with 955 ha (2,360 acres) of undulating pastureland dotted with ancient oak trees. Bridle paths pass ponds and meadows, and you can see rabbits and squirrels scampering in the undergrowth while fallow and red deer graze peacefully nearby.

Richmond wasn't always a park. For hundreds of years the land was occupied by small farmers, until it caught the eye of Charles I. He decided it would make a great hunting ground so in 1637, regardless of the local outcry, he turfed out the farmers, enclosed the whole area with 13 km (8 mi) of brick wall and introduced more than 2,000 deer. At the time it may have been unjust but, thanks to King Charles, Richmond Park is now a protected rural paradise for Londoners to enjoy. The timeless pastoral landscape is the result of centuries of grazing; and there are still more than 600 deer here.

Riding is a traditional activity in the park and there are several well-established British Horse Society approved stables in the vicinity, one of which has been in business since 1790! They are used to riders of all abilities and will provide ponies for children aged three upwards. The promise of a ride in Richmond may give the kids just the incentive they need to tear themselves away from the computer screen and force them out into the fresh air.

Syon Park

For a wonderful slice of English heritage, visit the last surviving ducal residence in Greater London. Set in 80 ha (200 acres) of grounds on the north side of the Thames facing Kew Gardens, Syon Park was originally the site of a medieval abbey dissolved by King Henry VIII in the 16th century. The estate has been inhabited by the aristocratic Percy family for the past 400 years and is home to the present Duke of Northumberland.

The interior of the neo-classical mansion, all gilding and marble, is of jaw-dropping magnificence, but the real point of coming here is outside. The grounds were landscaped by the great 18th-century English gardener, 'Capability' Brown. Wander around the tree-lined ornamental lake and maybe spot a terrapin, explore 16 ha (40 acres) of Grade I-listed garden, renowned for its variety of rare plants and trees, and gaze across tidal water meadows to the banks of the Thames. The picture is completed by the Great Conservatory, a fantastical glass-domed building built in 1826 and the inspiration behind the design of Crystal Palace 25 years later.

When you've explored the garden, take the kids to the Snakes and Ladders indoor adventure playground, where you can hide away with a cup of coffee and a good book, while they let rip on the massive three-tiered climbing frame. There are also slides and tunnels, ball ponds and rope climbs, electric motor bike and air hockey rinks and an outdoor assault course with a separate soft-play area for under twos and a zone specially for two to fives.

A trip to Syon Park is as good as a day out in the country. You will be revitalized by the beautiful surroundings and the kids should be pleasantly tired out after burning off their excess energy.

WHERE:
West London
BEST TIME TO GO:
Anytime
DON'T MISS:
The ice house, where ice from the lake was stored to be used to cool wine.
AMOUNT OF WALKING:
Lots
COST:
Low
YOU SHOULD KNOW:
The garden at Syon Park is open daily throughout the year and you can see inside the house from March to October on Wednesdays, Thursdays, Sundays and Bank Holidays.

Children in the butterfly cage get up-close with the inhabitants.

Cycle along the River Thames between Teddington Lock and Shepperton Ferry

WHERE:
Southwest London
BEST TIME TO GO:
May to September
DON'T MISS:
Watching the boats going through the locks.
AMOUNT OF WALKING:
Little, but lots of cycling
COST:
Low
YOU SHOULD KNOW:
The Thames Path is a national walking trail that follows the course of the river for 294 km (184 mi) from its source in the Cotswolds all the way through London to the Thames Barrier. The section between Teddington and Shepperton is an official cycling route and there are plenty of other stretches along the river where, although cycling is not officially allowed, tradition has dictated otherwise; as long as you always give pedestrians priority and don't steam along, nobody seems to object.

Cycling along the banks of the River Thames.

There are few more painless ways of spending quality time with the kids than going out on your bikes together, but in London it's not that easy to find a route that's both safe and interesting. The Thames Path is the perfect solution, with long stretches of traffic-free cycling through idyllic rural scenery interspersed with dramatic cityscapes, vast reservoirs and intriguing bits of river engineering. There is an unexpected sight literally round every bend and masses of wildlife nestling in the river bank; and, of course, always the boats of all shapes and sizes chugging along the river and moored along the banks.

Teddington is the point where the Thames stops being tidal. It is the longest and lowest lock on the river, with more than 800 million litres (175 million gallons) of water pouring over the weir every day. You can cycle upstream along the south side of the river to Kingston, where you must briefly keep your wits about you crossing the busy Kingston Bridge before reconnecting with the path on the north side, which takes you along a beautiful stretch skirting the grounds of Hampton Court Palace. After crossing the famous Lutyens-designed bridge and passing Molesey Lock and the exclusive multi-storey houseboats of Taggs Island, you reach the 500-year-old Shepperton

Ferry. Ring the riverside bell to attract the ferryman's attention and he'll chug over so that you can pile your bikes aboard for a boat ride across the river.

A successful bike ride must be planned with military precision, complete with map, refreshments and repair kit. The stretch between Teddington and Shepperton is all of 18 km (11 mi), so decide what distance you think is feasible and work out how you're going to get home; you can always do the rest of the route another day.

Polka Children's Theatre

Originally established in the 1960s as a touring theatre under the directorship of professional puppeteer Richard Gill, the Polka has gone from strength to strength: the company was the first in London to open a permanent venue devoted entirely to children's theatre, and its productions are invariably greeted with rave reviews.

The Polka has gained an international reputation for outstanding children's entertainment, but the company had far more modest aspirations when in 1979 it made its home in a disused church hall in Wimbledon Broadway, simply intending to serve the local community. The venue still retains the informal, friendly atmosphere of a community centre and parents are encouraged to come here with their kids simply to hang out, without necessarily feeling obliged to attend a performance. The theatre has a loyal following among local parents, many of whom remember coming here as children themselves and are now returning with their own offspring. You can bring your kids to play in the books-and-toys corner or in the garden Wendy house, and there is a lovely café that serves freshly made food.

The interior of the church hall has been converted to house a 300-seat main auditorium for kids aged four to 13 and the smaller Adventure Theatre for infants and toddlers. Virtually every well-known children's storybook gets staged in one or other of these spaces and more than 100,000 children are entertained here every year. The Polka's stated mission is to 'spark the imagination and fuel a sense of discovery' and the company is particularly well known for its pioneering early years' work and infants' story sessions.

Taking your kids to a Polka production really is an inspiring experience – the delight in their faces as they get caught up in the drama says it all.

WHERE:
Southwest London
BEST TIME TO GO:
Any time
DON'T MISS:
The exhibition area where you can see props and puppets from previous performances and a teddy bear museum collection.
AMOUNT OF WALKING:
Little. Good wheelchair access.
COST:
Reasonable
YOU SHOULD KNOW:
The Polka runs after-school drama courses and theatre workshops during school holidays and half-terms, where kids can gain skills and confidence through acting, movement, puppetry and mime.

41

Even empty, Twickenham Rugby Stadium is impressive.

Twickenham Rugby Stadium tour and Museum Of Rugby

Anyone remotely interested in sport will enjoy looking round The Cabbage Patch (as Twickenham is known to aficionados – because the site was once used to grow market-garden produce) and rugby fans of all ages will be in seventh heaven to find themselves in the home of English rugby football. Enthusiastic and knowledgeable guides will show you round one of the greatest sporting venues in the world: you will see inside the England dressing room and injury room, then go through the tunnel out onto the pitch, where you can touch the hallowed turf of your heroes, then take in the spectacular view over the arena from the top of the stands.

After your tour you can look round the Museum of Rugby. Opened in 1998, this international museum has the largest collection of rugby memorabilia in the world, with objects from around the globe dating back to the founding of the Rugby Football Union by William Webb Ellis in 1871. You can learn all about the history of the ultimate in team games, discovering how it evolved out of schoolboy football, and how bootmaker Richard Lindon got into the business of making rugby balls and came up with the idea of making them out of rubber instead of inflated pigs' bladders, but failed to patent it.

There are loads of interactive exhibits and you can see action-packed highlights from historic matches, discover the origin of the Calcutta Cup and how the red rose became the emblem of the England team. And you'll get a chance to see the Twickenham Wall of Fame, opened in 2005 as a lasting tribute to rugby's greatest players. The wall celebrates the best players from all over the world who have ever played at Twickenham.

WHERE:
Southwest London
BEST TIME TO GO:
Anytime. There are four tours a day Tuesday to Saturday and two tours on Sundays, except on days when there is a match fixture or event.
DON'T MISS:
Testing your strength on the 'scrum machine'.
AMOUNT OF WALKING:
Moderate. The stadium has full disabled access.
COST:
Reasonable
YOU SHOULD KNOW:
Twickenham is the fifth largest stadium in Europe, capable of holding a crowd of 82,000.

Hounslow Urban Farm

Originating out of the idealism of London's early 1970s alternative sub-culture, city farms started as community-based projects on patches of wasteland and are one of the few good ideas that have survived from those heady times. Having received the stamp of official approval, they've become a permanent feature of the inner city with more than 30 in London alone. The farms are just about the only way that many urban kids ever get the chance to interact with farm animals, see how crops grow and make the connection between agriculture and the food they put on their plates.

Hounslow Urban Farm, established in 1990, is larger than most, extending over more than 11 ha (29 acres), and it has an exceptionally wide range of animals, including rare breeds, Exmoor ponies, rheas, alpacas, chipmunks and other small mammals. The atmosphere here is really relaxed and friendly – the kids can wander freely around the stables and paddocks, and feed the animals. All the animals are used to being petted and appear to genuinely like the attention they get from visitors, responding in kind. The goats are particularly cheeky and will stand around expectantly, quite happy to try and snatch the food out of your hand if they're given half a chance.

There is a children's playground with miniature tractors to ride, a duck pond and a farm shop selling fresh eggs, but the animals alone will almost certainly keep the kids fully occupied. In the spring they can see the new baby animals and even get to bottle feed a lamb, and during the school holidays there are plenty of extra activities laid on including animal handling sessions, pig racing and scarecrow making. This is a really great place to bring young children to have a picnic and learn about animals.

WHERE:
West London
BEST TIME TO GO:
Any day March to September or at weekends October to February
DON'T MISS:
Pig racing – a chaotic affair that the pigs obviously really enjoy, thriving on the attention.
AMOUNT OF WALKING:
Moderate. The farm is wheelchair-friendly with good paths.
COST:
Low. Hounslow is the only London city farm that relies on a small entrance charge rather than charitable donations, but it is well worth it.
YOU SHOULD KNOW:
Hounslow Urban Farm runs a volunteer scheme for teenagers who are interested in getting experience of working with animals and it has excellent facilities for children with disabilities, including a sensory soft-play area, complete with sound effects and smells.

A young girl pets a baby lamb at the farm.

London Wetlands Centre

A disused Victorian reservoir in Barnes may not sound very
promising but it's amazing what a bit of imagination can achieve. The
Wildlife and Wetland Trust has created the largest urban wetland
centre in Europe, more than 40 ha (100 acres) of lakes, ponds,
meadows and marshes with more than 3 km (2 mi) of boardwalks
and pathways winding through it. The London Wetlands Centre
opened in 2000, and by 2002 it had already attracted so much
wildlife that it was designated a Site of Special Scientific Interest.

The Wetlands Centre has been cleverly planned with different
habitats and breeding grounds – reedbeds, islands, marshy pools,
thickets and meadows – to sustain an incredible variety of wild birds,
waterfowl, insects, amphibians and small mammals. The centre is
dotted with bird hides from where you can watch all sorts of rare

species including bitterns, lapwings, grebes and cormorants.

Your kids don't have to be passionate nature lovers to get stuck in for the whole day here. Although they will enjoy the birdlife – especially the different species of exotic ducks and swans from all over the world – there are loads of activities apart from bird watching and it's a great place to come and have a picnic. As well as the state-of-the-art visitor centre, there's a waterside café and an Explore adventure area where kids aged three to 11 can go tunnelling, fly down a zip wire and clamber around on a bouldering wall. There are also raised ponds where the kids can go dipping to see what's lurking under the surface and they can watch the birds having their daily feed at 15.00. Free guided tours are on offer (daily at 11.00 and 14.00) and there's a full programme of activities and events.

COST:
Reasonable
YOU SHOULD KNOW:
You can access the Wetlands Centre from the Thames towpath, so you can combine your visit here with a walk or bike ride along the river. Children under 16 must be accompanied by an adult. No dogs allowed except guide dogs

The London Wetlands Centre is the largest urban wetland centre in Europe.

A Donald Duck cartoon on the fuselage of a North American P-51D Mustang that was piloted by Captain Donald R. Emerson during World War II.

Royal Air Force Museum

The RAF Museum stands on the site of what was once Hendon Aerodrome, the first London airport. You can learn about the entire history of aviation here – from balloon flight to the latest state-of-the-art fighter plane – and the important part that the RAF has played in it all.

The museum is absolutely vast, with six huge exhibition halls, so don't even try to look round the whole place in one day. As well as more than 100 aircraft and all sorts of intriguing aviation equipment and absorbing wartime memorabilia on display, there is an awesome Battle of Britain audiovisual show, a 3-D cinema and loads of interactive exhibits.

For first-time visitors, the Milestones of Flight exhibition is probably the best place to start, to get an overview of the past 100 years of world aviation. A graphic timeline displays all the key events from the pioneering days of the Wright Brothers to the present, and you can have a close-up look at historic flying machines ranging from an early airship gondola to the latest Eurofighter Typhoon. The exhibition includes a fabulous Blériot XI, a wooden

WHERE:
North London
BEST TIME TO GO:
Any time
DON'T MISS:
The Air Traffic Control Exhibition, which shows the mind-boggling complexity of handling the traffic in our crowded skies.
AMOUNT OF WALKING:
Moderate. Good access for pushchairs and people with disabilities.
COST:
Low. Admission is free.
YOU SHOULD KNOW:
The RAF Museum is so big that it is split into two sites – at Colindale and at Cosford in Shropshire, where there is a collection of warplanes and exhibitions of the History of the RAF and the Cold War.

monoplane of the sort in which French aviator Louis Blériot made his historic flight across the English Channel in 1909. Make sure the kids have a go on the Eurofighter flight simulator; and then, for more hands-on stuff, go to the Aeronauts Interactive Centre where there are more than 40 entertaining and informative experiments to demonstrate the science of flight.

The idea of flying has always gripped the human imagination, and the RAF Museum holds a universal appeal. Of course, small boys are bound to think they've landed in heaven here; but everyone, male or female, from the tiniest tot to the very elderly, seems to get drawn in with equal enthusiasm.

Morden Hall Park and Deen City Farm

For an instant taste of countryside, take the kids on a family adventure in Morden Hall Park, a curious National Trust property in the suburbs of London. The River Wandle, a tributary of the Thames, meanders through the estate and you'll find yourselves crossing footbridges and sploshing through wetland, strolling along tree-lined avenues and roaming through woods and meadows. Morden Hall Park is a haven for wildlife and you're likely to spot a heron or kingfisher among the weeping willows along the riverbanks.

You can wander through the impressive formal rose garden, sit in the walled kitchen-garden café and explore 50 ha (125 acres) of scenic parkland. You'll come across interesting old estate buildings – some of them occupied by local craftsmen – where you can discover the history of the estate. In the 19th century Morden Hall was bought by the Hatfeilds, a wealthy local family in the snuff trade. The Snuff Mill is still standing; it was in production until 1922 when the workforce went on strike and the business collapsed. You can find out how snuff was made, see the original waterwheel that turned the millstones used to grind tobacco, and investigate the weir and millponds.

The northernmost end of the estate is Deen City Farm, where the kids can amuse themselves amongst the farm animals, and see peacocks and even ferrets. The farm runs a horticulture project and has a wildlife garden and stables, with a riding school offering lessons for children aged eight and over and pony rides for the little ones.

The soothing sound of the river in the background, birds warbling and country scents in the air will soon brush away the city cobwebs, and the kids will be intrigued by the novelty of this little-known corner of London.

WHERE:
Southwest London
BEST TIME TO GO:
May to September when the Snuff Mill Environmental Centre is open and the roses are in bloom.
DON'T MISS:
One of the oldest yew trees in England in the garden of Morden Cottage. The trout on top of the weather vane at Clockhouse Gate.
AMOUNT OF WALKING:
Lots, but most of the paths are easy for wheelchairs and pushchairs.
COST:
Low. Admission is free.
YOU SHOULD KNOW:
Unusual ways of getting to Morden Hall Park include taking the tram from Wimbledon, or walking or cycling along the Wandle Trail, following the course of the river. Family events at Morden Hall Park (including guided walks and arts and crafts activities) are held on the first and third Sunday of each month. Deen City Farm is closed on Mondays.

Birdworld

WHERE:
Farnham, Surrey
BEST TIME TO GO:
On a decent day between April and October
DON'T MISS:
The Crocodile Swamp with its young crocodiles, alligators and caymans
AMOUNT OF WALKING:
Moderate. Birdworld has good access for wheelchair users – you can even book a chair in advance; the level pathways are also helpful for those pushing buggies.
COST:
Reasonable.
YOU SHOULD KNOW:
If you book in advance you can feed the penguins yourself. Be forewarned, however, though great fun to feed, they are extremely smelly creatures, so it's not for the faint-hearted.

Set in 11 hectares (26 acres) of landscaped gardens and parkland, Birdworld is Britain's largest bird park. Packed with things to see and do, this is a splendid place to come for a day that is both entertaining and educational.

The birds, kept in aviaries, look healthy and happy – and the whole family will be delighted by parrots that talk, impressed by peacocks displaying their finery and amused by kookaburras that laugh. Twice a day you can watch the penguins being fed. This is always quite an event – make sure you have a good view by getting there early. You can also take an interesting tour with a keeper as he feeds the birds of prey.

Visit the Heron Theatre – regular shows are held – and see a performance by young birds that have been raised here. The Safari Train will take you to see some of the larger species such as cranes and emus, and the accompanying keeper gives an informative commentary.

There are mammals and fish here, as well as birds, and the Jenny Wren Farm is great for younger children, with lots of domestic animals to be stroked and cuddled, including some rare breeds. Many of them are born here, and can be bought, so you never know, you might go home the proud owner of a guinea pig or a ferret!

Included in the price is a visit to the Underwater World – a journey that takes you past tanks of marine life in streams, mangrove forests, swamps, and reefs, and provides information about the fish, their habitats and the future they face.

If your little ones need a break there are plenty of places to sit down and have a snack, but this is also a great place to bring a picnic of your own.

A rainbow-billed toucan

Rural Life Centre and Alice Holt Forest

The Rural Life Centre is exactly what it says it is: a place devoted to 150 years of farming and village life, providing visitors with a really interesting few hours. Set in large gardens and woodland, farm machinery, tools, wagons and displays of trades and crafts are housed in buildings across the site.

The Rural Life Centre

Some have been specially made, while others have been reconstructed – for example, there's a schoolroom, a chapel and a village hall. The old village playground is popular with children, as is the narrow-gauge railway. Available on Sundays between Easter and October, a trip can be enjoyed for a small fee. There's a shop and a café – always useful – but this is a lovely place for a picnic, and by the time you've seen everything and taken the Woodland Walk, you'll need to re-fuel.

Alice Holt Forest, down the road, is a great place to spend the afternoon. Whether strolling through the woods on your own, or doing something more energetic and organized, you'll enjoy doing it here. There are way-marked trails of different lengths and difficulty, or if you prefer, bikes can be hired. The selection of cycle trails includes a track specially designed for beginners and people with special needs.

Many events are put on during the school holidays, some of which need to be booked in advance, and an orienteering course is always available – you just need to pick up an inexpensive Wayfaring pack from the Forest Office to get you going.

The forest is an ancient woodland, meaning it has been continuously wooded since the 1600s. Although famous for its oak trees – once used to provide timber for naval ships – conifers and broad-leafed trees have been added to the mix, making it a haven for birds and other wildlife.

WHERE:
Near Bentley, Surrey
BEST TIME TO GO:
On a fine day between March and October
DON'T MISS:
The Adventure Playground, Timberland Trail assault course and Habitat Trail at Alice Holt Forest
AMOUNT OF WALKING:
Lots
COST:
Reasonable – the forest is free to enter but there's a small parking charge.
YOU SHOULD KNOW:
Weyfest, an annual family-friendly festival, is held at the Rural Life Centre. It boasts a fabulous children's play area, with lots of special activities for kids — including music workshops — while adults can enjoy live music, stalls and other jollities.

A McLaren F1 car

Brooklands Museum and Mercedes-Benz World

Brooklands motor-racing circuit opened in 1907 – the first of its kind in the world. It was a banked oval shape surrounding a large grass airfield that was used by pioneering aviators. Pretty soon, small factories were set up to build these early aircraft, adding to the existing sheds that were used for fine-tuning the superb, record-breaking cars that were being raced around the circuit, some of which you can still see here.

Brooklands Museum puts on lots of special events each year, many of which have children in mind and, those apart, there is always something happening. As well as cars and planes there are motorbikes, which you'll probably see being tested.

On the flying front there is a fabulous collection of aircraft, from early planes like the De Havilland Tiger Moth through to an opulent VC-10 airliner that was donated by the Sultan of Brunei. Perhaps the most exciting plane is the Delta Golf, the first British production Concorde. The Concorde Experience shouldn't be missed, but book early as places are limited. Next door you'll find one of the most sophisticated aircraft simulators ever built, where visitors can experience the thrill of taking off and breaking the sound barrier.

If you and your family are petrol-heads and aviation enthusiasts, Brooklands provides a fascinating day out with the opportunity to discover the history of both motor racing and flying.

Mercedes-Benz World, which encompasses the entire history of the company, is situated in a marvellous new building next to Brooklands Museum. It's more than just a showroom: there's a luxurious cinema where you can watch the whole story of the company's development and there's a chance to sit in some of the latest Mercs.

Under 17s can get a head start on their peers by booking for young driver training on a private circuit or, for those who would rather be a passenger, there are various rides available.

WHERE:
A few minutes drive from Junction 10 on the M25, not far from Weybridge, Surrey
BEST TIME TO GO:
Apart from a few days over Christmas, the museum is open all year round. It's probably best to choose a rain-free day.
DON'T MISS:
The interactive Discovery gallery at Brooklands. Available to visitors when not booked by school parties, this a place where science is turned into fun.
AMOUNT OF WALKING:
Moderate
COST:
Reasonable
YOU SHOULD KNOW:
James May, of the BBC's *Top Gear* fame, is re-creating the historic Brooklands banked racing circuit in Scalextric track.

Bocketts Farm and Norbury Park cycle ride

Set in the bucolic Surrey countryside, the working family farm Bocketts is a lovely place to visit with younger children, and is within easy reach of both London and the southeast. This is a mixed farm where crops are grown and animals are reared, so there's always something going on.

The kids will see and feel the natural rhythm of life here: baby animals born in spring, seeds sown and crops harvested – including 2,000 pumpkins grown for Halloween. They will also meet all sorts of domestic animals from rabbits and gerbils, which can be stroked and petted, to donkeys and horses and even llamas and alpacas. There are pony rides for the over threes, goat milking to watch, and animals to feed. If the weather turns, or you just feel like a change, there's a great indoor play area with a huge jumping pillow, a giant Astroglide, trampolines and play areas for the smallest ones. You can eat on site or just bring a picnic and, if you feel like spoiling yourselves, take a tractor-and-trailer ride around the farm and enjoy the views from a different perspective.

The farm is also the starting point for a delightful family cycle ride through Norbury Park. At 11km (7 mi), this is too far for very little ones, who will still be happily occupied at the farm, but for older children, accompanied by an adult, this is a lovely, well-signed route on decent tracks, roads and cycle ways that eventually brings you back to your starting point. *En route* you'll pass Druid's Grove, which contains yew trees mentioned in the Domesday Book and a teashop that is open at weekends.

WHERE:
Between Bookham and Leatherhead, Surrey
BEST TIME TO GO:
On a dry day
DON'T MISS:
The twice-daily pig races at Bocketts Farm
AMOUNT OF WALKING:
Moderate to lots
COST:
Reasonable, though it might seem a little steep for those who intend to spend only half the day there.
YOU SHOULD KNOW:
On a clear day, the London Eye is visible from Bocketts Farm.

Kids get the opportunity to meet baby animals at Bocketts Farm.

Boating and exploring the river at Guildford

WHERE:
Guildford, Surrey
BEST TIME TO GO:
You can hire rowing boats from the Guildford Boat House and visit Dapdune Wharf roughly speaking from Easter to October. Check their websites for exact dates. Choose a fine day to see the River Wey at its best.
DON'T MISS:
Looking round the restored buildings on Dapdune Wharf.
AMOUNT OF WALKING:
Moderate to lots – there are nearly 32 km (20 mi) of towpath to be walked.
COST:
Low to reasonable, depending on how many hours you rent the rowing boat.

Unlikely though it sounds, if you are longing to escape the rat race and take some quality time out with the children, you could find just what you're looking for in central Guildford. Guildford Boat House, located near Millmead Lock, will rent you a rowing boat for a few hours, enabling you to mess about on one of the prettiest stretches of river around. If you'd prefer just to sit back and do nothing, take a little cruise. Starting from the Boathouse, climb aboard a jolly-looking boat which has open sides and roll down, see-through curtains that will protect you from any change for the worse in the weather.

Made navigable in the 17th century, the River Wey links Guildford to Weybridge, which is on the Thames. Barges carrying heavy loads of wood, coal, corn and even gunpowder were thus able to travel back and forth to London and in 1764, when the Godalming Navigation opened, a few extra miles were added to the waterway.

Guildford boathouse and rowers on the River Wey

Looked after by the National Trust, the waterway and its banks are a wildlife haven, and a world away from the hustle and bustle of everyday life.

Dapdune Wharf is the centre of this unusual National Trust operation, and is really interesting to visit. Here you'll find out all about the history of Surrey's waterways thanks to an interactive exhibition. Explore a large, restored barge, enjoy a hands-on discovery room, and find out about the life and work of those who lived here. There are children's trails to explore, guided walks along the towpath – the entire length is open to walkers – and you can even take a 40-minute ride on an electric launch. A day spent on this stretch of river really perks you up.

YOU SHOULD KNOW:
Some of the land by the river is being reinstated to meadow and the sculptures in the sculpture park were carved from trees felled in the clearing process. There's also a wonderful sculpture adorning the height barrier at the entrance of the railway viaduct. Since 2004, offenders serving community orders have been clearing, coppicing and maintaining the towpath.

Campaign Paintball Park

The Campaign Paintball Park, which opened in 1987, is probably the largest paintball venue in the UK. Known throughout the paintballing world for hosting some of the major annual events, Campaign prides itself on introducing newcomers to the sport and, with this in mind, it puts on junior paintballing days every weekend, with extra dates added during the school holidays.

Developed as a game by three friends in the late 1970s, paintball – originally known as Survival – took off in the 1980s. Since then, many different games have been invented, but the most common involves two teams, each trying to capture their enemy's flag and bring it safely back to their own camp. Players are eliminated when they are hit by a paintball.

Campaign has ten different game zones, each purpose built, so your kids could find themselves in the Wild West, a cowboy town complete with saloon bar, blacksmith, bank and jail, or perhaps in the Jungle, D-Day or even the mysterious Dark Tower. They will be teamed up with other children and will play up to nine games during the course of the day.

You can drop them off at 09.30, safe in the knowledge that they'll be given a thrilling, action-packed day under the eagle-eyed supervision of the staff. They'll be kitted out with battle suits, goggles and body armour if they want it, and taught the rules of the game – including rules of safety. After being organized into teams and shown how to use the paintball guns, they will get some practice on a target range before starting their first game. In between times there are tea breaks and a decent lunch is provided. At the end of the day, you'll pick up grubby, tired, happy kids who've thoroughly enjoyed themselves.

WHERE:
Guildford, Surrey
BEST TIME TO GO:
It's more fun if the weather is good.
DON'T MISS:
The thrill of eliminating your enemies with splatters of paint and the satisfaction of achieving your goal.
AMOUNT OF WALKING:
Lots, though there may well be more running than walking during the day – expect plenty of action.
COST:
Reasonable, although the cost of extra paintballs is quite steep.
YOU SHOULD KNOW:
Safety is paramount, and all the games are supervised. Goggles must always be worn during games. Children have to be at least ten years old, although outdoor lazer game parties can be organized for those who are younger.

Godstone Farm

Godstone Farm and Playbarn is a terrific example of just how good a day out at a farm can be. Open all year round, except for Christmas Day and Boxing Day, this is a great place to visit with your under tens. Open from 10.00 until 18.00, there's so much to keep the kids occupied that you really can spend all day here quite happily and, unlike many places, the only 'extras' that you'll need to pay for are bags of animal feed so your children can hand feed some of the animals they meet, and fun tractor-and-trailer rides around the farm.

As you enter the farm you find yourself in a vast playground, full of fantastic equipment. There are swings and slides, a climbing wall, a zip wire, bouncy castles, climbing frames, an exciting water sledge ride and even a maze. Nearby are two giant sandpits, full of buckets, spades and other suitable toys, and the whole area is set among open, grassy spaces where the kids can happily run about. There's a café nearby that serves reasonably priced meals and snacks, and there are also plenty of picnic tables so you can establish a base camp where you will always be found, and where you can enjoy a picnic at lunchtime.

Of course, playing on great equipment is not the only thing to do at Godstone – you can visit the animals, too. Children may cuddle the lambs, stroke fluffy little chicks and rabbits, see ponies, goats and llamas, go on a nature trail or a marsh walk, and enjoy making something crafty like dough models or papier-mâché. If the weather turns, there's also an indoor play area that you can visit for a small extra fee.

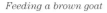
Feeding a brown goat

WHERE:
Godstone, Surrey
BEST TIME TO GO:
Springtime, when there are more baby animals to see.
DON'T MISS:
The toboggan run
AMOUNT OF WALKING:
As much as you want. But leave your buggy in the car if you can – some of the terrain isn't very buggy-friendly.
COST:
Low – they have an interesting pricing policy where adults get in for less than the children they bring with them.
YOU SHOULD KNOW:
Godstone Farm is easy to access by car, but much less so by public transport. The nearest station is at Caterham, and you'll need to check on bus routes and timetables to get you from there to Godstone village.

Dorking and the Surrey Hills

If you and your family enjoy old-fashioned pleasures and find walking in the beautiful British countryside a delight, then the next time you wake up to a sunny day, you should make your way to Dorking and the nearby Surrey Hills.

Dorking is an ancient market town and West Street, said to be the oldest street in town, is always fun to walk along – not only can you see historic buildings and the local museum, but also a wealth of antique shops, with windows like treasure chests. While you're in town, buy yourselves the makings of a picnic, plenty of bottled water and whatever else takes your fancy, and then get back in the car and drive to nearby Box Hill.

Looked after by the National Trust, Box Hill is a gorgeous area of woodland and downland, with many lovely walks to take and views to admire. Your kids might enjoy making a list of all the various trees, flowers and birds they see – even butterflies perhaps, since 40 of the 58 British species live here. At the summit you can pick up information about the hill and a quiz to play.

You could easily spend hours here, but you shouldn't miss Leith Hill. Situated to the southwest of Dorking, it boasts the highest summit in southeast England. Also belonging to the National Trust, Leith Hill has woodland, parkland, farmland and open heath, again with fabulous and extensive views. As at Box Hill, you can take a guided walk or, for a small fee, you can pick up a leaflet that gives you two circular trails to follow on your own. The summit here is crowned with a Gothic tower which you may climb and from which, on the clearest of clear days, you can see 13 counties.

WHERE:
Dorking, Surrey
BEST TIME TO GO:
On a sunny day between April and October
DON'T MISS:
The River Mole, below Box Hill. Look for kingfishers, mandarin ducks, and an established flock of parakeets that have made this their home.
AMOUNT OF WALKING:
Lots, some of it is quite steep, too, so wear appropriate shoes.
COST:
Low – there are parking fees but little else.
YOU SHOULD KNOW:
If you visit Box Hill in May and June you'll probably spot several types of orchid in flower, and for a small fee you can see a magnificent display of rhododendrons in flower at Leith Hill during the same months.

The Summit Tower on Leith Hill

Frensham Common

Back in the mists of time Frensham Common was covered by forest.
It was gradually cleared by Bronze Age farmers so that they could
grow their crops, but the soil proved to be too thin and poor. As the
farmers moved on, heather and other plants took over – changing it
into heathland. Today Frensham Common is a gorgeous, protected
area of heath and mixed woodland covering about 405 ha (1,000 acres).
This habitat supports many rare plants and creatures and it's a
marvellous place to spend the day.

There are a number of different things to do here, but assuming
you are all at your most energetic in the morning, you might start
with a walk. Make your way to the Information Centre near the Great
Pond and pick up a route map. There are four way-marked routes,
including one that is wheelchair-friendly, so you can choose
whichever suits you best.

There are two ponds here, one of which, the Great Pond, comes
as an enormous surprise if you've never visited before. It is used by
the Frensham Pond Sailing Club, which is simple to join and a great
amenity, and you may also swim in it. What a treat it is to discover a
sandy beach in the midst of the Surrey countryside, complete with
shallow water that makes for perfect swimming, and kids with
buckets and spades busily making sandcastles.

The Little Pond, owned and managed by the National Trust, was
formed in 1246 and provided fish for the Bishop of Winchester's court
when it visited Farnham Castle. Fringed with reeds, iris and sweet
flag you may see snipe, great crested grebes, reed buntings and
warblers as well as dragonflies and damselflies as you stroll around it.

*Recycled rubbish makes
apocalyptic horses.*

Chessington World of Adventures

Only 19 km (12 mi) outside London, Chessington is one of southern England's biggest and best theme parks. It has fewer teenage thrills than its nearest rival, Thorpe Park, with a more family-orientated atmosphere and loads of attractions for younger children. In other words, be prepared for precocious pre-teens to make sniffy remarks about it all being 'childish', though in fact there's lots here they'll secretly enjoy once they join in with younger siblings.

World of Adventures is split into nine themed zones with rides rated at one of four levels – mini, junior, family or experienced – so you can easily see what's age-appropriate. Tiny tots are incredibly well provided for, while the star rides for older kids are the three big switchbacks – Rattlesnake, Vampire and Dragon's Fury – and getting drenched on Rameses Revenge. And then there's Bubbleworks – an extraordinarily popular soap-and-water ride. Despite the fact that it's really a subliminal advert for Imperial Leather products, everyone smiles at the memory of it.

There is the bonus of a rather good zoo and huge Sealife aquarium. The zoo contains lions and tigers, leopards, a gorilla colony and a great collection of snakes and creepy-crawlies; and there's a children's zoo where the kids can fondle pygmy goats, miniature pigs and cute bunnies. In Sealife, there are 20 great displays, and you can walk through a wondrous viewing tank where sharks, stingrays and hundreds of other marine species swim around you.

At peak season you can spend frustrating hours (yes, literally hours!) queueing for rides, so you need to be canny, avoid going at obviously busy times, and even resort to forking out for a fast-track pass. Despite provisos, if you want a special family day out with entertainment laid on and blow the expense, then Chessington is probably the answer.

Flying Jumbo's Ride

WHERE:
Chessington, Surrey
BEST TIME TO GO:
World of Adventures is open from late March to the beginning of November. Go on a weekday in term time for the fewest crowds. (The zoo is open out of season – check website for days and times.)
DON'T MISS:
Safari Skyway – an elevated monorail train that gives a brilliant bird's eye view over the theme park and zoo. The pygmy marmoset monkeys in the zoo – unbelievably adorable, if you manage to spot them.
AMOUNT OF WALKING:
Lots, with generally good disabled access.
COST:
Expensive. Every conceivable extra costs money, down to the charge made for the park map (so make sure you download one from the Internet). Food outlets are particularly pricey so come with your own provisions if you don't want to feel ripped off. Look out for the special offers and family deals that are frequently advertised, which will help lower the price.
YOU SHOULD KNOW:
If you want to make a proper holiday of your visit here, the safari-themed Holiday Inn hotel on the Chessington site offers special family packages and has views over the zoo.

57

Thorpe Park

If you and your kids are adrenaline junkies, you need look no further than Thorpe Park to provide you with a full-on day of thrills. The rollercoaster rides that are on offer here are some of the highest, fastest and most exciting that you can find anywhere, and as such are probably best suited to older children and teenagers.

Thorpe Park consists of six themed areas, each containing a number of different attractions, including roller coasters and water rides. Amity Cove, for example, is themed as a New England fishing village threatened by a tsunami. One of the rides within this area is the Tidal Wave, which carries you up high into the air and then shoots you down into the water below. This is great fun on a hot day, but be warned: you'll all get soaked. Each of the other areas, Canada Creek, Calypso Quay, Lost City, Neptune's Kingdom and Ranger County have their own, themed rides.

It's a good idea to arrive as soon after opening time as possible, partly because there's so much to do, and partly because the queues for the most-popular rides get longer as the day goes on. Some of the biggest rides – with names like Slammer, Detonator and Colossus you can guess how heart-stopping they are – are classified as 'extreme thrills', but there are other, less scary attractions that are either 'thrilling and fun' or for 'young thrill seekers'.

Minimum height restrictions apply to most of the rides, some are not recommended for the under 12s, and some need an accompanying adult. Thorpe Park is constantly adding new attractions to satisfy demanding young thrill seekers.

WHERE:
Near Chertsey, Surrey
BEST TIME TO GO:
On a warm, sunny day – especially if you like water rides.
DON'T MISS:
Colossus – this is the UK's only quadruple corkscrew, and it's an extraordinary, white-knuckle, hair-raising experience. Families should also try the Pirates 4D – a 4-D cinema experience that is good fun for adults and children alike.
AMOUNT OF WALKING:
Moderate. Thorpe Park is accessible to wheelchair users, but some of the rides are unsuitable.

Stealth – Europe's fastest rollercoaster!

COST:
Expensive. You should look online to see if there are any special offers. And although there are plenty of opportunities for buying refreshments, you might prefer to take your own.
YOU SHOULD KNOW:
If you can see that the queue ahead of you is tremendously long, you can always decide to pay extra and be fast tracked. Although this will make an even bigger dent in your pocket, you will at least be making the most of the day.

Hollycombe Steam Collection and the Mid Hants Railway

The romance of steam is evoked in this splendid day out in the middle of Hampshire. Steam power may be a thing of the past but partly thanks to the enduring popularity of Thomas the Tank Engine and friends it still exerts a strong hold over younger imaginations. The Steam Collection at Hollycombe, on the eastern fringe of the county, showcases the many applications of steam power. Thus you can take rides on both a miniature railway and a narrow-gauge railway drawn by steam locomotives once used in the slate mines of Wales. Hollycombe maintains a large collection of steamrollers, traction engines and steam-driven farming machinery, such as tractors, threshers and ploughing engines; if you are lucky you may see some being put through their paces.

If younger appetites have not been fired up by any of these, then they surely will be by Hollycombe's other main attraction – a traditional Edwardian fairground that is still powered by authentic showman's engines. Here you can experience the precursors of today's standard fairground rides – the Steam Yacht (Pirate Ship), Golden Gallopers (Carousel), Big Wheel and Razzle Dazzle, 100 years old and regarded as the world's first 'white-knuckle' ride.

A short drive west brings you to the Mid Hants Railway, a privately run service connecting the market towns of Alresford and Alton. Its nickname – the Watercress Line – reflects its origins in the mid 19th century when it would carry locally picked watercress to the markets of London and Southampton. Nowadays, having been reopened after its commercial closure in 1973, the line operates for pleasure purposes only. Six trains daily run in each direction, hauled mostly by steam engines. You can board at either end and there are two intermediate stations; an all-day ticket gives you 'freedom of the line'.

WHERE:
Near Liphook and near Alton, Hampshire
BEST TIME TO GO:
May to September (but note that Hollycombe is normally open only at weekends, except in August, and that both attractions are closed on Mondays, other than Bank Holidays).
DON'T MISS:
The Emperor at Hollycombe, the oldest surviving showman's engine in the world, built in 1895 and still powering fairground machinery.
AMOUNT OF WALKING:
Moderate (wheelchair access for the Watercress Line is best at Alresford station).
COST:
Expensive (children over two years old are charged on the Mid Hants Railway and over threes are charged at Hollycombe).
YOU SHOULD KNOW:
The steep gradients on the Watercress Line account for the surprisingly large locomotives you will see and for the local saying that the line runs 'over the Alps'!

A Thomas the Tank Engine event at the Watercress Line, Alton

Paultons Park

Paultons theme park occupies a site on the edge of the New Forest that was once a large country estate. Paultons has always billed itself as a family theme park and does not attempt to compete with the bigger parks and their white-knuckle experiences. Its primary appeal may be to younger children and their families, but what an appeal it is! With over 50 rides and attractions covered by the single admission price this is a great day out for the whole family. And Mum and Dad have the added reassurance that there aren't too many stomach-churners they have to subject themselves to for the children's sake!

Even young teenagers should be impressed by the Cobra, the park's largest and longest rollercoaster, and the Edge, Paultons' newest ride, in which you join 40 others to be strapped to a giant spinning disc that travels along a camel-back track at 69 kph (43 mph). Water rides include a log flume and a giant water slide, which you travel down in a rubber dinghy. But it is with the attractions for smaller ones that Paultons Park really comes into its own. They can drive their own diggers and tractors, enjoy the Rabbit and Ladybird rides and take a trip on a miniature railway. Some of the bigger rides, such as the vertical drop, have scaled-down versions for the younger ones; and Paultons may be the place where your children decide they are brave enough for their first rollercoaster and ride the Flying Frog!

Staff here take particular pride in the gardens, which are a visual treat throughout the season and provide a home for an interesting collection of exotic birds and animals such as African meerkats and red-necked wallabies.

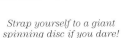

Strap yourself to a giant spinning disc if you dare!

WHERE:
Near Romsey, Hampshire
BEST TIME TO GO:
March to October
DON'T MISS:
The Floating Globe in the entrance area – 3.5 tonnes of solid granite, which you can move with the touch of a finger!
AMOUNT OF WALKING:
Moderate
COST:
Expensive. There is a small discount if you buy your tickets online, and children under 1 m (3 ft 3 in) go free.
YOU SHOULD KNOW:
You might want to bring swimwear and towels so the kids can check out the many different ways of getting a soaking in the Water Kingdom.

Fort Nelson and Winchester

Portsdown Hill is a high chalk ridge running parallel to the coast above Portsmouth and commanding spectacular views over the city and the Solent. Fort Nelson was constructed on this strategically important site in the 1860s and is still a massively imposing presence. Children will enjoy exploring the network of tunnels which enabled the garrison to reach the various parts of the fort under cover. Now part of the Royal Armouries (the national collection of arms and armour), Fort Nelson focuses on artillery: more than 350 big guns and cannon tell the story of ordnance down the ages, from rare examples of Tudor artillery to the present day. On most days there are firings as well as demonstrations of forging and casting techniques.

The county town of Winchester was once capital of the ancient kingdom of Wessex, whose most famous ruler was Alfred the Great. You can still see the foundations of Alfred's great church beside the present Norman cathedral, whose many treasures include the Winchester Bible, a priceless 12th-century illuminated manuscript thought to have been the work of a single scribe. A free trail helps children locate some of the building's more unusual features, such as the fine carvings of owls and monkeys on the choir stalls; the skeletal effigy on Bishop Fox's tomb; and the small statue commemorating the diver William Walker whose heroic efforts helped secure the cathedral's foundations.

Close to the city's West Gate, the 13th-century Great Hall is the only surviving part of the Norman Castle. On one end wall of the impressive interior hangs the renowned Round Table. Supposedly the original table that King Arthur and his 24 knights sat around, the 5.5-m (18-ft) diameter board is in fact a 14th-century creation, and the decoration you see today was commissioned by Henry VIII.

WHERE:
Near Fareham and Winchester, Hampshire
BEST TIME TO GO:
Any time of year
DON'T MISS:
Saddam Hussein's notorious 'Supergun' is one of the exhibits at Fort Nelson.
AMOUNT OF WALKING:
Moderate
COST:
Low (Winchester Cathedral has an entrance charge but it is free to children under 16 visiting with their family).
YOU SHOULD KNOW:
The Great Hall is sometimes closed for civic occasions and special events, so it is advisable to check in advance if you are planning a visit.

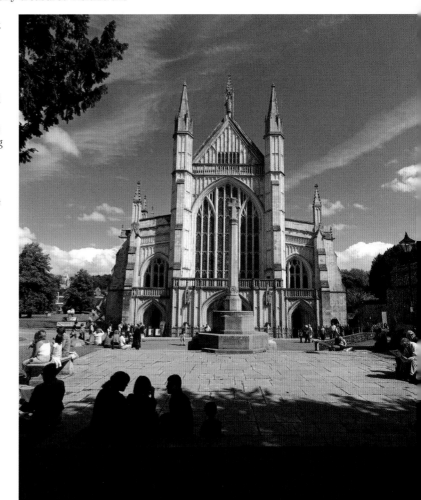

Winchester Cathedral on a summer's evening

Intech Science Centre and Planetarium

Taking the road east from Winchester towards Alton and Petersfield, you might be forgiven for thinking that aliens have already landed as you drive past Morn Hill, site of the Intech Science Centre. The striking white pyramid-shaped building houses about 100 interactive exhibits which have been designed to explain and illustrate basic principles of science and technology, and how these principles have found practical applications in the home, in commerce and in industry. Intech was originally conceived as an educational resource to support the curriculum work of Hampshire schools and colleges, but there is plenty here to interest and stimulate all ages, especially older minds whose science memories may be a little rusty. At Intech you can try your hand at designing a bridge, find out how to bend light, work out how much energy it takes to power a light bulb; you can even create your own tornado.

The adjacent spherical building is home to the Planetarium, Intech's newest attraction and the largest of its kind in the country. Using state-of-the-art digital technology, the Planetarium presents a changing programme of pre-recorded film shows and occasional live events with a presenter. As you relax in your reclining seat, it is easy to imagine yourself in other worlds as you gaze up at the enormous tilted screen on the dome. Kids will enjoy immersing themselves in the life of an astronaut in space, investigating those mysterious black holes, taking a journey through the cosmos, or simply finding out what's in the real-time sky above them.

Intech Planetarium, Winchester

Hayling Island

The Islander local special train service at Hayling Island beach

Hayling is a low-lying island near Portsmouth which divides Langstone Harbour to the west from Chichester Harbour to the east. In a coastline of mudflats, tidal creeks and saltmarshes the south shore of Hayling Island is a welcome exception, comprising an 8-km (5-mi) stretch of beach. Although mainly a shingle beach (sand is only exposed at low tide), Hayling is still a popular destination for families, thanks to the broad areas of grass flanking the beaches and a large sand bar. This extends into the Solent and acts as a breakwater to create gentle, safe swimming that is perfect for younger children. The beaches are clean and the islanders pride themselves on having two prestigious Blue Flags.

The conditions that make Hayling's beaches so good for younger bathers may make them less well suited for surfboarding. But the relatively sheltered waters, coupled with fairly constant sea breezes, make them ideal for windsurfing. Indeed, Hayling Island is credited with being the birthplace of the sport. This is as good a place as any for the adults and older children to have an introductory lesson. Or for something even more exhilarating, you might try your luck at kite surfing – the latest craze to hit the world of water sports.

If the family prefers solid earth beneath their feet, the seafront offers plenty of diversions. There are adventure playgrounds, designated areas for beach volleyball (bring your own ball!), public barbecue sites, a skate park and a BMX track. The Funland Amusement Park at Beachlands is a traditional fun fair with pay-as-you-go rides, including three rollercoasters and a range of indoor as well as outdoor amusements. Linking all the attractions is a delightful little narrow-gauge railway, which runs for 3 km (2 mi) along the seafront.

WHERE:
Near Portsmouth, Hampshire
BEST TIME TO GO:
May to September
DON'T MISS:
The exhilarating sight of kite surfers being lifted high into the air as they ride the waves.
AMOUNT OF WALKING:
Moderate (boardwalks provide good access for pushchairs and wheelchairs over the shingle banks).
COST:
Reasonable
YOU SHOULD KNOW:
The single road bridge connecting Hayling Island to the mainland can get very busy in the summer. An attractive alternative is to take the short ferry ride from Eastney across the mouth of Langstone Harbour (passengers only, though you can take a bicycle).

Fire torpedoes!

Royal Navy Submarine Museum and 1642 Living History Village

The life of a submariner, cooped up for days on end in a metal box hundreds of feet beneath the sea, is not easy to imagine, but the Royal Navy does an excellent job of helping the visitor appreciate its special character at its Submarine Museum in Gosport. The story of underwater warfare is told through various displays but the real excitement comes with going on board a genuine submarine – in this case, HMS *Alliance*, built at the end of World War II and the country's only surviving submarine from that era. Former serving sailors act as your guides on a tour of this self-contained world, so experts are on hand to answer questions about life in such cramped conditions.

The museum's other star exhibits include the Royal Navy's first submarine, launched in 1901 and known as the *Holland 1* after its designer; midget submarines used so effectively by both sides in World War II; and a more recent deep-sea submersible used in survey and repair work. An interactive zone gives the family a chance to command their own submarine or investigate the secrets of the deep.

In a nondescript suburb of Gosport you will come across the far-from-ordinary village of Little Woodham, where local enthusiasts have re-created as authentically as possible the living conditions of a 17th-century community in rural England. The site features buildings such as a blacksmith's forge, weaver's cottage and ale house, each constructed using materials and methods from the period. The village is 'frozen' in the year 1642, a time of growing unrest in the countryside that was to lead to civil war. The 'villagers' will happily chat to you about their lives and you can watch them engaged in activities such as turning wood, spinning wool and making charcoal.

WHERE:
Gosport, Hampshire
BEST TIME TO GO:
April to October (but note that the Living History Village has irregular opening times, so you are advised to check in advance).
DON'T MISS:
The section at the Submarine Museum devoted to torpedoes, still one of the most lethal and formidable weapons ever invented.
AMOUNT OF WALKING:
Little
COST:
Reasonable
YOU SHOULD KNOW:
The adoption of the pirates' traditional symbol of the Jolly Roger as the ensign of the Navy's Submarine Service arose out of the stiff resistance from the military establishment in the early 20th century to the submarine's introduction into naval warfare.

HMS Alliance *at the Royal Navy Submarine Museum*

Milestones and Basingstoke Canal

Old fire engine and shops at Milestones Living History Museum

Basingstoke's Milestones is very much a museum for the 21st century. Describing itself as a 'living history museum', it is anything but a collection of dry artefacts arranged neatly in glass cabinets. True, there are plenty of objects on display – over 20,000 of them – but all serve the museum's purpose of bringing the past to life for modern viewers. Milestones is Hampshire's premier museum of social history, providing an enthralling record of the working people of the county. Here you can walk down a Victorian street and another from the 1930s, seeing how shops and homes used to look. Characters dressed in period costume are on hand to tell stories about their lives. Children will find lots to amuse them: trails, activity boxes, Victorian clothes to try on, even a 1940s sweet shop where they can buy sweets with old pennies. A play post office caters especially for the under fives, while older members may welcome the refreshment on tap in the working pub!

The Basingstoke Canal opened at the close of the 18th century as a means of boosting trade between Hampshire and London. It took 200 men just six years to carve out the 59 km (37 mi) of waterway linking Basingstoke with Weybridge to the northeast. The canal was never a commercial success and soon lost out to the more efficient railway with the opening of the Southampton to London line. Rescued from total dereliction in the 1970s, the canal is once again navigable for most of its original length – only an 8-km (5-mi) stretch east of Basingstoke has been lost. Take a trip on a typical narrowboat from Odiham or the Visitor Centre at Mytchett; or if you fancy negotiating some of the 29 locks on the canal, hire your own boat for the day.

WHERE:
Basingstoke, Hampshire
BEST TIME TO GO:
April to September (note that Milestones is closed on Mondays, except for Bank Holidays).
DON'T MISS:
The chance to choose and listen to favourite tunes from yesteryear in the gramophone shop at Milestones.
AMOUNT OF WALKING:
Moderate (although this could be lots if you decide to walk along some of the canal towpath).
COST:
Reasonable
YOU SHOULD KNOW:
The Greywell Tunnel, which once formed part of the canal west of Odiham, is now closed to prevent disturbance to an important colony of bats.

The Hawk Conservancy and Charlton Lakes

WHERE:
Weyhill and Charlton, near Andover, Hampshire
BEST TIME TO GO:
March to October
DON'T MISS:
The two great bustards in their new aviary at the Hawk Conservancy. Famously shy and once native to this country, the great bustard is the world's heaviest flying bird.
AMOUNT OF WALKING:
Little
COST:
Reasonable
YOU SHOULD KNOW:
The great bustards are part of a programme to reintroduce the magnificent bird to the skies over Salisbury Plain.

The sight of a majestic bird of prey soaring towards you, and the sensation of its beating wings passing overhead are among the most thrilling experiences the natural world has to offer. Both can be enjoyed at the Hawk Conservancy outside Andover when many of their raptors are put through their paces and demonstrate their flying prowess. There are three different displays daily, each featuring different birds in the 150-strong collection, including hawks, owls and kestrels. The most spectacular is unquestionably the Valley of the Eagles display where the larger birds – eagles, kites and vultures – leave you in no doubt who is in charge in the skies. Those brave enough may hold a bird of prey on their hand, and Mum and Dad can try to impress the family by flying a Harris hawk.

Like many nature organizations nowadays, the Hawk Conservancy successfully combines the entertainment function of a major income-generating visitor attraction with its role as a serious conservation charity. Research, rehabilitation and breeding programmes are all key elements of the Conservancy's work. During your visit make sure that you look inside the site hospital, which each year treats some 200 injured birds of prey.

After the excitement of close contact with these formidable predators, unwind with a round of pitch-and-putt golf at the nearby Charlton Lakes. The children will certainly appreciate the 18-hole crazy-golf course at this outdoor sports-and-leisure centre on the outskirts of Andover. There is also a playground, BMX track and pedaloes for hire on the lake.

Ferruginous hawk

Royal Victoria Country Park

The Royal Victoria Country Park occupies a beautiful position on the shores of Southampton Water. As you soak up the peace and tranquillity of its fields and woods, it is hard to imagine that the country's largest military hospital once stood here. Conveniently located for troop ships returning to Southampton from throughout the British Empire, the Royal Victoria Hospital (from which the park takes its name) was built in the aftermath of the Crimean War, receiving its first patients in 1863. The main block was nearly 0.5 km (0.3 mi) long and at its busiest during World War I, providing some 2,000 beds. The hospital treated tens of thousands of wounded soldiers from both world wars but closed in the late 1950s. The main building was demolished in 1966, except for the chapel and its distinctive tower, which was retained as a memorial and now houses an exhibition telling the hospital's story.

Dozens of paths and trails enable you to explore the woods and parklands of this 81-ha (200-acre) site, but the family will undoubtedly clamour for a ride on the narrow-gauge miniature railway that makes a scenic loop around the central area. Drawn by a mixture of steam and Diesel locomotives, the railway forms a delightful introduction to the park as the 1.6-km (1-mi) circuit winds its way through its varying landscapes. Many of the unfamiliar trees and shrubs were brought here in the 19th century from various parts of the Empire.

The park is well provided with facilities, including a playground, tearoom and barbecue sites, but perhaps the most pleasurable activity is pottering about on the shingle foreshore and enjoying the grandstand view of the endless parade of ships, from simple yachts to cruise ships and tankers, passing along Southampton Water.

WHERE:
Netley Abbey, near Southampton, Hampshire
BEST TIME TO GO:
Any time of year (but note that the railway runs only at weekends and during school holidays).
DON'T MISS:
The view over Southampton Water from the site where a pier once stood to receive the hospital ships.
AMOUNT OF WALKING:
Moderate (the park offers good disabled access and facilities, including a sensory garden).
COST:
Low
YOU SHOULD KNOW:
Florence Nightingale was unimpressed by the designs for the original hospital but even her formidable powers of persuasion proved unsuccessful in getting them modified.

Royal Victoria Country Park

Butser Ancient Farm and Queen Elizabeth Country Park

For the past 30 years a group of archaeologists and ancient historians has been conducting a remarkable experiment on the downs south of Petersfield. At Butser they have reconstructed a working farm from the Iron Age using evidence gained from excavations at ancient sites. By re-creating as closely as possible the conditions in which our ancestors lived and worked the land, the experts try to learn more about agricultural and domestic techniques of the time.

This open-air research laboratory is open to the public and it's a great place for bringing the distant past to life for young people. Inside a fenced compound stand a number of farm buildings, including a substantial round house, built of wood, clay and thatch, which would have been home to the farmer and his family. The farm animals at the site include small Soay sheep and horned Manx sheep, both closely related to the ancient breeds found in 300 BC. Similarly, the crops under cultivation are authentic varieties of wheat, such as emmer and spelt. And you may be lucky enough on your visit to catch a demonstration of pottery making or weaving on a handloom.

Butser Farm lies just outside the Queen Elizabeth Country Park, Hampshire's largest, covering 570 ha (1,400 acres) of glorious chalk grassland and woodland on the South Downs. The park has miles of well-marked trails for walking, cycling and horse riding. Even if you are not feeling energetic enough for a long hike, the climb up to Butser Hill, the highest point on the South Downs, is amply rewarded by superb views which can extend on a clear day as far as Salisbury and the spire of its cathedral 65 km (40 mi) away.

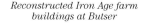
Reconstructed Iron Age farm buildings at Butser

WHERE:
Near Petersfield, Hampshire
BEST TIME TO GO:
April to September (note that Butser Ancient Farm is not open at weekends, other than for special events).
DON'T MISS:
The reconstructed Roman villa at Butser, complete with its underfloor heating system.
AMOUNT OF WALKING:
Moderate (or lots depending on how much of the Queen Elizabeth Country Park you choose to explore).
COST:
Low
YOU SHOULD KNOW:
Near the park's visitor centre a play trail for the under eights features wooden play equipment specially designed on animal themes by a local sculptor.

Portsmouth Dockyard and Spinnaker Tower

The historic home of Britain's navy, Portsmouth exudes the sea from every salty pore. The city has been the country's principal naval base for over 500 years, a heritage comprehensively explored in the Historic Dockyard. The dockyard is home to an array of maritime attractions, including three great ships from different eras of the seafaring past. The oldest, Henry VIII's favourite warship the *Mary Rose*, sank in the Solent in 1545 and its hull was famously raised from the seabed in 1982. Although it is not on public view until the museum being built around it is finished (scheduled to open in 2012), you can still visit the current museum. The many hundreds of artefacts retrieved from the wreck present a fascinating insight into life on board a Tudor fighting ship.

The Georgian era is represented by HMS *Victory*, one of the world's most famous ships, forever associated with Admiral Lord Nelson and his great victory at Trafalgar. A tour of this wonderfully preserved sailing vessel is an atmospheric experience, and knowledgeable guides help to recapture what life was like for the 800-strong crew. Built in 1860, the mighty HMS *Warrior* completes the trio; this was the world's first ironclad, steam-powered battleship. Your ticket also includes the Royal Naval Museum, a harbour tour, and children won't want to miss the excitement of Action Stations which showcases the modern Royal Navy in a series of interactive features and physical challenges.

Although there is more than enough to fill your day at the Historic Dockyard, you might like to start it with an overview from the top of the Spinnaker Tower, Portsmouth's stunning new 170-m (558-ft) high landmark which offers unrivalled 360-degree views of the coast and surrounding countryside.

WHERE:
Portsmouth, Hampshire
BEST TIME TO GO:
Any time of year
DON'T MISS:
The spot on the deck of HMS *Victory* where Nelson breathed his last, struck down by an enemy bullet.
AMOUNT OF WALKING:
Moderate
COST:
Expensive (but note that the all-inclusive ticket for the Historic Dockyard is valid for one year, so you do not have to visit all the attractions in a single day).
YOU SHOULD KNOW:
Although no longer a sea-going vessel, HMS *Victory* remains the flagship of the Commander-in-Chief Naval Home Command, making it the world's oldest ship of the line.

HMS Warrior *at Portsmouth dockyard*

Needles Cruise and Hurst Castle

WHERE:
Near Alum Bay, Isle of Wight
BEST TIME TO GO:
April to October
DON'T MISS:
The chance to hear how the extraordinary rocks of the Needles were formed.
AMOUNT OF WALKING:
Little (moderate if you visit Hurst Castle or if you walk out to the Needles' headland).
COST:
Reasonable
YOU SHOULD KNOW:
If you are looking for greater excitement you can do the same trip in a high-speed RIB.

The Needles are the Isle of Wight's best-known landmark and one of the enduring images of the UK's coastline. Lying at the extreme western tip of the island, these three chalk stacks rise like a line of jagged teeth out of the sea. In fact they are a continuation of its chalk downs, and if you are on the island you can walk out to the headland from either Alum Bay or Freshwater Bay to see the rocks. For the best views of the Needles and their lighthouse, however, you need to take a boat trip. The cruises that leave Alum Bay during the summer months also pass close to the famous coloured sands of Alum Bay and enable you to see the impact of coastal erosion on the 122-m (400-ft) high chalk cliffs. The live on-board commentary will draw your attention to any sea birds of note: guillemots, terns, gannets and cormorants may all be seen on this trip.

You can make this excursion from the mainland as well, with two-hour round-trip cruises that set off from Lymington on the Hampshire coast. Both cruises give you good views of Hurst Castle, strategically sited on a long shingle spit to guard the narrow western entrance to the Solent. Hurst Castle was one of the most advanced of the artillery fortresses built by Henry VIII towards the end of his reign, and it remained in use until the 20th century. Boat trips do not land at Hurst Castle so if you want to explore the fort properly you have a choice between a 2.4-km (1.5-mi) walk along the shingle spit from Milford-on-Sea, or else the ferry from Keyhaven (both on the mainland).

Hurst Beach, Hurst Spit, on the Solent

Amazon World and Arreton Barns Craft Village

It was one man's concern for the plight of the rainforest following a visit to the Amazon Basin that led to the establishment of the Amazon World Zoo Park. Even though this collection of some 200 different species of exotic animals and birds serves a serious conservation purpose (the zoo is an active participant in a number of international breeding programmes), its residents still manage to provide plenty of entertainment; who could resist a smile at the meerkats, for example, with their quizzical stare and bolt-upright posture? A series of scrupulously re-created rainforest habitats, complete with rivers, waterfalls and pools (beware the piranhas!) provide authentic settings for many of nature's more elusive and sometimes endangered creatures, including ocelots, lemurs, sloths, tapirs and the rare tamandua, a South American anteater that lives in the trees. As always the primates tend to steal the show; here they range from the tiny pygmy marmoset, the world's smallest monkey, to the aptly named black howler monkey, such a distinctive feature of the Amazon soundscape.

For a true Isle of Wight experience, leave your car on the mainland and take the high-speed catamaran ferry from Portsmouth to Ryde (20 minutes), and then catch one of the regular island buses to Arreton. Not far from Amazon World is Arreton Barns Craft Village, a collection of traditional buildings housing craft workshops and grouped around a 12th-century church and an ancient carp pond mentioned in the Domesday Book. Here you can see woodworkers, potters and glassblowers at work and browse through the shops that sell their wares. The site also has a small maritime museum featuring artefacts retrieved from the many shipwrecks that litter the seabed around the island.

WHERE:
Arreton, Isle of Wight
BEST TIME TO GO:
Any time of year (but note that the Maritime Museum is open only from April to October).
DON'T MISS:
The regular 'meet the animals' talks given by the keepers at Amazon World are a great opportunity to get a fuller picture of individual species.
AMOUNT OF WALKING:
Little
COST:
Reasonable
YOU SHOULD KNOW:
The black howler monkey uses its tail like an extra limb to help with climbing and balancing.

Maritime Museum, Arreton Barns

Isle of Wight Steam Railway and Butterfly World

WHERE:
Near Ryde, Isle of Wight
BEST TIME TO GO:
April to October
DON'T MISS:
The water tower alongside the 'up' platform at Havenstreet, where engines returning to Smallbrook Junction take on fresh supplies.
AMOUNT OF WALKING:
Little

It may be hard to believe nowadays but the Isle of Wight was once covered by an extensive network of railways. In its heyday at the start of the 20th century there were 86 km (54 mi) of track, but by the mid 1960s everything was gone save for the line between Ryde and Shanklin. Leave the train at Smallbrook Junction just outside Ryde to change on to the Isle of Wight Steam Railway, a private line running for 8 km (5 mi) westwards to Wootton. Vintage steam locomotives pull beautifully restored Victorian and Edwardian carriages on a 20-minute journey through the countryside. Your ticket gives you the freedom of the line for the day, so you can alight at any of its three stations. Havenstreet houses the railway's headquarters, where you can find a play area, woodland walk and a museum devoted to the island's rail history. A viewing gallery allows you to watch restoration under way in the carriage and wagon workshop.

You should return to Ryde or to Havenstreet in order to visit

Steam train at Wootton Station

Butterfly and Fountain World. Midway between Wootton and Newport, this attraction is entirely under cover, making it a good outing for a wet day. A large butterfly house offers the dazzling spectacle of tropical butterflies flying free, and there are colourful versions of an Italian and a Japanese garden. You may be lucky enough to see the world's largest moth, which has a wing span of 27 cm (10.6 in) but lives a mere ten days. Children have particular fun running the gauntlet of the Jumping Jets, a synchronized display of fountains and water jets which creates an overhead water arch – though you need to keep your wits about you to avoid a soaking!

COST:
Reasonable (if you are travelling from the mainland without a car, you can buy through tickets from the ferry office at Portsmouth Harbour which include unlimited travel on the Island line and on the steam railway).
YOU SHOULD KNOW:
The electrified Island line between Ryde and Shanklin uses old London Underground trains, brought over 40 years ago and still going strong.

The Living Rainforest

The British countryside holds no end of unusual delights, but few can be as surprising as coming across a swathe of tropical rainforest tucked away in the rolling hills of West Berkshire. The Living Rainforest is a meticulously researched re-creation of one of the planet's most important and diverse ecosystems. The whole thing is under cover, and well-marked trails mean that you can wander through the lush vegetation and get close to animals and birds that are allowed to roam freely. The aim is to present as natural an environment as possible; you may not know precisely what you are going to see on your visit, but the pay-off is the thrill of spotting an elusive fowl foraging on the forest floor or an exotic butterfly hiding in a plant.

The Living Rainforest dedicates itself to informing about the threats to the rainforest and other ecosystems, as well as to promoting new practices in sustainable development. This is a particularly good place to learn about human impact on the natural world and what people are doing to reduce that impact. Combating the illegal pet trade is one example, and the centre is home to a number of exotic animals confiscated by customs authorities, including geckos, chameleons, tortoises and frogs.

The rainforest may be a luxuriant habitat but competition for food and nutrients is intense and many of the jungle's more fearsome predators are on show here. Red-bellied piranhas and dwarf crocodiles hunt in the rivers and pools, while bird-eating spiders and giant millipedes lurk in the undergrowth. Even the plants can be deadly; look out for the carnivorous pitcher plant and the dumb cane, which in spite of the toxic chemicals contained in its leaves, is a popular houseplant.

WHERE:
Hampstead Norreys, near Newbury, Berkshire
BEST TIME TO GO:
Any time of year
DON'T MISS:
The giant leaves of the Amazon water lily which float on the pond during the summer months and can measure 2.5 m (8 ft) across.
AMOUNT OF WALKING:
Little
COST:
Reasonable
YOU SHOULD KNOW:
During holiday periods the centre offers a full programme of talks and workshops aimed at the whole family.

The Look Out Discovery Centre

You can mix fun with learning at this imaginative science centre. With more than 90 interactive exhibits, the centre enables children to enjoy the excitement of experimentation and finding things out for themselves, while adults get the chance to indulge the boffin inside. Activities are arranged in five themed zones. The sound and communication zone offers plenty of scope for devising your own sounds, whether on an electronic drum kit or by jumping around on a giant keyboard. In the force and movement section you can work out how to launch a hydrogen rocket and help get a hot-air balloon off the ground. The other zones are devoted to light and colour, woodland and water, and body and perception; in the latter there are opportunities to test your physical and mental reactions in various challenges and brainteasers.

The Look Out has something to interest every age, including the very youngest; toddlers have a great time in the play supermarket and messing around with boats in the 'stream'. Outside there is a specially designed play trail for three to six year olds, while the large adventure play area for older children boasts a handsome fort as its centrepiece. The centre is surrounded by 1,000 ha (2,470 acres) of woodland which offer a range of walks and cycle trails and the Look Out has mountain bikes for hire as an aid to exploration.

At weekends and during school holidays the Look Out presents special shows aimed at entertaining as well as informing on various facets of science; topics covered might include the brain, dinosaurs and being 'green'.

Children enjoying the interactive exhibits.

Beale Park

Beale Park boasts a lovely riverside setting on the Thames upstream from Reading. The 142 ha (350 acres) of parkland contain a wildlife park, three ornamental lakes, gardens and an extensive deer park. The wildlife collection concentrates on more unusual species such as the mara and capybara, two large rodents from South America, and delicate little marmoset and tamarin monkeys. Lemurs, raccoons and mongoose also make their home here; larger animals on show include the alpaca and the pygmy goat.

Beale Park is best known, however, for its bird collection and enjoys an international reputation for its conservation work and participation in captive-breeding programmes. Endangered species you can see here include the extremely rare Bali starling with its striking snow-white plumage and blue flash around the eyes. The caracara is a hawk-like scavenger native to Argentina and the Falkland Islands, and other birds from the southern hemisphere include the kookaburra and the flightless rhea, the largest in South America. Many of the birds can be viewed in a walk-through aviary, while others like the snowy and great grey owls have their own sizeable enclosures.

A narrow-gauge railway takes you on a ten-minute journey around the park where you should be able to spot the three species of deer. A good adventure play area has lots of ropes and webs for older children to clamber over, while under fives are well catered for too, with a play village, pets area, paddling pools and sandpit. On most days you will see local enthusiasts operating their model boats on the lakes. If you fancy being on the water yourself, short cruises on the Thames are available from the riverbank.

WHERE:
Basildon, near Reading, Berkshire
BEST TIME TO GO:
March to October
DON'T MISS:
The unusual sculptures dotted around the park, including a warrior on a charging horse, a monkey band and a very large crocodile.
AMOUNT OF WALKING:
Moderate
COST:
Reasonable (but note that the single admission price does not include the river cruise).
YOU SHOULD KNOW:
The park's founder, Gilbert Beale, had a passion for peacocks – by the time of his death at the age of 99 there were more than 300 on the site!

Beale Park children's swimming pool and play park

View of Cliveden from the garden

Cliveden Estate

Cliveden is a grand mansion surrounded by a large estate that once belonged to the 'fabulous Astors', the politician and newspaper magnate Waldorf Astor and his wife Nancy. The beautiful setting overlooking the river Thames is a haven of peace and tranquillity today but the gardens and terraces once echoed to the sounds of high society making merry. The parties that the Astors threw here in the early part of the last century were legendary for their extravagance and the calibre of their guest lists. Something of that atmosphere still remains as you wander through a series of formal gardens and admire the opulence of their plantings and the fine statuary. Now in the care of the National Trust, these stunning creations are no longer the preserve of the rich and famous but are there for all to see.

Cliveden's riverside setting and extensive woodlands provide plenty of walks and good spots for picnics. Children are encouraged to get into the spirit of the place not only with their own published guide to the property but also with a garden explorer pack; available on free loan from reception, this is a back pack filled with activity sheets and ideas for investigating the grounds. There is even a bow tie and a tiara, so two of you can dress as Lord and Lady Astor! If the splendid river views prove irresistible you can take a 40-minute round-trip cruise on the Thames or hire your own rowing boat (Thursdays and weekends only).

The house itself, built in a flamboyant Italianate style, is now a luxury hotel but parts of it are open to the public on certain days during the season.

WHERE:
Near Maidenhead, Berkshire
BEST TIME TO GO:
March to October
DON'T MISS:
There can be few more delightful places for a picnic than the benches beside the water garden.
AMOUNT OF WALKING:
Moderate
COST:
Reasonable (even allowing for the extra charge for the river cruise).
YOU SHOULD KNOW:
If you want to see something of the house as well, it is open on Thursday and Sunday afternoons from April to October.

Windsor Castle and the Giant Wheel

The lively but modest town of Windsor is dominated by its mighty castle. The original site beside the Thames was chosen by William the Conqueror over 900 years ago and has been continuously inhabited since, making Windsor not only the oldest but also the largest occupied castle in the world. It remains an official residence of the British sovereign and is a favourite weekend retreat of the present Queen. (The Royal Standard flies from the Round Tower when Her Majesty is in residence.)

A castle visit is a thoroughly rewarding experience but bear in mind that this is one of the country's top tourist attractions, so be prepared for crowds. Grown-ups will be suitably impressed on a tour of the magnificent state apartments, with their sumptuous furnishings and outstanding Old Master paintings drawn from one of the world's great private art collections. There is plenty to keep younger minds amused as well; activity trails and a family audio tour (included in your ticket price) help to bring the ancient stones to life by telling stories of some of the castle's characters. And children will certainly not want to miss Queen Mary's Dolls House, complete with electric lighting and flushing toilets.

If St George's Chapel does not impress as the burial place of ten monarchs, including the present Queen's father, George VI, and Henry VIII himself, then the Changing of the Guard in front of the main gate surely will. Time your visit to catch this colourful ceremony which takes place at 11.00 on alternate days. A popular recent addition to Windsor's attractions is the graceful Giant Wheel in Alexandra Gardens. Like the London Eye, this offers the comfort of enclosed capsules that convey you 50 m (170 ft) into the sky for panoramic views of the town and Thames valley.

Cartwheeling in the sunshine with Windsor Castle in the background.

WHERE:
Windsor, Berkshire
BEST TIME TO GO:
April to October (the wheel is not there during the winter months, but visiting the castle then means fewer crowds and more rooms to see).
DON'T MISS:
The pomp and pageantry of the Changing of the Guard in front of the castle gates.
AMOUNT OF WALKING:
Moderate
COST:
Expensive (if you ride on the wheel as well as visit the castle).
YOU SHOULD KNOW:
As Windsor Castle is a working royal palace, the state apartments and St George's Chapel are sometimes closed for state occasions and official functions, so you are advised to check opening times beforehand.

Legoland

WHERE:
Near Windsor, Berkshire
BEST TIME TO GO:
Any time of year
DON'T MISS:
The live-action stunt show – watch
Johnny Thunder take on the evil
Aztec Queen.
AMOUNT OF WALKING:
Moderate
COST:
Expensive (discounts are available if
you book tickets online or buy them
at the Windsor tourist information
centre).
YOU SHOULD KNOW:
To avoid misunderstandings, the park
recommends that you bring with you
proof of your children's ages.

A whole world built on the simple and versatile brick beloved of model-makers everywhere is celebrated at this theme park outside Windsor. Parents will be surprised to see how far both materials and technology have come since the days of their humble efforts on the kitchen table. Millions of bricks are put to all manner of uses throughout the Legoland site but the best place to see just what the medium is capable of nowadays is in the Creation Centre near the park entrance. Here you can see the park's largest single model – the near full-size cockpit of a jumbo jet. Outside, many famous buildings have been re-created in immaculately detailed scale versions.

However much all this may fill you with wistful memories, the

All systems go!

children are certain to be more interested in the rides – more than 50 of them – and in joining those queues early to make the best of their day. Legoland is aimed at children aged three to 12, and it seems that no type of movement has been overlooked in its mission to deliver a day out to remember – from the twists and turns of a classic rollercoaster and the catapults of a vertical drop ride to the more sedate pleasures of a jungle train ride or an ascent in a safely tethered hot-air balloon. And the Vikings' River Splash is just one of several opportunities to get a soaking.

There are daily indoor and outdoor shows, including a stunt spectacular. Younger children will enjoy being able to practise their driving skills and to operate the controls of a full-size mechanical digger. The park's latest addition is the Kingdom of the Pharaohs, featuring a new dark ride into the unknown terrors of a lost tomb.

California Country Park

California Country Park is a green lung in a heavily populated corner of Berkshire that is much valued by locals and visitors alike. The somewhat surprising name dates back to the early 1950s when one of the country's first holiday camps was established on this site and chose a name to conjure up West Coast American sunshine and glamour in contrast to the dourness and austerity of post-war Britain. The camp has long since gone, leaving the park to return to nature. Its 40 ha (100 acres) contain examples of two increasingly rare and threatened habitats in southern England: ancient bogland and lowland heath. The park is centred on Longmoor Lake, originally a clay pit excavated in the 19th century for use in the local brick-making industry. The 1.4-km (0.9-mi) walk around the lake takes about half an hour, though you are likely to find yourself stopping frequently to view the wildlife around the lake.

The more substantial Woodland Walk of 3.5 km (2.2 mi) includes a splendid boardwalk which takes you into the heart of the 8,000-year-old Longmoor bog. This is a good place to look out for butterflies and woodpeckers (though you are more likely to hear the latter than see them); this remarkable environment is also home to many unusual sedges and mosses. Back in the centre of California, an extensive adventure playground offers climbing and clambering opportunities galore, and a large paddling pool is very popular in the summer months. Assuming the family will tolerate it, day permits are also available for fishing on the lake.

WHERE:
Near Wokingham, Berkshire
BEST TIME TO GO:
Any time of year
DON'T MISS:
Keep your eyes peeled and you may be lucky enough to spot the delicate silver studded blue butterfly.
AMOUNT OF WALKING:
Moderate (the walk around the lake is a tarmac path suitable for wheelchairs and pushchairs).
COST:
Low
YOU SHOULD KNOW:
Bogland is now thought by environmental scientists to be as effective a carbon reservoir as tropical rainforest.

The River and Rowing Museum and a cruise at Henley-on-Thames

WHERE:
Henley-on-Thames, Oxfordshire
BEST TIME TO GO:
April to September
DON'T MISS:
The precious Iron Age hoard of 32 gold coins, an exciting local find, dating from about AD 50.
AMOUNT OF WALKING:
Little
COST:
Reasonable
YOU SHOULD KNOW:
The very first Boat Race between Oxford and Cambridge Universities was held at Henley in 1829.

The small town of Henley rejoices in its beautiful setting beside the River Thames. England's greatest river presents a tranquil picture here as it meanders past fields and meadows. This was the landscape which inspired Kenneth Grahame to create that classic of children's literature *The Wind in the Willows*. The riverside antics of Ratty, Mole, Badger and Toad are lovingly re-created in an exhibition at Henley's River and Rowing Museum. Based on E H Shepard's famous illustrations, the colourful three-dimensional models bring the timeless story to life with appropriate sound and light effects; join Ratty and Mole's picnic on the riverbank, see them lost in the Wild Wood, and enjoy their triumph as the Weasels are evicted from Toad Hall.

The River and Rowing Museum celebrates Henley's relationship with the river on which its fortunes have always depended. Life on and beside the Thames is explored in lively, imaginative displays which include various hands-on activities. One gallery is devoted to the history of rowing, the sport which has brought Henley worldwide fame. Every July the small town is transformed by the Royal Regatta, which is both a serious sporting event and a highlight of the English social calendar. At the museum you can see film footage of past races and also a replica of the Grand Challenge Cup, the regatta's main competition for rowing eights. A recent addition is Ratty's Refuge, a special garden that is part of a project to bring the water vole back to local riverbanks.

It would be a pity to leave Henley without a spot of 'messing about in boats', in Grahame's immortal phrase. One-hour river cruises depart from Henley every afternoon and travel the length of the Regatta reach between the two locks on either side of town.

Banbury Museum, Tooley's Boatyard and canal trip

The name Banbury is known to children everywhere for its Cross in the well-known nursery rhyme. The 'fine lady upon her white horse' may be just a statue today but Banbury is still worth a visit. Dating back to Saxon times, the town's long and interesting history is well documented in its modern museum. The story of Banbury is told using the latest ideas in museum display and interpretation. Find out about the devastating siege by Parliamentary forces during the English Civil War; how the manufacture of plush (a velvet-like fabric) helped revive the town's fortunes in the 18th century; and what life was like in the Victorian market town. There is a fine permanent collection of 17th-century costumes and a changing programme of temporary exhibitions.

The museum is attractively situated beside the Oxford Canal. A glass bridge over the canal allows you to look down into Tooley's Boatyard. This historic boatyard has been in continuous use for more than 200 years and is still active today, building and repairing the distinctive narrow boats used on the canals. The opening of the Oxford Canal in the late 18th century was a major boost to Banbury and the museum pays due tribute to this important aspect of the town's heritage. If you visit on a Saturday you can take a guided tour of the boatyard, including its two scheduled ancient monuments: a dry dock and a blacksmith's forge, both dating from the 1790s and still in full working order. The tours include a short boat trip on the canal but you might want to consider a longer ride (available any time) by clubbing together with another family and hiring a skippered boat.

WHERE:
Banbury, Oxfordshire
BEST TIME TO GO:
April to September – on a Saturday if you want to tour the boatyard; (the museum is closed on Sundays).
DON'T MISS:
The chance to sample Banbury cakes, a delicious local speciality, in the museum café.
AMOUNT OF WALKING:
Little
COST:
Low (though this will rise if you hire your own boat).
YOU SHOULD KNOW:
The present Banbury Cross dates from 1859 and is not the one mentioned in the nursery rhyme, which was pulled down in 1600.

Banbury Museum tells the story of the town's interesting history.

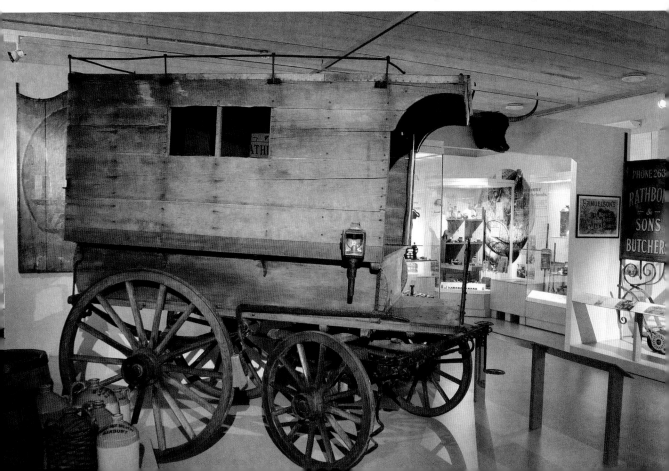

Pendon Model Village and Wallingford

For a vision of how the English countryside used to look take a trip to Pendon Model Village. For more than 50 years local model-makers have been re-creating miniature scenes of rural life with a concern for historical accuracy and an attention to detail that takes your breath away. It is easy to lose yourself in daydreams as you study the intricacies of a busy farmyard or a terrace of thatched cottages; you half expect the scenes before you to burst into life at any moment. Three contrasting landscapes are on show: the oldest is the imaginary Madder Valley, while the Dartmoor scene features working trains and some impressive railway bridges. The largest and most ambitious landscape is an as yet unfinished re-creation of the nearby Vale of the White Horse as it looked in the 1930s. This shrine to the modeller's art is under cover, so can be visited in any weather.

The town of Wallingford has an extraordinary history for its modest size. It was one of the 'new towns' founded by Alfred the Great in the ninth century and throughout the Middle Ages boasted one of the largest royal castles in the land. This history is colourfully told in the town's enterprising little museum, housed in a medieval building. Make your way through the Wallingford Story with an audio tour and learn how the mighty castle was finally razed to the ground on Oliver Cromwell's orders. The Victorian street scene features a walk-in shop, pub and workshop.

You may care to plan your outing on one of the weekends when the Cholsey and Wallingford Railway is running. This private line operates heritage steam and diesel trains between Wallingford and the main line at Cholsey 4 km (2.5 mi) away.

Oxford
Science Oxford Live, the Pitt Rivers Museum, the Botanic Garden and a punt on the river

The city that is synonymous with learning and the pursuit of knowledge is ever mindful that it has a duty to nurture future generations of scholars. The aim of Science Oxford Live is to demystify the principles of science and to popularize the spirit of scientific enquiry. Its Discovery Zone is an interactive area for children and families where young minds are put to work investigating phenomena and solving puzzles. Here they can play around with their own shadow, explore the effects of gravity, and find out how to send whispered messages across a room. For a complete contrast, head to the University's Pitt Rivers Museum. There may not be a touch-screen in sight, but this treasure trove of artefacts gathered from every corner of the globe is still a fascinating place to explore. With objects assembled by type and still in the original late-Victorian displays, the museum is full of surprises; familiar Western objects are often found alongside more exotic ones from foreign cultures. Be prepared to answer some possibly awkward questions when the children discover (as they are bound to) the collection of shrunken heads!

The University's beautiful Botanic Garden is the oldest in Britain and its seven glasshouses re-create a range of plant habitats, from dry desert to tropical rainforest. With 7,000 different types of plant on show, it claims to hold the most complex yet diverse collection of plants in the world. After your visit, cross the road by Magdalen Bridge and enjoy the quintessential Oxford experience of lazing in a punt on the river Cherwell. The family will have most fun if older members take turns on the pole propelling these flat-bottomed boats but, if your nerve fails, you can hire a chauffeured punt or settle for a rowing boat instead.

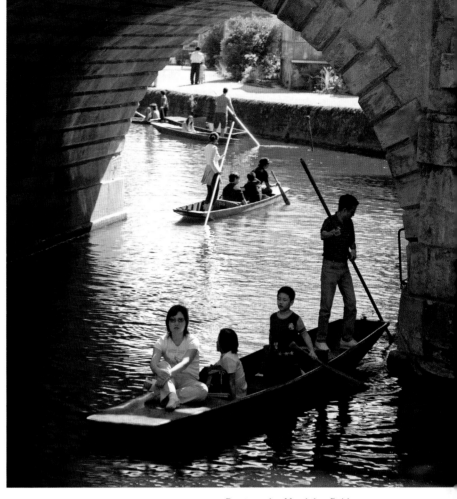

Punts under Magdalen Bridge

WHERE:
Oxford
BEST TIME TO GO:
March to September (but any time of year if you give the punting a miss).
DON'T MISS:
The complete skeletons of an iguanodon and a Tyrannosaurus Rex in the Museum of Natural History (you pass them as you make your way to the Pitt Rivers Museum).
AMOUNT OF WALKING:
Moderate
COST:
Reasonable (the Pitt Rivers Museum is free to all and the Botanic Garden is free to accompanied children who are in full-time education).
YOU SHOULD KNOW:
Concerns that the makeover of the Pitt Rivers Museum would alter its unique atmosphere were unfounded.

Blenheim Palace

Britain has no shortage of grand country houses but few can compare in scale and extravagance with Blenheim, the ancestral home of the Dukes of Marlborough outside Oxford. Not for nothing does it bear the title of palace, a designation reserved normally for royal residences. When in 1705 a grateful nation gave land and finance to John Churchill, the First Duke, for services rendered in defeating the French at the Battle of Blenheim, he and his formidable wife Sarah made the most of their opportunity to upstage not only the neighbours but all their fellow aristocrats. Visiting the opulent state rooms is usually by guided tour and you may decide the 40 or so minutes this requires is too much to ask of the children; it would be a pity, though, to deprive them of the sight of the magnificent Great Hall with its ceiling painting depicting the First Duke's battle feats, as well as the 55-m (180-ft) Long Library and the room in which Winston Churchill was born.

The main trade-off for doing the tour is the chance to see 'Blenheim Palace – The Untold Story', a state-of-the-art visitor experience where a virtual guide in the shape of Grace, the First Duchess's maid, gives you a below-stairs perspective on her masters and various episodes in the palace's 300-year history. With talking portraits and animatronic figures, this is an impressive addition to Blenheim's many attractions.

The formal gardens and vast parkland surrounding the palace are worth a visit in their own right. It is a 15-minute walk to the most popular section, the Pleasure Gardens, but it's quicker and more fun to take the miniature train. At the Pleasure Gardens you will find the Marlborough Maze, a butterfly house, a large adventure playground and the Blenheim Bygones exhibition.

Blenheim Palace

Roald Dahl Day

If you want to encourage your kids to read for pleasure, then there is no surer way than by introducing them to the works of Roald Dahl. He was an inspired storyteller with an extraordinary ability to see the world from a child's point of view and his gruesome characters have delighted generations of kids. A day spent exploring his world will stir your children's imaginations and send them diving straight into his books.

Dahl lived in the village of Great Missenden for 36 years, until his death in 1990. The award-winning Roald Dahl Museum and Story Centre was opened here in 2005 to store his archive for posterity and to be an inspiration for kids. You can find out all about his unconventional world, and the way he drew on his bohemian life to create his stories, in the two fascinating interactive galleries. Then go to the Story Centre to look round a replica of the garden hut where he did all his writing and take a peek inside his 'ideas notebook'.

Just down the road in Aylesbury, you'll find the Roald Dahl Gallery in the Buckinghamshire County Museum. The gallery has been brilliantly designed as a giant pop-up book, in which Dahl's stories have been ingeniously brought to life. There are all sorts of weird and wonderful sensory activities designed to awaken children's interest in literature, history, nature and science: they can crawl along Fantastic Mr Fox's Tunnel finding things from the past, climb inside the Giant Peach to meet James and his insect friends, play on the BFG's outsize pipe organ, and walk through a huge book into Matilda's library. Then you can all take a ride in the Great Glass Elevator to the Imagination Gallery where the kids can expand their minds among eye-boggling optical illusions.

WHERE:
Great Missenden and Aylesbury, Buckinghamshire
BEST TIME TO GO:
Anytime
DON'T MISS:
Having a snack in the Café Twit and taking the Village Trail through Great Missenden, identifying real-life local features that Roald Dahl incorporated into his stories.
AMOUNT OF WALKING:
Little
COST:
Reasonable
YOU SHOULD KNOW:
The Roald Dahl Museum and Story Centre runs workshops, events and storytelling sessions in the school holidays and at weekends. In 2008 it was rated 'Best small visitor attraction' by Enjoy England (the official English Tourism Authority).

A flushbunkingly gloriumptious day out!

A climber on the indoor wall at Xscape in Milton Keynes

Bletchley Park and Sno!zone

What's the connection between the British Secret Service and computer science? Find out at Bletchley Park, a Victorian country estate shrouded in secrecy for years before it was finally opened to the public in 1993.

Just before the outbreak of World War II, a mysterious 'Captain Ridley' took over Bletchley Park for a 'shooting party' – a cover for the fact that the mansion was being turned into an MI6 listening station. Here, throughout the war, the secret service eavesdropped on German signals while Britain's top boffins worked frantically to break enemy codes and build Colossus, the world's first proper computer.

Junior spies and budding computer buffs will be in their element at Bletchley as they get the low-down on intelligence gathering and the vital part played by computers, find out about the fathers of computer science Alan Turing and Tommy Flowers, see an original Enigma encryption machine and wartime wireless equipment, discover how messenger pigeons saved lives during the war, and have a go on the machines in the computer museum. In the estate grounds, follow the American Garden Trail to discover the links between US and British Intelligence and see wartime service vehicles and old cars in the 1940s garage forecourt.

After you've stretched their brains with code cracking, take the kids for some extreme sports fun in the award-winning Milton Keynes Xscape leisure complex. Go to Sno!zone for indoor winter sports – with real snow. They can ski, snowboard or toboggan down a 170-m (560-ft) slope piled high with more than 1,500 tonnes of fresh snow. Daredevils will demand a ride on the ice slide – keep your eyes closed as they rocket down the twists and turns in an inflatable ring. If there are any novices in the party, they can take a skiing or snowboarding lesson on the beginners' slope.

WHERE:
Bletchley and Milton Keynes, Buckinghamshire
BEST TIME TO GO:
Anytime
DON'T MISS:
The Home Front display at Bletchley Park, where you can find out about rationing, evacuation and domestic life in wartime Britain.
AMOUNT OF WALKING:
Moderate. Bletchley Park has full disabled access.
COST:
Reasonable at Bletchley Park. Expensive at Sno!zone.
YOU SHOULD KNOW:
Colossus was the first digital, programmable, electronic computer. For many years it was omitted from the official history of computing because it was classified under the Official Secrets Act. After the war all Colossus machines were destroyed. As a result, its inventor Tommy Flowers and his colleagues never got the recognition they deserved.

Treading the Thames Path and boating in Higginson Park

Marlow is a charming riverside town on the edge of the Chilterns where the family can enjoy a wonderfully relaxed outing, experiencing the best of both urban and rural worlds. Explore the narrow back streets, see the workings of the river locks and weirs, let the kids loose in Higginson Park, muck around in a rowing boat, and watch the river traffic and wildlife as you tread the Thames Path.

Of Marlow's many historic buildings, the oldest is the 14th century Old Parsonage in picturesque St Peter Street. From the other end of the road there's a wonderful picture-postcard view of Marlow Weir. And do stroll across Marlow Bridge, a 72-m (240-ft) suspension bridge built by engineer William Tierney Clark (designer of Hammersmith Bridge) as the prototype of his famous Széchneyi Bridge across the Danube – a Victorian wonder of the world.

Marlow takes justifiable pride in its town park, which year after year wins a prestigious Green Flag award. Higginson Park extends for 9.5 ha (23 acres) down to the riverside. Roam through immaculate formal gardens and let the kids run around on vast lawns dotted with 200-year-old plane trees. The park also has a wetland conservation area teeming with wildfowl and a great children's playground. Down by the river at the park moorings you can hire rowing boats and footle around having a family laugh while serious scullers fly past you.

The Thames Path leads through Higginson Park out onto a beautiful wooded stretch of the river bank. This is family-friendly country walking at its best and soon you'll find yourselves at Temple Lock, a tranquil haven far from the roaring traffic and madding crowds where you might see kingfishers in the willows, red kite swooping through the sky and even a vole scuttling along the water's edge.

WHERE:
Marlow, Buckinghamshire
BEST TIME TO GO:
May to September, when the ground by the river is drier for easier walking.
DON'T MISS:
The Millennium Maze, a multi-coloured brick maze path in Higginson Park showing the heritage of Marlow, designed by Adrian Fisher.
AMOUNT OF WALKING:
Lots
COST:
Low
YOU SHOULD KNOW:
The Thames Path is a National Trail following the course of the River Thames for 294 km (184 mi) from its source in the Cotswolds to the Thames Barrier. From Higginson Park to Temple Lock is less than 2 km (under 1 mi). Hurley (the next lock upstream) is a further 1 km (0.6 mi).

Marlow Weir

Chiltern Open Air Museum and the Chiltern Hills

WHERE:
Near Chalfont St Giles,
Buckinghamshire
BEST TIME TO GO:
March to October (the museum is
closed out of season).
DON'T MISS:
The exhibition at the Hawk and Owl
Trust Conservation and Education
Centre, housed in a 19th-century
barn at the museum.
AMOUNT OF WALKING:
Lots. The museum has limited
wheelchair access and some of the
paths can get very muddy. It is
working towards improving access.
COST:
Reasonable
YOU SHOULD KNOW:
The Chiltern Open Air Museum holds
different events each month, runs a
children's holiday club and lays on a
wide range of family arts-and-crafts
activities during school holidays,
including candle making, straw
plaiting and green woodwork.

*The resident Shire horse takes
visitors for a ride at Chiltern
Open Air Museum.*

The ancient pastoral landscape of the Chiltern Hills is an Area of Outstanding Natural Beauty (AONB), a 120-km (75-mi) chalk escarpment aligned southwest to northeast across five counties, under continual threat from urban sprawl. The Chiltern Open Air Museum was founded in 1976 to preserve the remains of the region's architectural and cultural heritage as the local old buildings started to be indiscriminately bulldozed to clear the way for new development. From small beginnings this wonderful museum, which is a real labour of love, has grown to be one of Buckinghamshire's biggest family attractions.

Sited on 18 ha (45 acres) of meadow and woodland bounded by thick hedgerows, a haven for England's dwindling wildlife, the museum makes history come alive with rural buildings spanning two millennia, from an Iron Age settlement to a 1940s prefab. There are picturesque cottages, a chapel, forge, and even a privy, all painstakingly transported from their original sites and reconstructed around a village green – and you can snoop round an old farmstead, peering into the outhouses, investigating the antiquated agricultural machinery and watching the animals, including a pedigree flock of Oxford Down sheep and the magnificent resident Shire horse.

Explore the rest of the Chilterns by car and on foot. Ramble among the historic oak trees of nearby Hodgemoor Wood or take a circular walk through the lovely countryside round Chesham, a 15-minute drive away. Then drive to the charming hamlet of Dunsmore, the remotest spot in Buckinghamshire, right next to Chequers (the prime minister's country retreat) and climb through National Trust land to the top of Coombe Hill, the highest point of the Chilterns. There are spectacular views across the Vale of Aylesbury and the Berkshire Downs, and the kids can have fun rolling down the grassy slope to the bottom of the hill.

Bekonscot Model Village and the Hellfire Caves

Bekonscot is the sort of unique place that etches itself into kids' memories, one of those magical childhood experiences that gets handed down from one generation to the next. This amazing real-life 'Lilliput' has six different 1930s towns to explore, each with its own peculiar character – from a market town to a coalmining village. Altogether there are more than 200 diminutive buildings as well as a miniature lake, harbour, racetrack, farm, castle and zoo, complete with perfectly matched scaled-down figures.

Bekonscot evolved out of a model railway enthusiast's folly. By 1929 Roland Callingham's railway had outgrown his house – so he set it up in the garden. And that was the basis of the world's first model village. The railway is still a central feature at Bekonscot: a complex network of main and branch lines criss-crossing the towns, with up to 11 trains at a time running through 0.6 ha (1.5 acres) of bonsai-style landscape. The kids will be captivated and so will you.

Near Bekonscot are West Wycombe's famous caves. Originally the site of ancient flint mines, the caves were extended in the 18th century by Sir Francis Dashwood, founder of the notorious Hellfire Club. He needed to find a way of providing work for unemployed villagers so he decided to create a 'feature' in his landscaped garden. It is awesome to think that these caves, which go down to a depth of 90 m (300 ft), were dug out entirely by hand, tons of chalky flint being carted off to be used as bedrock for the road between West and High Wycombe. Long winding passages lead through various underground chambers with waxwork figures and sound effects depicting the life and times of Dashwood's contemporaries, until you reach the Inner Temple, where the Hellfire Club supposedly gathered for meetings.

Bekonscot Model Village, Beaconsfield

WHERE:
Beaconsfield and West Wycombe, Buckinghamshire

BEST TIME TO GO:
April to October

DON'T MISS:
West Wycombe village, with its quaint old shops and 16th-century church loft.

AMOUNT OF WALKING:
Moderate, with pushchair and wheelchair access in most parts of Bekonscot

COST:
Reasonable, and all profits from Bekonscot go to charity.

YOU SHOULD KNOW:
As well as the model village at Bekonscot there are plenty of additional attractions: a ride-on train, remote-controlled boats, a playground, and an elevated walkway from where you can see the miniature world spread below you. At the Hellfire Caves regular children's events and activities are organized throughout the school holidays.

Admiring the trains at Buckinghamshire Railway Centre.

Buckinghamshire railway day

The world of railway travel is a perennial source of pleasure for both children and adults. You can pass an extraordinarily pleasant family day looking at old trains, finding out about the golden age of the railway and following the path of a long-forgotten railway line.

Spread over a 10-ha (25-acre) site, the Buckinghamshire Railway Centre has one of the largest private collections of engines and rolling stock in the country. The assortment of locomotives here is incredibly impressive, from lowly shunting engine to monster express, and there are railway wagons dating from the 1870s to 1970s, including a 1901 coach from the Royal Train. The mid-Victorian station building, with an imposing glass and cast iron entrance canopy reminiscent of the Crystal Palace, looks completely authentic . . . because it is. The old Oxford station of Rewley Road was dismantled, transported here in bits and reassembled. You can learn how the advent of the railways transformed the lives of our Victorian forebears, have a go at operating signals, see one of the driverless post office mail trains that used to run under the streets of London and, of course, take the kids for a ride on the miniature steam railway.

For an old-fashioned ride on a full-size steam train, drive a half-hour scenic route to Chinnor where the Chinnor & Princes Risborough Railway runs 11 km (7 mi) round trips, chuffing through beautiful Chiltern landscapes. Afterwards you can stretch your legs rambling along part of the Phoenix Trail, a track running from Princes Risborough to Thame, enjoying the wonderful views and seeing birds of prey circling in the skies. The kids can clamber on the extraordinary sculptures designed as resting places along the way, inspired by the trail's previous incarnation as a railway line.

Tiggywinkles Wildlife Hospital and Wendover Woods

Young children's hearts will be touched when they come to Tiggywinkles – even if your kids aren't particularly enamoured of hedgehogs, you can be certain they'll be completely smitten after a visit here.

The hospital evolved out of the goodwill of the Stocker family. In the 1970s they started using their garden shed to shelter injured animals they had found in the wild. Gradually, as other people started to bring rescued creatures here, nursing work became a full-time occupation and in 1983 Tiggywinkles was registered as a charity. The hospital is best known for its hedgehog care but in fact looks after any species. Every year some 10,000 wild animals are treated here, a third of which are hedgehogs.

In the Tiggywinkles Visitor Centre you can learn what to do if you come across an injured bird or animal and see behind the scenes, watching the day-to-day work of the hospital on CCTV. There is a charming museum devoted to hedgehog memorabilia and the kids will love looking round the nursery where orphaned baby animals and fledglings are hand reared. Animals too disabled to survive in the wild are given permanent sanctuary and you can meet these residents close up. There is also a toddlers' playground, a duck pond and a picnic area, complete with baby-changing facilities.

A lovely drive along country roads will get you to Wendover Woods, 325 ha (800 acres) of coniferous and broadleaf forest on the edge of the Chilterns. Kids will love exploring here. There are several sign-posted circular trails, a play area and a delightful café in the woods. The Boddington Bank Trail is the ideal distance for little legs, a beautiful walk among ancient beech trees with wonderful views over the Vale of Aylesbury.

WHERE:
Haddenham and Wendover, Buckinghamshire
BEST TIME TO GO:
April to October
DON'T MISS:
The Iron Age fort in Wendover Woods
AMOUNT OF WALKING:
Lots if you want. There is full wheelchair access to Tiggywinkles.
COST:
Low
YOU SHOULD KNOW:
Tiggywinkles Wildlife Hospital is regularly featured on TV and has an international reputation for its pioneering veterinary techniques in treating wildlife injuries.

Muntjac in hand

91

Diggerland Adventure Park

WHERE:
Strood, Kent
BEST TIME TO GO:
On a warm, sunny day. Diggerland is not open all year round, so check times and dates in advance to prevent disappointment.
DON'T MISS:
If your kids are over nine years old, make sure they get to drive the 4x4 Toyota Land Cruiser. Not only is this a pretty thrilling experience, but it's also safe – your child steers and accelerates but the staff control the brakes.
AMOUNT OF WALKING:
Little
COST:
Expensive
YOU SHOULD KNOW:
Wear comfortable clothes and sensible footwear, such as trainers. It would be wise to take a change of clothes if you think there's any chance of rain, for obvious reasons. There is a restaurant, or you can take a picnic, and there is a little indoor entertainment, too.

Diggerland is very different from your average adventure park – in fact it's quite hard to know how to classify it. However, if you have kids who are crazy about heavy construction machinery, this is the place to take them for an unusual day out.

To the untrained eye (Mums, whose idea of a good time is reading a good book) Diggerland doesn't look very inspiring; however, for those in the know, it looks absolutely great. How many places can you go to where everyone over the age of five can drive a truck or operate a full-size digger by themselves? The over threes are welcome, too, but they have to sit on your lap.

All the main rides are included in the entry fee and they can be enjoyed as often as you please. There's plenty going on here, from the Diggerland train which is pulled by a dumper truck and the Land Rover Safari which takes you on a wild, bumpy drive, to the Sky Shuttle where you sit in the scoop of a digger which raises you high into the sky. The most exciting ride is probably the Spindizzy, a JCB that scoops you up and swings you madly around in the air.

Forget the rides, the kids will want to do some driving themselves. Let them have a go at Dirt Diggers, where they compete with other drivers to see how much earth they can move, or they could try Skittles Alley. This last is really good fun and aids concentration and co-ordination as the over fives drive a JCB which has a ball and chain attached to the arm. Great big skittles await, and the kids compete to knock over as many of them as possible.

Chatham: the Historic Dockyard and Dickens World

WHERE:
Chatham, Kent
BEST TIME TO GO:
May to September (The Historic Dockyard is closed in December and January).
DON'T MISS:
A trip up the Medway on the *Kingswear Castle*, Britain's last coal-fired paddle steamer. The steamer operates from the Thunderbolt Pier at the Royal Dockyard throughout the summer.
AMOUNT OF WALKING:
Lots – the Royal Dockyard is a large site – but with plenty of opportunity for taking breaks.

A fascinating day can be spent in the Medway town of Chatham, exploring the Royal Dockyard and meeting classic fictional characters from the works of Charles Dickens.

Established by Queen Elizabeth I in 1568, Chatham Dockyard is one of the most important maritime heritage sites in the world. When it closed in 1984 32 ha (80 acres) of the original dockyard was preserved as a testament to 400 years of Britain's history as a great naval nation.

There is loads to interest everyone here. Look round the three war vessels in dry dock: *HMS Gannet*, a Victorian sloop; *HMS Cavalier*, a World War II destroyer; and *HMS Ocelot*, a Cold War 1960s submarine. In the Museum of the Royal Dockyard you can see model boats and learn about the Great Age of Sail. Costumed guides take you on a tour of the Ropery, to see the machinery in action and have a go at rope making. Join an apprentice shipwright at work in Wooden Walls, a vivid re-creation of the 18th-century dockyard. The kids can try their hands at flag signalling, brass rubbing and caulking, and there are two playgrounds for them to let off steam.

Charles Dickens spent his boyhood in Chatham and he often refers to the town in his stories. At Dickens World you can introduce the kids to this classic author's life and times. In an atmospheric reconstruction of a bustling Victorian courtyard you can go on a Great Expectations boat ride, see Scrooge's ghosts in the Haunted House and be subjected to Victorian strictness in a Dotheboy's Hall schoolroom. Go into the Britannia Theatre for an animatronic stage-show of Dickens's characters, and take a whirlwind 4-D film trip in Peggotty's Boathouse. The kids may also participate in the costumed courtyard plays, enacting scenes from Dickens.

COST:
Expensive
YOU SHOULD KNOW:
Due to slightly misleading advertising, many people go to Dickens World expecting a theme park and are consequently somewhat disappointed. It is in fact an accurate reconstruction with authentic Victoriana, and as such is extremely effective.

Dickens World

Thanet coast by bike on the Viking Coastal Trail

WHERE:
Ramsgate, Kent
BEST TIME TO GO:
May to October
DON'T MISS:
Salvage art on the beach at Pegwell Bay or the Viking ship *Hugin*, on the cliff-top at Pegwell Bay. In 1949 the *Hugin* sailed from Denmark to Britain to commemorate the 1,500th anniversary of Hengist and Horsa's invasion.
AMOUNT OF WALKING:
Little, but lots of cycling
COST:
Can be reasonable, but partly depends on bike-hire arrangements.
YOU SHOULD KNOW:
A detailed map of the Viking Coastal Trail can be downloaded from the Internet. Bikes can be hired in Ramsgate or Margate.

The Isle of Thanet peninsula is the most easterly tip of Kent, once cut off from the mainland by the Wantsum Channel until it finally silted up in the late 17th Century. The coastline of bays, caves, stacks and reefs has the best sandy beaches in Kent and the longest continuous stretch of chalk cliff in Britain. One of the nicest ways of exploring it is by bike.

The Viking Coastal Trail is a family-friendly cycle route round the peninsula. Altogether it is 33 km (21 mi) long, but is conveniently split into six themed mini-sections so you can limit yourself to one or two of them, depending on your family's stamina. One of the best sections for kids is the 7-km (4.5-mi) 'History, Art and Architecture' stretch of coast from Pegwell Bay to Ramsgate Royal Harbour.

Pegwell Bay is an inlet on the estuary of the River Stour, famously the landing place for three invasions that changed the face of Britain: the Romans in AD 43, the Jutes in 449, and St Augustine with his Christian missionaries in 597. Today the bay is part of Kent's largest nature reserve and the chalk cliffs and mudflats are one of Britain's most important havens for marine birds.

Ramsgate has the unique status of being the only Royal harbour in the country. The title was conferred by George IV in 1821 because he was so bowled over by the hospitality he had received there. The harbour is a major tourist attraction and after your bike ride you can take the kids to the Maritime Museum in the Clock House, stroll round the vast marina looking at the boats, and end your Thanet jaunt with a 'Sea Safari' boat ride to see the seals and the infamous Goodwin Sands.

Ramsgate harbour

A day by the sea at Margate

Like so many of England's fashionable Edwardian seaside resorts, Margate's fortunes declined from the mid-20th century and the town gained a reputation for being run down and seedy. But recently Margate has become trendy again, a town very much back in business as an unpretentious family destination for a day by the sea.

The great attraction of Margate was always its wonderful sandy beaches, three of which have won the coveted Blue Flag status. If your children are little, take them onto Margate Main Sands where they can have donkey and playground rides and swim safely in the tidal bathing pool. Older kids can go jet skiing, kite boarding or surfing at Walpole Bay, the main beach for water sports. And if you want some family fun, there's a great mini-golf course on Westbrook Bay promenade.

A trip to Margate has to include the Shell Grotto. This awe-inspiring Grade I-listed catacomb was discovered in 1835 and soon became a major tourist draw. You go along a 20-m (70-ft) long underground passage into a chamber decorated with more than 4.6 million shells arranged in a complex mosaic of intricate swirling patterns completely covering walls and ceiling. The effect is simply incredible. And it is a complete mystery – nobody knows when or why it was made.

In Dreamland, Margate's famous amusement park, you'll find Britain's oldest white-knuckle ride, The Scenic Railway. This Grade II-listed wooden rollercoaster has been restored to full working order after being badly damaged in a suspicious fire. And Dreamland has miraculously survived its battle with greedy property developers to become the world's first heritage amusement park.

Next time you're thinking of a day trip, make it to Margate to wallow in traditional seaside culture: buckets and spades, promenades and boardwalks, cockles and candyfloss – just like when you were a kid.

WHERE:
Margate, Kent
BEST TIME TO GO:
May to September
DON'T MISS:
The 16th-century timber-framed house in King Street or Draper's Mill – a four-storey 1840s mill that you can look round.
AMOUNT OF WALKING:
Moderate, or lots if you want
COST:
Reasonable
YOU SHOULD KNOW:
It is impossible to tell how old the mosaic in the Shell Grotto is, because carbon from Victorian gas lamps has rendered carbon dating techniques useless and the material used for gluing the shells is unidentifiable. Theories abound: some people argue that the grotto is a 2,000-year-old temple, others that it's a 17th-century folly.

Playground rides on Margate Main Sands

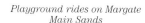

Romney, Hythe and Dymchurch Railway

WHERE:
Hythe, Kent
BEST TIME TO GO:
May to September
DON'T MISS:
The Martello towers at Dymchurch
and St Mary's Bay – part of the
coastal defences built during the
Napoleonic Wars – or Romney Marsh
Visitor Centre, an eco-building made
from straw bales, where you can find
out about the heritage and wildlife of
this unique wetland area.
AMOUNT OF WALKING:
Lots if you want
COST:
Reasonable
YOU SHOULD KNOW:
The bleak beauty of Dungeness has
attracted trend-setting artists and
writers in search of solitude, most
famously film maker Derek Jarman,
who created his beautiful shingle
garden here and brought Dungeness
to public attention.

Take the kids on a memorable eco-excursion on the Romney, Hythe and Dymchurch Railway from Hythe through Romney Marsh to the eerie shingle flats of Dungeness.

The 'world's smallest public railway' is a cute miniature railway, running on a 38-cm (15-in) track over a distance of 22 km (13.5 mi). It was built by a pair of wealthy enthusiasts, Captain Jack Howey and Count Louis Zborowski, as a public service and it has been in operation since 1927 carrying some 100,000 passengers a year between the historic town of Hythe and the remote headland of Dungeness, with a stop at the seaside resort of Dymchurch. There are several other stations along the way and you could hop off at Romney Warren Halt to look round Romney Marsh Visitors' Centre, or at New Romney, the railway's headquarters, to see the engine sheds and model-railway exhibition.

The landscape becomes increasingly desolate as you approach your destination – the shingle headland of Dungeness. You get off the train at one of the weirdest spots in England: it feels like you've just landed on another planet. An unimaginably bleak landscape stretches as far as the eye can see – the largest area of shingle in Europe, a 12 km (7.5 mi) by 6 km (3.75 mi) headland that continually changes shape, as more pebbles are deposited by the sea.

The only signs of human habitation are a cluster of fishermen's huts and converted-railway-carriage cottages, a lighthouse, and the forbidding outlines of the decommissioned nuclear reactors. The currents are far too dangerous for swimming, but do climb the 46-m (150-ft) high lighthouse for panoramic views.

View from the lighthouse of the Romney, Hythe, and Dymchurch line railway station on the Dungeness headland

Groombridge Place Gardens, the Enchanted Forest and a canal cruise

Groombridge Place is a historic country estate. The first manor was built here in the 13th century and the present 17th-century house is still enclosed by the original medieval moat. The grounds of Groombridge have been made into an award-winning magical world that is an absolute joy to explore.

The 17th-century formal gardens are incredible – a series of exquisitely planted 'outdoor rooms' that are works of art. Discover Peacock Walk where the peacocks roost in the wall, find the hidden door into a Secret Garden, marvel at the crazy topiary in the Drunken Garden, stroll along the multi-coloured Herbaceous Border and see a Giant Chessboard. Even the kids will be awed.

On the hillside at the end of the estate vineyard a door leads into the Enchanted Forest. Now the magic really begins. You find yourselves wandering through surreal woodland where nature has been transformed. The kids will love clambering along the Dark Walk – a raised boardwalk with rope swings, hanging tyres, scrambling nets and an aerial runway – and creeping through Tree Fern Valley to the Blue Pool. In the Serpent's Lair you may be unsure whether or not that branch is a snake and at Mossy Bottom be sure to look for fairy houses in the banks of the pond. See giant rabbits and a 'zeedonk' (a rare cross of zebra and donkey) in the Village of the Groms, and don't miss the dinosaur nest with its giant egg and monster footprints. The kids will be wide-eyed.

You can float gently back to reality by taking a boat ride along the willow-fringed canal. There are glorious views across the valley and the boatman may regale you with stories from the romantic history of Groombridge Place.

WHERE:
Tunbridge Wells, Kent
BEST TIME TO GO:
April to October
DON'T MISS:
The Raptor Centre, the largest conservation centre for birds of prey in southeast England in the grounds of Groombridge. You can watch flying demonstrations and go on the Hawk Walk to meet the birds on their perches.
AMOUNT OF WALKING:
Lots; there is wheelchair/pushchair access in some places but other parts are very steep.
COST:
Reasonable
YOU SHOULD KNOW:
A fun way of getting to Groombridge is on the Spa Valley heritage railway from Tunbridge Wells. Sir Arthur Conan Doyle was a frequent visitor to Groombridge and used it as the setting for his Sherlock Holmes story *The Valley of Fear*.

Life-size chess pieces at Groombridge Place

Canterbury tales

Britain's cultural heritage can be pleasurably diluted with plenty of family entertainment in the charming medieval city of Canterbury, a historic pilgrimage centre and a UNESCO World Heritage site.

The story of Canterbury Cathedral can be traced back to the 6th century when St Augustine landed in Kent and established his Motherchurch here. You can grab the kids' attention by showing them the spot where Archbishop Thomas Becket was martyred in 1170 and then point out the beautiful medieval stained glass in the Trinity Chapel shrine, the fabulous carvings in the Norman crypt, and the mind-blowing view upwards to the ceiling of the central Bell Harry Tower.

In the former church of St Margaret's in the city centre both you and the kids will be amused by the audio-visual exhibition of Chaucer's *Canterbury Tales*. Chaucer's pilgrim characters are presented in vivid waxwork tableaux as they wend their way to Becket's shrine while you listen to their stories of romance and skulduggery.

The Museum of Canterbury, housed in the medieval Poor Priests' Hospital, has loads of family-friendly activities and exhibits, especially the Medieval Discovery gallery and the Marlowe 'whodunnit' display. Attached to the main museum is the Rupert Bear Museum where you can learn about Rupert's connection with Canterbury, play giant snakes and ladders, and time travel with Rupert. Little children will love meeting Rupert, Bagpuss and other favourite TV characters.

Rather than battling your way through the packed town centre, it is a lot less stressful to see the city sights from the River Stour on the Historic Boat Tour. You are rowed down the river by knowledgeable and entertaining guides – and you can be sure the kids will be on best behaviour as soon as they find out that the boat trip ends at Canterbury's infamous medieval ducking stool.

The Old Weavers' House sits beside the River Stour in the centre of Canterbury.

WHERE:
Canterbury, Kent
BEST TIME TO GO:
April to September
DON'T MISS:
The World Heritage ancient ruins of St Augustine's Abbey
AMOUNT OF WALKING:
Lots if you want
COST:
Expensive. Although individual attractions are reasonably priced, there is so much to see and do that you'll almost certainly end up spending quite a lot. It's worth checking out the Canterbury Visitor Information Centre where you can get discounted combined tickets for the main attractions.
YOU SHOULD KNOW:
Canterbury is surrounded by lovely countryside with picturesque villages: Blean Woods, a few miles from the city, is the largest woodland in Kent, a great place for a country walk; or visit Howletts Wild Animal Park to see gorillas and elephants.

Kent and East Sussex Railway to Bodiam Castle

The kids will have a day to remember after a trip on the best steam light railway in the country to see one of England's finest medieval fortresses.

Originally known as the Rother Valley Railway, the Kent and East Sussex Railway was built by civil engineer and light-railway fanatic Colonel Holman Stephens and first opened in 1900. When in 1961, like so many other rural railways, the line was axed in the Beeching railway cuts, a preservation society was immediately formed. After a lot of hard work, this group of railway enthusiasts managed to get the K & E S R reopened in 1973 as a charitable enterprise. Since then, the line has been continually restored and improved.

The railway starts at Tenterden, a picturesque town known as the 'jewel of the weald'. The line snakes for more than 16 km (10 mi) through the lovely unspoilt countryside of the Rother Valley, following the contours of the land and stopping at stations on the way to the village of Bodiam at the valley's head. You chug along in a luxurious old railway carriage pulled by a vintage steam train, gazing out of the window and finally seeing the fairytale towers of Bodiam Castle rising before you.

Straight out of a storybook, Bodiam is the archetypal dream castle. Built in the 14th century by Sir Edward Dalyngrigge to protect the Rother Valley from a French invasion, the castle is surrounded by a wide moat. From the outside it looks completely intact, complete with drawbridge, portcullis and keep. The kids will have a ball exploring this amazing ancient building, strutting along the ramparts and climbing up into the towers, feeding the massive fish in the moat and running wild in the grounds.

WHERE:
Tenterden, Kent and Bodiam, East Sussex
BEST TIME TO GO:
May to September
DON'T MISS:
The Colonel Stephens Railway Museum in Tenterden where you can learn all about the K & E S R.
AMOUNT OF WALKING:
Moderate
COST:
Reasonable
YOU SHOULD KNOW:
The National Trust owns Bodiam Castle. Throughout the summer months there is a full family-friendly programme of organized events and activities.

Bodiam Castle

Hastings

The first written mention of Hastings is from the late 8th century, though evidence of prehistoric settlements has been found here. However most of us know it best because this was where the Normans launched their conquest of England in 1066. In reality, they landed at Norman's Bay, between Hastings and Eastbourne, and the famous battle

was fought eight miles to the north. William built himself a castle in Hastings, the remains of which you can still visit today. Ride on the West Cliff funicular railway – one of two funiculars in town – and take a look at the castle, making sure you don't miss the 1066 Story, a fascinating sound-and-light exhibit on the site.

There's a lot to see in Hastings. Apart from having fun at the beach, be sure to visit the Fishermen's Museum, which also looks after one of the famous net huts. Fishing has been important here for centuries and the museum is in the old fishermen's church on the Stade, as this shingle beach area is known. Hastings still boasts Britain's largest fleet of beach-launched fishing boats, which are fun to see. Have a walk round the fish market and buy something freshly caught to take home and cook for supper, or enjoy fish and chips at the nearby café.

In the afternoon you can explore the exciting St Clements Caves. Kids always seem to enjoy tunnels and caves and here they can discover the history of these sandstone caverns that were used by smugglers, bootleggers and gangs. Then, if you are all still raring to go, why not visit the Blue Reef Aquarium with its underwater walk-through tunnel, or the Shipwreck and Coastal Heritage Centre where you can watch an excellent audio-visual show that will tell you all about famous local shipwrecks.

WHERE:
Hastings, East Sussex
BEST TIME TO GO:
Any time, although of course it is nicer if it isn't raining.
DON'T MISS:
Hastings old town, with its historic buildings and winding lanes, elegant Pelham Crescent and Wellington Square. It's fun just to explore the area on foot.
AMOUNT OF WALKING:
Moderate to lots
COST:
Low
YOU SHOULD KNOW:
If you have time, try to visit beautiful Bodiam Castle, which is a National Trust property that can be found roughly 20 minutes drive away. This is a wonderful, moated castle built in 1385, and worth looking at even if you don't go in.

The beach at Hastings

101

Brighton Pavilion

Brighton

Everyone loves Brighton, and a day out there is always going to be fun. During the 1700s, the town was regarded as a rather up-market health resort, but with the arrival of the railway in 1841, it became accessible to day trippers from London, and it has remained a favourite destination ever since. This is a lovely town to explore, and there's lots to do quite apart from enjoying the beach itself which, on a warm summer's day, might provide more than enough amusement for you and your children.

There are, however, a number of iconic places to visit in Brighton, one of which is the famous Royal Pavilion. Built for the rakish Prince Regent, later King George IV, it was transformed from a straightforward farmhouse to an exotic Indian fantasy, complete with domes and minarets. The sumptuous interior has to be seen to be believed.

There are several fun museums to visit in Brighton. At the Toy and Model Museum, for example, over 10,000 exhibits – including toy theatres, puppets and marvellous model trains – will fascinate children. And down by the sea at the National Museum you can buy old pennies to feed into their fabulous, vintage penny slot machines.

Visit Brighton Marina, the largest in Europe, and admire the sailing boats as you potter along the boardwalk. There are restaurants and shops here, too, and you may be tempted to lunch

WHERE:
Brighton, East Sussex
BEST TIME TO GO:
Best on a warm, sunny day, though Brighton is great whenever you go.
DON'T MISS:
Exploring The Lanes – narrow alleyways crammed with interesting shops, restaurants and pubs.
AMOUNT OF WALKING:
Lots.

on fish and chips, or simply sit in the sun with a picnic brought from home or purchased in the town.

Of course you can't leave Brighton without a trip to the classic English pier, complete with amusement arcades, fairground rides, toffee apples and candyfloss. If you are on the pier as the sun goes down you will witness and enjoy the amazing sight of thousands of starlings swooping in to roost.

COST:
Reasonable for entrance to the Royal Pavilion and the Toy Museum.
YOU SHOULD KNOW:
Sometimes known as 'London-by-the-Sea', Brighton has eight million visitors per year and is packed with young people, being home to two universities and a medical school.

Bentley Wildfowl and Motor Museum and Spring Barn Farm Park

This is a day out designed to please everyone in the family, though not necessarily all at exactly the same time. Bentley Wildfowl and Motor Museum is an unusual attraction that promotes conservation of both water birds and cars – a strange combination that works well.

Since 1962, when the wildfowl reserve was established with 20 pairs of birds, it has become home to over 1,000 geese, ducks and swans from across the world – 125 of the 147 species in existence. The birds wander freely around the 9-ha (23-acre) park, and you can follow suit by exploring one of the many trails to get a good, close look at some of them.

The gardens here are fun, too. Yew hedges divide them into separate rooms and there are living-willow tunnels, bridges and domes to explore, plus pretty woodland walks to take in Glyndebourne Wood, including an Ancient Buildings Trail. At weekends and during the holidays a narrow-gauge steam railway operates and kids may enjoy joining an orienteering course for a small fee or trying out a quiz. Don't forget to look at the Craft Centre, where you can watch woodcarving, glass engraving and other crafts in action – and even buy yourself a souvenir.

Besides all this, there's a fabulous collection of vintage cars and motorbikes to be admired, and sometimes new and unusual cars, too. Most of them are privately owned and driven, which means the collection changes from time to time.

If your youngest children don't appreciate historic cars, you can whisk them off to nearby Spring Barn Farm Park where, during summer, the whole family will enjoy the Giant Maize Maze, and the little ones will love meeting and cuddling the baby animals, playing in the straw bales, go-karting and more.

WHERE:
Near Lewes, East Sussex
BEST TIME TO GO:
On a good day between May and September. Bentley Wildfowl and Motor Museum is closed during the winter months.
DON'T MISS:
The flamingos and cranes in the wildfowl reserve or the annual wood fair.
AMOUNT OF WALKING:
Moderate to lots
COST:
Reasonable, although you might find the entry fee for the farm park rather high if you only intend to spend an hour or two there.
YOU SHOULD KNOW:
The entry fee for Bentley Wildfowl and Motor Museum includes entry to the house, a beautiful, fabulously furnished, Palladian-style mansion.

Ashdown Forest

For a simple, old-fashioned family day out, take yourselves off to Ashdown Forest. Despite its name, over 60 per cent of the area is actually lowland heath, and its unusual ecology has earned it the accolade of SSSI (Site of Special Scientific Interest). Ashdown Forest is criss-crossed with footpaths and bridleways and there are a number of lovely spots to visit within it.

Alpaca on a farm in the forest

WHERE:
Ashdown Forest lies between East Grinstead, Uckfield, Crowborough and Haywards Heath, in East Sussex. The Forest Centre and the Llama Park are just off the A22, but there are 50 free car parks across the area.
BEST TIME TO GO:
The forest is lovely at any time of year, but choose a decent day to get the most from it.
DON'T MISS:
The absolutely beautiful views across the rolling Sussex countryside.
AMOUNT OF WALKING:
Moderate to lots. You can download several short, circular walks or buy maps or guides from the Forest Centre or the Llama Park.
COST:
Free, unless you visit the Llama Park, in which case it is low.
YOU SHOULD KNOW:
Cycling is forbidden in Ashdown Forest and dogs (other than guide dogs) are not allowed in the Llama Park. There are lots of picnic tables scattered about, but they are for picnics only – barbecues are forbidden because of the danger of fire.

For all those who have been brought up loving *Winnie the Pooh*, Ashdown Forest is the place to go. The book's author, A A Milne, lived here with his son, the real Christopher Robin, and many of the places described – such as the Pooh Sticks Bridge, Eeyore's Gloomy Place and the North Pole – can all be found near Gills Lap, where you can also see a memorial to both the author and E H Shepherd, the illustrator.

Evidence of the area's long history can also be discovered. There are the remains of two Roman roads, large Pillow Mounds where for several hundred years rabbits were bred and, from more recent times, the Airman's Grave and two World War II airstrips.

The forest contains plenty in the way of wildlife – foxes and badgers, fallow, roe, sika and muntjac deer, a flock of more than 100 Hebridean sheep that are brought out daily to graze on the heathland, and birds – lots and lots of birds – making it a magnet for twitchers.

In addition to all the indigenous fauna, there is also a Llama Park. Started in 1987, the Ashdown herd of llamas and alpacas has since increased to over 100 animals. In 1996 the park was opened to the public and in 2007 the herd was joined by three gorgeous female reindeer. You will find a coffee shop, an adventure play area and a visitor centre at the Llama Park.

Seven Sisters Country Park and Sheep Centre and Paradise Park

The Seven Sisters Country Park is named after the dramatic chalk cliffs, each with its own name, that drop down to the sea on this heritage coast. Beside them are 280 ha (2 sq mi) of superb open grassland and the Cuckmere River Valley. This is a marvellous area for walking and the views of the white cliffs, the estuary and in the distance Beachy Head, are absolutely stunning.

Start at the Visitor Centre, where you can pick up route maps and lots of interesting information about the park. There are several walking trails, including the Park trail, marked with purple arrows, and the Habitat trail, marked with green ones. However, the Easy Access trail is just what it says, and makes this park accessible to everyone as it traces the valley floor from the Visitor Centre to the beach, where the river and sea meet.

Close at hand, not far from Beachy Head, you'll find the Seven Sisters Sheep Centre, a family-run farm that is interesting to visit regardless of your age. Aside from sheep and, in the spring, lambs, there are other young animals to meet and stroke. In the summer you can watch sheep being milked, cheese being made, sheep shearing and their wool being spun. This is home to more than 40 different breeds of sheep, one of the largest collections in the world.

Should the Sheep Centre be closed on the day you're in the area (try to check opening times in advance), you can have a wonderful afternoon at Paradise Park instead. Walk through exotic gardens and plant-houses, enjoy the Dinosaur Safari, where life-size, moving dinosaurs lurk among the vegetation, or enjoy the adventure play area, the miniature train or crazy golf for a small, extra charge.

WHERE:
Seven Sisters Country Park is situated between Seaford and Eastbourne; the Sheep Centre is at East Dean; and Paradise Park is at Newhaven. All three are in East Sussex.

BEST TIME TO GO:
Between April and October, on a decent day. Check the opening times of the Sheep Centre in advance – it is closed for parts of the year.

DON'T MISS:
The rock pools at low tide at Seven Sisters Country Park; a whole little underwater world can be discovered there.

AMOUNT OF WALKING:
Moderate to lots

COST:
Free at the country park; low at the Sheep Centre; reasonable at Paradise Park

YOU SHOULD KNOW:
Apart from walking at Seven Sisters Country Park, you may cycle on the valley floor. You may also canoe at any time, although you must use the dedicated slipway. This is also a great place for birdwatching.

Seven Sisters Country Park, Cuckmere Haven

Drusilla's Park

WHERE:
Alfriston, East Sussex
BEST TIME TO GO:
Drusilla's Park is open every day
except December 24, 25, 26, but it is at
its best on a warm, summer's day.
DON'T MISS:
There's a swimming lagoon for children
so remember to bring swimsuits and
towels if it's a warm day.
AMOUNT OF WALKING:
Moderate. Drusilla's is excellent for
wheelchair users and has lots of
low-level interest and contact.
COST:
Reasonable to expensive, depending
on when you go. Once inside, almost
everything is free, although there are a
few activities that have to be paid for.
YOU SHOULD KNOW:
It is possible to organize special
birthday parties here, and you can also
arrange for your child to be a keeper
for a day.

Making friends at Drusilla's.

If your children are under the age of ten, Drusilla's Park is a
fantastic place to visit. Known as one of the country's best small
zoos, Drusilla's is home to lots of exotic creatures and has a policy
against keeping any of the large mammals such as lions, tigers
or elephants.

As they enter, the kids are given a 'passport' and, as they visit
different animals, complete a series of challenges and get their
passports stamped. At the end of the day, the passports are handed
in and the kids receive a certificate for their efforts. There is a
planned route that ensures you see everything on offer, but of
course you can just do your own thing if you prefer.

There is lots to do and plenty of interactive information.
Everything is quite close together, so there are no long walks, and
there is the opportunity for lots of close-up contact. You can walk
right through both the bat house and the meerkat's tunnel – which
is really good fun because as you pop your head up you find yourself
in the middle of the enclosure. Children may stroke some animals,
vanquish any fear of bugs in the bug-house, enjoy the primates and

walk right through the lemurs' enclosure. Along the way there are play areas with slides, swings and roundabouts, and you can take as many rides as you like on the Thomas the Tank Engine miniature railway.

Kids are fascinated by the Zoolympics, where they compare their physical prowess with that of various animals, and they always enjoy watching the penguins being fed. If they insist on a souvenir, you can either buy one from the shop or, much more fun, adopt any animal in the park for a year.

Pulborough Brooks RSPB Nature Reserve

The Arun Valley has some of the loveliest and most unusual countryside in southern England. Pulborough Brooks is part of the Arun flood plain, a region of wet grassland surrounded by scrub and woodland. The RSPB protects the reserve's biodiversity with controlled flooding, so that in every season it provides sanctuary to a full range of wildlife as well as birds. For visitors, it's a vision of nature's abundance.

The nature trail at Pulborough Brooks Reserve is famous for the intelligent care that informs it. It varies with the seasons so you don't miss anything important like the spring wading birds, or the huge winter flocks of geese, ducks and swans on the flooded meadows. The trail uses the cover of hedges to minimize disturbance to wildlife (the creatures of ditch, hedgerow and coppice, the bugs and butterflies and birds) and brings you to viewing points and hides where you might meet one of the RSPB volunteers who will be happy to answer questions or identify rare species. What you hear can be as exciting as what you see. Nightingales and warblers can raise the most jaded spirit.

The RSPB at Pulborough Brooks regards children as *bona fide* adventurers and scientists. They get free 'explorer backpacks' at the centre for use around the reserve. These contain binoculars designed for birdwatching, a bug box for collecting 'mini-beasts', and a seasonal 'spotting sheet' to record the expedition. There's even a play area with a wooden tractor and animal sculptures to clamber on (the giant grasshopper and mournful cow are a hoot) – but kids usually get distracted by the adjoining garden courtyard, designed to attract tits, finches, woodpeckers and nuthatches.

WHERE:
Wiggonholt, near Pulborough, West Sussex
BEST TIME TO GO:
Any time
DON'T MISS:
The winter flocks of teal and widgeon swirling over the reedbeds; in summer, the wildflower species, butterflies and dragonflies, newborn families hiding in ditches, waders on the ponds, swallows hurtling high and barn owls swooping over the brooks; the children's events, including guided walks in the Arun marshes and experiments to discover how animals and birds use their senses.
AMOUNT OF WALKING:
Lots. Wheelchair access is limited.
COST:
Free (Visitor Centre and play area); low to walk the nature trail.
YOU SHOULD KNOW:
The whole Arun Valley is a Ramsar site and Special Protection Area (SPA), and the RSPB manages the Pulborough Brooks Reserve for the benefit of wildlife well beyond its own limits. The range of natural habitats you can observe on a day out is truly colossal – and without parallel anywhere else in Britain.

A trip on the Wey and Arun Canal

Only a canal trip can make you feel peaceful and excited at the same time. On the Wey and Arun Canal, you get an environmental bonus as well. The canal's historic status is flagged as 'London's lost route to the sea'. It used to be part of the only inland water route from the south coast to London, connecting the River Arun at Pallingham in Sussex with the River Wey near Guildford (and thence to the Thames). It could be again. The whole 37 km (23 mi) of canal is being restored – and if you take a trip on its only substantial, navigable section, you'll be actively helping the restoration project as well as having a marvellous day out in the countryside.

The navigable section is the idyllic Loxwood Link on the West Sussex/ Surrey border. Less than 5 km (3 mi) long, it takes nearly three hours to cruise by traditional narrow boat if you go from end to end. There are shorter trips of 45 and 90 minutes, or you can hire your own little motorboat and spend all day pottering. You pass some of the loveliest vistas in West Sussex. Some reaches are lined, French style, with regiments of straight trees; others are overhung with branches, dappling the water and providing cover for furtive flurries of wildlife along the banks. The locks are always a thrill. The unfamiliar equipment is easy to use (if you have to do it yourself, or if you volunteer), but easily identifiable to children as a source of endless entertainment.

Everyone adapts to 'canal pace' very quickly. You'll see what the whole canal will look like when it's completed, and relish playing even a tiny part in bringing it back to life.

Canal boat on the Wey and Arun Canal near Loxwood

WHERE:
Loxwood, near Billingshurst, West Sussex
BEST TIME TO GO:
March to October
DON'T MISS:
The triumph of restoration at Drungewick Aqueduct (taking the canal over the River Lox) and Drungewick Winding Hole, a huge pool at one end of the navigable section where boats turn around – and so picturesque it's worthy of Constable. Also the outstanding land/waterscapes created by oxbows in the River Arun – sometimes only the width of the towpath separates the river from the canal.
AMOUNT OF WALKING:
Little. The Wey and Arun Canal Trust has yet to make its boats wheelchair accessible.
COST:
Reasonable (the longer boat trips); low (shorter trips)
YOU SHOULD KNOW:
The boat skippers volunteer their services free to the Wey and Arun Canal Trust. Do check on possible alterations to published timetables.

Tangmere Aviation Museum and the Sussex Falconry Centre

Tangmere is a hallowed name. As one of World War II's most important frontline RAF bases, it earned the right to host the most dramatic, interpretive display about the aircraft of that era that you'll ever see. In fact the museum covers the whole history of military aircraft up to the present, but all the major displays recall the heroism and sacrifice of those who fought in the Battle of Britain, in Bomber Command, in the Fleet Air Arm, in the SOE Lysander squadrons, and in the auxiliary and supply services. In context, it's no surprise that this museum has a much-used memorial garden.

There are interactive models galore, and they work. You can even bounce your own bomb at the Dambusters exhibit. There aren't many actual aircraft – but all of them are very special indeed, including world air-speed record-holders, and a full-size replica of Spitfire prototype K5054, built from R J Mitchell's own plans by the test pilot who flew it first. And dreams do come true – you can 'fly' a Spitfire in a special simulator, with the Merlin engines throbbing in your ears; or 'fly' a Hawker Hunter jet under Tower Bridge in London or a Gloster Meteor at low level across the Lake District. At Tangmere, the children will have a truly magical time and also leave with real respect and warmth for the people whose history it is.

The Sussex Falconry Centre illustrates the story of flight itself. Recently revamped, it still shows off its falcons, hawks and owls doing extraordinary things in free flight; but a first-class exhibition tracing flight development from Archaeopteryx onwards now lays out the information needed to consider fundamental questions of evolution and intelligent design.

Like Tangmere Aviation Museum, the Falconry Centre is good enough to leave the kids thirsting for more.

Young visitor holding an owl at the Sussex Falconry Centre.

WHERE:
Near Chichester, West Sussex
BEST TIME TO GO:
February to November
DON'T MISS:
A real flying lesson, on the Chipmunk trainer simulator – specially created so you 'fly' round RAF Tangmere and nearby Goodwood; 'flying' three different kinds of Spitfire, and the Hurricane – you can't do it anywhere else.
AMOUNT OF WALKING:
Moderate. Access is generally good, and better if you give the largely volunteer staff warning of any special needs.
COST:
Reasonable
YOU SHOULD KNOW:
To use the Tangmere simulators, you must be accompanied by one of the volunteer guides. They are very helpful and friendly, especially when younger children get frustrated because their co-ordination skills haven't yet developed.

Southwater Watersports Centre

WHERE:
Southwater, near Horsham, West Sussex
BEST TIME TO GO:
Any time (if you can deal with British weather, so can they).
DON'T MISS:
One of the best chances you'll ever have to learn a new skill that might become a lifetime pleasure. A day out at Southwater could eventually lead to enjoying holidays on rivers round the world, or a water-based job – or even the Olympics!
AMOUNT OF WALKING:
Nil (swimming is a different issue). Wheelchair access is easy, with purpose-built slipways, ramps and pontoons.
COST:
Reasonable (but can rapidly become expensive, unless you take advantage of course discounts).
YOU SHOULD KNOW:
The centre provides all the equipment you need, including wetsuits, spray-tops, buoyancy aids, boats, paddles and helmets. You need to wear appropriate clothes – old trainers or gym shoes, t-shirt and shorts, swimming costume, and take a change of clothes.

Child or adult, you'd be forgiven for feeling a tiny bit of apprehension on your first visit to Southwater Watersports Centre. There they teach you to kayak, canoe, windsurf, sail, build a raft or orienteer, and they do the job properly. But they're not really determined to make you into a commando – it's just their style, and probably why it works.

A day out at Southwater isn't really possible until you've qualified to go solo on one or more of the craft. Your first day will probably consist of a two-hour session under tuition; and though you can do more (at further cost), you'll likely be too tired to want to do so – though it's hugely pleasant after a session to lie on the grass with a picnic or drink and watch others practising at every level. Once you've absorbed the principles of your chosen craft, and tried them on the water, careful observation is the best way to learn.

When you're confident in your own basic skills, Southwater can do brilliant things for you, individually or as part of a group. On their 'home' lake, the centre organizes games and races between people of similar ability (age is irrelevant – a good six-year-old kayaker can demolish a 25-year-old athlete who's a novice). Days like these are enormous fun, and they can form part of qualifying hours if you're working towards a Royal Yachting Association or British Canoe Union certificate.

The best thing about Southwater is that they'll give you the chance to find out which kind of craft you most enjoy. You can go as a family or with friends (the centre will teach children as young as four accompanied by an adult, or six to 80 year olds unaccompanied). But do go – there's nothing like messing about in boats.

A day at Littlehampton

Littlehampton is a very English sort of resort. It reached its heyday in Victorian times, when it even had a ferry service to Honfleur in France, and by the 1920s was known as 'the children's paradise' because of its broad, sweeping beach and the classic entertainments to be found there. Most are still there, in much more strident, modern form.

Its 19th-century architecture still gives Littlehampton's seafront an air of gentility, but now it's dominated by Harbour Park – an amusement park which has the good faith to include something very like a traditional fun fair as well as a selection of up-to-date thriller rides. It's even got a special rollercoaster (the caterpillar) and an indoor cannon ball play zone for small kids. There's plenty of other indoor fun, too, including a skating rink and family arcade, but Littlehampton is about seaside favourites – the boating lake in the park, the seafront road train, miniature railway, crazy golf, and the wonderful old pier where the River Arun enters the sea.

You can try net fishing along Arun Parade by the riverside, and kite surfing or any other water sport; but most of the beach is reserved for families looking to make the most of the huge area of smooth sand that appears beyond the shingle at low tide. It's Blue Flag territory, and the most popular patch is around the East Beach Café, a preposterous and magnificent building that looks like a gigantic piece of driftwood turned on its side. It serves a mean cup of tea, but it's still highly controversial. The lifeguards on duty here operate a 'Kids Care' scheme – each child gets a free colour-coded wristband linked to a zone on the beach, so you can advise on sandcastle design or play beach games without needing eyes in the back of your head. Great day.

Holidaymakers in front of East Beach Cafe on the Seafront

WHERE:
Littlehampton, West Sussex
BEST TIME TO GO:
Any time
DON'T MISS:
The 360-degree panorama from the viewing tower of the Look and Sea Visitor Centre on Fisherman's Quay, opposite the Lifeboat Station, or boating on the Oyster Pond, beside the entrance to Harbour Park – it's where the fishermen used to store oysters
AMOUNT OF WALKING:
Lots – and much of it is wheelchair-friendly. Even the beach has flat, level access from the promenade.
COST:
Low to expensive – depending on what you do.
YOU SHOULD KNOW:
Littlehampton's thriving lobster industry in the 1930s inspired the famous Bauhaus artist Laszlo Moholy-Nagy to make the first known underwater film, a study of the lobsters' natural habitats, which also starred many local fishermen.

Worthing to Shoreham: the West Sussex coast by bike

WHERE:
Worthing, West Sussex
BEST TIME TO GO:
Any time (in good weather)
DON'T MISS:
A short detour to Lancing village and a glimpse of the lovely chapel at Lancing College; the French Market in Shoreham-by-Sea, if you're lucky enough to be there on the same day.
AMOUNT OF WALKING:
Little
COST:
Low
YOU SHOULD KNOW:
Even with a detour, you won't have to cycle more than 14 km (9 mi), and the stretch before the estuary is all downhill. If you time your ride to reach the footbridge at mid tide, you'll see the mudflat wildlife at its best.

Start from Worthing Pier, a classic English seaside pier opposite a very good ice cream stall. Adults may want to reflect that Oscar Wilde wrote *The Importance of Being Ernest* while in Worthing. Don't worry about the busy road; from East Worthing there's a dedicated bike track all the way to Shoreham – although it's not always easy to negotiate. The guesthouses soon thin out, enabling everyone to enjoy the vistas over the sea along to Brighton on one side, and the glorious Adur Valley on the other. As you pass Lancing, you'll understand why the hillsides on your left are a designated AONB (Area of Outstanding Natural Beauty), and a nature reserve within the South Downs protected region.

Sailboat on the mud of the River Adur estuary

The road dips sharply as it overlooks the fan-shaped Adur estuary. Here the famous fishing river cuts tidal channels of fast water, leaving huge mudflats for feeding plover, dunlins and lapwings and a roost for waders and gulls. The whole estuary is an SSSI (Site of Special Scientific Interest). You'll have to pause at the footbridge (you still can't cycle across), so take the time to wonder at the spectacular big sky effect. Landwards, the emergent flats are splashed with the fading colours of leaning boats; to sea, the Adur rushes away between two long piers that mark the entrance to Shoreham Harbour. The horizon would be a seamless blend but for a solitary, 106 m (344 ft) chimney, the tallest structure in Sussex. Coming into Shoreham you'll pass the Grade II* Shoreham Tollbooth, the last one to be used in Sussex. Keep peddling to Shoreham's beach, a Sussex classic of shingle and sand. Paddling will soothe your weary legs.

Fisher's Farm Park

When it was fairly new, Fisher's Farm Park was voted Farm Attraction of the Year. A few years later, it doesn't seem quite so certain about its identity. The farm is still very much there in the shape of cattle, pigs, goats, sheep, ponies and horses, but the livestock are now at one remove from the status of 'working farm animals'. Their function is to be enjoyed by small children hoping to stroke and pet them, as they do the orphaned animals that Fisher's accepts from all over the region. It's magic for the kids, but not much to do with farming. The animals have been absorbed as a living attraction into Fisher's family entertainment centre, a junior theme park for two to 10 year olds.

With no big kids to intimidate them, little kids thrive at Fisher's. They can climb, run, dangle, slide, swing, bump and jump in the same way as their older siblings at other parks, but in a much gentler mode. Even within Fisher's, most activities have 'big' and 'mini' versions. The Cresta Fun Toboggan Run offers two options to descend – spinning wildly on your 'doughnut' inner tube if you're brave, or sliding sedately. The Summit Plummet is the same.

It's a bizarre mix of fairground and farm fun. You're as likely to see animals perform in the theatre barn as puppets, and the pig racing is spectacular. There's a simulated 'beach' by the pond where tots soak up the sun and wait for the tractor-trailer and combine-harvester rides. Jolly Jumbos is an indoor, netted area where kids and adults are invited to sort things out with softball cannon fights. It may be a haphazard mixture, but Fisher's responds to the random likes and dislikes of real children. Adults can only approve.

WHERE:
Wisborough Green, near Billingshurst, West Sussex
BEST TIME TO GO:
Any time
DON'T MISS:
The barrel bug ride, jumping pillows, happy haunting ghost tunnel or the combine-harvester climbing frame (very different from the ride). The food is good – organic growing is big in this part of Sussex, and Fisher's does it well.
AMOUNT OF WALKING:
Moderate (but it adds up).
COST:
Expensive (but reasonable in the low season of term time).
YOU SHOULD KNOW:
Parts of Fisher's Farm Park are almost chic, others are distinctly rural. Some city folk are unaccustomed to rural sights and smells, however natural they may be. Be reassured that standards of hygiene and safety are high.

Dairyland Farm World and Blue Reef Aquarium

WHERE:
Near, and in, Newquay, Cornwall
BEST TIME TO GO:
All year. Dairyland farm is closed from November to March, but The Bull Pen remains open.
DON'T MISS:
Milking Clarabelle the cyber cow – her very realistic teats produce 'milk' when handled correctly. At Blue Reef, the columnar seahorse tank is home to several different species of these magical creatures.
AMOUNT OF WALKING:
Moderate
COST
Expensive. Under threes go free at Blue Reef; at Dairyland there are often special deals on admission and children under 92 cm (3 ft) tall go free. During winter opening at Bull Pen, adults go free.
YOU SHOULD KNOW:
Blue Reef is propagating its own hard coral; the coral display highlights the threats faced by coral reefs worldwide.

Dairyland's aim is to promote understanding of the countryside but it is also a place in which to have a lot of fun. The Heritage Centre features a Victorian kitchen, blacksmith and laundry alongside displays of historic implements and vintage tractors, while a farm nature trail around the lovely countryside includes informative displays. Animals for feeding, patting and petting include lambs, piglets and rabbits. Milking takes place in a space-themed parlour with the cows on a musical merry-go-round. A must for petrol heads of all ages is the hayride – pulled by a Lamborghini tractor. To let off steam – or if the weather turns nasty – take the kids to the Bull Pen, a huge undercover play area with lots of state-of-the-art equipment.

In Newquay's Blue Reef Aquarium, a huge variety of fish and marine creatures live in a range of underwater habitats, from the rocky Cornish coast to the enormous main display where sharks and rays patrol while brightly coloured reef fish drift like butterflies around a Caribbean coral atoll. This tank can be viewed from above or from a walk-through tunnel with glass caves. Multi-level viewing allows everyone a close-up view of all the tanks. Blue Reef runs a captive-breeding programme, and all kinds of baby fish may be seen in the 'nursery', while another display features the weird world of that strange and scary bunch of creatures, the deep-sea predators. Staff here are knowledgeable and enthusiastic and welcome questions. Daily Meet the Creatures sessions allow close encounters with rock-pool animals and there are frequent talks and demonstrations. Special events for children range from pirate weekends and mermaid parties to beach clean-ups.

Loggerhead turtle tank at the Blue Reef Aquarium

The Eden Project

Just the size of the Eden Project is thrilling. The biomes – the biggest glasshouses in the world – nestle in a vast, former china-clay excavation whose landscapes range from the neat hummocks of lavender fields and the profusion of 'wild Cornwall' to reconstructions of the Steppes, the Prairies and Chile on the steep upper slopes.

Inside one of the biggest glasshouses in the world

This extraordinary living theatre of plants demonstrates the interaction of man with nature and is packed with wonders and curiosities. Particularly for children are the hideaways, spy-holes and shortcuts, climbing frames in the shape of trees and ships, tube slides and giant musical instruments and junk percussion dotted around the site. A spiral maze of bent willow becomes a jungle in summer and a path made from recycled tyres offers a bouncy trip between rainbow flowerbeds. The project's interpreters also act as storytellers, while families can hire an Explorer Bag, packed with objects and clues for a discovery trail. School holiday activities include building dens and rafts and making bows and arrows, while at Christmas Eden becomes a winter wonderland complete with ice rink.

In the biomes, children can travel the world and learn how many everyday things – including tea and coffee, chewing gum and Coca-Cola – come from plants. Crops like olives and cotton grow in the Mediterranean Biome, where citrus orchards scent the air. Waterfalls maintain moisture in the enormous Rainforest Biome, and insects and small reptiles help out with pest control and pollination. The exotic plants are spectacular – water lily leaves as big as boats, bamboo thick and tall enough to be used as scaffolding and a fantastic range of luscious fruit, including dozens of different sorts of banana.

WHERE:
Near St Austell, Cornwall
BEST TIME TO GO:
Any time. Eden is very crowded in summer and the Rainforest Biome does get extremely hot.
DON'T MISS:
Scattered around Eden are some wonderful sculptures, many by local artists. In a Mediterranean vineyard, Dionysus plays his pipes to a leaping goat and a group of nymphs, while outside a charming herd of cork pigs snuffle about. A great favourite is Bombus, a gigantic bumblebee complete with striped fur.
AMOUNT OF WALKING:
Moderate or lots. This is a large and in places very steep site, though there is a mapped wheelchair/pushchair) route. The tractor-drawn land train, which tours the site, can be very welcome.
COST:
Reasonable; under fives go free. Check online for discounts.
YOU SHOULD KNOW:
There is probably too much information at Eden for very young children. In summer the Eden Project – and the roads leading to it – can become crowded. Regular bus services run to Eden from several Cornish towns; ticket prices include entrance to the Project, thus minimizing queueing.

The Monkey Sanctuary and Hall Walk

Now a Trust working to end trade in primates and protect their natural habitats, the Monkey Sanctuary was started over 40 years ago to care for Amazonian woolly monkeys and now also rescues and rehabilitates capuchins, patas monkeys and Barbary macaques. In beautiful woodland overlooking Looe Bay, the four species are housed separately in spacious enclosures with indoor accommodation. Enthusiastic keepers give regular talks adapted to the age of the listeners, and special children's activities include learning about 'enrichment' – keeping the monkeys happy and active by arousing their curiosity. Native wildlife is also protected, with ponds for fish and amphibians, wildflowers for butterflies and a Forest Garden where a permaculture plot provides year-round food for the monkeys (displays explain the nutritional and medicinal properties of the plants). There is also a play area and a café with views over the treetops to the sea.

Hall Walk is a hilly but fairly easy and well-maintained walk round the lovely woods, creeks and cliff tops near Polruan. After a ferry ride from Fowey to Bodinnick and a climb through the village, the signed path skirts oak woods, with views of the busy estuary. Next, the route follows Pont Pill, a peaceful creek, and swings southwards uphill past the little church of St Winwaloe and on to a glorious open coastal landscape above Lantic Bay. From here, it's down to Polruan and the foot ferry back to Fowey. This walk is about 6 km (4 mi); a shorter stroll, either from Polruan up to the cliff top or round Pencarrow Head from the National Trust car park near the church, can also be taken.

A gorgeous inmate at the Monkey Sanctuary, Looe

WHERE:
Near Looe and around Polruan, near Fowey, Cornwall
BEST TIME TO GO:
The Monkey Sanctuary is open from April to the end of September, Sunday to Thursday; Hall Walk is splendid at any time of year on a fine day
DON'T MISS:
The Bat Cave at the Monkey Sanctuary. Rare horseshoe bats live in the cellar where a camera link allows visitors to watch these tiny creatures. There is also a camera in a birds' nest and a 'beecam' in a hive.
AMOUNT OF WALKING:
Moderate or lots. Parts of the Monkey Sanctuary are very steep; Hall Walk is unsuitable for pushchairs.
COST:
Low; under fives go free at the Monkey Sanctuary.
YOU SHOULD KNOW:
The writer Daphne du Maurier lived for a while at Bodinnick; Sir Arthur Quiller Couch,'Q', lived in Fowey and used the town as a setting for his Cornish-based books; there is a memorial to him on Hall Walk.

Goonhilly Satellite Earth Station and The National Seal Sanctuary

On the windswept downs of the Lizard Peninsula stand the gigantic tracking dishes of Goonhilly, which received the first live transatlantic TV broadcast via the Telstar satellite in 1962. At one time this was one of the largest satellite earth stations in the world, with over 60 dishes.

A shuttle bus takes visitors around the main operations site. In the interactive exhibition area of the Visitor Centre, the tempting options include operating a satellite dish and emailing an alien. Here, too, is one of Britain's fastest cyber cafés. At FutureWorld@Goonhilly predicting the future and meeting and controlling a robot are among the popular activities; there is also an early years' trail. Outside, a new attraction is the Segway, a futuristic personal transporter, for which there is an extra charge.

The National Seal Sanctuary moved to its present large area of creekside woodland in 1972. Though other rescued animals – including ponies and otters – live here, the purpose of the sanctuary is to rescue and rehabilitate marine mammals. In the special hospital building, injured seals and orphaned pups are treated (children can have a go at feeding a model pup); in the convalescence pool the pups learn to interact with other seals, then they are tagged and returned to the sea (almost all successfully). Permanent residents are seals that would be unable to survive in the wild and Rocky, a blind sea-lion. At feeding time, talks are given and, from underwater observatories, the swimming skills of the seals can be watched.

WHERE:
Near Helston, Cornwall

BEST TIME TO GO:
Goonhilly opens from late March to the end of October; there are limited openings at other times. The seal sanctuary is busiest from late autumn to early spring; once the pups have been released there are few seals to see.

DON'T MISS:
The History of the Video Game sounds a little dull, but this room is a must for gaming fans of all ages who can play games such as Space Invaders, Pacman or the latest in PS3, Wii and Xbox; the only problem will be dragging them away!

AMOUNT OF WALKING:
Little

COST:
Expensive

YOU SHOULD KNOW:
It is worth checking with the seal sanctuary about numbers in residence to avoid expensive disappointments. Released in 1962 to coincide with the transatlantic broadcast, *Telstar* – a catchy twangy instrumental with space-age effects by the Tornados – was a huge hit and the first British single to top the US charts.

One of the impressive satellite dishes at Goonhilly Earth Station

Land's End and Geevor Tin Mine

WHERE:
Near Penzance, Cornwall
BEST TIME TO GO:
Any time of year, but Geevor closes on Saturdays.
DON'T MISS:
Underground tours (in overalls and hard hats) of the narrow (and in places very low) 18th-century tunnels of Geevor's Wheal Mexico workings are often led by former miners with lots of fascinating tales to tell.
AMOUNT OF WALKING:
Moderate. Neither site is suitable for very small children.
COST:
Reasonable – though if a lot of attractions at Land's End are visited, it can get expensive.
YOU SHOULD KNOW:
On Botallack Head, near Geevor, the old mine clings to the rocks close to the shore. Miners who worked in its tunnels, which ran far out under the sea, could hear pebbles rolling backwards and forwards over their heads as the tide ebbed and flowed.

Visitors to the dramatic, wave-lashed granite tip of mainland Britain have, for many years, been awestruck by the mystery and grandeur of the landscape and amused by the iconic signpost with worldwide mileages. Now this famous landmark is a brand, part of the heritage industry, and even a photo by that signpost costs money. Every year there seem to be more lasers, lights or themed exhibitions – from serious stuff about air-sea rescue to the entertaining jumble of history and legend that is The Last Labyrinth by way of Dr Who. However, each attraction at the Visitor Centre can be visited separately and it is still possible simply to park the car, walk along the cliffs to enjoy fantastic views, watch seals, dolphins and basking sharks around the Longship Rocks in calm weather, thrill to the power of the ocean in rough or, in summer, enjoy a firework display.

The tall chimneys and crumbling engine houses of Cornwall's derelict mines are a reminder of the fortunes made since ancient times from tin and copper. In 1800, three quarters of the world's copper was mined here – tin became predominant later. During the 20th century, these deep and dangerous mines gradually closed. Tin was mined until 1990 at Geevor and it is now a fascinating museum, where the children may pan for gold. Much machinery is preserved and exhibits include mineral samples, working models, a film show and a photographic archive on the history of the mine and people of the area. In the Mill, the process of transforming ore into tin concentrate is explained. Geevor stands in magnificent coastal scenery and offers picnic spots and a café with sea views.

Hard hats are the order of the day at the tin mine!

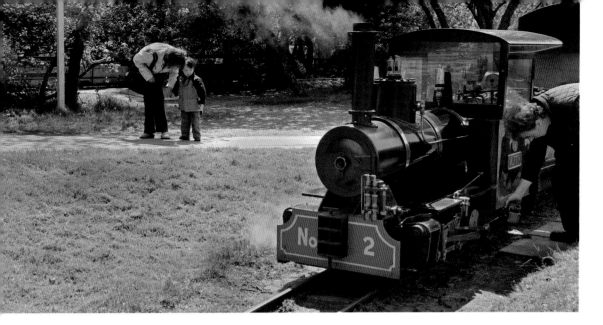

Keeping the loco in tip-top shape.

Lappa Valley Steam Railway

Three separate small-gauge railways run through the Lappa Valley, around an area of lakes that features games, mining history and walks. In the 19th century, East Wheal Rose silver-lead mine enjoyed great prosperity and a branch line of the Treffrey Tramway (which became part of Cornwall Mineral Railway) linked it to Newquay. The later passenger line operated until the Beeching cuts to the railway network in 1963. Eric Booth started the Lappa Valley Railway with 3.2 km (2 mi) of 38-cm (15-in) gauge track laid on cleared track-bed. A brand-new steam locomotive (*Zebedee*) arrived in 1974 and the whole area was drained by digging the lakes, and was then carefully landscaped. Since then more engines and carriages have joined the enterprise, an 18-cm (7.25-in) track – the Woodland Railway – has been laid to circle the smaller lake and, in 1995, a third, 26-cm (10.25-in) track – the Newlyn Branch Line – was added.

This is much more than a treat for train buffs; there are nature trails and walks through the valley – wildflowers bloom in profusion in this carefully protected, chemical-free environment, and nesting birds include buzzards, woodpeckers and owls. Stoats, badgers, foxes and deer are sometimes seen and, on early summer evenings, bats flitter by. Around the site there is crazy golf and putting, a brick-and-turf maze based on Richard Trevithick's engine, and various play areas. There are kayaks for use on the larger lake, while the small one acts as a nature reserve. At East Wheal Rose engine house, a viewing platform allows access to what was one of Cornwall's largest mine pumping engines, the 'Great Hundred'.

WHERE:
St Newlyn East, near Newquay, Cornwall
BEST TIME TO GO:
April to the end of September
DON'T MISS:
The Woodland Railway. This miniature train runs through a tunnel and round the nature pond. The rolling stock is, rather surprisingly, based on the 125 High-Speed Train and the Advanced Passenger Train.
AMOUNT OF WALKING:
Little or moderate
COST:
Reasonable; discounts may apply outside high season.
YOU SHOULD KNOW:
The size of Cornish beam engines was indicated by the diameter of their steam cylinders; the Great Hundred cylinder measured 2.54 m (8ft 4in) and, at its original installation in another mine, a dining table was lowered in with 13 people who enjoyed a feast while a band played on an upper floor.

An old cannon at Pendennis Castle

Falmouth Art Gallery and Pendennis Castle

Falmouth Art Gallery's proud motto is Family Friendly and Free. In its three galleries hang works from the excellent permanent collections and temporary exhibitions (about six a year) ranging from sea painting to Surrealism. An important collection of children's book illustrations has been set up at the gallery, and is a valuable resource for students of illustration. A winner of the *Guardian* Family Friendly Museum Award, the gallery runs regular workshops for children, drop-in family sessions, deliciously messy Baby Paint groups and school holiday activities. During the 2009 Darwin-themed exhibitions, workshops included Origin of the Species Zoetropes and Abstract Amoebas. In the gallery is a table where kids may sit and draw, an assortment of entertaining automata by local artists, and Paper People – quirky life-sized *papier-mâché* models. The gallery has produced a delightful activity story book which combines paintings from the collection (with comments by young critics), children's own artwork and a cartoon story – there is even space for readers' drawings.

At the other end of town on a rocky promontory stands Pendennis Castle, the last link of a coastal chain built by Henry VIII to counter the threat of invasion by France and Spain. Over the centuries, the castles were adapted to face new threats – Pendennis played a defensive role until the end of World War II. Now, every day in summer, the noonday gun is fired on the gun deck of the 16th-century circular keep and there are restored underground magazines and tunnels to explore. The Guardhouse has a World War I theme and in the refurbished Royal Artillery Barracks there is an interactive display on the castle's history. Events and activities take place during the summer.

WHERE:
Falmouth, Cornwall
BEST TIME TO GO:
All year. Access to some of the castle's buildings is limited from November to March.
DON'T MISS:
At Falmouth Art Gallery paintings by local children are hung during exhibitions. Young artists look at, copy, respond to or even improve on the professional works and a selection of the children's work is framed and displayed, close to the originals.
AMOUNT OF WALKING:
Little
COST:
Low
YOU SHOULD KNOW:
Pendennis's sister castle, St Mawes, stands on a headland across the harbour. It is a very fine example of Tudor military architecture and differs from Pendennis in that it is composed of three small circular bastions in a cloverleaf arrangement that enabled every angle of approach to be covered. St Mawes is just a quick ferry ride from Falmouth.

Trebah Gardens and Roskilly's Farm

Planted in the 1840s by Charles Fox and famous for rare and exotic plants gathered from all over the world, these beautiful gardens sadly suffered many years of neglect until the Hibbert family took on the enormous restoration and opened Trebah to the public in 1987. In the south-Cornish tradition, it occupies a steeply wooded ravine, tumbling alongside a stream down to a small beach on the Helford River. Trees and shrubs on the slopes include giant tree ferns and palms, and paths wind through hydrangeas and old rhododendrons. This 'garden of dreams' is great for children. There are two play areas – a sand pit and fort for under fives and exciting climbing and a zip wire in Tarzan's Camp. Permanent trails for different age groups include The Evolution of Man and the Hopalong Trail – a quest for bugs and beasties. Seasonal trails change frequently. Children may also feed the ducks, watch the koi carp in their shady pools, lose themselves in the Bamboozle and enjoy rock climbing and (very cold) bathing on the private beach.

No artificial chemicals have ever been used on Roskilly's dairy farm, and visitors here are welcome to follow paths and nature trails around ponds, old orchards, wetland withy woods, and the small irregular meadows with their shaggy uncut 'Cornish hedges'. Different areas provide habitats for wild flowers, fish and waterfowl, butterflies and insects, birds and small mammals. The old farmyard is home to friendly calves, ducks and hens, donkeys and cats, and afternoon milking can be watched. The rich, creamy milk of the large herd of beautiful Jersey cows is perfect for the clotted cream, fudge and ice cream for which Roskilly is justly famous.

WHERE:
Mawnan Smith, near Falmouth, and St Keverne, near Helston, Cornwall

BEST TIME TO GO:
Trebah offers variety all year; Roskilly's opens all year, but times vary in winter.

DON'T MISS:
The gunnera passage at Trebah – this tunnel through the towering giant rhubarb which looms above even adult heads is deliciously nerve tingling; children are warned to look out for 'things' that lurk in the tangle and in autumn the plants sink into a wonderfully loathsome mass of twisted, rotting and very hungry-looking stems.

AMOUNT OF WALKING:
Moderate or lots. Some parts of Trebah are very steep.

COST:
Low. Discounted winter prices apply at Trebah, and under fives go free.

YOU SHOULD KNOW:
From the large slipway on the Trebah beach, hundreds of men of the 29th US Infantry Division set off for Omaha Beach in 1944. There is a memorial to the many who died, and a small display about the part this tiny, peaceful spot played in the D-Day landings.

The beautifil Trebah Gardens

A boat trip up the River Fal

WHERE:
Falmouth to Truro, Cornwall
BEST TIME TO GO:
April to late September
DON'T MISS:
In the deep, secluded stretch of river near the King Harry Ferry, huge ocean-going vessels are laid up, sometimes for years. Some have been abandoned, some impounded, some await a last journey to the breakers. They tower above river traffic, enormous, sheer-sided, ghostly, rusting hulks.
AMOUNT OF WALKING:
Little
COST:
Reasonable
YOU SHOULD KNOW:
During World War II, Smugglers Cottage was requisitioned by the Admiralty. The concrete road to this remote riverside property was built for the embarkation of American troops and landing craft, and General Eisenhower visited before D-Day. There is an exhibition of memorabilia in the cottage.

Boats on the busy River Fal

Prince of Wales Pier in Falmouth is a fine spot to sit, watch boats in the harbour and eat ice creams or pasties. In summer, regular ferries to St Mawes and Flushing are joined by trip boats, and one of the most enjoyable is the journey up the river to Truro. It takes about an hour one way, and the timetable makes it possible to break the journey – the boats stop twice in each direction – and get on the next boat. There is a good commentary.

Carrick Roads is one of the world's biggest natural harbours, and around the shores villages bristle with moored boats while sails scud about. As the river narrows, steep, green, jungly hills plunge into the water – this lush area stood in for the Caribbean in an old film of *Treasure Island*. At Trelissick, a beautifully wooded estate almost surrounded by water, it is possible to disembark and enjoy a walk by the river or visit the National Trust property.

Just up river, the King Harry Steam Ferry Company has been transporting people and vehicles since 1888 – though Diesel now provides the power for this slow chain ferry. Next stop is Smugglers Cottage, a pretty thatched house with waterside gardens, for cream teas. After this, the river is tidal and a real wildlife haven, where the captain points out herons and seals. At low tide, the little village of Malpas is the last stop; an old blue double-decker bus takes passengers on to Truro, or a riverside pub makes a tranquil place to wait for the boat back.

Paradise Park and Hayle Towans Beach

Paradise Park, a collection of parrots and other birds housed in a spacious aviary in the gardens of Glanmor House in Hayle, opened in 1973. Since then it has become the base of the World Parrot Trust, with a successful breeding programme which owes much to the Parrot Flight – a huge aviary where birds live free, mate and flock in natural conditions. The aviaries have been extended with a medley of beautiful and rare birds including owls, other birds of prey and penguins as well as the parrots. Flamingoes occupy the lovely Victorian walled garden with its sub-tropical plants and elegant gazebos, and macaws fly free around the park. The park is also home to animals, with a variety of eminently 'pettable' miniature breeds in the Fun Farm, an otter pool, red pandas, and even a guinea pig village. Daily events include a free-flying bird show and feeding time for otters and penguins (keepers sometimes invite children to help). Little ones enjoy a ride round the gardens on the miniature railway, or playing in the indoor Jungle Barn.

Golden sands edge the whole of St Ives Bay; north of the Hayle Estuary, three miles of wide beach and turf-topped 'towans' – Cornish for dunes – sweep up to Godrevey Point. Though swimming, surfing and sandcastle building is possible everywhere, this top end of the bay is probably the most interesting. The Red River enters the sea, staining it with waste from the old tin mines and at Gwithian Towans there are rock pools and caves. There is a great walk to Godrevey over coastal grassland with views from the point right over the bay and down to inaccessible rocks where seabirds breed and seals bask.

Wind-swept dunes at Hayle Beach

WHERE:
Hayle, Cornwall
BEST TIME TO GO:
All year. Paradise Park closes early in winter.
DON'T MISS:
Feeding the lorikeets, little Australian parakeets, is a truly magical experience. The tiny, brightly coloured birds flutter around and land on arms, shoulders or heads, as they dart at the pot of special nectar the feeder holds.
AMOUNT OF WALKING:
Moderate
COST:
Reasonable
YOU SHOULD KNOW:
The red-billed chough, which appears on the Cornwall coat of arms, died out in the wild in the 1970s. A few have returned to the Cornish cliffs and the team at Paradise Park is now working on raising and releasing chough chicks.

The Camel Trail cycleway and footpath along the disused railway line on the estuary of the River Camel

The Camel Trail

WHERE:
Bodmin to Padstow, Cornwall
BEST TIME TO GO:
Any time of year
DON'T MISS:
The estuary of the Camel is important for over-wintering birds and at low tide, egrets and oystercatchers can be spotted. The golden plover is another resident. Out of season, there is real peace and an opportunity to watch wildlife – sometimes otters are seen.
AMOUNT OF WALKING:
Little
COST:
Reasonable – free if bike hire is unnecessary.
YOU SHOULD KNOW:
Sir John Betjeman was a regular traveller on the Atlantic Coast Express. He loved and was inspired by the river and the railway, and at the old Wadebridge Station, where the booking office and waiting rooms can still be seen, the John Betjeman Centre is dedicated to the popular poet.

Level and well-surfaced for all weathers, the Camel Trail follows an old railway track along the Camel valley through little-visited countryside. The original rail line from Padstow to Wadebridge carried sea-sand, and later slate and china clay, for shipping and fish for the markets. The Atlantic Coast Express brought holiday makers from London's Waterloo Station to the Cornish beaches.

The Camel Trail is provided and maintained by the County Council and allows riders, cyclists, walkers and wheelchair users safe and easy access to unspoilt areas. It links the towns of Padstow, Wadebridge and Bodmin and an extension follows the river towards Camelford. Car parking at Wadebridge, Bodmin and Poleys Bridge, makes it easy to break the trail into short sections with easy round trips of about 16 km (10 mi), and links with other cycle and walking trails. Cycle rental shops offer whole and half-day or evening hire of a wide range of bikes, from tandems to child's trailer bikes.

The most popular section of the Camel Trail is from Wadebridge to Padstow; the track crosses a fine, open estuary landscape, with opportunities for plant and bird spotting. Padstow is an excellent place to stop for an ice cream by the busy harbour, and perhaps a visit to the Lobster Hatchery. Experienced cyclists might try the longer circular route north of the river to Rock and, after a paddle, by ferry to Padstow. This route does get busy during school holidays. For a quieter ride, the track from Wadebridge towards Bodmin runs through narrow valleys and thick, shady woodland. North of Bodmin the woods give way to the wild, bare hills of Bodmin Moor, easily accessible from Poleys Bridge.

West Cornwall circular bus tour

The open-top double-decker summer service 300 makes a leisurely circuit of the far southwest of Cornwall. The timetable allows one or two stops, with time for a meal or exploration. The top deck is the perfect way to see this magnificent, empty countryside; the little roads wind between ancient stone 'Cornish hedges', through open moorland dotted with stone circles and Celtic crosses, past lonely villages and the relics of the mining heritage, often close to the wild cliffs, with sweeping sea views.

Porthcurno's beach, with white sand and the bluest water, lies below the remarkable Minnack Theatre. The bus stops at Land's End and Sennen and the granite village of Pendeen, where a little mining museum tells the story of the area. From here to Zennor the route crosses some of the finest coastal scenery in England, and the exhilarating Cornwall North Coast Path is easily reached from Morvah. Zennor, lying between moors and sea, is a lovely village. The Wayside Folk Museum is packed with artefacts, displays and stories of the lives of ordinary people, and nearby Zennor Quoit is just one of a number of ancient stone monuments.

In St Ives, the choices are numerous – paddling or bathing from the safe beaches, refreshment beside the bustling harbour, a brisk walk round the Island (actually a headland) where cormorants swim under the crystal water, or even viewing some art. The last stop on the return journey is at Marazion with its beach of wide, flat sand and St Michael's Mount rising like a huge sandcastle from the sea. For a cool-off back in Penzance there's the Jubilee Pool, an Art Deco lido.

WHERE:
Leaves from Penzance, Cornwall
BEST TIME TO GO:
May to the end of August – a reduced service operates in September.
DON'T MISS:
Zennor's church is famous for a medieval bench end carved as a mermaid holding comb and mirror. The local legend is that the mermaid fell for chorister Matthew Trewhella; he, enchanted, followed her down to the sea and now, sometimes, their duets can be heard rising above the sound of the waves. The story is retold by Charles Causley in *The Merry Maid of Zennor*.
AMOUNT OF WALKING:
Little or moderate
COST:
Low
YOU SHOULD KNOW:
The spectacular cliffs near Gurnards Head were used to train commandos in World War II and, in 1963, were climbed by Lord Hunt and Sherpa Tensing to celebrate the 10th anniversary of their conquest of Mount Everest.

First Western National open-top bus climbing out of Sennen Cove.

Restormel Castle and Charlestown

WHERE:
Lostwithiel and Charlestown, near
St Austell, Cornwall
BEST TIME TO GO:
April to end October
DON'T MISS:
At Charlestown the harbour and
beaches on either side are owned by
a company that operates a fleet of
tall ships. One or two are usually
anchored in the harbour and may be
visited. Their presence completes the
'time capsule' atmosphere.
AMOUNT OF WALKING:
Moderate
COST:
Low to reasonable; children under
ten go free at the Shipwreck
Museum.
YOU SHOULD KNOW:
Charlestown replaced a settlement
called West Polmear, which had a
population of nine. It was designed
by John Smeaton, who was
responsible for building the
Eddystone Lighthouse.

*Restormel Castle was built at
the turn of the 14th century.*

A perfectly circular castellated keep and its position crowning a mound, circled by deep moats, tucked into a bend of the River Fowey and backed by wooded hills, lends Restormel a fairytale appearance. One half expects a knight in shining armour to appear and rescue the princess languishing inside. It is a place of great peace and is delightful to explore. Edward the Black Prince stayed here in the 14th century – it was a stronghold of the Dukes of Cornwall – and it saw action in the Civil War. But it fell into graceful decay and now little is left but the ruins of a gate and traces of the great hall of the once-mighty fortress.

After the castle, visit the charming little town of Charlestown which was built by and named after local mine owner and china clay exporter Charles Rashleigh at the end of the 18th century. It remains a marvellously complete example of a late-Georgian working port. A basin was cut to allow anchorage for large ships, roads were widened and paved, and a pier built to shelter the fishing fleet. In the 19th century, fisherman's cottages and the warehousing for businesses like rope making and pilchard curing were added to the elegant Georgian houses. The Shipwreck Museum is a real treasure chest; as well as finds from wrecks, it houses records of maritime history and a large collection of diving gear. There are also animated scenes of village life, including a cooper and blacksmith. It is housed in an old china clay building, and visitors can walk to the docks through tunnels once used by clay trucks.

Surf school at Sennen Cove

A surf lesson at Sennen and the Porthcurno Telegraph Museum

Surfing is big business in Cornwall and surf schools have sprung up all round the coast – the beaches around Newquay sometimes seem more like Australia than England. The long west-facing beach at Whitesand Bay has superb surf and a couple of surf schools are based at Sennen Cove, a little harbour village at the southern end of the bay where steep slopes drop behind a huddle of cottages, a pub and beach restaurant. With sheltering cliffs, pale sand and turquoise waters, this is one of Britain's most beautiful surfing locations. Short one-day surf courses consist of a 'know-how' session on equipment and beach safety, and instruction on lying down and standing up on the surfboard before being pushed into small waves to put it all into practice. The small groups can be families, or just children. Longer courses are available for those who get hooked.

When the first undersea telegraphy cable was connected between Bombay and Porthcurno in 1870, the tiny village became the most important communication centre in the world. During World War II, secret messages were transmitted and the centre was moved into a bomb- and gas-proof underground building, now part of a fascinating award-winning museum. As well as exhibitions about the history of cable telegraphy (the 'Victorian Internet') and other methods of communication, and the lives of Cable & Wireless employees over the years, there are lots of working machines and equipment, and demonstrations. In the educational area, children can learn how to transmit Morse code.

WHERE:
Near Penzance, Cornwall
BEST TIME TO GO:
Surf schools operate from Easter until late September. The Telegraph Museum is open every day from April to the start of November, and on Sundays and Mondays for the rest of the year.
DON'T MISS:
The museum at Porthcurno has a maze of tunnels to explore and a look-out point on the evacuation stair. Interesting talks on the top-secret wartime work are given, sometimes by museum volunteers who actually worked there at the time.
AMOUNT OF WALKING:
Little
COST:
Expensive
YOU SHOULD KNOW:
Children must be over eight to join surf school. Proudly displayed in the lifeboat house at Sennen Cove is an August 1979 telegram from the Prime Minister, paying tribute to the work of the crew. Competitors in the Fastnet race ran into some very bad weather locally; several yachts and sailors were lost and the Sennen lifeboat men spent nine hours out at sea helping survivors.

The MS Oldenburg *passenger ferry for Lundy Island moored at the Landing Place.*

Day trip to Lundy

WHERE:
Off the North Devon coast
BEST TIME TO GO:
March to October. May – the nesting season – is the best time to spot puffins.
DON'T MISS:
In Lundy's village, as well as a church and a shop that sells Lundy stamps alongside general provisions, the Marisco Tavern is the hub of the island's social life. Here the visitor can enjoy a meal (there is a children's menu) and drink the Tavern's own Lundy beer.
AMOUNT OF WALKING:
Moderate or lots. The walking is very good, on springy turf tracks.
COST:
Expensive, unless visitors arrive in their own boats, in which case just a landing fee is due.
YOU SHOULD KNOW:
Sometimes return sailings are not to where they started from; in this case, coach transport is provided to the other town. Marisco Castle was once the well-defended stronghold of the piratical Marisco family. In 1242 William de Marisco was captured, taken to London and executed for allegedly sending an assassin to cut the King's throat; afterwards, the island changed hands frequently and the castle fell into ruins.

Over the centuries, rocky Lundy was held by Vikings, Normans, pirates and outlaws. Now the property of the National Trust, it is administered and maintained by the Landmark Trust, who run a ferry from Ilfracombe or Bideford. The two-hour mini-cruise allows views of the lovely North Devon coastline as well as preparation for the visit – the comfortable MS *Oldenburg* carries guides and leaflets on Lundy's history, wildlife and walks. The southeast tip is the only landing place. An imposing medieval castle (once the home of the lords of the isle) stands above it and from the village a little inland, paths lead to all parts of the island.

Lundy (its name means Puffin Isle in Norse) is tiny – just 5 km by 800 m (3 mi by 0.5 mi) – but its dramatic cliffs and scrubland provide habitats for a surprisingly large number of bird, animal and plant species. Puffins are less common now, though they still nest in burrows on the grassy cliff tops, while many species of raptor and migratory seabirds nest and visit. Resident mammals include Lundy ponies, Soay sheep and black rats, while around the coast seals and basking sharks may be spotted. The west coast is best for bird spotting and spectacular views, the east is for plant hunting – this is the only place where the Lundy cabbage grows. The central plateau is dotted with ponds and springs, and domestic animals wander, free-range and friendly, over the farmland.

This tranquil, traffic-free haven also offers diving opportunities, rock climbing the many soaring cliffs, and a few oddities including a chasm that opened as a result of tremors from the 1755 Lisbon earthquake.

Crealy Adventure Park

Although Crealy's lacks heart-stopping, state-of-the-art thrills, it has plenty of fun and excitement for younger children and for parents and grandparents who enjoy a slightly slower pace. Surrounded by a large area of parkland – where there is a campsite in the summer – Crealy's is divided into Realms, each with its own theme. Most of the bigger and faster rides and activities are found in the Adventure and Action Realms. Rides in the former range from a runaway train rollercoaster and water splash to a lovely Victorian carousel; energetic activities like reverse bungee jumping, tube slides, high-level walkways and climbing walls are cleverly transformed to magical worlds, with pirate ships, volcanoes, dinosaurs and caves adding just that bit extra. Action Realm is a place to drive and get wet, with activities like karting, bumper boats and water wars. For very small children, the Magic Realm, with its miniature railway and village, playground rides and sand games, is perfect, and the Magic Kingdom, an indoor adventure playground with soft, safe, netted play areas, combines fun and confidence building.

A little land train runs to the Natural Realm with its woodland and meadow walks and wildlife, river and lake, and the Farming Realm has farm animals, pony rides and glorious seasonal fields of sunflowers and pumpkins. Animal Realm provides a good range of small cuddly pets – and there is even a pet shop.

Special events include Easter egg hunts, a Halloween event with pumpkin carving and at Christmas a visit by Santa Claus. In the holidays, favourites from children's TV put in regular appearances.

WHERE:
Clyst St Mary, near Exeter, Devon
BEST TIME TO GO:
All year. Thursdays to Sundays only from November to late March but daily in Devon school holidays and in other months.
DON'T MISS:
Crealy's 'water features' are great fun. The little river is crossed by several bridges which offer a challenge – for example, stepping stones or wobbly logs. Dragonfly Lake is a haven for birds and there are ducks and carp to feed and radio-controlled boats and powered (with very small motors) canoes to play with.
AMOUNT OF WALKING:
Little
COST:
Expensive, though there is a whole range of discounts and reductions. Children under 92 cm (3 ft) tall go free while those up to 100 cm (3 ft 3 in) are eligible for reduced tickets which allow free re-entry. Other discounts apply during the winter season and for online bookings.

Enjoying the thrills of the runaway train rollercoaster and the water splash ride.

Babbacombe Model Village and Kents Cavern

The model village at Babbacome is set in extensive landscaped gardens featuring dwarf conifers and shrubs, streams and waterfalls – a tiny world complete with thousands of miniature buildings, people and vehicles, a peepshow on English life from medieval castle (with fire-breathing dragon) to Olympic building site. Around the garden are various trails, treasure hunts and competitions for families and children of all ages. A good range of under cover attractions includes a 3-D film show and a fine model railway layout. Special seasonal events include Halloween 'haunting' and a stunning winter wonderland with realistic snow effects and, of course, a visit by Santa Claus at Christmas.

Kents Cavern offers a contrast to the light-hearted little village. This complex of caves and passages is probably the oldest known 'residence' in Europe. It was first excavated in the 1820s, when a huge hoard of animal bones (including sabre-toothed cats and mammoths) was found; later digs unearthed a human jawbone more than 30,000 years old (now in Torquay Museum) and Britain's oldest flint axe heads. Nowadays, cave guides lead a journey through half a million years of intermittent occupation. Ice Age animals and Neanderthals were succeeded by the Romans, who left coins here, and in the early 20th century the cavern was used as a workshop for making beach huts for Torquay sea front. The tour passes through caves with stalactites and stalagmites and remarkable rock formations, and visitors see and touch some of Europe's oldest artefacts, experience total darkness, and hear tales of the cavemen. Above ground, children's activities include tribal face painting and digging for treasure; special events include ghost shows and Stone Age survival courses.

House of Marbles and Becky Falls Woodland Park

The House of Marbles is a complex of shops, workshops, museums and recreational areas in and around an old pottery near Bovey Tracey. From a viewing gallery, visitors watch the fascinating and highly skilled work of glass blowers, then learn about the history of glass making in the Glass Museum, where different processes are illustrated by examples from over the centuries. The Marble Museum houses a collection of unusual and historic marbles and explains their manufacture and history, while the Games Museum comprises marble-related and other games, old and new, from around the world. Beneath the old kiln chimneys, outside the restaurant, is the Games Garden, where games like skittles, giant chess and (of course) marbles can be played.

Visitors have enjoyed the peace and beauty of the hidden, wooded valley of Becka Brook, high on Dartmoor, since Victorian times. Now, Becky Falls Woodland Park at Manaton, with its waterfalls, huge granite rocks, thick oak canopy and rugged landscape, animals and all-weather activities, is a favourite with adults and children. Animals here include Dartmoor and Shetland ponies, rescued owls and other birds of prey and a delightful collection of small, cuddly creatures. A full weekend and school holiday programme includes meeting and petting the little animals and the very popular and informative Scary Animal Encounters with boa constrictors, tarantulas and the like. Carefully planned walks around the extensive park offer something interesting around every corner. A short walk incorporates a nature trail competition, longer routes pass waterfalls and a very energetic 'boulder scramble'.

A walkway in Becky Falls Woodland Park

WHERE:
Bovey Tracey and Manaton, Devon
BEST TIME TO GO:
House of Marbles is open all year. Becky Falls opens from February until November, and occasionally in winter.
DON'T MISS:
The Marble Runs, where a descending marble delicately trips a switch to send another down a different route, to what is possibly the biggest marble run in the world. Here, snooker balls take 20 minutes to complete a cycle and make the descent down something like the height of a house.
AMOUNT OF WALKING:
Moderate. Walks at Becky Falls are unsuitable for wheelchairs or pushchairs. Good footwear is recommended for the longer walks.
COST:
Reasonable. House of Marbles is free; all activities are included in the Becky Falls ticket price.
YOU SHOULD KNOW:
The two-tonne 'floating marble', centrepiece of the Games Garden, 'sits' on water and can be set in revolving motion with a firm but gentle push.

A Dartmoor walk and the Finch Foundry

Walking on Dartmoor

A huge expanse of windswept granite uplands, Dartmoor remains a true wilderness. Its most recognizable natural features are the tors – granite stacks towering above the eroded moorland – while stone circles and deserted quarries and mines bear witness to human presence since prehistoric times. Wild ponies still roam and the untouched landscape is habitat to many rare bird and plant species. This is challenging long-distance walking country; paths thread the moor and Tourist Information Centres provide advice and routes, but all walkers should have a good map and, for longer walks, water, waterproofs and stout footwear. Haytor Rocks gives a taste of Dartmoor – one of the most dramatic tors, it stands, visible for miles, close to the road. A longer – about 5-km (3.25-mi) – walk, starting at Bennets Cross on the B3215, uses heathery and grassy tracks and stretches of a narrow lane leading south towards Widecombe and is not too rugged. Walkers head east along the Two Moors Way, down the lane and up to Grimspound, a Bronze Age settlement. Next, the path westwards between Challacombe Down and Headland Warren passes the remains of Golden Dagger Mine, where there are information boards, and returns northwards to the starting point.

The pretty village of Sticklepath clings to the northern edge of Dartmoor along the River Taw. Here, the Finch Foundry is a rare survival – a working, water-powered forge that produced a wide range of edge tools for mining and agriculture from 1814 until 1960. Now it's a museum, home to the last authentic trip hammers in the UK. Regular demonstrations show how the foundry men fashioned their implements. The sluices power three wheels – one powers hammers and metal cutters, one grinds and polishes, and the third works the bellows. The size and ponderous action of the enormous beams, hammers and grindstones is awe inspiring.

WHERE:
Dartmoor and Sticklepath, near Okehampton, Devon

BEST TIME TO GO:
The Finch Foundry is open March to late October (closed Tuesdays).

DON'T MISS:
Grimspound is a remarkable site. Inside a huge, roughly circular enclosing wall, the remains of 24 houses show evidence of sleeping platforms, lintels and passages to keep out the weather. It is easily accessible from the lane.

AMOUNT OF WALKING:
Moderate or lots

COST:
Low

YOU SHOULD KNOW:
Never underestimate the weather on Dartmoor. It can change very quickly. Dartmoor Letterboxing began in the 19th century; now hundreds of 'letterboxes' are hidden across the moor; 'letterboxers' use stamps and inkpads to prove they have found them. Maps and clues can be downloaded, or provided by Dartmoor Tourist Information centres.

Cycling the Tarka Trail

Henry Williamson's famous 1927 book *Tarka the Otter* took inspiration from the glorious countryside around the Rivers Taw and Torridge, west of Exmoor, and this fertile, rural landscape remains wonderfully unchanged. In all, the Tarka Trail, part of the Devon coast-to-coast cycle route, is around 290 km (180 mi) long; the most popular stretch, the 48 km (30 mi) of easily accessible traffic-free track from Braunton to Meeth, uses the old passenger and mineral railways of North Devon, and follows the journey of the fictional otter. Cycle hire is available at Braunton, the delightful riverside towns of Barnstable and Bideford, and the historic hilltop market town of Great Torrington. The route is furnished with frequent information boards detailing the history and wildlife of the area.

From Braunton to Barnstable, the trail follows the banks of the river and Taw estuary, where many wildfowl over-winter. Barnstable can be bypassed over the new bridge, and from here to Bideford there are wonderful views over the river and the mouth of the estuary. Fremington Quay, with waterside pubs and restaurants, and Instow, with a sandy beach and a historic signal box, make good stopping places. The trail then cuts through the pretty village of East-the-Water, linked to Bideford by a bridge, and runs on to Torrington through cuttings and tunnels, along causeways and over bridges. The riverbank in the shadow of Beam Aqueduct near Weare Gifford is described as Tarka's birthplace, but riders are very unlikely to see otters. Though rare, they do still inhabit the rivers hereabouts but they are very shy and are usually only spotted after nightfall. The trail from Torrington to Meeth is more roughly surfaced and suitable only for mountain bikes, but this is a tranquil and scenic section through wooded and remote countryside with views of distant Dartmoor.

WHERE:
Braunton to Meeth, Devon
BEST TIME TO GO:
Any time of year in good weather
DON'T MISS:
Along the Tarka Trail are 30 lovely sculptural benches, part of the SUSTRANS Travelling Landscape programme. They include three wooden benches with sitting figures made from old railway sleepers, and four ceramic mosaic seats reflecting characters from *Tarka the Otter*.
AMOUNT OF WALKING:
Little (but plenty of cycling)
COST:
Low or reasonable – depending on the need for cycle hire.
YOU SHOULD KNOW:
Along the trail, riders may encounter volunteer groups working on clearing ponds, laying hedges and cutting coppices. Hazel coppice provides an ideal habitat for dormice and is augmented by special dormice nesting boxes.

Cycling on the Tarka Trail

Woolacombe beaches and Braunton Burrows Nature Reserve

WHERE:
Woolacombe, North Devon
BEST TIME TO GO:
Any time of year
DON'T MISS:
Barrican Beach is a rock-framed cove at the north end of Morte Bay where sands give way to rock pools. It is noted for seashells swept ashore by the incoming tide. Above, the cliff path leads to Morte Point which claimed so many ships in the age of sail – high above the rocks and reputedly once the haunt of wreckers.
AMOUNT OF WALKING:
Moderate or lots
COST:
Low
YOU SHOULD KNOW:
North of Braunton Village, Braunton Great Field is one of the few surviving relics of the open-field system of the Middle Ages, when land was communally farmed in long narrow strips. About 200 of the original strips survive.

The west-facing sandy beaches between Morte Point and the Taw estuary are some of the finest in the country. The popular resort of Woolacombe was just a fishing village until the 19th-century craze for sea bathing, and some Regency villas survive as a reminder of this elegant era. Now, over 3 km (2 mi) of clean sands, rock pools and sparkling water (the beach holds a Blue Flag award) appeal to families, while the great waves rolling in from the Atlantic attract surfers. Although it can get crowded in high season, there are walks along the gorse-clad downs and rocky headlands and it's usually possible to find relative peace. Croyde, the smaller beach to the south of Baggy Point, hosts the annual Oceanfest surf and music festival. Saunton Sands, with its colourful beach huts and 5 km (3 mi) of sands, is perfect for beach activities of all kinds.

Saunton sands are backed by Braunton Burrows, a wilderness of

A family walking on beach at the water's edge enjoying a perfect British summer's day.

sand dunes towering to 30 m (100 ft). This, one of the most impressive dune systems in Britain, forms the core of an extensive UNESCO Biosphere Reserve, which extends to take in the mudflats and salt-scoured creeks of the Taw Torridge Estuary and a verdant, flat area of marshland, drained by reedy dykes. The varied habitats – flower-rich grassland, scrub, and the flooded dune 'slacks' (damp hollows in the marram-clad sandhills) – are home to hundreds of flowering plant species and 30 or more butterfly species. Breeding birds in the reserve include wheatears, skylarks and meadow pipits, and many waterfowl over-winter here.

Combe Martin Wildlife and Dinosaur Park

A large area of steep wooded valleys, sub-tropical gardens and cascading waterfalls near the North Devon coast is home to a remarkable variety of wildlife. Here the visitor will see birds, from penguins to free-flying exotic species; animals, from meerkats and racoons to wallabies; plus primates and dinosaurs. In the Dinosaur Domain, life-sized models of the giants lurk among the trees, while another group, including the popular and terrifying *Tyrannosaurus rex*, comes alive every hour. The animatronic monsters stretch, roar and even spit, and small children shriek with delight – or alarm.

A miscellany of birds and animals lives around the hill park. Some are cute and cuddly, others – the timber wolves – are almost as frightening as the dinosaurs. There is a varied daily programme of talks, demonstrations and encounters. The falconry displays and the sea lion shows are particularly interesting and enjoyable and are introduced by informative talks, while Lemur Encounters allow visitors to hand feed the enchanting creatures. In the warm, humid tropical jungle garden of the Butterfly House, clouds of fluttering colour surround visitors, who may also be lucky enough to see butterflies emerging from chrysalises in the hatchery.

Other attractions that are under cover include a Dinosaur Museum for background information and a film show on evolution as well as unrelated options such as a space-themed light show, a large collection of brasses to rub and a trip round the Tomb of the Pharaohs, which is part history, part thrilling shocks. Outdoor activities and rides star the very exciting – and extremely wet – Earthquake Canyon.

WHERE:
Combe Martin, North Devon
BEST TIME TO GO:
March to November. The park is much more enjoyable in dry weather.
DON'T MISS:
The talk about wolves – there is only one a day – is absolutely riveting. Often given by TV's ' Wolfman', these talks engage with all age groups and allow the audience to get really close to the wolves.
AMOUNT OF WALKING:
Moderate, but neither easy nor level. The park is not suitable for pushchairs or wheelchairs, and some of the car parking is on steep hillsides which makes popping back for something a major trek.
COST:
Reasonable. Free entry for under threes.
YOU SHOULD KNOW:
In Combe Martin stands a remarkable building – the 18th century Pack O'Cards Inn, which has four floors, 13 rooms and 52 windows; it was apparently built by a local squire with the winnings from an evening's card playing.

Morwellham Quay

Morwellham historic copper ore mines

This fascinating open-air museum features restored copper-mine workings, a village and farm in an area of tranquil, rolling countryside backed by steep, thickly wooded valley walls on a bend in the River Tamar. Visitors are greeted by costumed villagers who introduce them to the 1860s, when the river would have bristled with the masts of merchant ships, the quays would have been heaped with copper ore, and the whole community would have bustled about their work.

Morwellham Quay provides an opportunity to explore the lives of the Victorians. Adults and children may dress up in period costume and children can try working – making rope, copper dressing, being in service and so on. Buildings in the village include a blacksmith's, Assay Office, sweet shop and (working) pub. Pretty cottage gardens are planted as they would have been in the 19th century and three of the cottages are fitted with furniture, domestic equipment and utensils, which give a picture of the lives of families in three very different income brackets. At the Quay, a restored Tamar sailing ship is berthed; children can sometimes get a taste of a cabin boy's life on board.

The Nature Reserve Walk passes kitchen gardens, woodlands, wetlands and hay meadows. Along the way are dipping ponds, mini-beast hunts and special hides with spotter charts for children. The Mine Railway runs alongside the river and deep into the George and Charlotte Mine, where the driver expertly explains the history and work of the mine and the lives of the miners.

Prickly Ball Farm and Hedgehog Hospital

Everyone loves hedgehogs; there is something irresistible about them, whether they are the heroes of the garden or, since Mrs Tiggywinkle, of favourite storybooks. The Hedgehog Hospital at Prickly Ball Farm rescues and cares for about 200 hedgehogs a year, with the aim of releasing them back into the wild when they are fully recovered, and a visit is a must for anyone with an interest in these charming and strange little creatures.

A baby hedgehog who is being looked after at the Prickly Ball Hedgehog Hospital.

There are informative sessions about the lives, habits and habitats of hedgehogs, and early arrivals can watch them being fed. A video presentation explains the valuable work of the hospital and there is a small collection of hedgehogs from around the world; here children learn to 'spot the difference' – such as the Egyptian hedgehog's huge ears.

Visitors can wander around the working farm, where children can see, and sometimes help with, pigs and chickens being fed. In the Big Barn there are miniature ponies, orphaned baby farm animals, and other animals including the entertaining and energetic chipmunks. Younger children adore Pets' Corner, where they can stroke a whole menagerie of small furry animals from mice to chinchillas. Other activities (timetabled, so that all get a turn) include walking goats and ferrets and collecting eggs and, at the end of the afternoon, helping to 'put the animals to bed'. The farm also has a children's play area, picnic benches and a beautiful wildlife garden with stunning views towards Dartmoor and lots of helpful information and hints about making gardens wildlife-friendly.

WHERE:
Near Newton Abbot, Devon
BEST TIME TO GO:
April to late October
DON'T MISS:
Meet the Hedgehogs sessions are offered several times a day in the Hedgehog Hospital. This is a carefully organized chance for children to ask questions, get really close to hedgehogs, and feel their spikes.
AMOUNT OF WALKING:
Little
COST:
Reasonable. Under threes go free and season tickets are available.
YOU SHOULD KNOW:
Nearby Newton Abbot is home to the UK's only working malthouse, which is open to the public. Brewery tours – and samples – are available.

The old kitchen in St Nicholas Priory

WHERE:
Exeter, Devon
BEST TIME TO GO:
The passages are open all week from June to September and during school holidays; and Tuesday to Friday afternoons and weekends from October to May. The priory is open Monday to Saturday during school holidays and on Saturdays the rest of the year.
DON'T MISS:
Most of the water piped into the city actually went to the cathedral precinct and householders had to collect their supply from conduits. Some acquired a direct supply by boring holes and lowering buckets; traces of this can be seen in the roofs of the passages.
AMOUNT OF WALKING:
Little. The tunnels have low vaults, uneven floors and dark areas; they are also constricted and not suitable for those who suffer from claustrophobia.
COST:
Low; children are admitted free at St Nicholas Priory.
YOU SHOULD KNOW:
Accompanied under fives are allowed free access to the exhibition, but not into the underground passages. Unusually, extensive buildings remain from the original Benedictine priory of St Nicholas. The story goes that a number of feisty Exeter women were so angered by the sacrilege of the Dissolution that they hurled stones and abuse at the workmen until they stopped demolition work.

Exeter's underground passages and St Nicholas Priory

The city of Exeter was founded by the Romans and flourished in succeeding centuries. Much of its old centre was destroyed by air raids in World War II, but one unique ancient monument untouched by bombs is the complex of underground passages, dating from the 14th century, constructed to house the lead pipes that carried clean spring water from outside the city walls. Much of the tunnelling was vaulted to allow workmen access to leaks, and the section running beneath Princesshay and the surrounding streets can be visited. Above ground a museum displays information panels, a full-size mock-up of part of the tunnels, a computerized link and a Fly Through experience, for those who are unable to go below ground. The tunnel guides explain the history and construction of the tunnels, and tell tales of hideouts and smugglers.

St Nicholas Priory was part of a medieval monastery which, after the Dissolution, became a Tudor merchant's home. A recent imaginative restoration project, which worked closely with local school groups, has refurbished it as an Elizabethan home. It is decorated with authentic rich colours and fabrics and with high-quality replica furnishings (which visitors can sit on, touch and use) as well as selected items from the museum collection. Rooms include the kitchen and fine parlour, with original Tudor plaster ceiling and painted panelled walls. The summer programme of Living History performances and hands-on activities concerning Elizabethan and Tudor life includes cooking and making herbal remedies in the kitchen, dance, and drama as well as meeting the Hurst family who lived in the house 400 years ago.

Sidmouth Donkey Sanctuary and Pecorama

Sidmouth Donkey Sanctuary has cared for old, sick and overworked donkeys for 40 years. The charity now owns several farms around the country where donkeys are homed, but Slade Farm welcomes visitors to learn about the work there, take walks in the lovely countryside and, most importantly, meet the residents. Around 150 donkeys live on the farm, many wandering the rolling pastures, others in the barn and main yard. Elderly donkeys need lots of extra tender loving care, and these and others in the yard are friendly and reliable and very happy to be talked to, hugged and generally made a fuss of. There are no commercial attractions here, but there is a hedge maze and a very pleasant walk to a Nature Centre with interactive displays on habitats and local wildlife. During school holidays, themed days are organized, with special activities for children.

On a hillside above the picturesque fishing village of Beer, Pecorama is home to the Beer Light Railway, a 184-mm (7.25-in) gauge, passenger-carrying miniature railway powered by steam or Diesel locomotives. The track meanders around the lovely flower-filled gardens, through cuttings and a tunnel and along embankments with glorious views over Lyme Bay. Here, too, is the undercover PECO Model Railway Exhibition, with all sorts of wonderfully detailed layouts in different styles and scales, some of which can be operated by children. The railway theme continues with an old Pullman car serving cream teas. The extensive gardens include the beautiful, celestially themed Millennium Gardens, planted to reflect their names – Sun, Moon and Rainbow – and linked by scented walkways and water features. There is a shell-decorated grotto to explore and daily summer afternoon entertainment in the Top Spot Garden Theatre, which includes clowns and magicians.

A lovely resident of Sidmouth Donkey Sanctuary

WHERE:
Sidmouth and Beer, Devon
BEST TIME TO GO:
Sidmouth Donkey Sanctuary is open all year. Pecorama opens Monday to Friday and Saturday mornings, April to late October; and on Sundays at Easter and late May to September. Closed Saturday afternoons.
DON'T MISS:
For donkey lovers, taking part in grooming and walking is a wonderful chance to get to know the gentle animals. The Welfare Department of the sanctuary also runs workshops on the care of donkeys.
AMOUNT OF WALKING:
Little or moderate
COST:
Reasonable. The Donkey Sanctuary is free, with a small charge for activities. Pecorama is free for the under fours and over 80s. Reduced price tickets are available for entry to gardens and model railways only.
YOU SHOULD KNOW:
Sidmouth Donkey Sanctuary charity is also involved in work abroad. The passionately committed staff (many of whom were regular visitors as children) are happy to talk to visitors about the international projects, which provide care and medication for over half a million donkeys worldwide.

Buckfastleigh Butterflies and Dartmoor Otter Sanctuary

WHERE:
Buckfastleigh, Devon
BEST TIME TO GO:
April to October. In March, only the otters may be visited (restricted hours).
DON'T MISS:
Visitors not arriving at Buckfastleigh by train can, for the price of a platform ticket, visit the Railway Museum, workshops, refreshment rooms and model railway in the Buckfastleigh terminus.
AMOUNT OF WALKING:
Little
COST:
Low, or reasonable if visitors choose to buy a combined ticket for butterflies and otters and the South Devon Railway.
YOU SHOULD KNOW:
The Valiant Soldier public house in Buckfastleigh hasn't sold a pint since the landlord called 'Time!' in 1965. Nothing has changed; it is now a Heritage Centre and a perfect time capsule.

The steam trains of the South Devon Railway follow the River Dart from Totnes to Buckfastleigh, where the Steam and Leisure Park with its children's play area, maze, riverside walks and occasional traditional fairground rides is also home to Buckfastleigh Butterflies and Dartmoor Otters. The Butterfly House was specially designed to exhibit exotic butterflies and moths; the environment in the flight area is carefully controlled with the high temperatures and humidity that suits the butterflies and sustains their food plants. For visitors who wish to learn more about the order Lepidoptera there are displays and information panels, but for most, the highlight of this lovely tropical garden is the butterflies themselves. These beautiful, ephemeral, delicate (and non-venomous) insects fill the air with colour and even settle on delighted visitors.

The outside landscape is a specialist otter park, so well adapted that wild otters from the River Dart occasionally 'break in' for a snack or nap. There are generous tanks, covered ways, raised viewing walks, underground observation windows and inclined mirrors above the holts, allowing non-intrusive viewing. Three species of otter live here – shy, elusive native otters, playful Asian otters and large American river otters. Some of the otters have been rescued, others were bred here. The park's owners and staff know each one by name and enjoy talking about them to visitors. Feeding time is when all otters are at their most active and playful, and it's a real joy to watch their antics. They dive, scamper, play-fight, and tumble with such verve that it seems they are putting on a special show for the onlookers.

An otter at the Butterfly and Otter Sanctuary

Dawlish to Teignmouth – beaches, tunnels and a pier

People leaving a tour boat moored at the Back Beach.

The highlight of a train journey down to the southwest is the stretch from Dawlish to Teignmouth. Spray lashed on wild days, sandwiched between red cliffs and the sea, the line runs through the arches and tunnels of rock that made the building of this part of the Great Western Railway so challenging. To the north of Dawlish, Dawlish Warren consists of a spit of land with sandy beaches, a resort and a nature reserve, where huge flocks of wildfowl and waders over-winter. Bright beach huts have made a welcome return to the Blue Flag beach here. Dawlish itself is an attractive Regency resort built along the seafront and up both sides of central gardens. It has several beaches and a quirky local museum.

Dawlish and Teignmouth are only a couple of miles apart and the South West Coast Path runs under the cliffs alongside the beach and railway line, except for a loop inland at Holcombe where a long tunnel runs through the headland called The Parson and the Clerk. Alternatively, there are local trains and frequent buses. Teignmouth has extensive and varied beaches and an outdoor swimming pool. The Grand Pier offers traditional amusements and good views; it originally marked the dividing line between male and female bathing huts. Around the point, the sheltered harbour and quay were once busy with the shipment of Dartmoor granite; they are still used by fishing boats and a ferry to Sheldon, where the Sheldon Wildlife Trust is a breeding centre for rare small mammals, reptiles and birds.

WHERE:
Dawlish to Teignmouth, Devon
BEST TIME TO GO:
In fine weather all year round
DON'T MISS:
The Lawn. Dawlish's delightful park in the middle of town is landscaped round a stream, with little weirs and pools where water birds live, including the Dawlish black swans brought here from Australia in around 1900.
AMOUNT OF WALKING:
Moderate
COST:
Low
YOU SHOULD KNOW:
At Starcross, between Dawlish and Exeter, is the remains of a pumping house, part of Brunel's Atmospheric Railway. Trains were operated by vacuum suction and ran quietly and quickly, but rats chewed at the leather valves and the system, one of the great engineer's few failures, was abandoned in 1848.

The Fairy Garden at Wookey Hole

Wookey Hole Caves

One of the most famous attractions in the West Country, Wookey Hole has been drawing visitors for centuries to marvel at its extraordinary show caves. The site lies on the southern edge of the Mendips, where the River Axe emerges from its subterranean passage through the hills. The simple action of water on limestone has formed a series of spectacular natural caverns and chambers in the rock, several of which can be visited on suitably atmospheric guided tours. Stalactites and stalagmites abound, the lighting artfully arranged to display the colours in the rock: vermilion stains from iron oxide deposits, and traces of black (manganese), grey (lead) and ochre. On your tour you will hear about the caves' prehistoric inhabitants; evidence of early man has been found, as have the bones of Ice Age animals such as mammoth, rhinoceros and hyena.

If all this isn't spooky enough for the young ones, then the guide can be relied upon to whip up a spell with the tale of the Wookey Witch. Legend has it that a fearless medieval monk entered the caves to exorcize the spirit of a resident witch; when she resisted his calls to repentance, he turned her to stone. Children will have fun spotting the witch in the cave – now known as the Witch's Kitchen.

There is plenty else to occupy all ages at Wookey Hole, including an Ice Age valley with life-size models of some 20 dinosaurs, the famous Wookey Bears (teddies), Edwardian penny arcade machines, displays of the ancient craft of making paper by hand in an authentic paper mill, and a huge indoor adventure playground for those wet days. The latest addition to the array of family attractions here is an adventure golf course, for which an additional charge is payable.

WHERE:
Near Wells, Somerset
BEST TIME TO GO:
All year round. The temperature inside the caves remains a constant 11°C (52 °F) throughout the year.
DON'T MISS:
The awe-inspiring space that is Cathedral Cave.
AMOUNT OF WALKING:
Lots. But note that the caves are not accessible to buggies or wheelchairs. A virtual tour is available for anyone unable to do the real thing.
COST:
Expensive (a small saving can be made on the cost of a family ticket if you book online).
YOU SHOULD KNOW:
The British record for the deepest cave dive was set here in 2004 when divers reached a depth of over 45 m (149 ft).

Weston-super-Mare

The bright and lively resort of Weston-super-Mare has lots to offer the family looking for a day out by the sea. The fine sandy beaches have designated areas that separate bathers from those seeking more active wind and water sports. Weston still remembers its Victorian and Edwardian heyday with traditional attractions like boat trips around the bay, tearooms and donkey rides on the beach. Younger appetites, however, will be handsomely catered for soon when the town's 100-year-old Grand Pier, one of two on the seafront, reopens following a serious fire; its centrepiece Pavilion will feature state-of-the-art indoor rides, including a surfboard simulator, a three-storey crazy house and what is billed as the country's longest electric go-kart track. An 85-m (279-ft) viewing platform will offer panoramic views over the Bristol Channel to the South Wales coast.

Also on the seafront, the Seaquarium invites you to get up close and personal with all kinds of sea creatures, from dainty seahorses to voracious sharks, in a series of cleverly re-created habitats. The daily feeding demonstrations are predictably popular with the children. Away from the beach and close to the town centre, Jill's Garden in Grove Park was created by the BBC *Ground Force* team as a memorial to Jill Dando, the popular TV presenter who was a native of Weston. And on the edge of town the world's largest dedicated helicopter museum, with over 70 full-sized aircraft on show, is also worth checking out.

Weston's sand has recently been found to be so good for building sand castles and the like that the town's beach now hosts an annual international sand sculpture festival throughout July and August.

WHERE:
North Somerset
BEST TIME TO GO:
Any time of year (though June to September is best for beach action).
DON'T MISS:
The resort's newest attraction, the Wheel of Weston, a 40-m (131-ft) observation wheel with weatherproof capsules.
AMOUNT OF WALKING:
Moderate
COST:
Reasonable to expensive (depending on how many paying attractions you want to fit in to your day).
YOU SHOULD KNOW:
At low tide the sea can be as much as 1.6 km (1 mi) from the promenade; if distance alone is not enough of a disincentive, signs warn of the dangers of crossing the exposed mudflats.

Building sandcastles on the sea wall.

Around Exmoor on an open-top bus

WHERE:
West Somerset
BEST TIME TO GO:
The bus only runs between the end of May and the end of September.
DON'T MISS:
If you break your ride at Wheddon Cross, the outstanding views from Dunkery Beacon, Exmoor's highest point, are well worth the 4-km (2.5-mi) walk.
AMOUNT OF WALKING:
Little (unless you do the walk to Dunkery).
COST:
Low (and the ride is free to anyone 60+ and/or with a disability who is on the national concessionary travel scheme).
YOU SHOULD KNOW:
An alternative open-top bus service (normally in modern double-deckers) runs along the Exmoor coast between Minehead and Lynmouth.

Although one of the country's smaller national parks, Exmoor packs a remarkable variety of landscapes into its compact area, from formidable cliffs along its coast to heather-clad moors and secluded, fertile valleys which appear in startling contrast to the barren uplands. Add to this rich mix man's impact on the environment – ancient packhorse bridges, charming little villages with whitewashed and thatched cottages – and it is easy to see why this has long been a favourite holiday destination.

One of the best ways to explore Exmoor is to leave your car and climb aboard the Exmoor Explorer, a vintage double-decker bus with an open top which makes a 50-km (30-mi) circuit of the park twice daily on summer weekends and also on Tuesdays and Thursdays during the summer school holidays. The children will enjoy the unusual excitement of wind on their faces and your higher vantage point gives you better views of the glorious scenery. The journey begins in the seaside town of Minehead; from here the route takes you inland via the medieval village of Dunster through Timberscombe and on to Wheddon Cross, the highest village on Exmoor, before it drops down to Exford, nestling cosily by the River Exe. Keep your eyes peeled and you may be lucky enough to spot red deer or an Exmoor pony as you head north over moorland to the coast at Porlock. The highlight of the actual ride, if your nerves can take it, is the descent down Porlock Hill, which claims to be the steepest main road in the country with a regular bus service.

Your ticket is for the whole two-hour round trip, but if you take the morning bus you can break your journey for three hours or so before completing it on the afternoon run.

Travelling along the cliffs above Minehead.

Exmoor Falconry and Animal Farm

Less than 2 km (1 mi) from the busy main road linking Minehead and Barnstaple, 15th-century West Lynch Farm enfolds you in an altogether different world that leaves the modern machine age far behind. This is now the home of Exmoor Falconry and Animal Farm, which pays entertaining homage to an era long before firearms when darting, swooping birds of prey were the hunting weapon of choice – if you had the means to keep them, that is. In medieval times hawking and falconry were very much the preserve of the aristocracy, the number of birds you maintained a clear symbol of your status. Nowadays, fortunately, you don't need a title or landed wealth to have your own close encounter with these magnificent birds as they are put through their paces at West Lynch in daily displays of flying and hunting prowess.

A buzzard at the Allerford Falconry Centre

As well as hawks, falcons, eagles and owls, the centre has a collection of tame farm animals, many of which children are able to handle. Bottle feeding the newborn lambs in season goes down particularly well. A miniature Shetland pony gives rides to very little ones (three to five years), while a Welsh cob is on hand for older children. If any in your party wants to immerse themselves more deeply in this lovely area, Exmoor Falconry offers full- and half-day 'experiences' where you get to fly a bird of prey yourself, or else you can go horse riding or trekking with the resident alpacas.

West Lynch lies in the huge Holnicote Estate, which was given to the National Trust by the Acland family in 1944. Nearby are the picture-postcard villages of Allerford and Selworthy, the latter largely built by Sir Thomas Acland for his estate workers and a great place for a cream tea.

WHERE:
Allerford, near Minehead, Somerset
BEST TIME TO GO:
Any time of year (but spring is a popular time to see the lambs).
DON'T MISS:
The new Owl Show, an unusual display inside the medieval barn featuring owls flying to music.
AMOUNT OF WALKING:
Little (and all areas of the farm are accessible to buggies and wheelchairs).
COST:
Reasonable
YOU SHOULD KNOW:
The birds of prey flying display is held indoors in bad weather.

145

WHERE:
Near Bath, Somerset
BEST TIME TO GO:
March to October (the museum is closed from November to February, except for a few weeks before Christmas. It is always closed on Mondays).
DON'T MISS:
The authentic covered wagon and other outdoor exhibits in the gardens.
AMOUNT OF WALKING:
Moderate (while the museum and galleries are fully accessible, the slope that the house is built on makes access to the gardens difficult for wheelchair users).
COST:
Reasonable
YOU SHOULD KNOW:
Pushchairs are not permitted inside the museum on account of the confined spaces. Baby carriers are available on free loan from reception.

The American Museum in Britain

Whether you have been to the United States or just dream of one day crossing the pond, the American Museum offers an absorbing and stimulating day out. The museum is housed in Claverton Manor, a fine country house on the eastern outskirts of Bath, 3 km (2 mi) from the city centre. Designed by Jeffry Wyatville in the 1820s, Claverton was acquired by three art-loving friends and Americophiles in the late 1950s to house a collection illustrating the early days of American settler and colonial culture. The museum opened its doors in 1961 and still bills itself as the only museum of Americana outside the USA.

If the carefully re-created period rooms illustrating the history of America from the days of the Pilgrim Fathers until the eve of the Civil War are likely to appeal more to the adult members in the family, the new American Heritage exhibition will keep younger minds amused with various interactive displays and opportunities for hands-on activities. Amid the outstanding collections of furniture, silver and glass you will find galleries devoted to folk art and to Native American art. The museum is particularly renowned for its magnificent collection of quilts. If you plan your visit for a Tuesday in the summer you may be lucky enough to pick up one or two trade secrets from local quilt makers who are on hand to demonstrate and talk about their craft.

True to its subject, the American Museum shows plenty of transatlantic showmanship and razzamatazz in promoting its strapline of 'education through entertainment'. During the summer months there are lots of special events in the extensive grounds, all included in the admission price; you might catch a historical re-enactment or the thrills of a Wild West weekend.

Plenty of fun activities take place in the American Museum's extensive grounds.

The Roman Baths

Few places provide more impressive evidence of the Roman presence in Britain than the city of Bath. Bathing was an integral part of Roman life, enjoyed as much for its recreational value as for hygiene, but the Romans also recognized the health-giving properties of the mineral-rich water that still emerges from the natural springs here at a constant temperature of 46°C (115°F). Having first built a pool to contain the spring, the Romans erected a prestigious temple alongside dedicated to Sulis Minerva, the goddess of the spring, who was believed to possess healing powers.

Today the uncovered remains of this vast bathing and temple complex, which used to attract visitors from across the Roman Empire, occupy an extensive site lying mostly beneath the streets of the modern city. Here you can marvel at the ingenuity of the Roman engineers and at standards of plumbing and heating which were not bettered until the last century. The museum's two most prized exhibits are the gilt bronze head of Minerva and the fearsome stone carving known as the Gorgon's head. And its most impressive sight is the Great Bath itself, lined with sheets of lead and originally covered by a 40-m (130-ft) high vaulted roof; the great drain still performs its original function, 2,000 years on, taking the overflow from the spring to the River Avon.

Considerable imagination has gone into bringing these ancient stones to life for modern visitors, through reconstructions, digital technology and guides in period costume. Your ticket includes an audio guide: adults have the benefit of the wit and perceptiveness of popular travel writer Bill Bryson, while children have their own audio tour which introduces them to the stories of Belator, a young Celtic boy, and Apulia, a slave girl who has accompanied her mistress from Italy.

A wide-angle view with Centurions and Bath Abbey

WHERE:
Bath, Somerset
BEST TIME TO GO:
Any time of year. There are special late openings in July and August when the torch-lit baths are open until 21.00.
DON'T MISS:
The remarkable collection of 2,000-year-old curses – messages inscribed on sheets of lead or pewter which were rolled up and cast into the spring.
AMOUNT OF WALKING:
Moderate. Note that pushchairs are not allowed in the baths but may be exchanged for courtesy child carriers at the entrance.
COST:
Reasonable. A family ticket includes up to four children.
YOU SHOULD KNOW:
There is some dispute about the designation of the Gorgon's head because the fabled monster of classical mythology slain by Perseus is also known as Medusa and is female, whereas the carved head from the temple pediment at Bath, sporting a full straggly beard, is most definitely male!

Montacute TV, Radio and Toy Museum and Ferne Animal Sanctuary

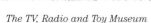
The TV, Radio and Toy Museum

WHERE:
Montacute, near Yeovil,
and Chard, Somerset
BEST TIME TO GO:
April to October (but note that the TV,
Radio and Toy Museum is closed on
Mondays and Tuesdays, except for
Bank Holidays).
DON'T MISS:
Chilli, the giant Friesian steer at
Ferne who at 1.98 m (6.5 ft) is as tall
as a small elephant and is thought to
be the country's largest bovine!
AMOUNT OF WALKING:
Moderate
COST:
Low. The Animal Sanctuary makes no
charge, but relies on donations.

If mum or dad can persuade the rest of the family that a trip down memory lane has something for everyone to enjoy, then a visit to Montacute's TV, Radio and Toy Museum is almost guaranteed to leave you misty-eyed with recollections of favourite programmes from childhood days. Housed in one of the village's many buildings constructed in the beautiful local Ham stone, the museum is a quintessentially British affair, a personal collection that bears testimony to one man's tastes and enduring obsessions.

The walls of this Aladdin's Cave are covered from floor to ceiling with memorabilia evoking the radio and TV programmes of yesteryear. Old toys, games and annuals add colour to a core collection of vintage television sets and more than 500 radios, featuring everything from primitive wirelesses to novelty transistors. There is even an area devoted to ventriloquists' dummies! And if the children start to tire of your reminiscences, a *Doctor Who* display featuring a full-size Dalek and the homespun truths of a talking Homer Simpson offer more contemporary diversions.

Some 30 km (20 mi) west of Montacute brings you to the attractive old cloth-making town of Chard. High in the Blackdown Hills nearby, the Ferne Animal Sanctuary has been providing a home for unwanted animals since 1939 when the Duchess of Hamilton recognized the need for a refuge where service men and women departing for war could bring their pets, knowing they would be cared for in their absence. This spirit is still very much alive at Ferne, which is now home to some 300 animals, rescued from neglect or maltreatment. Farm animals as well as domestic pets are looked after so you will see horses, cattle and pigs as well as cats, dogs and tortoises.

YOU SHOULD KNOW:
You need not worry unduly about coming away from Ferne Animal Sanctuary with more than you had bargained for, since Ferne's policy is to find new homes for their domestic animals within a strict 50-km (30-mi) radius of the centre.

Brean Leisure Park

The theme park at Brean, midway between Burnham-on-Sea and Weston-super-Mare on the north Somerset coast, may not be in quite the same league as Alton Towers or Thorpe Park but it still makes for an action-packed day out. In fact, having fewer of the white-knuckle rides that attract the dedicated adrenalin junkies means that it is probably a better experience for the whole family. Teenagers will enjoy scaring themselves on the Xtreme ride and will almost certainly try to persuade mum or dad to join them on the Shockwave Super Looper, the largest rollercoaster in the southwest. Brean features over 30 rides and attractions, and among the traditional favourites such as dodgems, waltzers and a log flume, rides specifically for younger children make a welcome and strong showing. Canoe River is an especially popular boat ride for the smaller ones.

Height restrictions are in force on all rides and the park operates like an old-fashioned fun fair where you pay per ride, although you can buy a wristband giving you unlimited rides for the day (not valid, though, for the go-karts, crazy golf or laser quest). If you want to combine a spot of sunbathing and swimming with the thrills and spills of Fun City, Brean also boasts a water complex comprising both indoor and outdoor heated pools. There is a separate charge for this but it gives you access to three water chutes and a rapids feature, which you can ride in an inflatable tube. For a cheaper alternative just head over the road for a fantastic 8-km (5-mi) stretch of sandy beach.

WHERE:
Near Burnham-on-Sea, Somerset
BEST TIME TO GO:
Any time of year (although some rides may be closed off-season and the outdoor pool is only open from May to September).
DON'T MISS:
The unusual lighthouse 'on legs' (wooden stilts) on Brean Sands.
AMOUNT OF WALKING:
Moderate. Brean Leisure Park is fully accessible to wheelchair users.
COST:
Expensive if the family plans to make full use of the park's various facilities (though you can reduce the cost by using 'pay as you ride' and rationing the number of rides per person).
YOU SHOULD KNOW:
If you don't mind the crowds in August, Brean Leisure Park is open late (until 22.00) throughout the month.

River Avon Trail

WHERE:
North Somerset, Bristol, South
Gloucestershire
BEST TIME TO GO:
Any time of year, though parts of the
trail become muddy after rainfall.
DON'T MISS:
Conham River Park is a lovely spot in
the Avon Valley Woodlands.
Wheelchair- and pushchair-friendly, it
has good walks, picnic areas and
opportunities for bird spotting –
herons may be seen on the river. In
summer, a ferry crosses the river to
Beese's Tea Rooms.
AMOUNT OF WALKING:
Little, for cyclists. Lots, for walkers
COST:
Low
YOU SHOULD KNOW:
The Bristol Channel has one of the
world's highest tidal ranges. In the
days when Bristol was a great port
Pill was famous for the skill of its
pilots, who used their knowledge of
tides and currents to tow ships safely
to the mouth of the Avon, from
where they travelled slowly up to
Bristol.

Bristol is a very 'green' city, the hub of a growing cycling network. The transformation of the Avon Walkway into the River Avon Trail, from Pill through Bristol to Bath, involved a remarkable co-operative project, which forged links between communities all along the river. Residents, local history and conservation societies and schools were consulted and worked on artistic and historical projects, contributing to a guide book, website and, along the trail, 15 interpretation boards which provide information on heritage, wildlife, geology and legend. Much of the 37-km (23-mi) trail is suitable for cycling, though at Hanham Lock cyclists continuing to Bath should join the Bristol and Bath Railway Path.

From the harbour village of Pill, the trail runs west, south of the river below Leigh Woods, through the spectacular Avon Gorge, whose limestone and sandstone cliffs and salty shores provide a unique habitat for plants and birds. The urban stretch through Bristol is surprisingly pleasant, making use of the historic waterfront, parks and off-road routes. East of Temple Meads, Nether Lock is first in the series of locks which made it possible to bring river traffic upstream – and uphill – from Bristol to Bath. There was an active brass and copper industry, powered by numerous water mills – at Troopers Hill a lone chimney is a relic of copper smelting – but this part of the trail along the northern river bank now runs through the beautiful Avon Valley Woodlands. In this local nature reserve, quarried rock faces and the spoil from metal-working enterprises are colonized and concealed by regenerated woodland. After Hanham Lock the trail follows the river below the Cotswold Edge to Bath.

Bristol Zoo

WHERE:
Clifton Downs, Bristol, South
Gloucestershire
BEST TIME TO GO:
Open all year
DON'T MISS:
Explorers' Creek is an all-weather,
all-age-group attraction. In Splash!,
streams and dams provide wet fun,
while in the Forest of Birds, after
following in the footsteps of jungle
explorers through exotic plants and
free-flying birds, the brave cross the
Wobbly Bridge above a waterfall. In a
clearing, tiny jewel-bright parrots flock
to feed from nectar in the Feed the
Lorikeets area.

Though elephants, giraffes and rhinos no longer live here – Bristol Zoo is committed to education, conservation and animal welfare and city zoos lack the space large animals need – hundreds of fascinating and well-presented animals, birds, reptiles and insects still do. Meerkats and prairie dogs are great comedians, weird and wonderful creatures such as tapirs and armadillos amaze with their strangeness, and the slithery and scuttling residents of the Reptile House and Bug World provoke pleasurable nervous shivers. The Butterfly Forest is a brilliant delight, in contrast to the dim and mysterious Twilight World, where nocturnal animals gaze, huge-eyed, at their visitors. A tunnel beneath the cleverly designed

Seal and Penguin Coasts allows underwater views of these playful favourites. Primates are well represented and marvellously housed – several species, including lemurs, gibbons and a wonderful family of gorillas, live on their own islands in the lake, where they can be watched getting on with life. The light and airy, open-topped Monkey Jungle contains a very popular walk-through area where lemurs scamper around, quite close up.

Regular daily events include talks by keepers, animal encounters and feeding times. In the summer, the zoo hosts evening performances and, at Christmas time, Santa Claus and carols. Highlights of the family fun and games are portrait boards, which allow visitors to be photographed with animal faces, and the Zoolympics Trail, where old and young compare running speeds, length of tongues and so on with those of various animals. A spectacular new attraction, ZooRopia, is a thrilling tree-top walk, part ropes course, part aerial nature trail. Harnessed and supervised participants scramble and balance, in some places high above the primates, and descend by zip wire.

AMOUNT OF WALKING:
Little or moderate. The zoo is pushchair- and wheelchair-friendly.
COST:
Reasonable. ZooRopia costs extra.
YOU SHOULD KNOW:
Age and height restrictions apply for ZooRopia. Some children may be alarmed by the lorikeets, which flutter around and land on people feeding them. In very wet weather, many animals retreat into their shelters. The lovely zoo gardens have one of Bristol's most important collections of plants. Unusual and rare trees, shrubs and plants from around the world are beautifully set out in formal beds, rock gardens and sub-tropical displays and, where possible, are used to enhance animal enclosures.

A keeper shows off a parrot.

Boat trip round Bristol Harbour and SS *Great Britain*

WHERE:
Bristol, South Gloucestershire
BEST TIME TO GO:
All year
DON'T MISS:
Several free MP3 walking tours of Bristol are downloadable. The Bristol Quays Adventure takes walkers on a journey through Bristol's pirate past as you listen to excerpts from *Treasure Island* while wandering around the waterside locations.
AMOUNT OF WALKING:
Little
COST:
Reasonable. Tickets for SS *Great Britain* include activities, audio tours and unlimited return visits for 12 months.
YOU SHOULD KNOW:
The Llandoger Trow, a handsome, half-timbered inn in King Street, was renowned as a haunt of pirates and smugglers in the 18th century. It is probably The Spyglass Inn in *Treasure Island*, and the meeting place of Daniel Defoe and Alexander Selkirk, the inspiration for *Robinson Crusoe*.

SS Great Britain *in Bristol Harbour*

Bristol was always a port and trading town, but after John Cabot sailed from here in 1497 to raise an English flag claiming the 'New Found Land' for Henry VIII, Bristol looked to the New World for imports. By the 17th and 18th centuries, rum, sugar, tobacco and slaves had made it one of the world's great ports. The construction of the Floating Harbour in the 19th century provided much-needed extra moorings, but subsequently trade waned, not just as a result of the abolition of slavery, but because manoeuvring bigger ships up the tidal Avon was too tricky. The port eventually moved to Avonmouth. Although the harbour is now used only by pleasure boats and small working craft, it is still very much the heart of the city, and seen most enjoyably from on board a boat. Ferry companies run regular guided tours all round the Floating Harbour, or trips through the centre of the city from Temple Meads Station. All give fine views of the quays and wharves, old warehouses, bridges and cranes that are reminders of Bristol's maritime history.

The centrepiece of the harbour is Brunel's SS *Great Britain*, the world's first great ocean-going liner. She was salvaged in the Falklands in 1970 and returned to the dock where she was built for restoration. Now visitors can explore the Docklands Museum, walk round the ship's enormous hull down in the dry dock and, on board, experience the life of Victorian passengers and crew. Audio tours range from First Class to Ship's Cat, while a year-round programme of activities and re-enactments include making sea-chests, meeting a Victorian surgeon, a Ratcatcher's Halloween and, of course, visits from Mr Brunel himself.

Cotswold Water Park

With more than 130 lakes around South Cerney and Cricklade and – though less developed – between Fairford and Lechlade to the east, this is Britain's largest water park. It was formed by the extraction of sand and gravel; when pits reach the end of their working lives, the pumps are turned off and they gradually fill with water, forming inland lakes which are put to many uses. A number of outdoor education centres offer activities and tuition, from open-water swimming and snorkelling to canoeing, sailing and windsurfing. Many people come to fish – both coarse and fly fishing is available on over 70 of the lakes – in peaceful locations with deep, clear waters. Day and club memberships may be arranged at one of the many fisheries.

The Cotswold Country Park and Beach at Somerford Keynes is very popular. The two scenic fishing lakes incorporate a large, man-made beach for paddling and swimming – lifeguards patrol at busy times. Other options include a fossil trail, toddlers' play areas with Teddy Bears' Picnics in summer, and an adventure playground. Dinghies, inflatables and barbecues are available for hire.

Most of the water park is in the care of the Cotswold Water Park Society and there is free access to a network of way-marked paths for walkers and cyclists – lakeside walks, canal towpaths and the long-distance Thames Path (the infant Thames runs through the park). The Society also owns and manages several nature reserves because the park supports large numbers of wintering waterfowl and breeding birds and there are colonies of water voles and otters.

Windsurfers and sailing boats at South Cerney Outdoor Education Centre, Cotswold Water Park

WHERE:
South Cerney, Gloucestershire (the park also extends south into Wiltshire).
BEST TIME TO GO:
Open all year. Some activities are restricted to school holidays.
DON'T MISS:
The Gateway Centre, between South Cerney and Cerney Wick, is a focal point for visitors and houses an Information Centre, café and exhibitions of local archaeology and geology. The building is constructed from sustainable green oak to an energy-efficient design. It has an enormous solar roof and heat pumps that recycle rainwater to create energy.
AMOUNT OF WALKING:
Little, moderate or lots. Many of the paths are suitable for wheelchair users.
COST:
Low, although some of the water-based activities are expensive. The country park is free to under 16s in winter.
YOU SHOULD KNOW:
Never swim in lakes that are not authorized – some are very deep, with dangerous currents.

WHERE:
Berkeley, Gloucestershire
BEST TIME TO GO:
April to October. The Castle opens on
Sundays only in April, May,
September and October; Sunday to
Thursday in June, July and August.
The Jenner Museum opens,
afternoons only, Tuesday to Sunday
from April to September, with
Monday openings in June, July and
August, and Sundays only in October
(and at half term).
DON'T MISS:
The pretty thatched summerhouse in
the lovely gardens of the Chantry,
where Jenner offered free
vaccination to the poor.
AMOUNT OF WALKING:
Moderate. The gardens, paths and
some of the staircases at the castle
are steep and uneven.
COST:
Reasonable. Joint tickets for the
castle and museum are available;
tickets for the castle gardens or
Butterfly House only are also
available.
YOU SHOULD KNOW:
Some of the photographs of smallpox
victims in the Jenner museum are
horrific. Dickie Pearce, a dwarf, and
the last Court Jester, died at Berkeley
in a fall from the minstrels' gallery.
He is buried in St Mary's churchyard.

*A family romp in the grounds
of the castle.*

Berkeley Castle and the Edward Jenner Museum

The castle dominates the handsome little town of Berkeley; from a distance, with its bastions and battlements, it looms above the green pastures, a fierce fortress, but inside the massive pinkish-grey stone walls is a treasure-filled family home. More than 24 generations of Berkeleys have lived here, making it England's oldest inhabited castle. Among its royal visitors were Edward II, who was infamously murdered here, and Elizabeth I, who hunted and played bowls.

Visits begin in the Norman keep, with its dungeon and the little room above it where Edward died – his tomb is in Gloucester Cathedral. Medieval rooms include the magnificent Great Hall, where guests have feasted since the 12th century, and the kitchen and buttery. The elegant State Apartments contain collections of furniture, tapestries, silver and paintings. The terraced gardens around the castle walls are beautiful; Queen Elizabeth's Bowling Green is edged by walls and ancient yews, and the peaceful lily pond was used as a swimming pool. In the walled kitchen garden, exotic butterflies flutter through tropical vegetation in the Butterfly House.

The Chantry, an elegant 18th-century house in Church Lane, once home to Dr Edward Jenner, is now a museum telling the fascinating story of the discovery of vaccination and the eradication of smallpox. Jenner, a country doctor with wide interests, including ballooning, noticed that milkmaids who caught cowpox never developed smallpox, one of the major killers of the age. Eventually – his work was initially greeted with derision – he developed the process of vaccination (*vacca* is Latin for cow). His first patient was his gardener's son, James Phipps, who, happily, became immune, and this was the first step in ridding the world of the disease that was finally declared eradicated in 1980.

Slimbridge nature reserve

Slimbridge

One of the world's finest wetland nature reserves, Slimbridge is the headquarters of the Wetland and Wildfowl Trust, dedicated to saving wetlands for wildlife and people across the world. The reserve – some of it protected by a fox-proof hedge – covers a large area of grassland, marsh, ponds and streams along the bank of the River Severn and is home to the world's largest collection of swans, geese, ducks and flamingoes and a multitude of wildlife from water voles and hares to dragonflies and grass snakes.

Slimbridge lays on a changing, year-round programme of events, lectures, workshops and wildlife encounters. At the Visitor Centre, Sloane Tower gives views over the reserve and the river, the cinema shows wildlife-related films, and there is an art gallery. Outside, a variety of special habitats allows close-up views of different species; Toad Hall is the realm of frogs, toads and newts, while the recently developed Back from the Brink is home to endangered wetland mammals such as otters, water voles and beavers. Hides offer bird-spotting opportunities – from the new, specialized Kingfisher Hide, the bright-blue flash of these elusive diving and skimming birds can be glimpsed. Exotic wildlife lives in the heated Tropical House – a good place to warm up on chilly days. Regular talks, walks, tours and demonstrations take place in all areas, allowing visitors to learn about, meet and sometimes feed the birds and animals.

Activities include pond dipping and Welly Boot Land, a lovely wet-play area. Family canoe safaris through reedy waterways are an exciting way to watch a variety of wildlife and guided Land Rover safaris explore the wild reserves. There are also seasonal events – the landscape and the residents of Slimbridge change with the year.

WHERE:
Slimbridge, near Gloucester, Gloucestershire
BEST TIME TO GO:
All year. Land Rover safaris operate in summer only. Canoe safaris are limited to weekends except in summer and school holidays.
DON'T MISS:
In winter, hundreds of thousands of migratory ducks and geese are joined at Slimbridge by families of Bewick's swans after their long journey from Arctic Russia. From November to February, daily floodlit swan feeds are a thrilling sight.
AMOUNT OF WALKING:
Little or moderate
COST:
Reasonable. There are additional charges for canoe and Land Rover safaris.
YOU SHOULD KNOW:
Canoe safaris are for over fives only. The Severn is renowned as a fishing river; elvers (young eels) swim up river in their millions and some salmon are still caught by traditional methods. Once it was also famous for the lamprey, a highly prized and expensive eel-like fish with a sucker mouth. Although Henry I died after 'a surfeit of lampreys', the City of Gloucester used to present a lamprey pie to the reigning monarch every Christmas as a token of loyalty.

Circular riverside walks at Arlingham and a trip on the Gloucester and Sharpness Canal

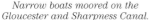

Narrow boats moored on the Gloucester and Sharpness Canal.

WHERE:
Arlingham and Saul, near Gloucester, Gloucestershire
BEST TIME TO GO:
Any fine day. The *Perseverance* operates (and the Heritage Centre opens) only at weekends and Bank Holidays from Easter until late September, but Saul Junction has good towpath walks, cafés, and lots of boats to look at.
DON'T MISS:
An excellent Wildlife Survey available at the Heritage Centre, with information on water safety, wildlife spotting and competitions and 'mug shots' of amphibians and reptiles, insects, fish, birds and mammals to look out for.
AMOUNT OF WALKING:
Lots. Arlingham walks are each about 8 km (5 mi), though there are shortcuts. The paths can get muddy, but it is all fairly easy going, though not accessible to wheelchair users.
COST:
Low
YOU SHOULD KNOW:
Arlingham walk leaflets are available at Tourist Information Centres and the Red Lion and Old Passage inns. The Severn Bore may be seen on the Arlingham loop, where the river starts to narrow. Bores – tide waves – appear in rivers with large tidal ranges; the river flows in the wrong direction, rolling up behind a head of foam at an average speed of 16 kph (10 mph) and, in the narrowest reaches upstream, with heights up to 2 m (6.5 ft). The name comes from the Scandinavian or Icelandic, *bara* meaning a wave or swell.

An unspoilt area of rich farmland, the Arlingham peninsula is surrounded on three sides by a great loop of the River Severn. Arlingham Parish Council has produced an excellent leaflet with detailed descriptions of four circular walks from a map-board near the Red Lion pub. They are named the Hare Walk, Salmon Walk, Skylark Walk and Gloucester Cattle Walk – and include stretches of the riverside Severn Way, with magnificent views over the wide silvery sweeps of the river to the wooded hills of the Forest of Dean, the Cotswolds, the Severn Bridges and, from Barrow Hill, Gloucester Cathedral and the Malverns. Though rarely spotted, hares are resident and the open fields of Skylark Walk ring with joyous birdsong. Salmon were widely fished below the Old Passage Inn, from where a ferry crossed to Newnham, and Gloucester cattle, a dark breed with a distinctive white stripe along their backs, can often be seen grazing the rich pastures. Their milk is used to make authentic Double Gloucester cheese.

At Saul Junction, the Stroudwater Canal, which once carried coal to the cloth mills of the Stroud Valley, meets the Gloucester and Sharpness Canal, which links the inland waterways with the Bristol Channel. There is a busy marina at Saul Junction now – the canal is used mainly by pleasure craft. Saul Heritage Centre provides education and information on the restoration of the Cotswolds Canals – Saul will be the western end of the link between the Severn and the Thames when this is completed – and from here the small traditional narrow boat *Perseverance*, skippered by enthusiastic volunteers from the Cotswold Canals Trust, runs short trips on the canal.

Gloucester Folk Museum and the National Waterways Museum

Gloucester Folk Museum is the oldest museum of its kind in Britain, with displays covering the social history, trades and industries, agriculture and fishing, crafts and pastimes of the region. It is housed in timber-framed Tudor buildings whose narrow, creaking stairs, uneven wooden floors and low-beamed ceilings add a sense of adventure and excitement. The toy room is reached up a wonderfully 'curly' stair; here, as well as displays of old toys, are a toy cupboard and playhouse. Up in the attic are a Victorian schoolroom and a cobbler's shop, and downstairs are displays on laundry and dairying, wheelwright and ironmonger's shops and a delightful cottage garden, with seats in and out of the shade. Dotted around the museum are some intriguing items, such as a huge, rather moth-eaten Gloucester Old Spot sow in the farming room, a 17th-century water main hollowed from a tree trunk and a board describing the fate in store for trespassers, including 'steel traps of the largest size' and 'spring guns . . . set to rake the walls'! The museum has regular temporary exhibitions, special events and school holiday activities for children.

Gloucester was once the most inland port in Britain and the National Waterways Museum now occupies one of the fine Victorian warehouses in the historic Docks. Here, an Ecology Gallery displays waterside wildlife, while the Move It gallery examines the history of the canals and the skills of canal workers. Among the excellent interactive displays are hoists and pulleys to heave, boats to race and model locks to navigate. Outside, the historic vessels moored at the quay include a narrow boat and a steam-powered dredger. The exhibition upstairs tells the stories of those who worked on the waterways, from bargees and their families, lock keepers and canal builders (the navvies) to clerks and ship owners.

WHERE:
Gloucester
BEST TIME TO GO:
Gloucester Folk Museum is closed on Mondays. The National Waterways Museum opens weekends only from November to March, then Wednesday to Sunday (except July and August when it opens daily).
DON'T MISS:
The Dymock Curse. This incised lead tablet is part of a folklore display in the attic. It bears the good and evil symbols of the moon, the figure 369 – the mystic number of the moon – and calls upon eight named demons to 'make this person to Banish away'. The unfortunate person's name, Sarah Ellis, is inscribed in backwards script and legend has it she was so affected that she killed herself.
AMOUNT OF WALKING:
Little. Gloucester Folk Museum's uneven floors and steep stairs make it only partially accessible to wheelchair users. Although the waterways museum is fully accessible, the quays are cobbled and uneven in places.
COST:
Low. Gloucester Folk Museum is free.
YOU SHOULD KNOW:
The spiral-topped bollards lining parts of Gloucester's pedestrian precinct represent the early stages of making pins by hand. Before the Industrial Revolution, pin making employed a fifth of Gloucester's residents, including women and children. The folk museum displays some of the complicated, hand-operated machines used in this industry.

The National Waterways Museum and children showing off their paintings of boats during an activity day.

Puzzlewood and the Forest of Dean Sculpture Trail

WHERE:
Coleford and the Forest of Dean, Gloucestershire

BEST TIME TO GO:
Puzzlewood is open for the February half term, weekends in March and daily from April until the end of October. The sculpture trail is open all year.

DON'T MISS:
One of the sculptures, *Melissa's Swing*, is a magical, musical piece, a sort of Aeolian harp high in a tree with a real swing hung below. A rope allows visitors who do not enjoy swinging to start movement even when there is no wind. Softly stirred, the sound is like wind in leaves, more vigorously shaken, and it thunders.

AMOUNT OF WALKING:
Moderate to lots. Puzzlewood paths, though tarmac surfaced, are unsuitable for wheelchairs or pushchairs. The paths through the sculpture trail are steep in places and can be muddy. The whole trail is about 6.5 km (4 mi) but there are two way-marked shorter routes. It can also be accessed from Speech House, for a shorter walk.

COST:
Low. The sculpture trail is free.

YOU SHOULD KNOW:
The Verderers are the sole remnant of an organizational structure developed to administer Forest Law; the Verderers' Court still meets in Speech House, in the middle of the forest. Built in 1676 and later used by Charles II as a hunting lodge, Speech House is now a hotel.

The Forest of Dean has been, over time, a royal hunting ground, naval timber reserve and an important industrial area – it was quarried for its hard-wearing stone and mined for coal and iron for many centuries. Puzzlewood is a fine example of a pre-Roman, open-cast iron-ore mine; the Victorians laid pathways over the weirdly eroded and overgrown workings and the surrounding ancient woodland and the site became a maze which continues to delight visitors of all ages. Narrow paths meander through dark passageways and deep ravines, over wooden bridges and past trailing vines, moss-covered rocks, luxuriant ferns and quaint grottoes, constantly teasing with dead-ends and loops. This is a place of magic: it was probably an inspiration for the forests of Tolkien's Middle Earth, and was recently used in *Merlin*. Outside the wood are farm animals, a picnic area and playground, and the indoor Wood Puzzle maze, with its own secret passageways.

The circular Sculpture Trail begins at Beechenhurst Lodge with a play area whose structures are based on timber production, mine workings and forest animals. Sculptures on the trail are site-specific, inspired by trees, wildlife and the area's industrial past, and are mostly built from materials found or mined here; several are slowly degrading, to rejoin the landscape. Among many striking works are a huge chair frame, like a giant's throne on a small hill; a steel-and-wire deer standing half-concealed by bracken; and a carved stone pine cone and acorn cup on a vast, surreal scale. High in a forest cathedral of towering tree trunks a stained-glass window catches the shifting light, and 20 evenly spaced railways sleepers are carved with images of nature and industry. The trail inspires walkers to look around them with new, observant eyes.

Sculpture Park Cathedral *by Kevin Atherton 1986 – a suspended stained-glass panel*

Snowshill Manor

From the outside, Snowshill looks like a traditional stone Cotswold manor house. Inside, it's a treasure chest, an eclectic array of thousands of objects from around the world carefully arranged in 22 rooms – one man's enormous 'cabinet of curiosities'. Charles Paget Wade began collecting as a child, filling his own room and

Part of the collection of Javanese and Balinese Wagang and Topeng theatre masks in Snowshill Manor

his father's outbuildings; after World War I he bought and renovated Snowshill and then augmented his collection of English household objects with colourful items from Europe and the Far East.

All the rooms are named, some appropriately – like 100 Wheels (an attic full of bicycles) and Admiral (nautical instruments and model ships). Other collections include clocks, musical instruments, spinning and weaving equipment, furniture and rugs. A special trail, The Amazing Ark, leads children around the house with clues for finding animals, but there is plenty to entertain in its own right. The Green Room contains a large collection of Japanese Samurai armour, arranged to give the impression of a group of warriors gathered, in slightly sinister gloom, around a camp fire. The toy collection – Wade believed that education stifled the imagination, while toys stimulated creativity – includes many of Wade's own toys, including the little shop in the large dolls' house. He named this room Seventh Heaven.

The gardens are laid out in walled terraces, 'outdoor rooms' which incorporate trees, outbuildings (some of which house yet more collections, including the model village that used to be outside), ponds and statues. Here is another very popular trail for children: Poos and Paws contains clues to locate (replica!) animal footprints and droppings.

WHERE:
Snowshill, Gloucestershire, near Broadway, Worcestershire
BEST TIME TO GO:
Snowshill is open from mid March to November 1 on Wednesday to Sunday afternoons.
DON'T MISS:
The Priest's House was Charles Wade's own cottage – there was no space to live in the Manor. He had no electricity and water came from a stream, driven by hydraulic ram; the cottage still has various gadgets he rigged up to make life comfortable, and its walls and ceilings are festooned with English domestic items and farm tools.
AMOUNT OF WALKING:
Little, though the Manor is 457 m (1,500 ft) from the car park. Wheelchair access is limited. Slings and infant seats are available.
COST:
Reasonable. Under fives go free but children's trails have a small charge.
YOU SHOULD KNOW:
Some of the dry stone walls used to divide the rolling Cotswold fields date back to the 18th and 19th centuries and the introduction of enclosure, but the earliest example of the technique is the Neolithic long barrow at Belas Knap.

Goats enjoy a special treat!

Cotswold Farm Park

In the 20th century, livestock breeding on British farms became increasingly selective and, between 1900 and 1973, 26 native breeds became extinct. With a passion for conservation, Joe Henson opened the family-run Cotswold Farm Park in 1971, since when it has become not only a wonderful day out for families but also an important breeding centre for rare breeds. Fifty flocks and herds now flourish in the beautiful Cotswold countryside, and walkways through small pastures allow visitors to get to know them. For visitors with an interest in history, there is lots of information. For example, the wide-horned, shaggy Highland Cattle are the ancestors of all domestic British cattle, golden Guernsey goats were only saved from being eaten to extinction during the occupation of the Channel Islands by being hidden in caves, and the small, semi-wild 'primitive' sheep of the Scottish islands shed their fleeces. There are also native ponies at the farm, and more than 20 breeds of poultry and waterfowl. Among the pigs are the popular Gloucester Old Spot, the 'orchard pig', and the friendly New Zealand kune kune ('fat and round' in Maori) which Adam Henson, the present director (and presenter of BBC's *Countryfile*) has taught to beg for treats.

Cotswold Farm Park has all kinds of activities for children; they can let off steam in a variety of play areas, find their way round a maze, drive pedal-powered tractors and take a farm safari. There are long and short wildlife walks around the farm, and a tower from which to survey the area. Under cover in the Touch Barn there are opportunities to meet the young animals, bottle feed lambs and kids and watch chicks hatching. Farm demonstrations include lambing, shearing and milking.

WHERE:
Guiting Power, near Cheltenham, Gloucestershire
BEST TIME TO GO:
Daily, mid March to early September, then weekends to mid October.
DON'T MISS:
The Iron Age pigs. These are in fact a 'reconstruction', created by crossing Tamworth sows and wild boar, originally for an Iron Age Village project. Since then, the Iron Age sows have appeared in films, which need quiet wild boar look-alikes.
AMOUNT OF WALKING:
Moderate
COST:
Reasonable. Admission prices are fully inclusive; no extra charge for demonstrations, rides etc.
YOU SHOULD KNOW:
The name of the Cotswolds, as well as the wealth of the area, derives from sheep farming. 'Cots' are sheep enclosures, 'wolds' the rolling hills. Cotswold sheep, also known as Cotswold lions, were so prized for their long, curling fleeces – they can produce up to 10 kg (25 lb) of wool a year – that their export was forbidden in the Middle Ages.

Longleat

Longleat House is one of England's most beautiful stately homes, but the real draw for children is the mass of attractions in the grounds and the Safari Park, well known from the BBC's *Animal Park* TV series. Longleat was the first place outside Africa to open a drive-through Safari Park, and the Longleat lions have been here since 1966, when their arrival in rural Wiltshire caused consternation. There is also a spacious tiger enclosure.

Other defined areas of the Safari Park include the Big Game Park, where large grazing animals include impressive white rhinos, and the East African Game Reserve, where giraffes, zebras and ostriches wander. Here, visitors can leave their vehicles (there is a safari bus for anyone without a hard-top car) to enjoy the Wallaby Walkthrough and climb the giraffe-viewing platform. Two popular animal-related attractions outside the park are Pets Corner, with snakes, tortoises and so on as well as small furry animals, Parrot Shows and Meet the Creature sessions; and Old Joe's Mine, a place of darkness where fearless visitors walk among free-flying fruit bats and staff are on hand to talk about bats – or reassure the nervous.

Rides at Longleat include a narrow-gauge steam train that chuffs through the woods and along the lakeside. Some of the most popular activities are Adventure Castle, a huge collection of towers and turrets, climbing frames and tube slides, the very extensive maze – it is quite a challenge to reach the central observation tower – and King Arthur's Mirror Maze, a tricky quest for the Holy Grail.

Feeding a deer from the car.

WHERE:
Longleat, Wiltshire
BEST TIME TO GO:
February half term and weekends from the end of February to the end of March; daily from early April to the end of October. Longleat House is open all year round.
DON'T MISS:
A safari boat trip on Half Mile Pond. Californian sea lions enjoy following the boat and leaping for food. Also Nico, the lowland male gorilla, who loves to watch the passengers from Gorilla Island, where he lives in a centrally heated miniature stately home.
AMOUNT OF WALKING:
Little
COST:
Expensive, though the Passport Ticket allows returns (one visit only to each attraction). There is an extra charge for the safari bus.
YOU SHOULD KNOW:
The safari bus has limited capacity, so early booking is advisable. At busy times, especially in the mornings, there can be long queues for everything. Lord Bath's family tree includes some colourful characters. Related not only to the Royal Family, but also to Old King Cole and Alfred the Great, his ancestor John Thynne, who built Longleat, was twice imprisoned in the Tower of London for alleged embezzlement.

Avebury

WHERE:
Avebury, Wiltshire
BEST TIME TO GO:
Any time of year. Facilities may not
be available at the Summer Solstice.
DON'T MISS:
The Barn Gallery (joint entrance with
the Alexander Keiller Museum) is a
fine 17th-century barn with
interactive displays – the Story of the
Stones – about the history of the
landscape and its people over the
past 6,000 years and the
archaeologist who pieced the story
together.
AMOUNT OF WALKING:
Moderate or lots. There is flat access
to the museums, but rough ground
and some stepped access in the
Stone Circle – an access guide is
available. This area has been grazed
since the Bronze Age and sheep are
still found among the stones; stout
footwear is recommended.
COST:
Low. Access to the archaeological
sites is free. Some special activities
carry a charge.
YOU SHOULD KNOW:
The huge stones used in the
megalithic (big stone) structures of
Wiltshire and Dorset are called
Sarsen stones. They are the remains
of a hard sandstone layer, which
once lay on top of the chalk of the
Downs, and can still be seen in some
places. One derivation is the
Phoenician *sarsen*, a rock, though the
name is popularly thought to be a
corruption of Saracen, which was
used for anything considered pagan.

Although Stonehenge is something of an icon, a day at Avebury is, in many ways, a more pleasurable experience. The complex site is enormous. The huge ring of ditches and banks encloses not only the remains of an enormous stone circle (at one time there were 98 standing stones), which contains two smaller circles, but also part of the village of Avebury. West Kennet Avenue, once lined with 100 stones in pairs, possibly representing male and female, leads to the Sanctuary, a ritualistic group of concentric circles. To the south lie the impressive West Kennet Long Barrow and Silbury Hill, the largest man-made mound in Europe, the purpose of which remains a mystery. This site lends itself to enjoyment as well as history lessons; these stones can be touched, hugged, leaned against, the banks can be climbed, the circles raced around, and a walk round the whole site takes about two-and-a-half hours. There is no queuing or herding here nor, apart from around Silbury Hill, any 'No Entry' signs. There is a pub in the middle of the ring and a very good museum just outside it.

The 'marmalade millionaire' Alexander Keiller, an amateur but excellent archaeologist, bought the site in 1930 and set about excavating and re-erecting the stones. Many of these had been broken up and used to build the present village inside the earthwork, or buried, because they were seen as evidence of pagan worship. Now the museum contains Keiller's outstanding collection of prehistoric finds from the area. There is an interesting programme of school holiday family events and activities like making sundials, wildlife trails, and winter storytelling.

Sunrise over the standing stones

Kennet and Avon Canal Trust Museum and Caen Mill Locks

The lock flight at Devizes on the Kennet and Avon Canal

It was during the wool boom of the 17th and 18th centuries that the town of Devizes expanded and the arrival of the Kennet and Avon Canal in 1810 increased its prosperity, making it part of the 'ribbon of industry'. Though the coming of the railways less than 30 years later effectively bypassed the canal, Devizes remains an attractive, busy market town. The Canal Trust Museum is located on the historic town wharf in an old warehouse. In the 1960s the trust started restoration of the canal – it was reopened by Queen Elizabeth II in 1990 – and the museum tells the story of this huge undertaking, with displays on the history of canals and canal artefacts, models and information panels telling the story of the Kennet and Avon.

During the Industrial Revolution, canals provided cheap transport of goods and raw materials, and the Kennet and Avon effectively linked Bristol and London. Caen Hill Locks was the last section to be completed by the teams of navigators – 'navvies' – who took 16 years to complete the canal, digging with hand tools. This remarkable piece of engineering is a watery 'staircase' of 16 very closely spaced locks, and is part of a flight of 29, with a total rise of 72 m (237 ft) in 3.2 km (2 mi). The whole flight takes five to six hours to negotiate, and watching boats (now mostly pleasure craft) make the slow climb is interesting and sometimes very entertaining. The towpath is also a popular and peaceful walk – long stretches beside the path are now nature reserves, and the deep ponds along the Caen Mill Locks – dug to hold enough water to operate the locks – are a haven for waterfowl.

WHERE:
Devizes, Wiltshire
BEST TIME TO GO:
All year
DON'T MISS:
A much-loved sight – and sound – in Devizes is the Wadworth's dray delivering beer around town, pulled by a pair of magnificent Shire horses. The brewery was founded in 1875 and still occupies its original town centre location. Tours feature not just the brewing process, but also the skilled job of barrel making, and a visit to the stables to meet the wonderful horses.
AMOUNT OF WALKING:
Little or moderate
COST:
Low
YOU SHOULD KNOW:
A plaque on Devizes' market cross recounts the story of Ruth Pearce, who came to the market and was accused by her friends of keeping back some money she owed. She called on God to strike her dead if she had cheated and promptly dropped down dead, with the missing coin in her hand.

Mother with her new bison calf at the centre

Bush Farm Bison Centre and Salisbury parks and river walks

WHERE:
West Knoyle and Salisbury, Wiltshire
BEST TIME TO GO:
The Bison Centre is open from Wednesday to Sunday, Easter to the end of September; the shop and gallery remain open in winter on Thursday and Friday. Salisbury walks are enjoyable at any time of year, though the Town Path tends to flood after heavy rain.
DON'T MISS:
Harnham Mill where there is a hotel and a pub and the River Nadder gushes over a weir into a large pond. Hundreds of hungry ducks potter about and children paddle and sometimes swim in the clean, cold water. The view of the cathedral over the water meadows (immortalized by Constable) is absolutely stunning in all lights.
AMOUNT OF WALKING:
Moderate. The Farm Trail at Bush Farm is accessible to wheelchair users.

Bison once roamed North America in such multitudes that early explorers described the plains as 'black and appearing as if in motion'. Essential to the life of the Plains Indians (they provided food, clothing and shelter), they were reduced almost to extinction by the settlers and their rifles. Happily, 20th-century conservationists have re-established them. Now, along with elk and red deer, these massive creatures roam the rolling Wiltshire pastures of Bush Farm. Here, a very enjoyable farm trail leads around the grazing herds and through peaceful woodland clearings and gardens. Near the lakes, waterfowl and other birds can be watched from a hide and, at the farmyard, rare-breed sheep and pigs keep company with a variety of American animals, such as chipmunks, racoons and prairie dogs. The Gallery shows pictures of American wildlife, a display on bison, and Native American artefacts of all kinds. In the farm shop, bison meat – very lean and low in cholesterol – is on sale.

The beautiful old city of Salisbury is criss-crossed by rivers and, as well as its famous buildings, has several enjoyable riverside walks and parks, with hordes of cheerful ducks waiting for crusts. Just south of the centre, Churchill Gardens are well laid out with mature trees and grass, a children's playground, skate park and walks along the banks of the River Avon. The Town Path crosses Harnham Water Meadows, an area rich in water birds, plants and insects; the grassland is still used for grazing and a llama may be spotted among the sheep – he keeps the foxes away. Queen Elizabeth Gardens, at the town end of the path, are charming and feature a sensory garden, ducks to feed and a chance to paddle in the clear stream.

COST:
Low
YOU SHOULD KNOW:
Water meadows are a sophisticated ridge-and-furrow irrigation system, used here since the 1600s. Diverted water runs along the tops of ridges, into the furrows and back to the river; the continually moving water keeps frosts off, and ensures plenty of early spring grass.

Trowbridge Museum, a walk at Bratton Camp and Westbury White Horse

Trowbridge, the county town of Wiltshire, has records dating back to the Domesday Book. The town's prosperity came largely from the wool trade – and several of the fine, 18th-century clothiers' houses are still standing, as are some of the mill buildings. There is a fascinating Industrial Trail around the town. The last working mill, Home Mill (Messrs Slaters) closed only in 1982 and now its upper floor (incorporated into the Shires shopping centre) is the Town Museum. This friendly little museum welcomes children with a Mouse Trail (mice concealed in displays) and various hands-on activities. These include trying out the old school desks, clocking on at a factory machine and dressing up as evacuees (Trowbridge welcomed many children during World War II) and finding out what life was like in wartime. There are extensive displays on the history of the clothing industry and, on Saturdays, there are weaving demonstrations.

The exhilarating open spaces of Bratton Downs are popular with walkers, picnickers and those with an interest in history. Bratton Camp is one of a series of fortified encampments on the edge of Salisbury Plain. Dating back over 2,000 years, the Iron Age hill fort has double-bank and ditch defences and its huge scale makes it very impressive. Just below the camp, the Westbury White Horse, dating to 1778, is the oldest of Wiltshire's famous hill figures. There was an earlier horse, which may have been carved as long ago as the Saxon period, possibly to commemorate Alfred's defeat of the Danes at Ethandum. The horse, which has been concreted and painted to counteract erosion, is visible for miles, and from it there are panoramic views of Wiltshire and Dorset.

WHERE:
Trowbridge and Westbury, Wiltshire
BEST TIME TO GO:
All year; the museum closes on Sunday and Monday.
DON'T MISS:
The Blind House, a curious little building with an arched roof and a knob on top, stands by the river in Trowbridge. 'Blind house' is the local term for a lock-up and prisoners were held here in two windowless cells. It was built in 1757 and used until a police station was built in 1854.
AMOUNT OF WALKING:
Moderate
COST:
Low. The museum is free.
YOU SHOULD KNOW:
Lanes leading to Bratton Downs are narrow and steep and are used by horse riders. Not all Wiltshire's chalk figures are horses; on the steep slope of Fovant Down, near Salisbury, a series of huge cap badge insignia have been cut. The first were created during World War I – the solders were camped locally – in honour of fallen comrades. Some have not survived but several are clearly visible from the A30.

Weymouth

The 5-km (3-mi) expanse of golden sands that sweeps around the bay is certainly Weymouth's principal attraction, and one that the town is careful not to underestimate. On a warm summer's day beneath a cloudless sky there are few better places for the family than this award-winning beach with its clean sea and safe bathing. Donkey rides, Punch and Judy shows, swing boats, pedaloes – the traditional seaside attractions are all here, as are more recent ones like trampolines and beach volleyball. And if after a full day on the beach you can't face the trek back to the car, then let the Land Train along the esplanade take the strain.

Like every British seaside resort, Weymouth has had to work hard at reinventing itself in order to win back the holiday makers lost to the overseas-package trade. There is now no shortage of all-weather attractions aimed especially at families. A top recommendation is the Sea Life Park and Marine Sanctuary, easily a day out in itself and sure to keep the most jaded appetites amused in some way or other. The displays of marine life include the customary stars such as sharks, rays and seahorses, but more unusually the park has a group of green sea turtles; watching these gentle giants swimming in their huge ocean tank is one of the highlights of a visit. Seals, otters and penguins entertain the crowds in outdoor enclosures, especially at the regular feeding sessions throughout the day.

If it's not beach weather, Brewers Quay is definitely worth checking out. This former brewery now houses craft shops, restaurants, a free museum and the Timewalk, where Miss Paws, the brewery cat, guides you through 600 years of Weymouth's history, re-created in a series of life-size tableaux.

Donkey rides on the beach!

Isle of Portland

Like Dorset's other 'Isle', Purbeck, and unlike those of Man and Wight, Portland is not surrounded by water on all sides. It is in fact a peninsula rather than a true island, connected to the mainland by a narrow strip of land which marks the start of Chesil Beach – the extraordinary pebble bank that runs 16 km (10 mi) west to Abbotsbury. Leave the car in Weymouth and cross the isthmus on the regular open-top buses to explore the many interesting features of Portland. The bus takes you down to its southernmost tip at Portland Bill, where the red-and-white lighthouse has been a prominent landmark for seafarers for some 300 years. The lighthouse helped guide vessels through the Race, a treacherous stretch of water separating the Bill from the Shambles sandbank offshore. You can climb the 153 steps to the top of the 41-m (134-ft) tower for panoramic views and the not uncommon sight of mighty waves smashing against the cliffs.

Portland is known far and wide for the quality of its silvery white limestone. Some of the world's most iconic buildings are faced with Portland stone; they include St Paul's Cathedral, Buckingham Palace and the United Nations in New York. Wherever you look on the island you will see evidence of the old workings. Nowadays the stone is extracted underground and many of the former quarries are being reclaimed by nature. One such abandoned area, Tout Quarry, in the northwestern part of the Isle, has been turned by artists into a sculpture park and an educational resource for learning about stone carving. This is a great place for children to wander around – as they explore the old trackways and hidden gullies they'll discover contemporary carvings and sculptures in the most unexpected places.

Sad face of a man carved in white stone with tear on cheek at Tout Quarry

WHERE:
Near Weymouth, Dorset
BEST TIME TO GO:
Any time of year (the lighthouse is open only from April to September).
DON'T MISS:
The Visitor Centre at the lighthouse has informative displays on the environment and history of the Isle.
AMOUNT OF WALKING:
Moderate
COST:
Low
YOU SHOULD KNOW:
The Isle and Royal Manor of Portland belongs to the Crown and there is an ancient meeting called the Court Leet, which still meets once a year to safeguard the rights of the 'islanders'.

Abbotsbury Swannery and Children's Farm

Visitors helping at feeding time at the Swannery which is protected from the sea by Chesil Beach.

At the western end of Chesil Beach the ancient village of Abbotsbury is home to one of the more unusual wildlife experiences in Britain. Abbotsbury Swannery is also one of the most historic, as it was established in the 14th century by the monks of St Peter's Abbey to rear swans for their table. The original function disappeared with the Abbey's dissolution by Henry VIII, and today the Swannery is a benign and conservation-minded enterprise. Mute swans enjoy the brackish waters of the Fleet Lagoon for the abundant supply of a favourite foodstuff (a type of seaweed). As spring approaches, the swans move to the Abbotsbury end of the lagoon where the reeds in the shallower waters offer good building material for their nests.

Abbotsbury claims to be the only managed colony of nesting swans in the world; certainly it is the only one where the visitor can walk so freely among the nests. Most years see more than 100 breeding pairs at the Swannery and if you visit in May or June the sight of hundreds of little bundles of grey fluff that are the newborn cygnets is simply irresistible. The swans may seem unfazed by the human attention but there are still discreet signs warning of the dangers of getting too near these powerful birds.

A short distance away in the village itself, the Children's Farm is housed in and around the magnificent Tithe Barn, the only substantial survival from the medieval abbey. Younger children especially love the many opportunities to stroke and cuddle a variety of farm animals, including rabbits, donkeys, cows and pigs. Pony rides and goat races are also on the menu and, after the racing, children get the chance to bottle feed the thirsty competitors.

WHERE:
Abbotsbury, Dorset
BEST TIME TO GO:
March to October (but May and June if you want to see the hatchlings and the nests).
DON'T MISS:
The spectacle of hundreds of swans being fed on the lagoon. Feeding sessions take place twice daily.
AMOUNT OF WALKING:
Moderate (and the Swannery is fully accessible to wheelchair users).

COST:
Expensive (you can reduce the cost by buying a passport ticket giving admission to both attractions plus the Sub-Tropical Gardens – they don't all have to be visited on the same day).

YOU SHOULD KNOW:
The Swannery at Abbotsbury is all the more remarkable when you consider that swans are by nature solitary and notoriously territorial in their breeding and nesting habits.

Dorchester Dinosaurs and Charmouth fossils

They may have been extinct for 65 million years but dinosaurs continue to exert a magnetic hold on children's imaginations. While in most museums the attention span of the adults proves longer than the children's, at Dorchester's Dinosaur Museum you may find yourself hard pushed to wrest the young ones away from its colourful displays about these prehistoric giants. Recently celebrating its 25th birthday, Dorchester Dinosaur Museum was one of the first to pioneer the hands-on and interactive experiences that are now such standard features of modern museum interpretation. The star exhibit among the fine collection of fossils and dinosaur bones is the complete skeleton of a carnivorous *Megalosaurus*. These authentic remains are complemented by life-size reconstructions of big-name 'dinos' such as *Stegosaurus*, *Triceratops* and, inevitably, *Tyrannosaurus rex* itself.

The museum actively encourages everyone to touch and feel the models and you are even able to handle some real dinosaur fossils. There are opportunities to hear the sounds dinosaurs might have made and to play around with the colourings they might have had (no one really knows). And, if you're brave enough, you can find out what a *Tyrannosaurus rex* felt like in the 'feely' box!

A good way to finish your day with the dinosaurs is to head 40 km (25 mi) west to Charmouth, where some of the exhibits in Dorchester were found. A designated UNESCO World Heritage Site owing to the importance of its geology, the exposed cliffs and rock strata of this stretch of coastline are one of the best places to look for fossils. Call in first at the Visitor Centre for advice and information on fossil hunting, before heading out to see if you are lucky enough to spot something exciting on the beach.

WHERE:
Dorchester and Charmouth, Dorset
BEST TIME TO GO:
Any time of year (though the Visitor Centre at Charmouth is open from April to October only).
DON'T MISS:
The reconstructed *Corythosaurus* in Dorchester was made by the BBC special effects team for an episode of *Doctor Who*.
AMOUNT OF WALKING:
Moderate. Note that only the ground floor of the Dinosaur Museum is accessible to wheelchair users.
COST:
Reasonable. You can obtain a small reduction at the Dinosaur Museum by downloading a voucher from the museum's website.
YOU SHOULD KNOW:
You should only search for fossils on the beach at Charmouth and not on or near the cliffs, as they are unstable and subject to erosion.

Fossil hunting on the cliffs at Charmouth

Royal Signals Museum and Maiden Castle

Good lines of communication have always played a key part in warfare, from despatch riders on horseback to the latest in electronic gadgetry. The Royal Corps of Signals provide this support function to the British Army and at its headquarters outside Blandford Forum the corps has a museum that tells the story of military communications from the Crimean War to the present. You don't have to be a radio ham to enjoy the displays here since the museum goes to impressive lengths to appeal to a general audience of all ages. Younger members of the family will enjoy testing their driving skills or sending a Morse code message in the interactive centre. And they can examine a suitcase radio and learn what life was like for a secret agent in occupied France.

The museum has a special section devoted to spying and code breakers, where children can try their hand at cracking codes. One of the famous Enigma machines is on show, reminding you that their use by Allied intelligence to break the German codes was decisive in ending World War II. Since then the Royal Signals have played a key role in many of the world's hotspots and the collection includes captured military equipment from the Falklands and Gulf campaigns.

A 45-minute drive southwest brings you to Maiden Castle on the outskirts of Dorchester, the largest Iron Age hill fort in Europe. Even 2,000 years on, the massive earthen ramparts present a forbidding spectacle, although entering the site now you will no longer be met with a hail of spears. Information panels dotted around this huge site explain how the earthwork defences were made ever more sophisticated but were ultimately no match for the Roman army when it stormed Maiden Castle in AD 43.

Museum of Electricity and Hengistbury Head

Do not let memories of those dry school physics lessons put you off the prospect of visiting Christchurch's Museum of Electricity. It may not set your world alight but it is well worth a couple of hours of anyone's time and you may be pleasantly surprised just how absorbed the children become. Housed in the handsome red-brick Edwardian building that was the town's generating station from 1903 to 1927, this free museum has a wide-ranging collection of electrical appliances and equipment illustrating the evolution in our use of the power source since Michael Faraday's trail-blazing experiments in the early 19th century. There are plenty of hands-on opportunities for the kids to learn more about electricity, and guides are on hand to help demystify the subject and explain the more complicated exhibits. The museum also features a collection of electric vehicles, including the ill-fated Sinclair C5 and a restored 1911 municipal tram from nearby Bournemouth.

If you need to clear your head of all those amps and ohms, head for Hengistbury Head on the south side of Christchurch Harbour. Evidence indicates that there was a settlement on the headland in prehistoric times but its glory days came in the era before the Roman occupation; the trading port that flourished may well have been Britain's first true town. You can still see signs of the Iron Age fortifications at the Double Dykes near the car park, a prominent ditch-and-bank system that crosses the narrowest part of the promontory. The gentle walk around the headland will take you an hour or so; it is well worth it for the superb views of the Isle of Wight and for the beach at Mudeford.

AMOUNT OF WALKING:
Moderate (you are asked to keep to the designated paths on Hengistbury, as the headland remains a fragile environment subject to erosion).
COST:
Low
YOU SHOULD KNOW:
If you don't fancy the full round walk on Hengistbury you can catch the road train from the beach back to the car park; a fun alternative is to take the little boat out from Christchurch Quay.

The Christmas Day walk on Hengistbury Head beach

Lulworth Castle

WHERE:
Lulworth, Dorset
BEST TIME TO GO:
End of July and August when the
Jousting Knights are performing
(although the castle is open
throughout the year, but not on
Saturdays).
DON'T MISS:
The unusual 18th-century Catholic
chapel built in the grounds for the
family's private worship.
AMOUNT OF WALKING:
Moderate
COST:
Reasonable (note that English
Heritage members get a 25 per cent
reduction on the full entry price).
YOU SHOULD KNOW:
The Lulworth Estate incorporates a
substantial stretch of the magnificent
Dorset coastline, including the
world-famous natural sights of
Lulworth Cove and Durdle Door.

Lulworth Castle looks the picture of a medieval stronghold with its massive keep-like appearance, battlements and corner towers – until you discover that it was in fact built as a hunting lodge at the beginning of the 17th century. Thomas Howard, the builder, was capitalizing on the vogue at King James's court for knights and chivalry and doubtless hoped to win favour by laying on lavish hunting parties for the monarch. Children will not worry unduly about this lack of authenticity as they explore the castle's reconstructed kitchen and cellars and climb to the top of the tower for some great views over the vast Lulworth Estate. Although much of the interior was never rebuilt following a disastrous fire 80 years ago, English Heritage has spent many years restoring the exterior and securing the whole structure for future generations.

There are plenty of things to entertain the family in the extensive grounds, including woodland walks, a pitch-and-putt course, a nature trail and a children's farm which is home to rare and unusual breeds of farm animal. Children can let off steam in the large adventure playground and there is even an indoor play area for rainy days. In the summer the world of medieval chivalry and knightly derring-do is brought to life when the castle provides an appropriate backdrop for spectacular jousting displays. These exciting tournaments between mounted riders in full armour form the centrepiece of a medieval village where you can learn how armour was made, watch demonstrations of longbow archery and enjoy the antics of Fiery Jack the Jester.

Lulworth Castle

Splashdown Poole

WHERE:
Poole, Dorset
BEST TIME TO GO:
Any time of year (though the full complement of rides, both indoor and outdoor, are only open from May to September).
DON'T MISS:
The chance to clock your speed on some of the flumes and stir up those family rivalries!
AMOUNT OF WALKING:
Little
COST:
Expensive. It is worth checking the website beforehand for any special offers or discounts.
YOU SHOULD KNOW:
The wristband you must wear is a 'smart band', which records the number of rides you go on, the distance you cover, and, if you want, works out your 'fear factor' rating!

There may be occasions when the appeal of even Dorset's fabulous beaches starts to pall and you find certain members of the family clamouring for a more intense kind of water action. If so, then Splashdown in the northern outskirts of Poole is the place to head for. Part of the Tower Park leisure complex, Splashdown is a water park for thrill-seekers which features twelve rides, including four outdoor rides open only during the summer months. Flumes with colourful names such as Colorado Coaster, Red River Roller and Zambezi Drop are guaranteed to get the adrenalin pumping, while the Screamer is an apt description for the reactions induced by its near-vertical drop. For a different but equally stomach-churning sensation the Spacebowl will hurl you around like a human pinball.

Ride the Mississippi Drifter in a rubber tyre while you decide if you've got what it takes to confront the Dragon's Lair – Splashdown's newest water attraction which adds sound and light effects to a daring ride into darkness. In summer the Drifter connects with an outdoor flume which makes for a terrific long ride as you shoot the rapids of the Grand Canyon. Children adore Splashdown but they do have to be at least 1 m (3 ft 3 in) tall and reasonably confident in water to use the flumes (although armbands are allowed). If they are not they can still enjoy Buccaneer Bay, a shallow fun pool, and in summer the Buccaneer Beach Lagoon, a beach-style outdoor pool that is perfect for parents and toddlers.

Should all this excitement become too much, there are always the more sedate pleasures of a spa pool and Jacuzzi where you can relax among the bubbles – as much at least as the soundtrack of shrieks and screams allows you!

Corfe Castle Model Village and the Blue Pool

WHERE:
Near Wareham, Dorset
BEST TIME TO GO:
April to October (but note that the model village is normally closed on Fridays).
DON'T MISS:
Keep your eyes peeled on the paths surrounding the Blue Pool and you may be lucky enough to see deer or even a green sand lizard.

Corfe Castle is one of Dorset's prettiest villages. The combination of a dramatic setting, a ruined castle perched on a hill and homes built in the harmonious local Purbeck stone has made it a favourite image on biscuit tins and fudge boxes. It is a delightful place to wander around but if the children prove immune to the charms of the real thing they are almost certain to appreciate the model village, a painstaking re-creation on a 1:20 scale of how the settlement would have looked 350 years ago. Stand on the lawn and enjoy the view of the real castle ruins as you compare them with the model showing its former pristine might before Oliver Cromwell's forces reduced it to rubble in 1646.

The attention to detail in the model is breathtaking. The roofs of the houses, for example, are made of real Purbeck stone, each tiny tile crafted by hand. And listen carefully at St Edward's Church for the sound of the choir. The model village is set in an old English country garden where you can also try your hand at croquet or play giant versions of draughts and Connect 4. The many plants and flowers attract plenty of wildlife and, if you've got the patience, a bird hide will help you to spot some.

A short distance away is the Blue Pool, one of Dorset's most renowned beauty spots. A previously undistinguished clay pit found a new lease of life after extraction ceased in the 1930s. The water which subsequently filled the pit was found to display striking variations in colour, from turquoise blue to shades of green, depending on atmospheric conditions. This remarkable phenomenon is due to the diffraction of light by a fine clay suspension in the water.

AMOUNT OF WALKING:
Moderate (there is a flat route around the Blue Pool that is suitable for wheelchair users).
COST:
Reasonable
YOU SHOULD KNOW:
Inviting though it may look, the water in the Blue Pool is neither safe nor suitable for bathing.

The model village at Corfe Castle

Adventure Wonderland and the Alice Maze

WHERE:
Hurn, near Bournemouth, Dorset
BEST TIME TO GO:
April to September
DON'T MISS:
See how many characters from the Alice stories the kids can spot during their visit.
AMOUNT OF WALKING:
Moderate
COST:
Reasonable. Children from two years old are charged; if you make a return visit within seven days you get half-price entry.
YOU SHOULD KNOW:
Alice Liddell, the real-life inspiration for the Alice stories, is buried not far away at Lyndhurst in the New Forest.

On the northern edge of Bournemouth the Adventure Wonderland children's theme park has grown up around the Alice in Wonderland Maze, one of the largest hedge mazes in the country with over 2.5 km (1.5 mi) of pathways. The spirit of Lewis Carroll's timeless classic still pervades the park and children should look out for Alice herself and the characters she encounters on her adventures. The Mad Hatter, White Rabbit, Queen of Hearts, Cheshire Cat, Mock Turtle – all are hiding somewhere in the maze and you may also be lucky enough to see them wandering around the park.

Adventure Wonderland is an amusement park designed for children from two to 14 years. Many old favourites are to be found here, including the Runaway Train rollercoaster, whirling Turbo Teacups and a giant swing boat called the Ghostly Galleon. More recent features include Snappy Croc, a bouncy inflatable which causes great excitement when it roars and closes its jaws, and Shark Island, an interactive water ride. Little ones can have a pony ride and handle guinea pigs and rabbits in the Cuddle Corner. And at Charlie Cool's Driving School they can start learning the rules of the road behind the wheel of a safari jeep.

The weather doesn't have to be fine for a visit to Adventure Wonderland because the Wild Thing! zone features an array of undercover rides and attractions themed around a Lost Aztec World. There are also daily magic shows in the Happydrome Theatre and regular special events throughout the main season; recent visitors have included a Cyberman from *Doctor Who* and birds of prey displaying their flying skills.

Fun with the Mad Hatter

Bovington Tank Museum

The tank was a British invention first used in 1916 in an attempt to break the deadlock in the World War I trenches. Although its introduction did not bring that war to the hoped for quick conclusion, the tank has nevertheless had a decisive impact on the nature of modern warfare, its brooding presence inseparable now from most conflict situations. If you want to learn how this brutally effective weapon has become such a symbol of power and oppression, be it in the streets of Prague in 1968 or Tiananmen Square in 1999, the Tank Museum at Bovington has one of the world's largest and most comprehensive collections of these armoured fighting vehicles.

Following a multi-million pound facelift the museum now has a new wing and improved facilities for its collection of more than 300 armoured vehicles from around the world. The collection has been rearranged into three main displays: the Discovery Centre, where you learn about the different uses of tanks in combat and what it's like to be a member of a tank crew; the Trench Experience puts you in the boots of a World War I soldier on his journey from recruiting office to front line; and the brand-new Tank Story tells the machine's history and features 33 of its most important examples – from Little Willie, the world's very first tank, to the current Challenger 2.

Other features include an excellent interactive trail for children, and an exhibition about T E Lawrence, better known as Lawrence of Arabia, who lived nearby. During the summer holidays your ticket includes an exciting display of tanks in action in the outdoor arena. For a small extra charge you may also experience riding in a tracked vehicle (though this is an armoured personnel carrier, not a tank).

WHERE:
Near Wareham, Dorset
BEST TIME TO GO:
Any time of year (but weekdays during the summer holidays if you also want to see the tanks in action).
DON'T MISS:
The Centurion tank that has been cut in half to reveal its inner workings.
AMOUNT OF WALKING:
Moderate
COST:
Reasonable
YOU SHOULD KNOW:
Bovington Camp is still the British Army's main tank-training area.

Tank Museum Bovington

Africa Alive

WHERE:
Pakefield, near Lowestoft, Suffolk
BEST TIME TO GO:
Spring for baby animals, and you'll
have more fun if it isn't raining.
DON'T MISS:
The feeding sessions
AMOUNT OF WALKING:
As much as you want; remember
that there are plenty of places to
stop for a while. There are facilities
for the disabled here.
COST:
Reasonable
YOU SHOULD KNOW:
No dogs are allowed in, including
guide dogs.

Ring-tailed lemurs

A successful re-creation of the African savannah set in coastal Suffolk seems very unlikely – however, the cleverly designed parkland that is Africa Alive! provides an exciting day out for the whole family. The 40-ha (100-acre) site is home to exotic birds and animals from the plains of Africa and here, as in their natural habitat, many of them roam the park together.

You can spend all day wandering through and around the various enclosures. The site is punctuated at regular intervals with look-out towers to give visitors a different and more intimate view of the many species which include lions, giraffes, hyenas, cheetahs and lemurs among many more. If the walking becomes too much, jump on the train for a while – the commentary will add to your understanding and enjoyment of the experience. At strategic points notice boards are to be found, detailing the times of feeding sessions – always fascinating to observe – and other activities such as the birds-of-prey display.

Africa Alive! is good fun for children of all ages. There's an adventure play area, crazy golf, a Farm Yard Corner where some of the animals can be stroked and fed, and a fantastic indoor play area for the under 12s. The Wild Zone, as this is called, features a splendid interactive rope bridge. As children make their way across the bridge it moves of its own accord and every so often a hail of foam balls erupts from below. These can be lobbed at fellow adventurers. Upper and lower levels are joined by snake slides and the walls themselves are lined with hands-on activities. There is also a special area for the under fives, so that even on a miserable day there's plenty to keep the kids happy here.

Beacon Rally Karts and Easton Farm Park

Many a young boy's dream!

Beacon Rally Karts is an off-road, outdoor karting centre in the Suffolk countryside and even if no one in the family has ever tried karting before, this is a great place to give it a go. With four different sized karts, all designed for maximum safety, and three separate circuits to use, Beacon boasts that it can accommodate everyone between five and 75 years of age.

Fully trained marshals kit out the protagonists and explain how to drive the buggies. Every kart for the over sevens can be remotely controlled to slow them down or even stop them completely and everyone gets at least ten minutes on the track, rather than just a dozen quick laps. There is a large spectator area, and food is available. Karting is a great way to introduce children to driving and helps develop quick reflexes, good decision-making and a competitive spirit.

Not far away is Easton Farm Park. A late Victorian Model Farm, the buildings themselves are architecturally distinctive. Specially designed for families with children under 11 years of age, this is an excellent place to spend the afternoon. The rides here are more traditional – pony back or pony and cart, on the Family Train or a Barrel Bug ride. Eight different activities, occurring throughout the day, are included in the entrance fee.

The children can meet, touch and even feed lambs, kids, chicks and rabbits. Many animals are born on the farm, which is also home to rare-breed cattle, Suffolk Punch horses and pigs. And there are gorgeous walks to take through the water meadows to the River Deben where you might spot herons, kingfishers, deer or even otters. If it turns rainy there's an indoor playbarn, or you can enjoy a cream tea at the Riverside Café.

WHERE:
Just off the A12, near Martlesham, Ipswich, Suffolk
BEST TIME TO GO:
Spring and summer – a sunny day is not essential, but it adds to the beauty of the countryside at Easton Farm Park.
DON'T MISS:
Feeding the lambs, kids and possibly even calves at Easton Farm Park.
AMOUNT OF WALKING:
As much or as little as you like
COST:
Beacon Rally Karts: expensive; Easton Farm Park: reasonable.
YOU SHOULD KNOW:
Beacon Rally Karts operates an 'arrive and drive' policy at weekends and school holidays – otherwise you must book. Rally Karts do not operate in wet weather. Lewis Hamilton and many other Formula One drivers grew up racing rally karts.

Sole Bay high-speed boat trip and crabbing at Walberswick

Separated by the River Blyth, Southwold and Walberswick are charming, old-fashioned seaside resorts complete with beach huts, buckets and spades. Start your day at the northern end of Southwold beach with a good breakfast in a café on the pier before enjoying the rest of this quirky spot. Watch the mechanical clock strike the hour, play with Tim Hunkin's extraordinary toys – hilarious for adults and children alike – and don't forget to read some of the messages on the brass plaques by the handrail; they are funny, moving and very, very British.

At the southern end of the beach, where the river meets the sea, buy tickets for a thrilling half hour of hurtling round Sole Bay on the high-speed *Coastal Voyager*. Built in New Zealand, the 400-hp boat is licensed to the UK Maritime Coastguard Agency and is always steered by one of the Southwold Lifeboat crew. Everyone is kitted out with waterproofs and life jackets and strapped securely into wraparound seats before blasting off into the bay.

After all that excitement, a calmer afternoon awaits you. Walk across the Bailey bridge or take the rowing-boat ferry across the river to Walberswick and discover the joys of crabbing. This is such a popular activity that the annual competition draws close to 1,000 entrants. It's easy to buy buckets, bait and lines here, and the crabs are remarkably obliging – you'll soon have several in your bucket. Your kids can compete with each other to see how many they can catch, but remember: the crabs have to go back into the water in the end. If it's hot, go swimming – Walberswick has one of the sandiest beaches on this coast – before having an ice cream or a cream tea to round off the day.

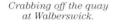

Crabbing off the quay at Walberswick.

WHERE:
The Suffolk Heritage Coast
BEST TIME TO GO:
You can speed around the bay any day apart from Christmas, but crabbing is best enjoyed during the summer months.
AMOUNT OF WALKING:
Little if you take the ferry both ways. It's about 2.4 km (1.5 mi) if you go via the Bailey bridge, so you might decide to walk there and take the ferry back.
DON'T MISS:
A tour of Southwold lighthouse, available on most Wednesdays, Saturdays and Sundays.
COST:
The high-speed boat trip is expensive; crabbing is cheap.
YOU SHOULD KNOW:
There are lovely walks along the beach and back through the marshes at Walberswick and the very pretty village boasts two good pubs with child-friendly gardens if you all get hot and thirsty.

Leiston's Long Shop Museum and Thorpeness Meare

Leiston, a small town near the Suffolk coast, is very different from any other town of similar size in the area. Its industrial history is apparent in the Victorian terraces of houses built for the workers employed by the Richard Garrett Engineering Works – manufacturer of agricultural machinery, steam engines and tractors plus, during both World Wars, ammunition.

The Long Shop Museum, housed in the original buildings of the engineering works, is well worth a visit. It explores the history of the town and the company and displays some fascinating old machines such as vintage fire engines and railway vehicles, among others.

A short drive from Leiston will bring you to Thorpeness, another unusual Suffolk destination that was developed as a model holiday village by Glencairn Stuart Ogilvie, a Scottish barrister, in 1910. A man-made lake, the Meare, was formed at the centre of this dream village, its inspiration drawn from J M Barrie's *Peter Pan*. Together with its islands, it covers some 24 ha (60 acres).

The Meare is no ordinary lake. No more than 1.2 m (4 ft) deep at any point, it's a marvellous place to go boating. You can rent many different types of boat: sailing boats, kayaks, canoes, rowing boats, punts and pedaloes, so there'll be something from which you can happily explore. Find your way down intriguing channels to Wendy's home or the Pirates Lair – small islands that kids love to play on. Take a picnic with you and eat it under a shady tree by the edge of the water. If you still have time and the energy, you can finish your day on the beach itself – or fly kites on the broad grassy sward that divides the beach from the road if it's too chilly to swim.

WHERE:
Leiston and Thorpeness are both near/on the Suffolk Heritage Coast, near Aldeburgh.
BEST TIME TO GO:
Any time of year, but the Meare is more fun when it's warm and sunny.
DON'T MISS:
The House in the Clouds and the windmill, both at Thorpeness
AMOUNT OF WALKING:
Little
COST:
Low to reasonable
YOU SHOULD KNOW:
Thorpeness holds a Regatta and nearby Aldeburgh holds a Carnival every August. Both these events are well worth attending if you have the opportunity.

Leiston Long Shop Museum patternmaker and blacksmith tool display

West Stow Anglo-Saxon Village and Country Park and the Museum of East Anglian Life

WHERE:
Near Bury St Edmunds, Suffolk
BEST TIME TO GO:
Any time of year, though preferably not when it's raining
DON'T MISS:
The interiors of houses dating back to the 1900s and the 1950s at the Museum – both are very different from what we are accustomed to today.
AMOUNT OF WALKING:
Moderate
COST:
Reasonable
YOU SHOULD KNOW:
The much-loved broadcaster John Peel, who lived in a nearby village until his death in 2004, brought many tourists to Stowmarket through his frequent mentions of the town on his programmes.

The site of the West Stow Anglo-Saxon Village has been home to different groups of people since about 5,000 BC – including Stone Age hunter-gatherers. Over 20,000 remnants of their flint tools and arrowheads have been discovered here, in 11 different locations. With funding from the local borough council and the Heritage Lottery Fund, an early Anglo-Saxon village was reconstructed and this provides an amazingly realistic picture of what life may have been like back in the mists of time.

Several different types of dwelling have been built, all of which can be entered and explored. Original artefacts are displayed, pigs and chickens wander freely, and a great many events take place. These include costumed theatre groups and storytellers as well as demonstrations of crafts such as weaving and basketry. The village is surrounded by a superb country park with plenty of trails and walks through woods, over heathland and by the banks of the River Lark.

Anglo-Saxon houses at the West Stow Village

Continuing the theme of East Anglian history, the Museum of East Anglian Life can be found in Stowmarket, just a few miles away. This wonderful museum depicts life as our great grandparents might have known it. Fifteen historic buildings have been rescued, including a blacksmith's forge and a working mill, and a fascinating collection of objects is on display. Look at the Victorian schoolroom, wonder at the old grocer's shop – it certainly differs from the average supermarket experience. Learn about Romany gypsy culture and traditional East Anglian crafts; admire unique working engines; meet Major, the resident Suffolk Punch horse; and enjoy the surrounding countryside. Many different events take place here, from performances by English folk groups and Morris dancers to beer and food festivals, but even on a 'normal' day there is much to interest people of all ages.

Canoeing the Bungay Loop

Part of the Broads National Park, Bungay is a handsome town in the Waveney valley largely surrounded by lush water meadows. There has been a settlement here for hundreds of years, indeed the name Bungay is said to derive from Anglo-Saxon times. The remains of Bigod's Castle overlook both town and river and it's worth a trip to the Visitors' Centre to learn more of the town's fascinating history. Crammed with splendid buildings, Bungay is a good place to have a hearty breakfast before you set out on your canoeing safari.

Outney Meadow Caravan Park, a short walk away, is where you can hire a Canadian canoe for a whole or half day. The canoes are easy to paddle, well balanced and stable so you don't need to be experienced to take to the river. The horseshoe-shaped loop takes at least three hours to navigate – longer if you like to dawdle and if you bring a picnic to enjoy somewhere *en route*. Although you are going upstream, there's usually very little current and you can make the day as strenuous or gentle as you please.

During the summer months you'll be astonished at the amount of wildlife you can see – swans, herons, various different warblers, dragonflies, butterflies and even, if you are very, very lucky, otters. The joy of being in a canoe is that you are close to the wildlife, most of which seems unperturbed by the presence of humans. In fact this is a heavenly way to travel: almost silent, you can slip through the water as slowly or quickly as you like, listening to birdsong and admiring gorgeous scenery as you go. Although this trip may not seem to be a particularly full day out, by the time you are back on dry land you'll feel happily exhausted.

WHERE:
On the Suffolk/Norfolk border
BEST TIME TO GO:
On a sunny day from spring through to early autumn
DON'T MISS:
The 'chicken roundabout' on the A143 at Bungay – scores of elegant, semi-wild chickens, cockerels and chicks inhabit the roundabout and nearby verges and are famous in the locality.
AMOUNT OF WALKING:
Low to moderate
COST:
Reasonable
YOU SHOULD KNOW:
On Sunday August 4 1577 a demonic Black Dog is said to have visited first Bungay and then Blythburgh church, killing members of the congregation in both places and leaving scorch marks on the door at Blythburgh. Today the Black Dog has become a symbol of the town, used on its coat of arms, the gate of the museum, on the annual marathon literature and other, commercial, ventures.

Family paddling a Canadian canoe on the River Waveney.

The Bressingham Collections

WHERE:
Near Diss, Norfolk
BEST TIME TO GO:
The main season runs from March 30
to November 1, but you'll find it more
enjoyable on a fine day.
DON'T MISS:
Check out the Special Event days at
Bressingham, which vary from Teddy
Bears Day, where children with a
Teddy get in free, to *Dads Army* Day
and Christmas Santa Specials.
AMOUNT OF WALKING:
Moderate; there is easy access for
wheelchair users.
COST:
Reasonable; one registered carer
gains free admission with each
paying disabled person.
YOU SHOULD KNOW:
It is possible to take a full- or half-day
course to learn how to drive one of
the steam engines here.

*Steam engine Alan Bloom at
Bressingham Gardens*

The small village of Bressingham in Norfolk, which can be found just a couple of miles from Diss, is home to two remarkable attractions that, between them, will appeal to everyone in the family. In 1947 Bressingham Hall was acquired by Alan Bloom, a man with twin passions: gardens and steam. During the course of the following 50-plus years, he and his son not only established magnificent gardens but also collected a fantastic array of steam engines, which he placed within them.

Take a turn on the Victorian steam carousel known as the Gallopers and visit the official *Dad's Army* exhibition, set up in a re-creation of the main street of Walmington-on-Sea. During the 1960s and 1970s *Dad's Army* was such a popular television series that repeats are still shown today, and the exhibition includes familiar props, uniforms and even some of the scripts from the show. Bressingham Steam Museum occasionally supplied the series with vehicles, such as the fire engine and the steamroller.

A day spent at Bressingham is full of interest: there are four

railways here and over 8 km (5 mi) of different narrow-gauge tracks, as well as some standard-gauge track. Enjoy chuntering through the gorgeous gardens, being pulled by a magnificent steam engine complete with toots and whistles and clouds of steam. Each railway takes you on a different route, occasionally crossing another line and sometimes apparently racing another train. This is also the home of the 6100 Royal Scot locomotive, finally back in full working order. There are more than 40 other engines to be seen and admired, each one beautifully restored. Children always enjoy the vintage signal box and, unusually, they are encouraged to play on many of the engines, too.

Redwings Horse Sanctuary and Bewilderwood

Established in the early 1980s, Redwings is now the largest charity in the country dedicated to rescuing horses, ponies, donkeys and mules. With eight centres across the UK, the Caldecott Centre at Fritton is one of only three visitor centres, and it is a joy to explore. Its 28 ha (70 acres) of paddocks provide a peaceful haven for numerous equines.

Take a tour of the stable yard and paddocks and meet some of the scores of rescue animals, including Denise, a much-loved, attention-seeking donkey, and Victor, the handsome Shire horse. You can watch demonstrations, learn about horse care, and visit the Horse Wise Education Centre with its interactive games and excellent displays. This is a delightful place to spend a few hours and, if you are in need of a break, there's even a good café.

Less than an hour's drive away, Bewilderwood is an unusual and imaginative attraction aimed at families with children of up to 11 years old. Many will already know the book of the same name and will recognize all the places to be explored in this magical forest. This is a hands-on, outdoor adventure park. From the moment they enter, your kids will be on the go – boating along the Dismal Dyke to the Scary Lake, or walking through the swamp, building dens, swinging through the trees on zip wires and crossing wobbly suspension bridges, using huge slides and climbing up to visit tree houses.

There's a special area for the under fives, which ensures that they can have as much fun as their older siblings in a very safe environment. As you'll all be using up masses of energy it's a good idea to bring a picnic along – there are lots of places to stop and re-fuel – and you might be advised to bring a change of clothes for the kids, in case of rain.

WHERE:
Redwings Horse Sanctuary – Fritton, near Great Yarmouth; Bewilderwood – Hoveton, near Norwich, Norfolk.
BEST TIME TO GO:
On a fine day – both places are very out-doorsy.
DON'T MISS:
The broad, sandy beach, two piers and amusement arcades of Great Yarmouth's 'Golden Mile'.
AMOUNT OF WALKING:
Moderate. The stables and first paddocks are easily accessed by wheelchair users. There is even a wheelchair available to borrow if you need one.
COST:
Redwings is free, though you may want to make a donation. Bewilderwood is reasonable.
YOU SHOULD KNOW:
Redwings is open from April to October – check opening times in advance.

Banham Zoo

The award-winning Banham Zoo is a terrific place to take your kids for the day. Just the right size, it is large enough to keep the whole family busy all day while still being easy to get around. Its friendly, helpful staff are there to point you in the right direction.

On your arrival, make for the information boards – you can then plan your day around the many activities on offer. Try to catch the Amazing

Lots of hands-on at Banham Zoo

WHERE:
Banham, near Diss, Norfolk
BEST TIME TO GO:
Anytime, but it's best on a fine day.
DON'T MISS:
The bird-of-prey display
AMOUNT OF WALKING:
Moderate
COST:
Reasonable
YOU SHOULD KNOW:
Banham Zoo is open every day except for Christmas Day and Boxing Day. It is home to about 1,000 animals from around the world and proud of its breeding programme for endangered species. A special scheme enables children to feel involved in conservation by sponsoring or 'adopting' an animal.

Animals presentation: 30 minutes of insight into the intimate life and behaviour of many of the animals you can see here. A fabulous new giraffe enclosure, opened to coincide with Banham's 40th anniversary, includes a high walkway and feeding platform. If you arrive early you may be able to book a place to help feed the giraffes by hand.

The bird-of-prey display is another must. It takes place twice a day and you will be delighted by the experience of a variety of splendid birds flying low over your head, and surprised at the sight of vultures walking calmly amongst the audience. Make sure you catch as many of the feeding talks and demonstrations as you can. They feature large cats such as tigers and snow leopards as well as small mammals such as meercats, plus otters and the ever-popular penguins.

Children are always thrilled to climb on board the tiger-striped road train for a trip around the zoo, complete with an entertaining commentary. Small children are well catered for. While their siblings are learning and encountering small animals at the Activity Centre, they are kept amused in a soft-play area. There's also a small playground for the under fives as well as a much larger one for older children.

Jet skiing and sailing on the North Norfolk Coast

The North Norfolk coast lies close to England's most easterly point. Much of this long coastline is an Area of Outstanding Natural Beauty and once you come here you'll see why. You could spend the best part of a lifetime exploring the creeks and mudflats, saltmarshes and pine forests, estuaries and bays, and marvelling at the vast sweeps of pale sand. As you travel further south, the cliffs gradually become dunes covered with marram grass and seawalls, breakwaters and man-made reefs provide defences against the expected rise in sea levels.

Not surprisingly, this coastline is a popular holiday location – its broad beaches and gently shelving seas are perfect for family fun. However, it is more than simply a great spot for buckets and spades because from Hunstanton all the way around to Sea Palling and beyond, this coast attracts attention from water-sport enthusiasts, including jet skiers and sailors.

Jet skiing is to water what motor biking is to roads, except that there are two types of jet ski – one you sit on and one you stand on. It became popular throughout the world in the 1980s and '90s, and today many traditional Norfolk seaside villages have made provision for devotees. Sea Palling is very popular with jet skiers – and even if your role in all this is to drive your teens to the beach and wait for them, it's exciting to be a spectator – though not as exciting as it is to be an active participant.

Sailing is a popular activity all along the North Norfolk coast, and in many places such as Blakeney, Wells, Cley and Hunstanton, courses are available to suit all ages and abilities. A day's sailing with the family is almost the epitome of an English summer holiday, the kind of experience your children will remember forever.

WHERE:
All along the North Norfolk coast
BEST TIME TO GO:
Summer, although spring and autumn can be lovely, too
DON'T MISS:
The stunning coastline
AMOUNT OF WALKING:
Little
COST:
Expensive, unless you are already fully equipped and experienced.
YOU SHOULD KNOW:
Jet ski courses are available for children over 12, but children of any age can be passengers. Sailing courses are available for those over eight but, again, children of any age can be passengers. These are just two of the many water sports that can be enjoyed along this coast.

Learning the basics of sailing on the Norfolk coast.

Visit the Blakeney seals and Holkham Bay

WHERE:
Blakeney and Holkham Bay, Norfolk
BEST TIME TO GO:
May to September
DON'T MISS:
A walk along Holkham Beach
at sunset
AMOUNT OF WALKING:
As much or as little as you choose
COST:
Reasonable
YOU SHOULD KNOW:
Gwyneth Paltrow famously walked
across Holkham sand at low tide
towards the end of the film
Shakespeare in Love and, more
recently, part of *The Duchess*,
starring Keira Knightley, was filmed
at Holkham House.

One of the classic things to do on the North Norfolk coast, enjoyed by generations of holiday makers of all ages, is to visit the seals at Blakeney Point. A long shingle spit that gives some protection to a large tidal area, the shape of which is in constant flux, Blakeney Point is also an important breeding place for a variety of birds, including large colonies of terns during the summer.

Although it's possible to walk out to the point at low tide, the best way is to take a boat from Blakeney or Morston Quay. The crew are full of pertinent information and you are guaranteed to see seals. This is a permanent colony of hundreds of both Common and Grey seals and you'll see them basking on the banks and popping up beside the boat to take a good look at you. You can just take the boat trip, but it's more fun to land on the point where you can visit the information centre in The Old Lifeboat House, enjoy a cup of coffee, watch the birds and experience this marvellous nature reserve for an hour or so before being ferried back to shore.

A hop, skip and a jump from Blakeney and you'll find yourselves on the magnificent swathe of pale sand that is Holkham Bay. Backed by pine forest and a nature reserve, this is one of the best and most unspoilt beaches in the country. The bay is long and wide – at low tide it can take 20 minutes to walk to the water's edge. There are no organized amusements here, so bring your own food and drink, buckets and spades, books and magazines, and settle down for a fabulous, relaxing afternoon of walking, swimming and collecting shells.

Blakeney seals turn out for the tourists.

Norwich Castle

Set upon a mound surrounded by gardens, Norwich Castle is an imposing sight and one of the city's best-loved landmarks. Built by the Normans during the 10th century, it was first a royal palace, became a prison in the 14th century and finally a museum in 1894. Today it is Norfolk's principal museum and art gallery and is a splendid place to visit with children of all ages.

A modern, glass lift transports you to the entrance. The site has two main sections – the Norman keep and behind it a rotunda with galleries on two floors that radiate out from it. The staff at the ticket desk will be able to give you a plan of the museum and tell you about any events and activities occurring during the day, including games and trails that will lead you around the galleries.

There is plenty to see and do here. Interactive displays and hands-on activities help kids to discover what it was like to live in the castle, or in East Anglia, during Anglo-Saxon times. Children can dress up in Anglo-Saxon clothes and learn to write their names in runes. They will learn about Boudicca, queen of the Iceni who rebelled against the Romans, and can even have a go on a re-created Iceni war chariot.

Don't miss a tour of the battlements if the weather is clement: you'll get a fantastic view of the city and beyond. Your children need to be over eight to join this tour as it's a long way up a 900-year-old spiral staircase. You can also take a tour of the dungeons – boys in particular seem to love learning about punishments such as the ducking stool and the gibbet iron, and there's even a suitably horrid collection of Victorian death masks.

A little girl takes a photograph at the entrance to Norwich Castle.

WHERE:
Norwich, Norfolk
BEST TIME TO GO:
Any time
DON'T MISS:
The Egyptian Gallery
AMOUNT OF WALKING:
Moderate. The battlements and dungeons tours are not accessible to wheelchair users.
COST:
Low. If you only have an hour at the end of the day, you can get in for £1 per person – a very good deal.
YOU SHOULD KNOW:
Norwich is the largest walled city in England and has the largest collection of medieval churches in Europe.

Tropical Wings, World of Wildlife

Tropical Wings is a rather unexpected and delightful place to spend the day. Spread over several acres of Essex countryside, it remains small enough to be able to see and enjoy everything and its scale and atmosphere makes it most suitable for children of 12 years and under.

As you enter Tropical Wings you are issued with a wristband, which allows you to come in and out as you please. This is a particularly good idea if you've brought a picnic or bought one at the attached farm shop. You can leave it in the car until you want it, rather than lugging it around with you.

The Tropical House is the pride and joy of Tropical Wings and one of the UK's largest butterfly houses. Here, hundreds of exotic butterflies fly freely through a hot and humid tropical rainforest. With a wingspan of 12 to 15 cm (4.5 to 6 in), the Owl butterfly is the largest you will see, but there is a myriad of these brightly coloured creatures fluttering about, landing on flowers, fruit-laden tables and even, if you're lucky, on you. Follow the path and you'll come to a bridge over a large pond full of shiny Koi carp – one of the few creatures you are encouraged to feed. Children usually love throwing food to them – it can be bought on entry – because of the way these large fish thrash and splash and jostle to reach the food.

Outside you'll pass through aviaries containing parrots, cockatoos, chatty mynah birds, kookaburras and owls, some of which respond to the sound of their own names. Further on you can find birds of prey, maras, otters, giant tortoises and more. The lemur enclosure is very popular, as are the meercats, but the biggest stars of the show here are the wallabies. You can walk freely in their enclosure, getting so close you can sometimes see a joey popping its head out of its mother's pouch.

All around you will find information boards relating to the different animals and birds, and throughout the day you can enjoy animal-encounter sessions that might include feeding, owl-flying displays or explanations of conservation techniques. There's a café as well as plenty of places to enjoy a picnic, play areas for both toddlers and older children, and a number of special-event days that take place during the course of the year.

Colchester Leisure World

Colchester Leisure World is probably the largest sport-and-leisure complex in East Anglia and it's an absolute godsend if you need somewhere to take the kids on a bad-weather day. It's open all year round and there are special schemes available in the holidays and at half term.

The main choice of activity is swimming. Children under 16 years of age can swim free, providing they are in possession of a Swimming Card, otherwise there is a fee. There are three pools: a Fitness pool, for swimming lengths, a Teaching pool and a splendid Leisure pool with a pirate theme, complete with flume rides that go right out of the building before coming back in again. The centre offers lessons for children of all ages and abilities, including sessions for parents and toddlers. The poolside café enables you to have an ice cream or a juice while you take a break or wait for your child. Other features include river rapids, geysers, slides and spa pools.

However, there's more to do than swimming – you can turn up, take potluck and see if you can book a badminton court, or play table tennis or squash, though during busy periods it's probably safer to book in advance. For parents there's a health spa so you can pamper yourself while your significant other keeps an eye on the kids.

If you are spending the day here, you can have lunch either in the café or in the restaurant/bar. This not only has a family area but also a giant television screen, so you don't have to miss the Wimbledon finals or premiership football. There's plenty for the entire family to do here, and if you live locally you and your kids can sign up to use the gym as well.

WHERE:
Cowdray Avenue, Colchester, Essex
BEST TIME TO GO:
Any time but it's especially good on a grey, miserable day.
DON'T MISS:
The exciting, 13-m (43-ft) flumes in the Leisure Pool
AMOUNT OF WALKING:
Little
COST:
Low to reasonable
YOU SHOULD KNOW:
Children under the age of eight must be accompanied by an adult (over 16 years) while in the water. One adult can accompany three children as long as at least one of them is over five years old. Check pool timetables, etc, in advance.

Waterslide at Colchester Leisure World

Colchester Zoo

WHERE:
Colchester, Essex
BEST TIME TO GO:
Any time
DON'T MISS:
The Orangutan Forest and the Heights
Zone, home to rare Amur tigers and
Komodo dragons
AMOUNT OF WALKING:
Lots. If you have a pushchair with you,
or are a wheelchair user, the yellow
route is the easiest way around the
zoo. Bear in mind that the site is on a
long, steep hill.
COST:
Expensive

Getting up close to the penguins.

Open all year round, apart from Christmas Day, Colchester Zoo provides an exciting and rewarding day out for everyone. The animals are housed in themed zones: the Aquatic Zone, for example, features Cuban crocodiles, penguins that can be seen from an underwater viewing area and the Playa Patagonia – the largest straight underwater tunnel in Europe, where you can admire sealions twisting and turning above. In the Valley Zone you'll meet, among other creatures, Sasha the magnificent Bengal white tiger. There is also an African Zone and others. The enclosures are spacious, modern and designed with the animals' welfare in mind.

It is impossible to see everything in a day, so do some advance research and work out your priorities. There are about 50 different displays and feeding sessions each day, so check on the times and make a plan. The train that chunters around the zoo is included in

your ticket price and you can go round more than once. Be sure to take a ride as the the black-backed jackals can only be seen this way. There are lots of interactive experiences to enjoy, so you might find yourselves feeding an elephant or a giraffe. If your children are young, visit the Kidz Zone. This includes the Wild About Animals Theatre, where you can see displays or possibly stroke a python, as well as meet and pet more familiar, domestic animals.

There are plenty of lovely spots where you can enjoy a picnic, as well as numerous food outlets. Many areas are under cover, so it doesn't matter if it starts raining. Including mammals, reptiles, birds and fish, there are over 2,500 creatures in this collection. But if by any chance your children suddenly get fed up, there are adventure playgrounds dotted around, too.

YOU SHOULD KNOW:
As well as being an entertaining and educational day out, Colchester Zoo is deeply involved in conservation projects and breeding programmes for endangered species. It was the first British zoo to set up a reserve in South Africa that protects endangered species in their natural habitat.

Stubbers Adventure Centre

Whether your children are sporty types, bursting with energy, or more inclined to sit in front of their computer playing games, you will almost certainly find something to appeal to them at Stubbers Adventure Centre. As long as they are nine or older they can come and enjoy themselves for the whole day, from 08.30 to 16.30.

Stubbers runs a whole variety of courses during the school holidays, with a very clever colour-coded system from which your child chooses four different activities in advance. Each day, from Monday to Friday, your child can choose one of five different bands, each of which features four different activities. For example, the red band on Monday might include open canoeing, jet ski rides, a team challenge and climbing, while on Thursday it might include sailing, kayaking, archery and a high-ropes course.

There are so many options to choose from that your children will surely find something to interest them, be it quad biking or banana rides, archery or all-terrain boarding. As well as the multi-activity days there are also one-day, two-day and longer courses for specific activities such as kayaking, sailing and quad biking.

You need to make sure the kids take a change of clothes, a towel, a warm jacket, a waterproof jacket and, most importantly, a picnic lunch. There is a tuck shop that opens at lunchtime, but it is fairly basic. Children learn a whole range of new skills here and meet and make friends. It is good for their self-confidence, helps build team spirit and, of course, it gives you a day to yourself – knowing that they are having fun in a safe environment.

WHERE:
Upminster, Essex
BEST TIME TO GO:
The summer holidays
DON'T MISS:
Conquering fears – encourage kids to choose one activity they are a bit nervous about. They don't like heights? They might enjoy a climbing course!
AMOUNT OF WALKING:
Little, but plenty of other exercise
COST:
Reasonable
YOU SHOULD KNOW:
The documented history of Stubbers goes back to 1334 and the name derives from William Stubbers, a farmer who lived there in the 15th century. In the 16th century it belonged to one William Coys who pioneered the use of hops and barley in the making of English beer.

Mountfitchet Castle and Norman Village

If you are looking for a day out in Essex that combines an element of education as well as entertainment, consider spending the day at Mountfitchet Castle and Norman Village. Occupying its original site, the castle is a historically accurate reconstruction so well done that it is a national Historic Monument, protected by the Department of the Environment.

Wooden barricades and thatched buildings as they might have been in Norman times.

WHERE:
Stansted Mountfitchet, Essex
BEST TIME TO GO:
On a fine day between March and November. Check opening times.
DON'T MISS:
See if you can visit on a Special Event day or try to come on a day when the windmill in Stansted Mountfitchet is open to the public.
AMOUNT OF WALKING:
Moderate. Disabled access at Mountfitchet Castle is limited and no dogs are allowed because of the free-roaming animals.
COST:
Reasonable
YOU SHOULD KNOW:
A 'motte' is a wooden or stone structure or keep built on top of a mound or small hill that is often man-made. A 'bailey' is a courtyard, normally enclosed by a fence, often with an exterior protective ditch, which was the village. Often attached to the castle by a drawbridge, this is where the servants would live, as well as craftsmen, merchants and even farmers – everyone the lord needed to make his life pleasant.

With excellent views over the Stort Valley, this historic site was first an Iron Age hill fort, then a Roman signals fort, a Saxon and a Viking settlement. In 1066 William the Conqueror gifted it to Robert Gernon, the Duke of Boulogne, who built a wooden motte-and-bailey castle here. Several generations later, Richard Montfitchet II joined the barons opposed to King John, who took his revenge by destroying the castle. The villagers removed the stones for their own use and the site lay forgotten until its 20th-century restoration.

Today, Mountfitchet effectively transports its visitors back to Norman England. You can visit the Grand Hall, the Duke's bedroom, the kitchen and the prison, as well as the extensive Norman village. Walk in and out of various houses: the blacksmith's house, the brew-house and the pottery. Look at the catapult and imagine the damage it could do. You'll meet and interact with interesting people and you'll be walking amongst the chickens, ducks, sheep and goats that wander freely around the village as they would have done in times gone by.

If you need a break from the Normans, the House on the Hill Toy Museum is a great escape. Containing some 80,000 toys, it is the largest in Europe. It also has some exciting dinosaurs on guard outside, a Rock 'n' Roll exhibition and the opportunity to play on some wonderful Edwardian amusement machines.

Cambridge University Botanic Gardens and Kettle's Yard

This is a day out best suited to either young children or art-loving teenagers and, of course, their parents. The wonderful Botanic Gardens open at 10.00, so you can make a beeline for the café and a morning coffee on your arrival. Just a five-minute walk from the railway station, the location is very central yet seemingly a world away from Cambridge's crowded streets.

Here you will find yourselves in 16 ha (40 acres) of tranquillity and it's a marvellous place to come with younger children. Bring a picnic lunch with you and make sure you bring extra bread to feed the ducks. Carefully landscaped, the Botanic Gardens include fabulous glasshouses, a rock garden, a woodland walk, a lake, a water garden and a scented garden. Kids love Healthy Herbie, a person-shaped garden of medicinal plants – those that are good for headaches form his head, and so on. Different events and family days are put on throughout the year – these are both fun and educational.

Kettle's Yard, a department of Cambridge University, is no ordinary contemporary art gallery. Originally the home of Jim Ede, a one-time curator of the Tate Gallery, the house is a beautiful conversion of several small cottages, with an additional modern exhibition gallery. Family-friendly, Kettles Yard offers a variety of drop-in art sessions and workshops for kids and families – even for pre-school children. During the summer holidays, the education room is often open for people to make their own artworks, using a selection of different materials, all for free.

As the house has lots of steep stairs and everything is for looking at rather than touching, keep your younger kids busy elsewhere. The permanent exhibition, however, includes works by Henry Moore, Barbara Hepworth, Joan Miro and Alfred Morris, so budding artists will be enthralled.

WHERE:
Station Road/Hills Road and Castle Street, Cambridge
BEST TIME TO GO:
On a pleasant day
DON'T MISS:
The finest collection of trees in the east of England
AMOUNT OF WALKING:
Little to moderate. It's not difficult to push buggies around the Botanic Gardens.
COST:
Low. Children are free at both venues, although a small charge may be made for some of the special events and courses that are on offer.
YOU SHOULD KNOW:
Kettles Yard is closed on Mondays and some Bank Holidays and although the gallery opens earlier, the house is only open in the afternoons. Check their website before you go. If you need an alternative venue for members of your family who are not art-lovers, take them to the delightful Cambridge Folk Museum, conveniently located right next door to Kettle's Yard.

Looking out on the Botanic Gardens.

Sedgwick Museum and Spymasters

WHERE:
Central Cambridge and Bar Hill
BEST TIME TO GO:
When the weather is miserable and you can't be outside.
DON'T MISS:
A walk round the historic colleges in the city centre or possibly a stroll by the Cam, weather permitting. There are other university museums near the Sedgwick that you can visit if you have the time and inclination – the Whipple Museum of the History of Science, the Museum of Zoology and others.
AMOUNT OF WALKING:
Moderate. Check in advance with both the museum and Spymasters if any of you are disabled – they will do their best to help, though it may not be possible.
COST:
Reasonable
YOU SHOULD KNOW:
Sedgwick Museum closes between 13.00 and 14.00 on weekdays and all day Sundays. You should check Spymasters' website for special deals and book in advance. Each mission takes about one-and-a-half hours to complete. There is a café on the premises, and you can also book a party, complete with party food, which probably adds an extra hour to the schedule.

For more than 100 years the Sedgwick Museum of Earth Sciences has been the geology museum of Cambridge University. Built in honour of Adam Sedgwick, whose work helped underpin modern geology, the museum is in a rather splendid building and its collection is both large and impressive.

Charles Darwin was one of Sedgwick's students and in the summer of 2009 a permanent exhibition was opened, exploring Darwin's work on the samples he collected during his voyage on *HMS Beagle* – which were donated to the museum after his death. The museum is family-friendly and puts on plenty of events for children; as it is free to visit, it's a good place to drop into for an hour or two.

If your kids are keen on fossils, gemstones and minerals, they'll appreciate the 1.5 million or so specimens the Sedgwick holds. Must-see exhibits include marine reptiles from the Jurassic age, dinosaurs from Cambridgeshire, a scary reproduction of a Velociraptor and, extraordinarily, a 125,000-year-old hippopotamus that was found in the nearby Barrington gravel pit.

A visit to Spymasters in the afternoon will bring the kids sharply back to the modern era. This is a new and innovative adventure centre, where fantasies of being a spy can be fulfilled. Designed to look like a Russian embassy, on arrival the kids will be briefed on their secret mission and then sent off to rescue a kidnapped colleague, steal vital information or save the world. Along the way they may have to learn to crack safes and hack computers, and certainly have to avoid being caught. There are three levels of difficulty and children need to be over eight to attend – it is a bit too sophisticated for younger children to fully appreciate.

The Fitzwilliam Museum

WHERE:
Trumpington Street, Cambridge
BEST TIME TO GO:
Any time, but perhaps it's best suited for a day when you don't want to be out of doors.
DON'T MISS:
The scary Grasshopper Clock striking the hour at Corpus Christi College in the city centre. A wonderful mechanical monster that eats time, the clock was unveiled by Professor Stephen Hawking in 2008.

The Fitzwilliam Museum in Cambridge is probably Europe's finest small museum. Part of Cambridge University, it is housed in an imposing neo-classical building that was opened to the public in 1848. Since then the collection has been considerably enlarged by gifts, bequests and purchases funded by charitable bodies and the nation.

Don't be put off if you think this sounds too rarified for your taste – the 'Fitz' is a lovely museum and welcomes all comers

Grand entrance to the Fitzwilliam Museum

through its doors. It's the sort of place that you can visit over and over again and, of course, the fact that it's free helps. With one eye to the future, the museum has brought itself up to date with plenty of activities for families and children. While some are ongoing, others pertain to specific exhibitions, so it is definitely sensible to check the website in advance to see what's on and when.

Talks are often held in the galleries at lunchtime and music is sometimes provided on Sundays. But the fun begins the moment you reach the entrance desks and are handed a colour-coded activity kit. This leads you on an adventure tour of the galleries, with interactive puzzles and games to be enjoyed – don't panic, parents are given the answers separately. There are drawing materials available, too, and even special story books for the under fives which connect with particular parts of the collection. The Education Studio puts on excellent events that you can book your kids into, and for which there may be a small charge.

The Courtyard Café serves drinks, snacks, sandwiches, lunch and afternoon tea and is open all day, so you can take breaks here or use it as a meeting place. The museum shop next door has a good range of items for sale.

AMOUNT OF WALKING:
Moderate
COST:
Free
YOU SHOULD KNOW:
In January 2006 a visitor to the Fitzwilliam Museum tripped over his shoelaces and smashed to smithereens three Qing vases that had rested safely on a window ledge for some 60 years. Now restored, the beautiful Chinese vases are back on display – this time in a case.

Duxford Imperial War Museum

WHERE:
Duxford, Cambridgeshire
BEST TIME TO GO:
May to October
DON'T MISS:
The historic aircraft in flight
AMOUNT OF WALKING:
Moderate to lots. The site is suitable for parents pushing buggies and for wheelchair users. Wheelchairs are available for hire, but you must ring in advance to reserve one. Guide dogs are the only dogs that are allowed entry.
COST:
Free for children (up to 15 years), except for air shows and some special events. The cost for adults is reasonable.

The Imperial War Museum at Duxford is just one of the five first-class branches of the museum that you can visit and, for those who love aviation, it's the most exciting. If you are walking or driving and suddenly become aware that there's an amazing historic aircraft in the sky above you, there's every chance it will have come from Duxford. Located near Junction 10 of the M11 motorway, it is easy to find and there's plenty of free parking.

This must be Europe's best aviation museum. There are hangars full of fantastic exhibits, including aircraft, tanks, military vehicles and artillery as well as naval vessels. Discover the story of the Battle of Britain, watch hands-on conservation work and enjoy any number of special events, family activities and air shows that take place during the course of the summer. You might get a chance to taste typical World War II dishes, or discover how families managed to cope with rationing. The famous, annual Duxford Air Show features both modern and historic aircraft, which are put through their paces above your heads – the display put on by the Red Arrows is always absolutely amazing. There's a

American military aircraft in the American Air Museum at Duxford Imperial War Museum

playground, picnic places, cafés and a restaurant so you can take a break every now and again.

The aerodrome was built during World War I and in 1924 became a fighter station. During World War II the airfield was handed to the US 8th Air Force and the American Air Museum here is a memorial to the US airmen who lost their lives. Here you can see the greatest collection of American warplanes outside the USA, beautifully displayed with many suspended from the roof as though in flight. A special American Air Day is put on once a year.

YOU SHOULD KNOW:
The last operational RAF flight from Duxford was in 1961. By 1969 the MoD had announced that it was going to dispose of Duxford, and plans to build a prison or a sports centre on the site were discussed. Eventually, in 1977, the County Council, the Imperial War Museum and the Duxford Aviation Society joined forces, bought the aerodrome and established the world-class museum that it is today.

Mepal Outdoor Centre, Ely

The city of Ely is in a wonderful location, surrounded by the tranquil, low-lying, watery landscape of the Fens. The Mepal Outdoor Centre is situated to the west of the city, on the edge of a lovely 8-ha (20-acre) lake so, if you feel like having an active, adventurous day out with kids who are bursting with energy, look no further.

There are lots of options to choose from – hire a family-sized canoe or individual kayaks, rowing boats, pedaloes or even a sailing dinghy, and take to the water. If you are beginners, or just want to hone your skills, sign up for a Paddlepower course. Be aware that you are probably going to get wet, so make sure that everyone has a change of clothes available. Book yourselves an exclusive family activity session with an instructor and you can choose two different activities – such as rock climbing, target shooting, trampolining, orienteering and others – or use the entire two-hour session canoeing or on the high ropes.

The centre offers considerably more than simple water sports. Take archery for example: if you have your own equipment, you are given a map with which you follow a route around the site, finding and shooting hidden targets and scoring points for prizes. If your kids are over 12, how about an afternoon paintball game . . . or six? This takes some advance planning, but is well worth the effort – check details with the centre.

There is plenty of amusement for younger children, too – an adventure playground, a Scramble Zone, a ball pool, a paddling pool and a sandpit. Walk around the lake and, if you don't feel like carrying a picnic with you, repair to the centre's indoor café where you can relax, warm up and compare notes with other families.

WHERE:
Mepal, near Ely, Cambridgeshire
BEST TIME TO GO:
A sunny day, if possible, and not too windy
DON'T MISS:
A river cruise in Ely. Choose between a quick half-hour tour of the waterfront or a longer, afternoon tea cruise.
AMOUNT OF WALKING:
Low to moderate – it depends on which activities you decide upon.
COST:
Reasonable
YOU SHOULD KNOW:
Ely was once an island in the middle of the Fens, historically an area rich in eels. It is thought that the name Ely is derived from this fact and that, during the 11th century, the local monks paid their taxes using eels as currency.

An owl landing on a falconer's glove at the Raptor Foundation.

The Raptor Foundation

A day out at the Raptor Foundation is both fun and educational. A registered charity, the 12-ha (30-acre) site is home to more than 200 birds of prey including falcons, owls, hawks and eagles. The Foundation includes a hospital where injured birds are rehabilitated and, although they cannot always be released back into the wild, they will be cared for here for life by a knowledgeable and highly dedicated team.

Spend the day exploring the site, trying to answer the quiz, and possibly watching pellet dissection in the education room, as well as catching the flying displays. During summertime there are three flying displays daily. These are really exciting to watch and allow for a certain amount of audience participation. Just imagine how extraordinary it would be to have Elmo, a great horned owl, or Quark, a ferruginous hawk, fly directly to you . . .

There are at least 40 birds on the flying team, so each display involves a different group of birds – there's even an indoor flying arena so you won't be disappointed if the weather suddenly turns. In between times you can relax in the restaurant – a playground is situated conveniently close by, so younger children can expend any extra energy in a safe location. The well-stocked shop is full of tempting souvenirs.

The Raptor Foundation puts on Experience Days that need to be booked in advance. Book two Meet the Birds sessions: this would enable you to take two children with you at no extra cost. These sessions last for half the day and include an introductory talk, a guided tour, meeting and handling some of the birds and participating in a flying display. To finish up, you'll be photographed with one of the birds as a memento.

WHERE:
Woodhurst, Cambridgeshire
BEST TIME TO GO:
On a good summer's day
DON'T MISS:
The flying displays and a close encounter with a bird of prey
AMOUNT OF WALKING:
Moderate
COST:
Low, though the Experience Days are expensive.
YOU SHOULD KNOW:
It is possible to stay at the Raptor Foundation, either in accommodation units or on their campsite. This would be good fun if you decided to go to a twilight flying display. The admission price for these evening sessions includes a meal, and you must book in advance as places are limited.

Maple Street Dolls House shop and the Royston Cave

If you or your children are fans of miniatures and dolls houses, you must take a trip to the Maple Street Dolls House shop in Royston. The largest shop of its kind in Europe, Maple Street is an absolute treasure trove of every conceivable type of dolls house and dolls house accoutrement – a complete eye-opener for the uninitiated.

The houses range from very sophisticated affairs such as the Tudor Coaching Inn, aimed at adult collectors, and Daisy Cottage, a charming pink cottage with shutters, windows and doors that open and a roof that lifts off to reveal an attic space. If you go mad and buy a starter dolls house, you automatically receive a family to go with it and you can spend hours looking for furniture, lighting, kitchen equipment and everything you'd expect to find in a full-sized house – right down to the plasma TV set!

There's a wonderful exhibition to enjoy – glass cases contain typical rooms in many different styles: Georgian, Victorian, town house or rural retreat, as well as other collections that have been acquired over time. It's easy to spend hours enjoying these varied and enchanting miniature worlds.

The Royston Cave, which you can visit during the afternoon, is a big surprise. Who would have thought that a 13th-century man-made cavern of historical significance would be sited beneath Melbourn Street in Royston? Unique in Europe, this small, Grade I listed cave, shaped like a bell, is covered with religious wall carvings and esoteric symbols. Its origins are uncertain, though many believe it to be the work of the Knights Templar; others suggest it was connected to the nearby Augustinian Priory. Whatever the truth of the matter, it is exciting to descend the narrow staircase and find yourself in such a mysterious place.

WHERE:
Royston, Hertfordshire
BEST TIME TO GO:
The Maple Street Dolls House shop is open seven days a week throughout the year, but the Royston Cave is only open from Easter Saturday until the last Sunday in September.
DON'T MISS:
The Royston Museum – if you'd like to find out more about the town and its history.
AMOUNT OF WALKING:
Little
COST:
Low
YOU SHOULD KNOW:
In August 1742 the Royston Cave was uncovered. Noticing a millstone in the ground, workers were amazed to find that beneath it was a narrow, vertical shaft with toeholds cut into the chalky sides. A small boy was sent down to see what might be there, but instead of a smuggler's hoard he saw a cave full of debris. The shaft was widened, the debris cleared and only then were the carvings discovered.

Royston Cave is under the junction of Icknield Way and Ermine Street.

Children sketch the exhibits at Tring Natural History Museum.

The Natural History Museum at Tring

Now part of the Natural History Museum, this extraordinary place was previously known as the Walter Rothschild Zoological Museum and housed Rothschild's private collection – the largest single accumulation of zoological specimens ever collected by one man. If your kids are keen on natural history, they'll enjoy it here although, unlike most zoos, these animals are all stuffed and mounted in lifelike poses. The collection is enormous: over 4,000 specimens from across the globe include large predators such as polar bears and lions, fish and crustaceans, birds, insects and even extinct species such as the quagga.

The museum is very popular with families. Gallery trails and activity sheets are available for a very small fee and clipboards, paper and pencils can be borrowed. There are six main galleries devoted to different types of creatures as well as temporary exhibitions. Gallery 6, for example, has a fascinating display of domestic dogs, and there's a collection of Mexican fleas dressed up in national costume that children always find highly amusing.

There are plenty of hands-on activities, too – try the Discovery Room. It was designed for children, but is enjoyed by people of all ages.

Walter Rothschild, who had a carriage drawn by zebras, was particularly interested in flightless birds and the park around the museum – which was then the family home – had many such birds roaming in it. These included cassowaries, some of which are now mounted in the Rothschild Room.

During the summer months lots of activities and drop-in sessions are put on with children in mind. Check the website to find out what's on and book in advance – it might be mask making, specimen sketching, bug hunting or pond dipping – whatever it is, it will be enlightening, entertaining and unusual.

WHERE:
Tring, Hertfordshire
BEST TIME TO GO:
Any time – the museum is open all year round apart from December 24–26.
DON'T MISS:
The Wildlife Photographer of the Year exhibition, shown here before moving to the Natural History Museum in London.
AMOUNT OF WALKING:
Moderate
COST:
The museum is free to enter, but small charges are payable for some of the special events. There is a café but also plenty of space in the surrounding park to enjoy a picnic.
YOU SHOULD KNOW:
Walter Rothschild was a serious zoologist and there are many birds, insects and mammals that carry his name. He travelled on many expeditions and was the first person to describe the *Giraffa camelopardis rothschildi*. This most endangered of camel sub-species has five horns instead of two and originates from Kenya and Uganda. In 1932 he was obliged to sell most of his bird collection after being blackmailed by a woman.

Knebworth House, Gardens and Park

A trip to Knebworth offers much more than simply a visit to a stately home, even one as interesting as this. With its high Gothic exterior and rooms reflecting English history from the Jacobean period to the 20th century, a tour of the house is both fascinating and informative.

Most children, however, are more likely to enjoy the gorgeous gardens and the vast park. Walk down avenues lined with pollarded limes, visit the formal rose garden, the herb garden designed by Gertrude Jekyll and the walled kitchen garden, and enjoy trying to find your way to the centre of the maze. Have a good look round before making your way to the Wilderness Walk, where you'll discover the Dinosaur Trail. As you follow the trail through beautiful redwoods you'll come across 72 life-sized dinosaurs hunting, fighting and grazing – don't miss the enormous T-Rex. Information boards along the way tell you everything you want to know about the dinosaurs you spot.

Your kids might be too young to want to spend much time in the house, but you can buy tickets that exclude it and just spend your day out of doors. The 101-ha (250-acre) deer park includes a miniature railway as well as a giant adventure playground where there are endless amusements ranging from Fort Knebworth, an enclosure with swings, climbing frames and bouncy castles, to a four-lane giant astroglide slide.

Bring your own picnic and wander into the park proper to enjoy it in peace – you might even spot some of the deer that roam here. Alternatively, buy snacks, ice creams and drinks on site. Keep an eye on the website – there are often special events during the summer that can be enjoyed by all the family.

WHERE:
Knebworth, near Stevenage, Hertfordshire
BEST TIME TO GO:
On a good day during the summer. Knebworth is open to day visitors at weekends and during school holidays from March to October. Check the website for precise dates.
DON'T MISS:
The pet cemetery, with its charming tributes to the Lytton family's dearly loved pets.
AMOUNT OF WALKING:
As much or as little as you want. Much of the gardens and the Dinosaur Trail are accessible for wheelchairs and buggies, but there is only limited access to some of the ground floor of the house.
COST:
Reasonable, but check in advance as the special-events weekends often cost more.
YOU SHOULD KNOW:
Home of the Lytton family since 1490, Knebworth House was given a major makeover in 1843. Edward Bulwer-Lytton, author and statesman, transformed the original red-brick Tudor manor house into the high Gothic fantasia that it is today, complete with griffins, gargoyles, turrets and domes. Edward Bulwer-Lytton wrote the famous words 'The pen is mightier than the sword'.

Knebworth House

Lee Valley riverside walk and boat trip

On either side of the River Lee, between Waltham Abbey in Essex and Broxbourne in Hertfordshire, lie 404 ha (1,000 acres) of beautiful countryside, lakes and waterways all linked by cycle paths, footpaths and walkways. This is the Lee Valley Regional Park and it's a wonderful place for a day out, offering all sorts of opportunities to enjoy the great outdoors.

Some of the most beautiful areas can be found right in the heart of the Lee Valley, at Broxbourne. There's a wonderful, four-mile-long riverside walk that you can take, starting and finishing near the station. If you enjoy nature you'll love this. The area teems with wildlife and, apart from the usual ducks and moorhens, you might spot kingfishers, terns and waders. If you are very lucky, you will glimpse a water vole or even an otter.

After about 15 minutes you'll reach Carthegena lock, one of the prettiest around. Further on you'll find Dobbs Weir. Here there's a tearoom and a pub, so you can stop and have a little rest in the sunshine. Further on you'll notice Admiral's Lake on your left, and further still you'll come to the banks of the New River – actually a man-made waterway – with lush gardens stretching right down to the waterside. Before long you'll pass the Victorian pumping station and then find yourselves back at the train station.

In the afternoon you can either hire a boat and take to the water yourselves, or enjoy a river trip. There are regular, hour-long trips that you can join, or longer cruises that include cream teas and need to be booked in advance. Whatever you choose to do, this is a peaceful and delightful way to spend a day.

Cruising on the River Lee.

Aldenham Country Park

The Country Park at Aldenham is a 71-ha (175-acre) area of woods and parkland set around a large, man-made lake. This tranquil location offers a splendid day out, with attractions for everyone in the family. All the paths here are surfaced and well maintained, which is ideal for those using wheelchairs or pushing buggies, and the usual amenities are available.

In 1984 the Rare Breeds Survival Trust Centre set up a farm in the Park, breeding rare livestock. Today you can see many unusual species, including a herd of Aldenham Longhorn cattle. There are also several different breeds of sheep, goats – including Bagot goats brought back to England by the Crusaders – pigs, poultry and Shire horses.

The Park prides itself on its on-going conservation programme, which has made it a wildlife paradise. Swallows swerve and swoop high in the sky and meadow pipits and skylarks trill as you wander through shady woodlands and open meadows bright with wildflowers. Take the Nature Trail or walk beside the lake to watch swans, ducks and all manner of other water birds. If you have budding fishermen in the family, day permits can be obtained from the bailiff. Members of the Aldenham Sailing Club may sail every day of the week and those who enjoy horse riding can do that, too.

If your family is very energetic, there's an assault course for older children and a toddlers' play area – but the most popular facility is Winnie the Pooh's '100 Aker Wood'. This is a trail that leads to the homes of Winnie the Pooh and all his friends. Each of their wooden houses has a sturdy doorknocker, which younger children love banging to see who's at home.

Berkshire rare-breed pigs at the Country Park.

WHERE:
Elstree, Hertfordshire
BEST TIME TO GO:
The Park is lovely whenever you go, and it's open all year except for Christmas Day. Obviously as it is an outdoor venue, it's better to go when the weather is fine, and probably spring, summer and early autumn are the best times.
DON'T MISS:
The occasional special event that is held here – there's an annual craft fair as well as interesting talks. Check the website for details.
AMOUNT OF WALKING:
Moderate
COST:
Low. You pay a small fee per car rather than per person; cyclists and pedestrians go free.
YOU SHOULD KNOW:
The 26-ha (65-acre) reservoir was created by French prisoners of war during the Napoleonic period.

Woburn Safari Park

WHERE:
Woburn, Bedfordshire
BEST TIME TO GO:
Any time, but preferably when it's not raining. If you can avoid school holidays you'll also avoid the crowds and queues.
DON'T MISS:
Some of the endangered mammals – including Przewalski horses and Rothschild giraffes. Both of these animals have been bred here successfully, as have the Pere David deer that roam the park beyond the wildlife enclosures.
AMOUNT OF WALKING:
As much or as little as you want
COST:
High
YOU SHOULD KNOW:
The rules that apply to the Road Safari are for your own benefit: many of the animals you'll see are dangerous. You should remain in your car no matter what, and sound your horn if you need help. Convertibles are not allowed in several enclosures, dogs and BBQs are not permitted anywhere for obvious reasons. Even on the Foot Safari you are liable to have your sandwich taken from your hand, and possibly your hair pulled – keep it tied back for the duration.

You won't forget your visit to Woburn Safari Park in a hurry – this is an exciting place where you can see animals roaming free and at very close quarters. Although the entry price may seem quite high, there's so much here that even if you arrive on the dot and leave only when you have to, you will not have seen it all.

At the gates, don't forget to pick up the very useful information leaflet that comes with the ticket – it includes maps and timetables detailing the various different feeding times, demonstrations and talks that you can attend. These are also included in the price, as are the Road Safari and the Foot Safari, both of which can be repeated as often as you like – you'll see different things each time, of course.

Take the Foot Safari first to wear off some excess energy. The animals you'll encounter range from penguins and sealions to lemurs and wallabies. Feed sips of nectar to the brightly hued lorikeets at Rainbow Landing, take the train journey through some of the enclosures, enjoy the adventure playgrounds or take a swan-shaped pedalo onto the water.

Later on, rejoin your car and take the Road Safari – for some, the highlight of the day. Each circuit takes about an hour and the trick is to drive steadily through the various enclosures, stopping only for a particularly irresistible sight. You'll see elephants, white rhinos, zebras, lions, tigers, wolves and monkeys among others, and they will often be very, very close. Beware of monkeys: they can clamber all over your car and have been known to dismantle chrome trimmings, break off wing mirrors and generally cause chaos if given the chance.

An afternoon nap in the park!

Whipsnade Zoo

Many of us have fond memories of being taken to Whipsnade in our childhood, so taking one's own children or grandchildren there is a curious experience – a mixture of nostalgic reminiscence, pleasurable memories in the making, and an acute awareness of the passage of time.

Begin the day at the fabulous Children's Zoo. Here kids can climb the lookout towers and swing in the Treetop Village – home to red pandas and coatis; explore a network of underground tunnels and the creatures who live there; meet and greet donkeys, llamas and kune-kune pigs in the Touch Zone; and learn about the importance of water in the Splash Zone.

Every year changes take place at the Zoo. New babies arrive, new enclosures open and new experiences thrill the public. Famous for its commitment to conservation work and breeding programmes both on-site and around the world, the innovative new cheetah enclosure is a result of Whipsnade's 30 years of conservation work with cheetahs in Tanzania, and is designed to put you up close and personal to these beautiful animals. The fastest things on four legs in the world, cheetahs can equal the speed limit on British motorways – 113 kph (70 mph).

Whipsnade is so large that lots of people use their cars to get about, enabling them not only to drive between enclosures but also through the Asian area, where animals roam free. However, there's a train that can be taken, as well as a safari bus, both of which transport you to all parts. Don't forget the large mammals – watch lions with their cubs, elephants and rhinos, and try to catch some of the feeding sessions – the sealions put on a particularly good display.

WHERE:
Whipsnade, near Dunstable, Bedfordshire
BEST TIME TO GO:
Any time of year, though a rain-free day is best. School holidays and Bank Holidays tend to be very busy.
DON'T MISS:
The excellent walk-through lemur enclosure.
AMOUNT OF WALKING:
Moderate. Most of the park is accessible to wheelchair users. No dogs are allowed.
COST:
Expensive, but your entry fee helps pay for conservation work and keeps Whipsnade going.
YOU SHOULD KNOW:
Take a walk with some of the Children's Farm animals and their keepers – this is not only exciting and educational, but also really good exercise for both animals and children. The time and route, which changes daily, can be found on the Children's Farm noticeboard.

A giraffe rests his long legs while the visitors look on.

Mead Open Farm

Mead Open Farm provides a brilliant day out for the little ones in particular, who will be absolutely thrilled to be able to feed and touch a number of domestic animals. Every day is packed with activities, and during the summer even more events are organized – ferret racing, for example, which is always good fun, and a sheepdog show, which is rather more unusual.

In these days of large farms and complete automation,

Pretty wellies and bunnies – perfect!

WHERE:
Billington, near Leighton Buzzard, Bedfordshire

BEST TIME TO GO:
Between April and October. A fine day is probably best, but there are things to do indoors if the heavens open.

DON'T MISS:
The sheep racing. Kids can bet on their favourite and cheer it on as a dozen sheep race round a track with teddy bear jockeys on their backs. Those who backed the winner will get a badge.

hand-milking is a dying art, but here's a chance for your kids to learn how to milk a cow and to bottle feed a lamb. For many this will be the closest they've been to farm animals and the experience will be memorable. If you have a pony-mad daughter, she'll be able to practise grooming skills on the farm's Shetland ponies. But if your kids are still too young for that, they'll certainly enjoy cuddling up with a rabbit or a fluffy guinea pig. Children may help walk the goats every afternoon during summer or, if they're getting tired, you can take them on a tractor ride around the farm instead.

Apart from the animals, there are plenty of other activities. Shaggy's Playworld is a large indoor area full of play equipment, including drop slides and net climbs, that can be enjoyed by everyone – including adults. There's also a special soft-play area for the under fives. If you prefer, there's an outdoor adventure playground and a large maize maze, too. Watch your kids race each other in go karts, and don't forget to visit the crazy golf course. If everyone gets tired and hungry, there are several places to stop for a break – or you can take a picnic.

AMOUNT OF WALKING:
Moderate
COST:
Reasonable – and once you've bought your tickets there's nothing more to pay. Every activity is included.
YOU SHOULD KNOW:
Mead Farm puts on lots of special events throughout the year, not just during the summer holidays, and is open almost all year round.

The Lodge RSPB Nature Reserve

At first glance, the idea of spending the day at the RSPB's headquarters, The Lodge, seems rather unlikely, but if you plan well, you and your children will have a brilliant day out. Your first stop should be the Lodge itself – a rather splendid, Grade II listed 'Swiss' cottage, where you can pick up useful information. Special activities are put on with children in mind during the school holidays, and a different activity sheet is available each month. Here you can borrow Wildlife Explorer backpacks full of things to help you enjoy the day – bug boxes, ID charts so you can make notes of everything you've recognized and, of course, binoculars.

The Lodge has fine formal gardens, a Victorian terrace and a modern landscaped fishpond, but the RSPB reserve is a large area of heathland and woodland. A network of trails has been established throughout, some (though not all) of which are suitable for buggies and wheelchairs, and hides are dotted about. From these you can spot a variety of woodland birds, such as tree pipits, treecreepers and all three British woodpeckers. Kingfishers and herons are often seen at the ponds and the Eurasian sparrow-hawk can often be spotted hunting over the reserve.

For a very small fee you might want to join a guided walk, a minibeast safari, a bird watching course for beginners or even a spinning demonstration – there's a flock of Manx Loghtan sheep on the Reserve that you may come across during your explorations. If your kids are happy running about, looking under leaves for insects or toads, making collections of found objects and seeing what birds and beasts they can spot, this is a great day out.

WHERE:
Sandy, Bedfordshire
BEST TIME TO GO:
A sunny day during the spring, summer or early autumn
DON'T MISS:
The special events – if you take a guided walk in the morning, you can spend the afternoon using the knowledge you have acquired.
AMOUNT OF WALKING:
Moderate to lots
COST:
Low – there's a small fee for car parking if you are not a member of the RSPB.
YOU SHOULD KNOW:
You'll need to bring your own picnic. Although drinks and sweets are available at the shop, there is no café.

Castleton and its Caverns

Long famous as one of the loveliest villages in Britain, Castleton might have been designed to appeal to children. Deep in the Peak District National Park, it's set in woodlands between the steep limestone hills of the Vale of Hope. It is fascinating to explore, with the ruins of a Norman castle, a medieval bridge and ancient narrow lanes of stone houses to inspire adventurous imaginations. The dramatic landscape all around is a reminder that Castleton lies above one of Britain's biggest cave and tunnel systems, and provides access to some of the country's best show caverns. The caverns are breathtaking, but pose a problem. It's quite expensive to visit them all, and few children want to spend most of the day underground. Instead, enjoy a family walk from Cave Dale, the beautiful gorge on the edge of the village, round the limestone bluff on which Peveril Castle stands. Follow the stream through the heart of Castleton, and pause at the Castleton Museum. It's full of interactive exhibits about local geology and village life down the ages, and has displays on potholing and climbing that are so vivid you feel you are part of the action. Both you and the children will be glad to have seen them before deciding which cavern or caverns to visit in the afternoon.

Each cavern is exciting in a different way. Peak Cavern, underneath Peveril Castle, has a spectacular entrance once used for rope making; Speedwell Cavern is accessible only via 105 slippery stone steps and a (thrilling) boat ride through a dark tunnel (unsuitable for small children); while Treak Cliff Cavern offers a tour of subterranean wonderlands including Aladdin's Cave, Fairyland Grotto, and the Witch's Cave. Everyone is guaranteed a fabulous day out – but Castleton is one of those rare places where you have to measure the children's ages and stamina against the possibility of entertainment overload.

A child exploring a cave in Winnats Pass.

WHERE:
Castleton, near Bakewell, Derbyshire
BEST TIME TO GO:
Any time
DON'T MISS:
For older children: the massive stalagmite formation of the Waterfall Cavern, and the Grand Crystallized Cavern at Blue John Cavern. For younger children: the showmanship of Treak Cliff Cavern, where the galleries and passages are superbly lit for spooky drama and dazzling effects.
AMOUNT OF WALKING:
Lots – and very little of it is wheelchair- friendly.
COST:
Free (around Castleton village)
Reasonable (for each show cave)
Expensive (two or more show caves)
YOU SHOULD KNOW:
Castleton's cave system is the only place where the rare 'Blue John' fluorspar is found, and it is still mined there. But above and below ground, Castleton's location, wildlife and geology make it a Site of Special Scientific Interest (SSSI) several times over.

Creswell Crags Museum and Education Centre

Creswell Crags boggles the imagination. It's a cave system full of 13,000-year-old rock drawings left there by our Palaeolithic ancestors. They are Britain's only known Ice Age art, comparable to the cave paintings at Lascaux in France. You can see them on a cave tour, but their fragility means some of the caves are barred for their protection.

There are two kinds of tour. Life in the Ice Age describes the cultural significance of the artefacts and drawings, and leads you round the lakeside information points. The Young Travellers tour is the most fun for families and younger children: an expert guide dramatizes the daily struggle of living in the caves. In Robin Hood Cave, the biggest at Creswell Crags, you need the torch on your helmet (the guide will lend you one) to appreciate the chiselled roof and wonder how people made a fire and lived there. Be prepared with flat shoes for difficult and slippery rock passages – unfortunately the geography means it's not very suitable for under fives or for wheelchairs. Luckily there's an even more dramatic version of the story of Creswell Crags in the Museum and Education Centre. Here you can examine the images of bison, deer, horses and birds in their astounding detail, along with the carved bone artefacts found with them. The Age of Ice exhibition tells the story of what it was like for our Stone Age forebears, from choosing a cave and making food to collecting bracken for a bed. It'll make you shiver.

The museum also knows just how to win young minds. The Virtual Ice Age display confronts visitors with a series of interactive challenges to survive Ice Age trials and tribulations. You have to hunt, make clothes, form tools from stone or bone, and carve out a life for yourself.

WHERE:
Creswell, Derbyshire
(near Worksop, Nottinghamshire)
BEST TIME TO GO:
Daily February to October, and Sundays from November to January
DON'T MISS:
The engraved bone from an extinct species of woolly rhinoceros, one of 4,400 bones unearthed at the Pin Hole Cave, including a piece of bison rib carved with the figure of a masked man.
AMOUNT OF WALKING:
Lots, including a stroll round the lake. The museum area is fully accessible to wheelchair users.
COST:
Free (Creswell Museum and Education Centre and the Crags gorge site); reasonable (guided tours)
YOU SHOULD KNOW:
Unlike Cheddar Gorge in Somerset, where there have been several cases of forged 'rock art', the Creswell drawings have been proved to be genuine by analysis of the thin film of stalagmite called 'flowstone' which has formed over the engravings since they were made.

Creswell Crags

Chatsworth Farmyard and Adventure Playground

Part of the magnificent Chatsworth House Estate, the Chatsworth Farmyard and Adventure Playground are run with real flair and imagination. The farmyard activities started years ago to show visitors how the estate used land to produce food and manage timber. Now they are designed primarily to foster children's enthusiasm for the hands-on practicalities of a working farm. There are dairy cows and beef cattle, poultry, sheep, pigs, birds and game fish plus a Shire horse, Shetland pony, and various goats and dogs. They all need feeding, milking or grooming – and friendly staff encourage participation at levels matched to every age group. Activities (like lambing) vary with the seasons, but there are daily animal-handling sessions, a favourite with smaller kids. Fascinating talks and walks highlight the interdependence of farmers, wildlife and the environment, and you can round off your visit with a trailer ride (for a small extra charge) round the farm and part of Chatsworth's woodlands.

The adventure playground is just as inspired as the farmyard (and just as safe – both incorporate the highest safety measures). It spreads through woodland, with a café and shop discreetly placed so you can see the children clambering excitedly on the towers, ropewalks, spiral slide and commando wire; or, if they are very small, absorbed by experiments in the gloriously huge sandpit and water-play area. There's a trampoline, a secret passage, and for bigger groups, a party house built around a tree. In fact the playground as a whole is so spectacular, it feels like the family has been let loose on a Hollywood film set – and you can even make your own accessories, like decorations, cards or hats, in the family craft cottage on site.

Conkers

Any time of year, in any weather, Conkers spoils you for choice. The 49-ha (120-acre) estate of woods, lakes and themed gardens calls itself 'the hands-on experience at the Heart of the National Forest' – a description that pinpoints its location near Swadlincote, but fails to do justice to its terrific range of indoor and outdoor activities. Conkers is a huge environmental pleasure park, with a mission to provoke environmental curiosity and concern through entertainment. You can measure its success in bright eyes, and faces flushed with excitement and healthy exercise. Outside, there are nature and sculpture trails you can follow either with a friendly and informative ranger, or with an activity sheet. In the woodlands and by the lakeside you'll find various play areas, craft workshops, a wildflower glade, a waterside café and restaurant, a viewing platform for treetop vistas, a superb adventure playground, and an 18-stage assault course (for over-13s only). You can also ride a steam train, get your face painted or risk a ducking at the gizmo-enhanced Waterside water-play area. You could even witness a re-enactment of a Civil War battle by the Sealed Knot or hear a concert – both are part of a programme of regular events throughout the year.

Inside, the Discovery Centre is an interactive paradise for even the smallest children – but you have to be aged four or more to explore the Enchanted Forest. It's a stupendous, all-interactive simulation of woodland life from the perspective of leaf litter. Adults and children alike enter the forest through giant worm tunnels. It's hundreds of metres BIG: you traverse a gigantic spider's web, climb giant acorns, slide down caterpillar tubes, avoid the eagle's nest (at all costs!) and clamber up to the Tree Top Adventure Walk, high in the 'night time' woodland canopy. It's nothing short of sensational fun and the kids will love it.

WHERE:
Swadlincote, Derbyshire
BEST TIME TO GO:
Any time
DON'T MISS:
The seasons – it's easy to let the woodlands and gardens pass you by. They are managed to make the best of each season, both in colour and planting layout. Children love the chance to create their own make believe, to play hide and seek, and just to explore the natural world
AMOUNT OF WALKING:
Lots – and everything that possibly can be (like the train ride) is wheelchair-friendly.
COST:
Reasonable
YOU SHOULD KNOW:
If you need temporary help, especially with very small children, look for Billy Bonkers near the indoor children's play centre – he's there to make sure you all have a great day.

Tackling the assault course at Conkers.

Crich Tramway Village and The Heights of Abraham

WHERE:
Crich and Matlock Bath are both near Matlock, Derbyshire
BEST TIME TO GO:
April to October
DON'T MISS:
The fossilized remains of the 3-m (10-ft) giant *Ichthyosaur* at the Heights of Abraham's Fossil Factory exhibition; testing your nerve on the cable car emergency vehicle simulation; the indoor Discovery Depot at Crich, a tram-themed soft-play area.

The new cable cars at the Heights of Abraham

Trams used to be one of the world's most popular forms of urban transport. Long gone from our cities, you can still see them in Britain's only large collection, at Crich Tramway Village near Matlock. When you arrive, you'll get £0.0s.1d – one old penny – to use as the fare for unlimited rides on vintage trams that rumble up and down the cobbled streets of a period village re-created in minute detail. The National Tramway Museum understands how to grab and hold your attention.

You can spend hours riding single- and double-decker trams from different eras and far-flung countries. Some are tall, gaunt and Victorian. Some are rickety, wooden affairs with no window glass, built for the tropics. Best of all are the horse-drawn trams, with a little, brass-railed staircase curling to the upper deck. You can ride them through the 'village', past the working pub and period sweet shop, out into the countryside for the spectacular views. At the Workshop Viewing Gallery you can see restoration in progress, and children can follow the activity-based Leaf Track, which is part of the Woodland Walk and Sculpture Trail.

Leave enough time to scale the Heights of Abraham at Matlock Bath! It's a 24-ha (60-acre) woodland and wildlife park, nearly 300 m (1000 ft) up on Masson Hill, accessed by a dramatic cable-car ride across a deep gorge. There are superb panoramas across the Derwent Valley, but underground, the old mine workings, galleries and show caves burrowed into the hill are even more breathtaking. Guides tell you thrilling stories about 17th-century mining families' subterranean lives, using soundtracks, brilliant lighting and sensational animatronics to bring them alive. Have tea afterwards on the terrace of the Hi Café while the children test the giant slide, wrestle for answers at the Who + Why + What interactive exhibition, or take on the Explorers Challenge.

AMOUNT OF WALKING:
Moderate. Crich Tramway Village has 'wheelways' for wheelchairs and buggies, and a 1960s tram from Berlin specially adapted for wheelchair users. The alpine cable car at the Heights of Abraham takes wheelchairs, and most of the attractions are accessible.
COST:
Expensive
YOU SHOULD KNOW:
The Heights of Abraham is an ideal venue for flying kites.

Gulliver's Kingdom

Adults must be accompanied by a child to visit Gulliver's Kingdom. Gulliver's is a theme park in Matlock Bath specifically designed to entertain children aged between two and 13, and two features distinguish it from super-slick, ultra hi-tech versions. First, Gulliver's goes to great lengths to encourage children to be children, and to enjoy everything at their own level; and second, all the rides, activities and attractions are exciting but – deliberately – not scary.

Gulliver's Kingdom appears compact for its size because its six zones are built into the woods of a steep hillside. The location helps create thrilling illusions of height and danger, like the switchback which seems to head straight off a precipice, or Bob's Biplanes whose innocent, cartoon-like 'aircraft' send you in a vertical whirl high above the trees. Each zone is named to suggest a different imaginative appeal, but you can't depend on the names for guidance: why Palais Royale should include the Log Roller Coaster, Switchback or Talking Apple will provide you and the family with hours of amusing speculation, and so will the Dodgems in the 'magical woodland' of Fantasy Terrace, or the Crazy Barrel, Veteran Cars and Rio Grande Train rides in the 'ultimate fairytale' of Lilliput Land. It's even more puzzling that the superb, designated under-fives play area, with great attractions like the Pirate Ship, Fire Brigade ride, Ferris Wheel and classic Horses Carousel, should be called Bourbon Street. A child under five could probably tell you, and the lack of logic is what makes Gulliver's Kingdom so good. Everything about it appeals intuitively to children, who have no trouble hurling themselves into its higgledy-piggledy world. Their enthusiasm will make you love it too.

One tip: with small children or a buggy, take the chair lift from the entrance to the top of the hill when you arrive. Then you'll be mostly walking downhill.

WHERE:
Matlock Bath, Derbyshire
BEST TIME TO GO:
March to October
DON'T MISS:
Getting 'wet and wild' on the Log Flume and flying an elephant in the Little Switzerland zone; the Jumping Star, Jungle Ball Crawl and other indoor attractions for smaller children in the Party House zone.
AMOUNT OF WALKING:
Lots, and it can be very steep and difficult for those pushing buggies or wheelchairs.
COST:
Expensive, but good value because even the smallest children can enjoy nearly all the rides. Children under 90 cm (2 ft 11 in) get in free.
YOU SHOULD KNOW:
Besides its more conventional action attractions, the fairytale castle at the heart of Gulliver's Kingdom and Lilliput Land provide adults and children with a much-needed break in tempo, with storytelling and the gentler arts to be enjoyed.

215

The National Trust Museum of Childhood at Sudbury Hall

WHERE:
Sudbury, near Ashbourne, Derbyshire
BEST TIME TO GO:
Mid February to December
DON'T MISS:
The Betty Cadbury Collection of Playthings Past, and the museum's own collection of fabulously colourful, intricately detailed dolls houses, toys and exotic mechanicals like the Trick Cyclist and Smoking Chinaman
AMOUNT OF WALKING:
Moderate (unless the family decides to wander through the adjoining meadows for a picnic), and nearly everything is accessible to wheelchair users.
COST:
Reasonable
YOU SHOULD KNOW:
As you might expect, facilities for looking after infants and children are comprehensive and first class. They extend beyond reins and hip carrying-seats to the traditional sweets and divine homemade fudge available at the museum shop in the stable yard.

It's debatable whether children or adults have more fun at the National Trust Museum of Childhood. It's captivating and completely charming – but it's not about nostalgia, although there are lots of things to stir your deepest memories. It's about enjoying being a child and enjoying being a parent – and the changing attitudes towards childhood in different eras and contrasting circumstances.

Sudbury Hall itself is a beautiful 17th-century stately home. The museum is in a vast Victorian service wing with a separate entrance (and entrance charge – don't pay for both unless you want to visit the Hall as well!). It has eight galleries. The Outdoor Adventure Gallery is an entire Victorian city street where you can play jacks, marbles or hopscotch. Inside, the history of modern childhood is colourfully set out to create great opportunities for participation. You can squeeze up the Chimney Climb like Victorian child sweeps; test for yourself the difficult tasks given to children in domestic service; or be a Victorian schoolchild (the playground games make up for strict rules in the classroom!). At the Home Gallery you look up to see an entire bedroom stuck to the ceiling – an ingenious method of suggesting the topsy-turvy world of family life in a World War II home – and ponder the virtues of simpler, pre-computer toys and board games.

You can dress up, walk in space or a magic forest, work puppets, and write and perform your own play in the Stories and Imagination Gallery; choose a teddy to take with you on the Teddy Bear Trail through the cornucopia of the Toy Gallery; and make friends in Mouseworld or with Trusty the Hedgehog. Unlike television, everything in the museum is intrinsically fascinating or delightful, and an irresistible invitation to join in. It's one big treasure hunt for joy, which everybody wins.

The classroom at Sudbury Hall

Nottingham Castle, City of Caves and the Galleries of Justice

The children will be so delighted by a day out in Nottingham that for weeks they'll be putty in your hands. It doesn't matter that the medieval castle has gone, replaced by a superb 17th-century mansion. Now it houses a museum and art gallery, including a special gallery designed for under fives in which the pictures come to life, plus a number of ingenious activity-led displays for children of all ages. History is not forgotten – the outdoor playground has a medieval theme (you'd think the kids were in a tilting yard!); and deep in Castle Rock you can visit some of the original dungeons, which connect with one of Nottingham's famous caves, the enormous Mortimer's Hole, from which Roger Mortimer was dragged to his execution by Edward III's men in 1330.

Nottingham's subterranean maze of tunnels and caves hasn't been fully explored. The City of Caves exhibition demonstrates what an endless labyrinth it is. Cleaned up and cleverly lit, you'll find (on their original sites!) a working medieval tannery, a catacomb of Victorian slums including the standing basement walls that connected to the world above, and other dramatic illustrations of how the caves have been used since Anglo-Saxon times. Children love the spooky sensation of meeting the caves' inhabitants (played by actors in costume) in the dark shadows.

Leave time for the best interactive history lesson of all, at the Galleries of Justice. You get three centuries of crime and punishment, played out with you as the star, in the actual buildings used during the period. Costumed staff make the handcuffs-on authenticity of arrest, sentencing, and the harsh conditions of imprisonment particularly vivid. Of course, older children relish the grim and gruesome true stories – but parents can take comfort in the knowledge that it's brilliant aversion therapy.

A young boy playing on the Robin Hood statue outside Nottingham Castle.

WHERE:
Nottingham
BEST TIME TO GO:
Any time
DON'T MISS:
The *oubliette* – a bottle-shaped hole in the castle dungeons where you were thrown and 'forgotten'; or the HM Prison Service Collection in the 1833 wing of the Galleries of Justice – artefacts from prisons all over the country, collected over more than150 years and now displayed in public for the first time.
AMOUNT OF WALKING:
Lots. Wheelchair and buggy access is impossible at the caves, but generally excellent elsewhere.
COST:
Low (Nottingham Castle) Reasonable (joint ticket for the caves and the galleries). It pays to check on other joint ticket offers.
YOU SHOULD KNOW:
The attractions are so fascinating and involving, it might be a good idea to reverse the order in which you visit them: that way you end up in the castle café, and the tired little legs end up in the playground.

217

People sledging in the snow at Wollaton Hall.

Wollaton Hall and Park

To see all the delights on offer at Wollaton Hall would take planning of military precision, quite contrary to the enlightened spirit of the place. Wollaton is one of England's greatest Elizabethan houses. It sits in incredibly flamboyant Grade I-listed splendour on the top of a hill on the outskirts of Nottingham, cushioned from urban noise by formal gardens and a 202-ha (500-acre) park where you can walk by a lake in mature woodlands among free-roaming herds of deer, perhaps to the 19th-century Camelia House, the oldest cast iron building in Britain. Idyllic doesn't do it justice.

The hall's most magnificent interiors have been restored, and children particularly enjoy the thoroughly interactive experience of the Tudor kitchens – but for years the house has doubled as Nottingham's Natural History Museum, comfortably distributed through the central 'keep'. The displays were recently refurbished to enable visitors to trace common themes among 750,000 specimens of geology, botany and zoology. The Bird Room now looks exactly as it did in 1932; the famous, stuffed animal collection has been reorganized as the Natural Connections Gallery, dealing primarily with the theme of extinction; and they and the stunning Insect and Mineral Galleries have all been raided to form the Africa Gallery, an unmissable waterhole scene featuring George the gorilla and an amused-looking giraffe.

In the vast 18th-century stables you'll find the Visitor Centre, Industrial Museum and Yard Gallery. The Industrial Museum alone has five major divisions, including the earliest specialist looms that made the lace for which Nottingham was famous. It also houses fantastically complex steam engines which you can see in operation on the last Sunday of each month. Or you can chat on a 1940s telephone exchange, mesmerized by the blinking lights of its system plot. Eventually, the children will point you at the café for a fuel stop, before planning a return visit.

WHERE:
Nottingham
BEST TIME TO GO:
Any time
DON'T MISS:
The bicycle and motorcycle collection, including the series of children's bikes donated by Raleigh, the Nottingham bicycle manufacturer; the duck-billed platypus and maned sloth; the Basford Beam Engine.
AMOUNT OF WALKING:
Lots, but access for wheelchair users is generally very good.
COST:
Free. There are low charges for parking (bring change), for (very good) guided tours, and for some of the special events and Yard Gallery exhibitions.
YOU SHOULD KNOW:
Wollaton Hall and Park offers such a variety of things to see and do that you need not hesitate to take the whole family and let them get on with it. It's one of the most interesting civic amenities in the country, on aesthetic, scientific, historical and industrial grounds.

Southwell Minster and The Workhouse

Green vales and woodlands enfold the small market town of Southwell, and the serene beauty of Southwell Minster seems to encapsulate the kind of England where there'll always be 'honey still for tea'. The tranquil atmosphere masks the tempestuous history etched into its very stones. Saxons, Normans, Plantagenets, Tudors and even Stuarts helped to piece together the 'Cathedral of Nottinghamshire'. Its patchwork of styles spans at least five centuries – from the Conquest to the Reformation and the Civil War. When school parties visit, they call it Time Travelling – spotting the hallmarks of different eras, tracking down the 28 wooden mice carved into the church's furniture, finding the dragons in the stone foliage, or creating stories about the gargoyles and grotesques leering down from the minster's unique, pointed 'pepperpot' twin towers. The closer you look, the more you discover. Learning to 'read' the magnificent architecture and fittings brings the minster bustling into life.

If Southwell Minster represents the great affairs of church and state, Southwell's Workhouse shows you how Victorians dealt with poverty and social failure. The Workhouse is a red-brick palace of grim deprivation. Its ultra-harsh regime was once the model for over 600 workhouses built across Britain. You can follow audio-guided trails round the spartan, prison-like yards and dormitories. Children can pretend they are ten year-old Victorian twins 'Emma and Sarah', or 11-year-old orphans 'Henry and William', dress up in workhouse uniforms, and play a game of punishments and rewards (a bit like Snakes and Ladders) called Master's Punishment as they go. At the end of the tour there are interactive games, which give you the chance to become 'prime minister' and 'end poverty'. If only! At least The Workhouse provides children with a graphic and entertaining introduction to what are still the essential questions of social welfare.

WHERE:
Southwell, Nottinghamshire
BEST TIME TO GO:
Any time of year
DON'T MISS:
The 'Leaves of Southwell' – the foliage beautifully carved in wood and stone that covers most of Southwell Minster's Chapter House, full of concealed, grimacing faces and mythical creatures; the fully furnished 1970s bedsit at The Workhouse – it's a shocking reminder that the building was still in use in the late 1970s.
AMOUNT OF WALKING:
Moderate. Wheelchair access at Southwell Minster is good, but at The Workhouse is restricted to the ground floor.
COST:
Officially free – but the minster 'suggests' small donations. Low, at The Workhouse
YOU SHOULD KNOW:
Perceptions change: the deliberately severe conditions in The Workhouse were originally applauded as a deterrent, to distinguish the 'Blameless and Deserving Poor' (the old and infirm) from the 'Idle and Profligate Poor' (the able-bodied). Now it is ranked with Russia's Gulag Museum in Siberia, and the Czech Republic's Terezin Holocaust Transit Centre, as a model of oppression.

Southwell Minster

Jumicar Children's Driving Experience

WHERE:
Hoveringham, near Nottingham
BEST TIME TO GO:
Weekends and Nottinghamshire
school holidays
DON'T MISS:
Getting your free 'driving licence';
the indoor play area for small
children; the homemade food at
Ferry Farm (Jumicar itself doesn't
offer refreshments).
AMOUNT OF WALKING:
Little
COST:
Reasonable. In fact, the admission
fee is for Ferry Farm. The Jumicar
supplement is for the car itself (with
up to two people) plus guaranteed
tuition.
YOU SHOULD KNOW:
The maximum speed of the Jumicar
cars is 16 kph (10 mph), Jumicar's
safety record is 100 per cent, and the
content and method of their driving
tuition is supported by the police and
fire services in Nottinghamshire and
Derbyshire.

As every parent knows, children want to learn to drive almost as soon as they've learned to walk and talk. Before they open negotiations on borrowing the family car, take them to the Jumicar Children's Driving Experience at Hoveringham. Jumicar is gentler than its name suggests. There's no speedway with pre-teens screeching past each other in Darth Vader helmets. Jumicar's appeal is that it introduces children to the rules and safeguards of driving in the real world. You use special, junior-sized petrol-driven cars (there isn't a hybrid model yet!) on a miniature circuit of real roads. There are traffic lights, roundabouts, zebra crossings, and the full range of road markings and street signage. Children learn proper road awareness skills, like judging distance and speed, noting road hazards, and why it pays off to obey traffic rules and be considerate to other road users. In the end you'll wonder why they can't get so excited about perfecting other essential life skills . . .

Of course, age is important. You must be at least six years old to drive solo, though five- and even four-year-old prodigies have been permitted after proving their co-ordination skills. With an adult or staff driver actually in control, one year olds can also take the wheel – so nobody in the family need feel left out.

In any case, there are other things to do. Jumicar is part of Ferry Farm Park and Restaurant in the lovely Trent Valley. Besides its range of farm activities, Ferry Farm has rare breeds, pony rides, a wildlife pond, and an adventure playground designed for under tens. The zip slide, assault course and trampolines will absorb any spare energy – but save yourself for a go-kart race with the children. Unlike Jumicar's authentic motors, the go-karts are pedal-powered, and hilariously good fun because you can make up the traffic rules.

Attenborough Nature Reserve

Sir David Attenborough opened the Attenborough Nature Centre in 2005 and called it 'a lifeline to the natural world'. It's got even better since. The centre provides everything visitors need to make the most of the reserve, and it's a model of how to build and organize an ecological centre. The offices, education facilities, interactive displays, nature shop and café are designed so that on both sides you get an uninterrupted view of the wildlife on the surrounding water. Behind it is an outdoor education area, where staff are regularly on hand to explain features of the special pond, the bird feeding stations and a 'sensory' nature trail where you can observe wildlife at very close quarters.

As an SSSI (Site of Special Scientific Interest), the reserve ensures that wildlife comes first. Sailing, water sports and horse riding are restricted to one end of the complex of former gravel pits; and at the other, the huge reed beds of Delta Pond provide a monitored sanctuary for breeding birds. In between is a tranquil maze of paths (some muddy) winding past ponds, waterways and lakes, divided by drier ground of scrub and grassland. There are lots of viewing hides. You might see kingfishers or woodpeckers among the willows, or any of the 250 other bird species recorded there. In season there are butterflies, dragonflies and damsonflies basking on lily pads – and otters have returned.

The reserve is lively throughout the year, and winter birds are as noisy as anything in summer. It runs on the seasons, but no two visits are the same. The centre collects much of its important research data from the observations of families and children on a day out. You know how children love to contribute – make the Attenborough Nature Reserve their lucky day.

WHERE:
Attenborough, near Nottingham
BEST TIME TO GO:
Any time of year. Weekends can be busy with walkers and cyclists, but in summer the reserve stays open until 22.00, so there are always quiet periods.
DON'T MISS:
The wildlife exhibits at Reflections, the centre's solar-powered, eco-lodge café; using a hide to see the thriving birds at the 'estuary' area of Delta Pond; the Wildlife in Art sessions for children, at the outdoor education area.
AMOUNT OF WALKING:
Lots (but only if you feel like it). The Attenborough Nature Centre is fully accessible to wheelchair users – the reserve as a whole is only gradually becoming wheelchair-accessible.
COST:
Free. There is a small charge for parking.
YOU SHOULD KNOW:
Attenborough Nature Reserve is in fact named after the nearby village of Attenborough, not Sir David; the reserve was voted ninth in a *BBC Wildlife Magazine* list of the world's top eco-destinations – and it deserves its high rating.

Lincoln Castle and the Bishop's House complex

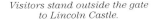
Visitors stand outside the gate to Lincoln Castle.

WHERE:
Lincoln
BEST TIME TO GO:
Any time – but if you can't go on a warm, sunny day, try and go during the four days of the Medieval Christmas Market.
DON'T MISS:
Magna Carta; walking the castle walls; the self-locking cubicles in the Prison Chapel, spitefully designed so prisoners could not see one another; the vineyard, thought to have been the most northerly in Europe.
AMOUNT OF WALKING:
Moderate
COST:
Low – especially the family tickets
YOU SHOULD KNOW:
The audio tour is recommended for its vivid portrait of the immensity and palatial magnificence of the Bishops' House.

Lincoln is a proper Norman castle, with a motte and bailey and the remains of a barbican. Its battlements, towers and keeps, backed by Lincoln Cathedral and the ruins of the Bishop's Palace, are spectacular. You'll need a map to explore them – or you can join a free, guided tour that includes 900 years of gossip with the history. In any case, the garden courtyards, flowery paths and swathes of lawn make strolling a pleasure, with archery, jousting, concerts and other events an incidental treat.

Since it was built, Lincoln Castle has been a court and prison. You can ogle 13th-century Cobb Hall (the northeast tower) used for 'the drop' (executing prisoners by hanging), but not the early 19th-century courtroom, because it's still in use. What you must see, as a matter of self-respect, is the Lincoln Magna Carta, one of only four surviving original copies of the charter sealed by King John at Runnymede in 1215. A well-pitched exhibition explaining its importance to all of us leads to a darkened room with the Great Charter dramatically illuminated. You can't fail to be moved, and even children feel the accumulated weight of 'something special' and know they should try and fix it in their memory.

If the sight of Magna Carta means anything at all, the Bishops' House is the place to think about it. Once the palace of Prince Bishops with authority over everything between the Humber and the Thames, the ruins are heroic in scale. The vaulted undercroft of the East Hall range gives you some idea – and with the heritage garden tucked into the walled terrace of the adjoining cathedral, it's a great place for contemplation and games of historical speculation. Lincoln Castle is for playing Saxons versus Normans. The Bishops' House is for thinking about what it all means.

Tattershall Castle and RAF Coningsby

Ralph Cromwell was Lord Treasurer to Henry VI. He built Tattershall Castle between 1434 and 1445 to show off his wealth and power, and he would have been delighted that nearly 600 years later it would be described as 'medieval bling at its best'. Its outer defensive walls have disappeared, but Tattershall was always more country mansion than military stronghold. Each floor has a magnificent chamber plus smaller rooms. The lowest floor was for storage and estate business; and you climb the 150 stairs to the top on a metaphoric ascent through society. By the time you get to the fabulous views (over RAF Coningsby and as far as the Boston Stump or Lincoln Cathedral) from the battlements, you are monarch of all you survey – just like Lord Cromwell. Unfortunately, apart from some wonderful tapestries, there's not much furniture. The audio guide more than compensates. Children love the climb, but have more fun in the grounds, where they can dress up as medieval magnates (or villeins) and play with Tudor toys.

For many people, RAF Coningsby is, and should be, a place of pilgrimage. It is home to the RAF Battle of Britain Memorial Flight (BBMF). Unless they're flying at a display, you'll see a Lancaster, five Spitfires, two Hurricanes, two Chipmunk trainers, and a Dakota DC3, every one of them a wartime original and in flying order, thanks to the volunteers who have serviced and restored them since 1957. Do take the guided tour – the guides know these aircraft backwards, and tell brilliant anecdotes of self-effacing derring-do. Some of them may even be aircrew as well. There's an interesting exhibition centre, and a shop with highly desirable aviation souvenirs/gifts – but it's the aircraft that send your pulse racing. You might get really lucky and see them fly.

WHERE:
Tattershall and Coningsby, near Boston, Lincolnshire
BEST TIME TO GO:
Any time (but check in case the BBMF is away).
DON'T MISS:
Showing the children the defensive secret of Tattershall Castle's clockwise circular staircase (if you're retreating upstairs from a medieval attacker, only you can wield your right, sword, arm; and the same is true when you're fencing him back down the stairs).
AMOUNT OF WALKING:
Little – but the circular staircase makes Tattershall's interior inaccessible to wheelchairs and pushchairs. Outside is no problem.
COST:
Low (Tattershall Castle)
Free parking and access to RAF Coningsby BBMF Exhibition and shop – but a very low charge for guided hangar tours.
YOU SHOULD KNOW:
Don't be ashamed to cry when you see the Battle of Britain aircraft. It's not at all unusual.

Tattershall Castle

Natureland Seal Sanctuary and Gibraltar Point Nature Reserve

WHERE:
Skegness, Lincolnshire
BEST TIME TO GO:
Any time
DON'T MISS:
At Gibraltar Point the mostly free children's events like sea dipping, scavenger hunts, wildlife art and Kid's Gang activities that take place frequently, but for which you may have to book. The supervising nature experts give playtime an extra dimension (and there aren't any play areas at Natureland).
AMOUNT OF WALKING:
Lots, probably. Natureland is fully accessible to wheelchair users (and very helpful); Gibraltar Point has hard paths wherever possible.
COST:
Reasonable (Natureland Seal Sanctuary). Free (Gibraltar Point – but there is a small charge for parking).
YOU SHOULD KNOW:
Gibraltar Point is one of Britain's increasingly rare, major marine wetland sites, with outstanding wildlife. Its importance is recognized by its designation as an SSSI, RAMSAR, NNR and SPA (the EC Birds directive). Please keep disturbance round habitats to a minimum, and respect any temporary or permanent prohibitions.

The Natureland Seal Sanctuary at the north end of the Skegness seafront may not be big, but it's serious about its work. The sanctuary is world famous for saving abandoned baby seals and returning them to the wild; and its inventive treatments have also helped dolphins, whales, and many seabirds and birds of prey. Its dedication includes making a special effort to open minds to the bigger picture of wildlife welfare. Visitors, and especially small children, are encouraged to participate in feeding times (ring ahead to check the times) – not just of the seals or the jackass penguins (named for their braying voices), but of rabbits, guinea pigs, sheep, goats, ducks and even koi carp. The idea is to get close to all kinds of wildlife, so there are quail running between your feet, and birds and iridescent butterflies fluttering free in the tropical house. It's true that sometimes the crocodiles won't budge and give you a thrill, but the general effect is to make you feel privileged to be in an anteroom of nature.

You get nature in the raw at Gibraltar Point Nature Reserve, a 5-km (3-mi) stretch of coast immediately south of Skegness, and Lincolnshire's biggest complex of saltmarsh and dunes. Go for an early lunch at the Visitor Centre – the Wild Coast Exhibition and Nature Discovery Centre will help you plot your afternoon adventures among the ponds, lagoons and reedbeds you can see through the picture windows. Gibraltar Point has huge wader roosts and spectacular, seasonal migration flocks (30,000 swallows, one year), unusual marine flora and fauna, and over 200 species of visiting birds. Its paths lead you to every kind of habitat, and there are hides and information boards to identify what you see. But do keep the children within sight, and please don't bring the dog unless you have to.

A Common Harbour baby seal

National Space Centre

The moon landing of 1969 was one of mankind's greatest technological achievements. It inspired two generations to pursue the dream of new adventures in space. The National Space Centre is intended to inspire the next one. On the basis that amazing facts are stranger than any fantasy fiction, the first thing you see looks like a beehive made of tubular bubble-wrap. It could be out of *Star Trek*. In fact it's the 42-m (136-ft) Rocket Tower display, built with internal glass lifts so you can get close to the two full-size space rockets it contains.

You're encouraged to indulge your spirit of enquiry in all the five exhibition galleries, pushing buttons and levers to operate satellites, rockets and capsules. You can create your own alien while learning about the solar system; test your command skills running a 'mission' to the ice-moon Europa; land an interplanetary capsule; 'train' as an astronaut; build a lunar buggy and test it on the terrain of Mars; and feel like you're actually flying through space on a 360 degree multi-media voyage under the Planetarium's dome. There are literally hundreds of ways of getting the best out of the National Space Centre – and sometimes it pays to spend longer on one exhibit at the expense of another. For example, the mission control simulator can offer a five-minute sampler, or a one- to two-hour mission that combines maths, science and technology with team skills of problem solving and decision making. You don't need to be part of a school visit to want to get stuck into something so meaty.

The real point about the National Space Centre is that it functions like most interactive exhibitions, but it doesn't deal in fantasy, only fantastic facts. The reward is the lasting pleasure of having your imagination massaged by new knowledge about our world and universe.

WHERE:
Leicester
BEST TIME TO GO:
Any time
DON'T MISS:
Taking the lift to the nosecone of the Thor rocket in the Rocket Tower; the full-size replica module of the ESA (European Space Agency)'s International Space Station, including the way an astronaut's food is wrapped; the rock samples from Mars and the Moon.
AMOUNT OF WALKING:
Moderate, and there's access for wheelchair users.
COST:
Expensive, but under fives go free.
YOU SHOULD KNOW:
Children have to think and work a little harder to get the most from the National Space Centre, and few of the thrills are physical as they are at other theme parks. Probably best for seven to 12 year olds, confident in their basic button-pushing skills.

Two rockets from the 1970s

Snibston Discovery Park

For chutzpah, effort and imagination, museums don't get better than Snibston Discovery Park. It's a big site with such a profusion of good ideas that it seems small. The park achieves two things. The first is to confront visitors with the technologies and scientific inventions that have shaped their daily world. The second is to demonstrate that there is life after technology, and regeneration is easier than most people think. Having any philosophy is unusual in a place of entertainment; having such a positive and practical philosophy makes Snibston a place of joy, wonder, and big laughs about gritty truths. What's more, apart from the teenies' soft-play area, everything at Snibston is pitched so that every adult or child can enjoy it at their own level, from the Toybox of bygone toys to the colliery tour with real miners.

Snibston used to be a colliery. Unemployed local miners saved the pithead buildings and some workshops. Now they act as some of the most amusing (and blunt) guides you'll find in any museum. Many are also family men and women, willing to coax shy children into eager participation. There's plenty to do: 20 extremely interactive demonstrations of technology in the Extra Ordinary gallery alone, including lifting a Mini, bamboozling a robot and using electro-magnetism to make things fly. There are at least another 70 indoor things to do spread across transport, mining, engineering and fashion industries. Outdoors, you can operate waterwheels, pumps and canal lock gates, go down a real mine, ride the former colliery train, help out in the range of 1740s workshops, or just enjoy the nature reserve, reclaimed and restored from former slagheaps. A day out at Snibston should be prescribed as a beneficial stimulant.

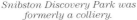

Snibston Discovery Park was formerly a colliery.

WHERE:
Coalville, near Leicester
BEST TIME TO GO:
Any time
DON'T MISS:
Lifting half a ton with one hand (Engineering); the reconstructed medieval mineshaft, with timbers and tools in use at the time of the (nearby) Battle of Bosworth, in 1485 (Extractions); the couture collection from the world's best classic and contemporary designers, like Galliano, Chanel, Dior, Westwood, etc (Fashion).
AMOUNT OF WALKING:
Lots, in the end. Not everywhere is wheelchair-friendly, but the staff certainly are.
COST:
Reasonable (there are occasional, low, supplementary charges for events).
YOU SHOULD KNOW:
Many places claim to be 'making science fun'. Snibston is so good at it that many children come away denying that they had an educational experience because it was much too enjoyable.

Twinlakes Park

Up to the age of 11, there's not much danger of anyone's attention flagging at Twinlakes Park near Melton Mowbray. You know it's designed for smaller children because there are lavatories right by the gate, and a lot of the signage has primary school colour schemes. It lives up to your expectations, too. The play zones include family rides, a huge indoor play centre, an animal farm, falconry centre and themed zones like Excalibur Adventure, Labyrinth and Lakeland. It's a fairly standard combination, and of course rides and activities vary with the seasons and technical improvements – but most attractions come with a twist of extra imagination, like the ferret racing which galvanizes visitors to the petting and feeding sessions at the animal farm, or the topically themed mazes open between July and September. They come in 'family' and 'junior' grades of difficulty, and information boards with clues you have to solve to find the exits.

Twinlakes used to trumpet its permanent 'ice skating' rink (it's not ice, but a special plastic), and attracted unfair criticism for not being the 'real thing'. Little kids love it for the opportunity to experiment safely. The principle applies to many of the rides and activities. They may not be sophisticated, but they provide real thrills calibrated to children's ages. Kids can swing, bounce, fly, climb, scramble, run, contort and do battle with accompanying adults (the Volcano in the Lakeland zone shoots thousands of foam balls at the pirates' stronghold – and guess who the pirates are . . .). From the Cherubs Play Palace for tots to the Trauma Tower's four levels of multiple slides (in the Labyrinth), and the '40 ft of Fear' promised by Shark Bite, the landscaped grounds and lakes are filled with eager little monsters having a good time.

WHERE:
Thorpe Arnold, near Melton Mowbray, Leicestershire
BEST TIME TO GO:
Any time
DON'T MISS:
Bumper Boats – waterborne dodgems in giant inner tubes; exploring the Wild West, a miniaturized town complete with swing-door saloon, bank, farrier, etc; the spooky Dungeon Quest at the Black Knight's Castle.
AMOUNT OF WALKING:
Lots. Twinlakes claims to be fully accessible to wheelchairs users. It is, but most of the paths are laid with coarse rubble that is very difficult for anything wheeled, including pushchairs.
COST:
Reasonable (with no extra parking charge). Wheelchair users and anyone under 92 cm (just over 3 ft) tall enter free.
YOU SHOULD KNOW:
Twinlakes makes a special effort to provide entertainment in winter. The indoor fun is mammoth in variety and energy consumption, and most of the time there are winter extras like the Wizard's storytelling, firework displays and reindeer.

Go-karts are great fun!

Ashby Castle and Rockingham Castle

WHERE:
Ashby de la Zouch and Market Harborough, either side of Leicester

BEST TIME TO GO:
Any time (Ashby Castle); afternoons from June to September (Rockingham Castle)

DON'T MISS:
The secret kitchen tunnel used in the year-long Civil War siege of Ashby Castle; the furnishings and decoration of the Panel Room at Rockingham, originally part of the Great Hall, and the most complete witness to centuries of continuous occupation; the 'outdoor' quiz for younger children featuring Wentworth the Gallant Guardian of Rockingham.

AMOUNT OF WALKING:
Lots, in the end. Wheelchair access is difficult (across grass) at Ashby, and only partial at Rockingham. Advance warning will guarantee assistance.

COST:
Low (Ashby); Reasonable (Rockingham). Tickets combining castle entrance with a special event are much better value at both castles.

YOU SHOULD KNOW:
Charles Dickens, a regular visitor at Rockingham, wrote much of *Bleak House* there; and performed his own plays in the medieval/Tudor/Victorian magnificence of the Great Hall.

Ashby de la Zouch is steeped in picturesque history. Not many places still boast a broad main street lined with half-timbered Elizabethan houses and bow-fronted, Georgian shopfronts – let alone the ruins of a spectacular medieval castle. Ashby Castle stands at the town's heart. A Norman and late medieval fortress, regularly visited by royalty, and used by the first Earl of Huntingdon as a prison for Mary, Queen of Scots, its battered remnants are still so impressive that Sir Walter Scott re-created them as the setting of the tournament in *Ivanhoe*. Nowadays, there are frequent military pageants and historical re-enactments on the trimmed lawns spreading around 24-m (78-ft) Hastings Tower – shattered by Civil War bombardment, but still climbable for the views and the sensation of command – but even without them Ashby Castle is a great place to explore and to make connections across 800 years of history.

Those connections take you to Rockingham Castle near Market Harborough. Enjoy the drive (about one hour), because it doesn't open until the afternoon. Built on the orders of William the Conqueror on a commanding site going back to the Iron Age, Rockingham was a royal fortress for 450 years, and home to just one family for another 450 years since. Richard the Lionheart loved Rockingham Castle, and King John's iron 'Treasure' Chest lies in the Great Hall. The centuries are jumbled in the architecture, furniture, pictures and objects that make up what is still a family home. The owners and staff treat you like visiting friends, telling fascinating anecdotes and explaining things. Children are enthralled; and they are presented with an *I-Spy* book to help them play detective round the house. That's typical of Rockingham: it's got all the grandeur of other stately homes, but none of the pretension. You're made to feel you're participating in the great affairs of state.

A misty morning at Rockingham Castle

Belvoir Castle

The sheer enormity and magnificence of Belvoir Castle is best appreciated from outside. Inside, you get a disjointed sense of its long and dramatic history. The tour (guided or otherwise) takes in the Chapel, Regimental and Military collections, and a selection of galleries, saloons and state rooms. They exude grandeur, pomp and colossal extravagance as well as beauty of fabric and design – but you can't really connect with them. What you're allowed to see beyond the heavy ropes doesn't have much coherence as a place to live, even on a ducal scale developed over 500 years.

Let children be your guide – the real fun is below stairs. The Old Kitchen and Bakery is 'dressed' for the year 1825, and the smell of fruit pies and spices is intoxicating. The housekeeper, cook and staff are (usually) in costume, playing out 19th-century roles to break down everyone's inhibitions. It's really gratifying to see children cotton on to the contrasts between early 19th-century Belvoir and their own lives; the castle doesn't seem so alienating, for them or for you. That's why the Regency School Room and Nursery are so entertaining. The children sit at desks, actively participating in lessons and a disciplinarian regime they'd scream at if they weren't laughing so hard. They also love playing with the vast collection of period toys, including a wonderful rocking horse, as well as dressing up in the period costumes.

Outside, the natural amphitheatre containing the formal gardens is full of features to whet everyone's curiosity. Among them are Britain's tallest – at 29 m (94 ft) – yew tree, a statuary garden and the Summer Pavilion, the best of several 'root and branch' rustic summerhouses made with living tree roots. For all the landscaped woodland, topiary, lawns and formal displays, the gardens are intended to frame a variety of panoramas over the lovely Vale of Belvoir, the castle's domain. Children will be grateful for the adventure playground.

Belvoir Castle

WHERE:
Near Melton Mowbray, Leicestershire
BEST TIME TO GO:
April to September
DON'T MISS:
Checking the programme of events – your visit may coincide with a theatre performance or concert, medieval jousting, Teddy Bear's Picnic, steam engine day, Civil War re-enactment, children's archery, birds of prey flight display, or something else on the regular programme that you wouldn't want to miss.
AMOUNT OF WALKING:
Moderate – but the gardens include some steep climbs. It makes wheelchair access difficult; inside, only the ground floor is accessible to wheelchair users.
COST:
Expensive – the reasonable entrance fee masks the compulsory extras for parking, permission to photograph and for a guidebook, and the restaurant mounts up, even at teatime. 'Garden only' tickets are half the cost.
YOU SHOULD KNOW:
The Duchess Garden refers to Elizabeth, the 5th Duchess of Rutland, who designed the park and gardens in their entirety from 1799.

The adventure play area at Stanwick Lakes

Stanwick Lakes and Harrington Aviation Museum

WHERE:
Stanwick and Harrington, on either side of Kettering, Northamptonshire
BEST TIME TO GO:
Any time (Stanwick Lakes); March to October (Harrington)
DON'T MISS:
The children's assault course at Stanwick; the high-priority Red Stocking mission papers at Harrington; the genuine World War II aircraft remains (Lancaster, Hurricane, B17 Flying Fortress, etc) in the Northants Aviation display next door to the Carpetbaggers; the Cold War display – from when Thor rockets were based at Harrington.
AMOUNT OF WALKING:
Moderate to lots. Major paths and activities are accessible to wheelchair users at Stanwick but only partially at the museum.
COST:
Low. Access is free at Stanwick Lakes; the charges are for parking and some of the events and children's activities.
YOU SHOULD KNOW:
Harrington is known in Air Force circles simply as the Carpetbaggers Museum. Among the 995 agents dropped by the 801st/492nd was Violette Szabo (in June 1944), the agent posthumously awarded the George Cross, whose story was filmed as *Carve Her Name With Pride*.

Stanwick Lakes total 263 ha (650 acres) of gravel pits and railway sidings, reclaimed as part of the River Nene Regional Park for conservation and recreation. The reserve looks like nature at its most haphazard, but there are nine distinct zones of lakes, ponds, sandbanks and small islands dropped into a quilt of open grassland, heath, woods, marsh and waterside reedbeds. At one end, six lakes are set aside for fishing. Three more are for 'non-motorized water sports'. The biggest are bird and wildlife sanctuaries of increasing international significance.

The lakes are a fabulous amenity, recently developed to provide every worthwhile environmental and ecological recreational facility. The trails lead to hides and lookouts. The spectacularly modern Visitor Centre includes a moated children's adventure play area constructed in wood, with a waterwheel, climbing tower, giant slides and 'action sandpit'; a separate, water-themed Hideaway indoor interactive play area; displays to help you make the most of your visit – like where you might see the herons or otters; and the terraced Café Solar. Events include storytelling, theatre and music as well as wildlife forays. Best of all are the 11 km (7 mi) of paths winding through the 'back country' where it's just you and the birds and the water.

About 15 km (9 mi) away, on the other side of Kettering, the

Harrington Aviation Museum stands in the fields where Harrington airfield once lay in World War II. In 1944, it was from this very spot that the USAF 801st/492nd Bomb Group carried out Operation Carpetbagger – delivering secret agents and supplies to resistance fighters in Nazi-occupied Europe. Inside, first-hand memoirs, artefacts, equipment and mementos of OSS and SOE courage are hair raising and incredibly moving. Children don't always fully understand, but are captivated by the physical evidence – aircraft, parachutes, etc – of real action heroes and heroines fighting a secret war.

Wicksteed Park

The spirit of philanthropy that created Wicksteed Park in 1921 lives on. As you arrive, you'll find one of Europe's biggest and best playgrounds. All year round, it's free and it's open. Take a picnic and you can have a wonderful day's entertainment for the price of parking. But there's more.

Wicksteed's Amusement Park is one of Britain's oldest, with over 80 years' experience of keeping children and families thrilled, entertained and fed. It understands the value of open space, of grassy parkland and woods by a lake to run about and play in. You can go rowing among the swans or follow the nature trail round the lake. You can ride the narrow-gauge Wicksteed Railway, running since 1931 and a vintage treat for everyone. Then there are 35 rides grouped in three, themed areas. Smaller children (up to 12 or 13) are drawn to the Fairground, full of colourful, storybook-style attractions like the Double Pirate Ship, Carousel, and Cups & Saucers as well as the more modern Laser Tag or Wicky's Inflatable. It's also the place to find all-family fun like the dodgems and crazy golf.

The water-themed activities at the Lakeside include an early white-knuckle ride, the Water Chute created by Charles Wicksteed himself in 1926. It's been described as 'like a builder's skip on a rope' hurtling into the lake to yelps of excited satisfaction. Other rides – Bumper Boats, Nautic Jets, Splashing Seals or the Monorail of pedal-powered 'helicopter' pods all provide great fun – but the spirit of Wicksteed is its Vintage Cars ride, designed so that a child believes he or she is at the wheel, although an adult is actually in control. It's a Willie Wonka style of make-believe.

Teenagers head for the conventionally 'big' rides in The Arena. They get scared witless because the rides are fun – but they're not what make Wicksteed great.

WHERE:
Kettering, Northamptonshire
BEST TIME TO GO:
April to September (Amusement Park rides); any time (Wicksteed Park and playground)
DON'T MISS:
The Water Chute and the moment of actual flight just before hitting the water in Nautic Jets (Lakeside); the inflatable Chair-o-Planes (Fairground).
AMOUNT OF WALKING:
Lots (including queuing for rides, lakeside walks, etc). Wheelchair access is necessarily limited, but better than you might expect.
COST:
Expensive – most people buy a 'wristband' for unlimited rides, but there are several alternatives. Parking charges are separate. Wheelchair users and children under 0.9 m (just under 3 ft) tall enter free. In comparison with many other Amusement Parks, Wicksteed is good value.
YOU SHOULD KNOW:
Charles Wicksteed bought the land in 1913 to provide a public park for children and families who had no garden and were forced to play in the streets.

Cadbury World

Chocolate fantasies rule at Cadbury World. As one of Britain's biggest chocolate manufacturers, Cadbury's take their fans seriously. For health and safety reasons you can't tour the actual factory, but Cadbury World goes one better anyway. It's attached to the factory, and you get plenty of opportunities to see how different kinds of chocolate are made. You also get umpteen chances to have fun with chocolate, and even to invent your own choc-themed games.

There's a life-size street called Advertising Avenue which you reach, like Indiana Jones, through a curtain of melted chocolate. The houses all look (and smell) like they're made of chocolate, but each is built in a different architectural style. Inside you can see the appropriate contemporary advertising, jewels of Cadbury's past including old posters, the Flake girls, Creme Egg, Milk Tray Man, the Fruit 'n' Nut Case and the all-chocolate *Coronation Street* set that once introduced Cadbury's as the sponsors of the TV soap. The Avenue is the climax of an imaginative account of chocolate itself, from its Aztec origins to John Cadbury's first (1824) shop, the Quaker beliefs that governed the company's growth, and – more to the point – how Cadbury's actually makes its products. The interactive 'Manufacturing' section is great – it's fun to punch Turkish Delights, Crunchies and Roses into shape, and to 'oversee' genuine factory wrapping procedures. If you're lucky, you should also get the chance to style your own fantasy chocolate bar, play in chocolate rain and grow your own cocoa tree.

Cadbury World is predictably popular, but for little kids it's worth the queues. It's just a pity automatic doors prevent you skipping sections if the need arises: they don't open until each presentation is completed. On the other hand, you won't go hungry!

Cadbury World is a popular tourist attraction at the Cadbury's chocolate factory.

The Back-to-Backs and the Pen Museum

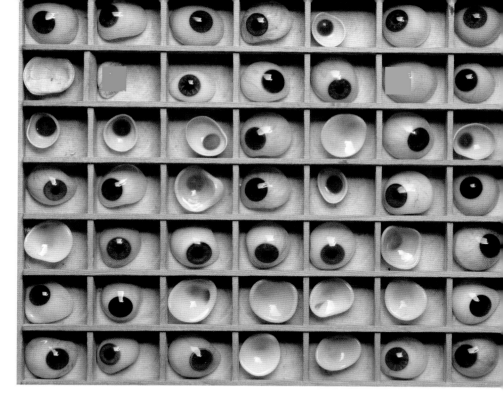

Trays of glass eyes in what was the optician's house

Once Birmingham had 20,000 'courts' of back-to-back houses, the cheap solution to the problem of accommodating the 19th century's rocketing industrial workforce. This is the only survivor – saved by the National Trust as a reminder of a way of life nobody would tolerate today. Grouped round a communal yard, with just one room on each of three floors, no plumbing and an outside lavatory shared by them all, the back-to-backs were both crowded and insanitary, despite the best efforts of the families who lived in them. Three of the 11 houses in this court have been restored to reproduce the authentic conditions of different periods – the 1830s, 1870s and 1930s. A fourth has been preserved as it was in 1977, when it was occupied by a tailor who only moved out in 2001. You'll need a timed ticket to visit, but the guided tours are led by people who lived and worked in the back-to-backs (including the tailor). Their anecdotes make your hair stand on end, though they tell their stories with endearing humour. Their insight makes the Back-to-Backs educational in the broadest sense, by encouraging children to identify the life games played by previous generations trying to survive poverty and squalor, to understand why they are still important, and how to have fun playing them.

Strike while the iron of revelation is hot: a bus ride from the Back-to-Backs, the Pen Room Museum at Hockley gives everyone bred in the computer age a chance to try the old ways of writing – with quills and steel pen nibs. The Pen Room tells the story of how the mass manufacture of cheap pens contributed to the spread of literacy everywhere in the world; and the whole family will have fun comparing their keyboard wizardry with traditional skills of handwriting and special calligraphy.

WHERE:
City centre and Hockley, Birmingham
BEST TIME TO GO:
Any time
DON'T MISS:
Searching for mousetraps in the Back-to-Backs, and the drawers of glass eyes in what used to be the optician's house; the 1930s sweetshop, selling period sweets like humbugs and striped mint balls; making your own steel pen nib on the original factory presses at the Pen Museum.
AMOUNT OF WALKING:
Little
COST:
Low. Free at the Pen Museum, but 'donations are welcome'. Free to under fives at the Back-to-Backs.
YOU SHOULD KNOW:
The cultural snapshots of the Back-to-Backs can provoke strong emotions at the thought of rats and mice in the bedding, or 15 families sharing the privy. But for those who lived in them, they were not slums, but home.

Birmingham Museum and Art Gallery and a canal boat trip

Gas Street Basin

WHERE:
Birmingham
BEST TIME TO GO:
Any time
DON'T MISS:
The flight of 13 locks at Farmer's Bridge; the lovely iron bridge in Gas Street Basin over the junction of the Worcestershire Canal and the Birmingham Main Line; the beautiful paintwork and designs on the narrow boats moored in the Oozells Street Loop.
AMOUNT OF WALKING:
Moderate (followed by a long rest on the boat).
COST:
Free for the museum; reasonable for the canal trip
YOU SHOULD KNOW:
The hidden perspective of Birmingham revealed by sailing its canals will change forever the way you think about the city and its historic contribution to industrial invention and progress. It also makes the city much more fun to be in.

The extraordinary collections at the Birmingham Museum and Art Gallery are a curiosity-seeker's goldmine. Beautifully organized under comfortable headings like social history, archaeology, ethnography, and fine and applied art, the exhibits come from all over the world and represent pretty well all known human history. You can browse happily for hours among spectacular, extended displays about Victorians, Romans, World War II, Egyptians, and the internationally famous collections of pre-Raphaelite pictures. Each of them offers children the chance to hold and examine costumes, masks and replica statues; and as a plus, you may find yourself in the middle of one of the regular storytelling, face painting or craft activities held at weekends and throughout school holidays. As a further encouragement to their thirst for discovery, the museum offers an interactive website on which children of all ages can play games with the exhibits (like creating landscapes or finding 'messages' hidden in paintings), and which includes useful pre-visit print-outs. Happily, Birmingham Museum is free, so you can go as often as you like.

A good day out in Birmingham has to include its canal system. As the hub of the entire West Midlands, the city's canals outnumber those of Venice, and include long reaches of a tranquil nature as well as fabulous industrial heritage and a few hotspots of waterside bars and cafés. Just a short walk from the museum, canal boats stationed close to the ICC (International Convention Centre) and the Gas Street Basin offer boat trips of every kind. There are long trips far afield, to Bournville or Dudley; drinks or meals on a waterborne diner; or – best by far – the 'heritage' trips with just enough commentary to help you understand Birmingham's alternative landscape, and the furious business rivalries that created it. It's a riveting story – and the ride is a real breath of fresh air.

Cannon Hill Park and Birmingham Nature Centre

It's no wonder Cannon Hill Park is Birmingham's flagship park. In the heart of the city, it's a huge green refuge of beautiful woodlands and meadows with a river running through its length. Few city parks anywhere can compete with its variety of landscape and amenities. There's boating and fishing on the lakes, putting greens, tennis and plenty of room to throw, kick or bat a ball without annoying anyone else. One of the woods – the 2.2-ha (5-acre) RSPB Centenary Plantation – is managed as a conservation area to provide habitats and attract unusual bird species; every year, the riverside wild-flower meadow is filled with field poppies, marigolds, and cornflowers. The river walks are havens for wildlife, and throughout the year the park puts on spectacular flower displays, culminating in the Tropical Plant Display House with its banana plants, mahogany trees and the luscious colours of floral meat-eaters – the flowers children always want to take home!

Sited conveniently at the edge of the park, the Birmingham Nature Centre is a 2.4-ha (6-acre) concentration of animals and plants from all over the world. It doesn't pretend to be comprehensive, so you won't see Africa's 'big five'. Instead, you'll find the animals that children most enjoy finding out about, in their appropriate woodland, wetland, farm or garden habitat. There are red pandas, meerkats, monkeys and duck-billed platypuses; goats, sheep and farmyard animals that children can feed and pet; deer, owls and otters; and the research facilities for which the centre is scientifically famous – the reptile house specializing in endangered species; the darkened rodent house you tiptoe through so that the nocturnal creatures don't freeze in fear, and the invertebrates house (insects, spiders, gastropods and crustaceans) of perpetual creepy-crawlie fascination. With a play area for under fives called Lilliput Village, Birmingham Nature Centre exactly complements Cannon Hill Park. They make entertaining children easy.

WHERE:
Edgbaston, Birmingham
BEST TIME TO GO:
Any time, though the Birmingham Nature Centre is only open at weekends from November to March.
DON'T MISS:
Ming Ming, the very rare red panda, and Guinea Pig Village, a favourite with little children.
AMOUNT OF WALKING:
Lots, and there's full access for wheelchair users.
COST:
Low
YOU SHOULD KNOW:
Birmingham Nature Centre bans dogs (except guide dogs), balls, balloons, bikes and scooters – any of which you might want to use in Cannon Hill Park. But parking is easy, so it's no problem to leave them in the car.

Cannon Hill Park

Sarehole Mill and Blakesley Hall

WHERE:
Yardley, Birmingham
BEST TIME TO GO:
April to October
DON'T MISS:
The Tolkien displays explaining Sarehole Mill's imaginative hold over the author during his childhood; the 16th-century wall paintings upstairs at Blakesley Hall, discovered in the 1950s during repairs to wartime bomb damage.
AMOUNT OF WALKING:
Moderate. Wheelchair access at both Sarehole and Blakesley is restricted by period authenticity – cobbles, uneven floors and steep staircases.
COST:
Free
YOU SHOULD KNOW:
It's easy to imagine the rolling landscape of fields and woods that surrounded Sarehole Mill before it was engulfed by suburban Birmingham – but once you enter what remains of its charmed enclave of natural beauty, there's no Visitor Centre or café to remind you of the modern world of concrete. When you visit, please support the local campaign to keep it that way.

The medieval dining room at Blakesley Hall

For anyone who has enjoyed *The Lord of the Rings* books or films, Sarehole Mill is a place of pilgrimage. The mid-18th century industrial marvel, with its mill pond and delightful woodland setting, was the inspiration for The Shire where the Hobbits lived in their rural utopia. The author, J R R Tolkien, could see it from his childhood bedroom window. Now it is a vital link in the Tolkien Trail, and attracts many visitors from all over the world to its sylvan tranquillity.

Sarehole Mill has an even better claim to fame. It's been a mill of some sort since at least 1542 (this one dates to 1768), and it's the only working survivor of Birmingham's 70-odd water mills. In its time it has been used to grind tools, wire, gun barrels and flour; and it's earned a special place in Birmingham's industrial history as the mill used by Matthew Boulton from 1755 for rolling sheet metal. You can see the mill's north waterwheel and the massive gears on the first floor in action on frequent demonstration days, and the bakehouse with its original bread oven and 'proving bin'. Costumed staff contribute – often hilariously – to the illusion of stepping into history, but the mallards and herons of the surrounding, classically English landscape rival them as entertainers.

There's another oasis with Tudor origins in Yardley. Blakesley Hall is a showpiece of half-timbered and decorated, wood-framed, Elizabethan aspiration. It's a yeoman's manor house built like a miniature of a much grander mansion. The layout and function of all the rooms, including the Great Hall, is the same but half the size. Furnished with authentic pieces to match an inventory of 1668, the house is brought to vivid life by the expertise of the guides. They've even stocked the 16th-century kitchen with realistic, raw chickens, meat and vegetables made of papier-mâché and rubber!

The Sea Life Centre

The promise of fun with virtual fish in 4-D Sensorama is almost irresistible, and it's only one of dozens of equally spectacular displays at the Sea Life Centre. Each of them is a stepping-stone in a continuous narrative, telling the story of freshwater and marine creatures along an approximate course following a river from its source into the shallow seas and deepest oceans.

The Sea Life Centre is built over several floors. You pass touch pools re-creating various watery habitats. It's worth pausing to get a detailed look at creatures and plants that later look infinitesimal in the Big Tank. It's your best chance to clock the tiny seahorse, a comical chess-piece look-alike – especially because the centre has become a major breeding laboratory for the species, and the breeding tanks are next to the habitat display. Then there are luminescent jellyfish, otters with long claws, a lagoon of sharks and a bay of rays; and set-piece dramas like the Mangrove Swamp, Nemo's Kingdom and the Red Sea Wreck where pulsing colour and swirling water turn lessons about the threat to the environment into exciting adventures. One favourite is the interactive Quest to discover the treasures of Atlantis amid 'a magical maze of ancient ruins and mysterious sea creatures'.

Everything comes together in the gigantic, one million-litre, ocean tank. Suddenly you're in the middle of it, literally. You walk through a 360-degree transparent tunnel, with black-tip reef sharks, candy-striped tropical fish and giant green sea turtles weaving over your head and under your feet. You are immersed in magic, with eyes wide open. Take a tip and go from the big tank to the 'Sensoramic' 4-D cinema. The films change but always include something to make you feel the wind and spray, and have dolphins and other creatures leaping out of the screen at you.

WHERE:
Birmingham
BEST TIME TO GO:
Any time
DON'T MISS:
Molokai and Gulliver, two of the giant sea turtles; the Shallow Seas 4-D 'experience' in which visitors dive into the waves and swim with whales and dolphins.
AMOUNT OF WALKING:
Moderate, and access is good for wheelchair users.
COST:
Expensive, with few concessions – but the ticket is All Day Come and Go.
YOU SHOULD KNOW:
Seahorse infants are tiny – roughly the size of a grain of rice. It is not thought to be anything to do with the fact that male seahorses get pregnant and carry the baby.

Thinktank

WHERE:
Birmingham
BEST TIME TO GO:
Any time
DON'T MISS:
Exploring your senses with a giant tongue; finding out who bit the Jurassic crocodile; racing against the clock to distribute chocolate around Britain.
AMOUNT OF WALKING:
Moderate, and there is full access for wheelchair users.
COST:
Reasonable. There are many ticket discounts available in conjunction with other Birmingham attractions, including the IMAX cinema.
YOU SHOULD KNOW:
Keep an eye on Thinktank's developing programme of regular special events; in the Kids Wet Play Area, Thinktank supplies children with protective aprons – but take a change of clothes anyway.

Thinktank does exactly what it says on the label – it makes you think. Birmingham's uncompromisingly modern museum of science, Thinktank presents science to visitors in an entirely new way. It's a proactive museum, meaning that you have to engage directly with the exhibits to discover all their secrets. For example, you don't just look at a model of a DNA spiral: instead, you try to solve a crime using pollen and fibre-matching as well as DNA profiling. Thinktank is about scientific relationships – and its biggest achievement is to show how the vital spark of imagination fires the dry logic of facts into sustained progress. Effectively, Thinktank makes its visitors into scientists.

Nothing illustrates the success of Thinktank's novel policy better than Kids City, where younger children can perform 'dentistry' on their elders, change a car's sump oil, and try their hand at mending pipes in the road. The Street is about the science we take for granted every day, and you can work a hydraulic digger as part of a project to find out what happens to your recycled household waste. You can join an interactive travel adventure through the human body in Things About Me, and make life-and-death decisions while exploring a space station. There are displays and adventures pitched at every age group and every level of interest.

Then there are the machines – robots used in modern medicine, Spitfires that won the Battle of Britain, trams that carried Birmingham's industrial work force, and the mighty engineering beasts that powered the Industrial Revolution. Looking into the future, Thinktank's digital Planetarium promises a 'totally immersive science experience', and matches it with an inspirational account of our galaxy and deep space. Probably, one day soon, Thinktank will have the means to offer weightless 'space walking' – it's that kind of innovative place.

Moseley Old Hall and Wolf Mountain climbing

WHERE:
Bushbury, Wolverhampton
BEST TIME TO GO:
Any time
DON'T MISS:
Timing your visit to Moseley Old Hall to include events like the Gentleman and Allied Skills Group re-creation of 'the sights, sounds and smells of a busy, upper class, 17th-century home'.

The mellow brick Victorian façade of Moseley Old Hall is only skin-deep. Underneath it is a timber-framed Elizabethan house of spectacular design, with an interior barely altered since it was built around 1570, and original fixtures and fittings that Charles II would recognize from his 'visit' in 1651. Charles Stuart arrived dressed in rags and exhausted, straight from hiding in the Boscobel Oak after defeat at the battle of Worcester, and on his way to exile in France. You can see the secret panel in the wainscoting of one of the bedrooms, and squeeze into the unlit priest's hole where Charles hid while Parliamentarians searched the house.

It's a super house for a family visit. Younger children love the gardens – but it is older children who appreciate the period authenticity of box parterres and the knot garden, and the 17th-century plants. Older children also appreciate more fully the insight the elegant interior of the house gives you of the conflict between Roundheads and Cavaliers, and the history of Catholic persecution. In Moseley Old Hall's atmosphere of intimate domesticity, history really comes alive.

Wolf Mountain Indoor Climbing and Caving Centre (to give it its full name), will absorb any excess energy. Close to Moseley Old Hall, it also teaches mountain biking and archery. Ability and previous experience aren't necessary to have a great time, though everyone has to do an induction course in basic rules and safety before moving onto the climbing walls. They include every kind of rock face you'll ever encounter, plus an indoor caving structure that replicates complicated natural cave systems. Everything is graded to age and skills, so it's the perfect place to sample what could become a lifetime's hobby. There's also a licensed bar and a café, if it ever feels like hard work.

AMOUNT OF WALKING:
Moderate. There's wheelchair access to the ground floor and gardens of Moseley Old Hall, but uneven paths and narrow doorways make it difficult.
COST:
Low (Moseley Old Hall)
Reasonable (Wolf Mountain – but equipment hire is extra, and the charges can mount up. Helmets are free).
YOU SHOULD KNOW:
Children must be at least five to climb at Wolf Mountain, and up to the age of 18 must be accompanied by an adult. That said, it's the kind of activity that works best if you get a whole bunch of children to go together for mutual encouragement.

Moseley Old Hall

Black Country Living Museum

The Black Country Living Museum is a heritage park on a heroic scale. It contains over 40 buildings, some of them massive, relocated brick by brick from their original locations across the Black Country, to a 10.5-ha (26-acre) site in Dudley. Reassembled as a village with every amenity, including a working mineshaft and canal system, all connected by working trams, trolleybuses and roads, the museum incorporates every industry that contributed to the region's wealth, and all the secondary services that enabled them to function. You don't so much 'visit' the museum – you come and live in it for a few hours.

You'll be fascinated just to find out where everything came from – the entrance building used to be the Rolfe Street Baths in Smethwick, and the Bottle and Glass Inn (real ale and good food) by the canal once backed onto the Stourbridge Flight of 16 locks – but you'll want to participate as much as possible, because every shop, trade workshop or facility is occupied by demonstrators in costume, ready to explain, define, describe or just chat about the 'world' they live in. Nothing is simulated. The huge lime kilns burned limestone quarried from underneath Dudley Castle until 1926, and the museum's canal complex was built to serve it. For a small supplement, you can take a 40-minute underground tour into the mine as it would have been in 1850, or a ride on a narrowboat onto the main canal and through the famous Dudley Tunnel.

You can eat with period authenticity at the 1930s fish and chip shop or the 1822 pub. Children can make their own sweets at T Cook's, and scoff them at the 'Old Tyme' fairground, typical of the small fairs that once thrived in the area. There is no end to the ways you can enjoy yourself, or the amazing things you can discover.

The traditional baker's and confectioner's shop

Dudley Zoological Gardens

It began in 1071 as a medieval fortress, and developed into a colossal Tudor palace where Elizabeth I stayed in 1575. Razed by fire in 1750, Dudley Castle remained a romantic ruin on a hill, until co-opted in 1937 as the centrepiece of the Dudley Zoological Gardens. Now you can see lots of the world's most exotic animals in one of Britain's most exotic heritage settings. The animal enclosures are set into the wooded slopes of Castle Hill, using the topography to hide the containing fences. The sight of snow leopards, lions and giraffes, apparently free to roam, in the middle of really spectacular medieval ruins (worth a visit in themselves) is unique, and amazing.

Female red panda at the zoo

There's a third strand of entertainment, too. Spread around the hill, between macaques and flamingos and tigers and toucans, are a series of children's events – interactive games and stories, dressing up and face painting, bird displays and animal feeding – that provide the day with an extra dimension. They all take place every day to a timed schedule, so you need never miss anything. Eventually you reach the Castle Courtyard at the top of the hill (or you can take the land train direct from the main entrance by the children's fairground), where you might see one of the regular historical re-enactments or animal events for which the huge expanse of grass is so perfect. Next to it is the Discovery Centre, bursting with displays and interactive games which explain (in a roundabout way) the important role played by Dudley Zoo in protecting endangered species. It's also the place to play the hilarious family adventure I'm a Visitor, Get Me Out of Here!

The best advice is: go early. It's a huge site, and there's so much to do and see (and good places to eat) that you'll be spoiled for choice and wish you had more time.

WHERE:
Dudley, near Birmingham
BEST TIME TO GO:
Any time
DON'T MISS:
The Ghost Tour in the castle; the parrot aviaries; penguin feeding time.
AMOUNT OF WALKING:
Lots, much of it on fairly steep gradients or up steps. Don't forget you can ride to the top and work your way down. Most things are accessible to wheelchair users.
COST:
Reasonable but there is no family ticket reduction.
YOU SHOULD KNOW:
The Dudley Zoological Gardens is one of the strangest places you will ever visit. It's a children's pleasure park and gameland, a first-class zoo with a dramatically good sense of presentation, and a really splendid medieval and Tudor ruin. Any way you look at it, it's stimulating and fun.

Alton Towers

Alton's ruined, Pugin-designed Towers make a scenic backdrop to Britain's best-known amusement park. It's only right to expect a little bit more of everything from the place that claims to be Number One – and to be prepared to put up with the queues and crowds that come with the position. Alton Towers is the benchmark used by other amusement parks to measure

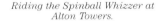

Riding the Spinball Whizzer at Alton Towers.

WHERE:
Alton, Stoke-on-Trent, Staffordshire
BEST TIME TO GO:
Any time
DON'T MISS:
Ug Land, the virtual-reality cave game; Toyland, a collection of rides for smaller children; the white-knuckle hair-straightener called Oblivion.
AMOUNT OF WALKING:
Moderate (though it might feel like lots). Practically everything is accessible to wheelchair users.
COST:
Expensive
YOU SHOULD KNOW:
Alton Towers is certainly one of Europe's great amusement parks. If it's not perfect, it would like to be. Let the management know if you have even a flicker of disappointment about anything at all. That's if you can speak after the rides.

their own performance. Occasionally, one of Alton's superlatives gets 'borrowed' by a competitor with something temporarily faster or dizzier – but from year to year, Alton Towers is still the place for technological innovation and ever bigger, better thrills.

To make the most of a day out at Alton Towers, use their website to plan your day. It's hard to choose attractions that you haven't tried, but everybody knows if they like being whirled upside down and drenched in a water splash or rocketed at white-knuckle speed – or not. You'll find out about height, age restrictions and when children must be accompanied by an adult (over 18), and with the site map you can actually have a lot of fun in anticipation, plotting who's going to go on what and in which order. Smaller children will be saved potential tantrums of on-the-spot indecision, and you'll save time and money, because it's cheaper to book ahead, and you can also get priority tickets to beat the queues. If you team up with other families, there may be further reductions for group activities.

Expect to be exhausted by the adrenaline rush of excitement and laughter, tinged (as it will be!) with moments of sheer terror. You can easily escape to the lovely gardens, or exile on a rowing boat in the middle of the lake, but you probably won't. Alton Towers really does deserve its reputation as doyen of thrills, spills and crazy amusements. Ask any child.

Trentham Gardens and Trentham Monkey Forest

Trentham Gardens is the kind of place that reminds you that Indiana Jones was a botanist. Though originally created by Capability Brown and Charles Barry, whose magnificent Italian Gardens form its central core, now Trentham's twelve show gardens have been revamped to engage the most adventurous visitors as well as the most demanding aesthetes. Adults are perhaps more likely to enjoy the experiments in scent and colour, and spatial illusions of the Sensory and Natural Intervention Gardens; but the serious fun is in the Hide and Speak hedge maze or the Trentham Barefoot Walk. It's amazing how many squeals and laughs you can generate from the texture of wood, mulch, pebbles, bark, mud, grass, rock, soil and cool water. The walk is part of a big Adventure Playground that includes a JCB track. There are also woodland walks with bird hides, aerial tree trails, the 60-m (195-ft) Potter's Wheel (with fabulous views from its cabins across the Potteries) and the Fern Miniature Railway around the lake.

You can row a boat on the lake, or take a ride on the wonderful L/V (Lake Vessel) *Miss Elizabeth*, which will also drop you off at the far end, at the entrance to Trentham Monkey Forest. The 24 ha (60 acres) of forest belong to 140 Barbary macaques, which suffer no restrictions whatever within that area. You are the alien species; the monkeys just get on with their lives. Despite the human crowds, you get a very real sense of the macaques' forest origins. Their personalities start to show in the mutual grooming, energetic prowling, and patterns of branch swinging; and if you look closely you see how every shrill screech has a meaning, and how important manners are in monkey society. Happily, there are two playgrounds for kids who want to practise their 'monkey moves'.

WHERE:
Trentham, near Stoke-on-Trent, Staffordshire
BEST TIME TO GO:
Any time
DON'T MISS:
The wild 'prairies' on the east side of the lake called Rivers of Grass, including the Floral Labyrinth; the special 'talking pipes' hidden in the hornbeam hedge maze, which can help you find your way.
AMOUNT OF WALKING:
Lots. Most of it is accessible to wheelchair users, including the Monkey Forest.
COST:
Expensive for a single day – but there is a huge variety of entertainment.
YOU SHOULD KNOW:
Trentham Gardens have been planted to offer distinct seasonal displays – always beautiful and always slightly different. As the project continues throughout the Trentham Estate, the gardens will incorporate more and more playful family adventure features.

A Barbary macaque at Trentham Monkey Forest

Biddulph Grange Garden and Rudyard Lake

WHERE:
Biddulph, Stoke-on-Trent, Staffordshire
BEST TIME TO GO:
March to December
DON'T MISS:
The chance to inspect the five different miniature narrow-gauge locos run by the Lake Railway. Their names all come from Arthurian legend (like *Merlin* and *Pendragon*) and each of them is a triumph of steam engineering.
AMOUNT OF WALKING:
Lots. Wheelchair access is limited, but still worthwhile.
COST:
Low. At Rudyard Lake there is a small parking charge, and the cost of boat or train rides, or equipment hire (such as a canoe) is reasonable.
YOU SHOULD KNOW:
The author Rudyard Kipling was named after the lake – his mother came here as a child.

The Chinese Temple at Biddulph Grange

There are very few surviving examples of a garden inspired by Victorian eccentricity. Biddulph Grange Garden is one of the best. It's conceived on a huge scale according to the most extreme Victorian ideas about landscaping – of creating studied views out of natural features and contrasting the 'wild' with formal arrangements. Restored to its full intensity by the National Trust, Biddulph Grange Garden is divided into a series of individually themed and enclosed areas, gardens within a garden including a Chinese Temple, Egyptian Court, Italian Terraces, American Gardens, a Pinetum, Dahlia Walk, Rhododendron Glen and typically Victorian oddities like the 'upside-down tree'. The planting and the architecture are full of surprises and even humour; and the stunning views are brilliant configurations of reflections on ponds, topiary, tall trees and huge bursts of floral colour. Clever banking and rock terracing hide each 'compartment' from the others, and they connect via winding paths, tunnels and artful passageways. It's a place of magic and genius which makes wide-eyed explorers of the whole family.

Rudyard Lake, next door to Biddulph Grange, was created even earlier (in 1797) as a reservoir. It's doubled as a popular amenity for

over a century, so its store of recreational activities is both bursting and well established. It's big enough to provide utter peace in the meadow clearings along its steeply wooded banks; and still have plenty of room for walking, swimming, sailing, rowing, fishing and boating (you need a lake licence for some kinds of boat). The Visitor Centre is free, and provides interactive panels to help you identify the abundant wildlife and birds you're likely to see. If you're not feeling energetic, the Rudyard Lake Steam Railway will take you in miniature narrow-gauge glory on a 5 -km (3-mi) return trip down the lake. Do it in style, and have proper, homemade tea and scones at the café afterwards.

Waterworld

Waterworld is the UK's biggest 'indoor tropical aqua park'. Including its outdoor 'California beach'-themed water garden, lazy-river ride, and Bar-B-Q area, Waterworld covers 4.9 ha (12 acres). The heart of the complex is an enormous lagoon, kept in continuous motion by a wave machine strong enough to thrill teenagers without threatening toddlers at the other end. Ramps and stairways lead to the aerial frames holding huge twisting water sluices and multiple slides in a confused riot of primary colours and waterfalls. There are more than 30 major rides, ranging from the Black Hole whirlpool flume (13 seconds of blacked-out, spinning vortex) to the white-water frenzy of the Rapids (restricted to strong swimmers over the age of eight), the Space Bowl and Nucleus, an indoor water-rollercoaster. Happy shrieking is a sure sign that visitors enjoy being thrown, spun, catapulted or just tipped into the chain of pools, and that there are rides graded to every age and temperament.

The Aqua Splash Jungle House is a section reserved for smaller children. Adults aren't even allowed, except to watch. It's a water-play area with a Shipwreck slide, a little waterfall called the Mushroom which toddlers love, a Frog climbing slide and a log raft. Of course, small children can easily manage family attractions like the water cannon and multiple slides you go down together, but the rules on age and height vary enormously, and are strictly enforced by the lifeguards stationed at each ride. Some rules concern dress – like t-shirts and armbands – so be prepared for on-the-spot changes.

Even when the weather's bad and the outside section closed, Waterworld can promise something like a beach to laze on. With a licensed bar and café among the clumps of palm trees, and the children safe under the lifeguard's gaze, it makes a convincingly tropical day out.

WHERE:
Stoke-on-Trent, Staffordshire
BEST TIME TO GO:
Any time
DON'T MISS:
The adrenaline rush of Twister; the holograms projected inside the flumes of Python and Superflume – as if the dizzying descent wasn't enough! – and the traffic lights at the start of the major rides, telling you when, and when not, to go.
AMOUNT OF WALKING:
Moderate (surprisingly, but it's a long way between some of the rides).
COST:
Reasonable
YOU SHOULD KNOW:
At less busy times, attention to detail in the changing rooms and around the pools can get slack. If you're going to keep Waterworld's rules, you have the right to ask them to keep yours.

Warwick Castle

Warwick Castle is a bit daunting – and it's supposed to be. It's one of Europe's very best medieval strongholds, and an absolute treasure house filled with the secrets, stories and legends of a thousand years. When you're in it, it seems almost disrespectful to treat its history as entertainment – but on the other hand, very few places offer such infinite potential for fun.

To begin with, you can't help just gawping at Warwick Castle's immense bulk. The stone face of its towers, battlements and fortifications is redolent of real power and truly bloody battle. Inside (largely rebuilt in the 16th century), pageantry vies with a magnificent display of wealth from a time when the Earls of Warwick were richer than the Crown or Kingdom. You may well wonder whether they still are. Once you cross the drawbridge, you have the freedom to explore the ramparts, the dazzling State Rooms, and authentic displays pinpointing different eras – like the preparations for a Victorian Royal Weekend party or the Kingmaker exhibition. Everywhere you'll find actors in armour or appropriate costume, eager to help you find out what it's like to get ready for battle, try on a jousting helmet, heft a medieval sword, or just show you how electricity was generated to light the castle over 100 years ago.

The number-one attraction is of course the Dungeon. Please be advised: the Dungeon is frightening. Fifteen people fainted in the first month of its recently created display, and not even children are immune to churning stomachs. The combination of atmosphere, live actors and brilliant special effects brings the terrors of torture and 'the foul pestilence of the Plague' to vivid and bloodcurdling life, or perhaps death. As scary, fright fun, the Dungeon is tops – but it may not be suitable for children under ten, and children up to 15 must be accompanied.

Jousting in front of the trebuchet.

Coventry Transport Museum and Brandon Marsh Nature Centre

An early penny farthing at the Museum of British Road Transportation

At its zenith, Coventry was the centre of a transport industry that catered to half the world, and influenced the rest. The factories may have gone, but the Coventry Transport Museum now guards the heritage of the roughly 600 companies that made bicycles, motorbikes, cars, buses and even milk floats in the city. All the exhibits have a connection with Coventry (if only as competitors), and they include legendary names like Triumph, Rudge, Talbot, BSA, Daimler (buses), Massey Ferguson (tractors), Humber and Norton. The sheer volume of vehicles – two or four-wheeled, vintage or modern – tells a fascinating story of technical and design development. There are plenty of famous cars and bikes, like a DeLorean from *Back To The Future*, the Mini Metro Prince Charles bought for Lady Diana, and the two Thrust Project cars that held world land-speed records. There's even a simulator in which you can experience breaking the sound barrier and there are loads of interactive displays or games that enable you to design your own car or imagine travelling into the future. For children, the museum is a brilliant chance to play with genuinely grown-up toys.

Just outside the Coventry bypass, Brandon Marsh is a nature reserve created from former sand and gravel quarries. Its lakes and wetland habitats cover 81 ha (200 acres), studded with woodland copses. The reserve is an SSSI (Site of Special Scientific Interest) and attracts migrating waders and breeding warblers to its resident kingfishers, coots and moorhens. The eco-zone at the Visitor Centre Welcome Desk is all you need to persuade children that real adventure lies along the Onyx Nature Trail around the reserve's wildlife habitats. Save the centre's other activities for teatime, after exploring the five birdwatching hides and a healthy tramp round the lakes.

WHERE:
Coventry
BEST TIME TO GO:
Any time
DON'T MISS:
At Coventry Transport Museum Queen Mary's State Limousine; the Tiatsa collection of die-cast models, one of the world's biggest, and full of rare Dinky and Corgi models; the 19th-century bicycle designs.
AMOUNT OF WALKING:
Lots. Access everywhere is good, including a wheelchair-friendly nature trail at Brandon Marsh.
COST:
Free at Coventry Transport Museum, but donations are welcome. Low at Brandon Marsh.
YOU SHOULD KNOW:
Coventry was badly bombed in World War II. The museum has a realistic Blitz Experience, which re-creates the raid of November 14 1940 when Coventry Cathedral was almost completely destroyed. With sirens, explosions and obvious suffering, it's probably unsuitable for small children.

Ragley Hall

Ragley Hall

WHERE:
Alcester, near Stratford, Warwickshire
BEST TIME TO GO:
April to October
DON'T MISS:
The collection of carriages dating back
to around 1750 – including the
horse-drawn limousines and sports
cars of their day; the Woodland Walk –
full of surprises and a reminder how
special an English landscape can be.
AMOUNT OF WALKING:
Moderate to lots, and almost all of it
fully accessible to wheelchair users
COST:
Reasonable

There's a very special atmosphere at Ragley Hall. It's not the grandeur, though Ragley is one of the earliest and loveliest Palladian masterpieces in Britain. It is the sense you get of it being a genuine family home, despite the baroque splendour of its interiors and the dazzling furniture and fittings it has acquired over several centuries. You can feel it even if you never enter the house itself (though you'll love it if you do), in the range of facilities and activities provided for family entertainment in the park and gardens.

No less a maestro than 'Capability' Brown laid out Ragley's 162 ha (400 acres) of park and woodland, with the hall set in formal gardens at its heart. The Kids' Zone is incorporated expertly into the harmonious topography, disguising its size and making the most of the views in every direction (a plus for accompanying adults). The Adventure Woodland has one playground for tots and another for toddlers, with sandpits, wooden forts, scramble nets and the like; and the woods around them are filled with tyre swings, aerial slides, trampolines, tunnels fashioned from the real tree trunks, and lots of other inventive equipment. You need to keep an eye open in case smaller children are attracted into the over-12s area, where the tree houses and rope ladders are very much higher, and bravado is greater. For all ages, the main attraction is the brilliant, 3-D wooden maze. Within its high containing fences, it includes swing bridges, complicated scramble nets, and climbing walls that you scale by pulling yourself up a rope. You may need to give smaller kids a helping hand.

The vast Ragley estate also offers a boating lake, wildlife rambles, an unusual sculpture park (with lifelike sculptures like a girl, reading on a bench), and Bodger's Cabin – a café and shop next to the playground.

YOU SHOULD KNOW:
Not many stately homes welcome visitors with such enthusiasm and sympathy, and fewer still work so hard to entertain children. There's so much for them to do and see at Ragley Hall that you may have to leave the house and formal gardens for another visit. The children, of course, will be delighted to go again.

Hatton Farm Village

You can't miss the tiny village of Hatton. It's signposted from every direction as the site of the Stairway to Heaven flight of 21 locks on the Grand Union Canal, and the home of Hatton Country World. Country World is primarily an adult attraction of small craft and farm shops. It's free. Once inside, what parent could resist a child's entreaty to visit its subsidiary, Hatton Farm Village? It costs – but if the children are 12 or under, it's one of the most engaging, hands-on, farm activity centres anywhere in England.

Hatton is a working farm set in lovely countryside, and though there's a good adventure playground full of slides, trampolines and climbing frames, the farm-related activities are more interesting, better fun and much more popular, especially with the three- to eight-year-old children for whom they have been devised. Most involve animals. There are babies to pet; goats, cows, reindeer, sheep, pigs and guinea pigs to feed; and ponies to ride. The guinea pigs have their own miniature village which entrances toddlers (perhaps they relate to the scale!). Bigger porkers have a Pig Palace with a royal mud wallow and throne made of straw. Farmyard sporting prowess is put to the test in the Sheepstakes sheep races, the Bird-o-Batics falconry display, the Daft Duck Trials in which farm dogs round up Indian runner ducks, and equally hilarious ferret racing. Older children may be more intrigued by the rare breeds conservation programme; or they can operate child-size mechanical diggers in a giant Build n Play sandpit, play Frisbee golf, pan for gold in a stream or ride Tristan the Runaway Tractor. And if you visit at the end of summer (mid July to early September, when the corn is high before harvesting), the enormous A-maize-ing Maze will give the whole family the giggles for months to come.

WHERE:
Hatton, near Warwick
BEST TIME TO GO:
Any time
DON'T MISS:
Panning for gold – there's a reward for finding ten 'nuggets' in the water; checking the programme of daily special events (like the one-off Penguin Olympics or the week-long Halloween pumpkin-carving competition) before your visit.
AMOUNT OF WALKING:
Lots – and the Farm Village is wheelchair accessible except for the steepest gravel paths.
COST:
Expensive (under twos enter free – but there's a supplement for the Bouncy Barn soft-play area).
YOU SHOULD KNOW:
Your ticket entitles you to come and go during the day, if you want to do other things like walk the canal – but under 14s must be accompanied at all times within the Farm Village. And don't forget the farm has plenty of lovely spots for a picnic, besides its own café and restaurant.

Ironbridge Museums

WHERE:
Ironbridge, Shropshire
BEST TIME TO GO:
Any time
DON'T MISS:
Blists Hill Victorian Town and
Enginuity, the best for children, with
the story of smelting at the Museum
of Iron, and the social history of the
Museum of the Gorge close behind.
AMOUNT OF WALKING:
Moderate; wheelchair access is very
variable – please ring the museums
in advance of your visit.
COST:
Reasonable. It's very expensive to
pay for each museum, but a
Passport Ticket gives you repeat
admission to all ten museums and
you can come back as often as you
like for a full year.
YOU SHOULD KNOW:
All ten museums are fascinating and
contain plenty to amuse and
entertain children. Sadly, even
though they are very close to each
other, it's unlikely that you could visit
them all in a day.

The Severn Gorge is where the Industrial Revolution began. Its symbol is the filigree work of iron struts and braces forming the sweeping arch of the Iron Bridge that gave the town its name, and its technology to the world. Now nature has reclaimed the gorge from the furnace flames and sulphurous smoke of factories in the white heat of the new technologies. Ten museums remain on its wooded banks to celebrate the superhuman achievements of the industrial pioneers who changed the way we live. Each museum tells a different story of exploration and discovery – challenging visitors to participate with hands-on activities that bring history to spectacular life. There's so much to see, you'll need to prioritize.

Blists Hill Victorian Town is more theatre than museum. It's a 21-ha (52-acre) Victorian community of real streets, shops, banks, workshops and pubs, where you use old money (pounds, shillings and pence). Costumed performers encourage you to join in their daily lives. You can ride a horse and cart to a genuine fairground, go to the bank, help Victorian housewives run their cottages, and maybe ride a penny-farthing bicycle. These were the people whose work was dominated by the exhibits you can see at the Museum of Iron, the Darby Furnace and Darby Houses; and the nearby Brosely Pipeworks Museum is a complete time capsule of that era.

The Ironbridge Museums were created to save the original buildings, forges and factories of the Severn Gorge. The latest addition, Enginuity, goes a big step further. It encourages children (and adults, if the children let you) to become apprentice engineers. It's a collection of amazing, interactive machinery, plus activities like testing your speed and accuracy against a robot, generating power from water, or pulling a locomotive by hand. It's certainly educational – but it's also the greatest fun.

Enginuity museum in Ironbridge

Severn Valley Railway

The Severn Valley Railway is such a treat it ought to be reserved for special occasions. For steam railway enthusiasts of any age, it is among the most admired in Britain; and those who have never experienced it before are likely to acquire a new passion. The Severn Valley Railway (SVR) is unusual on two counts. It operates full-size trains; and its 26-km (16-mi) track connects directly with the national railway system at Kidderminster. Its third claim to fame is pure serendipity: running alongside the Severn the railway passes through some of England's loveliest landscapes. You can get off at any station to explore, and then catch the next train onwards, or back.

The SVR is based in Bridgnorth, where you can see some of its amazing vintage locos and rolling stock up to 80 years old. Besides the railway's regular schedule, they are used for themed rides and excursions, like the 1940s weekend, the Classic Car and Bike Day, the Murder and Mystery ride and Thomas the Tank Engine's Christmas Special – but the service is at its best just doing what it does. From Bridgnorth, the stops are Hampton Loade, where there are lovely riverside walks; the Halt, which looks like the middle of some sylvan nowhere, and is in fact the Severn Valley Nature Reserve; Highley, where you can visit the SVR Engine House full of gleaming, hissing locos; the idyllic village of Arley; Bewdley, once an important inland port, and with a magnificent river frontage of grand houses; and Kidderminster.

The SVR inspires as much affection as nostalgia, not least because it is run largely by enthusiastic volunteers, happy to answer, especially children's, questions. It also fulfils its promise, to make every minute of every ride special to all its passengers.

Schoolchildren looking at a steam engine on the Severn Valley Railway.

WHERE:
Bridgnorth, Shropshire
BEST TIME TO GO:
May to October (plus weekends throughout the year and local school half-terms)
DON'T MISS:
Taking full advantage of train-hopping to visit some of the wonderful places along the route, including Bridgnorth's eccentric cliff funicular and the Wyre Forest.
AMOUNT OF WALKING:
Little. With prior booking, special coaches can take up to 15 wheelchair users at a time.
COST:
Reasonable. Charges vary according to the length of your journey, but a ticket from Bridgnorth to Kidderminster buys you unlimited SVR travel for the day.
YOU SHOULD KNOW:
The SVR is wonderful at any time. On a sunny day, hopping from train to train, none of the family will want to touch earth again. It's one of the best days out in Britain.

Onny Meadows Country Park and the Shropshire Hills Discovery Centre

As an introduction to the region, the displays at the Shropshire Hills Discovery Centre are ingenious. They start with the ecological adventure of the centre itself. Its galleries are blended into the contours of the land with a living grass roof that matches the hill forts and ancient barrows that dot the countryside. It's just as innovative inside, with old photographs, oral histories, artefacts and geological models illustrating the influences that shape the region. How these forces evolved is a story reserved for the Secret Hills exhibition, the Discovery Centre's *tour de force*. Secret Hills is aimed principally at inquisitive children, and explains landscapes like Long Mynd and Wenlock Edge using the latest forensic science to show the changes since the last ice age. There are buttons to press and levers to pull, culminating in a simulated hot-air balloon ride over the hills from the Wrekin to the Stiperstones Ridge. You control the 'flight', and it's enormous fun to make navigational aids out of scraps of geographical or literary knowledge acquired in the previous half hour.

In bad weather, you could happily spend all day feasting on local folklore and legend (and tea and cake), but Shropshire Hills Discovery Centre is also the anteroom to the 10 ha (25 acres) of Onny Meadows Country Park of which it is part. Outside, the river Onny meanders through water meadows thick with wildflowers, the haunt of kingfishers, herons, butterflies and a host of waterside flora and fauna. Children are encouraged to run and play in the ponds and fields, and there's a prize for anyone who follows the Little Mammoth Discovery Trail and answers all the questions on the trail sheet. It's only one of many clever and unobtrusive ways the centre transforms serious scientific nuggets of geology, ecology and culture into healthy entertainment for children.

Acton Scott Historic Working Farm and Wroxeter

Once the home farm of Acton Scott Hall, the Acton Scott Historic Working Farm is an unlikely survivor from the late Victorian era. It's never been touched by modern farming practice. All machinery is horse-drawn, and the farm workers use traditional husbandry to raise traditional breeds of poultry and stock. It's a self-contained community that owes nothing (except regulation) to the 20th and 21st centuries: a living history which the heritage industry and environmental movement have refashioned as a pioneer not just of farming methods, but of the interdependence of individual skills for everybody's benefit. It may be an unsubtle way of saying 'the old ways are best', but children get the message and go dotty at the way it's delivered.

It's a working farm, but you can get involved in every process of the daily chores and seasonal ploughing, sowing and harvesting. You can get close to the animals, and watch (and listen to) the farrier, wheelwright, blacksmith, woodsman, dairymaid and other experts whose patience with children matches their skilled labour. Show and tell at Acton Scott Farm is enthralling, and of apparently infinite variety. Every day there are extra events or demonstrations, like sheep shearing, lambing, cider making and threshing, that run with the seasons; but you might find yourself in a scarecrow-building competition or making pottery, or some other activity that contributes essential functions to the farm community. Children and adults both find rich satisfaction in helping to churn butter, which they can later eat as part of the famous Acton Scott cheese-and-pickle sandwich.

If you have any energy left, you can follow the Roman road more or less from the farm gates north to Viroconium (Wroxeter). Once the fourth largest city in Roman Britain, only the baths and a massive chunk of Basilica walls are visible. Much more is promised.

Shire horses at work

WHERE:
Acton Scott, Church Stretton, Shropshire
BEST TIME TO GO:
April to October
DON'T MISS:
The oral histories – real Shropshire folk memories, recorded over a long period and collected here. You can listen to people from the farming community recalling their rural lives at the end of the 19th century, listed by subject: working horses, fleecing, 'hiring day', haymaking, children at work, cider making and so on. A rare opportunity to hear authentic voices and feel directly connected to the land.
AMOUNT OF WALKING:
Moderate. Wheelchair access is patchy.
COST:
Low
YOU SHOULD KNOW:
If you like what you see, you can sign up for short courses in anything from Corn Dolly Making to Smocks and Smocking, Ploughing with Heavy Horses, Butter Making, and Introductory Blacksmithing. It's a measure of the fun and interest excited by Acton Scott Farm that you really, really want to.

Land of Lost Content and Bog Mine & Visitor Centre

WHERE:
Craven Arms and Stiperstones, Shropshire
BEST TIME TO GO:
February to October – any day except Wednesdays.
DON'T MISS:
The nylon stocking dispenser and the winklepickers; the comfortable chairs placed so you can really stare and make sense out of the piles of dazzling bric-a-brac; the sound and smell of the old-fashioned seaside, part of the holiday-themed section and typical of the evocative genius of the collections.
AMOUNT OF WALKING:
Little to lots (if the Stiperstones Nature Reserve lures you in). Wheelchair access at Land of Lost Content is restricted to the ground floor.
COST:
Low
YOU SHOULD KNOW:
Check out the 'Passport to Craven Arms', which will get you discounted entry to a number of local attractions. The real secret of the 'blue remembered hills' is the Shropshire Hills Shuttle, which provides service to all the best places for starting walks, and to regional attractions. Think of the freedom of not having to drive!

The National Museum of British Popular Culture is the formal name of one of Britain's most informal collections. Its theme is nostalgia – so it's appropriate that the museum is better known as the Land of Lost Content, a line from A E Housman that continues '. . . the happy highways where I went/And cannot come again'. Crammed into three floors of Craven Arms' former Market Hall is a riotous assembly of the banal and the curious everyday items which together make up the immediate past. They constitute nostalgia on a national scale, though the exhibits are mainly just the throwaways of the past three or four generations. The colourful jumble is organized with enough coherence to show how life – packaging, technology, kitchen gadgets, communications (a word that jars horribly in this context), music, clothes, cooking, bathing – changed between our grandparents' day and our children's. The exhibits are our memories, and even the smallest toddler will find plenty of excitement. There's lots you can touch, hold or operate, and far too much to take in. This brilliant, exhilarating, dismaying, sympathetic, wonderful museum is somewhere you will really want to return to.

The nostalgic Land of Lost Content

The matchless beauty of the Stiperstones, one of Shropshire's best-known landmarks, makes it a lovely place for reflection afterwards. The Shropshire Hills Shuttle will drop you at the door of the Bog Visitor Centre (or you can drive) on the edge of the Nature Reserve. The gas-lit Old School House is almost all that's left of Bog, a lead-mining village, but it serves great tea and sympathy and it's a crossroads for long, short, and circular walks across the hills. You might see red grouse or buzzards in that wild, dramatic landscape, but the green and blue pockets between the hills have an ancient serenity. It's a place for running free.

Park Hall Countryside Experience

Park Hall is a farm activity centre on a department store scale. It is spread across 53 ha (130 acres), but most of the farm action is contained in a series of restored Victorian farm buildings bunched round two giant barns, and half a dozen adjoining paddocks. The arrangement is good for kids – the whole place is designed for small children up to the age of 13 – to see what's happening, and for adults to keep tabs on them. Park Hall's 'menu' of attractions is endless, and distinctly hands-on. There's a daily regimen of horse grooming (Shetland ponies and Charm the Clydesdale 'heavy'), lamb coddling, pig petting, hand milking, rabbit tickling and llama spitting contests (now wash your hands!). Interspersed with all that is the driving school, junior Land Rovers, tractor rides and mechanical diggers. These activities take place at the same times every day, so you can plan in advance exactly where you want to be. One of the best participatory activities is the Victorian School Lesson: it turns the rather dull museum into a sparkling demonstration of living history (and discipline – you will be reminded 'Lateness will not be tolerated!'), based on the authentic toys, furniture and artefacts in the Victorian farmhouse.

The two giant barns in the centre of the farm are in fact gigantic play areas. Children still scratching their heads for something to do have a choice between Soft Play, Monkey Business Adventure Play, Woodland Adventure Play or the Crazy Fun Adventure Course; not to mention the wildflower walks in Sycamore Wood, the nearby Iron Age Roundhouse, the (late summer) maize maze, and the official Welsh Guards Collection of uniforms, honours and memorabilia. Park Hall must be the only place where children can dress like sentries at Buckingham Palace, be thrown in a cell, get a driving lesson and milk a cow.

WHERE:
Oswestry, Shropshire
BEST TIME TO GO:
March to September
DON'T MISS:
The Driving School for three to ten year olds – anything to foster their road sense; Charm, the Clydesdale heavy horse – not a toy to be taken out and put back in a cupboard; Water Blaster, spinning windmills with water cannon, etc; Crazy Fun – two parallel obstacle courses, so friends and family can race each other.
AMOUNT OF WALKING:
Moderate, and there's good wheelchair access everywhere.
COST:
Reasonable, but there are various supplements for some activities.

Arrow Valley Countryside Park

WHERE:
Redditch, Worcestershire
BEST TIME TO GO:
Any time
DON'T MISS:
The drop-in workshops for anything from nest building, drumming and face painting to assorted crafts. The Countryside Centre acts as a neighbourhood bulletin board, so the only way to find out about them is to go there.
AMOUNT OF WALKING:
Lots. The Countryside Centre and one lakeside path are tarmaced for wheelchair access; the wilder woods are not so easy.
COST:
Free – and low when you do have to pay for an event or service.
YOU SHOULD KNOW:
Other than play areas, most of the children's activities (like storytelling or pond dipping) assume that children will be eight or older. Younger children are welcome if accompanied by an adult.

For sheer contrast, the Arrow Valley Countryside Park must be one of Britain's most inspired municipal creations. Surrounded by urban developments and major roads on the edge of Redditch, the park's 364 ha (900 acres) have complete rural integrity. There's a 12-ha (30-acre) fishing lake with water-sports facilities, round which there are way-marked trails through woodland and meadows, and on both banks of the Arrow itself. The river runs the length of the park: you can go skating at one end, walk or cycle the Woodland Trail until it crosses the Miller's Trail, then follow it in pastoral tranquillity to the park's biggest attraction, the Forge Mill Museum at the north end.

Redditch once produced 90 per cent of the world's needles, and much of its fishing tackle. The Forge Mill is where they were tempered and polished. A series of tableaux re-creates the whole process in the original workshops and forges. The water-powered machinery still works, and the scouring mill is the only one of its kind left in the world. The museum is a vivid tribute to the Victorian Midlands' embrace of industrial technology. Next to it are the ruins of the medieval Cistercians' Bordesley Abbey, with its own Visitor Centre in a wonderful 16th-century barn. You can see artefacts excavated from the ruins, including a 15th-century skeleton, and with any luck, hear 'Brother Nicholas', a demonstrator dressed as a cowled monk, explain the abbey practices and medieval way of life.

The Arrow Valley Countryside Centre is the lakeside fulcrum of the park, where all the activities are organized, and where you can sit with a drink on the balcony overlooking the water. The two children's play areas are here, and it's where you can find out about the events programmed for the park, from theatre to charity runs, and craft workshops to children's wildlife expeditions.

The lake at Arrow Valley Countryside Park on a frosty autumnal morning

Witley Court and Gardens, and Mortimers Cross Water Mill

Like some English 'Xanadu', Witley Court has the intriguing glamour of a palace ruin. Until it was gutted by fire in 1937, it rivalled England's greatest houses. Now its roofless shell is a magnificent reminder of transient glory – and a great opportunity to see how a vaulted medieval house mentioned in the Domesday Book could evolve via Tudor and Jacobean expansion into the grandest kind of Italianate palace that Victorian taste could conceive. You can take special 'hard hat' tours (hats supplied) to the cellars and kitchens that sprawl underground below the huge, empty staterooms and galleries; and go Victorian 'time-travelling', dressing up and playing out life below stairs or in the Stable Yard. These tours are quite expensive, and most children are satisfied with a trot round the towering porticoes before heading into the fabulous park and gardens.

Witley's gardens were the creation of the mid-Victorian legend W A Nesfield, who called them his 'Monster Work'. Adults will appreciate the scale of his surviving parterres and terraces, blocks of colour leading the eye to grand gestures like the Perseus and Andromeda Fountain. Children are entranced by its cascade, which fires a water jet up to 37 m (120 ft); and for them the other highlights are the ponds and woodland walks of the rhododendron-filled North Park.

Head west from Witley to the beautiful border country south of Ludlow. At Mortimers Cross in Herefordshire, the site of a famous battle in which Edward IV won his crown in 1461, there's a rare, working water mill built in 1750. With their contribution to many kinds of history, the water mill and riverside battle site are great places to explore. The River Lugg's clear water runs fast and its banks are slippery and steep, so look out for small children (and wear boots or wellies).

The fountains against the south facade of Witley Court

WHERE:
Great Witley, Worcestershire; and Mortimers Cross, Herefordshire
BEST TIME TO GO:
Any time
DON'T MISS:
The Wilderness garden; traditional games in the park; the stone weir on the Lugg at Mortimers Cross.
AMOUNT OF WALKING:
Lots. Wheelchair access is restricted by steps at Witley Court.
COST:
Reasonable
YOU SHOULD KNOW:
The Perseus and Andromeda Fountain's central stone block is made from a single 20-ton chunk, and is 8 m (26 ft) high. With its high cascades and spectacular central jet, it was once the biggest fountain in Europe.

West Midlands Safari and Leisure Park

You can see the African 'big five' at the West Midlands Safari Park. The green, domesticated landscape may not have much in common with the heat and dust of the Rift Valley, but at least you get close to the animals. The dead-slow drive-through brings them right up to the car windows, and you can feed them if you dare. Be advised that giraffes in particular like to stick their heads inside the car, and they drool (experienced visitors suggest bringing a towel). The park is heavily involved in the IUCN (International Union for the Conservation of Nature) programme for saving endangered species. Many animals have been bred in captivity, so even rarities like the white lions and white tigers won't run away. And if you're worried that wallabies, wild dogs, or monkeys will damage your car (windscreen wipers are popular), for a small fee you can take the park minibus drive-through, with the advantage of being able to go off-road and seek out any temporarily shy species.

On foot, the park's Discovery Trail leads you on to the sea lion theatre, a walk underwater at the Seaquarium, the hippo lakes, reptile house, Twilight Cave and Creepy-Crawlies; and you'll meet a Bengal tiger, Amur leopard, Rodrigues fruit bat, bantang, aye-aye and Bactrian camel, not always with glass between you and them. Get the children to look out for question boards as you go – there are prize opportunities for filling in the free 'trail planner'.

Beyond the hippos is the huge Leisure Park, with 30 rides to make you wince, whimper and cheer. The New Venom Tower Drop isn't as spiteful as its name, but you do get drenched on the Zambesi Water Splash. Smaller children have nine of their own rides in Cubs Kingdom, including the interactive Fire Rescue Rangers in which they play the firefighters, among lots of other equally thrilling attractions.

Visitors feeding a giraffe from their car.

WHERE:
Bewdley, Kidderminster, Worcestershire
BEST TIME TO GO:
February to December
DON'T MISS:
Latabe, the 15-year-old football-loving African elephant; the aye-aye in the Twilight Cave – discover why the world's biggest nocturnal primate, a species of Madagascan lemur, fills the same ecological niche as a woodpecker.
AMOUNT OF WALKING:
Moderate
COST:
Expensive, though your ticket is valid for a return visit. Effectively, you pay twice: for the Safari Park and for the Leisure Park.
YOU SHOULD KNOW:
You can check height restrictions on the rides and other rules before your visit. Pre-booking may reduce your costs. The Leisure Park will give you an armband to save queuing to pay.

Small Breeds Farm Park and Owl Centre, and Longtown Castle

The Welsh border country is a beautiful place to indulge a passion for unusual animals and birds. The Small Breeds Farm Park and Owl Centre near Kington makes the most of its site in the shadow of Hergest Ridge and close to Offa's Dyke. The main display area is typical of the local landscape, except that there are Dexter cattle, Soay sheep and alpacas beneath the copsed trees and shrubs, and pygmy goats and kune kune pigs rooting in the ancient hedges between the fields. Grouped around the main paddock are the Owl Garden, the Waterfowl Enclosure, the Pheasant Aviaries and the Pet Animal House. The Owl Garden is full of the friendliest owls you could hope to meet, like Numpy the giant milky eagle owl and Mini Digger, a burrowing owl. Even children can get very close to them, and at the right time of year you can share the baby owls' hand rearing. Getting close is the whole point of the park, and there's a boardwalk across the waterfowl ponds to see the ducks, geese and swans. Whenever possible, you'll be given the chance to feed these and all the animals, including the miniature horses and donkeys, as well as the chinchillas, rabbits and delightful red squirrels.

From Hergest Ridge, a 40-km (25-mi) drive southeast takes in some of the loveliest and least known Marcher country. After crossing the Wye, you skirt the Black Mountains along the glorious Golden Valley to Abbey Dore. Turn south on the backroads, and suddenly you'll see Longtown Castle revealed above you. Still intimidating as a ruin, the once mighty Marcher castle is a picturesque reminder of harsher times in these green, green valleys; but you still wish Ivanhoe would come lance a-flutter through the gatehouse.

WHERE:
Kington and Ewyas Harold, Herefordshire
BEST TIME TO GO:
Any time
DON'T MISS:
The rare opportunity to see all of Britain's native owls in one place, plus several others – you'll never be closer to these magnificent birds; Folly Flights – the rare breeds of bantams and doves.
AMOUNT OF WALKING:
Moderate. Wheelchair access to the Small Breeds Farm Park is excellent, but very difficult at Longtown Castle.
COST:
Reasonable (free at Longtown Castle).
YOU SHOULD KNOW:
The Small Breeds Farm Park covers about 7 ha (18 acres), so the animals have lots of space to gambol in. Children, especially if they are under ten, seem to respond to the general air of cud-chewing content by getting more involved than usual; and the animals sense that, and respond in turn.

Remains of the 12th-century Longtown Castle

Goodrich Castle and canoeing on the River Wye

WHERE:
Goodrich, Symonds Yat, Herefordshire
BEST TIME TO GO:
April to October
DON'T MISS:
The defensive 'murder holes' in the castle ramparts; the Goodrich Visitor Centre, which is very good but out of sight of the castle so it doesn't impinge on the view; the riverside pubs accessible by canoe.
AMOUNT OF WALKING:
Moderate – and wheelchair access only extends to the castle Visitor Centre.
COST:
Low (Goodrich Castle).
Expensive (canoeing).
YOU SHOULD KNOW:
There's no need to worry about safety for smaller children in canoes. Broad Canadian-style canoes are both stable and easily controllable, and they come with all the proper safety devices. There are several canoe companies at Kerne Bridge.

Arriving at Goodrich Castle, you go weak in the presence of beauty. The 13th-century Norman castle stands sentinel on the old Roman road from Monmouth to Gloucester. With a drawbridge, a square keep, and unusually complete, surviving buildings, Goodrich is impossibly picturesque. Its site, above the 120-m (390-ft) Symonds Yat gorge, where the River Wye winds in a 10-km (6-mi) loop between wooded slopes and golden meadows, is internationally famous as one of the loveliest views in Britain. You can see forever, melting into a horizon of blue hills.

There's a good audio accompaniment to the castle, with vivid descriptions of its martial history, and you can still see 'Roaring Meg', the huge Civil War mortar that eventually smashed the castle walls and ended its military career. Even better are the colourful re-enactments among the ruins of Normans versus Saxons, the Medieval Knight's Trail, the English Civil War, and the timeline show *2,000 Years of the Sword* which are held very regularly, interspersed with occasional dramas like *The Railway Children* or *Romeo and Juliet*. It is no criticism to say that part of their attraction is the fabulous backdrop.

Directly below Goodrich Castle is Kerne Bridge, one of the best places along the Wye to hire a canoe. From the water, you understand why Symonds Yat and the Upper Wye Gorge is an SSSI (Site of Special Scientific Interest). Dragonflies and damselflies shimmer on the riverbanks; peregrine falcons soar above the cliffs and deer peep out of rare, lime and yew woodlands among the oak and beech. A short afternoon in a canoe will take you in an almost complete circle, effortlessly downstream, to the other side of Goodrich; and you won't even have to take the canoe back.

Canoeing on the River Wye at Brockweir

The aMazing Hedge Puzzle and Wye Valley Butterfly Zoo

Created for HM the Queen's Jubilee (and called the Jubilee Maze), the aMazing Hedge Puzzle changed its name by popular acclaim after maze experts recognized the fiendish cunning of its apparently simple design. Now it's the central attraction of a whole maze culture devoted to the fun and games you can have with mazes. It includes a Museum of Mazes where you can explore the history, philosophy, evolution and even the future of maze making – but the museum itself is an information maze, which you can only solve interactively. There's no point just looking: you have to get physically involved! It's riveting stuff, especially learning to create your own mazes, either for yourself or on a computer which has access to ideas drawn from the ancient Egyptians and Greeks. The most wonderful thing you learn is that mazes are nothing without games, and the aMazing Hedge Puzzle itself provides plenty. There's an adjoining balcony from which you can misdirect friends or family inside the maze; and young and old can have equal fun deceiving each other, and solving maze puzzles.

In the 21st century, the aMazing Hedge Puzzle represents a rare form of (non) commercial innocence. It's no surprise to find it shares some functions (like a bookshop) with its neighbour, the Wye Valley Butterfly Zoo. Here you can wander among some of the world's most exotic butterflies flying free in beautifully designed habitats. There are displays to show you how to identify butterfly survival strategies, colour-coded warning systems, mimicry and flight patterns – useful information when you follow the butterfly breeding cycle of supping nectar from tropical flowers, attracting a mate and laying eggs. The butterflies are certainly magic, and your visit will directly help their long-term survival.

A butterfly lands on a leaf at the Wye Valley Butterfly Zoo.

WHERE:
Symonds Yat West, Herefordshire
BEST TIME TO GO:
Any time
DON'T MISS:
The aMazing Puzzle Shop, full of action-packed puzzle books and games that most people don't know exist; Mazes and Mysteries, an interactive account of mazes as mystic and moral symbols hiding ancient magic; the delicacy of butterflies emerging from their chrysalides.
AMOUNT OF WALKING:
Moderate. Everything except the balcony – including the paths of the Jubilee Maze – is wheelchair accessible.
COST:
Low (the combined ticket is especially good value).
YOU SHOULD KNOW:
Even though maze games can (and should) get quite raucous, this is a gentle day out. The opportunities for contemplation, for children as well as adults, are multiplied by the setting: Symonds Yat is one of the greatest beauty spots in all Britain, and utterly appropriate for thinking about hedge mazes and butterflies.

Northumberland Seabird Centre and Coquet Island

WHERE:
Amble, near Alnwick,
Northumberland
BEST TIME TO GO:
April to September
DON'T MISS:
The long, sandy beaches, dunes
and cliffs stretching out along the
coast on either side of the mudflats
of the Coquet estuary in Amble
itself – they're teeming with birds
and wildlife.
AMOUNT OF WALKING:
Little. There's full wheelchair access
at the Centre and on the boat.
COST:
Reasonable
YOU SHOULD KNOW:
This is the only Seabird Centre in the
UK or Europe where you can watch
live CCTV images of roseate terns at
their nest sites – and operate the
cameras yourself!

It takes the exhilarating thrill of seabirds, swooping and diving under the vault of the sky, to bring alive the rugged drama of Northumberland's beautiful coast. In spring and summer especially, the Northumberland Seabird Centre at Amble is the place to see tens of thousands of Britain's most colourful seabirds, and some of the rarest. Eider ducks, puffins, guillemots, razorbills, greylag geese, fulmars, shags, cormorants and four kinds of terns gather to breed on Coquet Island, a 5.7-ha (14-acre) sanctuary just 1.4 km (1 mi) offshore from the Coquet River estuary at Amble.

The island is a nature reserve run by the Royal Society for the Protection of Birds. Only RSPB wardens may actually walk among the huge colonies competing for nesting space on every tussock, rock, burrow or building crevice – but the explosion of numbers among different bird species means that you can study them close up, without ever setting foot on Coquet itself. The Northumberland Seabird Centre operates its own catamaran to take you around the island. Powerful enough for close inshore work, it has seating arranged so that everyone gets an uninterrupted view forward, and a stable platform for watching the birds and for taking photographs. It also has RSPB volunteers aboard to answer questions and point out the birds' often quirky and bizarre behaviour. You'll also get an escort of grey seals bobbing up around you, and perhaps see dolphins as well. But sailing around Coquet is only half the adventure!

Back at the Seabird Centre, you can use the solar-powered CCTV system that monitors activity on the island to zoom in on puffins in their nesting burrows, or to watch the roseate terns – one of Britain's rarest species, of which the 70 pairs on Coquet represent 90 per cent of all those in existence.

Chillingham Castle and Alnwick Garden Tree House

Chillingham Castle has been called the finest medieval fortress in Europe. Austere and imposing, it looks just like a 'proper' castle should, a testament to the bloody deeds, battles and tragedies that pepper its history. Not even its beautiful formal gardens and dappled woodlands can dispel its aura of spookiness. Chillingham is said to

be one of England's most haunted houses, with at least six ghosts that include a 'glowing' Blue Boy whose eerie moaning comes from within the thick medieval walls where he was bricked-up.

Its history is so rich in bloodthirsty derring-do that Chillingham can never disappoint your imagination. Deep in the castle bowels you'll find the ancient dungeons, carved with the piteous graffiti of the doomed and damned. Next door, the torture chamber still contains its original 'Iron Maiden', rack and thumbscrews. It's a stark reminder of the ruthless means by which 20 generations of nobility maintained the gorgeous apartments, minstrel galleries and sumptuous halls that fill the castle – and an invitation to pretend to be a great medieval thane or a rebellious vassal as you go round it.

Don't let a long morning at Chillingham put you off an afternoon visit to Alnwick. Not to Alnwick Castle, but to the wonderful wooden Tree House in the Castle Garden. It's every child's fantasy brought to life – no fewer than 16 trees support a network of aerial walkways, hanging platforms, balconies, wobbly rope bridges and spiral staircases between the different levels. There are five rooms (including a café and even a proper restaurant!), capped with turrets and steeply pitched roofs. It's made for adventure – sprawling but safe for would-be brave knights rescuing distressed damsels, or just playing cards in the treetops.

The world's largest tree house at Alnwick Gardens

WHERE:
Chillingham, near Alnwick, Northumberland
BEST TIME TO GO:
May to September
DON'T MISS:
Chillingham Wild Cattle Park – for over 700 years, a unique herd of white cattle has prospered here. Also, it's fun dodging the water jets at the Grand Cascade near the Alnwick Treehouse.
AMOUNT OF WALKING:
Lots. Disabled access inside Chillingham is partly restricted but wheelchairs can roam among the treetops at Alnwick Tree House.
COST:
Reasonable (for adults); low (for children). At Alnwick Garden/Treehouse, with an accompanying adult up to four children may enter for 1p each.
YOU SHOULD KNOW:
There's an enormous play area at the base of the Alnwick Treehouse, but the nearby Bamboo Labyrinth is best for playing hide-and-seek.

Whitehouse Farm Centre and Morpeth Small Pipes Museum

WHERE:
Stannington, near Morpeth, Northumberland

BEST TIME TO GO:
Any time of year. During January and November Whitehouse Farm is only open at weekends.

DON'T MISS:
The Wild Willow maze at Whitehouse Farm or the Musette de Cour at Morpeth. It's a 17th-century bagpipe once played at the French Court – and has been identified in a painting from Versailles.

AMOUNT OF WALKING:
Moderate to lots. There is excellent wheelchair access to both places.

COST:
Reasonable – especially the family ticket at Whitehouse Farm. Morpeth Pipe Museum is free.

YOU SHOULD KNOW:
Music is made on bagpipes all over the world. It's worth taking the time to discover the astonishing range of totally different sounds made by the instruments in the museum.

The only worry you'll ever have at Whitehouse Farm Centre is choosing what to do. Whatever the weather, there's a variety of animals to see (and possibly feed, groom or play with); crafts to try; games to play in the straw play area; and real adventures to undertake, either in the adventure playground, or on tractor-and-trailer rides, farm walks or go-karts. Every activity has an indoor and outdoor version, is supervised by qualified adults, and (where relevant) divided into appropriate age ranges.

There's a Guinea Pig World, Rabbit Village, Chick Nursery, duck and wildfowl pond, and Farmer's Den soft-play barn for small children to pet animals. You can also see exotics like meerkats, wallabies and llamas, rare breeds of sheep, cows and pigs, and a variety of insects, reptiles and creepy-crawlies. It's a sizeable 16-ha (40-acre) working farm, so there's plenty to see and the non-farming attractions are just as compelling. Tots (up to six years old) love the pedal tractors, swings and animal rockers while the go-karts provide an irresistible challenge to older family members. The Centre is arranged so that everyone can easily do exactly what they want.

As it's close, try to take the opportunity to visit a real oddity – the Bagpipe Museum at Morpeth. It's housed in Morpeth's Grade 1 listed 13th-century Chantry Chapel and tells the story of pipes from all over the world. Ingenious headphones bring each exhibit to life as you approach it, flooding your head with awesome music. It's one of the most inventive, instructive, entertaining and delightful museums in Britain – and especially relevant to Northumbria, famous for its heritage of regional pipe music.

Poppy the donkey with an Easter chick

Seahouses Marine Life and Fishing Heritage Centre

Fishing boats in the harbour of the popular seaside resort of Seahouses

Set in the middle of one of Britain's most beautiful stretches of coastline, Seahouses is a colourful, bustling fishing harbour to which, throughout the summer, a steady stream of visitors comes to take a boat to the Farne Islands' wildlife reserve. Few linger in the town, yet Seahouses itself makes a wonderful, low-stress destination for a day out. It may not be sophisticated, but it's full of things guaranteed to fascinate children of all ages and will stimulate curiosity and even provide answers to their inevitable questions.

Just watching the boats coming and going is fun. But the town is proud of its history as 'the herring capital of Northumberland' and tells its tale at the Marine Life and Fishing Heritage Centre. The influence of the sea on the town's development and the demands of a sea-going life are explained alongside fascinating old photographs and artefacts. Learn about the trade in crushed limestone exported for fertilizer and about the lives of the 'herring lassies', who cleaned the fish brought in by the huge herring fleet that followed the shoals from Orkney in spring to Lowestoft in August.

There's a waymarked walk (amble is more accurate) from the harbour that takes you through typical early 19th-century 'squares' of houses built for fishermen around three sides of a courtyard, thus providing shelter for communal mending of nets and baiting of lines. The Tourist Information Office will give you a (free) children's quiz to accompany this and several other walks.

Smaller children are entranced by the fishy things in the salt-water aquarium, and by the darkened rooms of the Haunted Kingdom attached to the Heritage Centre. Innocent pleasures like these, enjoyed in lively seaside surroundings, make Seahouses an idyllic day out with the children.

WHERE:
South of Bamburgh Castle, Northumberland
BEST TIME TO GO:
March to October
DON'T MISS:
The building where kippers are said to have been invented (accidentally, in a fire) and where fish are still smoked; the charming ghost stories and legends recounted in the Haunted Kingdom; or the dunes next to the harbour.
AMOUNT OF WALKING:
Lots, because Seahouses is full of interesting seaside things to be explored – but most of it is accessible to wheelchairs.
COST:
Low
YOU SHOULD KNOW:
During the summer strains of Northumbrian folk music or sea shanties may be heard around the town, and local artists use shop fronts and cafés to show off their work. There's a festival, too, and frequent events and displays for children. Activities range from nature exploration to street theatre, dancing and crafts.

The Discovery Museum and the Centre for Life

Close to each other and to Newcastle Station, these are two of the most ingenious and innovative museums in Britain. Both are jam-packed with colourful, hands-on exhibits and jaw-dropping demonstrations devised for a huge range of interests at every age level.

The Discovery Museum brings Tyneside alive. It tells the story of its maritime and social history, and of fashionable and regimental life in the area since Roman times. Ten galleries – treasure troves of the imagination – surround a central atrium filled with the dramatic, 34-m (108-ft) bulk of the *Turbinia*, the world's first steam-turbine ship and the fastest of its day. It's a powerful symbol of Tyneside's invention. Another is Live Wires, which features robots. The Science Factory, Fashion Works, Pioneer Gallery and A Soldier's Life all offer opportunities to dress up, experiment and control exhibits with levers and buttons. On a practical level, the museum also provides pleasant spaces for families to enjoy packed lunches or teas (the café is good but costly for a family).

The Centre for Life celebrates the whole spectrum of human versatility. It is dedicated to real science (it's attached to working laboratories of international fame) and, most of all, to involving children in the magic of scientific surprise. From moving models of dinosaurs and mythical beasts, to evolutionary processes, to the journey through the stars in the huge Planetarium and Lifeseeker (an interactive multi-media 'research voyage' in which you make continual choices that determine how your notional world will develop), exhibits are gauged to different ages (there's plenty even for tots) to feel, smell, hear, handle, manipulate and enjoy. In addition, there is a constantly changing programme of scientific demonstrations and temporary shows. The Centre is a unique, revolutionary new kind of museum. You'll have to drag the children away.

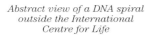

Abstract view of a DNA spiral outside the International Centre for Life

WHERE:
Newcastle upon Tyne, Tyne and Wear
BEST TIME TO GO:
Any time
DON'T MISS:
The Motion Ride at the Centre for Life where a panoramic screen synchronized to computerized seating offers an enthralling trip at breakneck speed through a variety of physical situations such as an urban car chase, a journey through a derelict mineshaft or a mountain road in the desert where you feel every bump, jolt, and stomach-churning lurch.
At the Discovery Museum, A Soldier's Life is inspired, unsentimental and moving.
AMOUNT OF WALKING:
Lots (but fully accessible).
COST:
The Discovery Museum is free. The Centre for Life is reasonable and family tickets are available. Under fours go free. Note that the Newcastle Discovery Card allows one child to enter free for each paying adult at a large number of venues.
YOU SHOULD KNOW:
Throughout the Centre for Life you can identify the staff called Explainers by their bright-red shirts. The Explainers are real scientists who often work in the laboratories elsewhere in the Centre, or who are studying for higher degrees. They believe it is a privilege to interest people in the sciences of the world around them and, most of all, to make science fun for children.

Seven Stories Centre

Seven Stories is dedicated to children's imaginations, and to celebrating the books which stimulate them. It's a seven-storey Victorian warehouse ingeniously converted into a literary adventure playground. Part bookshop with a vast range of children's books, part archive of the manuscripts and original illustrations of major children's authors like Philip Pullman, Edward Ardizzone, Quentin Blake and Michael Rosen, Seven Stories is also a creative workshop full of changing exhibitions, interactive games and performances, storytelling, animation workshops and author sessions. There's also a big, colourful reading room full of cushions.

Seven Stories uses every possible means to introduce children (from the smallest to mid-teens) to the idea of words, texts and illustrations as building blocks. The centre's name refers to the received wisdom that there are only seven basic stories in the world and all stories are a version of one of them. Knowing that, children are unafraid to experiment, and Seven Stories makes it easy. There's an activity table on each floor with a 'challenge' on it. In the basement, the Engine Room supplies pens, paper, clothes and props for children to create their own stories and dress up as the characters in them. More formal story-telling, readings, and poetry performances take place (usually at weekends) under the wooden beams of the Artist's Attic. It's also where you can sometimes meet authors like Jacqueline Wilson, or see how J K Rowling corrected each Harry Potter chapter.

The exhibitions are fabulous interactive trails. The recent From Toad Hall to Pooh Corner had everyone tooting car horns and racing their Pooh sticks, then sitting in a replica of Badger's Kitchen listening to a narrative from the book. It's typical of Seven Stories' continuous effort to demonstrate the magic of the written word and drawn image. It's a place that creates – and often fulfils – children's wildest dreams.

WHERE:
Byker, Newcastle upon Tyne, Tyne and Wear
BEST TIME TO GO:
Any time. (Seven Stories' boast is 'seven hours a day, seven days a week, seven storeys'.)
DON'T MISS:
While the children are off (very possibly with Kingsley's Fairies) being creative, adults will revel in the archive: it includes illustrations for *Narnia*, *The Borrowers* and *Ballet Shoes*. You can also raid the digital book collection in the Story Lab.
AMOUNT OF WALKING:
Little – and the centre is fully accessible to wheelchairs. However, there will be more jumping up and down in excitement than is usual in a bookshop.
COST:
Reasonable
YOU SHOULD KNOW:
Contact Seven Stories in advance if you can. With so many events, exhibitions and author visits, you'll want to make sure you're not going to miss something you could have gone to.

A giant foot from Jack in the Beanstalk *at Seven Stories*

Washington: WWT Wetlands Centre

So close to the conurbation of Newcastle, Gateshead and Sunderland, the Washington Wetlands Centre is as much a refuge for families as it is for wildlife. In fact the Wildfowl & Wetlands Trust (WWT)'s 45 ha (111 acres) of wetland and woodland provides the kind of sanctuary that has made the wildlife reserve one of the northeast's most successful conservation schemes. There aren't many wetlands left in Britain so, whatever time of year you visit, you'll find a series of unusual habitats and correspondingly rare plants, wildflowers, wildfowl and birds. Spring sees bluebells among the ancient oaks of Spring Gill Wood, plaintive lapwings, and rare nenes on Wader Lake. In summer dragonflies flash across the insect ponds, butterflies crowd the wildflower meadows full of bee orchids, cuckoo flowers and yellow rattle, and children are thrilled at close encounters with fluffy chicks at the Waterfowl Nursery. Migrating southbound waders ignore the jays squabbling for autumn acorns, the wheeling bats, and birds whose plumage changes with the leaves; and flocks of curlews roost next to redshank at winter dusk. Then, you'll see bullfinches and woodpeckers in the frosts of Hawthorn Wood – and on the meres the throng of water birds restart the annual cycle with their ritual of courtship displays.

Children love being so close to so many colourful living creatures, including the exotic Chilean flamingos, avocets, Eurasian cranes, grey herons, goldeneye, wagtails and widgeons. There are hides to encourage really close observation, a 'sustainable garden', a discovery centre and a Splash Zone adventure play area for three to five year olds.

Even with the birds in constant motion and the breathless excitement of children encountering new worlds, the Wetlands Centre is a place of infinite tranquillity – a day off as much as a day out.

Stephenson Railway Museum and the Toy Museum

The Stephenson Railway Museum is named after George and Robert Stephenson, the father and son who pioneered the steam railway on Tyneside. They were visionaries in a wider sense, aware that the machines developed from their inventions would have a profound effect on their community, country and, eventually, the whole world. The Museum is about those changes as much as it is directly about trains – so there's plenty to interest girls and boys in addition to the gleaming brass intricacies of the early machines.

You can see George Stephenson's *Billy*, the precursor of the world-famous *Rocket*; engines from steam's golden age (including the *Jackie Milburn*, named after one of Newcastle United's footballing legends); and a rare electric loco from 1909, once used to haul coal wagons at Harton colliery and now the fully functioning centrepiece of The Electric Century interactive multimedia display.

It's the story of how electricity transformed first transport, then our whole lives. Using hands-on exhibits, young visitors learn both how trains work and how they changed Victorian lives, bringing seaside holidays and encouraging mobility. Wonderful Wheels offers them a chance to make pop-up models; or they can learn about the wildlife colonizing railway verges. Trains and history form the displays, but children quickly realize that the real subject is themselves and their world.

After stretching their minds, it's only a short walk to the palace of hilarity and fond recollection called Childhood Memories Toy Museum. It's noisy and fun, as visitors rush from the familiar to the novel among the 7,000 clockwork and mechanical toys, dolls, teddies, pedal cars, prams, puzzles, games and memorabilia that fill the walls, floor and ceiling with colour, sound and movement. In this democracy of toyland, disposable plastic is as treasured as an early 20th-century tinplate classic. Surrender to the joy of the place.

WHERE:
Tynemouth, Tyne and Wear
BEST TIME TO GO:
June to September (also open April, May, October and November at weekends and school holidays).
DON'T MISS:
Riding a real steam train and the 1950s passenger coaches at the Railway Museum or the fabulous artwork of some truly bizarre board games and the vintage soundtracks that lend swagger and fun to the Toy Museum displays.
AMOUNT OF WALKING:
Moderate (and access is very good).
COST:
Nil at the Stephenson Museum; low at the Toy Museum
YOU SHOULD KNOW:
Because both museums are seasonal, check they are open before you go and find the best deal for your family or group and any restrictions (like height or age) that may apply to some of the exhibits. At the Stephenson Museum, most of the mechanical exhibits are in working order. They are necessarily kept well oiled, so beware sticky hands spreading grease and watch the children's clothes!

HMS Trincomalee and Hartlepool's Maritime Experience

Few things invoke glamour or glory more romantically than the Royal Navy in the era of Nelson. The centrepiece of Hartlepool's Maritime Experience is *HMS Trincomalee*, the oldest British warship still afloat. It's the real thing – a Leda-class sail frigate built in 1817 (to a design familiar to Nelson himself) for speed and superiority over anything of a comparable size. Now it's been revived as living history, with costumed guides to help you explore every rat-infested bilge and beeswax-polished Captain's sideboard. Pigtailed 'sailors' will show you how to tie important knots, haul on the rigging, take the quarterdeck wheel, avoid the recoil of the great guns, and dance a hornpipe.

Of course you'll want to jump ship to look at the quayside – all part of the HME's authentic 18th-century harbour. There's a chandler, gunsmith and naval tailor among the shops and gabled houses spread along the 'hard', with the Admiral's grand mansion in-between. You can go inside all of them, perhaps to try on a uniform or see a fowling piece demonstrated by a crack shot. Everywhere, guides in the clothes of the period – including passers-by – will be ready to explain procedures like operating a sextant. Keep your wits about you and listen for the tramp of a file of red-coated Marines on the cobbles. You could be 'press-ganged' – seized and sent to sea whether you like it or not. See the film about it instead and look out for the regular displays of musketry, cannon fire and sword fighting.

Hartlepool's Maritime Experience is the best kind of 'total museum'. *HMS Trincomalee* on its own is inexhaustibly fascinating. In the context of a miniature 18th-century society, complete in all essentials, it's just the dominant feature of one of the most imaginative, satisfying and good fun days out you can have in Britain.

WHERE:
Hartlepool, County Durham
BEST TIME TO GO:
Any time of year
DON'T MISS:
Hands-on maritime skills at the Children's Maritime Adventure Centre, or Fighting Ships – a multimedia narrative by a 'powder monkey' of weevils, grog and the 'cat-o-nine-tails' which ruled his life on board the frigate *HMS Prosperity* in 1800.
AMOUNT OF WALKING:
Lots, up and down – but wheelchair access is excellent, with a hoist between the *Trincomalee*'s decks.
COST:
Reasonable to expensive. Instead of a discount, there's a supplement to the entrance fee for groups of 20 or more.
YOU SHOULD KNOW:
Smaller children, especially, will enjoy the Playship and Skittle Square. With its crow's nest and captain's cabin, the adventure playship immediately transforms them into pirates and they can play quoits, hopscotch or skittles instead of computer games.

HMS Trincomalee, *an 18th-century restored warship in Hartlepool's Maritime Experience*

Killhope Mining Museum and Hamsterley Forest

The outstanding natural beauty of Upper Weardale makes the secret history of Killhope all the more vivid. Park Level Mine at Killhope is the north of England's Lead Mining Museum, restored and preserved as a testament to the region's paramount industry. Above ground, in the shadow of a massive Armstrong water wheel, you get the chance to dress up in Victorian clothes – children dress as 'waterboys' – to get in the spirit of historical adventure. Mining experts show you the machines that powered the mine, and how to enjoy the opportunities for hands-on participation. Then, with a hard-hat, lamp and stout wellies, you can descend into the mine itself! It's a real adventure that justifies Killhope's proud claim that 'It's Dark, it's Wet, it's Wonderful'. It's brilliant going down – but most visitors are just as glad to come up again. Suddenly, the surrounding woodlands, streams and wildlife look more intensely lovely and benign. They are – and you might see red squirrels, too.

After being underground, the perfect antidote is Hamsterley Forest, a short drive away at the eastern end of Weardale. Run by the Forestry Commission, Hamsterley is a 2,023-ha (5,000-acre) Area of Outstanding Natural Beauty catering to the widest possible range of interests. It's a paradise of wildlife, seasonal flowers, and tranquillity; and also an exciting resource for mountain bikers of every level, for whom a section of the forest is reserved, with marked trails. There's also a programme of regular events for children, such as Adventure Challenge, Play Day, Wild Creations, Den Making and Halloween Hauntings.

Or you may decide to just sit in the café or enjoy a picnic. You don't have to join in the organized activities at Hamsterley. Really, it's just a giant playground for families to do exactly as they choose.

WHERE:
Killhope is near Cowshill, Upper Weardale, County Durham; Hamsterley Forest is off the A68 near Witton-le-Wear, County Durham

BEST TIME TO GO:
April to September, and weekends in October

DON'T MISS:
The discomforts of the reconstructed Victorian miner's house and the collection of marvellous, coloured spar crystals retrieved from the mine; red squirrel spotting from the special hide along Killhope's Woodland Walk; or birdwatching in the magical oak and broadleaf woodlands along Bedburn Beck in Bedburn Valley, at Hamsterley.

AMOUNT OF WALKING:
Little to lots. Both sites have partial wheelchair access. At Hamsterley, friendly staff will point out or even assist you to the best places in the forest for views.

COST:
Reasonable at Killhope; under fours go free, but they are not allowed down the mine – there's a play park for them instead. Low at Hamsterley, where there is a small charge per car. Charges for organized activities are reasonable.

YOU SHOULD KNOW:
The Children's Adventure Challenge events at Hamsterley are designed primarily for eight to 13 year-olds but lots of other events are suitable for both younger and older children. Most of them involve getting messy and physical to some extent – so make sure everyone has suitable clothes. Remember that Killhope can be quite chilly, even in summer, because it's high in the Pennines.

A group of mountain bikers rides past foxgloves in Hamsterley Forest.

Broom House Adventure Farm and Beamish Wild Bird of Prey Conservation Centre

WHERE:
Near Witton Gilbert (Broom House Farm); near Stanley (Beamish Hall) – both close to Durham City
BEST TIME TO GO:
Any time of year
DON'T MISS:
Broom House Farm's Woodland Challenge, which includes climbing, hanging, zipping and balancing, and a constantly evolving range of 'problems' to be solved *en route*; stocking up on produce from the farm's shop and butchery.
AMOUNT OF WALKING:
Lots
COST:
Reasonable
YOU SHOULD KNOW:
In case of really vile weather, Broom House Farm has indoor activity provision. At any time, it has a very good coffee/lunch shop, with a play area attached for small children to enjoy while overseen.

On the open hillsides just outside the City of Durham, Broom House is an uncompromising working farm dedicated to achieving complete organic status. The owners are passionate in their belief that they can only be truly successful if they are transparent about what they do and how they do it, and the power of that transparency to get children onto the farm so they can learn about the relationship of farming and the countryside as a whole to the food they eat. The lovely surprise is that they've made what sounds like a strictly educational (for adults as well as children) outing into so much fun.

Going organic means performing heroic tasks like planting new hedges (to improve wildlife diversity), restoring ponds, and finding ways to sustain the countryside's natural beauty, as much as changing crop-growing methods and the ways of raising livestock. Rain or shine the work goes on, and visitors are welcome to help. Children love mucking in – carrying hay, chucking pellets, sluicing out buckets. Broom House also has an Adventure Trail, which requires participants to become 'nature detectives' and to join activities that involve some real orienteering and teamwork, with the family or their peers. Smiling faces and excited babble show that it works.

Afterwards, there's time to visit Beamish Wild Bird of Prey Conservation Centre. The Centre tries to replicate natural habitats for captive-bred species like eagles, African vultures, snowy owls, hawks and vultures. Under guidance, you can get close to and sometimes handle them. Baby barn owls are everyone's favourite!

Beamish Hall provides a really beautiful woodland setting for all these magnificent birds. Their soaring displays and lightning flight demonstrations will thrill you for years to come. At Broom House and Beamish Hall, you see and participate in two very different sides of conservation at its best.

Meeting the inhabitants of Beamish Wild Bird of Prey Conservation Centre.

Richmond Castle and the Green Howards Regimental Museum

The mellow North Yorkshire market town of Richmond can't ever escape its history. The town is dominated by its magnificent Norman castle, rearing 30 m (100 ft) above its perch on a steep bluff overlooking the River Swale. Children love it because it looks like something from a storybook. They quickly discover that the real history is even better – Richmond Castle was built by Alan the Red of Brittany on land given to him in 1070 by William the Conqueror, who took it from its Saxon owner, Earl Edwin of Mercia.

Armed only with a leaflet from the English Heritage kiosk, you can explore the huge site, imagining the battles, sieges and bloody deeds it has witnessed, from the Scottish raids of the 14th century to its use during World War I as a base for non-combatant conscientious objectors. The Great Courtyard used to have barracks where Lord Baden-Powell, founder of the Scouting movement, lived when he commanded the Northern Territorial Army from 1908 to 1910. They've gone now, but there's a programme of events, including re-enactments and exhibitions, to help children get the most from their visit.

Richmond's close association with Britain's military history is reinforced, and made more personal, by the Regimental Museum of the Green Howards. One of the best of its kind in the country, it houses a collection of artefacts and memorabilia covering 300 years of service in the Crimea, India's northwest frontier, the Boer War, and World Wars I and II. There are interactive displays specially designed to involve children, along with an object-handling area and a safari quiz. The Museum is careful to glorify regimental service and self-sacrifice instead of gruesome war itself.

Richmond Castle

WHERE:
Richmond,
North Yorkshire
BEST TIME TO GO:
Any time of year
DON'T MISS:
The massive keep, commissioned by Conan the Little, Earl of Richmond circa 1175; the Collins Collection of rare uniforms and head dress from 1768 to the present; the 3,750 medals and decorations presented to the Green Howards – including 16 of the 18 Victoria Crosses won by the Regiment, 'For Valour'.
AMOUNT OF WALKING:
Moderate, with good wheelchair access
COST:
Low
YOU SHOULD KNOW:
Richmond Castle was the HQ of the Honour of Richmond – a huge collection of different estates throughout Yorkshire and further afield.

The Forbidden Corner, the Dales Museum and the Wensleydale Creamery

Inside the Wenslydale Creamery

Full of fun and surprises, the Forbidden Corner near Leyburn is an invitation to stroll through a really beautiful park and gardens arranged as a labyrinth. It is endlessly good-humoured, a practical joke of an interactive maze where at any corner you might be faced with a bug-eyed gargoyle, a revolving floor, forest, waterfall, or a cherub armed with a well-aimed jet of water. There are tunnels and chambers, animated follies and sudden surprises. Children adore it – though it has to be said that some small tots (perhaps three or four years old) may be a little scared by grotesque carvings or noises in the dark that others find hilarious. There are always alternative paths. It takes about two hours to get round, though most visitors take a lot longer. The Forbidden Corner is a completely original kind of adventure playground that entertains children by provoking their imagination in the most delightful ways. Forget computerized special effects – they can enjoy this kind of inventiveness again and again.

The 20-km (12-mi) drive up Wensleydale to Hawes is one of Britain's loveliest – and a chance to recover from the fun at Forbidden Corner. Hawes is home to the Dales Countryside Museum, full of interactive displays that tell the history and culture of the Dales and their people. It's the kind of museum that quickly involves you in local life, and gets you participating in 'choosing' its potential future.

And you can't leave Hawes without stopping at the Wensleydale Creamery on the edge of town. It's where you can see how Wensleydale cheese (beloved of Wallace and Gromit) is made according to the most authentic practice – and you can sample it either in the demonstration room or in the restaurant/coffee bar. The cheese tasting comes as a perfect finale to the day.

YOU SHOULD KNOW:
You must book in advance for Forbidden Corner (though you can do so on the day), because its creators believe overcrowding would spoil the many surprises. And if the children are in a buggy, you'll miss out on many of the best bits, though you'll manage steps and other obstacles if you take them in a sling or papoose.

Big Sheep and Little Cow Farm, and Aerial Extreme

Across Bedale Beck from the ancient market town of Bedale, what was once Aiskew Water Mill is now called Big Sheep and Little Cow Farm. It's a working farm with a difference. All its livestock are chosen for their ready appeal to children, and for their friendly disposition when they are being fed, cleaned, or simply petted. The dairy herd is of Dexter cows, Britain's smallest breed and quite unthreatening to the curious eyes and hands of even the smallest children. Visits begin in the farm's Victorian kitchen with an explanation about health and safety, followed by a short tour to see what's happening in the fields and pens and a chance to meet and play with some of the smaller animals. Kids may bottle-feed the lambs, bathe a pig, cuddle a goat, tickle a hedgehog, pet a mouse and (for a small extra charge) ride a pony under friendly and informative supervision. The farm staff are happy to show children how to make the most of animal magic and the kids are fascinated by this intimacy with other species.

If the animals get too much for them (after all, proper farmyards are supposed to smell fruity!), there's Wooly Jumpers, a play barn full of slides, rope swings, climbing towers, spinning tops and bouncing nets. Adults can sit in the comfortable café with peace of mind.

From the farm it's no distance to Kirklington, where Aerial Extreme promises advanced versions of jumping, climbing, swinging, bouncing and balancing. Expertise isn't necessary – staff will check hard hats and safety harnesses, and launch everyone into an exhilarating, aerial world where they can be an eagle or swallow as easily as a Tarzan or Indiana Jones. The Junior Adventure Course, for six year olds up, makes the thrilling rides accessible to the whole family.

WHERE:
Bedale, Yorkshire
BEST TIME TO GO:
February to October
DON'T MISS:
The quad bikes at Big Sheep Farm – it's one of the few places where children (over six) can ride them in the fields and paddocks; the delicious homemade ice cream made from the farm's Dexter cows; defying gravity on the climbing walls and speeding down lengthy zip wires at Aerial Extreme.
AMOUNT OF WALKING:
Moderate – but both places inspire energetic participation. Wheelchair access is adequate at the farm, but only partial (for observation) at Aerial Extreme.
COST:
Reasonable at the farm (low if you only want to visit the play barn); expensive at Aerial Extreme.
YOU SHOULD KNOW:
There are some age and height restrictions at both sites. At Aerial Extreme you must be at least 1.4 m (4 ft 7 in) tall and 1.1 m (3 ft 7 in) for the Junior Adventure Course. New facilities may mean a change in requirements, so you should ring first to find out. Both sites offer all-weather entertainment and you could spend long periods outside – so don't forget to dress wisely in anticipation.

The Yorkshire Law and Order Museums at Ripon, and Newby Hall

WHERE:
Ripon, Yorkshire
BEST TIME TO GO:
Any time of year
DON'T MISS:
The audio-visual presentation of
actual cases, played while you stand
in the courthouse dock; the feeling
you get when the door slams on your
miserable cell in the prison; or the
Hard Times Gallery that describes the
deprivation of lives on both sides of
the workhouse gate.
AMOUNT OF WALKING:
Moderate, with good disabled access
and facilities, including parts of the
Adventure Garden.
COST:
Low at Ripon (one fee covers all
three museums and accompanied
children under 16 go free);
Newby Hall is fairly expensive just
to visit the gardens
YOU SHOULD KNOW:
Besides the many opportunities to
dress up and physically sample life in
prison, court or workhouse, the Ripon
Museums are notable for the
ingenuity of their interactive displays.
Initially reluctant and fearing
boredom, many children are reported
by their families as having had to be
dragged away.

Once they get inside, children become Ripon's Law and Order Museums' biggest fans. There are three, linked by themes of crime, its causes, and its retribution and punishment. The Prison and Police Museum building was Ripon's 17th-century House of Correction for Vagrants, its 19th-century Prison and 20th-century Police Station. Now, you can be (literally) 'banged up' in a cell, dressed in Victorian prison uniform, strapped in a restraint chair, or pilloried in the yard. The Courthouse Museum (restored to its original Georgian decorative scheme of 1830) will put you in the dock for sentencing – perhaps to transportation, as described in the exhibition One Way to Botany Bay. The grim severity of the Workhouse Museum was easy to create – the cells they lock you in (for a very short while) are part of the original 1854 Workhouse complex.

The authenticity of the buildings, the detail of the displays, and the appropriately horrid and stern atmosphere created by the costumed staff play to children's sense of fun (and adults' growing alarm at the little outlaws). Maybe the history of suffering and justice (merited or not) shouldn't provoke excited hilarity – but the museums make their point very successfully. Take a camera to record the children's many interactions with the Law!

Being so close to Ripon, it would be cruel to deprive yourself and the children of an afternoon at magnificent Newby Hall – at least to enjoy one of England's finest gardens, stretched along the River Ure. Among its many splendours is the children's Adventure Garden – a match for the Adam mansion of which it's part. It features the Tarantella interactive water play area and a wonderful miniature railway that tours the gardens (adults welcome, too). With pedaloes, climbing frames, a timber fort, slides and a swing pontoon, it is comprehensive, safe and superb.

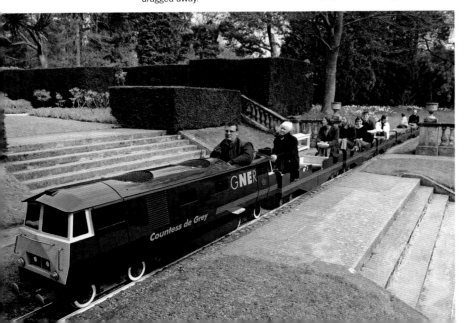

*A model train passing through
the garden at Newby Hall.*

Nidderdale Museum and How Stean Gorge

A re-creation of a local general store at Nidderdale Museum

The dramatic landscapes of the Area of Outstanding Natural Beauty surrounding Pateley Bridge in the Yorkshire Dales easily merit a special visit. Head for the Nidderdale Museum opposite St Cuthbert's Cross in the centre of Pateley Bridge. It's on the first floor of what was once the Victorian workhouse, and its 11 rooms are a vivid celebration of every aspect of Dales-folk life and history in that era. You see a series of tableaux, illustrating a Victorian parlour, kitchen, schoolroom, chemist's shop, haberdasher's, joiner's workshop, solicitor's office, general store and cobbler's shop – perhaps the best of them all. The artefacts and costumes are completely convincing and the imaginative displays inform you of not just how ordinary people lived, but how their lives influenced – and were influenced by – wider attitudes to religion, industrial progress, agriculture and even the development of transport. Children explore it like a treasure trove and launch themselves into hands-on games of 'let's pretend'.

Even the museum can't do justice to Nidderdale's natural beauty. It's only 11 km (7 mi) from Pately Bridge to How Stean Gorge, one of Nidderdale's, and Yorkshire's, greatest natural wonders. Almost completely hidden in lush pastureland and dense, broadleaf woods, How Stean is a spectacular limestone gorge about 1 km (0.62 mi) long. Its rock walls drop sheer for up to 20 m (65 ft) into deep pools, flattening out in places where the water rushes across huge boulders, carving them into slick whorls and u-shaped tunnels. It's paradise for all but the smallest children. Older ones can try abseiling, gorge scrambling or caving.

You can stick to the path and the footbridges, admiring nature at its most inspired from on high, or go adventuring down among the mosses, ferns, trees and lichen by the rushing beck. Afterwards, there's a café for exchanging travellers' tales and an adjacent children's play area.

WHERE:
Pateley Bridge, near Harrogate, Yorkshire
BEST TIME TO GO:
Any time of year. How Stean Gorge can be most impressive in winter, when How Stean Beck becomes a torrent.
DON'T MISS:
The cobbler's shop, and going down the mine at the Nidderdale Museum or the dripping stalactites in Tom Taylor's Cave at the gorge where a long underground passage leads to a chamber shaped 'like the belly of a whale' (you must carry a torch).
AMOUNT OF WALKING:
Lots – and the uneven ground at How Stean Gorge is unsuitable for wheelchairs. A hoist lift makes the Nidderdale Museum freely accessible.
COST:
Low at Nidderdale Museum; expensive at How Stean Gorge – but parking is free if you use the café, and there are other kinds of discount.
YOU SHOULD KNOW:
Wellies, hard hats and torches are available for hire at the gorge if you forget to take your own – whatever the weather, some places will be slippery and wet.

277

Plenty of interactive displays at Eureka!

Eureka! Museum for Children and Shibden Hall

WHERE:
Halifax, Yorkshire
BEST TIME TO GO:
Any time
DON'T MISS:
Scoot the Robot's giant teeth; the Ideas Garden, where (obviously!) you 'plant' ideas; the Early Years Activity Room, open only in the afternoons and with special staff.
AMOUNT OF WALKING:
Moderate (unless you take off at Shibden Hall)
COST:
Reasonable at Eureka! and a percentage of what you pay goes direct to the charitable foundation on which it depends; low at Shibden Hall.
YOU SHOULD KNOW:
On busy days at Eureka! your visit may be limited to three hours. Keep an eye on the special events at weekends and during school holidays; they include some wonderful 'screamers' like Blast Off!, Clowning Around and School for Witches and Wizards – but they change all the time.

Eureka! is simply inspired. Carefully and thoroughly thought through, from its easy access next to Halifax railway station to the intelligence and range of its exhibits and displays, it is a rare museum designed specifically to introduce children to the life sciences at work in the world about them.

The displays 'advertise' knowledge in the best sense, by promoting curiosity and a desire to find out more by pressing buttons, flipping switches or guiding a machine. Each age group 'grows' into the next band of understanding and participation, testing and being tested by the constant imaginative appeal of having fun.

There's lots for under fives – SoundGarden and Desert Discovery are just two galleries; even more for primary school children; and a huge array for pre- and early teens. Major themes, interpreted at different levels, include Me and My Body, Our Global Garden, SoundSpace and Town Square in which children play out imaginary 'realities' between the bank, supermarket, post office, kitchen and garage. Almost everything coaxes them into more engrossing interaction and participation. It's clever, compelling, and such fun.

The museum also has all the extras, such as a picnic area (in a railway carriage), storytelling and other events, a shop and an outside playground. The kids can't fail to have a really good time.

Afterwards you can cool pulses by winding down at Shibden Hall on the edge of Halifax. It's a beautiful 15th-century house full of glorious panelling and furniture. But at this point you may prefer the 37 ha (91 acres) of parkland, bluebell woods, meandering stream and lawns with boating lake, pitch-and-putt and a miniature train. Or you could marvel at the skills of the craftsmen working in wood and iron at the electricity-free barn of the Folk Museum. Have a cup of tea while you decide.

Ingleton Waterfalls trail and Ingleborough Cave

This is a spectacular day of crashing waterfalls, craggy ravines, dappled forest glades and the fresh, sweet green of one of Britain's most entrancing woodland walks. It's a circular trail of 8 km (5 mi) from Ingleton, deep in the Yorkshire Dales National Park, up the River Twiss as far as the old Roman road leading into Kingsdale. Here the woods open to reveal a vast panorama of the Southern Fells, with the bulk of Ingleborough – one of the Yorkshire Dales' celebrated Three Peaks – filling the skyline. Then you turn south and follow the River Doe downstream, back to Ingleton. The footpath is good, easy to follow, and though it twists and turns, is never more than a moderate incline up or down. It's easy going, too, for all but the smallest children (unless you carry them); and if distance is a problem, you can walk a shortened trail.

There are nine major waterfalls *en route*. Singles, doubles and triples as high as 30 m (100 ft) cut into deep ravines or cascade in series through the broadleaf woods and ancient oak forests. Local geology (limestone alternating with sandstone and slate) has created a series of dramatic landscapes full of rare flora and fauna. In fact much of the trail is designated as a Site of Special Scientific Interest, and if you pick up a leaflet with explanations of the trail's ecological importance before you set out, you'll enjoy the adventure all the more. Better still, get the children to 'interpret' the geology for you as they go.

You'll even have time for the stalactites and stalagmites of Ingleborough Cave afterwards. You can go up to half a kilometre inside the nearby complex – which connects to the 17-km (11-mi) Gaping Gill system – to marvel at its staggering natural wonders. It's a day for being awestruck by Nature.

WHERE:
Ingleton, near Settle, Yorkshire
BEST TIME TO GO:
Any time of year
DON'T MISS:
Thornton Force, the most famous of the Ingleton waterfalls, complete with an ideal picnic spot; the viewing bridge, spanning the sheer rocky drop of Baxenghyll Gorge; or the expert and anecdotal commentary at Ingleborough Cave, explaining its curious origins.
AMOUNT OF WALKING:
Lots. Patches of rough ground, steps, and changing levels mean there is no wheelchair access.
COST:
Low to reasonable – the leaflets, parking charges, etc, mount up.
YOU SHOULD KNOW:
Rain or shine, throughout the seasons and whatever the age group, the elemental forces brought together on the Waterfalls Trail touch the very soul of being. Children feel it instinctively as bubbling excitement.

Beck Isle Museum and Ryedale Folk Museum

WHERE:
Pickering and Hutton-le-Hole, Yorkshire
BEST TIME TO GO:
March to October (Beck Isle Museum); any time of year (Ryedale Folk Museum)
DON'T MISS:
The witch post at Stang End Cruck House (one of only 20 known examples and supposed to prevent witches entering a house) or the working forge – both at Ryedale.
AMOUNT OF WALKING:
Lots. Both museums have good wheelchair access to most exhibits.
COST:
Low
YOU SHOULD KNOW:
The Beck Isle Museum and the Ryedale Folk Museum complement each other perfectly – your day is half indoors and half out. You see two sides of North Yorkshire's loveliest countryside, one of its most interesting market towns and one of its prettiest villages – a doubly wonderful day out.

Just about the first thing they do at the Beck Isle Museum in Pickering is to get the children dressed up in a hat, waistcoat or smock. It transports them into the spirit of the museum's interpretation of Victorian life in Ryedale's rural culture. The galleries are dressed as rooms which you enter. Life-sized figures are frozen in mid-movement and conversation in tableaux of shops, workshops, businesses and domestic rooms. Crammed with accessible artefacts with obvious stories to tell, these rooms are entrancing to touch and explore. Learning is by sympathetic osmosis, and it's fun. There's a complete market town community to visit; a chemist's shop, nursery, village pub, gents' outfitter, cobbler's shop, Victorian parlour, and children's room are among the 27 display areas. The accuracy of these creations can be verified by the Sydney Smith collection of photographs of old Ryedale, in another room. Beck Isle Museum sends you away enlarged by its warm embrace and direct appeal to children.

Drive up the moors a short way to the stunning and ancient village of Hutton-le-Hole. Here you can explore a much bigger version of Ryedale's history and culture. The Ryedale Folk Museum is Yorkshire's best open-air collection and tells the story of the region's evolution as an agricultural community. There's an Elizabethan manor, a cruck house, shops, cottages and barns that illustrate Ryedale's development from Neolithic times to the early 1950s – whole rural 'streets' of real buildings from various eras, rescued and reconstructed, and it's full of artefacts to handle and operate. There are rare breeds and other livestock, craft demonstrations, music performances, medieval re-enactments, archaeology trails for children and a regular programme of special events. Children love its variety, rushing around, and the vintage sweet shop.

Medieval re-enactors at the Ryedale Folk Museum

A cruise boat on the River Ouse with the Guildhall and Lendal Bridge in the background

A boat on the River Ouse and York Model Railway

Many visitors to York are taken aback by the crowds wanting to see the same sights, but you can tour quite a bit of the city in comfort and style by boat on the River Ouse, York's principal river. If you've got children, this is a good option.

Boat trips start from King's Staith or Lendal Bridge, which is beautifully decorated with iron scroll work and the city's heraldic emblems. The standard journey lasts about an hour and includes a commentary. You may prefer to retreat to the onboard lounge and bar, but then you won't see where the Saxons fought the Vikings in 1066, or where witches were ducked in the Middle Ages. There are different kinds of trip, too. One goes through York all the way to Bishopthorpe Palace, the Archbishop of York's home. Another is timed for spring and autumn evenings, when the twilight creates the right atmosphere for some of the most eerie, weird, and occasionally gruesome tales in York's colourful history. You can even hire your own little motorboat and sail the river to your own timetable. Whatever kind of trip you choose, you get a really privileged view of York's historic buildings and the children get an adventure.

From the river, you only have to walk as far as the railway station to find the York Model Railway. It's next to, but distinct from, the Railway Museum with the big locos. The Model Railway is a child's idea of Hornby 00 gauge heaven. Central to it are four oval track systems, 320 m (1,000 ft) of track, and 14 trains running through beautifully constructed landscapes of town and countryside. They include an Intercity 125, the Orient Express, the Royal Train, and a whole Thomas the Tank Engine display which children are allowed to operate.

WHERE:
York
BEST TIME TO GO:
April to October
DON'T MISS:
The tree-lined avenue of New Walk, which runs by the river from Tower Gardens (downstream) to the Millennium Bridge. Created in 1730, it was one of the first acts of deliberate gentrification in Britain. If you're lucky you might see a longboat full of Vikings, raucously practising for one of their frequent 'dragon boat' races on the river.
AMOUNT OF WALKING:
Almost none – and there's full access to the river boats.
COST:
Reasonable (and for a family, hiring your own motorboat is very competitive)
YOU SHOULD KNOW:
The Ouse is perfect for boat trips. From it you can see across the heart of York and in a short time it can take you, however briefly, into really lovely countryside. It makes a welcome change of medium and pace for the whole family.

Abbey House Museum and Leeds Industrial Museum at Armley Mills

WHERE:
Leeds, Yorkshire
BEST TIME TO GO:
Any time
DON'T MISS:
Stephen Harding Gate, the 19th-century equivalent of a modern high street; a real Humpty Dumpty (one of several popular storybook characters to come alive), falling off a wall to entertain toddlers – both at Abbey House; or the awesomely big machinery at Armley Mills – water wheels, steam engine and huge, spinning 'mules', preferably in action.
AMOUNT OF WALKING:
Moderate, and there is wheelchair access almost everywhere.
COST:
Low
YOU SHOULD KNOW:
Working mills have occupied the same site at Armley Mills since the 17th century. Perhaps the presentations and activities of the museum are sympathetic and engrossing to children because they are the real thing and are imbued with the joys and hardships of all those who lived and worked there in the past.

The oldest part of Abbey House was once the inner gatehouse of 12th-century Kirkstall Abbey, the ruin across the road. It is fitting that now it's a museum of Leeds' social history and one of the finest of its ilk. The museum is laid out as a reconstruction of everyday life in the Leeds of 1880. Complete, named streets (rescued in the 1950s and now refurbished) of houses, shops, offices and businesses, peopled by costumed guides and posed mannequins, create a past of sound, smell and touch that is spookily convincing. They brim with life, as children in authentic costume (they are encouraged to dress up) rush happily from one activity, role-play or re-enactment to another. The separate Childhood Gallery includes Victorian toys and games in a collection of national importance and, like everything else at Abbey House, its primary function is learning through interactive fun. The street reconstructions are used in a rota of regular activities, targeting different age groups (like the Early Years programmes). Check in advance to get the ones you want.

The Leeds Industrial Museum at Armley Mills, just down the road from Abbey House, describes the origin and development of the industries that made Leeds great. It's a heavyweight museum – with stone buildings, cobbled paths and vast, complex machines ready to spit fire in memory of the 'dark, satanic mills' that crushed men, women and children in pursuit of wealth for a few and power for an elite – relieved by a light touch. Who would predict that the story of heavy industry could be made so exciting, or elicit children's enthusiastic participation? Full credit to friendly staff and imaginative planning: at Armley Mills they make serious industrial history a joy to learn, with non-stop, interactive displays and events for every age group.

National Coal Mining Museum and underground pit tour

Caphouse Colliery near Wakefield is the National Coal Mining Museum for England. The Colliery opened in the 18th century, and though it now incorporates every 21st-century safety requirement, you can't help being aware that the basic hardships of miners' lives, and the inherent dangers of the mining industry, haven't changed at all in over 200 years.

It's a real tribute to the friendly guides (all ex-miners) that they can inspire visitors, and especially children, to have such fun and excitement, and simultaneously reinforce the dignity and social importance of an industry that once undervalued its personnel.

Kids respond to the social history of mining quicker than adults. They are fascinated to learn how children like themselves were exploited at every phase of the mining process, but excluded from the few celebrations that raised adult mineworkers' morale – like the parades and galas where dozens of colourful colliery banners proclaimed local allegiances. Visitors can participate with costumed staff in role-playing.

Hope Pit, also within the museum, is a complex of historic pit buildings full of interactive exhibits about mining communities. Kids giggle at the pit baths (adults shudder), and want to adopt the pit ponies. If you stop at the café, or for a picnic, you may need the adventure playground to calm them down. The highlight, of course, is going down the pit. Hard hats and 2-kg (4-lb 7-oz) light-packs are compulsory: it's the real thing and there are a lot of tunnels. It's worth travelling a long way just for this. The guides bring out all the drama and threat, and the humour of the men, women and children who have toiled alongside pit animals in the dripping darkness, often in cupboard-sized spaces. It's a tour no child will forget, and nor will you.

WHERE:
Wakefield, Yorkshire
BEST TIME TO GO:
Any time
DON'T MISS:
Going down the mine – numbers are necessarily restricted, so you need to book your (free) tickets early in the day; the mini-train that runs (most of the time) between museum installations – there's a small charge to ride it, but like the Mini-Miners indoor play area, it's a treat for the under fives who are not allowed down the mine.
AMOUNT OF WALKING:
Lots. All the mine headgear and exhibition buildings are ramped for wheelchair access.
COST:
Free, though there are small charges for the mini-train and some of the special events.
YOU SHOULD KNOW:
It's 140 m (435 ft) in a cage to the bottom of the mineshaft. Even in summer wear warm clothes; the underground tour lasts 75 minutes.

The famous Davy Lamp is explained to these visitors.

Say cheese!

National Media Museum and IMAX

There aren't many places where you can unconditionally guarantee that you'll have a great time. The National Media Museum at Bradford is one of them. Children probably need to be five years old to absorb activity information independently, and there's plenty to captivate younger ones (and facilities to deal with them) – but the older they are, the more fun they'll have. There are seven floors of archives, galleries and exhibition spaces. Experience TV is just one, an almost symbiotic hands-on participatory adventure into television history. TV Heaven provides nothing less than your favourite programmes from the past, and a host of TV characters 'in the flesh' – you could meet Gordon the Gopher, Captain Scarlet or a rather stern Dalek.

In the Magic Factory you get the chance to play with light, colour and lenses and you can find out how different kinds of animation work as well as watch a professional animator at work, before trying out techniques for yourself, in the Animation Gallery. Everywhere, you can plug into world-class resources like the BBC to retrieve or play with film and television materials. In addition, at any time you can join in a non-stop schedule of children's festivals, sleepovers, special events, cult film showings, talks and exhibitions.

Then there's IMAX. The first time you experience its gigantic magnificence, you just gasp. Some IMAX films are in 3-D for which you wear special glasses to get the full effect. Especially popular films are the dripping rainforest, and the lions prowling a Botswana waterhole with their pride, so vivid you cower in your seat when they leap at you – but you may prefer to see an IMAX version of the latest Hollywood blockbuster (for which there will be an extra charge). One tip is not to take young children too close to the front: they can feel overwhelmed.

WHERE:
Bradford, Yorkshire
BEST TIME TO GO:
Any time
DON'T MISS:
Iconic objects made by BBC's *Blue Peter* presenters, especially the Thunderbirds Tracy Island; the Cinematography Exhibition of equipment used by the pioneers of filmmaking; or the historic photographs of the William Henry Fox Talbot Collection.
AMOUNT OF WALKING:
Moderate – and the wheelchair access is excellent.
COST:
The museum is free, except for certain events; IMAX is reasonable.
YOU SHOULD KNOW:
The museum is one of Britain's greatest days out for kids – and everyone else, too. You can go again and again and it will never be the same. The Bradford IMAX was the first IMAX cinema in Europe and the screen is so big that it had to be lowered into the auditorium through the roof.

Weston Park Museum and the Tropical Butterfly House, Wildlife and Falconry Centre

Going to Weston Park Museum is a bit like wandering round the gigantic attic of someone's family house, accompanied by a charming member of that family to make sense of the different treasures accumulated by its many generations. Recently reorganized to make its collections more accessible to children, the museum has six main rooms, each a hive of interactive treats.

The displays tell fascinating stories, illustrated by often-bizarre combinations of whatever exhibits Sheffield possesses. Sheffield Life and Times includes a re-creation of a period butcher's shop (with smell-o-vision), a Bronze Age pottery from the Peak District, a model hedgehog, and videos of the great flood and World War II. The History Workshop allows children to dress up as Anglo-Saxon 'maidens' and 'yeomen' to play time-travelling historical detectives on slick electronics. The Activity Rooms are busy with Little Explorers Art Time or Under 4s Explore sessions with toys and storybooks associated with the major displays. There are family trails for four to 11 year olds (and their parents!) such as What's Bugging You? and Opposites Attract – quests for the weird, the rare and the (sometimes) disgusting objects on display. A rolling programme of events and children's activities is guided by staff with the same imaginative flair they bring to the museum as a whole.

Sheffield's determination to give children every opportunity to discover their world is equally evident at the Tropical Butterfly House, Wildlife and Falconry Centre, a short bus ride or drive away. Allow several hours for gawping at creepy-crawlies as well as gorgeous butterflies, parrots and other magnificent birds, the alligator and the Baby Bunkhouse; playing with free-roaming farm animals; gasping at the birds of prey; and taking the Walk On The Wild Side. The Family Fun House, packed with big and little games equipment, is the icing on the entertainment cake.

WHERE:
Sheffield, Yorkshire
BEST TIME TO GO:
Any time of year
DON'T MISS:
Snowy, the polar bear with ideas, and the very old and rare Native American (Indian) shirt at Weston Park. Meerkat Mansion and the leaf-cutter ants above your head (behind glass) on the march with their enormous loads at the Tropical Butterfly House.
AMOUNT OF WALKING:
Moderate, with very good wheelchair access
COST:
Free, at Weston Park Museum (but you may have to book for certain regular events or activities, because of their popularity); reasonable at the Tropical Butterfly House.
YOU SHOULD KNOW:
Though both these collections are organized for their maximum appeal to children of different age groups, and both are proud of their fabulous toys and indoor and outdoor play areas, children are still expected to be accompanied by an adult – who will enjoy both places just as avidly.

The Yorkshire Planetarium

WHERE:
Harewood House, near Leeds, Yorkshire
BEST TIME TO GO:
Mid March to early November; the Planetarium operates every day during school and Bank Holidays, but is closed to the public on Mondays and Fridays during term time.
DON'T MISS:
Admiring the clarity of the Milky Way (our own galaxy!) in a pure night sky, with a meteor shower diving through it; using the opportunity to link up with YESnet (Yorkshire Education and Space Network) which promotes numerous activities for children in conjunction with the Planetarium.
AMOUNT OF WALKING:
Little
COST:
Expensive – you may have to buy a Harewood House Below Stairs/Gardens ticket, and pay an extra charge to enter the Planetarium. Check in advance – the method of charging for the Planetarium has changed each year it has been open.
YOU SHOULD KNOW:
Children must be at least six years old to enter the Star Theatre – the darkness and the length and content of the presentation make it unsuitable for the very young. But if your ticket includes the Harewood House Gardens, you can take them to the superb adventure playground or try boating on the lake.

To visit the Yorkshire Planetarium, you must go to Harewood House, near Leeds. Originally planned as a temporary attraction, the Planetarium's three linked geodesic domes proved an instant success with both visitors and professional boffins. Now they form the heart of a permanent installation, expanded and redesigned to appeal more directly to children, with a variety of interactive discovery trails. Actually, they boggle the imagination whatever age you are. One dome holds the Star Theatre, with the only Zeiss projector of its kind in the UK, which enables you to see the night sky without light pollution or atmospheric interference – they give you a mat so you can lie on the floor gazing upwards while an expert gives a magical presentation explaining the stars and galaxies above. Next door the kids can scale the Rocket Tower, a behemoth of a climbing frame 8 m (26 ft) high with a slide from its highest point. It's the same size as a real booster rocket, and already legendary among Yorkshire schoolchildren.

The third dome houses a giant screen where many short interactive presentations about astronomy, space travel, and the way the galaxies function may be enjoyed. One eerie and fascinating presentation involves the astounding images downloaded daily from the Hubble Telescope Team in California. Increasingly, too, you can watch 3-D films here, some of which inspire the workshop projects you may be able to try when you visit (rolling programmes mean you need to check what's on in advance). The Dark Sky Yorkshire project of 2009 offered air rocket construction and 'space origami' so that visitors could create and test their own rockets or models. Justly called the Futuredome, this space is where children get primary wonder to fuel their curiosity.

Magna Science Adventure Centre

Children can hardly believe their luck when they get to Rotherham's Magna Science Adventure Centre. Inside it's all walkways, platforms, scissor lifts, stairs and tunnels threading between 3-D screens and ascending many levels within the 32-m (100-ft) high building. This is the setting for the 'ultimate interactive experience', an invitation to explore the latest technology and life sciences using all five senses to follow trails, play games, test ideas and speculate on possible answers to big questions.

Deep inside the novel structure (a huge former steelworks) are four pavilions full of challenges and activities relating to the four elements. They go far beyond the usual 'hands-on'. You can explode a rock face and shunt rocks with a real JCB (earth); fire giant water cannon (water); go spinning in a gyroscopic chair (air); or create a terrifying 5-m (20-ft) fire tornado and a virtual fireball (in complete safety). There are over 100 interactive exhibits – provocative, stimulating, dramatic and enormous fun. The Centre's pyrotechnic and acrobatic bravura extends as well to its two permanent displays, which commemorate South Yorkshire's glorious steelmaking heritage. One of them, Big Melt, is set around the steel mill's original arc furnace. You feel its heat, hear its roar and squint through the fiery intensity – only the river of actual molten steel is missing from the experience.

Outside, the Sci-Tek and Aqua-Tek play areas are equally inspired by science but pitched at a younger clientele. But there's nothing didactic about the unusual playground equipment, or any of the Magna Centre's inspired showpieces. It's enough that merriment provokes youthful curiosity – and there are good people on the spot to answer questions. The Magna Centre is in every way a first-class treat.

The Magna Science Adventure Centre

WHERE:
Rotherham, Yorkshire
BEST TIME TO GO:
Any time
DON'T MISS:
Getting your hands on the life-size JCB or bringing history to life on the giant audio-visual set-ups of the Face of Steel displays.
AMOUNT OF WALKING:
Moderate – and although there are stairs, there is excellent alternative wheelchair access to the pavilions (and even to the zeppelin-shaped pod housing the 'Air' display, which is suspended from the ceiling).
COST:
Expensive, but worth it
YOU SHOULD KNOW:
Adults can join in everything – and will want to. The Centre deserves a high rating for novelty, interest, fun, adventure and participation.

The Deep, the *Arctic Corsair*, and the Streetlife Museum of Transport

WHERE:
Hull, Yorkshire
BEST TIME TO GO:
Any time
DON'T MISS:
Putting your head in a bubble at the top of a ladder in the Lagoon of Light – you'll be face to face with hundreds of dazzling tropical fish, with a periscope for all-round vision; the astounding interactive marine games in the Submarium; the soft-play area for under eights, called Hullaballoo – invaluable for winding down their excitement; the Laughing Policeman and many other vintage mechanical games at Streetlife.
AMOUNT OF WALKING:
Moderate. Wheelchair access is excellent at the Deep and at Streetlife, but not the *Arctic Corsair*, because of raised thresholds on its watertight doors in the narrow companionways.
COST:
The Deep is reasonable. Visiting the Corsair and Streetlife is free.
YOU SHOULD KNOW:
Growing popularity means there are sometimes queues at the Deep. Book online and you save 10 per cent and avoid queuing. A visit there lasts from two to three hours, though children sometimes want to stay forever.

The Deep does for the marine world what the Eden Project does for earth sciences. Inside what looks like a giant ship's hull on a slipway next to the water is a 10-m (35-ft) tank holding 2.5 million litres of salt water, a revolutionary kind of aquarium which tells the story of the world's oceans. It's spectacular to the point of being shocking: you walk among the sharks, rays and 3,500 fish of all species and all continents, through a series of acrylic and glass tunnels spanning the water at different depths. They lead to themed spaces like the Ocean Planet, the Coral Realm, Slime!, The Lagoon of Light, the Industrial Seas, the Twilight Zone, the Kingdom of Ice and Deep Blue One, in which you 'take command' of a deep-ocean research station of the future and its three 3-D screens, and where you can 'pilot' a submarine. If you're not hypnotized by the real marine world before you, there are numerous games to play and buttons or levers to operate.

It gets better. After descending through these fishy worlds, you walk through the deepest viewing tunnel in Europe, right at the bottom, before ascending to the surface via the world's only underwater lift. You are literally 'in' the teeming ocean! You'll be as enraptured as the children – and the Deep acknowledges this by suggesting you keep your tickets so you can return for a free visit within a year. Before or after you visit the Deep, don't miss boarding the *Arctic Corsair*, the last surviving 'side winder' deep-sea trawler, and witness to Britain's fishing heritage. You'll find it moored behind the Streetlife Museum of Transport in Hull's old town. Streetlife is also worth visiting – it re-creates an old street scene to show off trams, tricycles, carriages and cars from 200 years of transport evolution.

Children enjoying the Deep.

Seaside fun at Bridlington

Bridlington is, above all, a family resort – a perfect balance between natural beauty, heritage interest, and award-winning promenades full of carnival sideshows, fairground rides and old-fashioned amusements. It's a bucket-and-spade, ice-cream-cone delight of a town where you do things on a whim and the only bother is choosing. Bridlington really does have it all. Immaculate sandy beaches curve away either side of an historic harbour, bustling with colour. Squawking seabirds compete with the Wurlitzer crescendos and flashing neon of funfair rides. There's a Kiddies Corner, donkey rides, sandcastles and beach rounders. The Beside the Seaside Museum records Bridlington's most fashionable era with terrific photos and memorabilia, and its most popular era with life-sized models in string vests, knotted handkerchiefs and rolled-up trousers. The museum is by the harbour, from which you can take a speedboat trip across the bay, or a cruise up the spectacular coast to the nature reserve at Flamborough Head, which is clouded by soaring birds.

If Bridlington makes you feel you're in another world, it's because of its integrity in continuing to have faith in simple entertainments. Old Penny Memories is a collection of antique slot machines which use old money, available on the spot. An old penny isn't much to see What the Butler Saw, and these machines are historic. Children will prefer the Bondville Model Village or John Bull's World of Rock, a paradise of chocolate, biscuits, nougat and rock with letters through it. You can tour the factory and even make your own rock and lollies, for a small fee.

In between everything else, the beach comes into its own. You can race on it, flop in the surf, build a wave-filled moated sandcastle, sunbathe, or volunteer to be buried in sand up to your neck. Bridlington is a waiting invitation to have fun.

Old-fashioned seaside fun at Bridlington

WHERE:
Bridlington, Yorkshire
BEST TIME TO GO:
April to October
DON'T MISS:
Grumpy Len in the 1950s boarding house display at Beside the Seaside or the pleasure-boat cruise – for just an hour, it transports you into a different, marine world and you see the magnificent heritage coastline in a completely novel way.
AMOUNT OF WALKING:
Little or lots, according to your energy. Wheelchair access varies greatly – but there is at least one circular beach walk designed for the purpose.
COST:
Low in general, but the total can easily mount, depending on which activities you choose.
YOU SHOULD KNOW:
Of course Bridlington is just as well equipped as other resorts with attractions like swimming pools with water slides, wave machines and rain effects, a big wheel ride, aqua-blaster and dodgems. But it's the offer of an alternative, slower pace that makes it a great resort for a day out

Spurn Point National Nature Reserve and RAF Holmpton bunker tour

WHERE:
Withernsea, near Hull, Yorkshire

BEST TIME TO GO:
Any time (Spurn Head); March to October (RAF Holmpton – which is only open in the afternoon and, by arrangement, in the evening).

DON'T MISS:
At Spurn Head the orchids in summer and the yellow birds foot trefoil known locally as 'egg and bacon'; at Holmpton the massive Blast Doors deep in the tunnels of the Command Bunker – an indication of the anticipated level of threat during an attack – as well as the audio-visual presentation (in the original Radar Operations Centre) to explain why the base was necessary.

Spurn Head forms a natural breakwater between the Humber and the North Sea. It's the long, sandy spit that arcs 5 km (3.5 mi) from Yorkshire across the Humber estuary, with sandy beaches on its seaward side and mud flats on the other. The ancient grey dunes and chalk grassland in between narrow to just 46 m (150 ft) in places, but provide habitats and feeding grounds for a huge variety of resident and migrant bird species. The area has been protected as a National Nature Reserve for 50 years, and now it's a birdwatcher's paradise. Even if you're not one of them, you can't help getting excited by the thousands of waders and raucous squadrons of sea birds wheeling between flights of brightly coloured visitors. Walking there is like exploring a marine-scape wilderness. It feels elemental and exhilarating.

In every season there's plenty of thrilling wildlife. You can look for fossils, too: the beach is littered with them. If you get that far (you can drive, for a small toll fee), Spurn Head itself has both a lighthouse and a lifeboat station – the only one in Britain to have a full, salaried crew. They may be the only other people you see. Spurn Head's remoteness makes it a fabulous place to forget the world and open yourself to nature.

On the way home you can go from the sublime to the simply alarming at RAF Holmpton near Withernsea. It's too good to miss – a chance to see a genuine post Cold War Warfare Command Centre, recently declassified and restored. The presentations are slick and military: this is the real thing, from its beginning in 1953 as an Early Warning Radar Station to its intended role as Experimental Electronic Warfare Operations Centre (CCIS) in the 1990s. It's a chilling, but illuminating, two hours and the nuclear warhead is real.

AMOUNT OF WALKING:
Lots, and wheelchair access is very limited at both Spurn Head and RAF Holmpton.
COST:
Low at Spurn Head; reasonable at RAF Holmpton
YOU SHOULD KNOW:
Children's fact packs (full of things to do at Spurn Head) are available on site. Check the tides before you go – with a rise of up to 7 m (26 ft), the mid-point of the spit can be breached. With the Cold War now a subject on the national curriculum, a visit to RAF Holmpton is a valuable inspiration for older children, as well as being strangely good fun.

Walking the dunes at Spurn Head.

Windermere and the World of Beatrix Potter

WHERE:
Windermere, Cumbria
BEST TIME TO GO:
Any time of year (but note that during the winter months there are half as many scheduled cruises on the lake).
DON'T MISS:
The virtual dive bell at the Lakes Aquarium for an interactive (and dry) encounter with hippos, sharks and crocodiles!
AMOUNT OF WALKING:
Little
COST:
Expensive (but you can save money with a combined cruise and Lakes Aquarium ticket).
YOU SHOULD KNOW:
If you want to add some authenticity to your Beatrix Potter experience, you can also visit Hill Top, the small farmhouse bought by the writer on the western side of Windermere where many of her tales first saw the light of day.

The largest of the English lakes is the focus for this day out which begins in the bustling resort of Bowness-on-Windermere on the lake's eastern shore. Here you can immerse yourself in the fictional realm of one of the Lake District's great literary figures. Long before the exploits of young master Harry had fired youthful imaginations, another Potter was leaving her indelible mark on the world of childhood. Beatrix Potter fell in love with the Lakeland countryside as a young girl on family holidays from London, and the tales she later composed and illustrated about her family of animals – 23 in all – are lovingly re-created in three-dimensional form at the World of Beatrix Potter. It may be unashamedly aimed at younger audiences, but grown-ups would be hard-hearted indeed not to be moved by the looks of delight on children's faces as they encounter Mrs Tiggy-Winkle in her kitchen or Jeremy Fisher on his pond. The cheeky little bunny that started it all off is commemorated in Peter Rabbit's Garden, where pride of place among the varied plants goes naturally enough to the lettuces and carrots.

When you've had enough of the crowds in Bowness, escape to the lake itself for a gentle cruise down to its southern end. This is what prompted the first wave of mass tourism to The Lakes in the mid 19th century, and the appeal of gliding past vistas of wooded hills backed by grandiose fells and crags remains undimmed to this day. Disembark at Lakeside to have a look at the Lakes Aquarium, which concentrates on the wildlife of freshwater habitats. Its most spectacular feature is an underwater tunnel that gives you a lakebed view of perch, carp and diving ducks; keep your eyes peeled, too, for the giant catfish that lurks on the bottom.

The World of Beatrix Potter with Peter Rabbit

Ravenglass and Eskdale Railway

Looking at the toytown colours of the steam trains that chug up and down the valley of the river Esk, it is difficult to believe that this delightful little railway started life as a grimly industrial line, ferrying iron ore from the mines of upper Eskdale to the coastal port of Ravenglass. The latter years of the 19th century were boom times for West Cumbria, as the extraction of iron and other minerals from the Lakeland hills fed an apparently insatiable demand for construction materials. You can still find evidence of the old workings up in the fells, but down in the valley all traces of the line's commercial origins are long since gone, quarrying operations in the area having ceased over 50 years ago.

Instead, what you have is one of the country's most spectacular narrow-gauge railways, lovingly maintained nowadays by enthusiasts. Most people begin their journey on La'al Ratty (as the line is affectionately known) on the coast at Ravenglass, where a small museum covers the line's history and where there is a connection to the main West Cumbrian line. Take time before you set off to admire the locomotive that is going to pull you on the 11-km (7-mi) route up the beautiful Esk valley to the terminus at Dalegarth. Most trains are steam-hauled and the weather determines if you travel in open-top or covered carriages. The whole journey takes some 45 minutes and a day ticket allows you to hop on and off at stations along the route. A favourite among the many walking options is the short trail from Dalegarth to the waterfall at Stanley Force. There are other more surprising sights, too, such as the Japanese garden at Eskdale Green and the well-preserved 16th-century flour mill outside Boot.

WHERE:
Ravenglass, Cumbria
BEST TIME TO GO:
April to October
DON'T MISS:
The interior of the Ratty Arms, the pub next to the station platform at Ravenglass, is an extraordinary evocation of the 1950s.
AMOUNT OF WALKING:
Lots
COST:
Reasonable (children get a free scratch card game with their ticket to help while away the time if the scenery gets boring).
YOU SHOULD KNOW:
You can take bikes on the train but they have to be pre-booked. A good alternative to the round trip is to take bikes up to Dalegarth and then return along the cycle trail that is suitable for all ages.

The River Esk Steam Engine

Cars of the Stars and Honister Slate Mine

Have you ever wondered what happens to the four-wheeled stars of film and TV – vehicles like the DeLorean in *Back to the Future* and Mad Max's Interceptor, which generated as much excitement as the stars driving them? Well, these and many others have ended up in the Cars of the Stars Motor Museum

The Batmobile – one of three in the museum

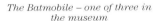

in Keswick. As so often, what started as one man's obsession has evolved into a major collection of many of the most iconic motors of the silver screen; thus alongside the DeLorean and the Interceptor you will see perennial favourites such as Herbie the Love Bug, Mr Bean's Mini, Chitty Chitty Bang Bang and the A-Team van. There are no fewer than three Batmobiles and *Thunderbirds* fans will adore the pink extravaganza that is Lady Penelope's FAB1 Rolls, which Gerry Anderson took to the movie premiere.

The museum's impressively large collection of James Bond cars, featuring everything from 007's customized Aston Martins to the tuk-tuk taxis from *Octopussy*, has outgrown its original home in a converted garage and is now housed in its own building ten minutes' walk away.

A drive along the shores of Derwent Water takes you south into Borrowdale and classic Lakeland scenery. Little prepares you for what follows – a steep, snaking climb up to the bleak and rugged Honister Pass. This isolated, inhospitable place was once a hive of commercial activity, where the region's distinctive grey-green slate was quarried. The old slate mine has been re-opened as a heritage enterprise where you can watch demonstrations of 'riving' (splitting) the slate and shop for slate products. What you should not miss is the guided tour of the old mines, which gives you a sobering – and chilly – insight into working conditions during their Victorian heyday.

WHERE:
Keswick and Honister, Cumbria
BEST TIME TO GO:
April to October
DON'T MISS:
The chance to see slate being shaped and processed by expert hands.
AMOUNT OF WALKING:
Moderate
COST:
Reasonable (expensive if you visit the James Bond cars as well).
YOU SHOULD KNOW:
Even if you are already prepared for visiting this famously wet part of the country, you are advised to wear special clothing for the cold and wet conditions underground.

Easedale Tarn

For all its many attractions tailored to families, the Lake District's primary appeal has always been the great outdoors. With some of the country's most inspiring scenery it has long been a Mecca for walkers and nature lovers alike. If you want to show the more reluctant members of the family what all the fuss is about, the walk from Grasmere to Easedale Tarn is an easy, non-threatening introduction to the delights of Lakeland. Although close to the tourist hotspot of Grasmere village with its Wordsworth connections, Easedale Tarn benefits from having no road access, which has helped to preserve its air of tranquillity and raw beauty.

Take the Easedale road out of the village and turn left to cross a bridge over the Easedale Beck. The route runs over fields with a clear view in the distance of the waterfalls at Sour Milk Gill – so called because in full flood the water looks like churning milk. Keep heading towards the falls for a short scramble up the left side (the only serious climb on the walk). At the top you are rewarded with fine views down the valley to Grasmere. From here it is a short distance to the tarn itself which sits in a splendid crater-like bowl, ringed by steep hillsides and fell-tops. The grassy hillocks around the little lake make excellent picnic spots. You could also take a dip, but be warned: the water in these high-level tarns never really warms up and temperatures drop sharply just below the surface.

You can return the way you came but for a change of scenery and a more interesting route, cross the stream at the tarn and head back down the valley of Far Easedale.

WHERE:
Grasmere, Cumbria
BEST TIME TO GO:
April to October
DON'T MISS:
The views of the fells surrounding the tarn – Castle How, Blea Crag and Tarn Crag.
AMOUNT OF WALKING:
Lots (the basic walk is 6.4 km (4 mi) there and back).
COST:
Low
YOU SHOULD KNOW:
A tarn is a small mountain lake that is usually found in valleys carved out by glaciers.

Easedale Tarn

Ullswater and Aira Force

For many people Ullswater is the quintessential English lake. As it winds its distinctive serpentine way from Glenridding north to Pooley Bridge, the 12-km (7.5-mi) long lake reveals strikingly contrasting landscapes, from the gentle hills and woodlands of its western shores to the rugged grandeur of the eastern fells. The best way by far to see all this is from the water, so it is not surprising that pleasure boats have been plying the lake for over 150 years. Indeed, two of the vessels – *Lady of the Lake* and *Raven* – have been in service for nearly as long; originally paddle steamers, they have since been converted to Diesel power (but are known still as the 'steamers').

There are lots of options at Ullswater and a Freedom of the Lakes ticket allows you a day's unlimited use of the regular sailings. You might want to begin, for example, with a cruise around the whole lake, which takes some two-and-a-half

A steamer glides across Ullswater.

hours; you can start at either end. Then drive along the road hugging the western shore to Gowbarrow, where a comfortable one hour round walk from the car park takes you to Aira Force. This waterfall, where the Aira Beck drops 21 m (70 ft) down a rocky chasm before flowing into the lake, is one of Lakeland's most celebrated beauty spots. Stone bridges at the top and bottom of the falls present an almost alpine aspect as the water makes its tumbling descent between slopes dense with spruce and pine. A walk along the lakeside is also recommended, especially if you are here in the spring and the Lenten lilies are in bloom; known more popularly as wild daffodils, these are the flowers immortalized in Wordsworth's famous poem.

WHERE:
Ullswater, Cumbria
BEST TIME TO GO:
April to October
DON'T MISS:
You may spot red squirrels in the woods around Aira Force.
AMOUNT OF WALKING:
Lots
COST:
Reasonable
YOU SHOULD KNOW:
For a longer walk (three to four hours) take the boat to Howtown and walk back along the shore to Glenridding for beautiful lake views with the awesome backdrop of the Helvellyn range.

Eden Ostrich World and the Upfront Gallery

The African black ostrich is an unexpected sight in the middle of the English countryside but a working farm in the beautiful Eden Valley a few miles east of Penrith is home to a flock of the giant birds. Nor are they the only unusual creatures to be found here, for as well as rare breeds of domestic farm animals there are zebras, porcupines and racoons. The ostriches know that they are the stars of the show, though, and the sight of large numbers in their enclosures is an impressive one. If you visit in the summer months you could be lucky and witness the hatching of an ostrich egg. There are lots of activities for children, including free quiz sheets, an adventure playground, an indoor soft-play area and tractor-and-trailer rides. On most days children can help with feeding the animals. And if you've never seen sheep being milked, this is your chance.

A former farm in the tiny hamlet of Unthank, northwest of Penrith, has been stylishly converted into the Upfront Gallery, which displays the work of contemporary artists and craft workers in four separate spaces and a small sculpture garden. The gallery presents changing exhibitions of painting, sculpture, ceramics and textiles. Dating from the late 17th century, its main building follows the layout of a classic Lakeland yeoman farmhouse. The gallery owners also run a puppet theatre and you might catch a daytime show if you visit at Easter or during the summer holidays. As well as selling the work of artists featured in the gallery, the shop has a well-stocked section devoted to puppetry, with smaller items such as finger puppets available for pocket-money prices.

WHERE:
Lanwathby and Unthank, near Penrith, Cumbria
BEST TIME TO GO:
Any time of year (but note that the Gallery is closed on Mondays, except Bank Holidays, and that Ostrich World is not open on Tuesdays during the winter).
DON'T MISS:
Pozee the zebroid at Ostrich World – a cross between a zebra and a Shetland pony.
AMOUNT OF WALKING:
Little
COST:
Reasonable
YOU SHOULD KNOW:
The strange placename Unthank is thought to refer to a clearing on the edge of a wood that had been occupied by unwelcome settlers.

Talkin Tarn Country Park

WHERE:
Near Brampton, Cumbria
BEST TIME TO GO:
April to October
DON'T MISS:
Look out for red squirrels in the woods.
AMOUNT OF WALKING:
Moderate
COST:
Low
YOU SHOULD KNOW:
Talkin Tarn was a popular recreation area in Victorian times, when it used to have a bathing house and even a wrestling ring.

The farmlands of the Eden Valley east of Carlisle may not offer the natural highlights of the Lake District but a visit to this lovely area does guarantee tranquillity and an escape from the crowds of its illustrious neighbour. A couple of miles south of the small sandstone market town of Brampton lies one of the region's hidden gems, Talkin Tarn Country Park. At the heart of the 75-ha (185-acre) park is Talkin Tarn itself, a lake formed by the action of an ancient glacier and fed by underground streams. Unlike the tarns of the Lake District, Talkin Tarn is not surrounded by fells and crags but by woods and meadows, with the Pennine Hills a distant backdrop. This is a great place to come and chill out on a nice day with a picnic and a ball or two. A sandy bay beside the lake is popular with

swimmers and there are numerous walking trails in the surrounding woods, where you should keep your eyes peeled for wildlife, including red squirrels, roe deer and woodpeckers. The tarmac path all the way around the lake is an easy one-hour stroll and is suitable for pushchairs and wheelchairs.

The lake provides a setting for various water activities, including sailing, windsurfing and canoeing. Rowing boats can be hired at weekends and during school holidays, and day permits are available for fishing (the lake has pike, perch and eel). The old Victorian boathouse has been converted into an exhibition space. A popular café and children's play area complete the facilities at this delightful spot.

Grizedale Forest

WHERE:
Near Hawkshead, Cumbria
BEST TIME TO GO:
April to October
DON'T MISS:
The chance to 'play' the giant wooden xylophone in the sculpture park.
AMOUNT OF WALKING:
Lots. Note that the 1.6-km (1-mi) Ridding Wood trail is fully accessible to wheelchair users and suitable for all ages and abilities.
COST:
Low (but expensive if you go on the Go Ape! course).
YOU SHOULD KNOW:
The two-hour sessions on the Go Ape! adventure course must be pre-booked. Children must be over 10 and at least 1.4 m (4 ft 7 in) tall.

A hundred years ago the rolling hills between Windermere and Coniston Water were stripped almost bare of trees, owing to timber being used in coppicing, iron smelting and charcoal making. Today, thanks to replanting and the stewardship of the Forestry Commission, Grizedale is once again an extensive forest. The thick stands of oak, spruce, larch and pine make a great place for a day's exploration, whether on one of the eight way-marked walking trails (ranging from a one-hour all-ability path to a demanding five-hour hike) or one of five mountain-bike routes (not for little ones!).

Whichever method you choose, you will encounter along the way many of the 80 or so sculptures that set Grizedale apart from most other forests. For over 30 years professional artists have been creating their own sculptural responses to the environment; the result is one of the country's largest outdoor sculpture parks. Although you can buy a location map, one of the pleasures of a walk here is coming across an artwork by chance. Because the sculptures make use of natural materials only they are not always easy to spot,

The Ancient Forester in Grizedale Forest Park

though this is not the case with the dry-stone wall that snakes through the conifers or the giant 'man of the forest'. The use of organic materials means that the display is constantly changing; new works are added as older ones decay back into their woodland surroundings.

If you are reasonably fit and looking for an adrenalin buzz, then you won't want to miss the Go Ape! high-level adventure course in the woods. Give vent to your inner Tarzan as you swing through the forest canopy on an obstacle course of rope bridges, ladders, nets and slides. It's exciting stuff, and perfectly safe as you're attached to a line at all times. The kids will love it.

Rheged Centre

Here are two important facts about the Lake District: it has some of the most beautiful and inspiring scenery in Britain, and it is one of the country's wettest places. Sadly, the two are not terribly compatible, but the region's tourist industry has done a good deal in recent years to boost the number of all-weather attractions suitable for those seemingly inevitable rainy days. An outstanding example is the award-winning Rheged Centre outside Penrith. What is claimed to be Britain's largest grass-covered building, Rheged has been cleverly designed to blend in with the surrounding landscape; in fact, from the nearby motorway you would hardly know it was there.

Inside there is a wealth of activities to keep children amused. There is an impressive permanent exhibition devoted to the history and traditions of Cumbria, including information about the ancient 'lost kingdom' of Rheged which once stretched from Strathclyde in Scotland as far south as Cheshire. The centre houses a number of speciality shops that showcase the best of Cumbrian products – arts, crafts and produce. Younger children can create their own designs in the pottery painting workshop or let off steam in the indoor soft-play area (and even more so, if weather permits, in Turrets and Tunnels, a terrific outdoor play complex).

The main draw at Rheged, though, and what most people come for, is the huge IMAX cinema. A giant screen as big as six double decker buses shows a changing programme of one-hour films throughout the day. Subjects are chosen for their popular appeal and to showcase the state-of-the-art technology, which now embraces films in 3-D; you might find yourself, for example, on a journey beneath the waves, into space, or back to the world of the dinosaurs.

WHERE:
Near Penrith, Cumbria
BEST TIME TO GO:
Any time of year
DON'T MISS:
The opportunity for your children to decorate and take home their own piece of painted pottery.
AMOUNT OF WALKING:
Little
COST:
Reasonable (entry to the Rheged complex is free, but you pay for the cinema and specific activities).
YOU SHOULD KNOW:
If you are tempted to see more than one film on your visit, the ticket price drops considerably.

301

Cycling around Coniston Water

WHERE:
Coniston, Cumbria
BEST TIME TO GO:
March to October
DON'T MISS:
Look out for the elegant steam yacht
Gondola, an immaculate replica of
the original Victorian vessel that plies
the lake between Coniston and John
Ruskin's home at Brantwood.
AMOUNT OF WALKING:
Little (but lots of cycling!)
COST:
Low (assuming that you have your
own bikes).
YOU SHOULD KNOW:
The Coniston launches run on solar
power and the steam yacht *Gondola*
now burns waste-wood logs rather
than coal.

Although only a few miles west of Windermere, Coniston Water feels like a different world and one where the hustle and bustle of its big sister is left far behind. The unspoilt shoreline and surrounding landscape of low fells and woodlands make for excellent cycling country, with minor roads and tracks that cater for a range of abilities and fitness levels. The obvious starting point for most excursions is the village of Coniston itself, situated at the northwestern end of the lake. From here an easy family cycle ride takes you south along the old railway line, which once carried copper and slate from the local mines to the coast. (You need to take care over two short sections along the main road.) Outside Torver the route turns onto a track to the western shore

and back past 16th-century Coniston Old Hall.

For something a little more ambitious than this two-hour trip, head for the eastern side of Coniston Water, where a quiet minor road hugs almost the entire shoreline and various points along it give access to the extensive network of tracks (colour-coded according to difficulty) in Grizedale Forest. The ride from Coniston village down the length of the lake to High Nibthwaite and back is 19.2 km (12 mi). If you want to avoid the initial section on the main road a recommended alternative is to take the cruise boat on the lake (bikes carried for a small extra charge) and ride back from the landing point at Water Park. A more challenging return involves the bridleway that climbs up onto the fell side behind the lake; the difficult terrain is more than compensated for by spectacular views of the Coniston range.

*Mountain biking at
Parkamoor above
Coniston Water*

Manchester United Museum and Tour

WHERE:
Old Trafford, Manchester
BEST TIME TO GO:
Any time of year (but note that tours do not run on match days).
DON'T MISS:
At the end of the tour you get a special certificate to commemorate your visit.
AMOUNT OF WALKING:
Little
COST:
Reasonable
YOU SHOULD KNOW:
This is an understandably popular attraction, so it is advisable to book in advance.

The appeal of this day out will depend entirely on your loyalties, nowhere more intense than in the world of football. Even so, unless you are a die-hard opponent of the 'Red Devils' the prospect of a visit to the home of Manchester United at Old Trafford is likely to be an alluring one for most children. As the world's most famous football club, 'Man U' manages to soak up interest among even those who are indifferent to the charms of a large round ball being kicked around by 22 players. Unsurprisingly for a club of this stature and means, Manchester United has a handsome museum dedicated to its 130-year history. Here you can recall past triumphs and tragedies, including the poignant display about 'Busby's Babes', the brilliant young players who lost their lives in the 1958 Munich air crash. Interactive exhibits allow you to re-live classic goals or to have an 'audience' with Sir Alex Ferguson in his private office. For many, the highlight is the trophy room where the club's jaw-dropping collection of silverware is on proud display.

You can just visit the museum, but the kids will get the real atmosphere of the place if you combine your visit with a stadium tour. Tours last an hour and take you from the heights of the stands via the home changing room and the players' lounge down to the pitch-side dugout, where you can experience Sir Alex's view of the game. Although you cannot walk on the hallowed turf itself, there is no denying the visceral thrill of treading the path taken by so many famous boots as you make your way through the tunnel to emerge into one of world sport's great arenas.

A stadium tour guide showing guests around Old Trafford, home of Manchester United Football Club.

Heaton Park

At the time Heaton Park opened to the public in 1902 it was the largest municipal park in the country. Manchester Corporation had purchased the Heaton estate from the Earl of Wilton the previous year in order to provide a recreational area for the rapidly expanding population in the northern suburbs of the city. Today this vast urban lung offers a setting for a range of sports and outdoor activities. There are football pitches, bowling greens and a lake where you can hire rowing boats. Serious golfers can enjoy an 18-hole championship course but the par three pitch-and-putt course is likely to prove more suitable for a family round. For younger children there are two play areas and an animal centre where they can get close to various farmyard friends, including a flock of Hebridean sheep and quaint little kune kune pigs from New Zealand. They should keep a respectful distance, though, from the trio of alpacas.

Donkey rides are occasionally available in the park and you can also arrange to go horse riding. You may be lucky enough to catch a more unusual mode of transport in the course of your visit: two vintage trams which were once in service in the city have been carefully restored and now give rides to passengers along a short stretch of tramline in the park. The depot where the trams are maintained also doubles as a small museum, which includes a working model tramway.

At the heart of the park stands Heaton Hall, regarded as one of the finest neo-classical houses in the country. It costs nothing to have a peek inside at the fine 18th-century interiors, which have been beautifully restored by staff from the city's art gallery and fitted out with period furnishings.

Let's take a picture!

WHERE:
Prestwich, Greater Manchester
BEST TIME TO GO:
Any time of year (although many of the activities are only available between April and September).
DON'T MISS:
Look out for the pair of handsome Highland cattle in the fields.
AMOUNT OF WALKING:
Moderate
COST:
Low
YOU SHOULD KNOW:
The area of the boating lake was once occupied by a racecourse, the setting for the famous Heaton Park Races in the 19th century.

Urbis and the Manchester Museum

As the city that kick-started the Industrial Revolution, Manchester is no stranger to the pioneering spirit; and proof that this is as vibrant as ever can be found at Urbis, the trendy and ultra-modern museum which celebrates the cutting edge of urban culture and city life. Urbis is the place to come if you want to get the pulse of contemporary Manchester. The building itself, situated in a new urban park close to Victoria station, is an object of wonder, as well as a testament to local innovation since it was Manchester architects whose design won the international competition. The dazzling glass triangle rises like a ship's prow to overlook the city centre, and it is well worth visiting the bar and restaurant on the top floors for the panoramic views of the skyline. Inside, displays on five floors examine the multiple facets of life in a complex 21st-century city. Permanent and changing exhibitions focus on the latest trends in contemporary art and design, fashion, popular culture and the urban environment. One of the best features is the interactive videos where you can listen to ordinary Manchester citizens telling their own stories.

A short distance south from the city centre along Oxford Road stands Manchester Museum. This treasure trove of a collection has a bit of everything – archaeology, anthropology, natural history, geology, social history. The museum is particularly noted for its

WHERE:
Central Manchester
BEST TIME TO GO:
Any time of year
DON'T MISS:
Look out in the Manchester Museum for the skull of Old Billy, thought to be the world's oldest horse when he died in 1822 at the age of 62.
AMOUNT OF WALKING:
Little

The Urbis building

collections of fossils and of mummies and other objects from ancient Egypt. The fossilized remains of Stan, a *Tyrannosaurus rex* unearthed in the USA as recently as 1992, should satisfy the serious dinosaur fan. The skull is the most complete yet found and the teeth are a sobering reminder of how it acquired its fearsome reputation.

COST:
Low (entrance to Urbis is free, but there may be charges for some of the temporary exhibitions).
YOU SHOULD KNOW:
The Manchester Museum is the work of the Victorian architect Alfred Waterhouse, who was also responsible for Manchester's Town Hall and London's Natural History Museum.

Boggart Hole Clough

Tucked away in the suburbs of northeast Manchester, Boggart Hole Clough is a rare surviving example of the ancient woodlands which once covered much of the country. Clough is a northern word for a deep wooded ravine and Boggart Hole has a number of such valleys and gullies, where it is easy enough to leave behind the stresses of city life. The council-owned land is managed by a local community group as both a public recreation area and a nature reserve, with a commitment to maintaining the Clough as a sustainable and thriving environment for the benefit of people as well as wildlife. The group cares for and helps protect a number of important habitats, including broadleaved woodland, wildflower meadows and wetlands.

Going where the mood takes you is the best way to appreciate this surprisingly wild place, and its many crannies and hidden spots make this a great location for adventures of the imagination. If you are after something a little more structured, the site offers courts for tennis and basketball, an athletics track and play areas for children. Boggart Hole also has a lake where fishing is permitted. Concerts, fun days and other special events are regular features throughout the year; many are held in or near the old boathouse, which has been converted into a café.

If you are wondering about the colourful name, it refers to a legendary creature called a boggart that was supposed to have made its home here (hence the 'hole'). Boggarts were mischievous spirits which liked nothing better than to cause havoc in human households; many are the stories that are told about their pranks and misdeeds.

WHERE:
Blackley, Greater Manchester
BEST TIME TO GO:
Any time of year
DON'T MISS:
Look closely and you'll be surprised how much wildlife there is in this relatively compact area.
AMOUNT OF WALKING:
Moderate
COST:
Low
YOU SHOULD KNOW:
Boggarts are an important element of the folklore of Lancashire and Yorkshire. They were believed to have inhabited the bogs and mossland, which once covered large parts of the north.

Stockport Air Raid Shelters and Staircase House

As a major industrial centre Manchester was a prime target for German bombers during World War II. The early 1940s were dark years indeed for those on the home front. When it came to finding shelter from the air raids, communities that lacked London's existing underground network found they had to create their own. In Stockport a labyrinth of tunnels was carved out of the red sandstone beneath the town centre to provide a refuge for some 6,500 people. These tunnels have been re-opened and they offer an authentic glimpse into life during the Blitz. This subterranean world was fitted out to enable people to spend days at a time there if necessary. It may not have matched the comforts of home but nevertheless there was electric lighting, bunk beds, first-aid facilities and even flushing toilets. You can choose between exploring the shelters on a self-guided tour or you can book for one of the special family tours held at weekends.

Five hundred years further back in time saw the construction of an imposing new residence in the centre of Stockport. Gracing the historic market place, Staircase House is a rare survival of a late medieval town house. Like all good homes, though, it has had its fair share of makeovers down the centuries, reflecting changing tastes and fashions. Staircase House is now a living history museum where an audio guide invites you on a journey through time. The atmosphere is refreshingly relaxed and children are actually encouraged to touch many of the objects – pull back the bedclothes on the four-poster bed, for example, or try their hands at the 17th-century skill of writing with a quill pen.

Anderton Boat Lift and Marbury Country Park

The country north of Northwich used to form the heart of Britain's salt-mining industry. First worked by the Romans, the mines are long since exhausted and the scars of the industrial past are gradually being concealed, as the area is transformed into a rich new environment of woodlands and parks. Not every trace of its commercial heritage has been lost, however. The Boat Lift at Anderton is a superb reminder of the great days of the canals. This marvel of Victorian engineering was constructed in 1875 to lift the heavily laden salt barges 15 m (50 ft) from the River Weaver to the Trent and Mersey Canal, so they could continue their journey to the Mersey ports. Towering over the river, the 'Cathedral of the Canals' has been restored to full working order. The modern Visitor Centre tells the history of the lift and you can also watch it being operated from the control centre.

Although there is a viewing platform overlooking the site, you won't want to come here without taking a trip on the lift itself. The experience of being raised in a glass-top boat high above the surrounding countryside is a memorable one, enhanced by the on-board commentary explaining the mechanics of the operation. A half-hour river trip on the same boat is also available.

A short distance away lies Marbury Country Park, once a large private estate with a manor house at its heart (now demolished). On the park's many walks and trails you will come across raised terraces, an arboretum and, best of all, some splendid lime avenues, all of which bear testimony to its grand past. Marbury is a haven for wildlife and a great place to while away the time over a picnic, as the children enjoy the play area.

WHERE:
Near Northwich, Cheshire
BEST TIME TO GO:
April to October
DON'T MISS:
The children's maze at Anderton Boat Lift, which has been made from old metal counterweights.
AMOUNT OF WALKING:
Moderate
COST:
Reasonable
YOU SHOULD KNOW:
Marbury is renowned for its bluebell displays in spring and for its autumn colours.

Anderton boat lift near Northwich

*Looking out from
Stormy Point.*

Alderley Edge

Rising 180 m (600 ft) above the flat expanses of the Cheshire Plain, Alderley Edge is a dramatic 3-km (1.9-mi) long escarpment of red sandstone. Its distinctive profile is somewhat concealed beneath the thick woodlands which now cover much of its surface, but there is still an unmistakable sense of a world unto itself when you stand on its slopes and ridges. The National Trust, which owns much of the land here, produces a range of guides and maps to help you explore the many paths through the oak and beech woods and identify the best places for the spectacular views over the plain towards the Peak District. They also have a children's trail and tracker packs for loan, filled with activities to liven up the family's experience of the area.

It is not surprising that such a striking natural feature should

have spawned a rich tradition of folk tales and legends over the centuries. One legend tells of a wizard leading a farmer and his horse deep inside the hill to a large cavern filled with sleeping knights. The obvious Arthurian associations are in part what inspired Alan Garner to use Alderley Edge as the setting for *The Weirdstone of Brisingamen*, his story of two children guarding a magical stone from evil powers which has become a classic of children's literature. Alan Garner still lives in the area and continues to draw inspiration from the Edge. The caves, gullies and hollows you will notice as you wander around are evidence of the old copper mines which were worked as far back as the Bronze Age and Roman periods; there is no question but that they enhance the mysterious appeal of this remarkable place.

WHERE:
Alderley Edge, Cheshire
BEST TIME TO GO:
Any time of year
DON'T MISS:
The village of Alderley Edge, with its handsome villas and houses built by wealthy Victorian merchants from Manchester, following the arrival of the railway in the 1840s.
AMOUNT OF WALKING:
Lots
COST:
Low
YOU SHOULD KNOW:
The old mine workings are opened to the public twice a year on tours organized by the local caving club.

Stockley Farm

WHERE:
Arley, near Northwich, Cheshire
BEST TIME TO GO:
April to September
DON'T MISS:
A gallery gives you a great overview of the milking operation in the impressive computerized parlour.
AMOUNT OF WALKING:
Moderate
COST:
Reasonable
YOU SHOULD KNOW:
Unlike many attractions featuring animals, Stockley Farm welcomes dogs, provided of course they are kept under control.

You don't want to wear your best clothes for this day down on the farm but, unless the weather looks very uncertain, you don't need to wear your wellies either. Stockley Farm is well used to receiving visitors who may not be there for the mucking out but still want to get an idea of life on a busy working dairy farm. You enter the rural spirit as soon as you leave the car park and take the tractor-and-trailer ride down to the main yard. Here you can inspect the farm animals at close quarters and, depending on the time of year, see newborn calves, lambs, piglets and baby goats. There is a pets corner where children are able to handle rabbits, guinea pigs and, sometimes, chicks and ducklings. There is both an outdoor and an indoor play area, the latter boasting a huge sandpit which is hard to resist.

Highlights of a day at Stockley for the children include the opportunity to bottle feed some of the animals, like baby goats and lambs, and watching the 200-strong herd of dairy cows being milked in the hi-tech milking parlour. Sheep racing makes an entertaining alternative to horse racing; you'll notice that it's even harder to pick the winner! You may also be lucky enough to catch a birds-of-prey flying display.

The 300-ha (750-acre) farm is set in lovely countryside on the extensive Arley Estate north of Northwich, and there is a woodland nature trail that is well worth exploring. Before you leave, treat the family to some of the farm's own organic produce available from the on-site shop.

Rixton Claypits and Fun2B Play Centre

At Rixton on the eastern outskirts of Warrington intensive extraction of clay during the first half of the last century has left a sizeable area pockmarked with a number of deep pits. These have filled with water and the resulting ponds and lakes are now havens for wildlife, supporting a diverse range of habitats. So significant has the reclamation by nature been that the old claypits are now a classified local nature reserve and a designated SSSI (Site of Special Scientific Interest). Easy-to-follow paths take you around the water features and through woodland and wildflower meadows. The industrial past of the area has made the ground quite uneven in places and created numerous slopes and drops, so you should take care when you are walking, especially in wet weather.

Among the profusion of plant life, including all sorts of ferns and mosses, you may catch sight of water voles, weasels and foxes, all of which frequent the area. Bats are also present and some 20 types of butterfly have been observed, including the rare purple hairstreak and the holly blue. Not surprisingly, this waterland is home to a large dragonfly population (18 species have been noted to date).

Rixton is an important and fragile site and to help protect it you are asked to keep to the designated paths. You can reward the children for following the rules by taking them afterwards to the Fun2B centre in Warrington. This large indoor play centre is just the ticket for under 11s with energy to burn; watch them mess around to their heart's content on an enormous multi-level climbing frame, complete with rope swings, ladders, slides and tunnels.

WHERE:
Warrington, Cheshire
BEST TIME TO GO:
Any time of year
DON'T MISS:
Rixton's star attraction, the rare great crested newt – the claypits support one of the largest breeding populations in the country.
AMOUNT OF WALKING:
Moderate
COST:
Low
YOU SHOULD KNOW:
It is a good idea to use insect repellent if you are visiting Rixton Claypits during the summer months.

Southport, Formby and Crosby Beach

Southport has always promoted itself as a genteel seaside resort, in contrast to Blackpool, its brasher neighbour up the coast. Although the town keeps a solicitous eye on its Victorian heritage, the modern family will also find plenty to entertain them. Southport boasts the country's oldest iron pier; it is still in use, thanks to a recent major refurbishment, and is so long that it has its own tram line taking visitors out to the pavilion. Just back from the seafront, the large Marine Lake offers rides on a Mississippi-style paddle steamer and on a lakeside miniature railway. For an even smaller railway experience visit the Model Railway Village; children may not be able to ride in the trains themselves, but they can get hours of enjoyment from watching the model trains that run continuously around the 500 m (1,640 ft) of track in this miniature outdoor landscape.

If the sea doesn't tempt you, you might want to consider Splash World, an all-weather water park that is guaranteed to set pulses racing with a number of high-speed water rides and flumes; there are also quieter paddling areas for toddlers and a regular pool.

Further down the coast, the extensive sand dunes and pinewoods at Formby offer walking opportunities and the chance to spot red squirrels. The most unusual sight on this coastline, though, and one that you will have no trouble spotting, is Another Place, Antony Gormley's extensive sculpture project on Crosby Beach. Another Place comprises 100 life-size iron casts of the artist's own body scattered along the 3-km (2-mi) long foreshore. The sculptures present an intriguing and slightly unnerving spectacle as they stand silently on the sands, looking out to sea.

*Antony Gormley's haunting
sculptures at Crosby Beach*

Knowsley Safari Park

WHERE:
Knowsley, near Liverpool, Merseyside
BEST TIME TO GO:
Any time of year
DON'T MISS:
The three white rhino calves born at
Knowsley in 2008.
AMOUNT OF WALKING:
Little
COST:
Reasonable (but note that the
amusement rides cost extra).
YOU SHOULD KNOW:
The name white rhino has nothing to
do with the animal's colour but
comes from the Afrikaans word *weit*,
meaning 'wide-lipped'.

*A monkey sitting on a car
mirror – it's safer to keep the
windows shut.*

When the 13th Earl of Derby started his private menagerie of exotic animals in the 19th century, he could not have imagined that 150 years later his estate at Knowsley would be open to upwards of half a million annual visitors eager to see a collection that has grown to some 500 creatures. Knowsley Safari Park is now one of the north west's leading attractions. As you steer your car around the 8-km (5-mi) safari drive to view the animals in the surrounding parkland, it is hard to believe that you are only a few kilometres from the centre of Liverpool. All the big players are here: lions, tigers, buffalo, bison, rhinos, wildebeest, antelope. There is a walk-around area, too, featuring elephants and giraffes. Back in the main park, the real scene-stealers tend to be the baboons; no respecters of personal possessions, they are inclined to give cars a thorough makeover (of the destructive kind); so much so in fact that Knowsley now offers an alternative route around the monkey jungle, which still gives you good views of the baboons without exposing your vehicle to the risk of attack.

The daily show where the park's two sea lions show off their

tricks is a sure-fire hit with the children, as is the Bug House and the domestic animals in the children's farm. The park is involved in various captive-breeding programmes for endangered species; among the rare animals you will see are the bongo, an antelope from the forests of central Africa, the scimitar-horned oryx, a pack of African wild dogs and the majestic white rhino. And if all this fails to keep the kids amused, Knowsley plays it safe by offering a range of amusement park rides as well.

316

The Beatles Story and Magical Mystery Tour

Its history as a major port with a window on the world makes Liverpool a fascinating and multi-faceted city. Whatever your reasons for visiting, however, you are unlikely to escape reminders of the local mop-headed foursome who propelled British pop music into the international limelight and themselves into everlasting glory. If you want to discover the stories behind the legends and the childhood influences that shaped Liverpool's most famous sons, The Beatles Story in historic Albert Dock is the place to start. The story is told from humble beginnings on Merseyside to the band's break-up and subsequent solo careers; on the way there are the Hamburg gigs, the Abbey Road recordings, the trips to the USA and the later albums on the Apple label. The museum has treasured artefacts such as George Harrison's first guitar and John Lennon's iconic round spectacles; it also features a full-size replica of the Cavern Club (surprisingly small) and a re-creation of the Abbey Road studio. An audio guide narrated by John's sister helps bring it all to life and there's a special version for younger visitors.

The memories here may all rest with the grown-ups but there's plenty designed for younger generations. As well as enjoying the large Yellow Submarine in the main display, children can try out various activities in the discovery zone, such as choosing a song in a 1950s record store or playing a Beatles tune on a giant piano.

When you've mugged up on the story, take a trip to the real locations on the colourful Magical Mystery bus, which departs every afternoon from outside the museum. The two-hour tour covers the principal Beatles landmarks – childhood homes, schools and sites such as Penny Lane and Strawberry Field – before finishing up at the Cavern Club itself in Mathew Street.

WHERE:
Liverpool, Merseyside
BEST TIME TO GO:
Any time of year
DON'T MISS:
The Fab4D cinema experience at The Beatles Story's subsidiary site at the Pier Head ferry terminal.
AMOUNT OF WALKING:
Little
COST:
Expensive (there is no reduction for children on the Magical Mystery Tour).
YOU SHOULD KNOW:
Although not the original (and not quite on the original site), the Cavern Club you see today is a faithful enough reconstruction. It remains a busy venue for aspiring local bands.

The entrance to The Beatles Story Exhibition in Albert Dock

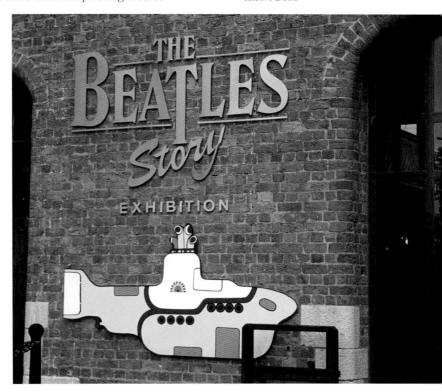

Witton Country Park

WHERE:
Blackburn, Lancashire
BEST TIME TO GO:
Any time of year
DON'T MISS:
If you visit during the summer season
there are horse-and-cart rides
available from the Visitor Centre.
AMOUNT OF WALKING:
Moderate or lots, depending on your
energy levels.
COST:
Low
YOU SHOULD KNOW:
Witton has a number of low mobility
tramper buggies available for a small
hire fee. These are specially designed
for use on off-road terrain to enable
people with limited mobility to have
access to the countryside.

The sprawling country park at Witton on the western edge of Blackburn is a great place for escaping from the hustle and bustle of urban life and for reconnecting with a gentler pace. The 195-ha (480-acre) park was once a private estate belonging to the Feilden family. The grand house they lived in for 150 years had to be demolished in the early 1950s, not long after Blackburn Corporation had bought the estate for the benefit of its citizens. The outbuildings survived, however, and the former coach house and stable blocks have been renovated and converted into a lively Visitor Centre. As well as displays about the history and ecology of the park, the centre maintains a collection of small British mammals such as voles and harvest mice, and a pets corner with goats and rabbits. There is also the chance to try making some pottery.

Getting out into the great outdoors is what Witton is really about, though, and there are lots of well-marked trails and paths through the lovely parkland and woodland areas. The Darwen and Blakewater rivers both flow through the country park and a riverside walk enables you to make the most of the important and distinctive wetland habitats. Trail guides and leaflets are available from the Visitor Centre, including several aimed at children and families. The kids won't want to miss the latest addition to Witton's facilities – a splendid adventure playground, complete with a large awning to shelter users from the worst of the elements. The country park lays on a full programme of (mostly free) special events throughout the year so it's worth checking what's on in advance of your visit.

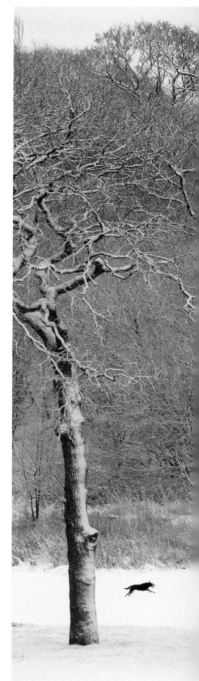

Witton Country Park as a winter wonderland

The World of Glass and Rumble Rumble

WHERE:
St Helens, Merseyside
BEST TIME TO GO:
Any time of year (but note that both attractions are closed on Mondays, except for Bank Holidays).
DON'T MISS:
The magnificent two-ton chandelier of Venetian glass hanging in the World of Glass foyer, one of four created originally for Manchester Airport in the 1960s.
AMOUNT OF WALKING:
Little
COST:
Reasonable
YOU SHOULD KNOW:
The World of Glass includes a heritage gallery devoted to the broader industrial history of St Helens.

The World of Glass museum in St Helens

The Merseyside town of St Helens is famous for rugby league and for being the home of Pilkington Glass. Now a global brand, Pilkingtons began life as the St Helens Crown Glass Company in the early 19th century. The multi-national is still one of the area's largest employers and continues to have a major impact on the local economy. Ten years ago it gave St Helens an attraction to be seriously proud of: a brand-new museum and visitor centre devoted to glass. The World of Glass tells you everything you want to know about one of the planet's most durable and versatile substances. The history of glass is told through displays featuring artefacts from ancient history and medieval times, culminating in spectacular examples of the art of the legendary glass makers of Venice. *Glass Revolution* is an exciting film show with special effects, and there are live demonstrations of glass blowing. The Level One gallery presents interesting work by contemporary glass artists, much of it for sale.

Children will have fun wandering around the intriguing mirror maze (but watch out for Wizard Filigrano!). They will also enjoy exploring the underground tunnels running beneath the Victorian Cone House. This unique example of a 19th-century glass making furnace is reached by crossing a glass bridge (what else?) over the canal.

Youthful exuberance may be somewhat constrained by all the glass around but there are no such concerns at Rumble Rumble, St Helens' largest indoor play centre where children can work off pent-up energy to their hearts' content. From the comfort of a ringside seat in the café watch them get stuck into the biff-bash bags, crawl tunnels, garbage rollers and giant slides.

THE
WORLD
OF
GLASS
ST HELENS

EXCELLENCE
IN ENGLAND
Awards for Tourism 2002
GOLD WINNER

Curraghs Wildlife Park and Onchan Pleasure Park

Curraghs Wildlife Park is situated in the northwest of the Isle of Man, on the edge of the Ballaugh Curraghs, an important wetland habitat. The park has been cleverly designed to make use of this, and enables the visitor to 'take a walk around the world' – for about 80 minutes rather than 80 days. Curraghs is definitely more park than zoo – you won't find large, dangerous mammals here.

Divided into continents, the enclosures mimic the appropriate habitat, and all but a few of the animals mingle freely within them. Paved pathways lead the visitor through the enclosures, ensuring a really good look at all the different creatures here. For example, in the Asian swamp area you'll see red pandas, fishing cats, crab-eating macaques and various water birds, while in the North American wetlands you'll find Canadian otters, racoons, and trumpeter swans. There are two types of wallaby in the Australian section, as well as emus, cockatiels and cockatoos.

Other attractions here are the Orchid Line miniature railway, a butterfly trail and a large covered aviary that you can walk through while birds fly freely overhead. There's a hands-on area for small children, a toddler's playground and an adventure playground, and you can either buy a snack or take your own picnic.

Just 30 minutes drive away lies Onchan Pleasure Park and boating lake, which offers a number of activities suitable for all ages. Here you can play crazy golf, miniature golf, or try the battery-operated kiddie cars. The bumper boats always prove popular, as does the amusement arcade. There's even a stadium for karting. You'll find a café here too, so if you like you can sit peacefully in the sun with a newspaper and a cup of tea while your kids amuse themselves.

WHERE:
Near Sulby, in the northwest, and at Onchan in the east, Isle of Man
BEST TIME TO GO:
During the spring, summer or early autumn, on a pleasant day
DON'T MISS:
Penguin feeding at Curraghs Wildlife Park
AMOUNT OF WALKING:
Moderate
COST:
Low to reasonable. Many of the activities available at Onchan Pleasure Park have to be paid for, and although nothing is very pricey, it all adds up.
YOU SHOULD KNOW:
In 1781, Captain William Bligh, who subsequently became famous as a result of his voyage on *The Bounty* and the mutiny that took place, married Elizabeth Betham in Onchan. He sailed with Captain Cook on Cook's final voyage, and eventually became a Vice-Admiral in the Royal Navy.

WALES

Electric Mountain

WHERE:
Llanberis, on the edge of Snowdonia National Park, Gwynedd
BEST TIME TO GO:
Open all year round; times vary.
DON'T MISS:
The close-up view of the world's fastest response turbines, which can go from idle to full power in just a few seconds.
AMOUNT OF WALKING:
Little. The tour is not suitable for children under four years old. For reasons of security no bags or cameras are allowed on the tour. Some buses are fitted for wheelchair users, check when booking. Advance booking is recommended.
COST:
Reasonable; family tickets are available.
YOU SHOULD KNOW:
The plant works by pumping water up to a reservoir at night when demand for power is low and then releasing the water to create electricity when demand is high.

When the need for a hydroelectric plant in North Wales was identified, to avoid spoiling the area's great natural beauty, it was built deep inside Eldin Mountain. The result is Europe's largest man-made cave, big enough to house St Paul's cathedral. The subterranean workings make the place feel like the *Island of Doctor Moreau*, but happily no mutants are being produced, only clean electricity. The first port of call is the free-to-enter visitor centre, which details the operation of the power station. Though interesting enough, the centre alone would not make this a great day out. It is the tour that is the star turn, as you get to see the inside workings of this huge and hugely impressive site.

The tour starts with a short film whose realistic evocation of the plant whets the appetite before your very own journey to the centre of the Earth. Then it is all aboard a bus that speeds you through spookily dark tunnels into the bowels of the mountain. Once through the tunnels, the vastness of the operation leaves you with the feeling that you and the bus have shrunk to almost nothing and at any moment a giant mouse might appear from behind one of the massive turbines. Thankfully it doesn't and the tour finishes with an audio-visual display describing the construction of the site, before the bus whisks you back through the tunnels and returns to its normal size.

This is an excursion with a whole range of 'wow factors'. Though the plant's primary purpose is to cater for surges in the national grid, at peak output it can power the whole of Wales. While theme parks often promise the ride of your life, this really is a journey you will never forget.

The reservoir by the power station at Llanberis

*Green in colour and nature:
fun but without a
guilty conscience!*

GreenWood Park

While winning few prizes for originality of name – GreenWood Park is both ecological and verdant and, yes, there is a lot of wood around – it wins many awards for its innovative and forward-thinking approach to providing a fun-filled day for the whole family. From the wonderland that is the toddlers' village through to the archery and jungle boat adventures, the park caters well for children of all ages. This fabulous and unique attraction makes use of the abundant energy of its young visitors to power the rides. Ropes are used to haul the boats through a dense faux jungle, while its 70-m (230-ft) gravity-powered sledge run is the longest in Wales. The most ingenious ride of all is the funicular railway, which uses the weight of the queuing crowd to lift it to its full height, before releasing the already boarded passengers on a thrilling rollercoaster ride.

The park has activities for all tastes and abilities, the only prerequisite being that you should want to have fun and possibly get a little bit dirty. The Crocodile Maze is specially designed for assisted wheelchair users, while the barefoot trail gives you a chance to take off your shoes and socks and walk over the varied terrain of the forest floor. While some attractions have minimum height restrictions, over sevens are barred from the Tunnel Warren – a collection of rope bridges, slides and tunnels – so no one should feel left out. The park pays great attention to reducing its carbon footprint by recycling, planting trees and using local materials. In this field it is an industry leader. While the staff of GreenWood keep one eye on reducing energy consumption (at present it is an astonishingly low 0.75 kw per visitor), they never take their foot off the pedal when finding new fun things to do.

WHERE:
Midway between Bangor and Caernarfon, Gwynedd
BEST TIME TO GO:
Closes from November to January. Open on selected dates in February and March – fully open for the rest of the year.
DON'T MISS:
The stilt-walking arena, where you can try your hand (or feet) at walking tall.
AMOUNT OF WALKING:
Moderate. While some areas of the park are inaccessible to wheelchair users, there is plenty left to enjoy. The staff are well trained to advise on any special needs when booking.
COST:
Reasonable – family tickets are available. Disabled visitors and their carers get a 50 per cent reduction on single-ticket prices. Under threes and over 80s get in free.
YOU SHOULD KNOW:
The park plays host to several diverse events and workshops throughout the summer, giving you a chance to take part in a medieval festival or to meet Ken the stick maker.

Alyn Waters Country Park and Minera Lead Mines and Country Park

It may be slightly unfair to Wrexham to say that the best bits of the town lie just outside it, but in the Alyn Waters Country Park residents of Wrexham have on their doorstep a wonderful outdoor experience aimed at making exercise fun. The park itself is situated in the beautiful Alyn Valley and has a series of well-crafted riverside, woodland and grassland trails, easily navigated on foot or by bicycle. The best place to start is the very welcoming visitor centre which has exhibitions of the resident wildlife and the history of the park. It is also the place to pick up a map and start your exploration.

The highlight of the park is a 3.2-km (2-mi) cycle path and sculpture trail which, aside from a short stretch, is kind on the legs, while the sculptures are staggered to offer ample opportunities for tired limbs to stop, rest and enjoy.

The Minera Country Park offers further chances to roam in the pretty countryside, but its best feature is a wonderful picnic site offering great views over the valley. Having scoffed the scotch eggs and quaffed the lemonade, it is now time to delve into the area's industrial past with a visit to the restored lead mines. The name Minera means 'ore' and there has been mining on the site since medieval times. The attached museum charts the often-problematic history of the mine, through the Black Death to the time when Owain Glyndwr frightened off English mine owners. Increased mechanization saw excavation reach its peak in the 19th century, before a collapse in the price of lead left the mine derelict by the time of World War I. Since the early 1990s much of the mine has been restored and it now provides an entertaining and informative glimpse into our past.

WHERE:
Near Wrexham, Clwyd
BEST TIME TO GO:
Alyn Waters is open all year. The Visitor Centre is open from 10.30 to 16.30 daily. The mine opens from Thursday to Monday from Easter to late September.
DON'T MISS:
The Pedal Power Project – a traffic-free 1.6-km (1-mi) circuit aimed at making cycling accessible to children and adults with disabilities.
AMOUNT OF WALKING:
Little if you cycle, moderate if you walk. Alyn Waters has excellent access for wheelchair users and those with pushchairs. Minera Mines has good access to most of the site.
COST:
Low – by donation at the mine
YOU SHOULD KNOW:
In the Middle Ages, when a new seam of lead was discovered, the miners elected an official to ensure that the bounty was divided up fairly. A proportion was payable to the landowner and those caught trying to keep the lead for themselves were subjected to gruesome punishment.

The waterwheel at the Minera lead mines

Snowdon Mountain Railway and a walk down the mountain

Any day that begins with the words 'we can do this the hard way or we can do this the easy way' does not usually bode well. Thankfully, the whole family can plump for the easy option and let the train take the strain for the toughest bit of this exploration of the highest mountain in the UK outside of Scotland.

Snowdon has long been the scene of human exploitation, first for minerals and then for tourism, and this has not been without cost to the landscape. The summit has variously been home to two pretty ropey hotels and a visitor centre/café that was described by the Prince of Wales as 'the highest slum in the world'. Now with their demolition and the erection of a new visitor centre, built fittingly of Welsh oak and granite, Snowdon's summit is once again a place to savour.

The Snowdon Mountain Railway is Britain's only rack-and-pinion railway and this system allows smooth passage on inclines that are greater than 1 in 5. The uncoupled engine pushes the carriage up the mountain, affording its passengers ever more astounding views. Snaefell on the Isle of Man and Ireland's Wicklow Mountains are two of many highlights of this fabulous emerging panorama. The summit station is the highest in Britain and at 1,065 m (3,493 ft) you are only a short walk from the summit.

Having breathed in the pure air, inspected the visitor centre and taken in the spectacular views once more, it is time to make the descent. Though it is longer than most, the suggested route for less experienced or younger hikers roughly follows the route of the train. The Llanberis Path, as it is known, has no really steep inclines and benefits from having a café at its half-way point.

WHERE:
The railway starts at Llanberis, 13 km (8 mi) from Bangor (the nearest mainline station), Gwynedd
BEST TIME TO GO:
The railway runs to the summit from mid June to the end of October.
DON'T MISS:
On a clear day the views across to Ireland are most spectacular.
AMOUNT OF WALKING:
The hike down should only be attempted by adults and fit teenagers. Those with younger children or restricted mobility should take the train both ways. Some trains are fitted to accommodate wheelchair users, so check when you book. The train may be cancelled in bad weather. The walk down the mountain should take between three and four hours.
COST:
Expensive, although a half-price 'earlybird' fare is available on the 09.00 train. Discounts are available for under 16s and seniors; children under five years can travel free provided they sit on a lap.
YOU SHOULD KNOW:
The weather on Snowdon can change rapidly, so come prepared. Conditions at the top may be cold and blustery even in high summer. You can insure against a sudden change in the weather by buying return tickets (the only way of guaranteeing a downward passage).

Snowdon Mountain Railway

Llangollen Motor Museum and a boat trip along Llangollen Canal

WHERE:
Southwest of Wrexham, Clwyd
BEST TIME TO GO:
Both attractions are open from Easter to September.
DON'T MISS:
The Pontcysyllte Aqueduct, an amazing feat of engineering
AMOUNT OF WALKING:
Little; both have good disabled/pushchair access.
COST:
Reasonable; family tickets are available for the barge trips.
YOU SHOULD KNOW:
Advance booking is recommended for the canal trips. If you take the trip across the Pontcysyllte Aqueduct, make sure that everyone in your party has a good head for heights. Those who don't should remain inside the boat and look out of the window on the towpath side.

On the way to this double header of a day out, ask the question what is horsepower? You might get blank looks or perhaps the answer 'what a horse can pull'. Anyone who gives the answer '33,000 lb ft/minute' should go to the top of the class immediately. Put into plain English, if you were to lift 33,000 lb one foot off the ground for one minute, you would be working at the rate of one horsepower. The day starts at a quirky little museum, dedicated to the history of the motor car, and finishes with a quite astonishing demonstration of one horse's power when harnessed to a barge.

Any child who can't wait to rip open the box of a newly purchased toy car will love the full-sized exhibits at the Llangollen Motor Museum. Aside from more than 60 gleaming vintage exhibits, there is a faithful re-creation of a 1950s garage. You can watch restoration in progress and there is a model exhibition detailing the development of the British canal system, which gives you a nice preview of the afternoon's outing.

The Llangollen canal is probably the finest in Britain. It has crystal-clear water, expansive aqueducts and pretty scenery, which make it the perfect location for a leisurely glide through the countryside. When pulling a barge, the angle of the horse to the boat and its distance from it allows the animal to pull around 250 times the weight that it could do on land. This 45-minute sampler takes you silently and sedately from Llangollen Wharf, through leafy countryside to the beauty spot of Horseshoe Falls. If this has whetted your appetite, there is also a two-hour trip which takes you over the Pontcysyllte Aqueduct, dizzyingly high above the River Dee.

Horse-drawn narrow boat on the canal at Llangollen

The Ffestiniog Railway and Portmeirion

Established by Act of Parliament in 1832, the Ffestiniog Railway stands proud as the oldest independent railway company in the world. Originally it was a horse-drawn affair before turning to steam. Its founding purpose was to carry slate from the quarries to ship for export, but its star faded by the end of the World War II, only to be revived later by enthusiasts.

Starting at Porthmadog, the railway takes you on a thrilling 31-km (19.5-mi) journey, through woodland and meadows, past lakes and waterfalls, climbing to 213 m (700 ft), deep into the mountains. There are three intermediate stations along the way before you arrive at the old market town of Blaenau Ffestiniog – a good place to lunch before returning. A day pass allows you to hop on and off and the rail staff can offer advice on local walks and attractions. One place you will certainly wish to see is the fantasy village of Portmeirion, a short walk from Minffordd station.

The brainchild of one Clough Williams-Ellis, this Italianate village contains such improbable follies as a castle, a lighthouse, several grottoes and a watchtower. All are painted in brilliant candy colours. Pinks, yellows and turquoises mix to give the impression that the whole place has jumped out from the pages of a children's storybook. Portmeirion is definitely not a place that takes itself too seriously and some of the whims of its creator can certainly raise a chuckle. Things are not always what they seem – what appears a substantial building may only be a façade and where else in the world would you find a statue of Buddha under a pantiled portico? Full of far-fetched fantasy and fun – a visit to Portmeirion will live in your children's memories forever.

Steam engine at Tan-y-Bwlch, on the Ffestiniog Railway

WHERE:
The train starts at Porthmadog, Gwynedd
BEST TIME TO GO:
Though the train runs all year round, a full timetable is only in place from April to October. Portmeirion is open all year.
DON'T MISS:
Llyn Mair, a beautiful lake, just a short walk from Tan-y-Bwlch station.
AMOUNT OF WALKING:
Little. The railway has carriages fitted to take wheelchairs – advance notice is required. Only part of Portmeirion is wheelchair accessible and a detailed map is available from the village's website.
COST:
Reasonable. On the railway under threes travel free and one child under 16 can go free for each adult fare paid. At Portmeirion under fives go free. Entry is also free if you dine at one of the village's eateries.
YOU SHOULD KNOW:
Don't be surprised if Portmeirion seems familiar. It has featured in many films and tv programmes. Most notable was the cult 1960s tv thriller *The Prisoner*. Also, Noel Coward wrote *Blithe Spirit* while living there.

The Great Orme Tramway above Llandudno

Llandudno and Great Orme

WHERE:
On the North Wales coast, Clwyd
BEST TIME TO GO:
Nice on any sunny day. The best
weather is from May to August.
DON'T MISS:
The scenic walk to the copper mines
at the top of Great Orme.
AMOUNT OF WALKING:
Moderate. The Victorian design of the
tramway means that motorized
wheelchairs cannot be
accommodated. There is room for
folding wheelchairs, but you have to
walk on. The pier has full access,
except for the rides.
COST:
The pier is free to enter. Family
tickets are available on the tram and
where under threes travel free.
YOU SHOULD KNOW:
Great Orme is home to wild Kashmiri
goats. These fine animals have lived
in splendid isolation on the hilltop for
over a century. At one time they
were considered too successful and
regular culls took place. A 'save our
goats' campaign successfully
defended their right to roam and
they are now allowed to live in peace
once more.

With its magnificent horseshoe bay, sweeping promenade and wide sandy beaches, Llandudno could not have been better designed as a coastal resort. Both genteel and gentle, it is far removed from the kiss-me-quick image of the British seaside. Ever since the railway brought the Victorian masses to this corner of North Wales, it has catered well for those wishing to escape the rigours of urban life.

The most immediately striking thing about Llandudno's 700-m (2,295-ft) pier is that it runs out to sea at a 45-degree angle to the shore. This quirk has no practical purpose, but it does allow you to view sea and shore simultaneously. Its other idiosyncrasy is that, unlike most other piers, the traditional amusements are located towards the shore and it becomes ever more peaceful the further out you go. There are no high-powered rides; rather more sedentary entertainments are on offer, like dodgems and merry-go-rounds – perfect for those with younger children. It is a place to saunter along the deck, picking candyfloss from your chin and munching on toffee apples, while taking the sea air. If you are not too full of sweets, both the pier and the promenade have many good eateries for a sit-down lunch.

For a different view of the town, you should journey up Great Orme, a promontory that sits high above the town. It can be reached by cycling, walking or driving, but the most relaxing way is to take the tramway or, if you have a head for heights, a cable car. The tramway uses a most ingenious system, whereby the gravity of the downward tram helps pull the one going up. Once at the top you can enjoy views of Snowdonia, Morecambe sands and the Lake District.

Anglesey Sea Zoo and Angora Bunny Farm

Founded in 1983 on the site of an oyster farm, Anglesey Sea Zoo has grown to become Wales's largest marine aquarium. The aim of the zoo is to be educational without ever being stuffy. It taps into children's fascination with the deep and the magnificent, and often curious, creatures that live beneath the waves. Located on the shores of the Menai Strait, the zoo has replicated the local natural habitat of Anglesey and is home to more than 50 species. The tour is bound to inspire, taking you through the Bone Free Zone – a collection of invertebrates – then on to a shipwreck, before finally leading over a shark pool. As well as displaying the animals, the zoo is actively involved in conserving stocks of lobsters and seahorses, while more exotic creatures include piranhas and Japanese oysters. The zoo caters for all tastes and in between learning about creatures of the deep, you can play with radio-controlled boats or have a round of crazy golf.

If the younger members of your party were at all perturbed by the sight of sharks and piranhas, then the rabbits of the Angora Bunny Farm at Llangefnis should calm them down. Bred for their astonishingly lightweight yet warm wool – it has eight times the warmth of sheep's wool – these oversized members of the rabbit family are fun to watch and feed. At the farm you can learn how this durable yarn is harvested and spun. But be careful, the bunnies are so cute and cuddly that you may have to bat away requests to take one home.

WHERE:
Anglesey, Gwynedd
BEST TIME TO GO:
The sea zoo is open all year round. The bunny farm opens from Easter to September.
DON'T MISS:
The zoo's big sea-forest display – a giant window on a world that is usually accessible only to deep-sea divers. It is also the perfect place for that family photo.
AMOUNT OF WALKING:
Little. The zoo has good wheelchair access but the farm isn't really suitable for wheelchair users.
COST:
Reasonable. Under threes get in free to the zoo, where family tickets are available.
YOU SHOULD KNOW:
Angora rabbits originate from Turkey. The name is a corruption of the word Ankara. Their wool can be obtained by combing them during their moulting season.

The big fish forest of Anglesey Sea Zoo

Bodelwyddan Castle

Bodelwyddan Castle

WHERE:
South of Rhyl, Clwyd
BEST TIME TO GO:
Open on weekends only from
October to May (except for school
holidays, when it opens all week).
From June to September the castle is
open every day, save for selected
Fridays.
DON'T MISS:
The medieval festival in August; it's a
most spectacular show, with music,
merriment and re-enacted battles.
AMOUNT OF WALKING:
Little. The house and grounds have
only partial wheelchair access.
COST:
Reasonable. Family tickets are
available; under fours go free.
YOU SHOULD KNOW:
If you are planning to take the ghost
tour, check that your children are old
enough to be entertained by ghost
stories, rather than being scared
witless. No dogs are allowed on the
site (except guide dogs).

As well as being home to such diverse events as an annual medieval festival and a ballooning spectacular, Bodelwyddan Castle has a multitude of permanent attractions. As a regional partner of the National Portrait Gallery it has a fine collection of art on display. It is also set within beautiful grounds, complete with formal gardens and a maze. The grounds of the castle were used for training during World War I, and the trenches have been maintained as an exhibit. All very interesting and certainly worth a look, but none of these is the main attraction. Bodelwyddan Castle is a real-life haunted house. Featured on television's *Most Haunted*, it has played host to more than its fair share of ghoulish goings-on.

Prepare to have your spines well and truly tingled by tales of weird spectres and ghostly shenanigans. Tour guides take you from room to room, each with its own story to tell. There is a blue lady who haunts the terrace tearoom, the sound of soldiers playing billiards in the games room is often heard and flying phantoms have

been sighted careering down corridors. Real-life tales include the castle's partial destruction by fire and the discovery of unidentified human remains near one of the chimneystacks.

There is much else besides the paranormal to make this the fullest of days out. There is an indoor games room, an adventure playground and several interactive displays. You can even dress up in Victorian attire and have your picture taken. In the grounds there is a well-marked woodland trail, which should use up any remaining energy before the journey home.

Gypsy Wood Park

If you have children still young enough to play with joyous abandon, untrammelled by the self-consciousness that comes with moving towards adolescence, then Gypsy Wood is the place for you. It is a place of fairies and of fluffy animals, of toy railways and of play. Located in the shadow of Snowdonia, it is a delightful open-air attraction guaranteed to captivate and enthral young children.

Home to Shetland ponies, miniature goats and diminutive Mediterranean donkeys, the wildlife is perfectly proportioned for the small child's eye. Those who hanker after a train set of their own can marvel at the workings of the UK's largest miniature railway. Be sure to bring along your Wellington boots to undertake the wetland walk – a must, especially for children who still like to walk through puddles.

Gypsy Wood is an 8-ha (20-acre) site crammed full of child-friendly delights. It is a place for feeding the ducks or cuddling up to a baby goat. Fabulous peacocks strut their stuff, llamas lollop and chipmunks chatter. It is a place where all the animals have names. This wonderful natural environment also encourages numerous non-domesticated animals. A host of wild birds and bushy-tailed squirrels take full advantage of the host's hospitality. If Noah had been a six-year-old child, the residents of Gypsy Wood would have been the only animals allowed onto the Ark. It is a place where carved fairies can be summoned to life by wind chimes and where every corner brings new surprises to light up young eyes.

WHERE:
South of Caernarfon, Gwynedd
BEST TIME TO GO:
Open from Easter to mid September
DON'T MISS:
If you wish hard enough the resident fairy godmother will appear. If she doesn't, the Vietnamese pot-bellied pigs are always amusing.
AMOUNT OF WALKING:
Moderate. There is good access to most of the site; however, the wetland walk has no wheelchair/pushchair access.
COST:
Reasonable – family tickets are available.
YOU SHOULD KNOW:
You should always wash your hands after touching animals. The park provides antibacterial hand wash and disposable towels at specially erected stations.

333

Newborough to Llanddwyn Island walk

WHERE:
Anglesey, Gwynedd

BEST TIME TO GO:
Any time of the year, but best in fine weather.

DON'T MISS:
Climbing the lighthouse. Even if your legs are a little tired, the views are worth it. You can always rest on the beach afterwards.

AMOUNT OF WALKING:
Lots – the walk should take around three hours. The full hike is not suitable for wheelchair users or pushchairs. There is a shorter round trip from the car park, which has good access. Dogs are not allowed on the island.

COST:
Free

YOU SHOULD KNOW:
Before setting out on the walk it is important to check on the tides. Even though Llanddwyn only becomes an island for a few days each year, it is better to be safe than sorry.

The coastal footpath runs through sand dunes.

If your kids are positively full of beans at the start of the school holidays, there are few better places to introduce them to the joys of hiking than this 8-km (5-mi) circular walk. Though it often gives you the feeling of remoteness, you are in fact never very far from civilization and there is ample opportunity to rest, picnic or play by the sea. Whether you arrive by bus from Bangor or by car, the starting point is the car park at Newborough.

The first part of the walk takes you through dense woodland – a managed forest planted at the end of the World War II. You then come to the tranquil sandy water's edge of Llanddwyn Island, an ancient place of pilgrimage, brim full of history. The island, which only becomes adrift from the shore at exceptionally high tides, takes its name from St Dwynwen, the Welsh patron saint of love – celebrated in much the same way as St Valentine.

Just past an eerie ruined church you come to the larger of two lighthouses where, by climbing up to the balcony, you get the best views of the hike. On a clear day the views out to sea and back towards Snowdonia are tremendous. The path then follows the rim of the island and a small detour takes you onto a wonderfully secluded beach, which provides a chance for a rest or even a dip, if the water is warm enough. You then follow the edge of the sand dunes and back into the forest for your return. This is a most rewarding hike, with enough of interest along the way to make the walking seem easy. Its varied terrain provides a good mixture of rambling, scrambling and ambling to test young legs, without ever being too hard on them.

Keep your eyes open for the monster of the lake!

Lake Bala

Technically speaking, Lake Bala is a mere interruption to the passage of the River Dee, but boy what an interruption it is! At 6.4 km (4 mi) long and 1.6 km (1 mi) wide, it is the largest natural body of water in Wales and has become its outdoor playground. Its shores are home to the largest concentration of water-sports teachers in the UK and, if it can be done on the water, you can probably do it here.

A good way to get a feel of this sumptuous environment is to take the hour-long return trip on the Rheilffordd Llyn Tegid (Bala Lake Railway). A steam engine plies its trade back and forth along the lake, offering great views across its tranquil waters and the mountains beyond. Then it is back to the information centre at the head of the lake to decide which activity is for you. If, as a family, you are experienced on the water, you will be pleased at the range available – offering you a chance to try something new or return to a tried-and-trusted sport. Novices are probably best advised to book a multi-activity package such as the one provided by the Bala Adventure and Watersports Centre. You can try your hand at sailing, white-water rafting, windsurfing, canoeing, kayaking and even gorge walking. Land-based activities include climbing, hiking and mountain biking. This potpourri approach gives the whole family a chance to test their skills under expert tutelage and, who knows, it could spark a lifelong interest.

Younger members of the family should keep their eyes open for Teggie, the benign monster of the lake. Though more elusive than its Scottish counterpart, Nessie, any sighting should be reported to the information centre.

WHERE:
Bala, south of Snowdonia, Gwynedd
BEST TIME TO GO:
The summer months (May to September); advance booking recommended during July and August.
DON'T MISS:
If you have never done it, gorge walking is a safe but exhilarating way to traverse difficult terrain.
AMOUNT OF WALKING:
Moderate. You should advise both the Bala Railway and the Adventure Centre of any special needs when booking.
COST:
Expensive, but you do get full use of some quite expensive equipment and expert guidance.
YOU SHOULD KNOW:
Legend has it that there is a palace buried under the lake. The story goes that a harpist tried to warn an evil prince of an impending flood, but the tyrant wouldn't listen. The musician was then carried up a mountain by a bird and the next day the valley was flooded and Lake Bala was born.

Teifi Valley – the National Wool Museum and Teifi Valley Railway

There is a lovely old term used to describe a daydreamer – 'woolgatherer'. Its origin is the somnambulistic appearance of those who collect stray wool from hedgerows. If the term could be applied to a physical feature, the Teifi Valley would be that place. Peaceful, sparsely populated, yet easy to access, it is a place to lose yourself in wonder. There is, however, no need to lay a breadcrumb trail to find your way back as the valley is wonderfully compact and, if you stick to the valley floor, the walking is easy.

Once the site of over 30 mills, the valley was the heart of the Welsh wool industry. The area is quieter now and the last remnant of a once-thriving trade can be found at Llandysul, in the shape of the National Wool Museum. Its caringly renovated buildings mix original machinery with modern adaptations, including a raised passageway that gives you a bird's eye view of the production process in the site's working mill. It is at the end of the tour that the fun really starts and you get to try your hand at carding – the first part of the process for turning fleece into wool.

The theme of restored heritage continues as you head along the dale to the Teifi Valley Railway. Though at 40 minutes for a round trip it may not qualify as a great railway journey, it certainly packs a lot in. You are transported through glades, past waterfalls and along this most verdant of valleys to make this a very satisfying trip. The line is staffed by volunteers and their enthusiasm for the robust little steam engines gives the railway the feel of an oversized toy train set.

A model shows the automation of sheep shearing.

Cardigan Bay's Marine Wildlife Centre and a taste of kayaking

The word 'coast' comes from the Latin costa, which means 'rib'. While it sometimes takes a leap of imagination to see the shore as a human body part, the Romans could have had Cardigan Bay in their minds. Perfectly curved and supremely protective of its most precious parts, this bay on Wales's west coast has some of Britain's finest coastal scenery and provides sanctuary to a huge array of marine wildlife. A well-maintained path makes for good walking around the coastline, but the full beauty of this nautical haven is best revealed by taking to the seas.

As seafaring nature-watching has grown in popularity, all too many operators speed you out to sea in the hope of you snapping a quick picture, and then return you to land to pick up some more punters. Not so with the Cardigan Marine Wildlife Centre, which offers you the chance to take part in a scientific survey by identifying species and monitoring numbers. As well as something that will look good on the school *résumé*, it is a fantastic experience to scan the waves for wonderful creatures like bottlenose dolphins and grey seals. A research assistant is on board every vessel to answer your questions and to collate the data from the sightings.

If the survey has whetted your appetite for the open seas, then you may wish to explore them with a little more independence. Invented by the Inuit people of North America and designed for speed and silence while hunting, the kayak is the perfect way to glide almost effortlessly through the water. The Cardigan Bay Watersports Centre provides supervised hour-long 'taste of kayaking' courses which take you around the edge of the bay and teach you the skills required for enjoying this supremely relaxing method of transport in the future.

Colourful canoes on the harbour wall at New Quay

WHERE:
On the west Wales coast, Dyfed
BEST TIME TO GO:
The Wildlife Centre is open all year; most dolphin sightings are from May to October. The kayaking is available from April to October – subject to cancellation due to bad weather.
DON'T MISS:
The playful dolphins – if you are lucky enough to see them group fishing, it is a most spectacular sight.
AMOUNT OF WALKING:
Little. You should advise both centres of any special needs when booking.
COST:
Expensive. The cost of the boat trip goes towards funding the survey.
YOU SHOULD KNOW:
The bottlenose dolphin is misnamed, as the protrusion at the front of its head is not really its nose. Its real nose is a blowhole at the top of the head. Children under 14 must be accompanied by an adult on the kayaking, where a good level of swimming is also required.

337

Llywernog Silver-Lead Mine and Devil's Bridge Waterfalls

WHERE:
East of Aberystwyth, Dyfed
BEST TIME TO GO:
The mine is fully open from March to October and open upon request at other times. The waterfalls are open all year round but are best in spring.
DON'T MISS:
The Devil's Punchbowl at the Falls
AMOUNT OF WALKING:
Moderate. Neither place is suitabe for wheelchairs or pushchairs. Sensible shoes should be worn at the waterfalls and great care taken as the stairway can get slippery.

Devil's Bridge

Until the 1840s, children as young as five worked in the mines for up to 12 hours a day. Jobs included loading minerals onto carts, leading ponies and staffing the tunnel entrances. In 1842 the Mines Act finally outlawed the employment of children under ten, though boys over that age continued to be exploited throughout the 19th century.

Thankfully child labour in this country is a thing of the past, but at the Llywernog Silver-Lead Mine you can get a sense of what things were like all those years ago. A good starting point is a self-guided tour of the site, which gives you a feel of the conditions the workers had to endure. Next, it is time to venture underground into the claustrophobic tunnels that run along the mineral seams, where you

learn how the miners drilled for silver. Back above ground you can then learn how to pan for silver and, most excitingly, anything you find is yours.

If all that subterranean foraging has left you gasping for air, then the afternoon's excursion to the Devil's Bridge Waterfalls will bring the blood rushing back through your veins. A steep stairway takes you down the side of the waterfall on a well-worn spiritual path that has for centuries been part of an important monastic experience. There are two walks, one of about ten minutes and the other of just under an hour. Either one takes you into a world that resembles a giant well. Water cascades alongside you as your descent is flanked by this magnificent natural wonder. At the end of the day the kids can try to work out the total distance you have travelled above and below the ground.

COST:
Reasonable; family tickets are available at both attractions. Under fives are free at the falls and under fours at the mines.
YOU SHOULD KNOW:
Legend has it that the Devil visited Wales, drawn there by its natural beauty, but could not cross the falls. He struck a Faustian deal with an old lady to build a bridge in exchange for the first living thing that crossed it, presuming it would be her or at least some prized livestock. The wise old stick tricked the devil by hurling a loaf of bread across the bridge; a dog then chased after the bread and so the Devil was thwarted – never to return to Wales.

Brecknock Museum and Art Gallery and the Play Barn

If you want to introduce your children to the delights of art and artefacts, then look no further than the splendidly diminutive Brecknock Museum and Art Gallery. Housed on three floors of an early Victorian mansion house, the museum takes you on a journey from the area's ancient Celtic roots, through Roman occupation and the Dark Ages up to the present day. By far the largest exhibit is a reconstruction of a Victorian courtroom scene, which is worth the visit alone. By pressing a button you bring to life 30 life-sized figures, which 'act out' the full drama of a trial set in the 1880s. The trial involves the theft of a cash box, and since potential punishments were particularly harsh at the time, the proceedings are full of tension.

If the morning is all about exercising the grey matter, then little limbs can be put to the test in the afternoon at the Play Barn. Promising 'adventure, exercise, exploration and excitement', it certainly delivers on all counts, providing a safe and rain-free environment in which to have fun. Parents and guardians can sit back on comfy sofas, sip their drinks and watch the fun. The most difficult decision of the day for the kids is just where to begin. Exhilarating slides, mind-boggling mazes and elevated 'crawl ways' are all waiting to be enjoyed. If the children grow tired of doing all the work, they too can take a rest at Storytime or participate in a craft session. Those with remaining energy to burn will want to get back to the aerobic attractions by clambering up the zig-zag climb or bouncing on the double see-saw.

WHERE:
Brecon, Powys
BEST TIME TO GO:
The museum is open all year round, but closes on some days from October to March. The Play Barn opens from Wednesday to Saturday, except for school holidays, when it is open all week.
DON'T MISS:
Viewing the early medieval log boat. Discovered by a local carpenter, it was one of the museum's first exhibits when it opened in 1928.
AMOUNT OF WALKING:
Little. The museum has disabled access throughout. You should telephone before visiting the Play Barn to discuss any special needs with their trained staff.
COST:
Reasonable. Admission to the museum is free for under 16s. The Play Barn is restricted to under 11s who are less than 144 cm (4 ft 9 in) in height.
YOU SHOULD KNOW:
The museum has a fine collection of love spoons. In a custom peculiar to Wales, these sometimes intricate wooden carvings were created by young men in a bid to entice young ladies into marriage.

Visitors are enthralled by a model of the planet Saturn.

The Spaceguard Centre and a red kite feeding station

It is all eyes to the skies, as we visit first a centre dedicated to the study of asteroids and then watch a sovereign of the air at feeding time. The Spaceguard Centre is the only place of its kind in the UK dedicated to the study of asteroids and their possible threat to Earth. The centre is well stocked with all the latest gadgets and software required to undertake its research and an expert team is on hand to answer any questions from visitors. While planetariums tread a fine line between entertainment and education, the practical *raison d'être* of the centre and its continual quest for new discoveries, puts it at the forefront of galactic research. You will learn that the asteroids that threaten us are called Near Earth Objects and though major strikes on our planet are few and far between, they can and have had devastating effects. If this exploration of our near universe kindles an interest, and if your kids are old enough, the centre opens in the evening, where you can experience the work live.

It is now time to head along the A44 to witness a display closer to *terra firma*, but no less extraordinary. At 14.00 GMT (15.00 BST) a whole host of our feathered friends descend on Gigrin Farm in what is surely the most spectacular avian display to be found on these shores. Once a common sight in the skies above Britain, the red kite was culled to near extinction. Thankfully, a few good farmers in these parts decided to protect and even encourage these magnificent creatures. Specially constructed hides give you a ringside seat as the farmers drop beef on the ground. Buzzards circle and crows descend on the meat, before the indomitable kites come and harry them and relieve them of their bounty on the wing. It's an unforgettable sight.

WHERE:
Near Llandrindod Wells, Powys
BEST TIME TO GO:
Both are open all year round. More kites come to feed when the weather is bad. A clear night is best for an evening visit to the Spaceguard Centre.
DON'T MISS:
The stars of the day are the kites so make sure you turn up on time, because they invariably do.
AMOUNT OF WALKING:
Little; both have good wheelchair/pushchair access.
COST:
Reasonable. Under 15s are half price and under fives are free at both venues.
YOU SHOULD KNOW:
If you are ever offered the chance to name an asteroid, turn it down. Only the International Astronomical Union can officially name these bodies, but there are several bogus organizations that will relieve you of your money by offering you a certificate with your name on it.

The Centre for Alternative Technology

In recent times there has been a discernible shift in the application of 'pester power'. It used to describe children's nagging of parents to make purchases, ranging from breakfast cereals right up to a new family car. In our more environmentally aware world, particularly amongst the young, the pestering has changed direction and now many children will switch that standby button off and insist on low-energy light bulbs – progress indeed. If your children have reached the age when saving the planet is important to them, there is no better place to take them than the Centre For Alternative Technology in Machynlleth.

Right from the word go, the centre practises what it preaches as you are whisked up to the complex by one of the steepest cliff railways in the world, powered only by the weight of water. The centre itself is packed full of useful gadgetry designed for green living, but the fun really starts when you go through the sliding doors into the main 3-ha (7-acre) site. Alongside more staid exhibits like wood burners and solar panels, there is a whole range of eco-friendly hands-on exhibits. There are wheels to turn, buttons to press and levers to pull in this perfect marriage of goodness and fun. If any little ones need a break from saving the planet, there are several children's play areas dotted around the site and a smallholding full of fluffy farmyard animals.

When it was founded by a group of scientists in 1973, CAT was seen as rather quirky, but over the years the centre has grown to become a place of international importance. It is a great educational resource and has proved time and time again that learning to be green can also be fun.

Everything at the centre is made out of recycled materials.

WHERE:
North of Aberystwyth, Powys
BEST TIME TO GO:
The centre is open all year round. The cliff railway operates from April to October.
DON'T MISS:
The Inventor of the Future workshop (summer only), where you get to use recycled materials to build your own machine, then hook it up to a solar panel or a wind turbine and watch it go.
AMOUNT OF WALKING:
Moderate. Most of the site is wheelchair accessible.
COST:
Reasonable; half price if you arrive by public transport.
YOU SHOULD KNOW:
The centre is so successful at producing alternative energy that even after catering for over 60,000 visitors a year it still has surplus power to sell back to the national grid.

Llanfair Light Railway

Lake Vyrnwy Sculpture Park and Nature Trails and Llanfair Light Railway

WHERE:
Near Welshpool, Powys
BEST TIME TO GO:
The park is open all year round but best weather-wise from March to September. The railway operates on most days from April to October. The area is most beautiful in April, when bluebells form a rich carpet around the railway line.
DON'T MISS:
The highlight of the day has to be the weird and wonderful sculpture trail.
AMOUNT OF WALKING:
Moderate. The Sculpture Park has good disabled access, the puzzle trail less so. Most of the trains have carriages that can hold up to four non-motorized wheelchairs.
COST:
Reasonable. The Sculpture Park and trails are free. Under threes go free on the train, while each adult fare allows one child under 15 to travel free.
YOU SHOULD KNOW:
The incline up to Golfa Bank is a pretty continuous 1 in 33 gradient, making it one of the toughest climbs on the British railway network.

The area around Lake Vyrnwy has a lot going for it. Its wide expanse of heather moorland brings in a varied population of birdlife, while the craggy mountains that embrace the lake are a haven for such diverse creatures as wild ponies and butterflies. It is this outstanding natural beauty that inspired the creation of a quite remarkable sculpture park and children's puzzle trail. Artists from around the world were invited to produce works using only local wood and stone. The result was an amazing assortment of shapes and figurative interpretations. As you wander along, prepare to be startled by a giant toad carved from a tree trunk or a wooden pig 'balancing' atop a beam.

The children's puzzle trail is a most ingenious way to get young children to engage with nature. Set beneath the dam that holds the reservoir's water in, the trail has ten wooden figures of animals hidden amongst the trees and the aim, with the help of clues on a supplied leaflet, is to find them all.

If all that rustic frolicking leaves you a little tired out, then you can take the weight off your feet and sit back and enjoy the sights from the comfort of the Llanfair Light Railway. Starting at the bustling market town of Welshpool, this narrow-gauge steam railway carries you at a sedate pace through the beautiful mid-Wales countryside. The sound of the engines being stoked up to full power evokes a bygone age as you travel up the particularly steep Golfa Bank. This 26-km (16-mi) round trip takes you over stone bridges, through forest and out over open heathland. It is here that you can put the skill learned earlier to the test as you look out of the window for the deer, otters and birds of prey that thrive here.

Llandovery and the Usk Reservoir

Llandovery is as delightful a market town as you will find anywhere in Wales. With the ruins of a Norman keep perched above it, the town spreads out along a green and pleasant valley. It is the perfect halfway house between town and country, and the ideal place to begin a journey up to the tranquil and secluded waters of the Usk Reservoir. If you leave the town taking the A40 towards Brecon, you will arrive at the Castle Coaching Inn at Trecastle. From here a single-track road takes you on a strikingly scenic drive up to the reservoir. The twin forested peaks of Mynydd Myddfai and Mynydd Wysg lie directly ahead, but as the road arcs round they appear to part, revealing the reservoir in all its glory. You have now arrived at one of the remotest parts of the Brecon Beacons and it's time to go explore.

The 9-km (5.6-mi) track that encircles the man-made lake is perfect for hiking or cycling, while the abundance of brown and rainbow trout in the area makes it an anglers' paradise. If you park up at the dam, you will see the reservoir snake round the valley before you. Save for a short bit of road, your journey takes you along dirt track on your circumnavigation of this sumptuous piece of water. The real joy of the walk is that the gradient is mostly gentle, making it suitable for relatively small children, and even a novice hiker will find it difficult to get lost, as you are never too far away from the water's edge. Whichever way round the lake you go, the Fedw Fawr end marks the halfway point of your walk. This is an ideal place to stop, as the views back across the water and into the mountains will make you feel that your journey has definitely been worth the effort.

WHERE:
Near Brecon, Dyfed
BEST TIME TO GO:
This really was the ideal place to build a reservoir as it rains a lot here. The best weather is to be found in June and July, but the walk is pleasant at any time of the year when it is dry and free from snow.
DON'T MISS:
The stone circles at Mynydd Bach Trecastell – a 15-minute detour from the north end of the reservoir.
AMOUNT OF WALKING:
Lots unless you cycle; the track can get quite muddy in places and the weather can change quickly, so wear walking boots and take a waterproof and a spare fleece. Wheelchair/pushchair access is possible only on the short road at the dam end of the reservoir and to a couple of fishing spots.
COST:
Free
YOU SHOULD KNOW:
Fishing on the lake requires a permit. Day permits can be obtained from a dispensing machine near the dam wall. You also need permission to take a boat onto the water.

Hay-on-Wye

You could be forgiven for thinking that Hay-on-Wye is all about books. True, it is home to a world-famous literary festival that attracts every man with his dog and even the odd ex-President. It is also home to dozens of fantastic bookshops, including a wonderful children's bookshop crammed full of kids' favourites. But Hay-on-Wye has a life beyond books, being positively brimful of artists, artisans and adventure centres. It has enough to give mind and body a thoroughly good workout.

You can unearth latent artistic talents at Fired – Creative Arts Workshop, where the instruction is to 'dress for mess' as you are guided towards producing your very own original masterpiece. Who knows, you might have the next Turner in the family! If not, you can always pass it off as a Jackson Pollock. Those crazy about horses can watch a blacksmith at his craft, while the more adventurous can hire a pony and explore the bridleways of the wide moorland around Hay Bluff.

As well as the comic creations on display at Brian Platt Cartoons, you can watch the artist at work and even commission a family caricature as a memento of your visit. Hay is reasonably compact and the perfect place to wander and browse on a sunny day. The fact that its main draw is the bookshops means that outdoors it never feels crowded, even in high season. A pleasant walk can be had along the River Wye, which provides ample opportunity for *al fresco* eating, while back in town the Norman castle is well worth an amble around. Hay is too well known to be called a 'hidden gem', but there are certainly many hidden gems within it.

Hay Castle outdoor bookshop

Felinwynt Rainforest and Butterfly Centre and West Wales Museum of Childhood

A close-up of a Tree Nymph Butterfly

Butterflies have established themselves across the globe and in a huge range of environments: hot and cold, dry and humid, from sea level to the highest mountains. Most butterfly species, however, are found in tropical rainforests. In order to cater for this range of spectacularly coloured Lepidoptera, the owners of Felinwynt Rainforest Centre have created a steamy environment in which to house these most magnificent species.

The centre offers many attractions with, at its core, a tropical house where you can have fun spotting amazingly camouflaged stick insects that live alongside brightly coloured birds, industrious leafcutter ants, as well as the centrepiece butterflies. A film show details the life stages of the butterfly and illustrates why they are such an important indicator of the planet's health. Astounding facts can be gleaned, such as if a human baby grew as fast as some caterpillars, it would weigh eight tons when it was only two weeks old. That is something to bear in mind when handing out the sandwiches at lunchtime.

If you then head to the Old Farmhouse on the outskirts of Llangeler, you will discover the delights of The West Wales Museum of Childhood. The place is positively bursting with toys and playtime accessories from down the generations. Starting with the plainest of wooden figures, the museum takes you on a journey ending with collectibles from modern television series. Five barns contain different exhibits, including the specifically Welsh Gallery (Oriel Cymru), which displays local costumes and dolls. Mothers and daughters can scrutinize dolls' houses in Gallery of Time (Oriel Amser), while fathers and sons can ogle toy trains in the Llangeler Junction Gallery. If you want to break down stereotypes, you can try this the other way round.

WHERE:
Towards the south end of Cardigan Bay, Dyfed
BEST TIME TO GO:
The museum is open all year round; the butterfly centre opens full-time from April to October and has limited opening for the remainder of the year.
DON'T MISS:
Meeting the curators at either attraction. They have turned what started out as hobbies into two fascinating, fun and informative showcases.
AMOUNT OF WALKING:
Little. The museum has good level access throughout. The Rainforest Centre has flat passage via a gravel and wood-chip track.
COST:
Reasonable. Under fours are admitted free at both attractions.
YOU SHOULD KNOW:
A common myth is that the word butterfly is an adaptation of the term flutter by. This would be convenient if it were true. The word actually comes from the Old English, buttorfleoge, and while the origins are hazy, it is most likely that they got that name because they appeared each year at the time in spring when people started churning butter.

Brinmore Tramroad

WHERE:
It runs into Powys from Gwent
BEST TIME TO GO:
March to September, though the road
is open all year round.
DON'T MISS:
Taking a look at the replica tram at
the Tramroads wharf in Talybont
AMOUNT OF WALKING:
It depends whether you are on two
wheels, four legs or two. Parts of the
Tramroad have good disabled access;
you can find a map of these sections
at the information centre in Talybont.
COST:
The road is toll free. Horse and
bicycle hire are available locally.
YOU SHOULD KNOW:
Despite its short length, the Tramroad
takes you through a surprising
variety of habitats – from woodland,
to peat bog, coniferous forest and
shaded outcrops – this diversity
makes the area home to hundreds of
varieties of wild flowers.

The Brinmore Tramroad, known in Welsh as Bryn Oer, stretches for 13 km (8 mi) from Trefil to Talybont-on-Usk, entirely within the strikingly beautiful Brecon Beacons National Park. It was originally a horse-drawn railway used to take coal and limestone from the valleys into mid Wales. More efficient means of transport, most notably the steam train, rendered it redundant by the mid 1860s. Now a public bridleway, the hawthorn-flanked Tramroad acts as a corridor for wildlife and a not-too-taxing little route through some of the best scenery Wales has to offer. Motorized transport is strictly forbidden, thus allowing you to soak up the sounds and smells of the countryside at a leisurely pace and with no distractions.

Whether you are on foot, pedal bike or even horseback, the Tramroad can be accessed from behind the White Hart Inn in Talybont-on-Usk via a short but steep bridge over a canal. The path then leads you gently uphill and away from the village. Though the gradient is on the whole relatively gentle, it is surprising how high up you get in a short space of time. Be sure to stop and admire the views along the way, particularly on the section that takes you high above Talybont Reservoir.

It was a simple twist of fate that has allowed the Tramroad to continue to exist. Created by Act of Parliament around the turn of the 19th century, the road was administered by the Brinmore Tramroad Company. Since there are no records of the company's dissolution, it is unclear who now owns the road. In 1999 a preservation society was formed and, with the help of local government and the National Park, the tramway is being preserved for all to enjoy.

*A cyclist makes his way up
the Tramroad.*

Cwmcarn Forest drive

At 11 km (7 mi), Cwmcarn Forest drive may seem on the short side, but anyone who has undertaken it will testify that it certainly packs a lot in. The road snakes around grassy knolls and verdant hills, taking you through this delightful urban forest. The one-way road has been specially designed by the Forestry Commission of Wales to maximize the views from the car and, on a clear day, you can see as far as the Mendips across the Bristol Channel.

The day is not all about driving, as there are seven car parks, each with picnic areas, barbecue spots, play areas and themed activities. There are also several hiking trails, a fishing lake and an invigorating mountain-bike trail; all you have to do is bring the energy and the equipment. The trail is well maintained and signposted, and maps are available at the well-stocked Visitor Centre to help your planning. All the car parks offer great views as well as being the starting points for various activities. Car park 1 (Giant's Court) is shaded by woodland and is home to some fabulous wood-sculptures. Be warned, however, that the area is stalked by the spectre of a Celtic warrior and those who see him are destined to have bad luck! Assuming he doesn't appear, you can journey on with confidence.

Other highlights include the fairy-tale-inspired Wizard's Walk at the Land of the Tylwyth Teg (car park 3) and replica story poles (totem poles) at Madoc's Place (car park 5). The real magic of the forest is that it makes getting away from it all trouble-free and accessible, being only a short drive from Newport, yet having the feel of somewhere far more remote. If you go down to these woods today you're sure of a very pleasant surprise.

WHERE:
Near Newport, Gwent
BEST TIME TO GO:
The drive is closed during December and January and opens from 11.00 to around one hour before sunset for the remainder of the year. Bad weather may cause its closure at any time during the year.
DON'T MISS:
The views across to the Brecon Beacons from Windy Ridge (car park 6)
AMOUNT OF WALKING:
Little or lots, it is up to you. The drive and car parks are designed to give disabled visitors good level access and unhindered views.
COST:
Low – a small charge is made per car.
YOU SHOULD KNOW:
During the summer the forest hosts special events such as bushcraft workshops, teddy bears' picnics and African drumming – so check ahead to see if there is something you would like to do.

Just the place for a picnic!

A former miner giving children an underground tour.

Abergavenny and the Big Pit in Blaenavon

Abergavenny is so solid a town that it gives the appearance of being hewn from the rocks that surround it. Nestled at the southern edge of the Brecon Beacons, it is a gateway for those wishing to explore the area by hiking, biking or on horseback. It has the splendid twin peaks of the Blorenge and the Sugar Loaf behind it and the clear waters of the River Usk flow through its heart. The verdigrised copper-roofed indoor market is the town's focal point and is a fine place to stock up for a picnic.

You can begin finding out about the area in the town's museum; founded in 1959, it chronicles the history of Abergavenny from ancient times to the present day. The highlight of the attraction is its Roman armoury and it also has a children's activity room with educational and fun workshops. Now you have learned a bit about the past, it's time to have a close-up look at a famous relic in the form of Abergavenny Castle. Thankfully you don't have to go far, as the museum is set in the only fully restored building within the castle's ruins. Built nearly 1,000 years ago, the castle has been razed and sacked on a pretty regular basis throughout history, and what remains is a ghostly assortment of craggy ruins.

Having had lunch – the Linda Vista Gardens are the perfect place for that picnic – it is time to take a look at the area's industrial past. At the Big Pit in Blaenavon you can learn about the history of coalmining, once the area's mainstay. This is a day that saves its best until last, as you are taken 90 m (295 ft) down into the bowels of the mine for a 50-minute tour of the coalface, guided by a former miner.

*Barges on the Monmouth
and Brecon Canal*

A cruise on the Monmouth
and Brecon Canal

A trip by canal boat is definitely not for anyone who wants to get anywhere in a hurry. Travelling at little more than walking pace, you are transported to a land where time is of little consequence and your only audience are the sheep and cows that graze the surrounding meadows. The Monmouthshire and Brecon Canal, known affectionately as the 'Mon and Brec', runs for 51 km (32 mi) from Newport to Brecon carrying you from docks, through the country's former industrial heartland and up towards the mountains of the Brecon Beacons National Park.

To navigate the entire length of the canal would take something near a week, but thankfully there are companies that offer day trips, giving you a bite-sized portion of this magnificent waterway. The best scenery is to be found at the Beacons end of the canal and several operators offer trips starting at Brecon, taking you down to Brynich and then returning. This mini-cruise packs in many of the best features of canal boating. There are two ways a canal system can deal with gradients, the first is by using locks to raise or lower the boat, the second is by traversing the terrain by way of an aqueduct – a water bridge. On this section of the 'Mon and Brec' you get to experience both.

For those new to this kind of boating, locks are the most exciting part of the journey. On a downward gradient, the barge is steered into the lock and the gates are closed behind it. The sluice gates to the bow of the boat are then opened, heralding a bubbling release of water and the slow lowering of the boat so you can continue your journey at the lower level. An equally effervescent filling of the lock is used on an upward journey.

WHERE:
The canal runs from Gwent into Powys
BEST TIME TO GO:
The canal is open all year round; the day trips are available at weekends throughout the year and all week during school holidays.
DON'T MISS:
The views as the Brynich Aqueduct takes you over the River Usk
AMOUNT OF WALKING:
Little; some barges have lifts to accommodate a limited number of wheelchair users. The towpath has good level access.
COST:
Reasonable
YOU SHOULD KNOW:
In spite of the hilly terrain, the canal has very few locks. Indeed a 37-km (23-mi) stretch of the canal is on level ground. Locks were expensive and of necessity slow traffic down. The engineers who built the 'Mon and Brec' used the contours of the land, navigating around the hills.

The Hidden Gardens and Grottoes of Dewstow

WHERE:
Near Caldicot, Gwent
BEST TIME TO GO:
The gardens are open from Easter to mid October.
DON'T MISS:
Walking through the Park Tunnel – it feels as if you're entering Fred and Wilma Flintstone's living room.
AMOUNT OF WALKING:
Moderate. The nature of the gardens makes access to the grottoes impossible for wheelchair/pushchair users; the management of the gardens ask that one adult should accompany each group of four children.
COST:
Low; accompanied children under ten can enter for free.
YOU SHOULD KNOW:
Oakley, who commissioned the building of the gardens, was so reclusive that very few people knew of the gardens' existence. It came as a huge surprise to the new owners, whose main business is the neighbouring golf course, when they stumbled across them. Even though there is quite probably a lot more that is still hidden, the proprietors felt they had to stop somewhere and open up the gardens for the public to enjoy.

In children's literature there is often a door or portal that leads to a hidden world where adults are excluded and where all things are possible. Of course these places don't exist in the real world – or do they? Dewstow is a place where fantasy and reality meet, but thankfully adults are not excluded, as there is the small matter of the entrance fee to be negotiated.

Constructed in 1895 and then neglected and buried by 1945, the Hidden Grottoes of Dewstow slowly gave up their secrets by the turn of the century. Careful excavation has since revealed a veritable wonderland of waterfalls and fern-lined caverns to delight and excite those who dare to explore these half-hidden recesses. The whole site is a subterranean fairyland that would grace any C S Lewis novel, as you are led through a watery labyrinthine world of rich greens and moisture-laden air.

Even after witnessing this amazing horticultural landscape, you may still be uncertain whether it is the work of a genius or a madman. Its creator, one H R K Oakley, was a renowned breeder of horses, many of which bear his name to the present day. However, his main legacy is these magnificent gardens, borne of a fantastic imagination and uninhibited by formal design. Above ground there were originally rock gardens, ponds and tropical greenhouses. Little of this remains, but below there is still a mysterious world waiting to be discovered.

Smaller children will take delight in pond dipping – searching the rock pools for tadpoles and the like – and there is a daily Teddy Bear hunt, where you try to spot Teddy and his friends hiding in the caverns.

The Hidden Gardens

Caerleon Roman Fortress and Legionary Museum

When the Romans came to Britain they met the fiercest opposition to their conquest from the Celtic fringes. Their arrival was greeted by dogged resistance from the local chiefs who banded together against them, and it was not until AD 78 that the whole of Wales was subdued. A tightly structured network of strongholds garrisoned by co-opted local troops was controlled by two formidable Roman legions based at Deva (Chester) and here at Caerleon – at a fort called Isca by the Romans.

Even though excavation has taken place on this home of the Second Augustan Legion for around a century, the gradual revealing of the site is still a work in progress. The 1930s saw a major breakthrough at the fortification with the unearthing of the Centurion's house, complete with patterned flooring. More recent discoveries have revealed just what a hive of activity Isca was. As well as eight barrack blocks used to house the ordinary soldiers, there were three granaries and a metal workshop where weapons were produced and repaired.

It does take a degree of imagination to look at this ruined site and picture it in all its glory, particularly when looking at the presumably once-grand amphitheatre, which is now just a series of scarcely revealed lumps of stone. Interpretative help is at hand, however, if you head to Caerleon town centre and visit its Roman Legionary Museum. The museum is full of Roman artefacts, from legionnaires' armour and burial caskets, through to decorative mosaics. Children can dress up in armour in the reconstructed Barrack Room or help out in the Roman Gardens (summer only). The most impressive part of the site is the Roman Baths Museum, which uses modern technology to bring to life the most complete relics of any Roman baths in Britain.

Sculptured Roman head outside the Roman Museum at Caerleon

WHERE:
On the outskirts of Newport, Gwent
BEST TIME TO GO:
Open all year round, with shorter opening hours in winter
DON'T MISS:
The pretty reclaimed mosaics now displayed at the museum.
AMOUNT OF WALKING:
Little; there is good level access at the museum and the baths; the fortress is rather bumpy in parts but can be viewed by wheelchair users from the surrounding grounds.
COST:
Free
YOU SHOULD KNOW:
There is evidence that Caerleon may have been the Camelot of Arthurian legend and the circular amphitheatre the original Round Table.

351

Pembroke Castle

Pembroke Castle

WHERE:
Pembroke, Dyfed
BEST TIME TO GO:
The castle is open all year round.
Check ahead for the calendar of
events.
DON'T MISS:
The wall walk, which gives great
views of the whole castle site and
the surrounding countryside.
AMOUNT OF WALKING:
Little.
COST:
Reasonable. Under fives go free and
family tickets are available. Some
events are available at additional
cost. Those with mobility problems
can access the ground floor of the
castle from the car park near the
main entrance.
YOU SHOULD KNOW:
It is no accident that the castle's
staircases arc round the way they do.
Their construction gave a natural
advantage to a right-handed
swordsman coming down the
stairs, defending the castle,
allowing a broad forehand sweep of
his sword. The attacker's angle of
attack is restricted to a short
backhand motion.

Perfectly located on the banks of the River Cleddau, which forms a natural moat, Pembroke Castle is an impressive stronghold that has stayed largely undamaged by the rigours of battle. The exterior is like a child's drawing of a castle, while inside a series of caverns, passageways and spiral stone staircases makes it fun to explore. The birthplace of Harri Tudor, later to become Henry VII, the castle has long been associated with some of the most powerful families in the land.

Coats of Arms together with carvings and re-creations of Tudor life are all on display inside, while outside you can take a walk along the castle walls or picnic in the sumptuous grounds. There are also fine views of the river mouth from St Anne's Bastion. You can bring the past to life by trying your hand at the craft of brass rubbing. This pastime, which gained popularity in the 17th century, involves laying a piece of treated paper on a monumental brass and rubbing the paper with a crayon until the images appear. As well as being great fun, it also gives you a decorative souvenir of your visit. You can practise your technique before you visit with a soft pencil, a sheet of plain paper and a coin.

The castle really springs to life in summer, when it plays host to a series of special events. You can variously marvel at displays of falconry, watch a re-creation of a Civil War battle performed by the Sealed Knot Society, or try on the armour of the Marcher Stuarts – a fearsome band of mercenaries. You can also extend your visit into the evening by taking in a Shakespearian play.

Castell Henllys Iron Age Fort and the Welsh Wildlife Centre

The Iron Age fort of Castell Henllys is a hybrid of excavation and reconstruction, which has slowly revealed how we used to live over 2,500 years ago. Once the foundations of an ancient circular house were discovered on this site in the 1980s, it was all systems go to re-create a living, breathing replica of our ancestors' lives. The result is a more than faithfully built model; as trustees, Welsh Heritage have sought to illustrate the full experience of our Celtic ancestors through dress and farming methods, as well as construction and craft techniques.

Resident storytellers are on hand to guide you around the site and explain what the ancient inhabitants were like and what they did for fun. These stories were essential to the propagation of knowledge long before the written word took over. Your fun really starts when you get to mix dyes using traditional methods, and have them painted on your faces.

Preservation of a different kind awaits you on the second part of this day out, as you head out to the Welsh Wildlife Centre, situated along the fertile emerald-green banks of the River Teifi. The reserve has tracks that lead you into the territory of badgers, otters and imported water buffalo. Inside the impressive wood-and-glass visitor centre there are webcam links to the setts and holts, so even on a rainy day you can enjoy the magnificent creatures that have made this reserve their home.

The more adventurous can take to the water for a guided canoe trip through the shallow waters of the River Teifi. The trip takes you alongside marshland, home to a whole host of wildlife, through the mightily impressive Cilgerran Gorge and then finishes off by traversing some rapids.

WHERE:
Near the Pembrokeshire Coast, Dyfed
BEST TIME TO GO:
The Wildlife Centre is fully open from March to October. Castell Henllys is open all year round, save for a couple of weeks around Christmas.
DON'T MISS:
The highlight of the day has to be the canoe trip, which gives a unique insight into the habitats of river-dwelling birds and mammals.
AMOUNT OF WALKING:
Moderate; maps of wheelchair-accessible routes are available at both venues.
COST:
Reasonable to expensive (depending on whether you take the canoe trip); family tickets are available at both attractions.
YOU SHOULD KNOW:
Water buffalo are one of the most important animals to humans. While the wild breeds are now registered as an endangered species, their domesticated cousins produce a twentieth of the world's milk and provide more than a fifth of the agricultural energy in southeast Asia.

A demonstration of the old method of spinning wool.

Cardiff Castle and the National History Museum

WHERE:
Cardiff, South Glamorgan
BEST TIME TO GO:
Both attractions are open all year round.
DON'T MISS:
The workshops at St Fagans, where traditional skills and crafts are faithfully demonstrated.
AMOUNT OF WALKING:
Moderate; at St Fagans wheelchair and pushchair access is only possible to some of the site. At the castle lifts are available to take you from floor to floor and onto the terrace, but some parts are not accessible for wheelchair users or those with pushchairs.

Cardiff Castle in the spring sunshine

The history of Cardiff is synonymous with the history of its castle and each dominant culture over the past 2,000 years has left its mark on the stronghold. The castle acts as both preserved fortress and museum of the Welsh capital's history. Guided tours take you from room to room and era to era, from its earliest Roman beginnings through to the Victorian expansion under the ownership of the Marquis of Bute. The castle is also home to the museum of the Welsh Regiment and houses many exhibits from the battle of Rorke's Drift, the famous battle of the Zulu Wars. If the yearning for learning wanes, there are always the magnificent surrounding gardens to play in and, by climbing the Norman keep, you get tremendous views of Cardiff and the surrounding countryside.

History is written by the victors, as the saying goes. It's equally true that heritage is all too often in the hands of the wealthy. The National History Museum at St Fagans has for over 60 years set out to redress this imbalance by re-creating the dwellings of the not-so-rich from earliest Celtic times, right through to the present day. Very often this has meant moving buildings brick-by-brick, with all their contents in tow. What seemed like a madcap idea in 1948 has seen the museum become the most visited attraction in Wales. More than 40 buildings – including a Methodist chapel, a schoolhouse, a bakery and a general store – were relocated from various parts of the Principality to find a new home here, all depicting a different epoch of Welsh life. Costumed guides are on hand to add to the authenticity and answer any questions prompted by this unique experience.

COST:
Reasonable. St Fagans is free to enter; under fives go free at the castle and those who live or work in Cardiff can gain free admission by applying for a Cardiff Castle Pass.
YOU SHOULD KNOW:
St Fagans is not just about buildings. Its Oriel 1 exhibition explores the 80 or so languages spoken in Wales today and throws up some startling hypotheses, such as the strong links between Welsh and Bengali.

Flat Holm

Flat Holm Island is just 8 km (5 mi) away from downtown Cardiff, but its peace and tranquillity make it feel far removed from the hustle and bustle of city life. It is therefore not surprising to find out that it was once used as a monastic retreat. As if to underline the contrast, the ferry to the island takes you first past the Cardiff Bay Barrage, an impressive feat of modern engineering, before heading out into the Bristol Channel to this serene isle.

Though small in size, the island has more than its fair share of history. Vikings and Saxons sought sanctuary here; it was home to smugglers and its isolation led to the building of a cholera hospital, the ruins of which can still be seen. Whatever its history, the island's current guardians – the Flat Holm Society – have ensured that it is a really pleasant place to visit.

Day trippers have just three hours to enjoy the island, but its compact size means that you can see most things without rushing. A self-guided tour pack is available to take you around the lighthouse, foghorn station and the island's many fortifications – just ask on the boat. For those with a more laid-back approach, picnic facilities (including benches and the use of the kitchen) are available. You can even work up an appetite by joining in a treasure hunt or taking a nature walk along the shore. Whether you come in search of nature or history, Flat Holm has both in abundance. It is home to innumerable seabirds as well as slow worms and common lizards and the island marks the point from which in 1897 Guglielmo Marconi transmitted the first wireless signal to go over the sea.

WHERE:
Directly south of Cardiff, South Glamorgan
BEST TIME TO GO:
The boat runs from April to October, weather permitting.
DON'T MISS:
Taking time to observe the wildlife, particularly the magnificent red-billed oystercatchers.
AMOUNT OF WALKING:
Moderate. The island is accessed via a long wooden jetty, making it difficult for those with mobility problems. The trip is not suitable for children under four years old.
COST:
Reasonable
YOU SHOULD KNOW:
The original lighthouse ran on coal and consumed over 23 tonnes (25 tons) each month, which all had to be carried by hand to the top of the tower. Thankfully the beacon is now solar powered.

Mountain bike trails of Afan Forest Park

WHERE:
Near Port Talbot, West Glamorgan
BEST TIME TO GO:
Open all year round and some might argue that it is more fun in inclement weather.
DON'T MISS:
The Wall Trail – it is long but rewarding and has an awesome final descent, fittingly called the Graveyard Section.
AMOUNT OF WALKING:
Little – unless you fall off a lot. It is difficult to give a minimum age for mountain biking, but on these courses you probably need to be over ten. Participants should already have some cycling skills and be reasonably fit.
COST:
Reasonable; you can bring your own equipment or hire bikes on a daily basis from Glyncorrwg Mountain Bike Centre.
YOU SHOULD KNOW:
With the thrills, inevitably come the spills and it is of paramount importance to wear the proper safety equipment. Try to stay together as a group.

Before venturing out make sure that you are not saddled with a rigid (a bike with bad suspension), put on your skid lid (helmet) and toe clips (toe clips!) and try not to corndog (become covered in mud after a fall). If you bonk (become tired) or washout (lose traction) you can always join a tea party (take a break with others) but it is best to bail (jump off) before you face shovel (taste the dirt). It is not every day out that requires its own glossary, but a whole language has evolved alongside the young and vibrant sport of mountain biking and, like surfing before it, the wonderfully descriptive terms add to the thrill of the activity.

If you fancy giving it a whirl, then look no further than the specially designed multi-track mountain biking nirvana that is Afan Forest Park. The 100 km (62.5 mi) of trails in the park cater for all levels from push-push (beginner) to can-can exponent (expert). There are four main trails ranging from 6 km (3.75 mi) to 46 km (29 mi) long, each with varying degrees of difficulty. If you are new to the sport or need any advice, then the Visitor Centre is the place to begin your two-wheeled exploration. One bit of universal advice is to get to know the terrain. Rather like a golfer who walks the course, it is important to know what hidden dangers lie ahead. This will allow you to tackle the tight twisted turns of the Penhydd Trail, negotiate safely the rocky White's Level Trail and survive Jetlag, the final descent on the Skyline Trail.

The trails in Afan Forest Park offer plenty of opportunities to get muddy!

Rhossili Bay and Aberdulais Falls

It may not sound like the most original suggestion, but the best place to start your exploration of this part of the Gower Peninsula is the Visitor Centre housed in the coastguard cottages in Rhossili. It has a fine exhibition detailing the history and ecology of the area, as well as being the ideal place to pick up maps or get advice on what to do and see. The views out over Rhossili Bay are pretty fabulous to boot. The area has something for every taste, as long as you have a love for the great outdoors. Wide sandy beaches, bracing cliff-top walks with ever-changing vistas and the eerie skeletal remains of the shipwreck *Helvetia* are all on offer. If the tide is low, you can stride out to the dramatic protrusion of Worms Head, named after the Norse word for dragon, 'wurm'.

Natural wonders, mixed with industrial heritage, await you as you head inland to Aberdulais Falls – just to the east of Swansea. For more than four centuries the power of the falls has been harnessed to provide energy for the smelting of copper and tin – an interpretive display details this history. The current waterwheel is the largest of its kind in Europe and continues the tradition of producing clean energy. The real stars of the show, however, are the waterfalls themselves. Their beauty and power have attracted notable artists, including Turner, who captured their full majesty in a painting of 1796. The combination of spectacle and ozone invigoration will keep the falls with you long after your visit

WHERE:
Either side of Swansea, West Glamorgan
BEST TIME TO GO:
The falls are open all week from March to October and from Friday through to Sunday for the rest of the year. The Visitor Centre closes on Monday and Tuesday from November to March.
DON'T MISS:
Walking along Rhossili beach, a 5-km (3-mi) long strand, which is one of the finest in Britain.
AMOUNT OF WALKING:
Moderate. The Visitor Centre has good disabled access, parking and a level picnic area. The waterfalls can be accessed via a lift.
COST:
Low; family tickets are available at Aberdulais Falls; National Trust members can enter free. The Visitor Centre is free.
YOU SHOULD KNOW:
In centuries past a group known as the Rhossili Wreckers would lure ships onto the rocks with the use of lanterns. Once the ships had run aground, this group of brigands would plunder the bounty.

The giant waterwheel at Aberdulais Falls

Dr Who Up Close and Techniquest

WHERE:
Cardiff, South Glamorgan
BEST TIME TO GO:
Both are open all year round.
DON'T MISS:
Playing a tune on the giant piano at Techniquest
AMOUNT OF WALKING:
Little. Both facilities have good disabled access.
COST:
Expensive. Family tickets are available at both attractions.
YOU SHOULD KNOW:
You can also enjoy the Techniquest experience at Techniquest Glyndwr in Wrexham in North Wales.

Being a traveller through space and time, Dr Who, the itinerant saviour of our planet, has no real home save for a surprisingly roomy police box. However, there is perhaps one place on Earth that could lay claim to being his spiritual home – and that's the Welsh capital, Cardiff, since the series these days is filmed there. As its title implies, this exhibition lets you get close up to the good doctor's friends and foes. You can meet the chirpy K9, get an icy reception from the Cybermen or run the risk of extermination by the fearsome Daleks. Because the *Dr Who* series relies less on computer-generated imagery than many of its genre, the models have a highly realistic feel. The centre is a shrine for devotees of the show and its spin-off series – *Torchwood* and *The Sarah Jane Adventures* – to enjoy. Many scenes from the shows were filmed with the magnificently modern Cardiff Bay as a backdrop and guided tours are available.

Science fiction segues nicely into science fact when, after lunch, you can head across the bay for a hands-on, fun and educational approach to science. At Techniquest there is a rolling programme of over 100 interactive and participatory exhibits, but you can invariably try your hand at launching a rocket or driving an electric car. Visitors fascinated by the far reaches of space are treated to a cloud-free simulation of our night skies through an informative audio-visual presentation. Science can seem somewhat staid when presented in the formal setting of the classroom, but while the time travel displayed in *Dr Who* is so far beyond us, the science of the possible is excitingly displayed at Techniquest.

The Science Centre also offers a wide-ranging education programme for the young, so if there is ever a dilemma whether to do homework or go out, you know where to come.

Barry Island and the Welsh Hawking Centre

Just as Brighton has earned the tag 'London by the Sea', Barry Island is the resort that embodies the spirit of the Welsh capital, Cardiff. While the turn of the millennium saw Cardiff's derelict docks transformed into one of Europe's biggest and finest waterside developments, Barry Island has lagged behind, only slowly shaking off its ramshackle image. Thankfully, change is afoot and the island's natural beauty, which drew holidaymakers here in the first place, is being rediscovered. The island's main beach, Whitmore Bay, is a fabulous long sandy strand book-ended by two limestone outcrops that provide a degree of shelter. It's the perfect place to just sit and soak up the sun, taking in the views across the Bristol Channel, while the kids build sandcastles.

For a more active experience of the island, there is a pleasant 3-km (2-mi) walk starting from the railway station, taking you along the promenade and out to the secluded beauty of Jackson's Bay. The walk then leads up onto a cliff-top path where views over to the twin islands of Flat Holm and Steep Holm are stunning. You then head back towards the station by way of the island's harbour. This short walk takes you away from the hubbub of the main drag and shows Barry Island at its natural best.

WHERE:
South of Cardiff, South Glamorgan
BEST TIME TO GO:
The island is good on any clear day; the Hawking Centre is open from March to November (weather permitting), but closed on Tuesdays.
DON'T MISS:
The walk round to Jackson's Bay, where you will find a cove beautiful enough to rival any on the Cornish coast.
AMOUNT OF WALKING:
Moderate; there is only partial disabled access on the walk around the island. The Hawking Centre can accommodate disabled visitors but advanced notice is required.
COST:
Reasonable; a discount is available for family groups at the Hawking Centre.
YOU SHOULD KNOW:
If a hawk ends a meal with its crop bulging, it probably won't need to eat for a couple of days. The crop is a pocket midway between the bird's mouth and stomach and food is slowly released into its belly to keep it nourished.

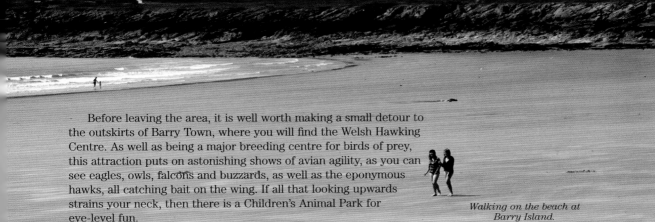

Before leaving the area, it is well worth making a small detour to the outskirts of Barry Town, where you will find the Welsh Hawking Centre. As well as being a major breeding centre for birds of prey, this attraction puts on astonishing shows of avian agility, as you can see eagles, owls, falcons and buzzards, as well as the eponymous hawks, all catching bait on the wing. If all that looking upwards strains your neck, then there is a Children's Animal Park for eye-level fun.

Walking on the beach at Barry Island.

Walking the Glamorgan Heritage Coast

WHERE:
West of Cardiff, South Glamorgan
BEST TIME TO GO:
Any sunny day between Easter and late September
DON'T MISS:
If you time it right, the sunsets across the Bristol Channel from Breaksea Point are simply stunning.
AMOUNT OF WALKING:
Lots. This walk is only suitable for families with reasonable experience of hiking.
COST:
Free
YOU SHOULD KNOW:
Great care is required while walking along cliffs and it is important to stick to paths at all times. Also, you should check tide notices before venturing along any of the walks on longer stretches of beach.

The Glamorgan Heritage Coast runs from Ogmore-by-Sea eastwards for 22.5 km (14 mi) to West Aberthaw. Unspoiled by any roads or development, this pedestrians' paradise takes you along cliffs and down to red sandy beaches, all the while offering spectacular views over the broad Bristol Channel. With only the noise of the wind, sea and birdsong as the soundtrack to your day, it is time to explore this natural wonderland.

Soon after heading east from Ogmore you will spot the strange ruins of Dunraven Castle. However things are not as they seem as this apparently ancient edifice is in fact a 19th century folly that has been left to crumble. The beach at Dunraven Bay gives you your first chance to take a break and even dip your toes into the water. The coastline then arcs round on the leg between Cwm Mawr and St Donat's (where guided tours of the famous castle-turned-school are available in June and July) until you come to the tranquil Tresilian Bay.

On the final leg, the town of Llantwit Major lies only a 20-minute walk inland, but such is the layout of this coast that you feel a million miles away from urban life. The climb around Pidgeon Point and Stout Point probably gives the best views of the walk as you look back towards St Donat's. It is from here that you can also see the brown sands of Limpert Bay and behind them Breaksea Point, your final destination. This is quite an arduous walk and, if you need to return to where you started, it will probably take you more than a day. You can, however, dip into the walk by following the B4265, which takes you closest to the path at Ogmore, Cwm Nash, St Donat's and Llantwit Major.

A stormy sea on the Heritage Coast

Cosmeston Lakes Country Park

Located just 8 km (5 mi) from the centre of Cardiff, Cosmeston Lakes Country Park offers a fine introduction to the great outdoors, without venturing too far away from the conveniences of town. Limestone was quarried on the site for 80 years, before the excavation stopped in 1970. There were plans to turn the area into a landfill rubbish dump, but thankfully it was transformed from several barren hollows into a fantastic mixture of lakes, fenland, copses and meadows.

The lakes have become a haven for birds and each season brings new visitors, from mating pairs of mute swans in summer to widgeons and bitterns in winter. A boardwalk takes you out onto the otherwise inaccessible marshland, home of the imperious Emperor butterfly, while the extensive woodland forms an ideal habitat for foxes, bats and badgers. A division of labour is required as lunch approaches. Parents and guardians can avail themselves of the facilities in the barbecue area to produce a sizzling feast, while children can head off to the wood-themed play area to work up an appetite.

While much of the development at Cosmeston has been designed to craft and bury a scarred landscape, one effect of the quarrying remains. The harvesting of limestone helped to unearth the remains of a mediaeval village, which was fully uncovered by archaeologists in the 1980s. The site is now home to a lively museum with costumed workers who guide you around the excavated buildings and reconstructed gardens. The scene is set in 1350, a time of great upheaval, disease and strife, and you can find out just how tough life was. Jousting, hawking and dancing are laid on to show that the people had fun as well. Nature and heritage combine well to make Cosmeston a wonderful place to visit.

Dinghies line up on the lakeside.

WHERE:
Penarth, South Glamorgan
BEST TIME TO GO:
Open all year round
DON'T MISS:
The village is home to several special events throughout the year, so check ahead to see this faithfully reconstructed piece of history in its full glory.
AMOUNT OF WALKING:
Moderate. The whole site has good wheelchair/pushchair access.
COST:
Reasonable. The park is free to enter; family tickets are available for the village.
YOU SHOULD KNOW:
Great care and attention should be taken when playing near the lakes, especially when accompanying small children. As the lakes are formed by quarrying, they are very deep in places.

Roath Park

Roath Park

If the British seaside can market itself as the new Costa del Sol, then the city park can fairly claim to be the new seaside. There are several advantages to urban dwellers in keeping it local. Less travelling is better for the environment, parks are generally less crowded than the often-narrow beaches found by our shores and you don't have to plan too far ahead. If the sky contains nothing more threatening than white cotton-wool clouds, it is time to pack the hamper, dust off the blanket, polish up on the rules of French cricket and venture out to enjoy your neighbourhood's best asset.

Cardiff is blessed with having a plethora of wonderful open spaces. Bute Park and Sophia Gardens are two of the best known, but if you want an *al fresco* frolic with the locals then head for Roath Park. Like much in Wales's first city, the creation of the park in 1894 owes a lot to the Marquis of Bute, once the world's richest man. With land donated by this mogul, the 53-ha (130-acre) site was transformed from swampy marshland into a fine Victorian park, complete with boating lake.

If you approach the park from the south, you first encounter an enormous greenhouse, home to a wonderful sub-tropical ecosystem, which is kept humid by a cute little waterfall feeding a pond that houses a school of glittering koi carp. A short walk through the rose garden takes you on to a large adventure playground where swings, slides and seesaws await those with energy to spare.

It is then time to hit the water as you are guided towards the lake by a lighthouse, a memorial to Captain Scott, who refuelled in Cardiff on the way to his doomed voyage to the Antarctic. Pedaloes and rowing boats are available to hire for a gentle exploration of the park's centrepiece.

WWT National Wetland Centre Wales

Can you imagine a subject on which practically the whole world is in agreement? Where Israel can concur with Iran, the United States with Russia and India with Pakistan? The Ramsar Convention, which concerns itself with the development and maintenance of wetland regions, is unique among international treaties in its diversity of members. Penned in 1971, the accord has gradually broadened to include over 150 countries, with more than 1,800 sites worldwide covering 181 million ha (448 million acres). Britain can be rightly proud of its role since, at 166 sites, it has more designated wetland areas than any other country.

This brings us on to this attractive corner of the mouth of the River Loughor, which has long been an important breeding ground for a wide variety of birdlife. Covering 100 ha (250 acres), the area provides an especially good habitat for ducks, wading birds, geese and little egrets. Boardwalks and paths take you out into this amazing environment, giving you a close-up view of the waterfowls' natural surroundings. If the weather is inclement, don't worry, the indoor discovery centre will provide hours of fun. Young ones can test their directional skills in the Swan Maze or crawl and slide about in a system of tunnels.

Don't fret if you don't own a good pair of binoculars, as you can hire some from the centre. It is also worth getting a demonstration on how to use them to best effect, so you can enjoy an intimate view of the wildlife. Then it's off to one of the many hides to observe the assorted feathered fancies. There are broadly two ways of watching birds. The first is to try to identify as many as possible and cross them off a list; the second, and far more relaxing, is just to look at them in all their glorious majesty – the choice is yours.

WHERE:
Near Llanelli, Dyfed
BEST TIME TO GO:
The centre is open all year round.
DON'T MISS:
Of all the residents, the pink flamingoes win the best-dressed prize every time.
AMOUNT OF WALKING:
Moderate; the site has good wheelchair/pushchair access. Only trained assistance dogs are allowed on the site.
COST:
Reasonable; under fours go free and family tickets are available.
YOU SHOULD KNOW:
Wetlands play an important environmental role. They are a first defence against flooding, as they act like a sponge. They are, however, under constant threat from chemical fertilizers which promote the growth of algae, which in turn denudes the wetland.

The vibrant flamingoes at WWT National Wetlands Centre

SCOTLAND

Archery and Jedforest Deer and Farm Park

Do kids still know all about Robin Hood and his legendary skills with a longbow? Of course they do – and a family session at Eastcote House Archery Centre will provide older children with the challenging opportunity to chance their arm under the supervision of qualified experts. The centre is just to the east of Hawick on the A698 Jedburgh Road.

Eastcote House is open six days a week (closed Tuesdays). It has heated indoor ranges for inclement Border days, plus an outside range, shop and workshop where arrows are made and equipment repaired. For fathers and sons (daughters too) who fancy having a go, booking a Come and Try session is the ideal way to sample this spectacular sport.

There should be time to fit some bowmanship into a day that is mainly focused on Jedforest Deer and Farm Park. This superb facility offers more than enough activities to occupy the family for a full day if archery doesn't appeal, or the kids are too young. Find it at Camptown, south of Jedburgh on the main A68 Newcastle road. The large working farm has splendid herds of deer (six species) and a major rare breeds conservation programme covering cows, goats, sheep, pigs and poultry. There are also favourites like wallabies and llamas to be seen.

Apart from fascinating livestock, there are numerous opportunities for children to amuse themselves – indoor and outdoor play areas, climbing frames, trampolines, slides and swings. For those making arrangements in advance there are ranger-led activities. It's a good idea to take a picnic to eat on site, after which a stroll along a choice of easy colour-coded walks or nature trails will appeal to some. The Deer and Farm Park has an Interpretive Barn and the whole experience offers an A+ blend of education and entertainment.

Young stag roe deer with velvet still on his antlers

Peebles Hydro Stables plus Osprey Watch

A view across the stunning Tweed Valley

The Peebles Hydro Hotel is an awesome building set in rugged landscape on the outskirts of town, amidst the extensive and beautiful landscape of Tweed Valley Forest Park. The grounds offer an unusual opportunity to give the kids a very different holiday experience – pony trekking for older children (suitable for beginners and novices) and forest pony walks for youngsters over four.

The latter involves a half-hour excursion with each pony being led by someone on foot. Either option is an excellent way to introduce children to ponies and, as the activity takes place entirely within Glentress Forest, there's no potentially dangerous road work. The excursions are supervised but parents are welcome to join in. For serious would-be equestrians, riding lessons may be booked at the Outdoor School.

(Incidentally, those parents who want to treat themselves to some holiday time off can book into the Hydro Hotel and turn their youngsters over to the Kids' Club – where energetic hostesses organize a wide range of stimulating activities for children up to the age of 12 while mums and dads enjoy extensive leisure facilities!)

Close encounters with Nature don't have to end when the ponies are back in the stables. One of the most interesting features of Tweed Valley Forest Park is Kailzie Gardens, just outside Peebles on the B7062 road. The impressive gardens are open all year round, but Osprey Watch is the undoubted highlight.

These rare and beautiful birds are slowly becoming re-established in Scotland. Breeding pairs return to the park each year, and their progress can be followed with the help of cameras that have been set up around nests in the forest canopy. This provides the opportunity for intimate insight into the lives of these magnificent birds, without disturbing them, and other species are also featured.

WHERE:
Peebles, Scottish Borders
BEST TIME TO GO:
Easter to the end of August for Osprey Watch
DON'T MISS:
The free School Holiday Nature Club for children on Wednesday afternoons at Kailzie Gardens, for three hours of entertaining hands-on activities.
AMOUNT OF WALKING:
Little
COST:
Expensive (if the whole family takes to the saddle)
YOU SHOULD KNOW:
If observing nature (from a pony or on screen) doesn't provide the required energy burn for older kids, Glentress Forest within Tweed Valley Forest Park offers some terrific mountain-bike trails, with suitable bikes available for hire within the park – the entrance to which can easily be reached by public transport from Peebles.

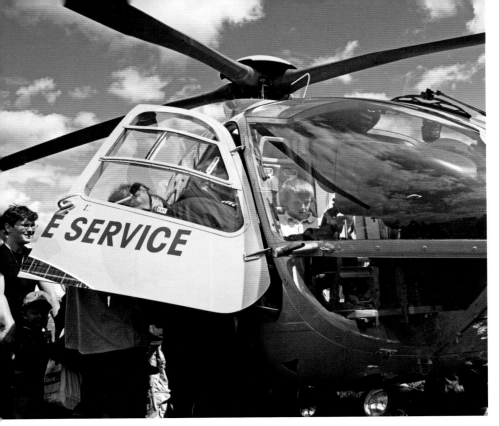

Mabie Farm Park plus an aviation museum

Take the A710 road from Dumfries and after 8 km (5 mi) find the well-signed entrance to Mabie Farm Park. The word farm suggests animals and there are plenty, from paddocks containing a wide assortment of appealing beasts including Oxford Down sheep, Britain's biggest breed, to a classic Pets Corner. Children are encouraged to feed the animals and donkey rides are another sure-fire winner.

But that's just the start. The park offers a sensational selection of activities that will encourage youngsters to let off all the steam they can raise. There's more than something for every age group, starting with indoor ride-on toys and outside sandpits for toddlers, and culminating with trampolines that adults may use. In between may be found the play park with classic swings and climbing frames, a barn with straw bales and rope swings (ideal for rainy days!), an aerial cable slide, a grass slide, Astroslide and bouncy castle. There's a boating pond for parents and kids, a pedal go-kart circuit (for children aged four and upwards) and quad bikes in two sizes for those aged six or older (helmets provided, tuition available).

The park can occupy a fulfilling day, but those who like to pack as much as possible into a holiday (especially those with older boys in tow) might find time to go on to Dumfries and Galloway Aviation Museum. Find it centred on the old control tower of an old World War II airfield, at Heathhill off the A701 roundabout on Dumfries bypass. It features fascinating displays relating to civil and military aviation past and present, over 20 classic aircraft and a re-created World War II living room. Open weekends from April to October, also Wednesdays, Thursdays and Fridays in July and August.

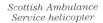

Scottish Ambulance Service helicopter

WHERE:
Mabie and Dumfries,
Dumfries and Galloway
BEST TIME TO GO:
Easter to the end of October
DON'T MISS:
The engine and prop from a hard-hit wartime Wellington bomber that crashed while trying to land at Dumfries in 1943, the recovery of which in the 1970s led to the founding of the aviation museum.
AMOUNT OF WALKING:
Little
COST:
Reasonable (with extra charges for some optional activities like quad bikes at Mabie Farm Park)
YOU SHOULD KNOW:
There are many covered and open picnic tables at Mabie Farm Park (though there is a tearoom) and families are welcome to bring their own portable barbecues and sizzle a hot meal. The whole site is pushchair-friendly and under twos get free entry.

Dumfries Museum and Camera Obscura plus Mossburn Animal Centre

There's nothing wrong with a little entertaining culture to give a Scottish day out that extra dimension for kids, and Dumfries Museum offers just such an opportunity (not to mention the fact that it provides an excellent answer to that awkward question 'Where on earth can we go today?' after the heavens have opened, as they more than occasionally do in Scotland).

The museum is based on an impressive old white-painted windmill high above the town and has interesting displays covering all aspects of southwest Scotland's history. These include prehistoric fossilized reptile footprints, tools and weapons left by the region's earliest inhabitants, early Christian stone carvings and a range of artefacts illustrating the way of life on a Victorian farmstead. But the highlight of the visit (literally) is the Camera Obscura that may be found on the top floor of the mill.

Kids will find this historical astronomical instrument fascinating, as it captures a full-colour image of the surroundings. This is then projected (upside down) within the camera chamber. On a clear day this one produces panoramic views of Dumfries and the countryside for miles in every direction.

To round off the day, visit the Mossburn Animal Centre, which is located off the B7020 road southeast of Dumfries between Lochmaben and Dalton. This is a very special place – a rescue centre that offers hope and a new home to a huge number of injured, abused, abandoned or neglected animals. The range of creatures to be seen is wide, from horses and cattle right down to the smallest domestic pets (including reptiles!). There are plenty of non-native 'exotics' like raccoons and ostriches, while Scottish wildlife – both animals and birds – is well represented. Children who love animals will adore the Mossburn Centre.

WHERE:
Dumfries and Lochmaben, Dumfries and Galloway
BEST TIME TO GO:
Any time
DON'T MISS:
The opportunity to sponsor an animal at Mossburn – not only will that generous gesture help to support a great cause, but there will also be a personal letter from the chosen animal, an animal photo ID card and regular updates on its progress.
AMOUNT OF WALKING:
Little
COST:
Low (both attractions have free entry, but there is a small charge for the Camera Obscura and the Mossburn Animal Centre welcomes donations that help support its good work).
YOU SHOULD KNOW:
It is speculated that clever artists from the great Leonardo da Vinci onwards used a camera obscura as their 'secret weapon', because this optical device enabled them to trace completely accurate landscapes or people as the basis for a painting.

Camera Obscura and cannon in Dumfries

Caerlaverock Castle and the Wetland Centre

WHERE:
Caerlaverock, Dumfries and Galloway
BEST TIME TO GO:
Any time (winter for thousands of migrating wildfowl and whooper swans at the Wetland Centre)
DON'T MISS:
The siege warfare exhibition at Caerlaverock Castle, which was twice taken – by 'Hammer of the Scots' Edward I in 1300 (the garrison surrendered inside two days) and in 1640 during a religious dispute between King Charles I and dissenting Covenanters (when it held out for 13 weeks).
AMOUNT OF WALKING:
Moderate to lots (the Wetland Centre is extensive)
COST:
Reasonable
YOU SHOULD KNOW:
The natterjack toad lurks along the Solway shoreline from April, when it emerges from hibernation – this extraordinary creature is nocturnal, but a Wetland Centre warden should be on hand to find one hiding beneath debris washed up by the tide for those who want to boast 'I've seen Britain's rarest amphibian'.

A 'must see' for kids is fabulous Caerlaverock Castle, a mighty fortress that once guarded the 'Gateway to Scotland' across the Solway Firth. Head south from Dumfries on the B725 road and find it some 13 km (8 mi) out of town, overlooking the water and England beyond. This substantial ruin has everything – a massive gatehouse towering above a wide moat, imposing battlements, a round corner tower and an unusual triangular shape. Within the walls is Nithsdale Lodging, a house built in 1634 within the older castle.

The setting is magnificent – the place stands amid unspoiled marshland dotted with willow woods (known hereabouts as a 'moss') that makes it easy to imagine this great edifice as it was in medieval times. To the joy of exploring a fairytale castle may be added a children's adventure park and a nature trail that leads to the remains of an older castle, ensuring that the kids really will enjoy their encounter with this special place. A picnic should round off the visit nicely.

The nearby Caerlaverock Wetland Centre delivers contrasting interest. The superb coastal habitat provides refuge for a wide variety of wildlife beneath big skies. The Salcot Merse Observatory offers great distant views of the English Lake District, plus a close-up look at thousands of waders on the salt marshes and avian hunters like peregrine falcons, hen harriers and short-eared owls.

There are intimate bird-watching hides dotted around the reserve and guided walks for parents and kids that cover the best wildlife at each time of year. From March to August it is possible to see on CCTV barn owls nesting, with ospreys following from April onwards. And of course there's also the unique opportunity to use the largest pair of binoculars in Scotland to complete a great kids' day out!

The ruins of Caerlaverock Castle on a summer's evening

Port Logan Fish Pond Marine Life Centre and Mull of Galloway Lighthouse

What better way to occupy the kids than showing them something unique that is both attention grabbing and entertaining? Port Logan is on the Rhinns of Galloway, the island-like peninsula at the western extremity of former Wigtownshire, looking out over the North Channel of the Irish Sea. Charming though it is, this little fishing port is not the day's special attraction. That honour goes to the Port Logan Fish Pond Marine Life Centre.

Take the A716 road from Stranraer Harbour towards Portpatrick then follow signs for Logan Botanic Gardens. The Marine Life Centre is about a mile past the entrance to the Logan Botanic Gardens, along a narrow road off the B7065. Entry to the attraction is via the public car park on the Stranraer side of Logan Bay. It features an extraordinary natural feature – a tidal pool created by a blowhole that was adapted as a fish pond around 1800, with a view to storing live sea fish. This extraordinary larder is reached through the original fishkeeper's cottage and visitors are amazed as they emerge above the dramatic pool. But kids are soon seduced by the excitement of feeding the fish, before going on to enjoy the Touch Pools and Cave Aquarium. There is an outdoor play area and the whole site is ablaze with wild flowers in spring and summer.

After enjoying the Marine Life Centre, it's well worth making the short trip to the most southerly point in Scotland. There the Mull of Galloway Lighthouse – approached through unspoiled countryside – stands in a dramatic clifftop setting. The 26-m (85-ft) tower may be climbed on certain days for awesome sea views to the Cumbrian coast and Ireland's Mountains of Mourne. There is an interesting exhibition in the Engine House that is open seven days a week. The lighthouse is within an RSPB reserve and there is a restaurant that provides meals and snacks (closed in December and January).

Mull of Galloway Lighthouse

WHERE:
Port Logan, Dumfries and Galloway
BEST TIME TO GO:
March to the end of October
DON'T MISS:
The restored bathing hut at Port Logan Fish Pond Marine Life Centre – find it on the rocks next to the main pond, near to the pool that used to provide a favourite outing for the family from Port Logan House in Victorian times.
AMOUNT OF WALKING:
Moderate
COST:
Low
YOU SHOULD KNOW:
The actual tower at the Mull of Galloway Lighthouse is open at weekends between Easter and mid October, plus every Monday in July and August. There are restrictions applicable to those climbing the tower, and it is advisable that anyone with mobility or breathing problems does not attempt the climb. The exhibition is in the engine room (which still contains the 1955 Kelvin Diesel engines) and there are 115 steps to the top!

Creetown Gem Rock Museum and Monreith Shore Centre

*Hypnotized by sparkling stones
at the Gem Rock Museum!*

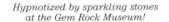

WHERE:
Creetown and Monreith,
Dumfries and Galloway
BEST TIME TO GO:
April to October
DON'T MISS:
The Gavin Maxwell Museum at
Monreith Animal World Shore Centre,
a tribute to the local author who
turned otters into celebrities in his
book *Ring of Bright Water*.
AMOUNT OF WALKING:
Moderate
COST:
Reasonable
YOU SHOULD KNOW:
An alternative to the Gem Museum is
The Tropic House at Newton Stewart,
with its amazing free-flying
butterflies and carnivorous plants.

Sometimes it's possible to combine a valuable educational experience with a thoroughly entertaining outing, and a visit to the Creetown Gem Rock Museum is just such an opportunity (especially if it's a wet day). Kids will be amazed by the variety of exhibits that cover a full range of rocks, minerals and gemstones . . . plus unusual items such as a genuine meteorite, fossilized dinosaur egg (and dung!) plus one of the largest gold nuggets to be seen in Britain.

The museum certainly contains some of Nature's most striking creations, but has much more to offer than well-filled display cases. There are various interactive features and the spectacular Crystal Cave is a wonderland of changing colours. The Professor's Study is a Victorian-themed room and the Fire in the Stones audio-visual presentation tells the story of man's quest to turn rough gemstones into beautiful objects of desire. Find Creetown on the A75 road between Castle Douglas and Newton Stewart.

After the Gem Rock Museum, the day can be rounded out with something completely different. Beyond Newton Stewart is an attraction that balances all those beautiful but inanimate minerals with living things that children never fail to appreciate – animals. Follow the A714 south from Newton Stewart through Wigtown and on past Kirkinner and find the Monreith Animal World Shore Centre and Museum signed to the left just before reaching Whithorn.

Here you will find a wonderful selection of happy animals, many in generous natural enclosures. The centre has – among other familiar creatures – cattle, ponies, goats, pigs and poultry. The otters are a particular attraction, as is the peaceful pond-side walk. There are reptiles, small rodents and many species of bird, including various owls, too. There is also the opportunity to study seashore life.

Museum of Lead Mining

There's lead in 'them thar hills'! Even though commercial mining of the heavy metal has long since ceased in Lanarkshire's beautiful Lowther Hills, it doesn't mean the family can't have a fascinating day out here. The Museum of Lead Mining is at Wanlockhead, famous as Scotland's highest village, and it provides real insight into a vanished industry.

Follow the trail that starts at the Visitor Centre in the heart of this historic settlement. Here you will find a walk-through exhibition that explains how lead was mined, and also see a great display of local minerals. From there, go on to take the amazing guided tour of the Lochnell Mine, which began life in the early 18th century and closed back in 1861. The experience gives a vivid impression of the harsh reality of mining in times gone by, as well as illustrating the methods by which the galena (lead ore) was extracted. It should be a sobering thought for the kids that boys as young as 12 actually worked long hours underground.

Finish off with a visit to the Wanlockhead Beam Engine – the only surviving example of a waterbucket pumping engine to be seen at any mine in Great Britain, this ingenious perpetual-motion machine is operated by water power alone.

If you make your family visit to Wanlockhead at the weekend or on a Bank Holiday, it's possible to nip across the county line into South Lanarkshire and enjoy the added bonus of a ride on the Leadhills and Wanlockhead Railway, a narrow-gauge adhesion railway created where the Caledonian Railway Company used to operate a line to carry refined lead from the local mines. The scenic ride up to Wanlockhead takes ten minutes and a single cheap ticket allows as many hop-on-hop-off journeys as you want to make.

WHERE:
Wanlockhead, Dumfries and Galloway
BEST TIME TO GO:
April to October
DON'T MISS:
The first piece of galena that was found in the South Cove vein of the Lochnell Mine, left in place by the original miners for good luck – see this plate-shaped piece of ore where the entrance tunnel joins the vein.
AMOUNT OF WALKING:
Moderate to lots
COST:
Reasonable
YOU SHOULD KNOW:
There's gold in these hills, too – much of the coinage during the reign of Mary Queen of Scots was minted from gold found in the Lowther Hills and the annual British and Scottish Gold Panning Championships are held here. Gold-panning equipment and treasure maps are available from the Visitor Centre!

Galloway Wildlife Conservation Park and organic ice cream

WHERE:
Kirkcudbright and Rainton,
Dumfries and Galloway
BEST TIME TO GO:
From April to the end of October
DON'T MISS:
The caracal lynx collection at the
Wildlife Conservation Park, housed in
a large purpose-built enclosure,
offering one of the few opportunities
in Britain to see a number of these
beautiful felines together.
AMOUNT OF WALKING:
Lots
COST:
Reasonable
YOU SHOULD KNOW:
For smaller children the Cream o'
Galloway Dairy has an extensive
outdoor play area suitable for under
fives, plus tempting features like
pedal go-karts, a 3-D maze and
viewing tower.

Close to Kirkcudbright on the B727 road may be found the Galloway Wildlife Conservation Park, overlooking the River Dee. This breeding centre for small animals allows some 150 species from all over the world to be seen in peaceful natural settings. Enclosures created within a large area of mixed woodland showcase an extraordinary collection of animals and birds, many rare and endangered.

There is constant turnover as new creatures arrive while others leave to contribute to captive-breeding programmes elsewhere, and the whole experience helps young visitors to appreciate the importance of protecting the world's natural heritage while enjoying the opportunity to study unusual animals at close quarters. There are regular guided tours and an informative nature trail winds through the woods.

The park is closed in December and January, but after winter loosens its grip the animals and birds start doing what comes naturally – producing the offspring that provide the park's rationale and in the process delighting visiting children, who always find the new arrivals enchanting. The park has a cafeteria, but families are welcome to use the picnic area if they choose. There is also a children's play area.

The park could occupy a leisurely day out but for something extra take a stroll around Kirkcudbright's attractive centre and waterfront. The main attraction for kids is MacLellan's Castle. Alternatively, make the short trip along the A75 to the Cream o' Galloway Dairy (pass the turn for Gatehouse of Fleet and follow the signs down Sandgreen Road). This started as the home base of Cream o' Galloway organic ice cream and frozen smoothies and has developed into a seriously child-friendly visitor attraction, with an irresistible ice cream parlour and a fantastic adventure playground complete with underground Smugglers' Warren where (up-for-it dads and mums take note) adults are also welcome.

Dean Castle Country Park and Garage Leisure Centre

Take your pick from three options for this potentially varied day out in Kilmarnock – strenuous open-air activity, frantic indoor fun . . . or better still both, enjoyed one after the other on an outing that will leave the kids tired but very happy.

Start at Dean Castle Country Park (find it off the A77 Kilmarnock bypass – from the north take the B7038 Glasgow Road towards the town centre and turn into Dean Road on the left). The Castle itself is seriously interesting, with a fantastic collection of weapons and armour and Europe's finest assembly of historical musical instruments. If the kids are too young to appreciate the ancient fortress/palace and its spectacular contents, there's plenty for them to do in the park.

The Visitor Centre explains all about local wildlife and a well-stocked Pets Corner has all the usual favourites like guinea pigs, rabbits, sheep, cows, pigs, pygmy goats and donkeys. There are aviaries stocked with exotic birds and ponds alive with wildfowl, while the modern adventure playground provides an exciting outlet for youthful exuberance. There's a good tearoom, too, should refuelling be necessary.

If there's any energy left after visiting the Country Park, or the rain comes down, it's but a short step to the Garage Leisure Centre – in Grange Street just down the road in the town centre. Here there is ten-pin bowling, indoor go-karting and – bliss for tiring parents – a safe Adventure Softplay Playground for kids aged up to 13. With secure supervision, it offers hours of fun with features like the terror slide, creepy house, jumps, swings, ball pools, climbs, bounces, tumbles, capsules, rollers, ladders, bridges, tubes, mazes, biff bags and much more. Meanwhile, as their kids go mad, parents can retreat gracefully to the tv lounge. Excellent!

WHERE:
Kilmarnock, East Ayrshire
BEST TIME TO GO:
Any time
DON'T MISS:
At Dean Castle Country Park's Visitor Centre – the opportunity to see fascinating pictures of wild animals and birds going about their everyday lives in the park, captured on remote nature cams.
AMOUNT OF WALKING:
Moderate (though it is possible to walk for as long as the children last out in Dean Castle Country Park).
COST:
Free (Dean Castle Country Park). Reasonable (Garage Leisure Centre, though endless laps of the go-kart track would rack up a hefty bill).
YOU SHOULD KNOW:
There are bumpers available for novices at the Garage's ten-pin bowling facility, to ensure that inexperienced kids actually get to knock down plenty of pins rather than getting disheartened by a succession of wasted balls down the gutters.

Suit of armour in Dean Castle

Dailly Paths and Girvan

WHERE:
Dailly and Girvan, South Ayrshire
BEST TIME TO GO:
Summer
DON'T MISS:
As many as possible of the numerous
birds and animals to be seen on
Dailly Walks – including herons and
dippers, curlew and buzzards,
kestrels and peregrine falcons,
squirrels and roe deer.
AMOUNT OF WALKING:
Lots
COST:
Free (unless a boat trip is taken,
which will be expensive)
YOU SHOULD KNOW:
Ailsa Craig was once the principal
source of the rare type of granite
used to produce the curling stones
used in that famously traditional
Scottish winter sport. After the
abandonment of the quarry and
automation of its lighthouse, Aisla
Craig is now uninhabited. Today the
island is managed as a nature
reserve by the RSPB and is a Site
of Special Scientific Interest as well
as being designated a Special
Protection Area.

This is one for kids who love (or are willing to be introduced to) the delights of the great outdoors, though it is not recommended for toddlers. Pack a picnic and head for Dailly Paths, centred on the small village of that name on the B741 road between Maybole and Girvan. This area was once a coalmining centre but is now at the heart of rural South Ayrshire. The village is pleasant, but the real attraction is the opportunity to choose from five waymarked nature trails.

The shortest is 4.5 km (2.8 mi) and the longest is over 10 km (6.2 mi). They go through fields and woods, along riverbanks and up hills. The scenery is magnificent and an abundance of wildlife should capture the interest of youngsters. There are numerous great spots to stop for that laid-back picnic and let the kids run riot, if they've got energy to spare.

If interesting country walks do not appeal, the old fishing port (and latterly resort) of Girvan has cliffs and good beaches. The latter provide an ideal opportunity for messing about at the seaside – always guaranteed to keep the kids happy. But those in search of more adventurous activities might consider taking a boat from the harbour to Ailsa Craig, an island in the outer Firth of Clyde some 16 km (10 mi) west of Girvan.

There are daily trips in season (weather permitting), either to circle the island to see its amazing bird colonies or actually land and explore this dramatic steep-sided extinct volcano (not for little ones). Alternatively, there are fishing trips on offer that might appeal to older children. Boat trips can be fully subscribed, so if the idea of taking to the water appeals, it's wise to make enquiries and book in advance.

Take to the waters to circle the island of Ailsa Craig and explore the bird colonies.

Loudon Castle Theme Park

WHERE:
Galston, East Ayrshire
BEST TIME TO GO:
The park is open from April to the
end of August, but check before
travelling – it's closed on certain days
in April, May, June and August.
DON'T MISS:
Flying through the air on the mighty
Plough – said to be one of the largest
chair swings in the world.
AMOUNT OF WALKING:
Moderate
COST:
Expensive
YOU SHOULD KNOW:
There are height restrictions on many
of the park's rides. These may stop
smaller kids from taking a particular
ride, or require a parent to
accompany each child. But there are
plenty of attractions that are suitable
for little ones at Loudon Castle.

The village of Galston is 8 km (5 mi) east of Kilmarnock on the A71 road, and just up the hill from Galston on the A719 is Loudon Castle Theme Park. Billed as 'Scotland's best family theme park', Loudon Castle offers a terrific day out for parents and kids of all ages.

The park isn't cheap, but offers some truly awesome rides. The Barnstormer launches high into the air, the Black Pearl is a ghastly galleon trip and there are two runaway roller coasters in The Rat and Twist N Shout. Too frightening? No matter. For scaredy cats the park also has some super family rides that will delight everyone, many centred on Pirates' Cove.

These include the spinning Stormbreaker, sinuous Wacky Worm, free-floating Drunken Barrels (beware of the shark!), Loggers Leap for a splashing time, a Regatta Ride around Pirates' Cove, the galloping Carousel, stomach-wrenching Milk Churn, bucking Rodeo Rider, twirling Crow's Nest and trying to drive around the madcap French Taxi area without crashing into a rival taxi (or three).

There are plenty of rides for smaller kids, the names giving a clue to the mini-thrills on offer: Pony Trek; McDougal's Tractors; Jammy Dodgems; Bug's Life; Junior Twist; Junior Pirate Ship; Freefall; Chair-o-Planes and Sea Patrol. They definitely deliver! The park also puts on sensational 'watch in amazement' stunt shows like Walk the Plank and High Dive, which will impress even the coolest of kids.

By way of a relaxing change of pace after all that frenetic action, there are several sit-down food outlets for a family meal, and afterwards a visit to the on-site Dougal McDougal's Rare Breeds Farm should slow the tempo nicely. The farm offers the opportunity to pet and feed a selection of animals. It's the perfect way to end an all-action day out.

*A Harris hawk at the
park's on-site farm*

Heads of Ayr Farm Park and Pirate Pete's

The combination of appealing animals and fun rides is potent when it comes to entertaining kids – and that's precisely what's on offer at Heads of Ayr Farm Park on the A719 coast road at Ayr, which has the added bonus of a seaside setting.

Those who like making furry friends will be delighted by the choice that awaits, with a variety of exotic animals like guanacos, squirrel monkeys, alpacas, wallabies, Asian otters, miniature zebu cattle and those oh-so-cute meerkats getting up to all sorts of antics. And of course those ever-popular occupants of pets' corners everywhere like rabbits and guinea pigs are waiting to be handled and fed.

Then it's Action Stations for thrill seekers, with a range of rides and numerous opportunities to burn off youthful energy, including various hairy sledges and slides, an activity tower and tricky tunnels, trampolines and bouncers, demon drops and a rope swing bridge, an Adventure Play Barn and Combine Castle. Children can also try their hands at electric quad biking, while adult quad bikes will appeal to get-up-and-go parents who are starting to feel left out of the fun. There are also working junior diggers and tractors to drive. This is really an outdoor venue, but covered play is available if the heavens open.

Should there be time to spare (or the weather misbehaves) Pirate Pete's awaits on The Esplanade near the sea front in Ayr. This is indoor entertainment guaranteed to stimulate adventurous children, with plenty to tempt both Mini-Mutineers (under fives) and Mighty Marauders (over fives). The ever-popular pirate theme is used to create four decks of climbs and tubes, slides and slopes, bouncers and ball lagoons, mainmast descent and plank walking, spook room and pool lagoon. There's a safe toddlers' area and – bliss – an adult chill-out zone.

WHERE:
Ayr, South Ayrshire
BEST TIME TO GO:
Heads of Ayr is open from Easter to October, Pirate Pete's all year round.
DON'T MISS:
The opportunity to impress the kids with your special parental powers at Electric Brae, south of Dunure on the A719 road close to the Heads of Ayr Farm Park – by letting the car coast up hill with the engine off (actually it's an optical illusion, but a very convincing one).
AMOUNT OF WALKING:
Little
COST:
Reasonable
YOU SHOULD KNOW:
There is a dedicated activity area for children aged between two and four at Heads of Ayr Farm Park, where parents can enjoy a cup of tea or coffee while keeping a discreet eye on their offspring.

Belleisle Park and Troon Beach

As an antidote to the frantic activity of Ayr's various action attractions, pack a nice picnic and a full set of beach paraphernalia. A stroll in the park provides a leisurely start to this different sort of day out, which can remind everyone that families don't have to spend lots of money to enjoy doing things together. Belleisle Park off Ayr's Doonfoot Road is just the place to start. This local-authority facility is a popular attraction, set in the superb gardens and tranquil parkland of the former Belleisle Estate.

Grown-ups will love the manicured gardens, conservatory with its exotic hothouse plants, fishpond and fountain in the walled garden, but children will soon demand more practical stimulus. This can come in the form of ball games on the extensive grassy areas provided for the purpose, or a good workout in the play area. This has balancing beams, climbing frames and some good old-fashioned swings. The park has a user-friendly Pets Corner that houses aviary birds, doves, ducks, rabbits, guinea pigs, chipmunks and pigs, and there are also deer, ponies and donkeys. Feeding most animals is generally permitted, with carrots, greens, grass and apples the favoured fare.

A morning at Belleisle Park can end with the picnic, or it can be saved to launch the second half of the laid-back day – an outing to easy-access Troon Beach, where there is a special picnic area. This long, sweeping stretch of sand is a terrific spot for classic activities like paddling, sandcastle building, beach cricket and ice cream consumption, with a popular outdoor play area and an esplanade to stroll along where (should making a picnic be too much trouble) some excellent fish-and-chip shops provide naughty-but-nice holiday fare. Find Troon off the A78 road north of Ayr.

There are plenty of activities available on Troon Beach.

Scottish Maritime Museum and Magnum Leisure Centre

A fascinating slice of history followed by some serious play can make for a great day out, and that's what youngsters can look forward to in Irvine. It all starts at the Scottish Maritime Museum, which may be found at the town's Harbourside.

It has a great floating collection of vessels to see, including an iconic Clyde Puffer, a harbour tug and classic steam yacht. Then there are informative presentations chronicling the important role Scotland's engineers and mariners played in building and sailing ships around the globe in times gone by. The Linthouse Engine Shop is a grand Victorian glass-roofed building, aptly described as 'Scotland's Cathedral of Engineering', that is sure to fill children with awe. But of course awe and interesting displays aren't enough to make the day for active kids, so happily the museum also offers the opportunity to build and test a model boat, plus the chance to become captain of a remote-controlled vessel on the indoor boating ponds.

A short step away the Magnum Leisure Centre, also located on Harbourside, offers a wide variety of activities to ensure that the kids with energy to spare will soon be in action. The two fitness centres (for younger and older children) combine structured exercise with entertaining games. There's a soft-play area for Tiny Tots and Mini Monsters with swings, slides and ball pools to cavort in, among other delights. To that may be added a leisure swimming pool with irresistible extras like fun slides, an elevated Jacuzzi and hot tub. For those with the necessary skills, or who are willing to try to learn them, the Leisure Centre's ice rink is a sure-fire winner. Spoiled for choice? Sounds like a perfect recipe for tired but decidedly happy kids.

WHERE:
Irvine, North Ayrshire
BEST TIME TO GO:
April to October (for the Maritime Museum); any time (Magnum Leisure Centre)
DON'T MISS:
The restored tenement flat at the Maritime Museum that will show the kids that life was harsh and very different for shipyard workers a century ago. It may even encourage them to count their blessings rather than their pocket money!
AMOUNT OF WALKING:
Moderate
COST:
Reasonable
YOU SHOULD KNOW:
At the child-friendly Magnum Leisure Centre under fives go free in the swimming pool and at the skating rink, while a Family Swimming Ticket represents excellent money-saving value for parents with two or more children.

Scottish Maritime Museum at Irvine

Kelburn Castle Country Centre

Kelburn Castle Country Centre is on the A78 coast road, just south of Largs, and this popular attraction is sure to deliver a worthwhile day out. The fairytale castle provides a perfect backdrop for the wealth of activities on offer

Kelburn Castle

WHERE:
Largs, North Ayrshire
BEST TIME TO GO:
Kelburn Castle Country Centre operates from Easter to the end of October. The Riding School and grounds remain open in winter.
DON'T MISS:
The Indoor Playbarn at Kelburn (especially if the rain comes down) – for a small extra charge, it offers supervised fun sessions for children up to 12 years of age while parents relax and observe proceedings from the gallery over a cup of tea or coffee.
AMOUNT OF WALKING:
Lots
COST:
Reasonable
YOU SHOULD KNOW:
Kelburn organizes a series of Ranger Events throughout the summer – typical subjects are Minibeasts and Creepie Crawlies, Bushcraft, Rustic Games and Save the Planet. Check with the venue for the current programme, and that super day out might just turn into a marvellous family weekend.

at the Country Centre and is actually open to the public in July and August, when a tour can add an interesting dimension for older children.

A walk through Kelburn Glen in one of Scotland's most beautiful woodlands leads to a wonderful vantage point overlooking the Firth of Clyde with its impressive islands. But this won't be a boring walk that has kids complaining – there are some wonderful water features along the way and The Waterfall Pool in its sandstone grotto will have adults and children alike itching to get their feet wet.

The Adventure Course is an exciting aerial challenge of walkways, rope swings, ladders, stepping stones and a high-wire crossing between two trees. This is one for parents and children together, as unsupervised kids are not allowed. The Stockade is a wooden fort that has a raised walkway round the battlements, plus a climbing tower, scramble net, slides, swings and a sand pit.

An undoubted highlight is The Secret Forest. This intricate complex of raised walkways and paths in a wild wood delivers lots of surprises. These include a Chinese Garden, Pagoda, Green Man Maze, Crocodile Swamp, Gingerbread House, Secret Grotto, Castle with No Entrance and delicious secret passage from the Woodman's Cottage.

For an extra charge, a visit to the Riding School will be a 'must' for horse-mad kids. There are 10-minute led pony rides for children aged two or more, or a one-hour trek for young riders who have mastered basic riding skills. This will mostly involve walking, but also some trotting.

Vikingar! and a trip out to sea

Pirates are a popular theme when it comes to entertaining children, but Vikingar! chooses to hang its helmet on different pillagers – the Vikings. In truth, these Norse warriors had much more influence on Scotland than buccaneers ever did, so the choice is entirely appropriate.

The story of these fierce invaders is brilliantly told with the help of costumed narrators, who dramatically bring the story of 500 years of turbulent history to life. Visitors can see a Viking longhouse and are introduced to Norse Gods and Valkyries in Valhalla as part of the unique 'Viking Experience'. Then it's on to the five-screen film presentation that chronicles the exciting lives of one Viking family though successive generations, culminating in the Battle of Largs (fought in 1263 between Norwegian and Scottish armies).

Find Vikingar! in Greenock Road, at the northern end of the Promenade in the coastal resort of Largs with its wonderful sea and island views. Getting up close and personal with that self-same sea is a great way to complete a memorable day out for the kids. Operating from Largs Yacht Haven (and Largs Promenade in high season), Cumbrae Voyages offers unforgettable wildlife adventures, with custom trips in special inflatable boats that explore the waters around the Cumbrae Islands in the scenic Lower Firth of Clyde.

Trips last for one, two or three hours and each trip is tailored to suit the particular interests of its passengers. These high-speed voyages are a thrilling experience in their own right, but can also introduce children to a variety of marine wildlife. Likely sightings depend on the season, but typically include the daily appearance of seals and assorted seabirds like gannets, oystercatchers and cormorants, while there are occasional sightings of dolphins, porpoises and whales. Experienced skippers and guides offer informed commentary.

WHERE:
Largs, North Ayrshire
BEST TIME TO GO:
March to October
DON'T MISS:
After all that axe-wielding Viking excitement, it's possible to cool down with a plunge into the main Vikingar! swimming pool, or treat the little ones to a frolic in the teaching pool for younger swimmers.
AMOUNT OF WALKING:
Little
COST:
Expensive (if a boat trip is undertaken).
YOU SHOULD KNOW:
If Vikingar! isn't for you, Cumbrae Voyages does offer a choice of full-day trips – one to the historic island of Little Cumbrae ('Wee Cumbrae' is the local name) and the other to spectacular Mount Stewart, one of Scotland's finest Victorian Gothic houses.

A replica Viking longboat at the Vikingar! centre

New Lanark and Falls of Clyde

WHERE:
New Lanark, South Lanarkshire
BEST TIME TO GO:
Any time
DON'T MISS:
The chance to get about as close as it's ever possible to peregrine falcons in Britain – these majestic birds of prey can be studied on the Wildlife Reserve with the help of an expert warden.
AMOUNT OF WALKING:
Lots (if the Falls of Clyde Wildlife Reserve is seriously explored).
COST:
Reasonable
YOU SHOULD KNOW:
On summer evenings it is possible to join ranger-led bat- or badger-watch walks on the Falls of Clyde Wildlife Reserve.

Sometimes a great day out for the kids involves stimulating the imagination by introducing them to living history. So pack a picnic and head for the New Lanark World Heritage Site, where just such an experience awaits. This beautifully restored mill village was built and managed by Robert Owen in the 18th century to take advantage of the fast-running waters of the Upper Clyde, which drove the machinery needed to produce cotton. The award-winning Visitor Centre offers a good-value family ticket for access to all New Lanark's attractions. The village itself is a fascinating slice of history that will reward a leisurely stroll, or the scene can simply be observed from the delightful roof garden atop Mill Number Two. But what will really entertain the children is The Annie McLeod Experience Ride, where the ghost of mill girl Annie magically appears to tell the tale of life at New Lanark in the 1820s. This can be followed by a visit to the historic classroom, to see how school kids were taught in Annie McLeod's time.

After a picnic by the river, move on to the Falls of Clyde Wildlife Reserve. This offers beautiful riverside walks that pass three wonderful waterfalls – Dundaff Linn, Corra Linn and Bonnington Linn. The reserve is home to over 100 species of birds, including the brilliant kingfisher, and it is sometimes possible to spot otters.

If the kids are too small, the Scottish Wildlife Trust's Visitor Centre in the old mill dye works at New Lanark offers the opportunity to use the Wildwood interactive guide to the surrounding countryside.

Jars of sweets and candies in a small grocer's shop in New Lanark conservation village

National Museum of Rural Life, East Kilbride

Wester Kittochside Farm off Phillipshill Road on the outskirts of East Kilbride provides compelling insight into a much older and less frantic way of life – country living as it used to be before the arrival of mass motoring and the wholesale modernization of farming. The National Museum of Rural Life is a unique partnership venture between the National Trust for Scotland and National Museums Scotland.

Start with the award-winning museum building, a huge barnlike structure. There are three galleries that look back at the rural past, but also illustrate the important point that agriculture still plays an important role today by helping to produce the food we take for granted. It's a point worth making to kids who often assume that food comes straight from the supermarket.

The galleries focus on the three essential ingredients needed to sustain agriculture – land, people and tools – and illustrate the way the land was gradually mastered by people with the help of tools and technology. There is an impressive collection of tractors and combine harvesters, many of the latter housed in an area that can be visited on request.

After exploring the museum's many displays, it's time for a tractor ride (or walk) to hilltop Wester Kittochside Farmhouse. Surrounded by original buildings and sheltered by trees, it is preserved as it was in the 1950s. The farm is still worked just as it was back then when serious mechanization was in its infancy and much work was done by horse – or people – power. As with every farming year, there's something different to see during each season, though the cattle, sheep and horses are always there. The whole experience is designed to educate, inform and entertain, and the result is a great day out that's different enough to surprise and delight the kids.

Heavy-horse Show at the Museum of Rural Life

WHERE:
East Kilbride, South Lanarkshire
BEST TIME TO GO:
Late April, for the irresistible newborn Scottish Blackface lambs.
DON'T MISS:
Milking time at the farm – the Ayrshires are generally to be found in the parlour at 15.00.
AMOUNT OF WALKING:
Moderate to lots
COST:
Low to reasonable (children under 12 are admitted free).
YOU SHOULD KNOW:
There is a rolling programme of special events at Wester Kittochside Farm, featuring such attractions as heavy-horse shows, sheepdog trials, demonstrations of country skills, horse-shoeing competitions, a toy fair and a Halloween party.

David Livingstone Centre and Hamilton Water Palace

If there's one saying that's as famous as Admiral Nelson's dying words 'Kiss me, Hardy' it must surely be journalist Henry Morton Stanley's 'Doctor Livingstone, I presume?' upon tracking down the intrepid explorer near Lake Tanganyika in the heart of Africa. It's a story every child should know and the David Livingstone Centre at Blantyre, just a short distance from Glasgow, duly commemorates the great Scottish adventurer's life and works. The centre is child-friendly, with pushchair access to all levels, babies' changing facilities and play areas.

Livingstone was of humble origins and the centre is housed in the tenement building where he was born, which was also home to over 20 other families at the time. Though set in urban surroundings, the centre's extensive wooded grounds and proximity to the River Clyde give it a rural feel and plenty of space to relax with a family picnic. Alternatively, kids' lunches are served at the centre.

Of course a little learning (however interesting) is often best followed by some serious R&R, and nearby Hamilton Water Palace (just down the A724 from Blantyre) will certainly deliver that. Find it in Almada Street, close to Hamilton's town centre. This popular swimming pool is always busy and offers a whole lot more fun than simply belting up and down the 25-m (82-ft) competition pool. The action really happens in the leisure pools that boast a tyre slide, flume and lazy river. The shallow pool reserved for under eights has a terrific pirate ship with tempting interactive features that are sure to impress the little ones.

Parents who prefer not to get their own feet wet can retreat to the Water Palace's coffee shop while their kids splash around to their hearts' content, hopefully wearing themselves out ahead of a blissfully dreamless night.

Summerlee Heritage Park

If you can't resist a winner, Summerlee Heritage Park must surely be on your top-day-out list, having scooped the 'Best Working Attraction' award to confirm its credentials. The accolade is well merited, for this vast heritage site (appropriately located off Heritage Way in Coatbridge) is a stunning tribute to Scottish working life, having recently seen a major updating. Allow a full day to get the most out of this fascinating place.

The vast main exhibition hall – an old crane works – has been completely revamped to show the park's major collection of industrial machinery to best advantage, and has allowed many treasures that were previously in storage to emerge into the light of day. The refurbished hall now contains incredible displays that bring Scotland's industrial and social history to life in a way that will entertain and inform the kids. These include working exhibits of heavy industrial processes.

But a tour of this amazing industrial treasure house is just the start of the entertainment. There's a re-created electric tramway (how many children have ever ridden on one of those?) that, for a modest fare, offers the sort of open-topped urban transport that once served millions of city dwellers throughout the industrialized world. A steam launch plies its trade on the Monklands Canal. There's even a coal mine that allows visitors to experience the dark and creepy conditions endured by bygone miners, while the way they lived may be seen at nearby Miners' Row, a set of cottages that illustrates how conditions changed for Scottish working people between the mid 19th century and the relatively affluent 1960s.

Other highlights include a boat shop, tram depot, railway locos, a steam crane and the intriguing archaeological excavation of the 1830s ironworks. There's even a children's play area where the little ones can unwind.

COST:
Free of charge
YOU SHOULD KNOW:
Summerlee Heritage Park stages a series of special events between Easter and the autumn half-term break, with the emphasis on entertaining children. These include occasions like an old-fashioned fun fair, a steam and model rally, plus kids' activity sessions during the summer holidays.

Passengers on a restored open-top tram

Motherwell Heritage Centre and M&D's Theme Park

The words 'Heritage Centre' don't necessarily set kids' pulses racing, but persuade them that a morning at Motherwell Heritage Centre will start a great day out. This modern facility in the town's High Road is anything but dull. This former burgh to the southeast of Glasgow was noted for steel production – Motherwell used to be called 'Steelopolis' until the giant Ravenscraig steelworks closed in 1992.

But that was just the latest chapter in a very long story, which is imaginatively brought to life at the Heritage Centre. The feature that will engage the kids is Technopolis, a terrific multi-media experience that explains the area's history from the time of the Romans, on through the rise and fall of industries like railways, mining and steel production to Motherwell's reinvention in the 21st century. Interactive technology delivers industrial and street scenes, insight into domestic life over the years and features the entertaining contribution of talking hologram figures. There is no admission charge.

That's good, because having saved those pennies in the morning they will soon be spent in the afternoon, with a visit to M&D's (Scotland's Theme Park) in Motherwell's Strathclyde Country Park. This boasts more than 40 rides and attractions to enchant children of all ages. Four awesome roller coasters – Tornado, Tsunami, Express and Bungee – are guaranteed to deliver white knuckles and churning stomachs (among other symptoms, as management boldly suggests that riders should bring a change of underwear).

But there are plenty of fun rides for smaller kids, too, and gentle family roller coasters like Flying Jumbos and Big Apple. There's also a sensational Cosmic Bowl (for extraordinary 'glow-in-the-dark' ten-pin bowling), the Krazy Congo soft-play area and a wide choice of themed eating places like Downtown USA and Guiseppe's for great coffee and ice cream. Sounds good!

Scottish Football Museum

In truth, this is really a day for families with boys, as girls may fail to appreciate the sporting delights of the Scottish Football Museum. That said, adventurous wee lassies might turn out to be as enthusiastic (and good) as the boys when it comes to enjoying the day's alternative treat.

It kicks off at Hampden Park, home of Scottish international soccer (and lowly Queen's Park Football Club). The Scottish

Football Museum is one of the country's most popular attractions and houses a vast collection of soccer-related exhibits (including the world's oldest national trophy, the Scottish Cup) and focuses on the history of Scottish soccer from the 19th century to the present day.

There are 14 galleries packed with football-related objects, ephemera and memorabilia. There is a rolling programme of themed special exhibitions, bringing an extra dimension to the experience – as does a visit to the well-stocked shop, which is likely to result in kids happily attired in Scotland football kit. There is parking available at Hampden (off Aikenhead Road).

If there's any time left after the soccer extravaganza, the rest of the day could see the kids going up in the world – at the Glasgow Climbing Centre on Paisley Road West. This is not an outing for the youngest children, nor does the centre offer play activities. But it does run great holiday programmes for children (during winter and summer, at Easter and on Bank Holidays).

There's a summer day camp for children over seven that offers a four-hour session either side of lunch (give the kids a packed meal) that provides stimulating exercise, improves co-ordination and encourages team building. It culminates in an exciting abseil down from the building's spire. Alternatively, there are numerous supervised activities for youngsters during the holidays, like Rock Ratz and Climbatize.

Hampden Park National Football Stadium

WHERE:
Glasgow South Side
BEST TIME TO GO:
Any time (summer holidays for day camp at the Glasgow Climbing Centre)
DON'T MISS:
The Hampden Park Stadium Tour – this is an extra that can be booked along with a museum ticket. It will excite every youngster who secretly (or openly!) dreams of achieving sporting success at the highest level – or is simply a football fanatic.
AMOUNT OF WALKING:
Moderate
COST:
Reasonable (children under five go free to the Scottish Football Museum) to expensive (if a couple of kids also do the climbing day camp).
YOU SHOULD KNOW:
Junior sessions at the Glasgow Climbing Centre tend to get booked up, so if climbing is to feature in this special day out, it's wise to check with the centre in advance, though drop-in places are sometimes available.

Bellahouston Park

Not far from Glasgow Rangers' famous Ibrox ground is another facility that attracts well over a million visitors a year, who don't pay a penny for the privilege. Bellahouston Park has everything needed for a great day out in the open air and is located off Dumbreck Road about 5 km (3 mi) to the southwest of the city centre.

For older kids with a lively interest in the world around them, there's a waymarked Heritage Trail that covers 31 sites of interest within the park. The self-guided trail takes around 75 minutes, or alternatively there are free tours conducted by park rangers, who provide running commentary on this impressive open space as the walk unfolds. There is an extensive network of asphalt paths that are ideal for those parents pushing their youngest ones in prams or buggies.

Otherwise, the park offers plenty of opportunity for *al fresco* entertainment that will amuse kids of all ages. Family ball games are an obvious starting point but there are also extensive sporting facilities within the park, which is sometimes described as 'the sports centre without a roof'. It has a ski centre and practice slope, cycling centre, an orienteering course, all-weather running track where dreamers can pretend they're competing in the Olympics and an 18-hole pitch-and-putt golf course. There are really good play areas,

LEFT: *A sculpture-themed play area in Bellahouston Park*
ABOVE: *Children enjoying the practise ski slope.*

including one that has an unusual sculpture theme.

Take food, as there are numerous tranquil spots where you can enjoy a peaceful picnic within open parkland. Should the rain come down (or the kids tire of all that fresh air), Bellahouston Leisure Centre within the park offers a range of enticing activities for non-members, including a climbing wall, swimming (the latter with the option of braving the water flume and rapids) and a children's play area.

Xscape

If it should rain (it has been known to happen in Scotland) then Xscape at Braehead, west of Glasgow, could be the ideal destination for family fun-seekers. It's adjacent to the M8 motorway and offers kids of all ages a great day out – parents too! This entertainment complex has an indoor ski slope, multiplex cinema, ten-pin bowling with ramps and bumpers for smaller bowlers and a large climbing wall, plus assorted rides and activities . . . not to mention shops and various eateries.

If there are lads (or tomboyish lassies) in tow, Soccer Circus is a sure-fire winner. This football shooting range has themed challenges, action replays and an exciting final game. Watchers are welcome and made to feel part of the action. Alternatively, it's possible to try Paradise Island Adventure Golf, playing entertaining mini-courses in the most exotic of surroundings. A rather more high-tech experience waits at the Laser Station, where youngsters with sharp reflexes can don body packs and phasers to fight for the future of the Galaxy.

Physical challenges await at Climbzone, a fabulous supervised adventure playground. The climbing wall offers vertical excitement and Skypark is an aerial adventure course that's 15 m (50 ft) above ground and 60 m (200 ft) long. A popular Climbzone attraction is Fan Drop, which allows kids to clip on and jump before being slowed to a soft landing below. The SNO!Zone is a ski slope (with 'real' snow) with special sessions for beginners and family fun activities like tobogganing and ice sliding.

Still got some energy (and cash) left to burn? Then try the Fun Station for out-and-out play in a bright and safe environment, or recover from all those extended exertions by taking the kids to a movie (choose from 12 screens), or a meal.

WHERE:
Renfrew, Renfrewshire
BEST TIME TO GO:
Any time (except Christmas Day)
DON'T MISS:
A wild, hold-tight ride on Robocoaster, the whirling robotic arm that lets riders programme the infernal machine for themselves.
AMOUNT OF WALKING:
Moderate
COST:
Expensive if the family has a full day at Xscape, though the actual cost will depend on the number of attractions used on the pay-as-you-go basis.
YOU SHOULD KNOW:
It's sensible to book in advance for Climbzone activities as these tend to be fully subscribed, especially during school holidays and at weekends. It's also cost-effective – bookings made online attract a discount.

Clydebuilt Scottish Maritime Museum

WHERE:
Renfrew, Renfrewshire
BEST TIME TO GO:
Any time
DON'T MISS:
The *QE2* Exhibition at the Maritime Museum, which looks at the life, times and retirement of the last great Clyde-built liner, one of the world's most famous ships of all time.
AMOUNT OF WALKING:
Moderate
COST:
Reasonable
YOU SHOULD KNOW:
Once the family skating session at the Braehead Rink is over, there is also an extensive curling facility that allows visitors to relax over a leisurely meal and watch this iconic Scottish sport being played, also enjoying a great view over the mighty River Clyde.

Xscape is terrific fun, but there's a less expensive day out to be found in Braehead that will prove both interesting and satisfying as far as the kids are concerned. The Clydebuilt Scottish Maritime Museum is close to Xscape and the Braehead Shopping Centre – find the Green Car Park and look for the towering masts.

The Maritime Museum focuses on the River Clyde's great trading and shipbuilding tradition, following the growth of Glasgow and its commercial and industrial heritage from the tobacco kings who made it big in the 18th century to construction of modern Royal Navy warships. An award-winning audio-visual display charts the rise and fall of Glasgow shipbuilding over three centuries. Another fascinating feature is the story of a typical build – of the MV *Rangitane* – through the eyes of those involved in her construction, from sweating riveters to bowler-hatted foremen.

But there's more to the Maritime Museum than interesting history, with the veteran Clyde-built coaster MV *Kyles* waiting to be explored and the chance for children to enjoy some exciting virtual reality – like piloting the MV *Clan Alpine* up the River Clyde or becoming an old-time wheeler-dealer Glasgow merchant buying and selling goods before transporting them around the world. There are also entertaining games in the interactive gallery for younger children.

The Maritime Museum probably won't take up the full day, so a contrasting activity could round things off nicely. The Braehead Skating and Curling Rink is also part of the Braehead Shopping Centre complex, offering safe, family-friendly skating for all ages. This Olympic-size rink offers ample room for skaters from rank beginners to confident speedsters, and there couldn't be a better place to sample this exciting activity for the first time – or hone existing blade skills.

Fossil Grove and the Museum of Transport

One of Scotland's most unusual attractions is the extraordinary Fossil Grove in Victoria Park – located in the Scotstoun area of the city's West End. The Grove consists of 11 fossilized tree stumps that were discovered in 1887 and represents a tiny fraction of the vast forest that stood here 330 million years ago, made up of long-extinct plants called giant clubmoss. An interpretive display explains this fascinating phenomenon for the benefit of parents and children alike. In addition to Fossil Grove, Victoria Park has a superb rock garden, arboretum, children's play areas and a boating pond, so it's easy to wile away a morning in one of Glasgow's prettiest open spaces.

The rest of the day can happily be spent at the Kelvin Hall in nearby Bunhouse Road – but don't expect to be alone. There, the Museum of Transport is a visitor attraction that draws over half-a-million people a year . . . with good reason. There is an extraordinary range of interesting exhibits ranging from the world's oldest surviving bicycle to a unique collection of Scottish-built cars. Original vehicles and models tell the tale of transport by land and sea, with emphasis on anything built or used in Glasgow – once known as the 'Workshop of the British Empire'.

The Clyde Room has over 200 model ships that testify to – and illustrate – the city's illustrious shipbuilding heritage. There are also some magnificent railway engines that reflect Glasgow's once-great locomotive industry. The re-creation of bygone Glasgow is always popular, featuring old trams, the Subway station and Kelvin Street.

The Museum of Transport is child-friendly, offering ride-on toy cars that parents can borrow to push youngsters aged three to six around the extensive displays, to save little legs from tiring – and tempers from fraying.

WHERE:
Glasgow West End
BEST TIME TO GO:
Summer for Victoria Park, otherwise any time (the Transport Museum is actually worth a day in its own right out of season or in inclement weather conditions).
DON'T MISS:
A free guided tour at the museum, with experts providing insight into the history and use of many exhibits. These flexible tours last for around an hour – ask at Reception for details upon arrival.
AMOUNT OF WALKING:
Moderate
COST:
Free
YOU SHOULD KNOW:
At weekends there are free screenings at Kelvin Cinema – historic footage on Saturdays and children's animation on Sundays.

Petrified trees at Fossil Grove, Victoria Park

Glasgow Science Centre

*Children playing on scientific
equipment at the Glasgow
Science Centre.*

If there's one destination that is guaranteed to delight kids with enquiring minds it's Glasgow Science Centre on Pacific Quay. This state-of-the-art facility is centred on the Science Mall, a gleaming titanium building overlooking the River Clyde that has three floors featuring endless interactive exhibits and displays that will fascinate children and encourage them to get involved in the magic of science.

Floor One features action tests like trying to beat the wiggly wire and a wonderful optical illusions section where seeing isn't believing. There are also interactive workshops, where kids can get to know creatures like hissing cockroaches or giant land snails. Here, too, is the Science Centre's Planetarium, allowing visitors to study brilliant night skies as they can rarely be seen in these days of pervasive light pollution.

Floor Two looks at the role of science in everyday life and explores issues that affect us all, though this educational dimension is merely the *hors d'oeuvre* before a raft of exciting hands-on activities like face morphing and 3D modelling, plus access to the Science in the Dock wall that lets kids post their own image and

comments, then explore space using the Who Should Go? feature. Workshops cover subjects like stilt walking, building and flying hot-air balloons and experimenting with tasks like building and launching a rocket or solving a crime as DIY detectives.

Floor Three features the amazing bubble wall and ever-popular exhibits like Whirlpool, Indoor Tornado and the giant plasma globe. This is also the place to see the current exhibition, throwing light onto a hot scientific topic of the moment. Outside, the Glasgow Tower (that only operates if conditions are suitable) allows visitors to be transported skywards for incredible city views. Actually, one day might not be enough to see and do everything!

The Tall Ship and Kelvingrove Park

There's something very romantic about the towering masts and intricate rigging of a great sailing ship, and The Tall Ship at Glasgow Harbour lets kids get up close to a magnificent survivor from the great days of sail. The Clyde-built barque *Glenlee* is one of Scotland's most popular visitor attractions. This three-masted ship with its steel hull was built at Port Glasgow in 1896, and after decades travelling the world's oceans ended up as a training ship for the Spanish Navy, before being laid up in Seville harbour. She was saved from the scrapyard, returned to her home port and restored, now being one of only five Clyde-built sailing ships left in the world.

A number of interactive exhibits will intrigue youngsters, there are on-board Discovery Trails and kids can join the hunt for Jock the Ship's Cat. A programme of exhibitions is organized on *Glenlee*, illustrating a facet of bygone life at sea or Glasgow's maritime heritage. The Kelvinhaugh Ferry No 8 is berthed alongside *Glenlee*, after transporting Glasgow folk to and fro across the Clyde from the mid 1950s. She can be inspected by prior appointment and makes river trips on special occasions.

Just north of The Tall Ship's berth is the green expanse of Kelvingrove Park. This grand Victorian public space is a great place for the family to relax and unwind after travelling the Seven Seas in their imagination. For the energetic (and curious) there is a Heritage Trail with 35 points of interest. Also on offer are a tranquil riverside walk, an orienteering course, a skateboard park and a children's play area. The park also contains recently refurbished Kelvingrove Museum and Art Galleries in their impressive building, with fabulous displays designed to appeal to all ages.

WHERE:
Glasgow West End
BEST TIME TO GO:
Any time (summer if visiting Kelvingrove Park)
DON'T MISS:
The opportunity to turn the children loose on the mock yardarm and rigging feature on *Glenlee*, which will give them some idea of the difficult tasks faced by the hardy but agile sailors of old.
AMOUNT OF WALKING:
Moderate
COST:
Reasonable (one child goes free to The Tall Ship with each paying visitor).
YOU SHOULD KNOW:
The *Glenlee* should be moved and berthed alongside Glasgow's Riverside Museum when this modernistic building is completed on the banks of the Clyde, opposite Govan.

Clyde Muirshiel Regional Park 1

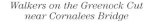
Walkers on the Greenock Cut near Cornalees Bridge

WHERE:
Renfrewshire (though parts of the park are in Inverclyde and North Ayrshire)
BEST TIME TO GO:
Summer
DON'T MISS:
The swallows busy nesting and raising their young in close-up detail on CCTV screens in the Cornalees Visitor Centre.
AMOUNT OF WALKING:
Low to lots (depending on the amount undertaken around Cornalees).
COST:
Free of charge
YOU SHOULD KNOW:
There is a pushchair-friendly mini trail starting at Cornalees Visitor Centre that even toddlers can manage comfortably.

It's best to allocate two days to the family delights of Clyde Muirshiel Regional Park . . . or face the hard choice between a pair of contrasting but equally satisfying outings. In fact, it's even possible to make this a great weekend by staying overnight at the campsite.

This splendid park is billed as 'The Great Escape' for those in search of healthy open-air activities on land and water, covering a vast area of attractive rural countryside 30 minutes west of Glasgow by rail or road. It consists of linked areas of unspoiled countryside on the South Clyde Estuary set aside for recreation. The park's various locations offer a huge variety of outdoor activities and the first day might start on the wonderful beach at Lunderston Bay. This is the nearest sandy beach to the great metropolis of Glasgow. Bring buckets and spades and simply do all those beach-day-out things, then sample the children's play area, have a stroll and enjoy a picnic in one of the scenic areas reserved for the purpose.

After lunch (if the kids can be dragged away from the beach) the Cornalees Visitor Centre offers a change of pace. This traditional building is located on the west side of scenic Loch Thom at the top of Shirehill Glen, south of Greenock. This is for walkers, but that doesn't necessarily require excessive effort. There is an easy 2.5-km (1.5-mi) woodland nature trail that should be well within the compass of all but the smallest children. Bolder walkers can find the historic Greenock Cut Aqueduct that has fantastic views over the Clyde. But even kids who don't like walking will be enthralled by the ever-changing contents of the Wildlife Tank and absorb lots of information on wildlife, flowers and fungi.

Clyde Muirshiel Regional Park 2

The second day at Clyde Muirshiel Regional Park can be set aside for a visit to the Castle Semple Visitor Centre & Country Park on the shores of Castle Semple Loch. This is a good day out for older kids with the get-up-and-go to enjoy a strenuous physical workout, although it's possible to include some laid-back relaxation on the greensward beside the loch as part of the outing – ideally with a picnic. Take a loaf of bread and indulge in an activity that never fails to delight children of all ages – feeding the loch's population of greedy ducks, swans and terns.

There's also some super strolling to be had in Parkhill Wood, with its maze of tempting trails, where the roofless 15th-century Collegiate church and medieval fishpond may be found, though children will probably be more interested in the intriguing grotto by the pond.

Meanwhile, back with the action, dads who fish can treat their offspring to an angling session (or lesson if they're beginners) with coarse fish such as pike, perch and roach to tempt. The park's Ranger Service organizes family-friendly activities and events throughout the year. If fishing isn't anyone's cuppa, a little advance planning should allow the kids to join a group taster session for an outdoor activity that will capture their imagination, like archery, kayaking, mountain biking, orienteering, sailing or windsurfing.

For those children big (or experienced) enough to do their own thing under parental supervision, there is mountain-bike hire (Castle Semple is on Cycle Route 7 from Glasgow to Irvine, so there's some ideal two-wheel terrain). Alternatively, if the water should beckon, rowing boats, aquatrikes, surf bikes and kayaks may be hired in season. This encourages a full spectrum of activity, from a leisurely family row to some uninhibited aquatic romping.

WHERE:
Lochwinnoch, Renfrewshire
BEST TIME TO GO:
Summer
DON'T MISS:
The chance to join together as a family and take the Parkhill Challenge – ask the Rangers at the Visitor Centre about this entertaining treasure-hunt-style activity.
AMOUNT OF WALKING:
Lots (optional)
COST:
Low
YOU SHOULD KNOW:
Castle Semple Loch is generally quite shallow so even if there should be an unfortunate capsize (deliberate or otherwise!), most kids will simply be able to stand up in the water.

Sailing boats on Castle Semple Loch, Clyde Muirshiel Regional Park

Waterfront Leisure Complex and Newark Castle

WHERE:
Greenock and Port Glasgow,
Renfrewshire
BEST TIME TO GO:
April to October for Newark Castle
DON'T MISS:
Parents who need pampering can
use the sauna and steam room next
to the leisure pool at the Waterfront
Leisure Complex, while also keeping
a watchful eye on their children as
they disport themselves in the pool.
AMOUNT OF WALKING:
Moderate
COST:
Reasonable
YOU SHOULD KNOW:
The upper floors of Newark Castle
are not accessible to little ones in
pushchairs and can only be reached
by steep stairs (including tight spiral
staircases). But there are great views
across the River Clyde from the top
of the tower for those who make it
all the way.

The proud boast of the Waterfront Leisure Complex at Greenock is simple: 'All you and the family have to do is turn up and enjoy yourselves'. This super-modern leisure facility offers wheelchair and pushchair access throughout and certainly delivers on that welcoming claim.

The place is paradise for water-loving kids, with a training pool and leisure pool to choose from. The all-action leisure pool has two flume rides, Scotland's longest tyre ride and a wave ride for those who want to try a little body surfing. The complex also holds regular Sea Scooting sessions, allowing children to thrill to an effortless tow from these lightweight personal water propellers.

After all that fun and frolic in the water, there's an opportunity to switch to the ice. The Waterfront Leisure Complex's large rink has four curling lanes that are used through the winter months. There are daily public skating sessions and the rink is entirely turned over to the public from Fridays to Sundays. There's skate hire for every session and it's possible to book weekend 'learn to skate' sessions for kids, while those who are confident on ice might demand to be treated to the early evening Ice Disco.

Just along the A8 road lies Port Glasgow, and here Newark Castle provides a change of pace – assuming the whole day hasn't somehow been used up exploring the delights of the Waterfront Leisure Complex. This well-preserved castle on the shores of the Clyde estuary dates from the 15th century, with substantial rebuilding around 1600. Highlights of the tour are below-stairs areas that provide a fascinating glimpse into the demanding working lives of the servants in times past and the late-16th-century Little Bedchamber that has retained its original fixtures and fittings, including a fine painted ceiling and bed-press (a bed that folded away into a cupboard).

Edinburgh Zoo

This ever-popular attraction is on Corstorphine Road, west of the city centre, and has been delighting youngsters and adults alike for around a century. Set in extensive sloping parkland, it provides a safe haven for 1,000 interesting, rare and endangered creatures. But Scotland's largest wildlife centre also offers imaginative attractions and great visitor facilities, plus a continuous series of activities and events throughout the year.

Get there as soon as possible after opening time (09.00) to make the most of a special day out – there's loads to see and do. That being so, it's sensible to get a site map upon arrival and have a family conference to plan a day that pleases everyone. As well as the incomparable range of animals and birds to be seen, there's a daily programme of talks on favourites like the koala, chimpanzees and penguins, plus entertaining activities like sea lion training.

Other highlights include the twice-daily (in summer) Animal Antics Show in Hilltop Arena, featuring animals and birds that demonstrate dazzling skills. The best way to get up the hill is to take the free Hilltop Safari, riding a bush-camouflaged trailer pulled by a matching Land Rover. And few kids can resist the walk-through Rainbow Landing, where brilliantly coloured Australian lorikeets fly down to perch and sip nectar from the hand.

There are cafés and kiosks offering drinks, snacks and food, including children's meals. Picnic areas allow those who bring their own to enjoy a leisurely feast in a super setting, and there are several play areas for kids who want to have some active fun. Incidentally, should that famous Scottish rain come down the day will not be a washout – the Zoo has 11 major indoor areas that house animals and there are also several sheltered observation areas.

WHERE:
Edinburgh
BEST TIME TO GO:
Any time
DON'T MISS:
The Budongo Trail, through a cleverly re-created natural habitat for chimpanzees – it presents a close-up look at these enchanting animals, as well as illustrating the zoo's vital work in the fields of wildlife conservation, scientific research and education.
AMOUNT OF WALKING:
Lots and lots (if you want to see everything). The site is generally suitable for pushchairs, though there are some steep paths and steps to negotiate.
COST:
Expensive (though still great value and children under three go free, with family tickets attracting a discount).
YOU SHOULD KNOW:
The zoo is easily accessible by public transport, with several low-floor bus services providing a frequent service from the city centre and Edinburgh's two train stations. Car parking is available but there is a charge for this facility.

Boy and Gentoo penguin examining each other.

Edinburgh Dungeon plus Camera Obscura and World of Illusions

What is it with kids and dungeons? They can't resist them, which should make this day a sure-fire ghoulish success. The Edinburgh Dungeon (on Market Street, parallel to Princes Street) boasts a wealth of gruesome discoveries, using phrases like 'horrifying myth', 'barbaric savagery' and 'inhumane medical practices'. Sounds perfect!

The dungeon has much dark Scottish history to feast on, and duly gorges on horrors like Mary King's Close, with its stench of dead plague victims. A blood-spattered Anatomy Theatre looks at 18th-century surgical experimentation that encouraged the city's infamous body-snatching trade. The Haunted Labyrinth explores Edinburgh's spooky underworld and nimble visitors may try to escape from repulsive cannibal Sawney Bean. But there's no evading a harsh fate as the Judgement of Sinners hands down cruel sentences that involve terrifying tortures. If those nasties are survived, the Extremis Drop Ride to Doom should finish everyone off nastily.

If there's one thing kids love nearly as much as dank depths, it's magic. So upon escaping the Dungeons head for the Camera Obscura and World of Illusions on nearby Castlehill. The Victorian Camera Obscura is a famous Edinburgh landmark and visitors (especially children) are always amazed and delighted by the moving images of the city projected onto a viewing table, finding it hard to believe that a simple arrangement of mirror and lenses can create such a compelling panorama.

But that's just the start. The associated World of Illusions offers a fascinating selection of interactive activities where seeing definitely isn't believing. How do they do that? The kids will love trying to find out in the Magic Gallery and Light Fantastic features. Fun, Games & Stairway at the World of Illusions presents some of the most fiendish and baffling optical illusions ever devised. It all adds up to an awesome day.

A girl stares into the infinity light tunnel.

National Museum of Scotland and Museum of Childhood

The National Museum of Scotland is in the process of transforming itself into a world-class venue, though in truth this grand old building in the heart of Edinburgh's Old Town is already a must-visit attraction. Find it in Chambers Street, off South Bridge. Ambitiously, the museum covers 'Life, the Universe and everything in it'. No problem in finding something for everyone, then.

Kids will be especially turned on by the interactive science-and-technology Connect Gallery, which features such delights as space travel and robotics. This is the place to try on a spacesuit, gawp at a Black Knight rocket and check out a genuine NASA Gemini space capsule. Alternatively, there's a Formula One racing car simulator to drive, the chance to launch a hydrogen-powered rocket or control a model robot as it explores an alien planet. Hours of happy fun await here. Other interesting possibilities include the Communicate! gallery (where kids can often outshine parents in mastery of the latest technology), and some fascinating insight into Scotland's colourful history.

Moving on from the National Museum, an irresistible attraction awaits. What youngster could ignore the opportunity to visit Britain's noisiest museum? Even parents will be enchanted by the Museum of Childhood on the High Street, part of Edinburgh's famous Royal Mile. The world's first-ever specialist showcase for children's-interest exhibits was opened in 1955, and this large facility is stuffed with objects relating to the lives, loves and upbringing of children.

There are toys and games galore from many countries and highlights include a re-created 1930s schoolroom (kids had better know their multiplication tables) plus the 1950s street games of Scottish children. Best of all, the sobering glimpse into the sometimes-harsh lives of kids in times past will enable harassed parents to play the 'aren't you lucky?' card.

WHERE:
Central Edinburgh
BEST TIME TO GO:
Any time
DON'T MISS:
Discovery Zones at the National Museum of Scotland, which allow kids to slip effortlessly into history, exercising their imagination as anything from a Roman soldier to a Viking invader.
AMOUNT OF WALKING:
Moderate to lots (depending how thoroughly both museums are explored).
COST:
Edinburgh's museums all offer free entry.
YOU SHOULD KNOW:
The Museum of Childhood only opens on Sundays during the summer season (July and August), operating for six days a week throughout the rest of the year.

Model of a grocery shop interior at the Edinburgh Museum of Childhood

*A red tourist bus travels along
Princes Street, Edinburgh*

Edinburgh bus tour

First-time visitors to Scotland's historic capital – and those returning to see more of this great city – should enjoy taking one of the hop-on-hop-off bus tours that cover Edinburgh's notable features. Edinburgh sprawls over seven hills and has a fascinating skyline and splendid old buildings. The four different tours that leave Waverley Bridge at regular intervals have 20 or more strategically placed stops where passengers can either disembark or jump aboard. Each takes around an hour to do a circuit on its appointed route.

However, this outing should absorb more time than that, as unlimited tickets are valid for 24 hours. The ideal way to play the day is to do the whole tour to see the principal sights, with a little help from a well-informed guide or audio commentary. The kids will enjoy this, as riding on an open-top bus is great fun and the novelty is slow to wear off. Having seen everything from the bus, it's then possible to start hopping on and off, checking out individual attractions that looked interesting first time round.

A typical itinerary will include all the city's notable landmarks, though of course these may leave the kids cold, even though they will greatly enjoy observing the bustling streets below from the open top of the bus. But the beauty of the flexibility provided by jumping on and off the bus at will is that it provides endless opportunities to explore things that children will enjoy. Especially recommended in this context is Edinburgh Castle, where history is brought to life. Let the kids romp in the playpark at West Princes Street Gardens or have a family picnic in Princes Street Gardens (failing which there are loads of fast-food outlets). In fact, there's so much to choose from that the day will fly by.

YOU SHOULD KNOW:
One unusual stop-off that should keep the kids quiet and busy for a while is the Brass Rubbing Centre in Trinity Apse, just off the High Street. Here youngsters (and grown-ups!) can make brass rubbings from a range of monumental brasses, featuring subjects as diverse as medieval knights and ancient Celtic designs. Open April to September.

Murrayfield Stadium and Our Dynamic Earth

The Scots are passionate followers of ball games and, while soccer is the nation's first love, there is an honourable tradition of successful competition in the rugby union arena. When it comes to home matches, the arena in question is Edinburgh's Murrayfield Stadium, located in an affluent suburb to the west of the city. Find it just up the road from Edinburgh Zoo.

The iconic home of Scottish rugby is recognized as one of the world's top stadia and the 75-minute weekday tour is a thrilling experience for parents and children with sporting tendencies. This behind-the-scenes peek at the splendiferous facilities is hosted by knowledgeable guides and takes in the Players' Entrance, dressing rooms, President's Suite, tv studio, hospitality boxes, Players' Tunnel, Royal Box and famous pitch. Just standing there looking round the empty stands is an awesome experience, so it's easy to understand the intense emotion that is generated on match days.

To round off the day it's possible to pop into adjacent Murrayfield Ice Rink for a skating session, but for non-skaters a swift return to the city centre can be followed by a visit to Our Dynamic Earth, close to Holyrood Park. This is one of those experiences that happily combines education and entertainment, giving the kids insight into our planet's beginnings, past, present and future with the help of interactive exhibits and the very latest technology.

Features include the Time Machine (ride it right back to the Big Bang), Restless Earth (smell the sulphur as the volcano prepares to erupt), Casualties and Survivors (winners and losers in the story of evolution including the biggest losers of all, dinosaurs) and the sweltering Tropical Rainforest. This is science made compelling, and kids just love it.

WHERE:
Edinburgh
BEST TIME TO GO:
Any time
DON'T MISS:
The Polar Adventure at Our Dynamic Earth, complete with freezing temperatures, howling winds, icebergs, polar bears, penguins and the shimmering Northern Lights.
AMOUNT OF WALKING:
Lots
COST:
Reasonable to expensive (if the family takes in both the day's main attractions).
YOU SHOULD KNOW:
Weekend and Bank Holiday tours of Murrayfield are by arrangement only and require at least ten participants. Tours do not take place on match days, or for two days before and after a Scotland home international.
To be sure of avoiding disappointment it is wise to book a Murrayfield visit 48 hours in advance.

Midlothian Snowsports Centre and Edinburgh Butterfly & Insect World

WHERE:
Hillend and Lasswade,
City of Edinburgh
BEST TIME TO GO:
Any time
DON'T MISS:
Friday afternoon at Butterfly & Insect
World, when the sinuous Royal
pythons are fed in the Snake Pit –
watch it go down!
AMOUNT OF WALKING:
Moderate
COST:
Reasonable to expensive
(depending on the amount of time
used at the Snowsports Centre's
assorted facilities)
YOU SHOULD KNOW:
It's possible to book weekend Easy
Ski lessons at the Snowsports Centre
for youngsters aged six or older who
have never skied but are keen to give
it a good go. There are also
snowboarding lessons available for
kids of eight and upwards.

Just outside the Edinburgh bypass to the south of the city is the Midlothian Snowsports Centre, nestling in the stunning Pentland Hills Regional Park at appropriately named Hillend. Here is Britain's largest artificial ski slope, so come aboard for some seriously slippery fun!

Actually, there are several slopes at the centre, so this isn't simply a day out for families who already ski. In addition to the two main slopes there are two nursery slopes, a jump slope and various freestyle features. There are chair lifts and tows, and beginners can tackle the nursery slopes as soon as they've mastered the tows. On certain days there are super tubing sessions when children under 12 can shoot downhill on round inflatable 'doughnuts'. On Saturday afternoons Super Slider sessions offer supervised skiing instruction. Whatever the chosen option(s), all essential equipment (including helmets) is supplied. Children under six are not permitted to ski but may take private lessons.

Round off the day with something completely different. Further to the east is Edinburgh Butterfly & Insect World, which transports visitors to a tropical rainforest inhabited by creepy, crawly and flying insects – kids just love 'em! Find it at Dobbies Garden World, Lasswade, just off the A772 road south of the Edinburgh bypass (Gilmerton exit). It's also on various bus routes.

All sorts of exciting encounters await, including animal handling (that'll be snakes, tarantulas and giant millipedes, so not for the faint-hearted), fish feeding (impressive Koi carp), the glowing scorpion display, leafcutter ant parade and beady-eyed iguanas. The tropical gardens are ablaze with thousands of colourful butterflies feeding on the exotic flowers and it's even possible to experience the fury of a tropical rainstorm first hand. And while the whole experience is highly entertaining, a visit also helps to support valuable conservation work.

*Children learn to handle
animals and conquer phobias
at Butterfly & Insect World.*

East Links Family Park, Dunbar

Travel east from Edinburgh on the A1, turning off at the Thistly Cross roundabout for West Barns, some 40 km (25 mi) from the city. Here, John Muir Country Park encompasses a beautiful stretch of coastline that should tempt any family that adores the great outdoors. It's well worth a visit but is not the principal location for today's outing. That honour goes to the adjacent East Links Family Park, which offers rather more structured entertainment. There is loads to do there, inside and out, so even adverse weather can't dampen the day.

The park has numerous animals for the kids to inspect, including long-horned Highland cattle, pygmy goats, sheep, deer, horses, Shetland ponies, pigs, donkeys and llamas. In spring there is sometimes the opportunity to assist in bottle-feeding newborn animals. There are plenty of birds, too – ostrich-like rhea, guinea fowl, ornamental chickens, peafowl, quail, pheasants . . . plus various geese and ducks. The small-animal section has favourites like chinchillas, chipmunks, rabbits and guinea pigs.

That's the gentle, laid-back part. After enjoying animal watch, the circular Train Safari by narrow-gauge railway never fails to please, and bold kids will want to try and beat the baffling woodland maze. But mostly it's the get-up-and-go activities that will appeal. These include pedal go-karts, an outdoor play area, hay barn soft-play, pirate ship, tractors, crazy bikes, the slippery Jelly Belly, trampolines, Ball Blast arena, climbing walls, bouncy castle, all-weather sledging, horse-shoe pitching and milk-can skittles.

There's a café for when that inevitable 'we're hungry' cry goes up – though visitors are welcome to bring their own picnics – and a shop that sells essentials like ice cream. More than enough action will ensure that this fun-filled day will seem to pass in a flash, satisfying even the most hyperactive offspring in the process.

Children handle a chick at the East Links Family Park.

WHERE:
Dunbar, East Lothian
BEST TIME TO GO:
Any time
DON'T MISS:
Pony rides at East Links – there's a small extra charge for this kids-will-adore-it activity but it's worth every penny (from April to October at weekends and during holidays).
AMOUNT OF WALKING:
Lots
COST:
Reasonable (tots under two go free and there's a discount on a family ticket).
YOU SHOULD KNOW:
Scottish winter weather can be harsh, but the consequent disincentive to enjoy the outdoor activities is more than compensated for by the Christmas Winter Wonderland feature (from early in December to New Year).

405

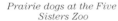
Prairie dogs at the Five Sisters Zoo

Five Sisters Zoo Park and Almond Valley Heritage Centre

Handily placed twixt Edinburgh and Glasgow is the Five Sisters Zoo Park near West Calder, off the A71 road at Polbeth. This is a serious attraction for animal-loving kids, as many mammals, birds and reptiles from all over the world are on display.

Highlights include a reptile house, mixed bird aviary, crocodile pool and monkey house. Among the many animals to be seen are cheeky meerkats, reindeer, wallabies, lemurs, bat-eared foxes, porcupines, otters, wild cats, prairie dogs, raccoons and micro pigs. The talkative African grey parrots are always popular and other splendid birds include snowy owls and kookaburras. After that, Jungle Tums Café may well tempt the inner family.

Following a tour of Five Sisters, nearby Almond Valley Heritage Centre offers more varied fare, though once again there are plenty of animals. This special attraction is on the outskirts of Livingston Village – find it just off the A705 road at Mill Roundabout, close to Junction 3 on the M8 motorway. The Heritage Centre has been thoughtfully organized as a family attraction that should appeal to everyone, with lots to see and do.

A range of farm animals is tended at picturesque Mill Farm, including Highland cattle, horses, ponies, goats and rare-breed sheep. Kids are encouraged to gain hands-on experience during regular tasks like milking, feeding and grooming and there is a regular programme of seasonal crafts, activities and games.

The large riverside site has woods and ample green space, containing a wealth of imaginative activities. These range from a peaceful nature trail to all-action pedal carts, toy tractors, trampolines, rabbit tunnel, adventure zone, simulated archaeological dig and play mine. There's also a narrow-gauge railway, working water mill and local history museum combining to deliver a day to remember, even if it rains – there are plenty of indoor attractions, too.

WHERE:
West Calder and Livingston, West Lothian
BEST TIME TO GO:
Spring to autumn
DON'T MISS:
Crocodile feeding at Five Sisters Zoo Park, which takes place three times a week in summer – in mid afternoon on Wednesdays (small feed) and on Saturday and Sunday (large feeds).
AMOUNT OF WALKING:
Moderate to lots. All the main pathways at the Almond Valley Heritage Centre are surfaced and suitable for pushchairs.
COST:
Reasonable
YOU SHOULD KNOW:
For a small extra charge, the Morag's Meadow soft-play area allows smaller children to romp safely while their parents enjoy a cuppa and watch the fun as the little ones leap from leaf to leaf or bounce happily on giant vegetables.

Beecraigs Country Park and Linlithgow Canal Centre

This super day only works at weekends, starting and ending at Linlithgow between Falkirk and Edinburgh. Nestling in the Bathgate Hills just south of town is Beecraigs Country Park, offering various outdoor activities from archery through kayaking to orienteering and gorge scrambling. Introductory two-hour courses are available, also day courses. These, along with trout fishing in the well-stocked loch, must be pre-booked.

But unless the kids are really keen on being introduced to one of these open-air skills the idea is simply a family visit to this beautiful place, to see the red deer herd which may be observed from pathways or a raised platform – expect calves from May and roaring stags during autumn rut. The Park Centre has a farm shop and crafts for sale, plus a restaurant with sensational views – a great place to end the visit with a snack.

After a leisurely morning, the day's main attraction may be found at Linlithgow's Manse Road Basin on the Edinburgh and Glasgow Union Canal. It's only open after lunch on Saturdays and Sundays, but well worth the effort of planning accordingly. There is a choice of boat trips – *Victoria* is a 12-seater replica steam packet that does half-hour stints on the Town Stretch, while *St Magdalene* is a 40-seater that does a two-and-a-half-hour round trip. This relaxing journey along the peaceful waterway culminates with the awesome stone-built Avon Aqueduct, 247 m (810 ft) long and 26 m (86 ft) above the river.

The Canal Centre is actually open on weekdays in July and August (boat trips on *Victoria* only). On the last Sunday of each month kids go free on boat trips – up to two with each paying adult. Well-heeled families who want to make a full day of it could even pre-book the *Leamington*, a small self-drive narrowboat.

WHERE:
Linlithgow, West Lothian
BEST TIME TO GO:
May to September
DON'T MISS:
The Canal Museum, housed in former canal stables at Manse Road, with an extensive display that focuses on the history and working life of the Edinburgh and Glasgow Union, plus coverage of the wildlife found on, in and around its waters.
AMOUNT OF WALKING:
Moderate to lots (if the Country Park's scenic trails prove irresistible).
COST:
Low to reasonable (depending on which boat trip is taken).
YOU SHOULD KNOW:
There are occasional special boat outings from the Manse Road Basin to the extraordinary Falkirk Wheel, which replaced 11 dismantled locks to connect the Edinburgh and Glasgow Union to the Forth and Clyde Canal by transporting boats up and down a vertical distance of 35 m (115 ft).

Autumn beeches at Beecraigs Country Park, Linlithgow

Seafari Adventure and Inchcolm Island

WHERE:
Leith and South Queensferry,
City of Edinburgh
BEST TIME TO GO:
April to October
DON'T MISS:
Rare survivors of ancient times at
Inchcolm Abbey – a 13th-century wall
painting and also medieval stone
screens in the bell tower.
AMOUNT OF WALKING:
Moderate
COST:
Expensive (if both boat trips are taken).
YOU SHOULD KNOW:
If two boat trips overstretch the
budget, the day could start at
Queensferry Museum in South
Queensferry. The museum focuses on
local history and children will be
impressed by a full-sized model of the
Burry Man, who wears a costume
covered in those irritating products of
the burdock plant and parades
through town for nine hours in early
August, for reasons lost in the mists of
time. The museum is closed on
Tuesdays and Wednesdays.

Forth Railway Bridge

Today's the day to go afloat and see some of the best sights offered by the Firth of Forth. Starting from Newhaven Harbour, close to the Royal Yacht *Britannia* in Leith Docks to the north of Edinburgh, the Seafari Adventure involves a one-hour exploration of the Forth's islands in a fully equipped RIB (Rigid Inflatable Boat), with a skipper who knows the best places to see seals, occasional porpoises or dolphins and the abundant seabird population. No two trips are ever the same and in addition to the sheer thrill of riding a high-speed RIB, the skip explains the many sights that may be encountered.

Next up another wonderful expedition awaits – a trip to historic Inchcolm Island, the source of endless conflicts between the English and Scots in medieval times. Fife's 'Iona of the East' lies off Braefoot Bay in the Firth and is so called because both islands are dedicated to St Columba. The historic religious significance of Inchcolm is underlined by the ruin of a 9th-century hermit's cell and the magnificent Inchcolm Abbey, Scotland's most complete medieval monastic house.

The Inchcolm ferry is the *Maid of the Forth*, sailing from Hawes Pier in South Queensferry in the shadow of the original Forth Bridge. The 45-minute cruise out to Inchcolm involves passing beneath this awesome structure and there's a lively running commentary. This is a top-notch wildlife area and seals plus many seabirds will be seen,

almost certainly including comical puffins, gannets, fulmars, cormorants, eider ducks and guillemots.

It's possible to remain aboard for the return leg to South Queensferry, but most prefer to land and explore Inchcolm. In addition to the hugely impressive historic abbey, this small island has a visitor centre, gardens, picnic areas and beach. The *Maid* will be back to collect the shore party after 90 minutes.

Museum of Communication and Beacon Leisure Centre

This is the perfect opportunity to shock – and intrigue – children who think communications technology began and ended with colour television, mobile phones and the Internet. The place to do it is the Museum of Communication on the High Street in Burntisland, on the north side of the Firth of Forth directly opposite Edinburgh.

The museum has a mission – to inform, educate and entertain the public with the exciting developments in communications technology that have given rise to the way of life we enjoy today. If this all sounds a bit worthy, the reality is actually rather good. The permanent collection encompasses an eclectic display that tells the tale of sound (from phonographs to MP3 players), information technology (from Babbages's difference engine to modern super computers), radio (domestic and commercial), radar (from World War II to modern air-traffic control), telephony (from Alexander Graham Bell's humble beginnings to universal usage), telegraphy and television. The old equipment that's on show may amuse the kids, but they'll definitely learn something.

Lessons entertainingly learned, the day can proceed with a short trip to Lammerlaws Road, at the eastern end of town. Here, the Beacon Leisure Centre makes that oft-repeated promise 'fun for all the family' – and it delivers. It has a great pool with the features that make kids leap into the water with gusto – a wave machine and two spectacular flumes.

There's a beach area beside the pool and a nice café overlooking the beach and sea. Smaller kids and non-swimmers can enjoy an extensive soft-play area. Should the day be warm and any time remain, the kids could stay in their swimming costumes for the short trip to Burntisland's famous Blue Flag beach. But you probably won't be able to prise them away from the Beacon Centre's flumes.

WHERE:
Burntisland, Fife
BEST TIME TO GO:
April to September (but note that the Museum of Communication is open only on Wednesdays and Saturdays).
DON'T MISS:
The replica of John Logie Baird's primitive Televisor of 1930 at the museum – the world's first domestic tv set used a noisy spinning disc and had a tiny picture composed of 30 vertical lines. From little acorns . . .
AMOUNT OF WALKING:
Little
COST:
Low
YOU SHOULD KNOW:
If none of the kids likes swimming (or technology!) an alternative attraction is the Burntisland Museum (behind the library in the High Street, closed on Sundays), which has a wonderful Edwardian fairground display.

Scottish Deer Centre, Cupar

WHERE:
Cupar, Fife
BEST TIME TO GO:
Any time
DON'T MISS:
A little parental self-indulgence at the Highland Smokehouse, which features shelves groaning with quality Scottish provisions – including an incomparable selection of single malts and blended whisky.
AMOUNT OF WALKING:
Moderate to lots (it's a big site with super walks but those trailer rides can cut down extended tramping).
COST:
Reasonable
YOU SHOULD KNOW:
It's now possible to see Scotland's rarest bird at the Deer Centre – the capercaille, which is now almost impossible to find and see in the wild.

More animals! West of historic Cupar in the Ancient Kingdom of Fife is the Scottish Deer Centre, in Rankeilour Park off the A91 road. This magical place offers a terrific day out, packed with interest and variety for families with kids who like being outdoors. It's quite possible to simply wile away the hours exploring the deer centre, though for those who prefer a more structured day there are numerous organized activities on offer.

The centre has around 150 deer, representing nine different species from around the world. Each species has its own spacious enclosure and may be observed from viewing platforms and scenic pathways that criss-cross the park. Then there are native foxes, Soay sheep, rare cattle, and European wolves in Wolf Wood – a highlight of the day being their feeding time at 15.00 every day except Fridays.

A typical programme might start in mid morning with a ranger-guided tour that introduces the different kinds of deer, followed by a snack in the coffee shop or picnic in any one of numerous peaceful locations overlooking deer enclosures. After lunch it's time to watch a falconry display as spectacular raptors are put through their paces, followed by another 'meet the animals close-up' session with a ranger, then wolf feeding accompanied by a presentation on these complex animals, and finally an extended trailer ride around the park.

Alternatively, there's an exciting treetop walkway to try, with the chance of spotting fellow travellers from the thriving population of red squirrels, or different ranger tours to choose from. For kids with energy to spare (and mums and dads who like to join in) there are indoor and outdoor adventure play areas. For parents with money to spend there's Courtyard Shopping for quality knitwear, country clothing and a selection of Scottish crafts.

Deep Sea World and Aberdour

WHERE:
North Queensferry and Aberdour, Fife
BEST TIME TO GO:
Any time (summer if the beach is included).
DON'T MISS:
The two large seal pools at Deep Sea World – not only home to the resident population of common seals, but also to rescue seals being prepared for a return to the wild.
AMOUNT OF WALKING:
Moderate

Yes, today Scotland's National Aquarium is the draw, dramatically situated beneath the world-famous Forth Railway Bridge at North Queensferry, close to the M90 motorway. Deep Sea World was created from flooded Battery Quarry, but nowadays it's an amazing facility that showcases a huge variety of marine animals, fish and reptiles.

A number of themed zones have been created, each with a unique environment in which to present its natural species. One unmissable highlight is the 112-m (370-ft) underwater tunnel, one of the longest in the world. Millions of litres of water teeming with fish life – including ever-popular Sand Tiger Sharks – are held back by a dramatically curved acrylic passageway that actually makes these large fish seem smaller than they really are.

Other areas include a realistic recreation of the Amazon rainforest experience (anyone dare be around for the frenzied weekly feeding time of the red-bellied piranhas?), the Krakatoa tank full of brilliantly coloured tropical marine fish, Lake Malawi's unique cichlid fish, Rocky Shores with three rock pools stocked with a huge variety of creatures from around Britain's shores and the Amphibian zone, where the world's deadliest vertebrate, the golden arrow frog, may be studied – from a safe distance.

If there's time after the extended aquatic safari, a swift drive along the A921 road can be followed by a visit to the picturesque village of Aberdour, just along the Fife coast opposite Inchcolm Island – a relaxing way to end the day. After exploring the picturesque village find Shore Road that leads down to West Sands and the pretty harbour. Take all the bits 'n' pieces required for a romp on the beach. Aberdour Silver Sands is a famously tranquil location with coveted Blue Flag status. The place is unspoiled but there are lifeguards and it has all the necessary facilities.

COST:
Reasonable to expensive (though a discounted family ticket to Deep Sea World eases financial pain and children under three go free).
YOU SHOULD KNOW:
For any child who deserves a special treat – or would appreciate an unusual birthday present – it is possible to pre-book a day in the school holidays where the lucky one becomes a temporary member of the Deep Sea World team, helping to prepare food and feed the animals . . . even doing a little presenting.

Looking up to sharks and other fish swimming in a tank at Deep Sea World.

Kinshaldy Riding Stables and Fife Animal Park

Tucked away in vast Tentsmuir Forest near Leuchars is Kinshaldy Riding Stables. It won't be easy to locate, but follow the signs for Kinshaldy Beach from Leuchars or the B945 road south of Tayport and locate Kinshaldy Farm on the right-hand side of the road within the forest. The effort will be more than worthwhile for children who ride, or would like to have a first experience on horse or pony back in an idyllic setting.

There are three large outdoor sand schools and a lunging paddock for lessons, and complete beginners (aged five or over) are welcomed by expert instructors. This friendly yard has some super horses for all levels of ability and there couldn't be anything more satisfying than a gentle family trot along the seemingly endless network of sheltered forest paths or (better still) along the vast

deserted expanse of sandy Kinshaldy Beach.

If riding doesn't appeal, it's actually possible to spend the whole day at the second port of call – Fife Animal Park on the B937 near Collessie east of Auchtermuchty, just south of the A91 Milnathort to St Andrews road. There are animals galore to look at and some great new experiences for the kids to try like cuddling a skunk, handling a zebra or being kissed by a cheeky Australian cockatoo.

Species housed at the park include alpacas, capybara, cats, cattle, chinchillas, chipmunks, deer, dogs, donkeys, ferrets, foxes, goats, guinea pigs, lemurs, meerkats, mice, monkeys, pigs, ponies, porcupines, rabbits, raccoons, reindeer, sheep and lambs, skunks, squirrels and wallabies. Feathered inhabitants include birds of prey, parrots, pheasants and rhea.

The animal park has a soft-play area imaginatively entitled Animal Anticz and Patsy's Pantry, an award-winning restaurant that offers everything from a quick snack to a three-course meal.

Horse riding on Kinshaldy Beach.

Bo'ness and Kinneil Railway

WHERE:
Bo'ness, West Lothian
BEST TIME TO GO:
July and August (when there's a full daily train service, which is otherwise restricted from the opening in mid March to closure at the end of October, with occasional specials at other times).
DON'T MISS:
The Birkhill Fireclay Mine – in the Avon Gorge close to Birkhill station. A visit can be co-ordinated with the railway timetable and offers a walk through beautiful woodland followed by a fascinating underground guided tour of the mine's caverns and old workings (not suitable for the very young).
AMOUNT OF WALKING:
Moderate to lots (if the mine tour is undertaken)
COST:
Reasonable
YOU SHOULD KNOW:
In addition to the regular tourist timetable, the Bo'ness and Kinneil Railway runs all sorts of special events like Diesel Galas, Tank Engine Days, vintage vehicle meets, Easter Egg Specials, the Halloween Steam 'n' Scream weekend, Santa Steam Trains and Hogmanay Black Bun Specials at year's end.

As heritage railways go, the Bo'ness and Kinneil on the southern shore of the Firth of Forth is something of a one-off. Unlike most such ventures, much of the track upon which it runs was laid from scratch by the Scottish Railway Preservation Society, which actually created rather than preserved in this case. That said, Bo'ness is the Society's home base and it has a superb assembly of authentic Scottish railway heritage, ranging from mighty locomotives to bygone tickets.

Bo'ness Station is in the town's Union Street, to the north of the M9 motorway (Leave at Junction 3 eastbound or Junction 5 westbound and follow the signs). It occupies a former industrial site but, new or not, Bo'ness looks the part. It has a number of authentic old railway buildings relocated from elsewhere, including the magnificent Caledonian Railway signal box dating from 1899. There is also a great assembly of locomotives, rolling stock, carriages, wagons and equipment.

To start the day, walk across a former Highland Railway footbridge over the line (a super vantage point to watch the bustle of Bo'ness Station and trains departing) and go past the goods shed to visit the Scottish Railway Exhibition that contains the SRPS's fantastic collection and that covers every aspect of railways in Scotland. There is also a demonstration workshop.

Seeing everything will take a while, but eventually it's time to ride the rails. Trains run from Bo'ness to Birkhill via Kinneil and plans are afoot to upgrade a further section for passenger traffic, giving access to the Glasgow main line at Manuel. After travelling along the shores of the Firth of Forth the train climbs through the woods along the route of an original branch line, before turning inland to Birkhill, a secluded rural location that's ideal for a picnic.

Steam train driver on the Bo'ness Kinneil Railway

Callendar House and Bannockburn

The magnificent Callendar House

Situated in magnificent wooded parkland, Callendar House on the eastern outskirts of Falkirk is a place where 800 years of Scottish history will capture the imagination of children, as it is brought to life by costumed role players in a setting familiar over the centuries to such luminaries as Mary Queen of Scots, Oliver Cromwell and Bonnie Prince Charlie.

This imposing house looks like a great French château and is a major heritage centre. The candlelit Georgian kitchens – dominated by a huge open fireplace with a mighty spit – have been restored to working order and busy staff show what life was like below stairs in the 18th century. It's even possible to eat the historic dishes they create for an added sense of authenticity. The splendid morning room sees staff in period dress at work doing the sort of domestic chores that made life easy for the privileged classes.

There is a printer's and a clockmaker's workshop to reflect the ownership of the entrepreneurial Forbes family during and after the Industrial Revolution and, outside, the gardens and extensive grounds shouldn't be missed. Plants are grown in the Georgian Garden using traditional methods and the parkland offers excellent walking with super picnic sites.

Just up the M9 motorway from Falkirk an even more significant slice of Scottish history is dramatically explored. The Bannockburn Heritage Centre south of Stirling (on the A872 road) is close to the site of the famous 1314 battle where Robert the Bruce finally won independence from England, following in the heroic footsteps of William Wallace. The displays bring the Scottish wars of independence to life and feature the coronation of Robert as undisputed King of Scotland. There is a model of the earlier battle of Stirling Bridge, where William Wallace routed the English, and a splendid audio-visual presentation on Bannockburn.

WHERE:
Falkirk and Stirling, Stirlingshire
BEST TIME TO GO:
Any time (but Easter to October is preferable for those taking advantage of the day's worthwhile outdoor possibilities).
DON'T MISS:
Outside Bannockburn Visitor Centre – the statue of Robert the Bruce on his warhorse at the spot where he is said to have defeated Sir Henry de Bohun in single combat, cleaving the unfortunate English knight's skull with his battleaxe. But be aware that opinions on where the actual battle took place do differ considerably.
AMOUNT OF WALKING:
Moderate
COST:
Low (Callendar House and gardens are free)
YOU SHOULD KNOW:
Those having a seriously entertaining Scottish heritage day should try and find time to visit the Wallace Monument on Abbey Craig. It's north of Stirling, offering a commanding outlook over the surrounding countryside for those willing to climb 246 steps to the top, with stops along the ascent to review tributes and exhibits chronicling the life and times of the 'Father of Scottish Freedom'.

Stirling Castle and Blair Drummond Safari Park

WHERE:
City of Stirling and Blair Drummond, Stirlingshire
BEST TIME TO GO:
Any time
DON'T MISS:
The fascinating regimental museum of the Argyle and Sutherland Highlanders within Stirling Castle, containing weapons, uniforms, medals, pictures, silver, tableaux, pipe banners and general militaria.
AMOUNT OF WALKING:
Moderate to lots (for those who must see and do everything).
COST:
Expensive (if both attractions are visited, though children under three go free at the Safari Park).
YOU SHOULD KNOW:
Allow at least four hours for the visit to Blair Drummond Safari Park, which involves driving through extensive animal enclosures before parking and taking advantage of the many adventure areas, watching sea lion and falconry displays, visiting Chimp Island and having a restaurant meal (or picnic).

If there's one castle in Central Scotland that must be visited, it's Stirling. This imposing structure mostly dates from the 16th century and has played an epic part in Scottish history – it was besieged on many occasions (the last time by Bonnie Prince Charlie who failed to take it in 1746) and three major battles took place in the immediate vicinity of this great fortress atop its volcanic crag.

Many Kings and Queens have been associated with Stirling Castle, and it was here that James II stabbed the Earl of Douglas to death and Mary Queen of Scots was crowned. Although there are excellent historical displays and the 16th-century kitchens have been re-created, the real purpose of a visit to the castle is to explore the magnificent buildings, including a vast Great Hall and the Royal Palace, Scotland's finest renaissance structure. There are tour guides on hand, plus an audio-visual presentation beside Queen Anne Gardens.

If the kids aren't turned on by the romance of history, no matter – Blair Drummond Safari Park can offer plenty of fun and frolic. The park is northwest of Stirling, well signed from Junction 10 on the M9 motorway. As with any good safari, there are numerous exotic creatures to spot, including some never seen on genuine African safaris. The menagerie includes antelopes, bears, bison, camels, chimpanzees, deer, elephants, giraffes, lemurs, lions, meerkats, ostriches, penguins, otters, rhinos, sea lions, tigers, wallabies and zebras.

It's not just a matter of looking, either, because there are great play opportunities. The names tell the tale – Adventure Playground, Giant Astraglide, Wooden Castle, Bouncy Castle, Flying Fox, Pirate Ship, Family Pedal Boats, Amusements and Dodgems. Then there's face painting and Pets Farm to entertain the little ones, plus a family barbecue and picnic area. Children simply adore the place.

Stirling Castle

Go Ape!

Parents who have occasionally accused over-active offspring of being little monkeys can prove the point in spectacular fashion by visiting the Go Ape! course at David Marshall Lodge Visitor Centre (though after this treetop family adventure they will be able to counter that the parents of little monkeys must be big monkeys). In fact, participants under 18 who Go Ape! are labelled 'baboons' and accompanying adults are 'gorillas'. This is one for older kids as children under ten cannot participate, and all youngsters must be supervised by adults. The course is physically demanding so participants also need to be fit.

Going ape at David Marshall Lodge Visitor Centre!

The Visitor Centre is in Queen Elizabeth Forest Park, and is located just north of the village of Aberfoyle on the A821 Dukes Pass road. The fabulous forest scenery provides a stunning backdrop for the six-zone course – and what a course. It will take around three hours to complete and involves a series of rope ladders, Tarzan swings, bridges, trapezes, stirrup crossings and zip wires – all happening 12 m (40 ft) or more above the forest floor. A highlight will be a whiz down Britain's longest zip wire that's 426 m (1,400 ft) in length, which makes it a seriously exhilarating experience.

For non-participants who sit out Go Ape!, or those who want to make an extended day of it, the David Marshall Lodge Visitor Centre does offer some less challenging but rewarding activities. There's a good outdoor play zone for smaller kids plus a café and shop. The picnic area has fabulous views of the surrounding countryside, known as the Trossachs for its wooded glens, braes and lochs. Pleasant walks can take in a nearby waterfall and the squirrel hide, while inside the centre CCTV cameras relay pictures of nesting ospreys and nest boxes (April to August).

WHERE:
Aberfoyle, Stirlingshire
BEST TIME TO GO:
April to October
DON'T MISS:
At David Marshall Lodge Visitor Centre – hilarious live pictures from the nut feeder, which show just how cheeky and inventive red squirrels can be.
AMOUNT OF WALKING:
Moderate (but lots of flying through the air)
COST:
Expensive
YOU SHOULD KNOW:
It's necessary to book for the Go Ape! experience, ideally in advance. Failing that, it's sensible to arrive early (opening time 09.00), preferably not at a weekend, and just hope there are some places available on the day.

Loch Lomond paddle steamer and Bird of Prey Centre

The bonnie bonnie banks of Loch Lomond offer many possibilities and this day out provides a gentle, unhurried look at history and wildlife. The *Maid of the Loch* is moored at Balloch Pier – the last (launched in 1953) and largest of a succession of paddle steamers that have plied the Loch since 1818. After being rescued from near-dereliction, she is the subject of an ongoing major renovation which should see her steaming Loch Lomond's waters again in the not-too-distant future.

For now, she may be visited at her scenic moorings. It's possible to have a meal or snack on board and there's a Local History Facility in the forward deck saloon that explores the loch's maritime heritage through slide and video presentations. Balloch's Steam Slipway has also been renovated. This magnificent example of late-Victorian engineering hauled boats out of the water for maintenance and repair. With restricted opening times, it's best to check in advance if this forms a 'must-see' part of your day – ask about live steam sessions, too.

Finish up with a visit to the Loch Lomond Bird of Prey Centre, at nearby Ballagan (just outside Balloch on the A811 Stirling Road, accessed through the Loch Lomond Homes and Gardens Centre where cars may be parked). The centre is run by dedicated enthusiasts, whose mission is the conservation of birds of prey for the appreciation of future generations. This encompasses vital captive breeding programmes and the rescue and treatment of injured wild raptors. It's possible to see a wide variety of birds and inspect the centre's extensive facilities, and there's a pleasant picnic area. For a special treat (birthday boy or girl?) it's possible to book activities like flying a hawk or meeting the owls personally.

Maid of the Loch on Loch Lomond

MAID OF THE LOCH

Admiring the view on the shores of Loch Lomond.

Loch Lomond Shores

WHERE:
Balloch, West Dunbartonshire
BEST TIME TO GO:
Summer (for outdoor activities, though the Aquarium is open all year).
DON'T MISS:
A magical journey at the Loch Lomond Aquarium – from the Falls of Falloch via Loch Lomond, then following the SS *Sea King* as it travels the world's oceans and eventually sinks in the Pacific.
AMOUNT OF WALKING:
Lots (plus plenty of pedal pushing or paddling for good measure)
COST:
Reasonable to expensive (depending on amount of boat or bike hire)
YOU SHOULD KNOW:
It's possible to make a worthwhile saving on a family ticket by booking for Sea Life's Loch Lomond Aquarium in advance. Mountain-bike hire offers bikes for all ages, plus toddler trailers for family outings.

There are days out for buying things, seeing things and doing things – but this one offers the best of all worlds. Loch Lomond Shores at Balloch (northwest of Glasgow on the southern tip of Loch Lomond) is a tempting visitor destination in a beautiful location that offers a range of activities guaranteed to send everyone home tired but happy.

Retail therapy could put the grown-ups in a good mood, with plenty of quality merchandise on offer along with little treats like local ice cream for the kids. But the latter will really engage when it's time to visit the Loch Lomond Aquarium. This magical marine world allows children to see an astonishing variety of fascinating sea creatures. There are rock pools filled with starfish, crabs and anemones, Asian otters, sharks, giant rays and shoals of colourful fish.

In addition to the visual treat provided by the aquarium's inhabitants, expert staff give informative presentations that add an interesting extra dimension to the visit – including the chance to handle creatures like crabs and starfish during Touchpool Encounters. Another popular highlight is feeding time – starring otters, rays and sharks. Feeding sessions usually take place early afternoon and vary, as rays and sharks are fed on alternate days.

After that it's on to the 'doing things' bit. This can vary, depending on the age of the kids, with the Can You Experience section at Loch

Lomond Shores offering a choice of activities from half-day mountain-bike hire (get out and about on mapped or self-chosen routes in magnificent countryside) through kayak and pedal-boat hire (go afloat on a sheltered lagoon patrolled by a safety boat). If gentle perambulation is preferred, the Gateway Centre has a splendid short woodland walk and offers delights like a bug-hunt pack. It also sells tickets to local attractions.

Scottish Owl Centre plus Carradale and a Scottish Wildlife Trust nature reserve

A foray onto the Kintyre Peninsula to the southwest of Glasgow (take the A83 road) can produce a wonderful day out with contrasting halves. Perhaps the first call should be to Campbeltown. This attractive waterside town is well worth exploring. It has a heritage centre and museum but the main attraction for kids must surely be the Scottish Owl Centre. From Campbeltown, take the B842 road (signed Machrihanish) and find the centre opposite Campbeltown Creamery.

This is an officially rated four-star wildlife experience, allowing visitors to get close to Scotland's largest public owl collection, featuring birds from all parts of the world. These range from little (the tiny Scops owl) to large (the huge Eurasian eagle owl) and there are daily flying displays in the early afternoon. A tour of the centre not only showcases these magnificent birds, but also explains about their habits, habitats and vital conservation work that is taking place in Britain and overseas. There's a great adventure playground where kids can let off steam and a good tearoom for those essential refreshments.

Later in the day (providing that the weather is set fair) head for the wilder east coast of the Kintyre Peninsula, and the village of Carradale with its charming working harbour. A quick stop at the Carradale Network Centre will provide an interesting glimpse of local heritage, including insight into Carradale's long relationship with the sea and the newer industry of forestry. There are numerous waymarked walks in the woods that surround the village, but the kids would doubtless prefer to spend this part of the day by letting it all hang loose on the great sandy sweep of uncrowded Carradale Beach, with its dramatic view across to the Isle of Arran and Ailsa Craig.

WHERE:
Campbeltown and Carradale, Argyll
BEST TIME TO GO:
The Owl Centre is open from April to September
DON'T MISS:
The ultimate keepsake from the Scottish Owl Centre – photographs of the kids (parents too?) holding a real live owl.
AMOUNT OF WALKING:
Moderate (to lots, if you also look round Campbeltown and explore Carradale village and harbour).
COST:
Reasonable (children under three go free at the Owl Centre).
YOU SHOULD KNOW:
If beach entertainment at Carradale isn't part of the family's ideal day out, an alternative would be a visit to the Scottish Wildlife Trust's Largiebaan reserve on the western side of South Kintyre – dramatic coastal scenery is spiced with abundant birdlife and a magnificent display of wildflowers in summer.

Sea Life Sanctuary and Cruachan Power Station

WHERE:
Barcaldine and Dalmally,
Argyll and Bute
BEST TIME TO GO:
April to October
DON'T MISS:
The unique shoaling ring at the Sea
Life Sanctuary, where an endlessly
moving procession of silver herrings
is a sight to behold – they are said to
travel non-stop for more than the
distance to the moon and back in an
average fishy lifetime.
AMOUNT OF WALKING:
Moderate
COST:
Reasonable (and there are usually
bargain deals on offer for
pre-booking the Scottish Sea Life
Sanctuary online)
YOU SHOULD KNOW:
Children under six get a free tour at
Cruachan, but while the Visitor
Centre is pushchair-friendly, the
Hollow Mountain expedition is not.
It is advisable to pre-book a tour to
be sure of seeing this engineering
marvel, especially at peak
holiday times.

*A common seal dries off
his whiskers!*

The Scottish Sea Life Sanctuary nestles in a spruce forest beside picturesque Loch Creran on the A828 road north of Oban. It's a compelling visitor attraction with a mission for, in addition to its splendid aquarium, the sanctuary serves as a seal pup rescue centre.

The place is home to an extraordinary variety of sea creatures living in natural marine habitats. There are daily talks and feeding demonstrations (kids are sometimes allowed to feed the fish). The multi-dimensional aquarium houses everything from shrimps to sharks, mainly species native to Britain. There are resident river otters and the rescued seal pups are adorable, being hand reared until they can be released into the loch-side pools to become acclimatized prior to release.

It may be hard to detach children from the Sea Life Sanctuary, but something different comes next. Not too far from Oban, amid stunning mountain scenery, Cruachan is a working power station hidden within the mountain of Ben Cruachan on the shores of Loch Awe. The Hollow Mountain Power Station surely ranks as one of Britain's most impressive engineering wonders.

The Visitor Centre is located 30 km (19 mi) east of Oban on the A85 road, close to the Falls of Cruachan Station. It has an interactive display that shows how the power station works and includes cutaway models of the turbines for little 'techies'. There is a restaurant overlooking the loch and a peaceful picnic area for DIY

diners, both offering a chance to see rare birds like eagles, ospreys and red kites.

But a guided tour lasting around 30 minutes is the highlight. The visitors' walkway is lined with subtropical plants that grow well in the humid atmosphere within Ben Cruachan and the gallery offers a breathtaking view of the vast subterranean cavern that houses four mighty turbines.

Perth Leisure Pool and Active Kid Adventure Park

This super day out in and around Perth is guaranteed to tire out even those children who have hitherto proved remarkably adept at keeping going . . . and going. It starts at the town's impressive Leisure Pool in Glasgow Road, which appeals to a much wider public than the people of Perth, being one of Scotland's premier tourist attractions – with good reason.

This superb complex has five pools to choose from. The free-form Leisure Pool has two flumes, whirlpools, a wild-water channel and poolside bubble beds that will keep older kids happily splashing around for ages. For little ones, the shallow Kiddies Lagoon provides safe bathing and an entertaining slide. The Outdoor Lagoon is another favourite.

Should one parent want to slip away for some swift pampering, there's a crèche for tots and a Health Suite with sauna, steam room, jacuzzi and needle shower. For non-aquatic youngsters the Boomerang Play Park is a constructive alternative and there's a picnic area where the morning's entertainment can be satisfyingly concluded with a homemade feast.

Moving on, Burnside Farm in Stanley (signed off the A9 road just north of Perth, at Luncarty) is the location of Active Kid Adventure Park. There are plenty of farm animals about, but the prime attraction here for children of all ages is the opportunity to engage in a wide range of energetic activities (parental supervision is required).

The large Play Fort is packed with climbing and sliding opportunities and there's target football, a tyre swing, climbing frame, swings, beams, a wobbly bridge, zip line, rope maze, trampolines and sports field. The pedal go-kart circuit is a winner, as is a play area for smaller kids with push cars, a sandpit and mini go-karts. Youngsters will eventually wear themselves out, but not before trying absolutely everything.

WHERE:
Perth and Stanley, Perth and Kinross
BEST TIME TO GO:
April to September (for the Active Kid Adventure Park)
DON'T MISS:
The exotic Monkey Jungle at Perth Leisure Centre – interacting with exotic birds, monkeys and the Cheery Snake is terrific fun for children under eight.
AMOUNT OF WALKING:
Moderate to lots (the Adventure Park covers quite a large area with plenty to see and do).
COST:
Reasonable (children under five can take to the water for free at Perth Leisure Centre, while infants get free entry to the Adventure Park).
YOU SHOULD KNOW:
The Adventure Park is alongside the Active Kid Toy Shop that stocks an amazing range of outdoor and indoor play stations and a huge variety of toys – children will love browsing through the large outdoor retail display area and shop, optimistically selecting what they would like for the next few dozen birthdays and Christmases.

Dunalastair Activity Centre

WHERE:
Kinloch Rannoch, Perth and Kinross
BEST TIME TO GO:
April to September.
DON'T MISS:
An imposing monument to the great 18th-century Gaelic poet Dùghall Bochanan (Dugald Buchanan) that stands in the village centre – he was a schoolmaster hereabouts and his memorial serves as a reminder that Celtic culture is alive and well in these parts.
AMOUNT OF WALKING:
Little
COST:
Very expensive (but worth it for those who can afford the outlay – the kids will remember the raft trip for ever).
YOU SHOULD KNOW:
Demand for white-water rafting places can be considerable and it is advisable to contact the Dunalastair Activity Centre in advance to book the day's exciting outing.

West of Pitlochry, at the eastern end of Loch Rannoch, is the village of Kinloch Rannoch. This remote but popular village on the banks of the River Tummel is a centre for outdoor activities and can deliver a day out to remember for families with children aged eight and older in stunning Highland countryside.

The Dunalastair Activity Centre is based on the Dunalastair Hotel in The Square at Kinloch Rannoch, proudly claiming to be 'Perthshire's Best Outdoor Activity Centre'. This is the place to book a white-water rafting trip on the turbulent River Tay, which is an awesome experience for first-timers. All necessary rafting equipment is supplied (wet suits, helmets, life jackets, etc) and there are stretches of calm water where instruction is given and paddling techniques may be practised before the rapids are reached. Then the thrilling surge down the Zoom Flume and the fearsome Washing Machine will satisfy even the most addicted adrenaline junkies.

It's best to wear a swimsuit (or shorts and t-shirt) beneath the wet suit and bring a towel – everyone will get completely soaked. The three-hour raft trip may be enough to make everyone's day, but those who like enjoying the maximum possible stimulation could also try the centre's quick-fire indoor laser clay-target shooting experience (suitable for children of 12 or older).

If the idea of a day out in this wonderful area appeals, but the family has one or more kids under eight and can't go rafting, it's possible to arrange a satisfying do-it-yourself day out by hiring a five-person motorboat from the Activity Centre (for up to five hours) to explore the scenic local waters at leisure (fuel, life jackets and oars supplied). For non-nautical types, mountain bikes can be hired for an alternative on-shore family adventure.

The Scottish Crannog Centre and Falls of Acharn

Who knows what a crannog is? Today's the day for those who don't know to find out, and for those who do to see one of these ancient dwellings for real. This is an outdoor excursion that will take in some fascinating early history and a wealth of beautiful Scottish scenery, starting at the Scottish Crannog Centre off the A9 road north of Perth at Kenmore, beside Loch Tay.

Crannogs were loch dwellings found throughout Scotland, Ireland and (occasionally) Wales. These timber-built circular houses for individual extended families were initially built on stilts and reached by walkways, but later stone versions were built on artificial islands. A number of crannog sites have been discovered by archaeologists beneath the waters of Loch Tay, and the centre has a reconstructed crannog with a guided tour that transports visitors back to 600 BC. On shore it's possible to try ancient crafts presented by experimental archaeologists and special events are put on that bring the Iron Age to life.

The Crannog Centre experience should take around two hours, and the day can be rounded out by doing the Acharn Falls Walk, enjoying a family picnic against a stunning scenic backdrop before or after the walk. This steep circular route is short enough – around 1.5 km (1 mi) there and back – for all but the youngest children. The signed start point is in the village of Acharn, just along the loch side from the Crannog Centre.

First stop on the ascent is the wonderfully atmospheric Hermit's Cave, which has a viewing platform overlooking the Lower Falls. The path then continues up to the viewing platform for the Upper Falls. From there, it is possible to return by the same route or cross over and descend the (somewhat rough) path on the other side.

WHERE:
Kenmore and Acharn,
Perth and Kinross
BEST TIME TO GO:
April to October
DON'T MISS:
From the Crannog Centre – the ancient crannog site close to the opposite shore of Loch Tay, visible as a group of trees that have sprung up on an artificial island that once housed a stone-built crannog.
AMOUNT OF WALKING:
Lots
COST:
Reasonable
YOU SHOULD KNOW:
To see the Falls of Acharn at their most impressive, it is preferable to visit not too long after there has been rain, when the burn will be in spectacular spate. It's also a good idea to take a small torch on the walk, as the interior of the Hermit's Cave is quite dark.
A reconstructed Iron Age crannog

Built for polar voyages,
RRS Discovery

Discovery Point and Sensation Science Centre

One of Britain's all-time heroes is Captain Robert Falcon Scott, the gallant Antarctic explorer who died amid the icy wastes of the Ross Ice Shelf on the way back from the South Pole in 1912. Every child should know his dramatic story, and Discovery Point (on Discovery Quay close to the city centre in Dundee) is the place where Captain Scott's tale is told with the help of audiovisual shows, computer-generated multimedia, hands-on interactive features and numerous genuine artefacts owned by Scott and members of his various expeditions.

The undisputed star of the show is RRS *Discovery* – the last wooden three-masted vessel ever built in Britain, at Dundee. She was specifically designed for polar research and conveyed Scott on his 1901 expedition, remaining trapped in Antarctic ice until 1904, when the crew finally succeeded in freeing her with the help of controlled explosions. Exploring the ship is both interesting and informative, starting with a tour of the deck and finishing with the lavish officers' wardroom and cramped crew's quarters below decks. It's a rewarding experience that will fascinate the kids, so allow at least two hours.

Also in Dundee, the futuristic Sensation Science Centre in Greenmarket will keep enquiring children enthralled for the rest of the day – as the centre's slogan 'Warning: high risk of serious fun' neatly suggests. The wonders of science are communicated with the help of over 80 interactive exhibits and helpful staff who explain how they work.

Highlights include a journey into Roborealm (where the robots use sensors to interpret and react to their environment) and a visit to the Mindball Arena (where two players compete to move a ball using only the power of their brain waves). If you ever thought science was boring, the Sensation Science Centre will make you think again.

WHERE:
City of Dundee
BEST TIME TO GO:
Any time (both Discovery Point and Sensation are open all year).
DON'T MISS:
Science-on-the-Spot at Sensation, which features demonstrations such as the amazing effects that may be achieved using everyday household ingredients, or the opportunity to try a little keyhole surgery (happily not for real, though it all looks realistic).
AMOUNT OF WALKING:
Moderate
COST:
Reasonable to expensive (if both attractions are visited, though under fives go free to Discovery Point and under fours go free at Sensation).
YOU SHOULD KNOW:
The RRS in *Discovery's* name stands for 'Royal Research Ship', a title earned in 1923 when she was rescued from retirement as the HQ of London's Stepney Sea Scouts and re-commissioned to work in the Antarctic and Southern Oceans, before being finally laid up in 1936. She returned to Dundee in 1986, after narrowly escaping the breaker's yard.

Camperdown Wildlife Centre and Mills Observatory

There's lots happening in Dundee but one thing that definitely shouldn't be missed is Camperdown Wildlife Centre, just 15 minutes from the city centre in beautiful Camperdown Country Park, the city's largest open space. This great attraction is suitable even for the smallest children, and has pushchair-friendly tarmac paths and baby-changing facilities.

The animals are in generous enclosures designed to reflect natural environments. The European otters may be seen basking in the sun or cavorting in their pools, and the observation building contains a spy camera that shows their sleeping quarters and offers a fascinating explanation of the lives these appealing creatures live in the wild. This is part of Camperdown's 'Wild about Learning' programme, designed to educate and inform visitors on zoological matters. Other favourites are acrobatic black-and-white and red-bellied lemurs, plus the impressive European brown bears. Camperdown also has an excellent picnic area.

On a wooded hilltop in another of Dundee's parks – Balgay Park – is the unique Mills Observatory . . . unique because it is Britain's only full-time public astronomical observatory and the only one built with the sole objective of encouraging general understanding of astroscience. Although not finally constructed until 1935, this special place was made possible by a Victorian bequest from keen amateur astronomer and local industrialist John Mills.

An informative visit first allows kids to explore the outdoor Planet Trail on Balgay Hill. This is a scale model of the solar system that leads to the observatory, where the pier supporting the main telescope represents Pluto, the outermost planet. Within the building is a display area that houses changing exhibitions plus an array of historic equipment. There is also a small Planetarium that introduces visitors to stars, planets and the Milky Way. The large dome houses two telescopes, the main one being an impressive 19th-century Cooke refractor.

WHERE:
City of Dundee
BEST TIME TO GO:
Any time (both attractions are open all year).
DON'T MISS:
Every day in the summer holidays Camperdown puts on special activities for kids, like face painting, safari trails and storytelling.
AMOUNT OF WALKING:
Lots
COST:
Low (generous family rates are available at Camperdown and the observatory is free).
YOU SHOULD KNOW:
On winter evenings with clear conditions the Mills Observatory shows visitors 'live' pictures of the night sky, as observed by the main telescope and dramatically projected onto a downstairs wall.

Verdant Works and the Frigate *Unicorn*

WHERE:
City of Dundee
BEST TIME TO GO:
Any time
DON'T MISS:
The *Unicorn's* splendid figurehead that is – surprise! – a magnificent white unicorn bearing the Royal coat of arms, intricately carved in Canadian pine.
AMOUNT OF WALKING:
Moderate. Verdant Works is pushchair-friendly with ramps between different levels and lift access to the first floor.
COST:
Reasonable
YOU SHOULD KNOW:
Both *Unicorn* and The Verdant Works are closed on Mondays and Tuesdays during the winter months.

An outing to the Verdant Works provides an extraordinary journey into Dundee's past. You'll find it at West Henderson's Wynd off Lochee Road. This old mill reflects the fact that jute was once king in these parts and Verdant Works resounds with the bang and clatter of original jute-processing machinery that was used to transform this natural fibre into versatile raw material for everything from sacks to sailcloth, rope to roofing felt.

To the sound and fury of a working jute mill may be added a fascinating examination of an industry that boomed in Dundee (Juteopolis) throughout the Industrial Revolution, before declining in the 20th century and of the harsh lives of tens of thousands of workers – mainly women and children – who toiled for long hours in the city's numerous jute mills. This is all brought to life with the help of computer-based multimedia and displays, an audio-visual show, hands-on interactive exhibits and a thought-provoking Social History Gallery. Guided tours are available, and a minimum of two hours should be allowed to appreciate the experience.

Another important aspect of Dundee's past is the city's maritime heritage. HM Frigate *Unicorn* at Victoria Dock was not actually a product of the prolific local shipbuilding industry, having been built at the Royal Naval Dockyard at Chatham, but she's been in Dundee since 1873. This magnificent 19th-century 46-gun warship was launched in 1824 and represents an important moment in naval ship design, when traditional wooden sailing ships were just starting to give way to iron steamships. She's the oldest British-built ship that's still afloat and a tour of the atmospheric interior reveals an authentic glimpse of the time when Britannia ruled the waves by force of arms – and the kids will certainly find those great cannons mighty impressive.

Monikie Country Park and Broughty Ferry beach

WHERE:
City of Dundee
BEST TIME TO GO:
Summer
DON'T MISS:
Broughty Castle – a splendid late-15th-century fortress on a rocky promontory close to Broughty Ferry Beach, now a fascinating free-entry museum that chronicles the history of the local area, along with the life and times of its people and wildlife.

The former fishing village of Broughty Ferry is now an eastern suburb of Dundee, and can offer a pleasant family day out in bracing sea air beside the scenic Firth of Tay. First stop is Monikie Country Park, just off The Esplanade. This is a wonderful open space around reservoirs built to supply Dundee's fresh water in the 19th century.

There's a huge choice of activities within the park, and it will be easy to keep the kids occupied. There are self-guided nature trails (collect details from the Ranger Centre) with a variety of wildlife to be spotted, and a super adventure play park occupies a woodland setting. Experienced users can hire rowboats, kayaks or windsurfers, while two-hour beginners' courses can be booked to introduce children to these exciting activities. Improvised rafting sessions and the high-ropes course are also great fun. The park has a nice café but it's a great idea to take a picnic or barbecue that can be fetched from the car at lunchtime to round off an active morning spent sampling a selection of the many attractions.

The rest of the day can be spent enjoying the pristine charms of Broughty Ferry beach, one of a mere handful in Scotland that enjoys coveted Blue Flag status. This splendid recreational facility nestles beneath a historic castle. It has a promenade and is backed by sand dunes. Volleyball nets are erected in summer for general use and there is a designated swimming area watched over by lifeguards. Windbreaks can be hired for those who want to sunbathe or have a sheltered picnic. There is a nature conservation site and excellent children's play area, while a nearby rock garden, shops and restaurants await, in the unlikely event that anyone should be tempted to stray from the sands.

AMOUNT OF WALKING:
Moderate to lots (depending on how thoroughly the country park and beach are rummaged).
COST:
Free (apart from a small car-parking charge at Monikie Country Park that is levied between Easter and the end of September).
YOU SHOULD KNOW:
During the school holidays the Ranger Service at Monikie Country Park organizes stimulating activity sessions for kids (advance booking required). The park's Ranger Centre, picnic facilities, bird hides, paths and nature trails are all easily accessible to pushchairs.

Sand dunes and beach at Broughty Ferry near Dundee

Around Arbroath

WHERE:
Arbroath, Angus
BEST TIME TO GO:
Summer (Kerr's Railway is open at weekends from April to September and daily in the first half of August).
DON'T MISS:
The chance to try (and also take home) a few delicious Arbroath Smokies – these golden-brown, sustainable line-caught haddock are oak-smoked using traditional methods and this cottage industry is centred on the town's harbour. You'll be in the best of culinary company – one local supplier has a coveted Royal Warrant.
AMOUNT OF WALKING:
Lots
COST:
Low
YOU SHOULD KNOW:
If the east coast's generally reliable summer weather should let you down, the Old Signal Tower off Ladyloan could provide an interesting refuge – once the signal tower for the Bell Rock Lighthouse, it is now a delightful little museum that brings the history of Arbroath and the surrounding area to life with the help of voices and life-sized models.

Sea stack and red sandstone cliffs near Arbroath

Arbroath's attractive old harbour district – known as Fit o' the Town – is the place to begin this laid-back day out, it being an ideal starting point for a leisurely ramble along the sandy beaches and impressive cliffs that stretch out on either side of town. Follow the Arbroath Cliffs Nature Trail Guide (available at the Tourist Office) and be sure to find the red sandstone cliffs of Whiting Ness, beyond Victoria Park on King's Drive to the north of town. Here, erosion has created a wonderland for kids with myriad inlets, arches and caves to stimulate the imagination, and with a little help from classic beach activities like paddling and sandcastle construction the morning should fly by.

A short drive up the A92 towards Aberdeen will produce the opportunity to explore one of the east coast's finest beaches. There is a newish car park behind the backing sand dunes at Lunan Bay that has made this wonderful spot more popular, but there's still more than enough beach to go round. The ruins of Red Castle on its grassy knoll above the beach will prove irresistible and the kids should enjoy prospecting for agates and other gemstones that can sometimes be found in patches of pebbles amongst the sand.

Alternatively, a return to town can provide the opportunity to try out Scotland's oldest miniature railway. This charming little attraction was created in 1935 and Kerr's Miniature Railway is still going strong, with small steam locos and Diesels that convey kids (and born-again dads!) along a seafront track in Arbroath. Find it right beside the East Coast Mainline, close to the A92 coastal road. There are also scale models of fire engines and coaches that give young passengers a ride to remember, while the line skirts a playground and paddling pool.

Kirriemuir and Mountains Animal Sanctuary

Every youngster grows up with *Peter Pan*, but how many know who wrote this enduring children's classic, and where the famous author was born? They will wise up as soon as they see the large statue of Peter Pan in the middle of Kirriemuir, a charming market town in Central Angus with narrow winding streets built in striking red sandstone.

J M Barrie's relatively humble childhood home is in Brechin Road. This enchanting 19th-century cottage was the author's birthplace and he was raised here along with nine brothers and sisters. The house has been returned to a state the young Barrie would have instantly recognized, and there is a wonderful collection of memorabilia in the next-door house. Children's activities are mounted during the summer holidays, held in the Peter Pan Garden and Pirates Workshop, and the Peter Pan Experience encourages kids to dress up like Peter Pan and associated characters (and even fly!).

The Peter Pan connection can be followed to another magical attraction that will intrigue the kids – a *camera obscura* within the cricket pavilion on Kirrie Hill, which was a gift from J M Barrie when he was given the freedom of Kirriemuir in 1930. This cunning optical device projects fantastic colour pictures of the surrounding countryside onto a large concave table within a darkened room.

After Peter Panning, a trip up the B995 road from Kirriemuir, followed by a right turn into the back lanes at Cortachy, leads to the Mountains Animal Sanctuary at Milton of Ogil. This horse-rescue charity has around 150 horses, ponies and donkeys, that were mistreated or neglected before being rescued. They are housed in 25 large paddocks and the sanctuary has a good Visitor Centre. A voluntary donation will help support the charity's good work.

Peter Pan statue and church spire in Kirriemuir

WHERE:
Kirriemuir and Milton of Ogil, Angus
BEST TIME TO GO:
April to October (for J M Barrie's birthplace, which is sometimes closed on Thursdays and Fridays).
DON'T MISS:
While in the area, it would be a great shame to ignore the Reekie Lynn Falls at nearby Alyth, to the southwest of Kirriemuir. There's a car park and picnic site close to the B954 road and a short walk leads up Glen Isla to the spectacular waterfall.
AMOUNT OF WALKING:
Moderate
COST:
Low
YOU SHOULD KNOW:
Witchcraft was a big issue in Kirriemuir in the 16th century, and old habits die hard – many of the town's houses have a 'witches stane', a hard grey stone set into the regular red sandstone designed to ward off evil spirits. There's a pond on the outskirts of town called the Witch Pool where, legend has it, witches were ducked.

Aberdeen Maritime Museum and Satrosphere Science Centre

WHERE:
City of Aberdeen
BEST TIME TO GO:
Any time (but there are great children's workshops at Satrosphere during the summer holidays).
DON'T MISS:
Great harbour views from the upper floors of Provost Ross's house. Built in 1593, it has been incorporated into the Maritime Museum. This ancient structure is full of displays featuring fishing, redundant lighthouses, diving equipment and whaling harpoons and has many splendid ship models.
AMOUNT OF WALKING:
Moderate
COST:
Reasonable (the museum is free and kids under three go free to Satrosphere).
YOU SHOULD KNOW:
The Satrosphere Science Shop sells a range of unusual gifts that include scientific toys, models and home experiment kits. Satrosphere's Tramsheds Café offers high chairs for babies and changing facilities. Both can be used without paying for entry to the main exhibition area.

Appropriately located in historic Shiprow, near the harbour, the award-winning Aberdeen Maritime Museum examines the city's long and fruitful relationship with the North Sea, ably assisted by great multimedia displays and fixed exhibitions on clipper ships, shipbuilding, fishing, tales of the city's port over the centuries and – more recently – the offshore oil industry. There is a fascinating photographic archive, a significant collection of portraits and memorabilia associated with the Great North of Scotland Railway. There are stunning harbour views from the Museum, which has a café and shop.

Museums can be very interesting, but kids can never resist some stimulating hands-on activity, and that's what awaits at the Satrosphere Science Centre in Constitution Street, near Beach Boulevard. This great facility for youngsters (oldies too!) is billed as Scotland's first Science and Discovery Centre. This fun learning environment brings science to life and explores its relevance to everyday living, with the help of over 50 interactive exhibits and live science shows.

There is a rolling programme of fascinating exhibitions and the Science on the Spot floor show features dramatic experiments that the kids CAN try at home without demolishing the house. Another ever-popular activity is the regular weekday afternoon bug-handling sessions. How many legs has a Giant Millipede got, and how loudly can the cockroaches hiss? Sign up on arrival for the opportunity to count and listen (but note that it's a case of first come, first served).

This all ensures that children will enjoy a highly entertaining outing, but there's a serious purpose lurking beneath the all-action exhibits. The Satrosphere Science Centre is a charity dedicated to promoting public understanding of science, which also aims to make youngsters aware of the exciting career opportunities that await those who pursue a scientific education.

Grampian Transport Museum and Alford Valley Railway

A treasure house of transport history awaits discovery at Alford, on the A994 road east of Aberdeen, along with an encounter with the real thing – the dinky Alford Valley Railway. But first the Grampian Transport Museum (with its entrance off Alford's public car park) that has recently expanded to offer ever-changing insight into the foundation and advance of vehicle technology.

This is a great trip down memory lane for oldies and an eye-opener for youngsters with motorcycles, cars and public transport from many eras on display. Highlights include the historically significant Craigievar Express steam tricycle, the beautifully restored Cruden Bay Hotel tramcar and an original trend-setting Raleigh Chopper bicycle. There are numerous climb-aboard exhibits like the traction engine, six-wheeled snowplough, buses, tramcars and a penny-farthing bike (ladder provided). Numerous interactive displays, DVD presentations and a rolling programme of special exhibitions enhance the experience. There is a children's play park, and entertaining organized activities in summer include events like eco-marathons on the museum's own track.

Close by is the Alford Valley Railway Museum, based at an old railway station. This has a re-created ticket office that has been returned to the early 1900s, which has an amazing collection of old tickets in wooden cabinets. The former waiting room now houses a number of relevant displays and some splendid large-scale models of steam trains.

The stone-built engine shed contains a number of narrow-gauge locomotives, including the steam engine *Saccharine*, built in Leeds in 1914 but so named because her working life was spent on a sugar plantation in South Africa. There is also a recently built steam-outline Diesel, *James Gordon*. Volunteers laid a new 3-km (2-mi) narrow-gauge line from Alford Station to Haughton Park in 1984. The half-hourly departures carry passengers on a scenic route that offers great views of the Bennachie Hills.

The AA exhibits at the Grampian Transport Museum

WHERE:
Alford, Aberdeenshire
BEST TIME TO GO:
April to September (but note that the Alford Valley Railway runs only at weekends during the off-season months of April, May and September).
DON'T MISS:
If possible, catch the Motorvation! annual cavalcade held in Alford on a Sunday in the middle of July each year, which not only offers an eclectic collection of interesting vehicles, but also numerous trade stands and all sorts of transport-related activities centred on the Grampian Transport Museum.
AMOUNT OF WALKING:
Moderate
COST:
Reasonable (children under five get in free at the Transport Museum).
YOU SHOULD KNOW:
A vast new Collections Centre at the Transport Museum is open to visitors every Wednesday, offering the opportunity to view the extensive reserve collection, observe current restoration projects in progress and talk to knowledgeable experts and engineers about their conservation work.

Archaeolink Prehistory Park

Put the words 'living' and 'history' together to summarize the attraction of this day out at the Archaeolink Prehistory Park in beautiful Aberdeenshire countryside. It's at Oyne on the B9002 road, off the A96 northwest of Aberdeen. This award-winning attraction justifies an extended visit, with the emphasis on fun, participation and education – more or less in that order.

Archaeolink Prehistory Park

It's the longest journey the family will ever make in one day, spanning 10,000 years from the Mesolithic period to the Roman era. This lengthy saga of human development is dramatized with the help of exhibitions (indoors and out), hands-on activities, guided tours and regular summer workshops featuring tempting titles like Bushcraft, Way of the Warrior, Fables and Folklore or Crafts from the Past.

The reconstructed Mesolithic hunter-gatherer encampment has a simple wood-and-hide hut and dugout canoe. Demonstrations include flint knapping, primitive antler and bone tool making, archery, basketwork, leather working and cookery. Moving on, see how Neolithic people became farmers, occupying fixed settlements and constructing henges, stone circles and burial cairns that dot the Scottish landscape.

The first metal workers arrived in Scotland from Europe around 2200 BC, dramatically changing the inhabitants' way of life. The Bronze Age area features a wattle-and-daub metal smith's workshop. Activities include pewter and bronze casting, charcoal production and jewellery making. The Iron Age is represented by a reconstructed roundhouse and farmstead. There are demonstrations of woodworking, cooking, pottery making, spinning, weaving and cloth dyeing. This working farm grows crops and husbands animals.

The last great historical phase covered at Archaeolink is the final confrontation between Romans and Picts, represented by a reconstructed section of a Roman marching camp, complete with embankment and protective ditch. It's a great ending to the day's fascinating historical journey.

Aberdeenshire Farming Museum and Arbuthnot Museum

West of Peterhead, off the A90 road between Mintlaw and Old Deer, is the Aberdeenshire Farming Museum, set within delightful Aden Country Park – itself worth a look before visiting the museum, as there are children's play areas and good walks.

The award-winning museum portrays farming practices in these parts over two centuries and more, and is based at a splendid semi-circular Victorian Home Farm building. Here, the tale of the Aden Estate – which once owned all the surrounding land – is recounted. A large number of displays and audio-visual presentations fill out the picture of local farming life and changing agricultural methods. There is a reconstructed horseman's house and costumed guides help bring the stories told in this atmospheric museum to life.

The next stop is the apparently authentic Hareshowe of Ironside farm steading – and indeed it is an authentic small farm from the Buchan area, though the buildings originally stood some distance away. They were transported here and rebuilt stone by stone in the early 1990s, before being returned to the character the place would have had in the 1950s. This is a working farm that still operates just as it did half a century ago.

Back in Peterhead, in Peter Street, the interesting Arbuthnot Museum (one of Aberdeenshire's oldest) focuses on the town's past and its colourful maritime history. As well as numerous ship models that show the development of Peterhead fishing boats over the centuries, there's an important collection of Inuit artefacts, mounted Arctic fauna including a polar bear, and major coverage of the whaling industry. The museum has one of Scotland's most extensive coin collections and displays a huge number of old photographs featuring bygone local people and places. A rolling programme of temporary exhibitions features varying aspects of life in Scotland's northeast.

WHERE:
Mintlaw and Peterhead, Aberdeenshire
BEST TIME TO GO:
May to September (for the farming museum, which is also open at certain weekends in April and October).
DON'T MISS:
The Weel Vrocht Grun (well-worked ground) exhibition at the Aberdeenshire Farming Museum, which uses dioramas, film and soundtracks to illustrate how rugged, boulder-strewn land was cleared over time to produce rich farmland.
AMOUNT OF WALKING:
Lots. The Arbuthnot Museum is not accessible to families with prams and awkward for pushchair users (it's on the first floor). Likewise, certain displays at the Farming Museum – those on the first floor of the main building and at Hareshowe Farm – are not pram-friendly either.
COST:
Both attractions are free of charge (but there is a parking charge at the Farming Museum).
YOU SHOULD KNOW:
In 1878 the crew of the whaling vessel *Eclipse* saw an amazing sight. While sailing at 80 degrees north they spotted a black-browed albatross, a species that has only rarely been seen north of the equator, let alone almost at the North Pole. In keeping with the attitudes of the time, the albatross was duly shot and later presented to the Arbuthnot Museum, where it was stuffed and is on display to this day.

Macduff Marine Aquarium

The traditional fishing town of Macduff is the site of a special attraction – the Macduff Marine Aquarium, situated on High Shore east of the harbour. It promotes awareness and enjoyment of the local Moray Firth marine environment, providing a unique opportunity to see hundreds of native fish and invertebrates in their natural habitat – an experience normally reserved for hardy scuba divers. The Moray Firth has over 800 km (500 mi) of varied coastline from Fraserburgh to Duncansby Head, and this vast bay encompasses many habitat zones that are represented at the aquarium, including coastal, shallow water, kelp reef, deep reef and muddy sea floor.

The aquarium's centrepiece – the only one of its kind in Britain – is the living kelp reef where divers may be seen feeding the fish. There is a regular feeding programme for the aquarium's many environments. The programme may vary, but generally follows this set pattern: Tuesday afternoons estuary and rock pool displays; Wednesday afternoons diving, main reef, ray pool and muddy sea-floor display; Thursday afternoons estuary and rock pool displays; Friday afternoons (summer only) ray pool; Saturday afternoons diving, estuary and rock pool displays; Sundays diving, ray pool, deep reef and muddy sea-floor displays. These add considerable interest to a tour, so it's wise to check that feeding will actually be happening.

The Marine Aquarium provides a rewarding day out for the kids, but those who like to pack a family outing with varied activities might consider taking the short drive along the A98 road from Macduff, through Banff to the village of Boyndie. Here, The Old School offers the chance for a family stroll in superb surroundings that feature woodland paths, ponds and an abundance of wildlife. The Visitor Centre has a café, shop and interesting craft workshops.

The Museum of Scottish Lighthouses and Willows Animal Sanctuary

Lighthouses have a mystique that rarely fails to excite children, so a day that starts at the Museum of Scottish Lighthouses is likely to be a great success. It's easy to find, being well signed from the centre of Fraserburgh. This is a purpose-built facility with a number of galleries containing a wealth of artefacts that relate to the technology of the lights that saved countless mariners' lives around the rugged coasts of Scotland for over two centuries. It also illuminates the lives of the hardy souls who manned these lifesaving towers and their long-suffering families. Audio-visual displays and interactive exhibits complement the main collection, engaging the kids in both science and history.

Good though the exhibitions section is, the children will hardly be able to wait for the exciting tour of Kinnaird Head Lighthouse – the first tower lighthouse ever built in Scotland (in 1797, revamped in 1823) and still the site of a powerful navigational beacon today. The timed tour, announced by the ringing of a bell, visits each room of the tower that – uniquely – rises above elements of a 15th-century castle.

For something very different, the Willows Animal Sanctuary will also delight the kids. Find it off the A981 road to the southwest of Fraserburgh (turn onto the B9093 New Pitsligo Road at Strichen) and visit over 200 abandoned or mistreated animals that have been rescued. These include horses, ponies, donkeys, cows, goats, sheep and pigs, plus assorted rabbits, poultry, reptiles and abandoned pets. Some suitable animals are available for re-homing.

In addition to assorted animals, the sanctuary has a gallery, coffee shop, gift shop, nature trail, a super Pets' Corner and the unmissable Beastie Hoose. A leisurely visit is a great way to end this special day in northeastern Aberdeenshire.

AMOUNT OF WALKING:
Moderate. The Kinnaird Head Lighthouse tour is not for pushchairs or tots – it involves climbing the many steps to the top of the lighthouse.
COST:
Low to reasonable (Willows Animal Sanctuary is free but requests a donation to support its rescue work that gives so many needy animals a new life).
YOU SHOULD KNOW:
Any kids sufficiently numerate to count the number of steps correctly to the top of the lighthouse will be rewarded with a handsome certificate.

The Museum of Scottish Lighthouses

The *Jacobite* steam train

WHERE:
Fort William, Highland

BEST TIME TO GO:
The *Jacobite* runs from mid May to early October (advance booking recommended, though some turn-up-and-travel tickets are reserved for sale each day).

DON'T MISS:
The railway museum in the station buildings when the *Jacobite* stops at Glenfinnan for 15 minutes on the outbound journey to Mallaig, giving passengers the opportunity to stretch their legs and take in sensational views of Loch Shiel, where Bonnie Prince Charlie landed in 1745.

AMOUNT OF WALKING:
Low to moderate (depending how much extra exploring is done before, during and after the railway trip).

COST:
Expensive (and upgrading to first class will make the credit card beg for mercy).

YOU SHOULD KNOW:
Don't take dad's word for it – this really is a terrific day trip for everyone, and has been voted 'Top Rail Journey in the World' by *Wanderlust* magazine.

The Jacobite steam train crossing the Glenfinnan Viaduct.

Is a day out that involves a steam train really for the children, or is it actually for dad's benefit? Let's be generous and say 'both', for a round trip to Mallaig on the West Highland Line out of Fort William, riding the *Jacobite* steam train, offers a great sightseeing outing for the whole family with the bonus of being romantically conveyed by that huffing, puffing steam locomotive.

The train departs from Fort William at 10.20 daily, arriving in Mallaig at 12.25. The return journey leaves at 14.10, getting back to Fort William at 16.00. This provides ample time to explore the charming loch-side town of Fort William before or after, and the bustling port of Mallaig at lunchtime – perhaps enjoying a picnic overlooking the busy harbour.

The *Jacobite* is the only scheduled steam service on Britain's national rail network and it travels through some stunning coastal scenery. During the course of the 135-km (84-mi) round trip, the train passes over the world-famous curving 21-arch viaduct between Fort William and Glenfinnan, as featured prominently in *Harry Potter and the Chamber of Secrets*, then *The Prisoner of Azkaban* and *The Goblet of Fire*.

After a stop at Glenfinnan it proceeds through Lochailort, Arisaig and Morar before reaching Mallaig. Along the way passengers see Britain's highest mountain (Ben Nevis), longest inland waterway (the Caledonian Canal that begins with Neptune's Staircase, a remarkable series of locks visible on the right), most westerly station (Arisaig), shortest river (River Morar), deepest loch (Loch Morar) and whitest beach (also Morar). On a clear day, there will be great views across to the Small Isles of Eigg and Rum and the tip of Skye.

Hot and cold snacks are available on the train, but taking a packed lunch is definitely a much more economical option.

Treasures of the Earth and Nevis Range

The gondola ride at Aonach Mor offers spectacular Highland views.

At Corpach on the outskirts of Fort William (take the famous 'Road to the Isles', the A830 along Loch Linnhe towards Mallaig), Treasures of the Earth is a truly amazing museum featuring geology and mineralogy. It has a spectacular collection of priceless gemstones and brilliant crystals, displayed in the atmospheric setting of convincing caves, caverns and mines. Among hundreds of exhibits there are gold and silver nuggets, aquamarines, diamonds, blood-red garnets, fiery opals and rubies. Also massive crystal geodes, fossils galore (be sure to see the sabre-tooth tiger skull) and a shop packed with gemstone giftware, jewellery and healing crystals.

On the other side of Fort William, the Nevis Range Mountain Experience is at Torlundy's Aonach Mor access road, signed off the A82 11 km (7 mi) northeast of Fort William. There are forest trails around the base station, but the attraction here is the gondola ride that effortlessly lifts the family up the mountain of Aonach Mor, starting at 90 m (300 ft) and ending at a height of 655 m (2,150 ft). Views of the Scottish Highlands and Islands – including the Great Glen, Ben Nevis and the Hebrides – during the 15-minute ascent are breathtaking.

Once up, there are some great mountain trails and panoramic viewpoints. During the summer months the Mountain Discovery Centre (beneath the Snowgoose Restaurant) has interpretation panels, displays on history, habitat and wildlife, video showing of year-round mountain activities plus colouring, a hands-on quiz and nature trail for younger visitors. There is also a good outside play area.

For active families with older kids, mountain-bike hire from Nevis Range base station is an active alternative to the simple gondola ride – the gondola does the hard uphill work and bold riders can then discover what true mountain biking is all about, with a little help from gravity.

WHERE:
Corpach and Torlundy, near Fort William, Highland
BEST TIME TO GO:
May to October
DON'T MISS:
The Dinosaur diorama at Treasures of the Earth – parents and teens may think it's a trifle naff, but smaller kids will love it.
AMOUNT OF WALKING:
Moderate to lots
COST:
Reasonable to expensive (though children under five do go free on the gondola).
YOU SHOULD KNOW:
The weather can change rapidly in the Scottish mountains, even in high summer, so it's sensible to pack weatherproof clothing when visiting the Nevis Range. Note that the gondola's operation can be restricted for safety reasons, particularly in high winds.

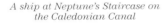
A ship at Neptune's Staircase on the Caledonian Canal

Neptune's Staircase and Seal Island cruise

Those lucky enough to have ridden the *Jacobite* steam train will have been intrigued by the sight of an extraordinary series of ascending canal locks from the train window, shortly after leaving Fort William. This is the day to explore Neptune's Staircase at Banavie (signposted off the A830 Mallaig road just before Corpach). A genuine engineering marvel designed by Thomas Telford and completed in 1822, the staircase consists of a series of eight locks that raises boats to 20 m (65 ft) above sea level over a distance of 460 m (1,510 ft).

The best way to appreciate the staircase is to follow a lock-full of boats from bottom to top, then the next batch down from top to bottom. After admiring Neptune's Staircase, make the short trip to Corpach, where the basin should be full of interesting craft. This is where the Caledonian Canal connects with Loch Linnhe and thence to the open sea, through a sea lock and two more canal locks.

Having arrived at the water's edge, it's time to get up close and personal with this impressive sea loch. Return to Fort William and find the town pier, where Crannog Cruises do a wonderful 90-minute boat trip down Loch Linnhe to Seal Island and back. The well-appointed *Souters Lass* departs at 10.00, 12.00, 14.00 and 16.00. Affordable tickets can be purchased at the pier.

This rewarding cruise delivers some terrific wildlife sights, including sea birds galore, running salmon, porpoises, an occasional golden eagle – and the abundance of grey and common seals that give Seal Island its name. This is all delivered against the stunning backdrop of dramatic Lochaber scenery, including stunning views of the southern slopes of Ben Nevis. The skipper's keen eye and cheery running commentary ensure that nothing is overlooked.

WHERE:
Banavie and Fort William, Highland
BEST TIME TO GO:
Mid March to October
(for Seal Island cruises)
DON'T MISS:
The magnificent vista seen from the banks of the Caledonian Canal, which stars Ben Nevis – it's infinitely better than the view of Britain's highest mountain from nearby Fort William.
AMOUNT OF WALKING:
Moderate to lots (it's easy to be tempted into taking a lengthy stroll along the banks of the Caledonian Canal.
COST:
Reasonable
YOU SHOULD KNOW:
Although *Souters Lass* has excellent all-weather facilities – including a cosy enclosed viewing lounge that serves snacks and drinks – sailings are cancelled if the weather turns nasty. There are occasional evening cruises in summer to watch the spectacular sunsets that occur in the Highlands.

Highland Folk Museum and Waltzing Waters

Newtonmore is a village above the River Spey within sight of the Cairngorm mountains, on the A86 road between Fort William and Aviemore. This is the proud location of the Highland Folk Museum, an extensive living history site that requires half a day or more to appreciate properly.

There's a huge amount to see. An outstanding feature is The Township – a painstaking re-creation of the ancient Highland settlement of Easter Raitts that once stood nearby, before being abandoned early in the 19th century. It has many cruck-framed buildings, ranging from the large dwelling occupied by the principal tenant down to the lowly Pigman's House, and costumed guides in this authentic setting make the reality of everyday Highland life in the 1700s easy to imagine.

Another major attraction is Aultlarie Farm – a real steading acquired by the museum and worked just as it would have been in the 1920s. A number of buildings round out the picture of the bygone Highlands, including a railway halt, post office, shepherd's bothy, school, church, tailor's shop and clockmaker's workshop. Again, costumed interpreters bring Highland history to life in a profoundly interesting way, even as a vintage bus runs from one end of the site to the other.

If there's time (and energy) left for something completely different, Waltzing Waters offers a stunning 40-minute show (starting on the hour) in a purpose-built theatre on the northern side of Newtonmore. This is guaranteed to be unlike anything anyone in the family has ever seen before and children will be entranced. An astonishing blend of technology and artistry generates a dynamic series of moving water patterns that move to music – creating a spectacular extravaganza of kaleidoscopic colours that is as good as – or better than – any firework display. This one really does justify the tag 'seeing is believing'.

WHERE:
Newtonmore, Highland
BEST TIME TO GO:
April to October
DON'T MISS:
Red squirrels in the pinewoods at the Highland Folk Museum, after a project to encourage these small charmers met with considerable success – watch them scampering along ropes between trees and using the numerous feeders.
AMOUNT OF WALKING:
Lots
COST:
Low to reasonable
YOU SHOULD KNOW:
In addition to the buildings and fixed displays, the Highland Folk Museum runs a programme of enticing child-orientated activities throughout the summer months, on subjects as diverse as traditional crafts, cooking in the 1700s and creating collages with natural materials found in the woods.

A replica of an old Highland bus

Highland Wildlife Park and Leault Farm

WHERE:
Kincraig, Highland
BEST TIME TO GO:
May to October (for sheepdog demonstrations)
DON'T MISS:
The beavers at the Highland Wildlife Park – serving as a reminder that the Royal Zoological Society of Scotland is a partner in the exciting project to reintroduce these long-extinct-in-Britain mammals to the wild in Knapdale Forest, Mid Argyll.
AMOUNT OF WALKING:
Moderate to lots (depending how much exploration of both attractions is undertaken).
COST:
Reasonable to expensive (a family ticket to the Highland Wildlife Park is not cheap, but includes a voluntary donation that helps support the valuable work of the Royal Zoological Society of Scotland).
YOU SHOULD KNOW:
Anyone who has trouble controlling the rebellious family pooch is welcome to discuss their canine problems with the shepherd at Leault Farm, who is happy to answer questions and offer valuable professional advice on dog training and handling. Ironically, dogs are not allowed at the Highland Wildlife Park, though free kennels are provided.

South of Aviemore, off the A9, is Kincraig. Turn off the main road and follow the B9152 through the village and find the Highland Wildlife Park. This has the wide-open spaces that allow the Royal Zoological Society of Scotland to present the country's native creatures – along with endangered species from the world's mountains and tundra – in the superb natural setting of the Cairngorms National Park.

The first part of a visit involves driving around the Main Reserve with its magnificent collection of animals living in conditions that mirror their natural environment as closely as possible. After this fascinating safari the next stage is a tour of the walk-round area.

This is a unique opportunity to see the full gamut of Scottish wildlife, covering both more common animals and many creatures that have become so rare that there is little chance of seeing them in the wild. The selection includes black grouse, capercaille, choughs, otters, pine martens, red deer, red grouse, red squirrels and wildcats. More exotic world species include lynx, wolves, macaque monkeys, red pandas, amur tigers, Bactrian camels and birds including snowy owls and eagle owls.

There's another amazing animal show at nearby Leault Farm – back towards Kincraig and up a track signed 'Working Sheepdogs' that crosses the A9. There, at 16.00 each day except Saturdays, it's possible to marvel at a 45-minute demonstration where canny border collies manoeuvre sheep and ducks through a testing obstacle course. The kids will be mightily impressed by this and also by the long-horned Highland cattle (including appealing calves) on the farm. In spring there will be lambs to bottle feed and, a bit later, the chance to try life as a sheep-shearer's assistant. Best of all, there are likely to be some adorable collie puppies about the place. Take the camera!

A young Scottish sheep farmer and his Border Collie demonstration team

Landmark Forest Adventure Park

Off the A9 road south of Inverness – just before reaching Aviemore – a left turn onto the A398, followed by a right turn to follow the B9153, leads to the village of Carrbridge. Here, in Main Street, is the entrance to Landmark Forest Adventure Park. This promises fun, discovery and adventure for all ages and deserves the best part of a full day.

Start with the Red Squirrel Trail, through an ancient woodland that has been standing for thousands of years. Red squirrels are becoming an endangered species as their grey cousins relentlessly colonize, but it's still possible to see this delightful native species. See them here, plus dozens of birds, close up in the wildlife feeding area. Another great experience is the Tree Top Trail, through upper branches on a raised walkway that's accessible to prams and pushchairs.

Next, the Timber Trail features Scottish logging as once it was, complete with terrific working steam sawmill and a sturdy Clydesdale horse to haul logs. Blow off some personal steam by having a go or doing some crosscut sawing in the Activities Area, which also offers climbing possibilities.

However, little monkeys really come into their own in Adventureland, where Spiral Tower has sensational slides, nets, tunnels and ladders. The Nest offers two floors of adventurous climbing, sliding and bouncing. For older kids, RopeworX is a testing high-level cable trek, Sky Dive is a simulated parachute jump and Pinnacle is a great climbing wall. Less demanding alternatives are the Wild Forest Maze with apparently endless paths testing patience and navigational skills, driving mini cars or directing radio-controlled trucks.

After all that the words 'tired but happy' should spring to mind . . . but that's just the parents. You'll find that the kids will probably want to keep right on going.

The Fire Tower at Landmark Forest Adventure Park

WHERE:
Carrbridge, Highland
BEST TIME TO GO:
Summertime
DON'T MISS:
The 105-step climb up the timber Fire Tower for sensational all-round views, brought into sharp focus with the help of a powerful telescope.
AMOUNT OF WALKING:
Lots
COST:
Reasonable to expensive (though the family discount does help a little).
YOU SHOULD KNOW:
Although the park is open all year round, bad weather can lead to winter closures, and some attractions only operate between April and October. There are a few restrictions on smaller kids – Skydive and RopeworX require a minimum height of 1.5 m (4 ft 11 in) and the Big Slide is not for children under five. Parents must supervise kids at all times.

In search of Nessie

Is Nessie real or a figment of endless fevered imaginings? Despite numerous claimed sightings and lots of photographs (some definitely exposed as hoaxes), repeated scientific investigations have failed to find proof that the famous Loch Ness monster actually exists. But the loch is long and very deep, containing enough water to fill every other lake and reservoir in Britain combined, so happily for lovers of unfathomable tales the jury is still out.

Whatever the truth of the matter, Nessie (real or imagined) is world famous, and the locals have taken full advantage of the fact. So the kids can have an exciting time probing the mystery at competing facilities in the village of Drumnadrochit, on the A82 along the loch's eastern shore, a road that goes from Inverness to Fort William through the scenic Great Glen.

The Loch Ness Centre & Exhibition Experience presents an overview that is not confined to monster matters, instead promising to reveal 'everything about Loch Ness that you can't see by looking at it'. Although there's a super-thorough examination of the Nessie legend, the amazing laser shows, digital projection and mind-blowing special effects explore the loch's geology and folklore, too, as well as covering various expeditions that have probed its depths.

The not so differently titled Loch Ness Visitor and Exhibition Centre presents all the known facts – from the first reported sighting of a mysterious creature in Loch Ness by St Columba in the 6th century – that help enquiring visitors make up their own minds (and enjoy themselves, the slogan here being 'brimming with fun, wonder and adventure'). A wide-screen cinema presents real-life accounts and footage of Nessie sightings. For those who've had enough of monsters for one day, the associated Braveheart Centre tells the story of Scottish hero Sir William Wallace and Robert the Bruce's great victory at nearby Bannockburn.

*Urquhart Castle on the shores
of Loch Ness*

Aquadome and WDCS Dolphin and Seal Centre

Find Bught Park off the A82 road in Inverness, where the Aquadome is guaranteed to surprise and delight kids who love the water. Forget the Competition Pool – that's for serious organized swimming. The place to be is Leisure Waters, the section packed with fun features for the family.

Here is a bubbling spa pool and wave pool with beach. There is a dramatic flowing 'river' and choice of flumes – the Ness Monster that plunges riders from top to bottom in a couple of seconds, Vortex with its whirlpools and the dramatic Dark Cyclone. There's even an outdoor pool for hardy little souls prepared to brave the Highland weather (contrary to popular belief, the sun shines quite often). There is a crèche where non-water-babies aged from four months to four years can be left to enjoy games, soft-play, sand pit, toys, painting and colouring. For adventurous kids who don't like water, beginners can sample the exciting world of indoor climbing.

After all that exertion, a more leisurely visit should complete the day rather well. Driving to the peaceful village of North Kessock, on the Black Isle a short journey up the northbound A9 road from Inverness, offer a small prize to the first child to guess what WDCS stands for (clues may be needed – the answer is Whale and Dolphin Conservation Society). The WDCS Dolphin and Seal Centre is signed shortly after crossing Kessock Bridge and it's a great place to see (and hear) dolphins.

The centre has a great viewing window and spectacular views, with every chance of spotting bottlenose dolphins racing through the waters of the Moray Firth. There's an interesting Dolphin Trail that encourages the kids to look for seals, harbour porpoises and dolphins, plus a great selection of assorted bird life. It's different, and the kids will be fascinated.

WHERE:
Inverness and North Kessock, Highland
BEST TIME TO GO:
June to September for the Dolphin and Seal Centre
DON'T MISS:
At the Dolphin and Seal Centre – listening to the intriguing clicks and whistles of dolphins as they communicate with one another, thanks to well-placed underwater microphones.
AMOUNT OF WALKING:
Little
COST:
Low to reasonable (spectators and children under 18 months old are admitted to the Aquadome without charge and the Dolphin and Seal Centre offers free entry).
YOU SHOULD KNOW:
At the Aquadome, an adult must accompany children under eight at all times. Kids must be at least five to use the flumes and there is a height restriction. A special toddler pool has exciting chutes and interactive features for the little ones.

Watching Bottlenose dolphins playing in the Moray Firth.

Culloden Battlefield and Loch Ness cruise

WHERE:
Inverness, Highland
BEST TIME TO GO:
April to September
DON'T MISS:
The panoramic view over the entire Culloden battlefield from the landscaped roof of the Memorial Centre.
AMOUNT OF WALKING:
Moderate
COST:
Reasonable to very expensive (depending which cruise is chosen).
YOU SHOULD KNOW:
For those with deep pockets, the Passion Cruise is the ultimate experience afloat on Loch Ness. With a coach pickup in Central Inverness this six-and-a-half-hour special takes in Urquart Castle, the Loch Ness Visitor Centre and Corrimony Cairn.

The last pitched battle fought on British soil was at Culloden Moor, by Inverness, when the troops of King George II routed Bonnie Prince Charlie's Jacobites in a short but bloody battle. The site has been restored to its original state and retains major historical significance, now emphasized by the magnificent new Culloden Battlefield Memorial Centre.

This modernistic building is set back from the actual battlefield and contains a series of exhibition spaces, educational areas, museum, restaurant and shop. There is an exciting interactive exhibition that explains events before, during and after Culloden. There are daily Living History presentations that bring interesting characters involved in the battle to life, plus an immersive film that puts visitors at the heart of the action and communicates the horror experienced by combatants. An original cottage on the battlefield itself, which survived the fighting, has been kitted out as a contemporary field dressing station.

After the historic Culloden experience, the ideal way to end the day is with a cruise on Loch Ness. Jacobite Cruises leave from the Caledonian Canal's Tomnahurich Bridge on the southern outskirts of Inverness, or Clansman Harbour further down the A82 road on the eastern shore of Loch Ness. There's little likelihood that the infamous Loch Ness monster will be spotted, but stunning scenery is absolutely guaranteed.

There's a tempting choice of cruises, of differing duration (and cost). Two start from Clansman Harbour – the one-hour Inspiration and the two-hour Freedom. Cruises from Tomnahurich Bridge are longer, reflecting the time taken to travel down the Caledonian Canal to Loch Ness. The Temptation lasts for two-and-a-half hours, the Reflection and Discovery each take three hours and the Sensation occupies three-and-a-half hours to include a stop at the Loch Ness Exhibition.

Fort George

There couldn't be a more impressive testament to the turbulent history of the Scottish Highlands than Fort George, one of the mightiest artillery fortifications in Europe. It was built to subdue the Highlands in the aftermath of the 1745 Jacobite rising, occupying a spit that juts into the Moray Firth 18 km (11 mi) to the northeast of Inverness, with its own harbour beneath mighty walls that could supply the place in the event of a siege.

But there never was a siege, for Fort George duly contributed to the final suppression of the Jacobite cause. Today, it remains a working

A jousting event at Fort George

barracks but is also a compelling attraction that deserves an all-day visit, covering a huge area containing much to entertain and excite the kids – starting with the initial approach across a raised walkway complete with drawbridge.

Fort George has hardly been altered since it was finally completed in 1769 after a long build that went way over budget (some things never change!). The garrison buildings and defensive positions bristling with cannons provide real insight into 18th-century military history – insight that is complemented and enhanced by the ability to inspect historic barrack rooms barely changed since the original occupants departed, illustrating the conditions in which Scottish soldiers once lived.

The splendid Seafield Collection of arms is displayed in the Grand Magazine, designed to hold 2,500 barrels of gunpowder, and includes bayoneted muskets, swords, pikes and ammunition pouches. Here, too, actors in period costume re-create scenes from the 1700s.

A 'must see' is the Regimental Museum of the Queen's Own Highlanders – the Seaforths and Camerons – one of Scotland's proudest and most illustrious regiments. Another unusual feature that will intrigue the kids is the dog cemetery, the resting place of regimental mascots and pooches belonging to officers.

WHERE:
Ardersier, Highland
BEST TIME TO GO:
Any time (but the large outdoor areas are obviously less welcoming in winter, and there is a programme of interesting special events throughout the summer months).
DON'T MISS:
The chance to spot dolphins disporting in the Moray Firth from the fort's seaward ramparts.
AMOUNT OF WALKING:
Lots
COST:
Reasonable
YOU SHOULD KNOW:
The Fort George complex was built by the Adam family construction company – and the garrison chapel is thought to have been personally designed by one of its greatest sons, the famous Scottish architect Robert Adam.

Gairloch

This open-air day out shows the west coast of the Scottish Highlands at its best. Gairloch is a collection of small settlements in Wester Ross, overlooking Loch Gairloch on the A832 road that loops off the A835 from Ullapool to Inverness. This remote and unspoiled area has been a popular tourist destination since Victorian times and it's easy to understand why. This scenic location is famous for magnificent views across to Skye and inland to the Torridan Mountains, and sunsets hereabouts can be awe-inspiring.

Take everything needed to enjoy Gairloch's renowned beaches, though there are a few shops if anything should get overlooked. Big Sand speaks for itself, and its wide sandy expanse may be found west of Gairloch on the B8021 coast road. A full day enjoying the delights of Big Sand may satisfy everyone in the family, but if not there are other things to do that can fill an entertaining day in Gairloch.

Visitors can try windsurfing or a round on the compact golf course (beware, the eighth hole is infamous). But perhaps the option that will be most appealing to the kids is a visit to the Gairloch Marine Life Centre. The centre overlooks Charleston, Gairloch's harbour, and is devoted to raising awareness of the marine environment. There are interactive wildlife displays and a resident biologist explains the centre's research and educational activities.

To prove that serious ecological work can be fun, the centre runs associated two-hour boat cruises on the well-appointed *MV Starquest*. They have the serious purpose of surveying the local marine wildlife, focusing on porpoises, dolphins, basking sharks and whales. There are also regular sightings of seals, otters and bird life including white-tailed and golden eagles. Identification guides and binoculars are provided for the convenience of passengers. Early booking is advisable.

The vast expanse of Big Sand near Gairloch invites you to play.

NORTHERN
IRELAND

Belfast Zoo and Belfast Wheel

WHERE:
City of Belfast
BEST TIME TO GO:
Any time
DON'T MISS:
The stunning views out across
Belfast Lough from the vantage point
of Cave Hill, and the relaxing picnic
area beside the lake inside the
entrance to Belfast Zoo, where there
is also a play park and farm to tempt
the little ones.
AMOUNT OF WALKING:
Moderate to lots
(the zoo is extensive).
COST:
Reasonable to expensive (there's a
discounted family ticket available for
Belfast Zoo, where children under
four go free).
YOU SHOULD KNOW:
Feeding time at the zoo can be most
entertaining, and Belfast's schedule
(pretty reliable but as always subject
to change) is as follows: Red river
hogs (11.15); chimps (indoors, 11.30);
Malayan sun bears (11.30); monkeys
(12.00); lowland gorillas (indoors,
12.00); spider monkeys (12.00); sea
lions (12.30); lowland gorillas
(outdoors, 14.00); penguins (14.30);
sea lions (15.00).

On the side of Cave Hill at the top of Antrim Road, Belfast Zoo offers a day out that kids will really appreciate. This thoroughly modern establishment plays an important part in captive-breeding programmes designed to safeguard some of the world's most endangered animals, but that doesn't stop it being a great place to visit.

The zoo is home to nearly 150 different species and a total population of around 1,200 creatures, including Barbary lions, elephants, giraffes, Malayan sun bears, Moloch gibbons, red kangaroos and spider monkeys, to name but few of many. The newly refurbished Bird Park houses some wonderfully colourful tropical birds, including many rare exotics. The giraffe and elephant enclosure has a healthy population of Rothschild's giraffes as the zoo's contribution to a successful European breeding programme. They live in harmony with natural African neighbours like elephants and zebras, while Cape porcupines and cheeky meerkats aren't far away. The steamy Rainforest House does just what it says on the tin, nurturing inhabitants like sloths, fruit bats, Nicobar pigeons and whistling ducks. If short legs tire there is a refreshment kiosk, plus the Mountain Tea House or Ark Café.

If a visit to the zoo isn't enough for one day, why not take to the skies? Where London leads, Belfast follows – or at least that was the way of it when it came to the Belfast Wheel. Northern Ireland's answer to the London Eye is located to the east side of Belfast City Hall, and this 12-minute ride gives spectacular views across the city from a maximum height of 60 m (200 ft). A daytime observation journey is excellent, but if bedtime can be postponed for a while the kids will love taking a spin as darkness falls, to enjoy a spectacular light show.

*Belfast City Hall
and Wheel*

W5 and Aunt Sandra's Candy Factory

Off Queen's Quay in Belfast's city centre is the Odyssey Arena, beside the River Laggan – home to the award-winning W5 science and discovery centre. This is an outing of two parts – and much as they'll revel in nearly 200 interactive exhibits at W5, it may be wise not to mention what awaits later in the day lest the kids start clamouring to move on in mid morning, long before getting the most out of this dynamic attraction.

The W5 experience is organized into zones, succinctly titled Start, Go, See and Do. Start is really designed for younger children, with a castle to explore, make-believe shopping, dancing, house building and water play. Go has elevated pulley chairs, tug of war, space exploration and cars to build and race. See includes optical illusions, lie detector tests, a sound wall, pro microscopes and lasers. Do involves design and build, robotics and animated film production. This all-action programme will entertain the kids, and only the snootiest of parents will fail to join in the fun.

In addition to permanent exhibits, W5 runs a programme of one-off exhibitions and there is a fascinating series of live shows and science demonstrations taking place throughout each day. There is also a special area for toddlers to enjoy. And after everything else there's Discover, the tempting shop.

When W5 has temporarily exhausted the kids, reveal the day's next destination and they'll soon recover. A visit to Aunt Sandra's Candy Factory on Castlereagh Road involves a history lesson of the best kind – illustrating the way sweets used to be made, using some recipes more than a century old. Explore the old-fashioned shop and take the hour-long factory tour . . . before enjoying some free samples of the handcrafted goodies. Yummy!

Thousands of sweets in jars line the shelves at Aunt Sandra's Candy Factory.

WHERE:
City of Belfast
BEST TIME TO GO:
Any time
DON'T MISS:
A taste of Aunt Sandra's delicious honeycomb, plus a slice of her famous chocolate macaroon cake, freshly baked on the premises since 1953. Her traditional fudge is pretty tasty too.
AMOUNT OF WALKING:
Moderate
COST:
Reasonable (with a family ticket at W5 offered at a discount, and no charge for children under three)
YOU SHOULD KNOW:
Children under the age of 12 must be accompanied to W5 by an adult and remain under the supervision of that adult at all times – this is not the place to let smaller kids run off and do their own thing.

Steaming through the countryside on the Downpatrick & County Down Railway.

WHERE:
Seaforde and Downpatrick, County Down
BEST TIME TO GO:
Summer
DON'T MISS:
The Thomas the Tank Engine model railway upstairs at Downpatrick Station that will surely delight kids of all ages (yes, that most definitely does include dads).
AMOUNT OF WALKING:
Moderate to lots (the latter optional, but there is a great deal to be seen at Seaforde Gardens).
COST:
Reasonable
YOU SHOULD KNOW:
Although the Downpatrick and County Down Railway runs mainly on summer weekends, there are specials at other times – like Christmas, St Patrick's Day, Easter, May Day and Halloween (ghost trains, naturally!). There are also special enactments like World War II weekend and Viking time travelling. Check online for current details and timetables.

Seaforde Gardens and Downpatrick & County Down Railway

Though there's plenty for kids to enjoy, this is a day to please parents too. Seaforde Gardens is signposted off the A24 road north of the village of Seaforde and a combined ticket allows the day to begin with a tour of the walled gardens. The fabulous plant collection will impress the adults, while children will enjoy the hornbeam maze and Mogul Tower with its spiral staircase and viewing platform. There is also a plant nursery specializing in exotic trees and shrubs.

But the highlight for kids will be the enchanting Tropical Butterfly House, a dramatic space that contains hundreds of exotic free-flying butterflies, colourful parrots and various reptiles. There is also a playground, shop and café at Seaforde Gardens.

If the time is right (weekends from late June to mid September), spend the afternoon discovering the wonderful world of steam. Travel the short distance along the A24/A7 roads to Downpatrick and find the brown Railway Museum sign near the bus station in Market Street – The Downpatrick & County Down Railway is across the car park in the shadow of picturesque Down Cathedral.

After a guided tour of the exhibition and workshops, it's all aboard for a spin on a restored section of the former Belfast and County Down Railway's old line, enveloped in steam and thrilling to the pulse of a powerful steam loco. The trip goes one way to ruined Inch Abbey and the other to the burial mound of Viking King Magnus Barefoot. It's possible to dismount and explore, returning on a later train. Afterwards there's a buffet carriage at the platform serving tea, coffee, soft drinks and buns for thirsty travellers. Even if trains aren't running, all is not lost. Visitors may tour the workshops and signal cabin to see behind-the-scenes activities in progress.

Lagan Valley LeisurePlex and Clementsmount Fun Farm

Based at Lisburn Leisure Park, just outside the city centre, Lagan Valley LeisurePlex offers a splashy morning's entertainment for the whole family. Northern Ireland's largest leisure pool has some thrilling water rides – long, fast and very wet!

The fun pool's centrepiece is a pirate ship, complete with water cannons to repel adventurous boarders. Around the pool are themed rides – not for the faint hearted, but appealing to thrill seekers young and older. The Falling Rapids is a 100-m (330-ft) white-water plunge. The Drag Race is a short but speedy flume. The Space Bowl is Ireland's fastest indoor flume, descending at a dizzying 65 kph (40 mph). Master Blaster and Tyre Ride combine to make Ireland's longest flume.

The village area allows families with children to get changed together, while ensuring that privacy is maintained. Start the morning with a Lazy River Family Session at 10.00, followed by the rides and flumes from 11.00. Younger kids will be entranced by the Sunken Galleon, Lazy River and Toddlers' Beach, and also enjoy poolside water attractions like whirlpool spas and bubble loungers.

After all that physical excitement, the afternoon maintains the active entertainment theme – this time at Clementsmount Fun Farm (up the A30/A26 roads from Lisburn, between Crumlin and Nutts Corner). This combination of working farm and children's nursery has grown into a serious attraction.

Animals include goats, sheep (kids can bottle feed lambs in spring), cows, calves, ponies (rides available) and chinchillas. There are also ducks and hens, plus a Petting Barn where small creatures like rabbits, guinea pigs and chicks can be handled. Outside is a host of activities like the Jumping Pillow, pedal go-karts, mini golf, trampoline, sand diggers, football challenges and there is an indoor soft-play area. Oh, and after all that activity you'll like the welcoming tearoom!

WHERE:
Lisburn City and Crumlin, Counties Down and Antrim
BEST TIME TO GO:
Easter to September (for Clementsmount Fun Farm, though it is also open at weekends in autumn and winter).
DON'T MISS:
The multi-coloured Barrel Train at Clementsmount, which allows little ones with tired legs (parents ditto) to tour the farm and see everything from the comfort of . . . one of half-a-dozen barrels on wheels towed by an ATV.
AMOUNT OF WALKING:
Moderate to lots (for those who explore the farm fields at Clementsmount thoroughly).
COST:
Reasonable to expensive (if both attractions are visited and extras like pony rides are enjoyed at Clementsmount Fun Farm).
YOU SHOULD KNOW:
Underwater cameras that are constantly monitored contribute to a comprehensive programme ensuring that LeisurePlex applies the highest possible safety and security standards for the benefit of users.

Streamvale Open Farm and Dundonald Ice Bowl

WHERE:
Dundonald, County Down
BEST TIME TO GO:
Summer holidays (July and August, when Streamvale Farm is open daily from 10.30, except Sundays when the opening time is 14.00, and there are rides, animal feeding and cuddle sessions every day).
DON'T MISS:
The sheep races at Streamvale Farm – they take place at 14.00 on every summer afternoon and the sight of greedy lambs racing round obstacles in pursuit of some extra food is highly entertaining.
AMOUNT OF WALKING:
Moderate
COST:
Reasonable to expensive (if all the activities at Dundonald Ice Bowl are sampled by the family).
YOU SHOULD KNOW:
Dundonald Ice Bowl's Olympic ice rink is large enough to accommodate over 1,000 skaters at any one time (with beginners and learners tending to stay safely around the edges!). The Belfast Giants ice hockey team can often be seen training on the ice, to the delight of those who follow this high-speed sport.

On Belfast's eastern fringes, Streamvale Open Farm is a family-run dairy farm situated where countryside takes over from urban sprawl, with views across to the city and its surrounding hills. The farm provides an opportunity to see the constantly changing daily life of a working farm, with bonus attractions thrown in. To find it, follow signs for the Dundonald Ice Bowl and, when you get there, Streamvale Farm is close by.

Spring at Streamvale sees the usual explosion of new life – calves, lambs, chicks, puppies and baby rabbits. If the timing is right, it's possible to be present while cows give birth and also to bottle feed newborn lambs. But there's also plenty to see and do later in the year. Pets Corner – where kids can enjoy cuddling and feeding sessions – houses a variety of creatures from a large Highland bull to tiny rabbit kits. The farmyard features fluffy yellow chicks, assorted creepie-crawlies and (shock, horror!) a mouse farm. Play areas are stocked with tempting toys for little ones, while older children should see plenty to interest them on the Nature Trail. Cows are milked at 16.00 every afternoon (there's a viewing gallery) and The Creamery is open all day for meals, snacks, milk shakes and homemade ice cream.

Streamvale Farm could occupy a full day, but those who want extra action can pop next door to the aforementioned Dundonald International Ice Bowl. This modern facility with its large rink not only offers capable skaters the opportunity to slide their stuff, but also has a Ten-Pin Bowling Centre for non-skaters, plus the spectacular Indianaland jungle-themed playworld for kids, with ball swamps, tunnels and assorted slides. If that's beneath them, older children might prefer the pool tables and live satellite TV. Something for everyone, then!

Ulster Folk & Transport Museum

One of Ireland's leading visitor attractions is just 11 km (7 mi) east of Belfast city centre, at Cultra near Holywood on the A2 Bangor Road. The Ulster Folk & Transport Museum is set in a large expanse of rolling countryside and offers a wonderful day-long journey down memory lane (grandparents and parents) or a stimulating voyage of discovery (kids of all ages).

The 'Folk' part involves an extended tour of Ballycultra, the museum's re-created town site that harks back to the early 1900s. Costumed guides bring the Northern Ireland of a century ago to vibrant life and make this seem like a highly authentic experience of times past. Around 50 buildings have been acquired from all parts of Ulster, then restored and furnished as they would have been in their heyday. The working buildings and exhibits hark back to activities that were once commonplace but are now rare, like open-hearth cooking, spinning, weaving, carpentry, wood turning, lace making, decorative needlework, basket making, blacksmithing and hand printing.

These are demonstrated and taught, and visitors are encouraged to get a hands-on feel for these once-vital folk skills. The open-air displays are complemented by Folk Galleries that illustrate how Irish farming, food production, everyday activities, jobs and lifestyles have changed over time.

It's easy to spend a lot of time exploring Ballycultra, but that would be to ignore the day's second historical treat – the 'Transport' element. The museum presents a magnificent transport collection – Ireland's finest – that ranges from an assortment of horse-drawn vehicles to Irish-built cars. There is also an award-winning gallery covering Irish railway history that contains some magnificent locomotives. Northern Ireland's long and honourable tradition of building ships and aircraft is not forgotten and, in addition, there's a rolling programme of special events that may be of interest.

WHERE:
Holywood, County Down
BEST TIME TO GO:
Any time, though the open-air displays will be more enjoyable in sunny weather.
DON'T MISS:
The *Titanic* and Flight X2 Experience exhibitions. The former illustrates this famous ship's construction, sinking and the legend that ensued with the help of original material, photographs, newsreels and recordings. The latter is an interactive exploration of the science of flight, with the chance to try a flight simulator.
AMOUNT OF WALKING:
Lots; the museum site is generally pushchair-friendly.
COST:
Reasonable (for both Folk and Transport sections, which may be visited separately – though there's a great family discount available for joint tickets, especially on days when major events are taking place, and children under five always go free).
YOU SHOULD KNOW:
Families with little ones who tire easily can drive from car park to car park to get around the extensive site with a minimum of effort. There are various refreshment facilities on site, plus numerous designated picnic areas.

Children are shown how to make scones.

457

Bangor Seafront Experience

Dust off those kiss-me-quick hats and head for Bangor, on Belfast Lough's southern shore. This is the day to enjoy some traditional seaside family fun at one of Northern Ireland's favourite resorts, which has been a popular holiday destination since Victorian times.

The town beach of Ballyholme isn't memorable, though it is perfectly adequate for sandcastle building and beach football. A much better place to do the whole beach thing is one of two wonderful stretches of golden sand to be found in Crawfordsburn Country Park, 5 km (3 mi) east of town. In addition to great beaches, the parkland has woodland, meadows, ponds and easy walking trails, so the morning will flash past.

After a picnic lunch in the park (or sit-down meal in one of Bangor's many family eateries) the self-proclaimed Bangor Seafront Experience awaits. In addition to sampling all the kitsch resort activities that kids can never resist, the afternoon's highlight should be a visit to Pickie Family Fun Park on The Promenade, close to the busy new Bangor Marina. The maritime-themed adventure playground with its impressive equipment is the perfect place for children to blow off some serious steam, while parents can enjoy a cold drink and watch from the terrace of the Windjammer Café. The paddling pool appeals to smaller children, as do the sandpits, soft-surface play area and kiddie rides.

But the one thing everyone will want to try – and remember for a long time – is a voyage on the shallow lagoon aboard Pickie Fun

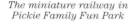

The miniature railway in Pickie Family Fun Park

WHERE:
Bangor, County Down
BEST TIME TO GO:
Easter to September
DON'T MISS:
If there's time, stroll through Bangor's splendid Marine Gardens to Wilson's Point and watch big container ships, tankers, fast ferries and a host of small sailing craft on Belfast Lough.
AMOUNT OF WALKING:
Moderate
COST:
Low

Park's iconic pedaloes, which take the form of giant floating swans. The Pickie Puffer is a delightful narrow-gauge railway that circles the site; there are mini go-karts for competitive types and entertaining live performers in the Arena for those who prefer watching to doing.

YOU SHOULD KNOW:
If it rains, the Bangor Heritage Centre tells the story of the town's past and the cinema in Castle Park (seven screens) can save the rest of the day.

Titanic's Dock & Pump House and Pirates Adventure Golf

Does any child grow up without knowing about the unsinkable *Titanic*'s unhappy end? For those who already know, and those yet to find out, a visit to *Titanic*'s Dock & Pump House will be exciting. So great is the doomed liner's fame that the modern redevelopment of the old shipyard area on Queen's Island has been christened Titanic Quarter.

The Thompson Dry Dock and Pump House was at the heart of the Harland and Wolff shipyard when the great White Star liners were built – *Britannic*, *Olympic* and *Titanic*. Take the guided tour (at 11.00 or 14.00) to appreciate the awesome scale of Edwardian shipbuilding in Belfast. The kids will be amazed when they realize just how massive *Titanic* actually was. The hour-long tour goes right round the huge dock and into the Pump House, with the guide explaining how this once-mighty shipyard operated.

The Visitor Centre in the Pump House uses audio-visual, archive film and computer-generated imagery to tell the tale of the people and technology that made the creation of these great ships possible, starting way back around 1600 when serious shipbuilding began in Belfast.

For more light-hearted nautical-themed entertainment, the day could be rounded off (literally) at Pirates Adventure Golf. Located on Old Dundonald Road around 5 km (3 mi) east of Central Belfast, it can be reached by bus or car. The whole family can enjoy Blackbeard's Adventure – a round of mini golf accompanied by waterfalls, fountains, a ghostly pirate ship and convincing sea battle as Cap'n Blackbeard prepares to come ashore. The Captain's Challenge features a water rapid into which the ball must be played and also encompasses the pirate battle. It's tremendous fun, and can even be enjoyed under lights in the evening. Why go to Florida when Florida has come to Ireland?

WHERE:
City of Belfast and Dundonald, County Down
BEST TIME TO GO:
Any time (both attractions are open all year round).
DON'T MISS:
A long look at *HMS Caroline*, berthed at Alexandra Wharf in the Titanic Quarter. This is the Royal Navy's second-oldest commissioned ship (after Nelson's *HMS Victory*) after being in service for nearly a century. This light cruiser served with distinction at the Battle of Jutland in World War I and is now a naval training centre.
AMOUNT OF WALKING:
Moderate to lots (if the full circumnavigation of the Titanic Quarter is undertaken).
COST:
Reasonable
YOU SHOULD KNOW:
The War Memorial on the side of the Thompson Pump House was designed and made by leading Irish artist Sophia Rosamond Praeger to commemorate men from the Workman, Clark & Co shipyard who died in action during World War I, notably Edward Workman – the only son of owner Frank Workman.

Exploris

Portaferry is on the Ards Peninsula south of Belfast, at the entrance to Strangford Loch, and it's a great place for a family day out. This ferry town is pleasant enough, with good Georgian houses and an impressive ruined castle, but the attraction here is Exploris – Northern Ireland's premier marine-life centre and aquarium.

Half a million people use the ferry to and from the opposite shore each year – so why not start the day in Strangford village and enjoy the 15-minute crossing to Portaferry? A visit to Exploris will be educational, but happily the kids will hardly notice the knowledge they're soaking up, so interesting will they find the whole experience.

The journey appropriately begins in Strangford Lough Hall, with tanks representing various environments found within this important sea loch. Species here include assorted fish, prawns, mussels, spider crabs, and dead man's fingers (a soft coral). The Irish Coast Zone houses creatures that live around Ireland's rocky shores and beaches, including many species of fish, plus the likes of crabs and cuttlefish.

The Open Sea Tank isn't outside, 'Open' referring to the sea rather than its own location, as this truly spectacular tank is actually in a cave and may be viewed from a bridge above or windows below. Here are species that commercial fishermen pursue, like cod and halibut, plus rays, sharks and conger eels. Divers can often be seen feeding the fish – not to be missed!

Demonstrations are held throughout the day at various Discovery Pools to show visitors the variety of marine creatures that are close to hand, and help children appreciate the natural world. And indeed that's the fascination of Exploris – seeing and appreciating an underwater world that is normally a closed book, with fabulous tanks housing a wealth of marine species in a re-creation of natural environments.

*Among the fishes, but
keeping dry!*

Castle Espie Wetland Centre and Drumawhey Junction

Newly refurbished Castle Espie Wetland Centre is on the shores of stunning Lough Strangford, and is a special place where the family can get up close and personal with Nature. The Centre may be found 4 km (2.5 mi) from Comber on the Ballydrain Road (off the A22) and to prove its ecological credentials those arriving by bike pay a reduced entry charge.

The wildfowl to be seen will vary from season to season, but almost the entire world population of light-bellied Brent geese is here in winter and there's a great resident collection of ducks, geese and swans (Ireland's largest). This tranquil place has hides and walks that allow visitors to see assorted wild birds and many captive endangered birds from round the world. There's a sustainable garden to raise ecological awareness, an interesting education area and wet woodland. There's also the Stoat Town natural play area, a play and picnic zone, gallery, gift shop and café. The views across Strangford Loch are superb.

If Castle Espie Wetland Centre isn't enough to fill the day, plan the outing to coincide with Drumawhey Junction being open. This charming narrow-gauge railway stretches for 1.5 km (1 mi) and includes realistic features like bridges, a twin-track tunnel, signals, cuttings, embankments and gradients. The 12-minute run is tremendous fun and the kids will adore it. Drive up to Newtonards and take the B172 road towards Millisle, and Drumawhey Junction is at Four Road Ends (Six Road Ends is just up the road – only in Ireland!).

Opening times should be checked in advance, but trains generally operate only on certain days – notably Sundays, Wednesdays and public holidays in the summer holidays. The Junction is also open on some Sundays after Easter, and for special occasions like Halloween, Christmas and New Year.

A white-faced whistling duck being fed at the Wetland Centre.

WHERE:
Comber and Donaghadee, County Down
BEST TIME TO GO:
Winter to see the huge flock of light-bellied Brent geese at Castle Espie, summer for the great resident collection of ducks, geese and swans and for Drumawhey Junction.
DON'T MISS:
The Plumbs – the local name for the ponds housing the wetland centre's extensive wildfowl collection, where kids can hand feed ducks, geese and swans.
AMOUNT OF WALKING:
Moderate to lots
COST:
Reasonable (Optional Gift Aid entry to Castle Espie Wetland Centre is slightly more expensive but makes a disproportionately large contribution to vital conservation work).
YOU SHOULD KNOW:
The importance of preserving Irish wetlands is underlined at the wetland centre by the on-going programme to restore saline lagoons, salt marshes, limestone grasslands and freshwater lakes on the one site, enhancing the reserve's flora and fauna.

Delamont Country Park

Off the A22 road, on the western shore of Strangford Loch, Delamont Country Park at Killyleagh offers a day out that combines the best of Irish countryside with some entertaining activities. Pack a picnic and prepare to get away from it all.

Check what's on offer at the Visitor Centre (various special events take place throughout the summer) then take a family stroll. There are five nature walks ranging from 1 km (0.6 mi) to 7 km (4.4 mi) in length, giving an option suitable for every age and fitness level – all accessible to pushchairs, all offering the chance to see assorted wildlife in tranquil surroundings.

If the mood (and weather) dictates, Tyrella Beach is worth a day in its own right. This enclosed dune complex on Dundrum Bay has a long, flat sandy strand with safe bathing, various amenities including a shop and tourist information, off-beach car parking, ranger service and lifeguards during the summer holidays.

The boat trip around Strangford Loch is another possibility, but requires advance planning – trips happen at irregular intervals and it's necessary to book in advance, reporting to the gift shop in Delamont Country Park 30 minutes before scheduled departure time. The effort is worthwhile – the 90-minute cruise not only takes place within an area of outstanding natural beauty, but also offers the chance of seeing seals, porpoises or even the occasional basking shark.

A shorter but equally entertaining journey involves riding the park's miniature railway – the longest in Ireland. Hauled by Freddy the Tank Engine (no relation) it potters round the meadow and passes through a tunnel, hooting loudly to the delight of passengers big and small. Who could resist riding a railway with the slogan 'Under the tunnel, around the track, you'll love it so much you'll want to come back'?

AMOUNT OF WALKING:
Lots
COST:
Low to reasonable (if the boat trip is included as a treat).
YOU SHOULD KNOW:
The prominent Strangford Stone was raised in 1999 as a Millennium celebration by 1,000 young people in teams hauling on ropes – quarried in the nearby Mountains of Mourne, it is Britain's tallest megalith.

Views of the Mourne Mountains from Delamont Country Park

Annaginny Park Farm and Armagh Planetarium

Some experiences provide a happy combination of entertainment and education, which is no bad marriage where kids are concerned. Both attractions on this interesting day fall into that category, though for different reasons.

Start off at Annaginny Park Farm, at Newmills near Dungannon. The visit can include a tour of the pet farm, which has farm animals and exotics like alpacas, llamas, wallabies and black swans. There is a nature reserve, woodland walks and a picnic area with barbecue facilities – which might come in handy if the rest of the morning is successful.

For the main activity at Annaginny Park Farm is fishing, in lakes generously stocked with rainbow trout – including some very big ones. These stock fish are not hard to catch, especially as various methods (fly for experts, spinning or bait fishing for beginners) are permitted. Kids will enjoy the fishing lesson, as this is the perfect opportunity to introduce them to the thrill of catching a hard-fighting fish (or to please those who fish already). Just be aware that the bill will soon escalate if too many fish are caught and kept, though a cheaper 'catch and release' ticket is available.

Rather more academic enlightenment awaits at Armagh Planetarium, just up the A29 road from Newmills on College Hill, Armagh. This is billed as 'Ireland's leading centre for astronomical education' but don't assume 'education' equals 'dull'. Instead, an exciting intergalactic voyage of discovery is in store, soaring away from Armagh in the Earth to the Heavens exhibition area and worshipping in the Celestial Cathedral with its stunning deep-space images taken by the Hubble Space Telescope. Armagh Planetarium mounts a variety of dramatic shows, at hourly intervals from noon, with titles like Invaders of Mars and Secret of the Cardboard Rocket, though these must be booked in advance.

Astronaut at Armagh Planetarium

WHERE:
Newmills, County Tyrone; Armagh, County Armagh
BEST TIME TO GO:
Summer (though both attractions are open all year).
DON'T MISS:
The opportunity to lay hands on the oldest thing anyone in the family will ever touch – Armagh Planetarium's amazing 140 kg (308 lb) nickel-iron meteor that is 4.5 billion years old.
AMOUNT OF WALKING:
Moderate
COST:
Reasonable to expensive (if the kids prove adept at catching trout).
YOU SHOULD KNOW:
Some shows at Armagh Planetarium are unsuitable for younger children (under six), because of the darkness and noise generated. Check that the preferred show is suitable when booking to be sure of avoiding disappointment – there are shows to choose from that are suitable for all ages.

Oxford Island National Nature Reserve and the Navan Centre

There are plenty of fun-packed family outings on offer in Northern Ireland, often costing a bit, but it would be a huge mistake to ignore one of Ulster's greatest assets – its outstanding natural beauty. Better still, this can be enjoyed without the need to spend any hard-earned cash.

Nowhere is that more apparent than at the Lough Neagh Discovery Centre, situated on the southern shore of Lough Neagh just off the M1 motorway at Craigavon, near Lurgan (leave at Junction 10). The centre is the jumping-off point for exploring breathtaking Oxford Island National Nature Reserve, a large unspoiled tract of land surrounded by water. The Lough Neagh Discovery Centre itself has a shop, café, paddling pool, children's play area and offers general tourist information.

But the natural world is the day's main attraction, with 8 km (5 mi) of easy walks and nature trails that reveal something different in every season. There are a number of bird-watching hides scattered around Oxford Island National Nature Reserve's wildflower meadows, woodland and shoreline, while strategically placed information panels throughout the site ensure that visitors can gain maximum appreciation of this magical place.

Those determined to spend some money can either seek out one of the many boat trips that ply the waters of Lough Neagh, or travel to the Navan Centre on the A28 road 6.5 km (4 mi) from Armagh. Here a superb archaeological facility interprets Emain Macha, the legendary Navan Fort. This is one of Ireland's most important historical sites – Ulster's ancient capital and royal seat of its kings. The fort's vibrant history is made child-friendly with the help of exhibitions, an audio-visual presentation, re-created period dwelling, costumed interpreters and a guided tour. The Navan Centre offers kids' activities and there is a pleasant picnic area (or a café for those who don't bring their own).

Kings Of Ulster Bronze Age visitors centre

WHERE:
Craigavon and Armagh, County Armagh
BEST TIME TO GO:
April to September to see Oxford Island at its best.
DON'T MISS:
The King's Stables at the Navan Centre – an artificial Bronze Age pool used to make gifts to the gods 3,000 years ago. A human skull and assorted animal bones have been recovered from its tranquil waters.
AMOUNT OF WALKING:
Lots (pushchairs can be used if necessary).
COST:
Free or low to reasonable (if the Navan Centre is included).
YOU SHOULD KNOW:
Clever clogs who point out that Oxford Island is a peninsula rather than a true island should know that it really was an island until the 1850s, when those resourceful Victorians lowered the level of Lough Neagh to prevent the surrounding farmland from being flooded in winter.

Castle Archdale Country Park and MV *Kestrel*

WHERE:
Lisnarick and Enniskillen, County Fermanagh
BEST TIME TO GO:
Summer
DON'T MISS:
The Castle Archdale at War exhibition, covering the role Lough Erne played in World War II – it was Britain's most westerly flying-boat station and Castle Archdale was the main base from which vital anti-U-Boat sorties were constantly flown during the critical Battle of the Atlantic.
AMOUNT OF WALKING:
Lots (optional)
COST:
The country park is free and the boat trip reasonable to expensive (though good value for money with a family ticket).
YOU SHOULD KNOW:
Devenish Island is one of Northern Ireland's best monastic sites. It has a 12th-century round tower, St Molaise's House (actually a small church), the 13th-century lower church and extensive hilltop remains of St Mary's Augustinian Priory. Kids will like the atmospheric ruins, especially as the tower can be climbed using internal ladders, so a visit would be worthwhile.

Some fabulous countryside may be enjoyed at Castle Archdale Country Park on the shores of Lower Lough Erne – once the demesne of 18th-century Archdale Manor House. Find it at Lisnarick village, signed from Irvinestown on the A32 road northwest of Enniskillen.

A family outing to this special place should begin at the Countryside Centre in the impressive stable courtyard – the only remaining evidence that Archdale Manor once stood hereabouts. The centre offers insight into the geography and history of the park, wildlife information and an old farm machinery display, together with washrooms and a café (the latter only open in season).

After that, it's a matter of sampling the many pleasures offered by the country park. It has a red deer enclosure, ponds alive with wildfowl, a butterfly garden, wildflower meadow, waterside or woodland walks and numerous nature trails. For those who crave action, pony trekking and bicycle hire are available, while boats may be hired for voyages of discovery to nearby White Island, Devenish Island, or even to venture further afield.

Speaking of boats, a great way to complete this special day out in the open air is to take a cruise from Enniskillen. The MV *Kestrel* departs from the Round O Jetty in Brook Park for a cruise of Lower Lough Erne that lasts for just under two hours. This well-fitted 56-seater waterbus (shop, bar and lavatories) provides luxury cruising and the trip includes not only panoramic views of the Lough's stunning scenery but also informative running commentary and a visit to the Devenish Island monastic site.

The fully glazed MV *Kestrel* runs from May to October, though with limited sailings in May, September and October, one or two afternoon sailings in June (the second depending on demand) and four daily sailings in July and August.

Getting ready to sail, Castle Archdale Country Park

Marble Arch Caves and Florence Court

Visitors are guided through the Marble Arch caves.

The first part of the day involves a place that would almost be worth visiting for the name alone – Legnabrocky, off the A32 road southwest of Enniskillen. Happily there's a bonus, in the form of Marble Arch Caves. They give their name to Marble Arch Caves European Geopark in Counties Fermanagh and Cavan, recognized by UNESCO as having exceptional geological heritage.

It would be possible to spend a rewarding week exploring the Geopark, but today's starter is Marble Arch Caves themselves. This is one of the most impressive show cave complexes in Europe, and the 75-minute tour reveals a fascinating subterranean world of rivers, waterfalls, passages, soaring chambers, stalactites and mineral deposits. Powerful lighting illuminates amazing rock formations and the tour involves spectacular walkways, and gliding through huge caverns and along underground rivers in electric boats. Those embarking on the tour should wear comfortable walking shoes and a warm sweater as the atmosphere can be chilly. The souvenir shop, café, exhibition area and audio-visual presentation can set the seal on a memorable morning.

Just a short hop along Marble Arch Road, Florence Court is a great place to spend the afternoon. One of Ireland's finest 18th-century houses, it is set against the dramatic background of the Cuilcagh Mountains and has sweeping grounds. This is anything but a dusty old stately home. The house does have superb rococo plasterwork and splendid Irish furniture, but the National Trust at its most innovative mounts 'Living History' tours that provide entertaining insight into life at Florence Court in the 1920s (Sundays in July and August). Outside, there's a children's play area, a quiz and trail for kids, an old sawmill, ice house, the unusual thatched Heather House and walks galore. There are regular events, including family fun days and a country fair in late May.

WHERE:
Near Enniskillen, County Fermanagh
BEST TIME TO GO:
Mid March to September
(for Marble Arch Caves)
DON'T MISS:
The famous Florence Court Yew, a freak of nature with an upright shape that's very different from the norm – dug up in the wild and gifted to the Earl of Fermanagh in the 1770s and commercially propagated from 1820 as the Irish Yew subspecies, this one is therefore known as 'The mother of all Irish Yew trees'.
AMOUNT OF WALKING:
Moderate to lots
COST:
Expensive (if both attractions are visited, though children under five go free at Marble Arch Caves).
YOU SHOULD KNOW:
Older kids inclined to get impatient with natural wonders and historic houses, however interesting, could be indulged with a high-tech alternative to one of the day's main attractions. Laserforce (off Forthill Street in Enniskillen) claims to offer the most advanced laser games system in the world. Players compete against each other in the exciting interactive arena and challenge the resident cyborg (The Silver Lady), using phasers and wearing illuminated battle suits.

Ulster American Folk Park and Sloughan Glen Riverside Walk

A spinning wheel demonstration at the Ulster American Folk Park

How many Irish people were forced to abandon their homeland and seek a new life in America before, during and after the awful 19th-century potato famine? The kids can find the answer in the most dramatic fashion at Castletown, outside Omagh, where the Ulster American Folk Park tells the story of those turbulent years. The emphasis is on the lifestyle and experiences of emigrants before leaving Ireland (the Old World) and upon arrival in America (the New). The park contains many restored or re-created buildings, where guides dressed in period costume illustrate aspects of Old World life, demonstrating everyday skills like cooking, crafts, weaving, spinning, farming techniques, blacksmithing and more.

Linking Old and New is a splendid full-sized replica of the brig *Union*. This typical emigrant sailing vessel may be seen at the Ship and Dockside gallery. The themed approach continues in the New World area, with log cabins and scenes from everyday lives of newly arrived immigrants. The impressive outdoor displays are complemented by the major indoor exhibition, Emigrants, that pulls everything together. The whole experience is fascinating.

The Ulster American Folk Park is more than just a fantastic open-air museum – it also serves as a major centre for the study of Irish emigration from 1600 and is a valuable resource for those trying to trace their Irish ancestry.

After all that thought-provoking history, a walk by the water should provide a relaxing return to the 21st century. Take a picnic and find the Sloughan Glen Riverside Walk, signed from the village of Drumquin (on the B84 road northwest of Omagh). This secluded stroll through woodland culminates in a delightful waterfall, is not overlong – about 1.5 km (1 mi) – and, though steep in places, is worth the effort. Then you can enjoy that laid-back picnic at one of the tables provided.

Ulster History Park and Gortin Glen Forest Park

If around 10,000 years of Irish heritage in one morning seems daunting, think again. The Ulster History Park at Cullion, on the B48 road just outside Omagh, delivers this comprehensive history lesson in the nicest possible way, so even the kids will thoroughly approve.

This open-air museum presents a chronological view of settlement and how people lived – principally in Ulster – from way back in the Stone Age until the Plantation era of the early 1700s, when Protestant incomers from Scotland and England were 'planted' hereabouts in an attempt to subdue the local Catholic population.

Authentically reconstructed buildings range from the flimsy huts of early Mesolithic hunter-gatherers, right though to the sort of fortified manor house favoured by the wealthiest of those unwelcome 17th-century settlers. In between are other fascinating sites, including a farmstead from the Early Christian period and a Norman motte-and-bailey castle. The Plantation Settlement has a working corn mill and the centrepiece of the history park is a typical early round tower. Vast stone monuments are scattered throughout the site, testifying to the capabilities of early engineers.

If little legs are tired after scampering through ten millennia, a visit to Gortin Glen Forest Park will allow flat batteries to recharge. The western gateway to the Sperrin Mountains is clearly signposted from Gortin village, further up the B48 from Cullion. Take a picnic and do the Forest Drive – an 8-km (5-mi) scenic route that has plenty of vista stops with breathtaking views where the picnic can be consumed at leisure. If the kids are sufficiently recovered, there are informal or way-marked walks to explore, including an interesting Nature Trail or the Polalan Trail that follows a burn down the mountainside and includes a great waterfall. Each is a manageable 2 km (1.25 mi) long.

WHERE:
Cullion and Gortin, near Omagh, County Tyrone
BEST TIME TO GO:
April to September
DON'T MISS:
The exhibition gallery and audio-visual theatre that stands alongside the main site at Ulster History Park, which helps put the extraordinary collection of buildings into context and flesh out the lives lived by their original inhabitants.
AMOUNT OF WALKING:
Lots (though the history park is pushchair-friendly).
COST:
Low
YOU SHOULD KNOW:
The Gortin Glen Forest Park was opened in 1967 and was the first such facility to add a leisure dimension to coniferous woodland that had originally been planted purely for timber production.

Barrontop Fun Farm and Gray's Printing Press

WHERE:
Donemana and Strabane,
County Tyrone
BEST TIME TO GO:
Easter to September
DON'T MISS:
In Strabane – the extraordinary sculpture group entitled 'Let the Dance Begin' at the Lifford Road roundabout, where these atmospheric giant figures symbolize a new 21st-century beginning for the once-divided community.
AMOUNT OF WALKING:
Moderate
COST:
Reasonable
YOU SHOULD KNOW:
Pony trekking is available at Barrontop but must be booked in advance – choose from a short trek on a lead rein, short trek, canter trek or full trek. Barrontop Farm also hosts occasional one-off fun days and exciting special events at Christmas, Easter and Halloween. Note that Gray's Printing Press is closed on Bank Holidays.

Ireland does open farms rather well and today's first visit proves the point. Set in picturesque hills at Donemana (near Dunnamanagh on the B49 road northeast of Strabane), Barrontop Fun Farm is a working farm with the usual attractions, ensuring that kids can pass several happy hours. However, the experience is not entirely about pleasure, as it also introduces children to the important relationship between farming and food – a lesson worth learning.

But 'Fun' is in the title and fun is the focus. Barrontop has a wide range of animals – including assorted farm animals and less common creatures such as llamas and pot-bellied pigs – and it specializes in providing hands-on experiences like irresistible opportunities for cuddling puppies, holding chicks and stroking lambs or calves. There is an excellent adventure playground and a bouncy castle – the latter being indoors, as is the soft-play area and face painting, so should the heavens open there will still be plenty to do. Outside, there are tempting opportunities like tractor, cart and fire engine rides plus pony trekking to suit different ages and abilities.

The short journey back to Strabane leads to an impressive experience that lurks behind the elegant original shop front of Gray's Printing Press at 49 Main Street. Strabane was a major printing centre in the 18th century and John Dunlap (printer of the American Declaration of Independence) and James Wilson (grandfather of President Woodrow Wilson) learned their trade here.

Gray's Printing Press is owned by the National Trust, and this historic building provides fascinating insight into Ireland's industrial heritage. Old-style printing is brought to life with the help of the informative guided tour, plus demonstrations and audio-visual displays. There is an excellent collection of 19th-century hand-printing machines that will amaze kids who think printing is done by desktop inkjets.

Creggan Country Park and Tower Museum

High above Derry is Creggan Country Park, opened as a fishery in the early 1990s and now offering much more than that – though if dad's a fisherman he can still wet a line in the Lower reservoir while the rest of the family enjoys a lively morning at this fabulous watersports centre. He might even come back with a couple of rainbow trout!

Located in Westway, a few minutes from the city centre, the elevated park has great views to the hills of Donegal and across Derry to the Lough Foyle estuary and Binevenagh Mountains. This is the day to choose a couple of taster sessions from the likes of sailing or windsurfing, canoeing or kayaking on the Upper Lake. There are also organized land-based opportunities like nature or treasure trails that kids can follow. Alternatively, it's possible to take to the water in the park's unique pedal craft (each carrying three) for a session afloat combining fun and healthy exercise.

After lunch (a picnic or a meal at the park's Lakeview Café), it's time to head back to town and the Tower Museum in Union Hall Place. Located within Derry's historic walls, this marvellous facility tells the story of one of Ireland's oldest settlements. But the feature that will really capture the imagination of children is the re-creation of *La Trinidad Valencera*'s story. This unfortunate Armada galleon – one of the largest in the Spanish fleet – foundered in nearby Kinnagoe Bay in 1588 during a violent storm. The wreck was discovered four centuries later, and the exhibition contains a host of interesting artefacts recovered from the seabed, including cannons and everyday articles like wooden bowls, pewter dishes and goblets. Kids will be fascinated by the audio-visual and interactive displays that tell this once-mighty warship's dramatic story.

Tower Museum

WHERE:
Londonderry/Derry,
County Londonderry
BEST TIME TO GO:
Summer
DON'T MISS:
If there's half an hour to spare, a quick visit to Derry's Foyle Valley Railway Museum (in Foyle Road, open from June to August with free admission) gives a flavour of the area's rich railway heritage, centred on a re-created station platform and containing the splendid County Donegal Railway's *Columbkille* steam loco.
AMOUNT OF WALKING:
Moderate (though lots is definitely a possibility in Creggan Country Park for those who like to roam).
COST:
Low to reasonable
YOU SHOULD KNOW:
Creggan Country Park is a non-profit-making enterprise that provides recreation, training and employment for the local community, with particular emphasis on introducing youngsters to a range of water-based activities and outdoor pursuits, supervised by professional instructors. The site was once a deer park and the reservoirs were built in the late 1840s as an unemployment relief scheme during the potato famine.

Giant's Causeway and Carrick-a-Rede rope bridge

WHERE:
Bushmills and Ballintoy,
County Antrim
BEST TIME TO GO:
During the week or off-season
DON'T MISS:
An audio-visual presentation at the
Visitor Centre explains the geological
origins and myths and folklore
surrounding the Giant's Causeway.
AMOUNT OF WALKING:
Lots
COST:
Low (the only charge at the
causeway is for parking).
YOU SHOULD KNOW:
Legend has it that Irish warrior Finn
McCool built the Giant's Causeway
so he could attack Scottish rival
Benandonner. He fell asleep *en route*
and his enemy came looking for him.
Finn's wife threw a blanket over her
husband and told Benandonner that
this was Finn's son. Assuming that if
the infant was so big the father must
be a giant, Benandonner fled, tearing
up the causeway behind him so the
supposed giant Finn couldn't follow.

*The rope bridge is not for the
faint hearted!*

There are some days out when the kids may be a little grumpy to begin with, because the itinerary doesn't instantly appeal to junior thrill-seekers. And this could be such a day, though it should swiftly turn into an outing that delights children despite initial reservations. For they will see one of Britain's most impressive natural wonders and later enjoy an exciting high-altitude adventure above the surging sea.

The Giant's Causeway is on a loop road off the main A2 coast road between Bushmills and Ballycastle. It's the most popular tourist attraction in Northern Ireland, so don't expect to have the place to yourself. This extraordinary phenomenon is made up of 40,000 basalt columns, formed by volcanic action some 50 million years ago. The causeway consists of interlocking stepping stones, mostly hexagonal, that lead out from the base of the cliff and disappear into the sea.

This World Heritage Site and National Nature Reserve is owned by the National Trust, but the local council runs a car park and Visitor Centre on the cliff top that serves as the starting point for a walk to this amazing piece of natural sculpture. Once there, the kids will surely be awestruck.

Just along the road towards Ballycastle, the National Trust's second star attraction is Carrick-a-Rede rope bridge. Originally constructed by fishermen who crossed to the rugged island of

Carrick-a-Rede, this now serves as an exhilarating challenge – spanning as it does a chasm 20 m (65 ft) wide and 30 m (98 ft) deep. Only eight people are allowed on the bridge at the same time, and once over it's possible to enjoy some spectacular bird life and stunning coastal views of Rathlin and the Scottish islands. Not for the faint hearted, but try stopping the kids!

Brunswick Superbowl and Riverwatch Visitor Centre & Aquarium

Don't worry if it happens to be raining in Derry – this terrific day out starts with a visit to Brunswick Superbowl and ends at the Riverwatch Visitor Centre & Aquarium, with absolutely no outdoor activity required (though that doesn't mean the kids will have a lazy day).

As the name suggests, the principal entertainment at Brunswick Superbowl (on Derry's Pennyburn Industrial estate) is ten-pin bowling. The Brunswick offers a 21st-century cosmic version that comes with fluorescent lights, luminous lanes and pins, plus an awesome sound system. For little ones learning the game, there is a computerized system that can automatically raise and lower bumpers for each bowler, so nobody suffers the disappointment of seeing a misdirected ball rumble away down the gutter.

Before, after or instead of a bowling session, Bananas Adventure Castle offers safe play, while mums and dads relax and observe proceedings from a safe distance. The adventure castle has two levels of general fun for toddlers and three more challenging levels for older kids. Exciting features guaranteed to burn off youthful energy include scramble nets, ball pools and various slides, while face painting provides a change of tempo.

Next stop, rain or shine, is The Riverwatch Visitor Centre & Aquarium on Victoria Road. Another suggestive name confirms that the place is right beside the River Foyle. This interesting and informative facility concentrates on local varieties of marine river and still-water life, with five stunning tanks representing typical environments – stream, lake, sea shore, pond and lough. The species on show are always changing, but expect to see a wide selection. There are plenty of short but interesting audio-visual presentations that cover more or less every aspect of the animals, birds and plants that live in the Foyle and Carlingford catchment areas.

WHERE:
Londonderry/Derry,
County Londonderry
BEST TIME TO GO:
Any time (but note that the Riverwatch Visitor Centre & Aquarium is not open at weekends).
DON'T MISS:
Feeding time at the Riverwatch Aquarium – be there at 15.00 on Mondays, Wednesdays or Fridays. If you can't make that, be sure to ask for activity packs that will keep the kids entertained for up to two hours.
AMOUNT OF WALKING:
Little
COST:
Reasonable (the Riverwatch Visitor Centre is free).
YOU SHOULD KNOW:
Worldly wise older children who find Bananas Adventure Castle beneath them may prefer the American pool tables and the latest interactive arcade games at Brunswick Superbowl.

Portrush Whiterocks Beach and The Dunluce Centre

Sandhill Drive in Portrush is the place to find The Dunluce Centre, but the day's first engagement is a visit to Portrush Whiterocks Beach, recent recipient of a coveted Blue Flag Award. It's possible to park on the coast road above the beach and take in spectacular sea views to the Giant's Causeway one way and rugged Donegal the other.

Whiterocks Beach stretches from Curran Strand in Portrush to Dunluce Castle near Bushmills, so there's plenty of space for the family to hang loose on the beach without feeling crowded. The

bonus is the opportunity to explore limestone cliffs that have been sculpted by the sea into an extraordinary labyrinth of arches, caves and headlands with names like Elephant Rock and Lion's Paw.

After making the most of the morning, it's back to Portrush and The Dunluce Centre. This family entertainment complex is a typical resort attraction, offering a variety of stimulating activities created with kids in mind. Finn McCool's Playground caters for Juniors (a soft-play area for children under four with features like foam steps, ball pool, rockers and slides) and Seniors (for under 12s, with thrillers like tumble steps, obstacle course, climbing wall, cargo nets, spiral tube slides, tunnels, rope bridge, aerial glide and suspended pod). Sessions last for 90 minutes and parents can allow kids to let rip in complete safety.

Other attractions include the Darklight Laser Drome – a must for young gamers over eight, who enter a world where speed and stealth are required to combat mysterious forces. Turbo Tours adds a fourth dimension in a theatre where seat movement synchronizes with screen action to deliver a unique experience. The Fun House Express is a hilarious underground ride through Jimmy the Clown's chaotic world. One way or another, the kids will have a ball.

AMOUNT OF WALKING:
Little or lots (there's plenty to explore on Whiterocks Beach, but it's also possible to have a great time in one spot).

COST:
Low to reasonable (it's a case of pay as you go at The Dunluce Centre, so costs are flexible).

YOU SHOULD KNOW:
If it's a beach tour to take in the full grandeur of the coastal scenery, rather than a quick family frolic on pristine sands, a visit to the spectacular ruined Dunluce Castle (open from Easter to September) at the far end of Portrush Whiterocks Beach would make for a great finale to the morning.

A stroll along Whiterocks Beach

Barry's Amusements and the Portrush Puffer

Certain things are essential when it comes to seaside resorts, and amusement parks guaranteeing 'fun for all the family' rank high on the list. Portrush is blessed with a fine specimen that really does fulfil the familiar promise – Barry's Amusements, founded by a member of the famous Chipperfield Circus family way back in 1925; but more of that anon.

The day starts with something unique to Portrush – the bright-blue Portrush Puffer. Technically this is a bus, but passenger carriages pulled by a look-alike engine make it look remarkably like an old-fashioned steam train and ensure that the kids will really enjoy a tour of the town's sights. Alternatively, an all-day family ticket allows unlimited hopping off and on. As the Puffer runs every half hour and stops at all the town's main attractions, this can be a good deal.

Hopping off at Kerr Street for Barry's Amusements is definitely worthwhile. This is Ireland's largest amusement park (which doesn't actually make it that big!) and it has both outdoor and indoor entertainment, so a visit needn't be spoiled if the heavens open. All ages are catered for and it has some terrific rides. These include classic fairground attractions like a vintage carousel, helter-skelter, ghost train and dodgem cars (full size and minis for smaller children).

To this may be added the excitement of big rides like Freak Out, Cyclone, The Experience, SRV motion simulator and the awesome Looping Star roller coaster. Toddlers and little ones are catered for with rides like Big Apple, Monte Carlo and Turtle Splash, supported by typical one-child coin-in-the-slot mini-rides. There are plenty of video games for indoor kids and active options like trampolines for those who prefer the great outdoors. Barry's isn't for hardened thrill-seekers, but it definitely delivers on the 'family fun' front.

Watertop Open Farm

High in the glens of Antrim, Watertop Open Farm offers a rewarding day out in the open air amid wonderful scenery. Find it off the A2 road 8 km (5 mi) southeast of Ballycastle, beside the entrance to Ballypatrick Forest.

Billing itself as a 'Family Activity Centre', Watertop Farm offers a variety of interesting ways to fill the day. Start with the gentle Waterfall Walk, which has great views of the valley and waterfall and sheep aplenty to be seen along the way. Next, the kids can burn off energy on the pedal go-karts – there are two tracks so little ones don't have to mix with bigger and stronger wannabe Lewis Hamiltons.

Then there's something to test the whole family – a low-ropes assault course amid the trees that will bring stamina and agility into play. After that, the Paddiwagon could give everyone the chance to recover – this yellow ex-army truck has been converted to give rides around the farm, providing a great vantage point from which to see the animals and enjoy the spectacular surroundings. The Quad Bike Train offers an alternative tour.

Pony trekking is a reliable favourite with boys and girls alike, offering an hour-long guided trek around the farm, mostly on gravel tracks. Helmets are provided and an adult must accompany children under 12. The whole family can take to the water on the boating lake, with assorted rowing craft to choose from and lifejackets supplied for children. To add variety there is also fishing, various play areas, a farm museum and a collection of small animals.

Don't arrive too long after opening time (11.00) as the hours will fly by, and it would be a shame to find there are still things left untried when the gates close at 17.30.

WHERE:
Near Ballycastle, County Antrim
BEST TIME TO GO:
July or August, though Watertop Farm is also open for the May Bank Holiday weekend.
DON'T MISS:
The sheep-shearing demonstration, which not only lets kids watch the sheep being shorn, but also explains the whole process of sheep farming and the wool process (not every day, check in advance to be sure of seeing this interesting demo).
AMOUNT OF WALKING:
Moderate (though as much as they want is available for active families).
COST:
Reasonable
YOU SHOULD KNOW:
It's possible to take a picnic to refuel the family, but the Lakeside Tea House does offer very tempting homemade food. Perhaps the best of both worlds would be a packed lunch followed by a farewell cuppa and cake in the Tea House at the end of the day.

Finvoy Fun Farm and the Ecos Centre

There's a choice of farm attractions in these parts, each having a distinctive character. Finvoy Fun Farm is off the B62 road, just outside Ballymoney, and the accent here is definitely on the 'Fun' part. The morning will include lots of tasty ingredients that cook up into great entertainment for the kids.

There are animals galore, some of which may be touched, petted or fed. The menagerie includes sheep, lambs, cows, calves, llamas, goats, pot-bellied pigs, reindeer, turkeys, ducks and chickens – plus furry friends in the animal shed. On the activity front, there is bouncing (trampolines and bouncy castles), a soft-play area, hay barn with tyre swings, traditional swings and a slide, table soccer, pedal cars and tractors, pony rides and a maize maze (July to October).

Moving on, all funned out, the Ecos Millennium Environmental Centre is a 'must see' for families with an interest in the environment, as it helps kids understand the importance of biodiversity, sustainability and caring for the world we live in – not by preaching, but by entertaining them in high-tech galleries that communicate important messages in the nicest possible way. Find the Ecos Centre down the A26 road from Ballymoney, off Broughshane Road close to Ballymena town centre.

A spectacular waterside Visitor Centre suggests ways in which humankind can live without destroying the planet, with the help of

*Ecos Millennium
Environmental Centre*

interactive displays that calculate the family's environmental footprint and illustrate how renewable energy cuts carbon emissions. It's also possible to see why it's vital to preserve wildlife, and take on board simple steps that would encourage birds and insects at home. The latest green technology is on show (and used to heat the building) while outside space offers light entertainment like mini-tractors, sand pit, play park, willow tunnel and duck feeding. Highly recommended!

Castledawson Open Farm and Moneymore Model Village

Off the A6 road at the top of Lough Neagh, Castledawson is the place to find the farm of the same name on Leitrim Road, north of the village. A warm Irish welcome is guaranteed at this family-run attraction and Castledawson Open Farm is definitely one for children who love animals. Here they will find Dexter cattle, Jacob and Soya sheep, miniature Shetland ponies, goats, dwarf pigs, chinchillas, chipmunks, rare breed farmyard fowl, peacocks, rabbits, guinea pigs . . . even comical emus.

The beautiful thatched cottage has a peat fire crackling in the hearth and contains a superb collection of bygone country artefacts – a treasure trove of weird and wonderful things sure to intrigue young and old alike. There is a working well and collection of water pumps in the garden, while a warming cuppa and slice of homemade cake provide the perfect end to a visit.

Complete a memorable day by making the short journey down the A31 to Moneymore (claim to fame – the first village in Ulster to have piped running water). Find the interesting Model Village in the centre, occupying a Victorian walled garden behind Manor House Lodge. Moneymore is one of Ireland's best examples of a Plantation village, built for Scottish and English settlers brought in to counterbalance restless locals in the early 17th century.

It is therefore appropriate that the Model Village represents Moneymore exactly as it was first created during that traumatic period. The layout is based on a map of 1622 and features two intersecting streets populated with figures, with a market cross and stocks at the centre. There is a manor house, stone and timber houses, a mill and thatched cottages.

Kids can sometimes feel dwarfed by their surroundings, and seem to love looking down on a miniature world.

WHERE:
Castledawson and Moneymore, County Londonderry
BEST TIME TO GO:
April to September (if visiting both attractions)
DON'T MISS:
The stunning hand-painted red, blue and yellow Romany caravan at Castledawson Open Farm, serving as an ornate reminder of a vanished way of life.
AMOUNT OF WALKING:
Moderate
COST:
Low (contrary to its name, Moneymore Model Village is not expensive and admission to the open farm is nominal).
YOU SHOULD KNOW:
There are plans for a second Model Village that will represent the Moneymore of 1880, in its Victorian heyday.

REPUBLIC
OF IRELAND

Dublin Zoo

WHERE:
City of Dublin, Dublin Region
BEST TIME TO GO:
Any time
DON'T MISS:
The critically endangered – and enchanting – golden lion tamarins. These small South American monkeys are part of a captive population of some 500 animals kept in zoos worldwide to ensure survival of the species, as the tamarins' forest habitat is being relentlessly destroyed.
AMOUNT OF WALKING:
Lots (and lots, but there are plenty of places to rest up and watch the animals).
COST:
Expensive (but great value, discounted family tickets are available and children under three get free entry).
YOU SHOULD KNOW:
The Phoenix Park Shuttle from Park Gate Street, beside Heuston Station, follows a circular route that takes in the major sights in one of Europe's largest and most magnificent city parks, including the Visitor Centre, Papal Cross, Farmleigh Estate and, of course, Dublin Zoo.

Off the aptly named Zoo Road in green and pleasant Phoenix Park is Dublin Zoo. Ireland's largest, it was founded in the 1830s and attracts nearly one million visitors a year. This fabulous place will keep children enthralled all day long as it not only offers a terrific selection of the world's most interesting (and often endangered) creatures, but also has imaginative extras to surprise and delight kids.

In a thoroughly modern approach, the zoo presents themed habitats like African Plains, Fringes of the Arctic, Kaziranga Forest Trail, World of Primates and World of Cats. This provides the opportunity to see groups of animals that would exist side by side in the wild, or

Alpha male orangutan hanging from the branch of a tree.

impressive collections of similar species, housed in enclosures that mirror their natural habitat as closely as possible. The Reptile House contains a wide range of cold-blooded animals, from Nile crocodiles to leopard tortoises, pythons to lizards. The South American House has charmers like squirrel monkeys and three-toed sloths.

Plan the day to include Meet the Keeper sessions and informative Keeper Talks. It's wise to check the schedule in advance to make sure nothing has changed, but the regular programme is as follows: Meet the Keeper – ring-tailed lemurs 11.30; orangutans 11.45; reptiles 12.00; penguins 14.30; giraffes 14.45; rhinos 15.00; Keeper Talks – Sumatran tiger 11.15; Elephant encounters 12.30; Chimpanzee chat 12.45; Sealion splash 14.15. It's also possible to see animals being fed.

A sure-fire winner is the City Farm and Pets' Corner, where kids are encouraged to interact with cows, goats, donkeys and ponies. There are rare breeds – including Kerry cows and Galway sheep – and all the small favourites like guinea pigs, rabbits and canaries, plus dogs and cats. Another highlight could be a snack in the Meerkat Restaurant, observing those inquisitive little meerkats watching the diners' every move.

Dublinia and the Viking World

Right beside Christ Church Cathedral, Dublinia and the Viking World is a heritage centre located in the heart of Dublin's old city. Its mission is to bring medieval Dublin to life in an entertaining and historically accurate manner. After a recent revamp there's even more to see, and kids will love it. The reconstructions and re-creations are truly awesome. Supported by graphic panels and electrifying soundtracks, they bring history to vivid life.

The Viking World explores the impact these Scandinavian raiders had on Ireland – including the fact that Dublin became northwestern Europe's most important slave market. Here it is possible to see what life was like on one of those infamous longships, experience the sights and sounds of a Viking street, be chained up as a slave, inspect a family house and understand burial customs.

Dublinia moves on to the medieval era, following the city's fortunes from its capture by Strongbow and his knights in 1170 to Henry VIII's violent dissolution of the monasteries in the 16th century. This is the place to see a bustling market, noisy street and the interior of a merchant's house. It's also possible to learn how felons were punished and crude dentistry was practised around 1300 (ouch!). There's also a shop with gifts inspired by the medieval period, plus books (for adults and kids), children's costumes and fun mementoes of the visit to Dublinia.

Should a couple of hours remain after time travelling into the past, the historic theme can be maintained by pre-booking a Viking Splash Tour. This will use an old World War II amphibious vehicle (a DUKW, pronounced 'duck') to provide an entertaining tour of Dublin's sights by land and water – just imagine the kids' delight when their open-topped tour bus drives straight into the river!

WHERE:
City of Dublin, Dublin Region
BEST TIME TO GO·
Any time
DON'T MISS:
The panoramic city view from the top of 17th-century St Michael's Tower, which is part of Dublinia . . . though it's only for those who have the energy to climb the 96 steps to the top.
AMOUNT OF WALKING:
Moderate
COST:
Expensive (if both attractions are enjoyed, though there is a worthwhile family discount ticket available at Dublinia – the more kids you have the more you save).
YOU SHOULD KNOW:
After visiting Viking and medieval Dublin it will be hard to resist a quick tour of impressive Christ Church Cathedral, where a discounted entry charge is available to those who have been to Dublinia.

A Viking Splash Tour

Imaginosity and The Chocolate Warehouse

WHERE:
Sandyford and Walkinstown,
Dublin Region
BEST TIME TO GO:
Any time
DON'T MISS:
The Art Studio at Imaginosity – great
fun, but be warned that it's not for
kids whose mums and dads get
upset when their little ones get
SERIOUSLY MESSY.
AMOUNT OF WALKING:
Little
COST:
Reasonable to expensive (should the
Chocolate Workshop be sampled by
all the family).
YOU SHOULD KNOW:
The Chocolate Warehouse holds
special events during December (meet
Santa, receive a gift, make a cracker
and see the mini-chocolate factory)
and in the month before Easter (meet
the Easter Bunny, see the mini-
chocolate factory and come away
with a personalized Easter egg).

This is a day to be enjoyed by families with children under ten, for Imaginosity has been created specially for them. The philosophy is simple – children learn best when they're having fun, so let's make sure they have loads of fun and learn lots. As the name suggests, the whole experience is about stimulating the powerful imagination of children. Imaginosity is at The Plaza in Sandyford, off the M50 motorway south of Dublin. Kids can be energized and have their confidence boosted through creative activity, ending up feeling just great about themselves.

The Kids' Stage allows children to try on costumes, operate lights, change scenery and even create little dramas. The Climber, over two floors, has almost endless opportunities to indulge in imaginative play. Town Centre is full of props and provides a structured environment for enacting everyday experiences, as created by the lively minds of participants. The Construction Company allows youngsters to don hard hats, load up with plastic tools and get building. The youngest visitors are entertained at Tir na nOg (the Land of Eternal Youth) and Little Me.

After enjoying the world of the imagination, the afternoon can be spent appealing to those other vital motivators of childhood – taste buds and stomachs. A short trip up the M50 and exit onto Naas Road towards the centre of Dublin will deliver eager learners to The Chocolate Warehouse (located in the Mulcahy Keane Industrial Estate off Greenhills Road).

This is wonderland for chocoholics, being Ireland's largest chocolate factory shop. Serious students can pre-book the ever-popular two-hour Chocolate Workshop (suitable for children aged six and upwards), which includes a film, demo of Easter egg manufacture and some tasty hands-on enrobing (that's coating chocolates and adding toppings to you and me), before boxing the result to be consumed later. Scrumptious!

Liffey cruise and National Aquatic Centre

Like many cities, Dublin sits astride a great river – in this case the Liffey – and a cruise on the comfortable *Spirit of Docklands* is a super way to see the river and waterside Dublin. This purpose-built vessel (fully enclosed, just in case it rains) can take 48 passengers from its base at Bachelors Walk, close to O'Connell Bridge.

An informative commentary tells Dublin's tale from the arrival of the Vikings a thousand years ago, through rapid development in the 18th and 19th centuries to emergence as an important European capital city. The rise and decline of Dublin Docks is charted, along with that of the Royal and Grand Canals, and the cruise passes landmarks like the majestic Custom House and Ha'penny Bridge. It's also possible to book cruises that further expand awareness of Dublin's fascinating history by combining a walking or coach tour with the river cruise.

The rest of the day can also happily involve water, as in 'having fun in' rather that 'cruising on', at the National Aquatic Centre in Snugborough Road, Abbotstown (close to the M50 motorway). As well as being the focal point for Irish national swimming excellence, the Aquazone is one of Europe's most exciting water parks. It has terrific rides like the white-water Flow Rider, assorted flumes that deliver high-speed descents, the pirate ship for smaller kids with lots of safe fun rides, or a wave pool that's just like swimming in the sea and also contains the Lazy River that lets riders drift around the perimeter on a leisurely 10-minute journey.

If river cruising sounds a little dull to lively rarin'-to-go kids, it would be very easy for them to spend the whole day testing the National Aquatic Centre's state-of-the-art fun facilities to near-destruction. After all, the slogan is 'Fantastic family fun'.

The Custom House which dates from 1791 and the River Liffey.

WHERE:
City of Dublin, Dublin Region
BEST TIME TO GO:
March to November (for river cruises)
DON'T MISS:
Master Blaster at the National Aquatic Centre – this sensational water ride involves being blasted up hill on jetted water, followed by a thrilling rollercoaster-style plunge with banked turns and surprise drops.
AMOUNT OF WALKING:
Little (unless the cruise plus walking tour is undertaken).
COST:
Expensive (if both attractions are enjoyed).
YOU SHOULD KNOW:
There are up to six sailings of the *Spirit of Docklands* every day in season, but it's still advisable to book in advance to be sure of a place on the chosen cruise on the chosen day – and online bookings attract a good discount on adult fares.

Croke Park and the Bram Stoker Dracula Experience

Even for kids with no sporting aspirations, touring any major sports stadium is an impressive experience. For sporty children it's awesome. Dublin's Croke Park Stadium in St Joseph's Avenue is the home of Gaelic Games and has been at the heart of Irish sporting life for over a century, providing a fascinating start to a very different day out.

The guided stadium tour (at least three daily, all year round except around match days) provides kids with insight into what happens behind the scenes at a mega-stadium. The tour encompasses dressing rooms, premium and corporate levels, VIP area, media centre and service sections. The climax is a visit to the pitch. The Gaelic Athletic Association (GAA) Museum is under the Cusack Stand at Croke Park and adds another dimension to the occasion. It has a vast collection of artefacts to remind visitors how passionately the Irish identity is tied up with Gaelic football and hurling.

Another type of passion – for a pint or two of warm blood – characterizes the day's second outing, to the Bram Stoker Dracula Experience in the West Wood Club on Clontarf Road. This ghoulish adventure takes full advantage of the fact that Count Dracula's Victorian creator was born in Dublin – exploring his life and (more significantly) that of his inspired invention, the un-dead star of over one thousand horror movies.

The kids will know what to expect, but this walk-through encounter with the fanged one (and horror in general) will still cause them to shudder with pleasurable terror as they experience the spine-chilling journey through Castle Dracula. This evil lair is full of scary enactments, cobwebs, blood that trickles down walls, bats, nameless creatures that creep and crawl in the night and – most horrifying of all – the gruesome torture chamber. Aaargh!

Malahide Castle

Set within wooded parkland, Malahide Castle offers a memorable day out. The seaside town of Malahide is north of Dublin and its imposing fortress has been standing tall for 800 years, home to the Talbot family from 1185 until 1975.

A castle tour reveals magnificent drawing rooms, beautiful furnishings and wonderful Irish portraits, though the kids may be more interested in hearing about Malahide's ghosts – like the shrewish Lady Maud Plunkett, who has been seen pursuing her hen-pecked spouse along gloomy corridors. Don't let the kids misbehave – Malahide's most famous ghost is 16th-century jester Puck, who is said to reappear if anything that he disapproves of happens.

Next stop is the Fry Model Railway, adjacent to the coach park. The extensive array of scale models was handcrafted by railway engineer Cyril Fry, who personally created all the Irish locomotives, rolling stock and tram models. Every piece was assembled with extraordinary attention to detail and together they tell the story of Irish railways. If the static models are impressive, the working railway layout is amazing. Kids will love the tour that features just about every era of Irish railways, all operating simultaneously on a huge life-like layout that contains many recognizable Dublin features.

Last but not least is Tara's Palace & Childhood Museum in Malahide's Courtyard. It's insulting to call Tara's Palace the world's finest doll's house, as it is at the very least a stately home. This masterpiece is built to one-twelfth scale and filled with exquisite contents. There are other important dolls' houses here, too, including 'Portabello' from around 1700, one of the oldest to survive. Also on show are antique dolls and toys. This may be one mostly for girls, but even the boys will be secretly impressed by those superb miniature artefacts, pictures and pieces of furniture.

DON'T MISS:
The castle's extensive parkland – it will be tempting to linger around the main attractions, but finding a little time for a stroll in the delightful gardens and grounds should be part of this special day at Malahide Castle. There is a children's playground if all that passive looking has allowed surplus energy to build up, plus a craft shop, restaurant and tearooms.

AMOUNT OF WALKING:
Moderate

COST:
Reasonable

YOU SHOULD KNOW:
When drinking in the atmosphere of the Great Hall during the Malahide Castle tour, just imagine the scene on July 1 1690, when 14 members of the Talbot family sat down for breakfast. By nightfall all were dead – killed at the Battle of the Boyne where the Catholic Jacobite forces were routed by those of the Protestant William of Orange.

Malahide Castle

National Transport Museum and Ye Olde Hurdy-Gurdy Museum of Vintage Radio

WHERE:
Howth, Dublin Region
BEST TIME TO GO:
June to August (the Transport Museum is open only at weekends and on Bank Holidays outside these months, and the Hurdy-Gurdy Museum is also restricted to weekends from November to March).
DON'T MISS:
A summer wander through the wild rhododendron gardens at Howth Castle – a 14th-century pile restyled by the famous English architect Sir Edwin Lutyens (no access possible to the building itself).
AMOUNT OF WALKING:
Moderate
COST:
Low
YOU SHOULD KNOW:
The Hurdy-Gurdy Museum is in an appropriate location – in 1854 the first underwater telegraph cable from the British mainland came ashore immediately below Howth's Martello Tower, which became a cable station. In the early 1900s it was used by the Marconi Company to conduct ship-to-shore wireless experiments.

Howth is a busy Dublin suburb, and the day's first stop is the National Transport Museum located at the Heritage Depot close to Howth Castle. This is the place to show the kids a wonderful assembly of vintage transport that was started in 1949 with an attempt to preserve three Dublin trams.

Nowadays the museum has nearly 200 interesting vehicles, recounting the story of Irish vehicular transport with a little help from old photographs and memorabilia. The oldest exhibits date from the 1880s, when horses provided the pulling power, while the most modern are from the 1980s when Diesel engines ruled the commercial roost. This was a century of astonishingly rapid change and development in the field, which is brilliantly illustrated by the museum's extensive collection.

This covers public service and commercial road transport and is organized into five sections: Passenger; Commercial; Fire & Emergency; Military; Utility. Included are sole survivors of once-familiar types, unique one-offs and many rarities. Unfortunately, only a proportion of the collection is on show at any one time because space is lacking and in consequence exhibits are quite tightly packed. But the balance is in storage and may be inspected by prior arrangement – and even without them the museum puts on a great display.

It takes nearly as long to say the name as actually visit the next attraction, not to mention the time taken to climb a steep path to the entrance (opposite the Abbey Tavern in Howth's Abbey Street). Ye Olde Hurdy-Gurdy Museum of Vintage Radio is in the historic Martello Tower overlooking Howth harbour, and it has an intriguing collection of radios, gramophones, music boxes and related items – the kids will be amazed by what people had to make do with before MP3 players and digital radio were invented.

National Sea Life Centre and Glenroe Open Farm

Plunging beneath the sea without getting wet – seeing wondrous sights in the process – is a good trick. It can be played at the National Sea Life Centre on the seafront in bustling Bray, south of Dublin. The centre has a huge collection of underwater creatures and not only gives visitors the opportunity to see this fabulous array of freshwater and marine life, but also offers interesting talks throughout the day on subjects including seahorses, piranhas, sharks and octopuses.

There is a selection of rewarding exhibits at the centre, including Tropical Shark Lagoon, Rivers of the World, Nemo's Kingdom and Lair of the Octopus. Feeding times are always popular, taking place on the hour from 11.00 to 16.00. Some – like sharks – are fed every day, but most species are fed less often, though there are feeding sessions of some kind every day.

Further down the N11 road, leaving at Exit 11 for Greystones and Kilcoole, Glenroe Open Farm is signed from the latter. This special place continues the day's 'all creatures great and small' theme, but this time the animals have their hooves, paws and feet firmly on dry land. The farm is one of Wicklow's most popular attractions for families with younger children (though teens can have fun, too). It follows the tried-and-tested pattern of combining lots of interesting and appealing creatures (from farm animals to the inhabitants of Pets' Corner) with exciting children's play opportunities.

However, Glenroe Farm offers unique features that can provide an additional dimension to the visit. These include a Sensory Garden, the magical Secret Garden in the woods, a Nature Walk through coastal marshlands teeming with wildlife, an old thatched Farmhouse Museum packed with interesting exhibits and an area displaying bygone toys. There's lots to see and do, so don't arrive late.

WHERE:
Bray and Kilcoole, County Wicklow
BEST TIME TO GO:
Any time
DON'T MISS:
A walk along the famous Victorian Promenade at Bray – followed by the easy ascent of dramatic Bray Head from the southern end of the Prom for families with energy to spare and a weakness for far-reaching sea views.
AMOUNT OF WALKING:
Moderate to lots
COST:
Expensive to reasonable (if advantage is taken of generous discounts that can be obtained by booking in advance for the Sea Life Centre online).
YOU SHOULD KNOW:
Glenroe Open Farm is pram- and pushchair-friendly. There is a café serving wholesome homemade food (indoors or on the patio outside) but there are also indoor and outdoor picnic areas for families who prefer to bring their own.

Brittas Bay Beach

Wicklow's Historic Gaol and Brittas Bay Beach

No dragons, but plenty of dungeons (well, cells mostly) to entertain the kids – that's the promise at Wicklow's Historic Gaol, built in 1702. They'll love an interactive experience that involves a visit to a spooky place boldly promising a story of crime, cruelty, exile and misery – billing itself as 'One of the most haunted places in Ireland'.

The ghosts are, of course, the legion of lost souls who passed through this forbidding place in over two centuries of use as a harsh prison. Many notorious characters that were incarcerated here are brought back to life with the help of costumed actors and dramatic set pieces housed in the old cells. This is the story of Old Ireland from the Rebellion of 1798 through the horrors of the Great Potato Famine to prison reform and eventual closure in 1900. A 'lowlight' that children always enjoy is the old dungeon, complete with flogging (no, not them!) and solitary confinement. The latter can be tried for a few minutes (sorry, mums and dads, it can't be several hours).

After all those scary enclosing walls, wide-open spaces and a breath of sea air are just the (free) ticket. And the place to find those is Brittas Bay Beach, one of the finest on Ireland's east coast. This 5-km (3-mi) stretch of powdery golden sand earns a coveted Blue

Flag year after year, and is just perfect for all those activities (including bathing) that can make a family outing to the beach such fun. For little explorers, the sand-dune system behind Brittas Beach is a great place for imaginative minds to create an exciting adventure. Access to this splendid open-air playground is from the R750 road (parallel to the N11) between Wicklow and Arklow.

Clara Lara Fun Park and Greenan Farm Museum & Maze

In the heart of the scenic Wicklow Mountains, between Rathdrum and Laragh on the R755 road, is an attraction that makes no bones about its role in the global scheme of things – Clara Lara Fun Park. This is one of Ireland's most compelling outdoor adventure parks, with so many stimulating activities to choose from that kids may have difficulty deciding what to do next.

Land-based fun comes in many forms. Should it be Tarzan swings or tree houses, rope bridges or balancing bars, mini-golf or pedal go-karts? There's plenty of water in the form of shallow artificial lakes and waterborne fun includes rafting, canoeing, rowing, Amphicats, an aqua shuttle, radio-controlled boats, an awesome water slide and ahoy-there pirate ship. Be aware that while general play facilities are included in the admission price, there is a small charge for specific extras – boats, go-karts and mini-golf. A 'gold' bracelet may be purchased that allows unlimited use of these facilities.

Complete the day with something different – a visit to Greenan Farm Museum & Maze, just up the road at the foot of beautiful Glenmalure Valley. It has all the animals (and more) to be expected on a working hill farm, while the restored farmhouse has a traditional interior and an unusual and extensive bottle collection and other historical artefacts.

The Farm Museum within a large barn is packed with interesting rural exhibits, while the attempt to beat the large hedge maze should keep the family entertained for some time. A stream flows through the maze and it also has a pond, while the adjacent viewing tower gives an idea of what's in store before tackling the afternoon's highlight. Greenan Farm also has a sculpture trail, nature walks and craft shop, with tearoom offering welcoming refreshments. Junior satisfaction guaranteed!

WHERE:
Rathdrum, County Wicklow
BEST TIME TO GO:
May until August for both Fun Park and Greenan Farm
DON'T MISS:
Greenan Farm's new Solstice Maze, set in a stone circle with paths that lead to four standing stones – not intended as a challenge, but rather offering a few quieter moments within the otherwise busy afternoon.
AMOUNT OF WALKING:
Lots
COST:
Expensive (if all the optional extras are purchased at Clara Lara Fun Park).
YOU SHOULD KNOW:
It's possible to use a free barbecue to cook a midday meal at Clara Lara Fun Park, where there are also scenic picnic areas for those who prefer to bring a packed lunch. Lazybones can take advantage of the park's picnic restaurant that serves burgers, chips, sandwiches, ice cream and soft drinks. Wear old clothes and bring a change of clothing – the kids will invariably get wet.

Straffan Butterfly Farm and Larchill Gardens

WHERE:
Straffan and Kilcock, County Kildare
BEST TIME TO GO:
June to August (for both butterfly
farm and Larchill)
DON'T MISS:
When in Straffan try to find time to
visit The Steam Museum, rather
bizarrely located in a former church
brought from a Dublin railway works
to Lodge Park. There is a wonderful
collection of model steam
locomotives and some great
(literally!) industrial steam engines,
including a huge beam engine. Open
Wednesday to Sunday in summer,
with live 'steam up' on Sundays.
There is also a splendid walled
garden in Lodge Park.
AMOUNT OF WALKING:
Lots (though it is perfectly possible to
enjoy an afternoon at Larchill
Gardens without doing the full tour).
COST:
Reasonable to expensive (if all
attractions are visited).
YOU SHOULD KNOW:
A number of special events are held
at Larchill to provide an added
dimension for those who preplan.
These include poultry shows, falconry
displays and archery demonstrations
(beginners welcome to chance their
arm). Larchill Gardens are open from
Thursday to Sunday (plus Bank
Holidays) from June to August.

Butterflies are special and always fascinate children. Straffan Butterfly Farm is the place to show them a wonderful selection of these brilliant creatures. It is located at Ovidstown near Straffan (signed off the R403 road between Celbridge and Clane). The farm grew out of its owners' passion for butterflies and the natural world. It was Ireland's first such attraction and remains one of the very best.

There is a large exhibition area housing extensive collections of butterflies from all over the world and a number of educational displays that explain everything about the life cycles of butterflies and moths. But the real draw is the butterfly house that creates a tropical environment in the heart of the Irish countryside. Here, exotic vegetation and colourful blooms form the backdrop for myriad butterflies that fill the hothouse as they forage and feed. As a bonus, there are plenty of creepy-crawlies to make the kids shudder (happily confined behind glass), including tarantulas, snakes, scorpions, geckos and iguanas. The tropical house is suitable for pushchairs.

Moving on from Straffan, take the R406 to Maynooth then turn left onto the R148 to Kilcock. From there, the R124 leads to Larchill's magnificent Arcadian Garden. This is Europe's only surviving example of an 18th-century *ferme ornée* – an ornamental farm that was really an excuse to create a wonderful romantic landscape. A 40-minute scenic walk links ten magical follies, including two on an island in the lake, while there is a decorative Gothic farmyard and a shell-lined tower.

The 'farm' element is fulfilled by an extensive selection of rare-breed farm animals and birds. The Toddlers Sandpit, Pets Corner and wooden Adventure Playground mean the kids won't get bored, while the tearoom (or picnic area) ensures they needn't go hungry.

Roll 'n Bowl and Portlaoise Pet Farm

Clonminam Business Park in downtown Portlaoise seems an unlikely location for brisk family fun, but that is where the day's action starts at 11.00. For this is the location of Roll 'n Bowl, an entertainment centre that offers ten-pin bowling . . . and more.

Young ten-pinners will be encouraged by the choice of balls (various sizes) and automated bumpers that deal with wayward efforts. Beyond that, there are three soft-play areas (for different age groups) with a conservatory and Coffee Dock for watching parents. What else will smaller people want to do?

There's a Roller Disco Arena where kids sprout wheels beneath amazing lights to the sound of disco music. Laser Quest is a high-tech game played in a multi-level arena with weird lighting, fog effects and pounding music – lasers are used to tag opponents' sensors to score more points than anyone else stalking the electronic jungle. Little ones can pick an unborn bear from the soft-toy range and fill it out on the Teddy Bear Stuffing Train, before naming the newcomer and creating a birth certificate. For those who fancy a whiff of fresh air, there's an outdoor crazy golf course.

Unless the day's sped by unnoticed at Roll 'n Bowl, slip away in the direction of Portlaoise Pet Farm. The journey will take you out on the M7 towards Mountrath, where the farm is signed to the left just after leaving the motorway. Set in beautiful countryside, this is the place for a leisurely stroll round the shortish all-weather walkway (no mud, even when it rains) to see over 40 different kinds of animal. In addition, there are indoor (beat that shower) and open-air play areas, sandpit, reptile house and indoor animal viewing area. Picnics are encouraged, but there is a café on site.

WHERE:
Portlaoise, County Laois
BEST TIME TO GO:
Any time (but the Pet Farm is closed in winter and never open on Mondays, except Bank Holidays, with restricted opening in March, April, May, September and October).
DON'T MISS:
A quick word with the star of the show at Portlaoise Pet Farm – that'll be colourful Jeffery the parrot.
AMOUNT OF WALKING:
Moderate to lots (optional). Portlaoise Pet Farm (including the farm walk) is pushchair-friendly.
COST:
Expensive (if additional activities are enjoyed at Roll 'n Bowl, though bowling itself is cheaper during the day than in the evening).
YOU SHOULD KNOW:
Bowling and soft-play at Roll 'n Bowl are charged by the hour. Players of Laser Quest must be 1.1 m (3.6 ft) tall and aged seven or older. Should a junior birthday be in the offing, Roll 'n Bowl offers some terrific party options.

Belvedere House, Gardens and Park

Standing in beautiful wooded parkland on the shores of Lough Ennell, Belvedere House, together with its gardens and park, offers a wonderful day of family togetherness in peaceful Irish countryside. Take a picnic (there are lakeside picnic tables), find this restored Georgian villa off the N52 road south of Mullingar and prepare to discover Belvedere's many intriguing features.

The house itself is a former (and rather impressive) hunting lodge and it's possible to stroll around the interior, which has notable rococo ceilings and restored rooms such as the kitchens, dairy, dining room and drawing room. There's enough here to interest children, including the story of Wicked Earl Robert Rochfort who kept his second wife Mary a prisoner for 31 years after wrongly accusing her of infidelity.

WHERE:
Belvedere near Mullingar,
County Westmeath

BEST TIME TO GO:
Open all year, but spring to autumn
shows Belvedere Gardens and Park
at its best

DON'T MISS:
The Garden Market – a recently
introduced area at Belvedere House
that sells exclusive garden products,
accessories and interesting plants.

AMOUNT OF WALKING:
Lots (if full advantage is taken of
Belvedere House's extensive
lakeside parkland and trails, though
lazybones or families with little ones
can take the Belvedere tram for a
parkland tour).

COST:
Reasonable (a family ticket comes at
a discount from accumulated
individual entry fees but the
Belvedere tram is extra).

YOU SHOULD KNOW:
There is a constant succession of
special events at Belvedere that can
be of interest to those looking for
something extra. Activities include
nature roadshows, steam train
outings from Mullingar, rare plant
fairs plus numerous food, design and
fine-art shows.

Outside, the parkland rolls down to Lough Ennell, offering numerous scenic walks and the opportunity to discover some of the many romantic follies dotted around the park. There's no missing the largest – the Jealousy Wall, erected in the form of a ruined medieval abbey by that self-same Robert Rochfort to hide the view of his brother's (larger) house. There are signed walks and the one children will enjoy most is the Narnia Trail through woods where various creatures lurk, all turned to stone by the White Witch, along with a beaver dam, stone table and Witch's Castle (in reality a Gothic folly).

There is a fabulous Victorian walled garden full of interesting plants, plus a recently created Fairy Garden, and Cherry Valley with exotic blossoming trees. But the features children will get excited about are the small animal sanctuary and two playgrounds close to the Courtyard Café. If they have any energy left after a day in the fresh air, this is where it will get burned off.

The Jealous Wall and Belvedere tram at Belvedere House and Gardens

Athlone Castle and Derryglad Folk Museum

WHERE:
Athlone, Counties Westmeath and Roscommon; Curraghboy, County Roscommon
BEST TIME TO GO:
The Derryglad Folk Museum is open from May to September only.
DON'T MISS:
The Famine Memorial Stone at Derryglad Folk Museum, recalling the sad tale of the Kelehan brothers who died of exposure after being expelled from Athlone Workhouse and left to find their own way home on a bitterly cold night.
AMOUNT OF WALKING:
Little
COST:
Reasonable
YOU SHOULD KNOW:
Athlone Castle featured in the 17th-century Irish Confederate Wars and Athlone was a Jacobite stronghold twice besieged by William of Orange's forces in 1690 and 1691 – the first time they were unsuccessful but duly emerged victorious the following year, shortly before Catholic resistance in Ireland was finally crushed.

Times past are brought to life in Ireland's heartland on this day out, with the first stop focusing on history and the second allowing mums, dads (and grandparents) to enjoy an extended wallow in nostalgia, while children are amazed by thousands of exhibits that illustrate bygone ways and folk culture.

The day begins at mighty Athlone Castle, standing beside the River Shannon in the centre of town. Its Visitor Centre provides riveting commentary on the story of this 13th-century fortress. An audio-visual presentation covers the Sieges of Athlone and The Story of the River Shannon explains the area's archaeology, its flora and fauna, plus transport on the Shannon and its role in generating hydro-electricity. Local celebrity tenor John Count McCormack is also featured and there are items of personal memorabilia on display, including his gramophone. A tour of the military and folk museums should occupy another interesting hour.

Then it's off to explore some more ordinary history – that experienced by working folk when Ireland was a relatively impoverished country, as they struggled to make decent lives for themselves despite hardship. Family-run Derryglad Folk Museum is appropriately situated in rural South Roscommon, signed from the N61 Athlone to Roscommon road. The effort required to wend through the lanes will be well rewarded, with a host of interesting items waiting to be inspected, from vintage machinery to old cameras.

An Irish country bar and grocery store from the mid 1900s has been re-created and almost everything ever used on the farms and in kitchens, sculleries, homes, shops and bars of Old Ireland is on display. There's even a sideways glance at other rural cultures, with exhibits featuring barn threshing on a Scottish croft and sheep shearing in the Australian Outback. It's a highly recommended eye-opener for grown-ups and kids alike.

Athlone Castle

Brú na Bóinne Visitor Centre and Grove Gardens & Open Farm

One of the passages of Knowth

West of Drogheda, blending into the landscape on the southern bank of the River Boyne, Brú na Bóinne Visitor Centre near Donore is the starting point for a voyage of discovery into prehistory. If this sounds dull, it isn't. Kids will find this outing fascinating, especially when they get to explore ancient passage tombs.

The Visitor Centre has a large interactive exhibition, including an informative audio-visual presentation, but this merely sets the scene for subsequent tours of Brú na Bóinne's most famous prehistoric monuments – Newgrange and Knowth. These atmospheric places may only be seen via the Visitor Centre, with tours leaving from the north side of the Boyne after each party crosses a footbridge.

Newgrange and Knowth date from around 3,000 BC (making them older than Stonehenge in England or Giza's Great Pyramid in Egypt). Newgrange has been restored and the mound has a white quartzite face on the entrance side. This fronts an 18-m (60-ft) passage that leads to a cruciform burial chamber with a high, corbelled roof. Knowth has two separate passages and wonderful rock art. There are other tombs in the Brú na Bóinne complex, mostly on private land.

The passage and chamber of Newgrange are illuminated by the rising sun at dawn on the winter solstice. Thousands of people enter a lottery to be there for this magical moment; 50 winners are drawn in September, each getting two places. It's possible to enter the draw at Brú na Bóinne Visitor Centre.

To round off the day with a change of emphasis from past to present, move on to Grove Gardens & Open Farm – find it on the R164 road between Athboy and Kells. There are extensive gardens to explore, plus lots of tropical birds and farm animals for the kids to enjoy. Take a picnic.

WHERE:
Donore and Kells, County Meath
BEST TIME TO GO:
Any time for the Visitor Centre and Newgrange (though Knowth is open only from Easter to October).
DON'T MISS:
The clematis walk at Grove Gardens, containing over 300 species of large and small flowering hybrids.
AMOUNT OF WALKING:
Lots
COST:
Reasonable (veering towards expensive if Visitor Centre entry is combined with both Newgrange and Knowth tours).
YOU SHOULD KNOW:
Access to Newgrange and Knowth is limited to 700 people per day. It is therefore wise to arrive at Brú na Bóinne Visitor Centre in good time, especially in high season, to be sure of getting a booking on an early tour to avoid a potentially long wait. Note that Newgrange (24 people) and Knowth (48 people) are separate tours, each lasting 75 minutes.

Dundalk Sportsbowl and County Museum

Once upon a time, ten-pin bowling was, well, just ten-pin bowling. Not any more. Nowadays, the places once known as bowling alleys offer a complete entertainment package. And so it is with Dundalk Sportsbowl in the town's Racecourse Road. Of course it's still possible to bowl, using computerized lanes with bumpers to redirect wayward balls for the benefit of beginners.

But that's just the start. Tumble Towers is a multi-level play centre, with sections for under and over fives. There are slides, ball pools and more, while parents can relax in Martha's Vineyard restaurant watching their kids at play. Bigger youngsters who wouldn't be seen dead in soft-play areas may have to be surgically separated from the pool/snooker tables and/or the numerous video and arcade games. The café will be a hit with all ages – it sells naughty-but-nice meals like an all-day breakfast and burgers or chicken nuggets with chips.

Staying at the Sportsbowl all day might break the bank, so bailing out to the County Museum could be a prudent move. This splendid facility is located in a restored 18th-century warehouse in Jocelyn Street's Roden Place, close to the town centre. It has permanent exhibitions, temporary themed displays, drama, music, film and lectures. Even if there are no special events to attend, a visit is still a most interesting experience – even for children, providing only that they have enquiring minds.

The ground floor features a display entitled from From Farm to Factory, with exhibits open for close inspection – including a locally built Heinkel bubble car. The first floor has fascinating historical artefacts including Oliver Cromwell's shaving mirror and the jerkin worn by William of Orange at the battle of the Boyne, complete with musket-ball hole. The top floor covers the area's extensive and significant archaeology.

Pirates' Den and Dundalk Ice Dome

Starting young, the Pirates' Den Adventure Centre (in Coe's Road off the Dundalk Bypass north of the town centre) offers stimulating supervised play for children – from babies upwards, though it's not for teens. The den is a large, child-friendly indoor play arena with three levels and a variety of energy-intensive activities to choose from.

Babes can crawl and roll to their hearts' content in a large area packed with tempting soft toys. Over twos have their own zone with slides, a ball pool, rope bridge and interactive sound equipment. Over fives graduate to the Kids' Zone with three-level climbing, a huge ball pool, rope bridges, an aerial runway, swing ropes and five slides. The café overlooks the play area for exhausted (by just watching the frantic fun) mums and dads. Play time is booked in 90-minute sessions.

For older children a good alternative to the Pirates' Den is the Dundalk Ice Dome, in Dundalk Retail Park off the town's Eastern Bypass. This is Ireland's only permanent indoor Olympic-sized rink, where the country's top figure skaters are trained and numerous ice hockey teams practise – but there is public skating available every day for those who know their way around the ice (in the afternoons during the week and all day at weekends).

If there are keen but untutored kids in the family, there are one-hour classes for beginners on Wednesdays from 19.30 to 20.30 and Fridays from 17.15 to 18.15 (mums and dads who are not ashamed to admit that they can't skate are welcome, too). Of course it's also possible to learn by trial and error during public sessions, though it's wise to stick to the perimeter of the ice, as many of the skaters are seriously fast. The Ice Bar and Bistro serves delicious fresh food.

WHERE:
Dundalk, County Louth
BEST TIME TO GO:
Any time
DON'T MISS:
Figure skaters at the spring, Halloween and Christmas shows at Dundalk Ice Dome offer spectacular entertainment. Others might be tempted by the Disco on Ice, held every Friday evening from 20.00.
AMOUNT OF WALKING:
Little (but plenty of sliding)
COST:
Reasonable (both attractions charge by the session so you only pay for what you want).
YOU SHOULD KNOW:
Although the Pirates' Den does offer supervised play, it is a requirement that parents keep a watchful eye on their kids as they hurl themselves into the activities on offer.

Ice hockey is all action with lots of thrills and spills.

Belturbet Station and Killykeen Forest Park

The day begins in the pleasing town of Belturbet on the banks of the River Erne, where the main attraction is the restored station in Railway Road. This used to be the meeting point for two lines – the GNR broad-gauge and the Cavan & Leitrim narrow-gauge Railways – until the station closed in 1959.

The historic stone-built station, completed in 1885, has been completely refurbished. The Visitor Centre provides fascinating insight into the important part Belturbet Station played in local life. There is a terrific display of memorabilia and railway-related artefacts, while the collection also includes rolling stock that is currently being restored. An audio-visual presentation features original footage of the Cavan & Leitrim Railway, while keynote displays cover the history of Belturbet Station and the people who worked there, the Great Northern Railway, Arigna Tramway and the steamship *Belturbet*.

The afternoon can be spent enjoying a relaxing family outing amid the stunning scenery of Cavan's lakelands, the county's enduring claim to natural fame. Stock up on picnic fare and head out of Belturbet on the N87 road, soon turning left onto the R201 that runs via Milltown and the shores of Lough Oughter to Killeshandra. From there, follow the R199 until finding Killykeen Forest Park signed to the left.

This magical place is woven around the waters and islands of Lough Oughter and cries out to be explored. There is mixed woodland and the remains of early fortifications such as crannog lake dwellings are scattered throughout the park. There are marked forest walks and nature trails to follow – from a manageable 1.5 km (1 mi) to 2.8 km (2 mi) in length – and this peaceful haven is alive with birdsong and wildlife. Enjoy strolling through leafy glades and having that picnic on the lakeshore.

Dunbrody Famine Ship and The Berkeley Costume and Toy Museum

WHERE:
New Ross, County Wexford
BEST TIME TO GO:
Easter to September
DON'T MISS:
In high season – the opportunity for children to take a ride in the Victorian goat carriage at Berkeley Forest House.
AMOUNT OF WALKING:
Little
COST:
Reasonable
YOU SHOULD KNOW:
The Irish Emigrant Wall of Honour at the Famine Ship pays tribute to the thousands of people who emigrated from their mother country in search of a better life over a period of two centuries to the early 1900s.

In 1845, the three-masted barque *Dunbrody* was built in Canada, though owned and operated by the Graves family of Wexford's New Ross. Although primarily a cargo carrier, she also took passengers. At the height of the Great Famine in 1847 over 300 starving Irish emigrants a time were crammed onto the ship, desperately seeking salvation in the New World.

Today, a precise replica of the 54-m (176-ft) *Dunbrody* may be seen and explored at her home port – and this will be an occasion the family will never forget, for it echoes the experience of those mid 19th-century emigrants hoping and praying for a better life. Today's visitors are first treated to an audio-visual presentation that tells the story of the Great Famine, a traumatic historical period that would shape the future of both Ireland and America.

Then it's all aboard, following in the footsteps of countless famine emigrants, using an 1849-style ticket that allocates the meagre space and food rations on offer for the voyage ahead. The *Dunbrody* is fitted out exactly as she would have been 160 years ago and actors, sound effects and smells transport visitors back in time. Emigrants explain the harrowing circumstances that have forced them to leave the land of their birth and a member of the crew talks about life on a sailing ship.

Moving on, another slice of history the kids will find interesting awaits at Berkeley Forest House, 5 km (3 mi) outside Wexford, signed from the N30 road. This fine Georgian house is home to The Berkeley Costume and Toy Museum, a fascinating private collection of 18th- and 19th-century carriages, costumes and dolls, plus toys dating from as far back as the 13th century. There is also a pretty garden and an area of raised bog where bog rosemary grows.

The Dunbrody *Famine Ship*

Ballykeenan House Pet Farm & Aviary and forest walk

WHERE:
Myshall, County Carlow
BEST TIME TO GO:
Summer for the mountain walking
DON'T MISS:
The tour of Ballykeenan House Pet Farm & Aviary conducted by a member of the McCord family. The owners are extremely enthusiastic about their charges and the tour is both entertaining and informative.

Animals and birds never fail to intrigue children and the chance to handle them is always a bonus, so pack a picnic and head for Ballykeenan House Pet Farm & Aviary. This hidden gem takes some finding but the experience that awaits the kids certainly justifies the effort. Ballykeenan House is signposted from the N80 Carlow-Rosslare road near Ballon and is on Kildavin Road close to Myshall village.

This 18th-century farm was once important, as numerous stone outbuildings surrounding the farmhouse testify. Nowadays the farmstead houses a host of animals and birds. Four-legged inhabitants include horses, ponies, deer, pigs, sheep, goats, dogs, chipmunks, hedgehogs, hamsters, gerbils, mice and guinea pigs.

Around 100 species of bird are also on display, from waddling

farmyard ducks and geese through turkeys and an assortment of poultry to colourful exotics in the aviaries. There is a feel-and-touch pet area where children can handle their little favourites, and also feed them. A pleasant picnic area provides just the spot for a leisurely *al fresco* meal, and should the rain come down, an indoor play area will keep youngsters happy until the sun comes out again.

Afterwards, that generous lunch can be walked off at the nearby Kilbrannish Forest Loop. Offering superb views of the surrounding Blackstairs Mountains, there are two signed trails to choose from. Both are pushchair-friendly and suitable for families with children. The Windfarm Loop is 3 km (2 mi) long and the name suggests the fact that four impressive wind turbines on Greenoge Hill fill the skyline. The 5-km (3-mi) Kilbrannish Forest Loop should take around two hours to complete and offers superb panoramic views from the summit of Croaghaun. Access the trails from Myshall, just up the road from Ballykeenan House, Borris or Bunclody.

AMOUNT OF WALKING:
Lots (if one of the walks is undertaken).
COST:
Low
YOU SHOULD KNOW:
Those aiming to be at Ballykeenan House on the last Sunday of the month not only get to enjoy all the fun of the farm, but also an unusual bring-and-buy car boot sale that features small animals and rare-breed poultry.

Walking the Kilbrannish Forest Loop.

National 1798 Centre and Ballymore Historic Features

WHERE:
Enniscorthy and Ballymore,
County Wexford
BEST TIME TO GO:
Summer (Ballymore Historic Features
has limited opening times – Sunday
afternoons in May and June, then
Fridays, Saturdays and Sundays in July
and August, plus Bank Holiday
Mondays).
DON'T MISS:
A themed 1798 play area the kids can
enjoy after visiting the exhibition area
at the National 1798 Centre, allowing
them to interact with the past in the
most entertaining of ways and
teaching them that great events which
shaped history are often themselves
determined by pure chance.
AMOUNT OF WALKING:
Moderate
COST:
Reasonable

The ancient town of Enniscorthy on the River Slaney is home to the National 1798 Centre. This commemorates the stirring events of that year, when Irish insurgents rose against harsh English rule and – assisted by French troops and ships – fought a series of skirmishes and battles against government forces.

The distinctive National 1798 Visitor Centre is in the shadow of Vinegar Hill, a location that played a significant part in an uprising which is seen today as the start of the Irish people's long march to self-determination and democracy. Children will be enthralled as the bloody events of 1798 are brought to life using the latest multi-media techniques. A spectacular audio-visual presentation puts this epic story's vital place in Irish history into the context of its time and a clever giant chess board explains the deadly game of strategy pursued by rebels and authorities alike.

After the most rewarding of history lessons in Enniscorthy, take a quick trip along the N11 road towards Dublin and find the signs for Ballymore Historic Features, near Camolin. Ballymore Historic Features is the place to go walkabout in an unusual open-air museum for a

The Tree of Liberty, a display in the National 1798 Centre

different slant on Irish history. This long-time home of the Donovan family has some intriguing historic sites to inspect, including a holy well, Norman motte and church complete with ancient graveyard.

The 18th-century farmyard has a hayloft museum containing a wonderful mixture of everyday country exhibits that include vintage clothing, old lace, embroidery, toys and old farm accounts. Traditional household items and dairy equipment are also on show, together with a waterwheel and a range of horse-drawn farm equipment. After enjoying the show, a cuppa and piece of cake in the tearoom, located within the reconstructed 19th-century glasshouse, is the perfect way to end the outing.

YOU SHOULD KNOW:
The 1798 Rebellion looms large in local history because the conflict was particularly brutal in County Wexford, with no fewer than 11 battles resulting in 20,000 people being killed in a four-week period – one sixth of the area's inhabitants. By way of sobering comparison, the contemporary French Revolution claimed 25,000 lives over six years out of a total population of 20,000,000.

Nore View Folk and Heritage Museum and Nore Valley Park

Overlooking magnificent scenery – with the Blackstairs Mountains and Mount Leinster as a spectacular backdrop – the charming village of Bennettsbridge beside the River Nore south of Kilkenny will provide any family with an interesting and rewarding day out. Contrasting attractions ensure variety that will appeal to children of all ages – as will the extraordinary display of bygones at Nore View Folk & Heritage Museum on the village outskirts.

Kids will be intrigued to see thousands of objects that once played a regular part in community living, together with re-creations of rural cornerstones like an old-time kitchen, dairy, pub, carpenter's workshop, forge, petrol station and horse-threshing area. Exhibits dating back to prehistoric times cover every aspect of local history and country life, with themed features on major events like the Great Famine and 1916 Easter Rising. Children used to seeing siblings in sleek buggies will think the old prams are hilarious and find it hard to believe that anyone ever had to make do with one of many vintage bicycles on display. Other strengths are old musical instruments and church-related artefacts. The museum offers a window on a vanished world that will be a real eye-opener for one and all.

After those fascinating but static displays, the kids may be ready to blow off some steam, and that's where Nore Valley Park comes into its own. This activity centre and open farm offers the appealing combination of animals galore (small pets to cuddle, lambs or kids to bottle feed and greedy poultry just waiting to be fed) with action (Wild West fort, giant chess, sandpit with diggers, pedal go-karts, crazy golf, swings, slides and straw bounce). The kids will just love sampling all the fun of the farm, which is just south of Bennettsbridge off the R700 road.

WHERE:
Bennettsbridge, County Kilkenny
BEST TIME TO GO:
March to October (though summer is best for open-air farm frolics).
DON'T MISS:
Bennettsbridge is an important craft centre with a number of quality outlets – find time to visit one of the best, the Nicholas Mosse Pottery with its colourful wares located in an old flour mill beside the River Nore, where it's possible to browse in the shop, have a snack and watch pots being thrown.
AMOUNT OF WALKING:
Moderate (to lots, if Nore Valley Park is thoroughly explored).
COST:
Reasonable (entry to Nore Valley Park is inexpensive but there are further charges for individual activities like pedal go-karts or tractor-and-trailer rides).
YOU SHOULD KNOW:
Nore Valley Park is closed on Sundays. There are indoor possibilities there, such as a three-level maze, to occupy the kids if the heavens open – plus picnic areas and a lovely riverside walk if the weather's set fair.

Kilfane Glen & Waterfall and Reptile Village

WHERE:
Thomastown and Gowran,
County Kilkenny
BEST TIME TO GO:
Kilfane Glen & Waterfall is open
during July and August only, from
11.00 to 18.00.
DON'T MISS:
An impressive display of modern
sculpture pieces in wonderful natural
settings beside the paths that wind
through the top part of Kilfane Glen.
AMOUNT OF WALKING:
Lots (and Kilfane Glen is definitely
worth the effort).
COST:
Reasonable
YOU SHOULD KNOW:
Reptile Village has a conservation
programme that involves captive
breeding of many species, including
some rare or endangered creatures.
Animals that have given birth or laid
eggs include boa constrictors,
white-lipped pit vipers, frilled dragons
and knight anoles (aggressive lizards
from Cuba, in case you were
wondering).

Children and open-to-the-public gardens may not seem like a recipe for the ideal outing, but the kids won't be disappointed by a day that starts at Kilfane Glen & Waterfall. This is one of the finest surviving examples of a late 18th-century romantic garden to be found anywhere, having been meticulously restored after a century and more of neglect, and there couldn't be a more impressive setting for the relaxed togetherness of a family stroll.

The whole idea was to inject drama into the landscape, and to that end Sir John Power and his wife created this wild garden in the 1790s. A wooded valley with towering rock faces and rugged outcrops was subtly transformed by changing the course of a stream to create a stunning waterfall that is the highlight of the walk. But there are other features that children will enjoy, like a thatched summerhouse beside the cascade and a grotto that cries out to be explored, plus rustic seats, bridges and fountains. Find Kilfane Glen signed from the N9 road north of Thomastown, opposite the Long Man pub.

Round off the day by zipping up the N9 to Gowran, where Reptile Village will soon have the kids oohing and aahing – in horror and delight. This fascinating facility is Ireland's only reptile zoo and it has around 50 cold-blooded species on display, from crocodiles to chameleons via snakes, geckos and iguanas. This is not only the place to marvel at the great selection of reptiles, amphibians and invertebrates, but also the place to handle (some of) them. Interaction with the animals involves only safe, vetted species under the direction of an experienced curator but that fact will not lessen the kids' excitement by one iota.

Castlecomer Discovery Park

WHERE:
Castlecomer, County Kilkenny
BEST TIME TO GO:
Any time (in addition to indoor
activities, the nature trails offer
something different in every season).
DON'T MISS:
The herd of sika and fallow deer,
together with a small flock of Jacob
sheep, that may be seen in the
walled garden near the Visitor Centre
at the Castlecomer Discovery Park.

Situated 16 km (10 mi) north of Kilkenny on the N78 road, Castlecomer – with 1,500 inhabitants – sits at the confluence of three rivers and is the unofficial capital of North Kilkenny. It also offers the promise of a wonderful family day out at Castlecomer Discovery Park, situated through impressive iron gates just north of the town. The park occupies the landscaped grounds of Castlecomer House, a now-vanished mansion that was once the heart of Wandesforde Estate.

Today, this special place offers a large expanse of parkland and mixed woodland as the setting for a variety of activities that will happily occupy a full day. The magnificent Visitor Centre is located in the estate's former farmyard, beside the kitchen gardens. The old buildings have been restored and now serve as units full of interesting craft work.

The Visitor Centre presents a fascinating interactive experience entitled Footprints in Coal, which not only tells the tale of three centuries of coal mining in the area, but also features insight into prehistory helped by the fact that miners discovered many important fossils during the course of their underground operations.

The extensive grounds adjoin the River Deen and have 6 km (4 mi) of splendid themed woodland walks, with three main colour-coded nature trails with interlinking paths around two fishing lakes linked by cascades. These routes pass a number of striking wooden sculptures and have secluded picnic areas for those who prefer to bring their own lunch rather than use the Visitor Centre's excellent Jarrow Café. Picnic tables are also provided beside the river and children's playground. The latter is sure to be a hit with kids under 14, offering hours of energetic fun on themed timber apparatus that reflects the prehistoric and mining themes of the Footprints in Coal exhibition.

AMOUNT OF WALKING:
Lots (but this can be appropriately tailored to the children's capabilities as there are options that require different amounts of walking).
COST:
Reasonable
YOU SHOULD KNOW:
The two lakes that now form the scenic trout fishery were – unusually for Ireland, which is not short of natural aquatic features – created by the Wandesforde family to enhance their estate. The lower lake is for experienced fly fishermen but the upper lake offers bait fishing – ideal for beginners – with tackle hire available for those who want to have a go.

The Visitor Centre at Castlecomber Discovery Park

Waterford Treasures and Bilberry goat herd

WHERE:
Waterford Town, County Waterford
BEST TIME TO GO:
Any time is right, though summer
weather can be a valuable bonus.
DON'T MISS:
In the Granary Museum – the splendidly
worked Magi Cope, part of the only
complete set of pre-Reformation
priest's vestments to survive in the
British Isles, after being hidden from
Oliver Cromwell in Waterford's Christ
Church Cathedral and rediscovered in
the 18th century.
AMOUNT OF WALKING:
Moderate to lots (the latter for those
who take that interesting stroll to meet
the goats).
COST:
Low (with very affordable family tickets
available for Waterford Treasures).
YOU SHOULD KNOW:
In the 19th century the Bilberry goat
herd was a valuable common resource,
as the women of Ballybricken would go
up via Lady's Walk to milk the goats.

In the Granary Museum on Waterford's Merchants Quay an extraordinary collection of historical artefacts has been assembled. If that sounds dull for children, it isn't – the magnificent Waterford Treasures are so impressive that curiosity will surely be piqued (and at the very least kids will climb a useful learning curve).

This award-winning museum's superb displays cover a millennium of ethnic, cultural and religious diversity, explaining the fascinating history of Ireland's oldest city. The story starts with 10th-century Vikings and travels forward to the present. Along the way extraordinary exhibits attest to the power and influence of Waterford over the years. The city's own historic memorabilia is combined with stunning finds made during excavations started in the 1980s and there are seven entertaining audio-visual presentations plus three interactive pods where children (and parents!) can do their own thing.

Thousands of exhibits range from the humble (like one of Ireland's earliest known dog collars, from the 1100s) through the devout (such as the carved 13th-century head of a Dominican monk) to the regal (notably the only surviving piece of Henry VIII's personal clothing, a cap of maintenance awarded to the Mayor of Waterford in 1536 along with a bearing sword).

After browsing through all those unburied treasures it's time for a walk on the wild side of Waterford, to see some living history. The area around the town's Bilberry Rock is the place to see a herd of feral goats that became established when persecuted French Huguenots brought the goats' ancestors to Ireland in the 17th century. With their long beards, shaggy coats and heavy crooked horns, the goats are unique survivors unlike any modern domestic goats. Having the opportunity to meet these striking creatures during the course of a leisurely walk is a great way to end the Waterford day out.

Copper Coast Mini Farm and Bunmahon Beach

The Copper Coast is so called because it used to be the historic centre of Ireland's metal-mining industry, and the relics of that era have become a major tourist draw. However, this is not the day to go walking along cliff tops seeking old mine workings. Instead, the children can be treated to the familiar but never-failing appeal of one of Ireland's most popular attractions, the open farm.

The one in today's frame is Copper Coast Mini Farm near Fenor on the Tramore to Dungarvan road (the R765), which is part of the scenic southeast coastal drive. The kids will have the opportunity to see a good selection of interesting animals including pot-bellied pigs, pet sheep, calves, llamas, alpacas, donkeys, miniature ponies, pygmy goats, chipmunks, chinchillas, wallabies and zebras. There is also plenty of poultry strutting about the place and petting baby bunnies in the covered pet area never fails to delight younger children.

WHERE:
Fenor and Bunmahon,
County Waterford
BEST TIME TO GO:
This is definitely a sunny summer
day out.
DON'T MISS:
The extra dimension that can
entertain children for some time – a
splendid children's playground just
behind Bunmahon Beach.
AMOUNT OF WALKING:
Moderate; the Copper Coast Mini
Farm is pushchair-friendly.
COST:
Reasonable (a family ticket offers
discounted admission to the farm).
YOU SHOULD KNOW:
Should it rain there are indoor play
and picnic facilities at the Copper
Coast Mini Farm, plus a Copper
Kettle Tea Room that serves hearty
homemade fare.

Other activities on offer include sandpits with buckets and spades, plus mini diggers and toy tractors just waiting to be driven. There are speedy pedal go-karts for older children (up to the age of 14) and green areas for football or Frisbee. The farm also has a great collection of vintage farm memorabilia to admire.

After doing some mini-farming, the rest of the day can be spent on Bunmahon Beach. The former mining village of Bunmahon (once home to 21 pubs) is also on the R765, towards Dungarvan from Fenor. Bunmahon's superb, sheltered beach is enclosed by headlands and is backed by a thin strip of sand dunes. There is lifeguard coverage and the kids will love the surf, which is exciting without being dangerous. If ever there was a place to enjoy uninhibited beach fun, this is it.

Bunmahon Strand Copper Coast

Around Cashel

The Rock of Cashel may be one of Ireland's most famous tourist sites, but a family day out in this historic town should begin at Cashel Folk Village, crouching at the foot of 'The Rock'. This splendid museum presents living history at its best, bringing times past vividly to life. A charming thatched cottage off the main road serves as a gateway to Old Ireland.

Cashel Folk Village contains reconstructions featuring traditional country premises such as a farmhouse, shop-cum-pub, butcher's shop and blacksmith's forge, together with a penal chapel (an example of the humble places of worship used by Catholics when practise of their religion was banned). There's also that essential element of the bygone country scene, a tinker's caravan, plus numerous artefacts and old signs.

Another important aspect of Irish history is covered – Ireland's struggle for independence, in which freedom fighters from Tipperary played a significant role. The village contains a Celtic cross erected in memory of the 1916 Easter Rising, together with an impressive collection of guns, medals, photographs of participants and general memorabilia.

But of course the mighty Rock of Cashel must be the day's highlight. This limestone outcrop in the Golden Vale is topped by a spectacular group of medieval buildings, with access from Dublin Road close to the town centre. The site is entered through the restored 15th-century Hall of the Vicars Choral and the huge complex includes a 12th-century round tower, High Crosses, Romanesque Cormac's Chapel with important early wall paintings, ruined 13th-century Gothic Cathedral, fortified 15th-century Archbishop's tower house and extensive graveyard.

Together, they form one of the most remarkable surviving examples of medieval architecture and Celtic art anywhere in Europe. The 45-minute guided tour and 17-minute audio-visual presentation will help children and parents alike to appreciate the historical context of this wonderfully special place.

WHERE:
Cashel, South Tipperary
BEST TIME TO GO:
March to October for Cashel Folk Village (but ideally not on a high summer weekend, when the Rock of Cashel is sure to be extremely crowded).
DON'T MISS:
The Rock of Cashel Museum, by the main entrance, which has many interesting Rock-related exhibits and explains the legendary origins of this evocative reminder of Ireland's medieval greatness.
AMOUNT OF WALKING:
Moderate
COST:
Reasonable (with a family ticket at 'The Rock' representing excellent value).
YOU SHOULD KNOW:
The Rock of Cashel is also known as St Patrick's Rock or Cashel of the Kings, as it was the seat of High Kings of Munster long before the Norman invasion and is said to be the place where St Patrick converted King Aenghus to Christianity in the 5th century.

Rock of Cashel

Mitchelstown Cave and Cahir Castle

Mitchelstown Cave

Halfway between Cork and Cashel off the N8 road, Mitchelstown Cave is one of the most spectacular cavern complexes in Europe. It's located in the foothills of the Galty Mountains near the village of Burncourt, signed from the main road at Kilbeheny, and the family will be awestruck by this extraordinary natural phenomenon.

The cave system extends to 3 km (2 mi) but the guided tour covers a manageable kilometre that's within the compass of even smaller children. Timeless sights within three massive caverns are breathtaking, encompassing dramatic showpieces like stalactites (down!), stalagmites (up!), dripstone formations, calcite curtains and glistening crystals. The Tower of Babel is one of Europe's most impressive subterranean columns, though the aptly named Organ Pipes runs it close.

Temperature within the dry caves is comfortable – cool in summer, warm in winter – so no special clothing is required. One family has owned Mitchelstown Cave since its discovery and their proud boast is that no words can do this special place justice – you have to see for yourself. On to the day's other attraction, then!

Some 15 km (10 mi) further up the N8, the charming Heritage Town of Cahir has one asset kids will find irresistible – Cahir Castle, an ancient fortress that seems to have grown from the living rock on an island in the River Suir, right in the centre of town. This imposing structure was built between the 13th and 15th centuries and it remains one of the largest and best-preserved castles in all Ireland.

It just cries out to be explored – but not before seeing the excellent audio-visual presentation that dramatically describes the castle's history (latterly somewhat ignoble – it surrendered to Cromwell in 1650 without a shot being fired). Take the informative guided tour or simply wander around this magical fortress at leisure.

WHERE:
Burncourt and Cahir, South Tipperary
BEST TIME TO GO:
Both attractions are open all year.
DON'T MISS:
When in Cahir it's the done thing to visit the famous Swiss Cottage, just outside town on the R670 road to Ardfinnan. This extraordinary thatched confection was designed by the famous Regency architect John Nash and is a perfect example of the then-popular cottage *orné*, a romantic folly designed to enhance the countryside (closed on Mondays).
AMOUNT OF WALKING:
Lots
COST:
Reasonable
YOU SHOULD KNOW:
Mitchelstown Cave was discovered in 1833 by a labourer who was quarrying limestone and dropped his crowbar into a crevice. When Michael Condon moved a few rocks in an attempt to retrieve it he found himself looking into a vast cavern that would become a major Victorian tourist attraction, as curious spectators were guided through the underground wonderland by candlepower and lamp light. Happily, electric lighting and proper footways were installed in the 1970s.

Nenagh Heritage Centre and Lough Derg cruise

WHERE:
Nenagh and Lough Derg,
North Tipperary
BEST TIME TO GO:
Summer
DON'T MISS:
In the old prison gatehouse at
Nenagh Heritage Centre – cells
occupied by condemned men and
the execution area where they
paid the ultimate price for their
(often fairly minor by today's
standards) crimes.

Prison governors must have been important (though not necessarily well-loved) people in Irish rural society – as the imposing 19th-century house in Nenagh that was home to the North Tipperary County Gaol's Governor testifies. Nowadays, it serves as a Heritage Centre that brilliantly recaptures the flavour of not-so-long-vanished Irish country life. This should be a real eye-opener for kids raised on fast food and computer games, proving fascinating to enquiring young minds.

This special museum provides a window into intriguing bygone places like a re-created 1913 schoolroom, a classic country bar and grocery store, a dairy that illustrates butter making the old-fashioned farmhouse way and the original 19th-century kitchen from North Tipperary Gaol. The Museum of Rural Life contains hundreds of old implements, utensils and equipment used every day in times past. There is a model of the old gaol complex and the Heritage Gallery in the Lough Derg Room hosts a rolling programme of art or

photographic exhibitions, or information shows on a variety of subjects with a Tipperary connection. There is also a genealogical research facility.

The afternoon can be spent enjoying a relaxing cruise amid the fabulous scenery of Lough Derg, with various comfortable waterbuses offering trips that pass pretty waterside villages and weave between the Lough's many islands, including the most famous of all – Inis Cealtra (Holy Island), the site of a 7th-century monastic settlement. There are sailings from Killaloe, Banagher and Dromineer, just along the R495 road from Nenagh.

The latter is home to the popular *Ku ee tu* (an excruciating pun based on the fact that this luxurious 53-seat waterbus used to be a tender belonging to the famous liner). The kids will love going afloat and an informed commentary will ensure that they appreciate all the interesting sights to be seen along the way.

AMOUNT OF WALKING:
Little
COST:
Free (Nenagh Heritage Centre) to reasonable (if Lough Derg cruise is included).
YOU SHOULD KNOW:
It is advisable to book the family's Lough Derg cruise in advance, as sailing times vary and demand for all sailings can be keen in high season.

Beara Peninsula

WHERE:
Counties Kerry and Cork
BEST TIME TO GO:
Any time (though winter wind and rain can be off-putting).
DON'T MISS:
The last cable car back from Dursey Island to the mainland, thus avoiding an unplanned overnight stay.
AMOUNT OF WALKING:
Lots
COST:
Low (there is a small charge for visitors making the return trip to Dursey Island).
YOU SHOULD KNOW:
The Dursey Island Cable Car service runs at the following times: 09.00 to 11.00; 14.30 to 17.00; 19.00 to 20.00. Sunday hours are slightly shorter, though the evening session remains unchanged.

For a wonderful family day out in the bracing sea air of Ireland's west coast, the Beara Peninsula takes some beating. It's south of the famous Ring of Kerry but lacks the latter's intense tourist pressure, making for an altogether more relaxing experience. There is plenty to see and do, with picture-book villages like Eyeries awaiting discovery along with the fishing port of Castletownbere and nearby Dunboy Castle. This is a trip to do by car, stopping to explore as the mood dictates – not expecting to hurry, as roads are narrow and local traffic can be slow moving.

For the kids, the day's highlight will be a visit to Dursey Island, because it involves a return trip on Ireland's only cable car. This 'flying biscuit tin' is a lifeline for the few remaining islanders and runs from Ballaghboy on the Beara Peninsula's toe.

It only carries a few people at a time and with islanders (and/or their animals) having priority there can be a wait for the ten-minute trip. A bottle of holy water in the car is for emergency use only, or perhaps to ward off untoward happenings to ensure that an emergency never arises. It's also necessary to take everything the family might need – like a hearty picnic – as there are no shops or facilities on Dursey Island.

Dursey Island cable car

The cable car soars above Dursey Sound, where rip tides make boat crossings a hazardous business. Once ashore, this rocky island must be explored on foot. Apart from scattered hamlets there are whales and dolphins to be seen from the cliffs in season, while the seabird life is awesome. There is a 200-year-old signal tower at the western extremity, plus a graveyard and the remains of its church. The well-marked Beara Way walking trail extends to the island and encourages exploration.

Perks Family Entertainment Centre and Blackwater cruise

Whatever the weather, one outing that rain can't spoil may be found at Youghal (pronounced 'Yawl' for the uninitiated) on the Blackwater estuary. This picturesque seaport is not as important as it was in medieval times, but that doesn't stop it being a great place for a family day out.

Proclaiming that it has recently celebrated '80 years of Glorious Fun', the Perks Family Entertainment Centre is where it happens. As with a traditional fun fair, entry is free and there's a charge for individual attractions and activities, so budget-conscious parents need to be made of stern stuff. The centre is designed to appeal to children of all ages and the only problem is deciding where to start – and keeping an eye on the kids as they dash from treat to treat.

Many fun-fair rides are offered, including a classic carousel and the Safari Train. A plethora of games includes the all-action Megazone Lazer Shots. This comes complete with special effects like swirling fog and darting light, as combatants seek to zap opponents to the sound of pounding music – junior heaven! Other tempters are Ball Blast, video games, snooker and pool. Blackbeard's Play Centre is a 'must' for smaller kids, with three decks of hands-on play.

For those who would like to put a limit on indoor fun, a cruise on the half-decker *Maeve* could be the answer. The kids will love this old-fashioned fishing boat that sails up the Blackwater from Youghal jetty, offering a 90-minute river tour that passes through an unspoiled area of natural beauty. Along the way are impressive sights like the remains of Templemichael Castle, Molana Abbey and the magnificent Ballnatray House. There's only one snag – in delightfully Irish style the skipper has to be tracked down in order to book the trip.

WHERE:
Youghal, County Cork
BEST TIME TO GO:
May to September (if going afloat, though Perks Family Entertainment Centre is open all year round).
DON'T MISS:
A quick family workout at the accompanying East Cork Superbowl, with computerized scoring and bumpers/light balls to ensure that smaller children have a great time.
AMOUNT OF WALKING:
Little
COST:
Expensive (even if the Blackwater cruise isn't added, as it's hard to resist the kids' pleas to try just about everything at the Perks Family Entertainment Centre).
YOU SHOULD KNOW:
If 'all the fun of the fair' is a phrase that resonates with the kids, the Perks family has a wonderful traditional-fair-cum-theme-park at Salthill in Galway City that would also make for a super summer day out. It's grandly titled Perks Leisureland Funworld.

*Plenty of hands-on at the
Lifetime Lab*

Lifetime Lab and Blarney Castle

WHERE:
Cork City and Blarney, County Cork
BEST TIME TO GO:
Any time (though kissing the Blarney
Stone can mean a rather frigid
encounter in winter).
DON'T MISS:
Rock Close at Blarney Castle – a
romantic ramble with impressive
features like the Head Druid's Cave,
Druid's Circle, Sacrificial Altar, Witch's
Kitchen, Wishing Steps and Fairy
Glade. The Blarney estate also boasts
wonderful gardens and woodland
walks for families so inclined.
AMOUNT OF WALKING:
Moderate
COST:
Reasonable (family tickets are
available at both venues, with the
Lifetime Lab being especially
good value)
YOU SHOULD KNOW:
The Blarney Stone is a block of
bluestone, said to have been
presented to Cormac McCarthy by
Robert the Bruce after the Battle of
Bannockburn in 1314 – having been
detached from Scotland's famous
Stone of Scone – as a gesture of
thanks for Cormac's military support.
It was first installed in an earlier
fortress then set into the tower of
the 'new' Blarney Castle in 1446.

A waterworks might not seem the perfect starting point for a rewarding family day out, but this is the exception that proves the rule. Imposing industrial buildings that stand at the Cork Waterworks in Lee Road beside the river are now home to the Lifetime Lab. Not only has an important historic site that supplied the city's water from the 1760s been restored, but an experience that will fascinate, educate and inform children and parents alike has also been created.

The Visitor Centre is a former coal store and boiler house dating from the 1860s, perfectly illustrating the Victorian tendency to endow even the humblest working buildings with the best materials, assembled with meticulous attention to detail. There is a reception area, coffee dock and exhibition where kids can enjoy becoming environmental detectives as they explore the interactive exhibits, picking up clues along the way. The themes are water, waste, energy and Nature.

The Steam Centre contains boilers and huge steam engines that once pumped Cork's water, marvels of bygone manufacturing and engineering skills. This building has an amazing decorative chimney that is a city landmark. In addition to the fine buildings, the Lifetime Lab has a picnic area with scenic river views, a playground, sensory garden and willow tunnels.

For those who aspire to the gift of the gab, Blarney Castle is the place to go next. From Cork, find Ireland's most famous castle off to the left 8 km (5 mi) up the N20 road, in the workaday village of Blarney. The partially ruined 15th-century castle has accessible rooms and battlements, but the day's main business is hanging upside down to kiss the Blarney Stone, thus acquiring (if legend is to be believed) instant eloquence. Never again be lost for words!

Fota Wildlife Park

Around 10 km (6 mi) east of Cork City, just off the N25 road, the Zoological Society of Ireland's Fota Wildlife Park delivers a super day out with lots to see and do. There are many familiar animals, but this conservation facility also has endangered or vulnerable species, including some that could soon become extinct in the wild. These include cheetahs (Fota is the world's leading captive breeder of these super-fast cats), scimitar-horned oryx, lion-tailed macaque monkeys from India (just 800 left in the wild) and white-tailed sea eagles (extinct in Ireland but being reintroduced in Kerry).

At Fota most creatures live in natural surroundings, and seeing the likes of giraffes, zebras, ostriches and antelope roaming together much as they would in the African savannah is impressive. Other chirpy characters with licence to roam include colourful macaws, kangaroos and lemurs, while assorted moneys swing through the trees on lake islands.

Children appreciate wandering among the animals but lazybones can take the *Awacachi* or Maxi Zoo Tour Trains. Animals are fed twice daily (early and late) while a programme of talks starts at 10.45 and continues at regular intervals until 16.45, giving insight into some of the most interesting inhabitants. There is a picnic area, though the park has a café for diners without a packed lunch.

If the day isn't entirely consumed by wildlife delights, a family romp on Garryvoe Beach could provide a pleasing footnote to a great day out. This is a mixed sand-and-pebble beach in a stunning location (head for Youghal and turn right off the N25 at Castlemartyr for Garryvoe village). A Blue Flag attests that it's one of the finest beaches in the area and lifeguard cover during the holiday season reassures parents with youngsters who fancy taking the plunge.

WHERE:
Carrigtwohill and Garryvoe, County Cork
BEST TIME TO GO:
Summer (for the beach, though Fota Wildlife Park remains open all year).
DON'T MISS:
Fota's daily cheetah run that takes place at 16.00, weather permitting, preceded in summer by an informative talk. These speedy animals may not get up to their full top speed of 105 kph (65 mph) but it's still wonderful seeing them chase their dinner as dead rabbits or chickens speed along, suspended from overhead lines.
AMOUNT OF WALKING:
Moderate (or lots for anyone who wants it).
COST:
Expensive (but Fota Wildlife Park's hefty entry charge is justified by the experience that awaits).
YOU SHOULD KNOW:
Unlike many an open farm, feeding the animals is not an option at Fota Wildlife Park, as they have special diets and can be harmed by unsuitable foods offered by well-meaning visitors.

Admiring the lemurs at Fota Wildlife Park.

Crag Cave and Oceanworld

WHERE:
Castleisland and Dingle, County Kerry
BEST TIME TO GO:
Any time
DON'T MISS:
For children up to 12 years of age a
session in the Crazy Cave at the
Crag Cave location is great fun, with
indoor and outdoor play areas
offering slides, mazes, rope bridges,
ball pools, laser disco room and
more besides. Parents can watch
the action from the comfort of the
coffee shop.
AMOUNT OF WALKING:
Moderate to lots (the cave tour is not
short but perfectly manageable even
for smaller children).**COST:**

Watching Molly the turtle.

Not many people knew about Crag Cave before the 1980s – none, in fact. But following its discovery in 1983 this cavern at Castleisland (just off the N21 road) has become a major visitor attraction. Better still, it matters not if the rain comes down, for this is a dry underworld journey.

The cave was developed with the help of a man-made entrance shaft, pathways, railings . . . and a music system. The 30-minute guided tour will amaze kids, passing side passages that echo with the sound of running water, monumental caverns and a succession of awesome limestone formations, including numerous stalactites and stalagmites. Children find caves irresistible and will really appreciate this voyage of discovery.

After Crag Cave, head along the N21 and N86 roads via Tralee to the beautiful Dingle Peninsula. In Dingle Town, find Oceanworld on the waterfront opposite the harbour. This splendid aquarium imaginatively presents a wide selection of marine life, ensuring that kids will be thrilled by the series of varied presentations.

Included is a surge tank that replicates the action of the sea,

containing the likes of crabs, anemones and shellfish. A major highlight is the Amazonian area, with seven displays that showcase South American species like deadly piranhas, pacu and catfish, plus nasty natives like poisonous frogs. The tropical marine tanks contain a startling selection of brilliantly coloured fish, there's a sea-horse tank and touch pool where kids can handle starfish and stroke rays.

The ever-popular shark tank is home to reef sharks, fearsome sandtiger sharks, Molly the turtle, large rays and thousands of smaller fish. But perhaps the most awesome experience is the Ocean Tunnel's fish-eye view, where an extraordinary array of fish may be seen swimming around and above visitors . . . children are especially delighted to be in among the fish.

COST:
Expensive (if both attractions are visited, though both offer discounted family tickets).
YOU SHOULD KNOW:
Take a good map and beware of the signposts – Dingle (sorry, An Daingean) is in the Gaeltacht area where the Irish language is spoken and English versions of local place names no longer appear on road signs, though helpful locals occasionally spray on former Anglicized names to help out tourists who are vital to the local economy.

Eclipse Centre and Kissane Sheep Farm

It's possible to spend a whole activity holiday at the Eclipse Centre (which has self-catering holiday homes) – so spending half a day or more there should mean that the family's spoiled for choice. Find it signed at Moll's Gap some 30 km (19 mi) along the R568 road, which branches off the N71 road from Killarney – part of the delightful Ring of Kerry that will make a great contribution to the day in its own right.

Eclipse's Equestrian and Activity Centre has horses and ponies suitable for all family members over the age of seven. It offers custom treks on scenic off-road routes that can encompass meadows, moorland, forests, rivers and streams. Lessons can be booked for kids who want to sample life in the saddle. For non-horsey types it's possible to select from a range of exciting supervised activities, with different options to suit individual family members. These include salmon and trout fishing, archery, rough-track cycling, climbing and kayaking.

If the day hasn't been activitied away at the Eclipse Centre, Kissane Sheep Farm will welcome the kids for a stopover on the way back. It's located on the N71 between Moll's Gap and Ladies' View. These are both famous for wonderful views so yet more spectacular scenery will be enjoyed. Once at the working Kissane Farm, a visit will combine sheep galore (plus lots of adorable lambs) with fun activities like a Puzzle Walk and Adventure Trail and possibilities like three marked mountain trails for families that like a walk on the wild side.

But the happenings that will really entertain the kids are sheep-shearing sessions and impressive sheepdog working demonstrations. End the visit with a tasty snack in the barn, where smaller children can get stuck into the ever-popular task of colouring in farm pictures.

WHERE:
Blackwater Bridge (near Killarney) and Moll's Gap (near Kenmare), County Kerry
BEST TIME TO GO:
June to August for Kissane Sheep Farm (closed Sunday and Monday, limited opening with some demonstrations in April, May and September).
DON'T MISS:
Bottle feeding the orphan lambs at Kissane Sheep Farm, an activity that never fails to delight children.
AMOUNT OF WALKING:
Moderate to lots (for those who choose to stride out).
COST:
Reasonable to expensive (depending on chosen activity/activities at the Eclipse Centre).
YOU SHOULD KNOW:
It's possible to 'Adopt a Sheep' at the Kissane Sheep Farm, to help preserve the longstanding Irish heritage of mountain sheep-farming in this beautiful area of County Kerry.

Beal Lodge Dairy Farm and Lartigue Monorailway

WHERE:
Asdee and Listowel, County Kerry
BEST TIME TO GO:
May to September (to ride the rail)
DON'T MISS:
The site of the original Listowel and Ballybunion Railway terminus in a park right next to the current Lartigue site, where the base of two turntables and foundations of the old engine house have been preserved. It's an ideal picnic area.
AMOUNT OF WALKING:
Moderate
COST:
Reasonable
YOU SHOULD KNOW:
The Listowel Ballybunion Railway opened in 1888, linking the two towns, and was the world's first passenger monorail. The system invented by French engineer Charles Lartigue was trialled in North Kerry, but sadly for lovers of quirky railways the idea didn't catch on elsewhere and the Listowel to Ballybunion line was never a commercial success. It closed in 1924.

Start and end the day with two things the kids have never seen before and should find rather interesting. The first falls under a heading that ought to be on every modern family's knowledge agenda – where the food really comes from. Yes, this is a valuable lesson that will be learned during a visit to Beal Lodge Dairy Farm, one of relatively few organic dairy farms in Ireland, to see farmhouse cheese making in progress.

This go-ahead rural establishment is in an idyllic spot at Asdee beside the mouth of the River Shannon. There's an opportunity to watch a video explaining how cheese is made, then see the process in action for real – before sampling the delicious result. Beal Lodge has Holstein cows, pigs, ducks and chickens. There's a children's play area, too.

Should the sun be shining and the opportunity of fitting in an hour or two of beach time appeal, Blue Flag Ballybunion North Beach is just 8 km (5 mi) down the road from Asdee – and it's as good a strand as any on Ireland's west coast. But don't linger for too long, as a trip on the extraordinary Lartigue Monorailway awaits back at Listowel and the last train leaves at 14.30.

Located in Listowel Town's John B Keane Road, this extraordinary piece of railway history is also unlike anything the kids will ever have seen. It's a unique creation – a Victorian train that runs on a raised track, with loco and carriages straddling one central rail. The Lartigue Monorailway's line and rolling stock are exact replicas rather than restored originals but there is a good stretch of track, plus three platforms and two turntables. Before enjoying the ride, the Museum and Interpretative Centre in an old goods shed explains all about this amazing railway.

Foynes Flying Boat Museum and Nature Trails of Aughinish

WHERE:
Foynes and Aughinish,
County Limerick
BEST TIME TO GO:
Summer allows visitors to see the beautiful butterflies of Aughinish, though birdwatchers prefer the winter months for the abundant estuary birdlife.

It may seem hard to believe today, but Foynes was once the centre of the world's embryonic airline industry. After being surveyed by aviation pioneer Charles Lindburgh, this quiet little town on the River Shannon became the focus of air traffic across the North Atlantic between 1939 and 1945.

During World War II flying was the only (relatively) safe way of getting to and from Europe and the USA, so many important people used Pan Am's service – including President Roosevelt's wife Eleanor (travelling as 'Mrs Smith'). The first non-stop passenger flight from Foynes to New York took place in 1942, with the Boeing Clipper's historic crossing taking a numbing 25 hours and 40 minutes. The pilot was Captain Charlie Blair, later husband to Hollywood star Maureen O'Hara, and he also piloted the last Clipper flight in 1945, after which the service was provided by conventional airliners flying into nearby Shannon.

A dozen Boeing 314 Clippers were built, though none of these classics survives. Happily, the Foynes Flying Boat Museum has an exact replica of a Boeing 314. This allows visitors to appreciate just what travelling on one of these famous aircraft was like while the museum in the original terminal building – complete with original radio room and weather centre – explains this brief but romantic chapter in aviation history.

Flight of an altogether gentler sort is the keynote of the day's second visit, to the Nature Trails of Aughinish on the south bank of the Shannon Estuary, close to Foynes. Here, a disused quarry has been transformed into a butterfly sanctuary by careful habitat management designed to sustain native Irish species. There's more – numerous tranquil trails through meadows, woodland, heath and beside the saltmarsh. This magical wild place is perfect for a rewarding family ramble, ideally prefaced by a tasty picnic.

DON'T MISS:
Hunt's Lough at Aughinish, where delights like the four-spotted chaser and blue-tailed damselfly may be seen disporting themselves at Ireland's first dragonfly sanctuary.
AMOUNT OF WALKING:
Moderate to lots (if all the nature trails of Aughinish are explored).
COST:
Reasonable (under fives go free at the Flying Boat Museum).
YOU SHOULD KNOW:
Irish coffee was invented by Brendan O'Reagan, who had a restaurant and coffee shop at the Foynes Terminal. In 1942 he came up with the idea of lacing hot coffee with Irish whiskey before pouring on thick cream, thus fortifying waiting passengers. Nowadays there's an annual Irish Coffee Festival at Foynes every summer to celebrate this classic concoction.

Foynes Flying Boat Museum

King John's Castle and Bunratty Castle & Folk Park

WHERE:
Limerick City, County Limerick and Bunratty, County Clare
BEST TIME TO GO:
April to September
DON'T MISS:
The Bunratty Walled Garden, built in 1804 to supply Bunratty House with flowers, fruit and vegetables and now refurbished to reflect its Regency origins and Victorian heyday.
AMOUNT OF WALKING:
Lots (but well worth the effort).
COST:
Reasonable to expensive (it's pricey if both attractions are visited by a large family).
YOU SHOULD KNOW:
As Lord of Ireland, King John had coins struck in his stronghold's mint – and today's visitors can receive their own newly minted coin as a souvenir of their tour of King John's Castle.

One of the many demonstrations at Bunratty Castle & Folk Park

This is the day when two terrific old castles make up the agenda, starting in Limerick City. There, King John's Castle is on King's Island overlooking the mighty River Shannon – a stronghold built around 1200 on the orders, as the name suggests, of England's infamous King John, would-be master of Ireland. The morning can happily be spent discovering history at its best, appreciating a major historical exhibition, excavated pre-Norman houses, siege mines and great views from the battlements.

Moving on up the N18 road from Limerick, Bunratty is signed to the right. Standing proud in the village centre is Bunratty Castle, a tower house in beautiful grounds that dates from the 15th century. Ireland's most authentic medieval fortress is impressive. Following restoration in the 1950s, the place was filled with an extraordinary collection of 15th- and 16th-century furniture, tapestries and works of art, underlining the fine quality of life enjoyed by Ireland's high and mighty.

The much less opulent lifestyle of toiling workers is illustrated by Bunratty Folk Park beneath the castle's walls, which vividly creates a later era in Irish rural life – the late 19th century. Actors in period costume (and character – what characters they are!) bring a village containing over 30 buildings to life, as visitors stroll around discovering the school, post office, hardware shop, doctor's

premises, printer's workshop, pawnbroker's and pub . . . among other typical establishments. Georgian Bunratty House serves as a reminder that landowners continued to live well.

This is living history children will identify with, combining the sights, sounds and village people of a bygone age. Note that Bunratty Castle closes at 16.00 each day so that staff may start to prepare for the nightly medieval banquet, though last admission to the Folk Park is at 16.15.

Doolin Cave and Moher Hill Open Farm

At Doolin near Liscannor, deep beneath the lunar-limestone landscape of Burren country, lies Doolin Cave. This magnificent cave complex was discovered by potholers in 1952 and the stunning one-hour tour will certainly impress the kids at the start of a great day out.

After donning hard hats and descending over 25 m (80 ft) into the first tunnel, visitors enter an eerie underground world carved by water – the Burren has many rivers, all but one of which follow a subterranean course. The journey through rough-hewn passages does not disappoint, with a stunning climax as a cathedral-like cavern is reached, bisected by a fast-flowing stream. After a moment of intense darkness, subtle lighting comes on to dramatically reveal Doolin's star attraction – the Great Stalactite, a monstrous spike hanging from the cave roof that measures 7.3 m (23 ft) in length. Having viewed this awesome natural phenomenon, the kids will be able to brag that they've seen the largest stalactite in the northern hemisphere.

At nearby Liscannor, in a magnificent setting overlooking the sea, Moher Hill Open Farm has a wonderfully Irish slogan: 'We can't guarantee sun but can certainly guarantee fun'. This boast seems justified by indoor facilities that include go-karts and a bouncy castle. But hopefully the weather will be in benign mood, for the open farm's outdoor attractions are compelling.

There is a huge selection of animals and birds to look at including deer, ponies, pot-bellied pigs, donkeys, cows, sheep, goats, peacocks and a host of rare farmyard fowl. Cuddly rabbits are among the creatures children can handle. To that may be added the opportunity to play a family round of mini-golf, a tree house for little climbers to explore, a fully equipped children's play area and display of interesting old farm machinery.

WHERE:
Doolin and Liscannor, County Clare
BEST TIME TO GO:
March to November, when up to nine guided tours of Doolin Cave take place every day.
DON'T MISS:
A visit to the stunning cliffs of Moher – one of Ireland's most awesome coastal features – which may be found just a few minutes away from Doolin Cave or Moher Hill Open Farm.
AMOUNT OF WALKING:
Moderate to lots
COST:
Expensive
YOU SHOULD KNOW:
With strictly limited availability (in order not to damage a delicate eco-system) it is wise to avoid the possibility of disappointment – or a long wait on the day – by booking in advance for a tour of Doolin Cave.

Cahermurphy Forest and Lough Derg cruise

WHERE:
Flagmount and Killaloe, County Clare
BEST TIME TO GO:
Lake cruises on *The Spirit of Killaloe* run from the beginning of May to the first week in September.
DON'T MISS:
The chance to stroll around Killaloe and Ballina, linked by a narrow stone bridge with 13 arches – these charming places have been awarded Heritage Town status, share a rich history and have some wonderful buildings like Killaloe's 13th-century St Flannan's Cathedral and Oratory.

This is a day to enjoy two of County Clare's beautiful loughs and their peaceful environs. Start in Cahermurphy Forest, adjacent to the village of Flagmount on Lough Graney – find it northwest of Ennis on the R476 road, off to the right of the N85. This unspoiled open space is a great place to explore woodland trails, wander beside the lake (or fish in it) and enjoy an *al fresco* lunch in the waterside picnic area.

For energetic families with older children the car park at Cahermurphy Forest serves as the trailhead for a 9-km (5.5-mi) way-marked circular route that can be briskly tramped in a couple of hours, with a service stop-off at Flagmount *en route*. This excellent walk takes hikers along the lakeside, beside the river, along woodland tracks and minor roads. It's not difficult though it does require a reasonable level of fitness.

After a morning spent at Cahermurphy Forest, a cross-country drive will transport the family to Killaloe, at the southern end of the day's other lough. Despite being long and relatively narrow, Lough Derg is Ireland's third-largest lake. This scenic marvel is bounded by three counties – Clare, Galway and North Tipperary – and lies to the south of the River Shannon's other two major lakes, Loughs Ree and Allan. A number of cruise boats operate on Lough Derg, offering passengers a waterborne tour with breathtaking views of this impressive expanse of water and surrounding countryside with its many interesting sights.

The largest passenger boat on Lough Derg is *The Spirit of Killaloe*, a luxury cruiser featuring a centrally heated lower space with seating for 50 and refreshments on offer. During fine weather, an upper viewing deck offers all-round views to go with the expert historical commentary during the hour-long excursion.

AMOUNT OF WALKING:
Moderate (lots if the loop trail at Cahermurphy Forest is undertaken).
COST:
The cost of a lake cruise is reasonable, with a discounted family ticket available for *The Spirit of Killaloe*.
YOU SHOULD KNOW:
In high season it is advisable to book in advance for a cruise on *The Spirit of Killaloe* and to arrive 15 minutes before the scheduled sailing time. Cruises depart daily (subject to weather conditions) at 14.30, with additional sailings at 13.00 and 16.00 if there is sufficient demand on the day.

Logh Derg

A dolphin swims alongside a ship in the mouth of the Shannon.

Dolphin Watching

WHERE:
Shannon Estuary, County Clare
BEST TIME TO GO:
Cruises run from April to October.
DON'T MISS:
The sound of dolphins having a natter – underwater hydrophones pick up the sound of these intelligent creatures communicating with one another by means of ultrasonic clicking.
AMOUNT OF WALKING:
None
COST:
Expensive (but worth every penny)
YOU SHOULD KNOW:
The weather is rarely perfect and can change rapidly – so take jackets and warm clothing whatever the season, plus binoculars, camera and sunscreen. Be aware that daily cruises tend not to have regular timetables but are scheduled according to tides and sea conditions. It is advisable to book in advance, though there are sometimes places available for those who simply turn up on spec.

Question: Where may Ireland's most famous pod of dolphins be found? Answer: Around the mouth of the River Shannon. So that's the place to go to enjoy a day on the water spent looking for – and almost always spotting – these most endearing and friendly of marine mammals. Most kids will have seen these sleek ocean racers breasting the waves in formation on TV, but will have no idea how thrilling it is to see dolphins in the flesh, as they cavort beside the boat in their natural habitat.

Dolphin-watching cruises may be booked from Kilrush Creek Marina, or down Loop Head Peninsula at the village of Carrigaholt, home to the Dolphinwatch operation run by passionate conservationists. The *Draíocht* (meaning 'Magic' in Irish) is their comfortable modern vessel, offering superb viewing for 48 passengers, with informed commentary from a qualified marine naturalist.

Those choosing Kilrush will sail aboard the state-of-the-art *Dolphin Discovery*, passing out into open water through the only lock gates on the Lower Shannon. There are three daily sailings in high season (June to August) to cope with demand, and this is the period when baby dolphins are most likely to be seen. Adult dolphins can swim at 40 kph (25 mph) and stay submerged for 20 minutes. Happily, they are always sufficiently curious to pop up to take a close look at passing boats.

The Shannon Special Conservation Area is home to around 140 of these delightful bottlenose dolphins, plus other marine and coastal wildlife including seals, numerous seabirds, rare choughs and peregrine falcons. Coupled with dramatic coastal scenery, this makes for an interesting voyage, even before the dolphins show up. When they do, it's an unforgettable experience that will provide the kids with a memory to treasure. Parents too!

The West Clare Railway and Heritage Centre

Boys will be boys (dads and sons both) so this is a day when mums and daughters must be prepared to indulge their loved ones. The West Clare Railway and Heritage Centre is twixt Kilrush and Kilkee on the N67, at riverside Moyasta Junction, and it serves as a romantic reminder of the days when narrow-gauge railways were vital to Irish rural life.

The line was closed in 1961, but grand plans envisage once more linking Kilrush and Kilkee by rail. Reinstatement has already progressed sufficiently to provide for a scenic 5-km (3-mi) train trip as the highlight of a West Clare Railway visit. Those wanting a steam-train ride should be aware that the weekday train service is Diesel-powered, with steam only taking the strain on Fridays, Saturdays and Sundays between 13.00 and 17.00 on the hour.

The Station House at Moyasta has been refurbished and contains a museum packed with railway memorabilia, plus numerous relics from West Clare's rural and musical past. There are informative display boards explaining the line's history and the role of narrow-gauge railways before and just after World War II, while assorted locomotives and rolling stock await restoration. The Railway and Heritage Centre is pushchair-friendly and serves refreshments in an old rail car.

If the girls have become impatient – or some time remains after riding the rails – a visit to nearby Poulnasherry Bay should please everyone. This is a scenic tidal estuary well off the tourist trail, beloved of anglers, and it's well worth exploring. From there, continue to the fishing village of Carrigaholt (N67 road towards Kilkee then left onto the R487) where a well-preserved 15th-century castle stands imperiously overlooking the Shannon Estuary, just waiting to be explored by anyone willing to cross a field to get there.

WHERE:
Moyasta Junction, County Clare
BEST TIME TO GO:
Easter to October
DON'T MISS:
The West Clare's star steam loco – the line's No 5 *Slieve Callan*, originally commissioned in 1892 and recently returned after a full overhaul in England. Most trains are hauled by a Diesel once used in the construction of the Channel Tunnel between England and France.
AMOUNT OF WALKING:
From none (railway only) to little or lots (if the afternoon is spent exploring a little or lots of the marvellously scenic Shannon Estuary).
COST:
Low (as modern train fares go!)
YOU SHOULD KNOW:
The West Clare Railway was made world famous by the song entitled *Are Ye Right There Michael?* – read the lyrics in the Museum at Moyasta Junction Station House for a hilarious description of an unfortunate train journey on the line in 1897, when performer Percy French was so delayed after leaving Sligo early in the morning that by the time he arrived for an evening recital the audience had departed. Timekeeping's better today!

527

The Craggaunowen Project

WHERE:
Kilmurray Sixmilebridge (near Quin),
County Clare
BEST TIME TO GO:
The Project is open to visitors
between (roughly) mid May and mid
September each year.
DON'T MISS:
The Brendan boat – constructed from
animal hides in the 1970s and sailed
from Ireland to Canada, proving that
St Brendan the Navigator could
indeed have reached North America
long before Christopher Columbus,
just as legend suggests.
AMOUNT OF WALKING:
Moderate to lots
COST:
Low to reasonable (with a very
affordable family ticket)
YOU SHOULD KNOW:
John Hunt's magnificent collection of
art, antiques and historical artefacts
was donated to the Irish people and
may be seen in the Hunt Museum,
now housed in the restored
18th-century Customs House at
Limerick City.

One man's vision is now everyone's terrific day out. He was John Hunt, a noted medievalist, and his vision of illustrating Irish history with reconstructions has become the striking Craggaunowen Project 10 km (6 mi) east of Quin, signed from the main N18 Limerick-Galway road. This living memorial to the man is an award-winning, open-air archaeological museum centred on a lakeside 16th-century tower house set in an expanse of idyllic woodland.

This is a day for relaxed exploration of a stimulating site – take a picnic and don't hurry. Enjoy the scenery and introduce the kids to the main features at a pace that allows them to appreciate and comprehend what they're seeing. The restored castle and authentic reconstructions of homesteads and monuments will throw light on Ireland's early heritage and illuminate its vivid past.

The crannóg is a splendid re-creation of the sort of secure island homestead first used around 1,000 BC in the Late Bronze Age. Built on natural islets where these were present, or artificial islands where nature hadn't provided a ready-made site, this impressive example is of a type used in Ireland during the Early Christian Period (AD 500–1,000).

Ireland's earliest field systems date from between 4,000 and 2,500 BC, but the Iron Age field at Craggaunowen dates to the period 600 BC to AD 400 and shows the primitive character of early farming techniques. The associated ring fort is a splendid enclosed farmstead from the same period. A rebuilt *fulact fia* is a mystery, with experts undecided as to the real purpose of these horseshoe mounds of stones – were they used for cooking, bathing sites, primitive breweries or leather-processing areas? There is also a dolmen (portal tomb) and various standing stones. The whole Craggaunowen experience is fascinating, and will be a valuable eye-opener for youngsters.

*Visitors at the reconstructed
ring fort*

Leahy's Open Farm and Blackrock Castle Observatory

A haven for young and old, Leahy's Open Farm is outside Dungourney on the R627 road in East Cork. Should it rain there are indoor activities, too, and as open farms go, this one has more than most to offer. Situated in the beautiful wooded area of Cnoc a Ceo, Leahy's offers a wonderful variety of things to see and do. There are numerous animals – including many exotic species like camels and monkeys – to look at and kids just love helping the farmer to feed the animals, collecting free-range eggs, cuddling baby rabbits and handling snakes.

Non-animal options include boat rides, go-karts, tunnels, kiddie and adult mazes, leprechauns' cave, indoor and outdoor play areas plus large sandpit. When it comes to 'seeing' rather than 'doing', visitors are spoiled for choice. There's an ancient crannóg dwelling, a water mill and museum areas that throw light on bygone Irish rural life, featuring an extensive collection of artefacts, horse-drawn farm machinery, early public transport and old cottages furnished as they would have been in centuries past. It really is an impressive display.

A brisk cross-country drive to Cork City will enable the day's outing to end on a cosmic note. Blackrock Castle Observatory on the banks of the River Lee has a state-of-the-art exhibition showcasing recent discoveries of extreme life forms and probing the possibility of similar organisms existing in outer space. Kids can send emails to space and track their navigation or use huge screens to explore the formation of the universe and development of life on earth, while Cosmo the friendly astronaut wants to hear weird and wacky ideas about alien life forms. Best of all, kids can turn into Comet Chasers in Ireland's first interactive theatre and try to save the (virtual) planet. Educational? Yes. Great fun? Definitely!

Blackrock Castle Observatory

WHERE:
Dungourney and Cork City,
County Cork

BEST TIME TO GO:
Leahy's Open Farm belies its name by closing between October and the following Easter.

DON'T MISS:
The gypsy caravan at Leahy's Open Farm for an idea of what life on the road used to be like for the legions of itinerant Irish travellers.

AMOUNT OF WALKING:
Moderate to lots (there is a working farm for curious visitors to explore).

COST:
Reasonable (under eights go free at Blackrock Castle).

YOU SHOULD KNOW:
Last admissions to Blackrock Castle Observatory are at 16.00, but it's wise to allow most of the afternoon if possible, to ensure the children get to see and do everything on offer.

Galway Atlantaquaria and Renville Park

Ireland's National Aquarium is on Seafront Promenade in Salthill, overlooking Galway Bay. Atlantaquaria is home to the country's most comprehensive collection of marine and freshwater life, with over 150 different species to be seen. Displays are organized to replicate different habitats – each populated by appropriate denizens of the deep – including estuary, harbour, open ocean, spectacular splash tank with regular crashing wave that replicates shore conditions, stream, weir and millpond. There is also a model of Mutton Island Lighthouse, complete with rock pools plus a dedicated ray pool.

In addition, the Aquaculture section has an ever-changing population, ranging from unhatched shark and ray eggs through shoals of growing baby fish to creatures collected from the wild that are being acclimatized. For a change from numerous finny friends and their offspring, Atlantaquaria's audio-visual facility shows wildlife films on a cinema-size screen. There are also a couple of boats to see – a Galway hooker and wrecked Long Island mackerel boat – plus a deep-dive submarine.

After all those fishy happenings some serious exercise shouldn't come amiss – and may be found at Renville Park, Oranmore, 12 km (8 mi) from Galway City along the R339 and R338 roads. Sited at the eastern end of Galway Bay, it has beautiful views of the sea and surrounding landscape, with more than enough for the kids to see and do.

There is a gate lodge, castle, medieval tower house, estate farmyard, pasture and woodland. A number of walking trails have been created, of various lengths to ensure that even the shortest legs can cope. An adventure playground ensures that any spare energy is burned off before going-home time. There are picnic and barbecue areas for those who wish to 'eat their own', while refreshments are available at the on-site eateries for those who do not.

Exploring Loughrea

Sometimes lavish spending isn't necessary to achieve a great family outing and this qualifies. Children will learn a lot about Ireland's heritage, be introduced to inspiring old buildings and earn some uninhibited fun and frolics. Like most Irish towns, Loughrea has seen much new development in recent times, but it remains a charming place in a beautiful situation beside – as the name suggests – lovely Lough Rea.

The town cries out to be explored, with wonderful discoveries to be made – notably superb medieval features including Ireland's only functioning ancient moat, St Brigid's Church, a well-preserved Carmelite Abbey with graveyard and the Town Gate. There are also fine 18th-century buildings within a street pattern true to medieval origins. All sorts of interesting establishments are to be found in Main and Barrack Streets and seven narrow side streets that connect the two main thoroughfares.

But Loughrea is the self-appointed 'Centre of the Celtic Revival' and this proud boast has substance. St Brendan's Catholic Cathedral is regarded as a major contributor to 20th-century European art and must be visited. The building has unusual double transepts but its true glory is the internal decoration. Designed by William Byrne and completed in 1902, the 'Celtic Revival' tag is amply justified by art and craftsmanship of amazing quality, reflecting that period's growing interest (and pride) in Ireland's Celtic heritage – soon to be crowned with national independence. The stained-glass windows are world famous and the cathedral has magnificent sculpture, woodcarving, metalwork and textiles.

After all that impressive culture, the kids should be ready for some uncomplicated action, which may be enjoyed on one of Ireland's more surprising Blue Flag beaches – scenic Loughrea Lake Beach. It's not every day that a family can throw itself into the uninhibited delights of a beach outing without going near the sea.

WHERE:
Loughrea, County Galway
BEST TIME TO GO:
April to September
DON'T MISS:
The museum in the grounds of the cathedral containing early chalices, medieval carved wooden figures and banners or hangings produced by the Dún Emer Guild, founded in the year the cathedral was completed to revive traditional Irish arts and crafts.
AMOUNT OF WALKING:
Lots
COST:
Free
YOU SHOULD KNOW:
The small islands near Loughrea boathouse are remains of crannógs – lake dwellings constructed to offer the occupants some protection from marauders, human or animal.

The prehistoric Turoe Stone showing Celtic La Tene style curvilinear carving on a white granite boulder.

Arigna Mining Experience and Lough Key Forest & Activity Park

WHERE:
Arigna and Rockingham (near Boyle), County Roscommon

BEST TIME TO GO:
Any time (both attractions are open all year, though summer is best for outdoor activities at Lough Key Forest & Activity Park).

DON'T MISS:
For an extra payment, a two-hour session at the exciting Boda Borg at Lough Key Forest & Activity Park is the ideal solution if the weather is foul. It involves the whole family in puzzling their way through 47 rooms – each containing fun-filled challenges, imaginative puzzles and enjoyable tasks with no instructions.

AMOUNT OF WALKING:
Moderate to lots (there's much optional perambulating to be done beside Lough Key if the family fancies exercise with a scenic backdrop).

COST:
Expensive if both attractions are visited (though the once-in-a-lifetime Mining Experience is well worth the outlay and children under five get in free at the Forest & Activity Park).

YOU SHOULD KNOW:
The Lough Key Experience (including the Tree Canopy Walk) is suitable for little ones in buggies or prams. The Visitor Centre has all necessary facilities, including a café and baby-changing room.

The words 'coal mining' and 'Ireland' aren't natural bedfellows, but the land of peat fires did once have a thriving coal industry. The Arigna Mining Experience preserves that heritage, providing riveting insight into the realities of the mining way of life in Arigna Valley from 1700 until the mine's closure in 1990.

The ultra-modern Visitor Centre's exhibition area contains a tour that explains the origins and history of the Arigna coal industry and its local mining community. There is also an in-depth exploration of renewable energy systems. These are demonstrated – and their vital contribution to reducing global warming explained – in the Energy Centre Building and Energy Playground.

This is both interesting and educational, but the highlight is undoubtedly an underground mine tour that graphically illustrates the challenges of working some of the world's narrowest coal seams. Visitors reach the coalface and learn about methods used here to extract coal, with lighting and sound effects adding to the atmosphere.

After the confines of Arigna Mine, a healthy dose of fresh air will blow away any claustrophobic cobwebs. The Lough Key Forest & Activity Park is near Boyle, a half-hour drive from Arigna across country to the N4 road (turn right there and find the park signed after the Boyle turn off). A lakeside Visitor Centre gives access to large expanses of parkland and forest, where the family can roam at will.

However, it would be a sin to miss the thrilling Lough Key Experience – a magical self-guided audio tour explaining the local landscape, flora and fauna. Highlights include old underground tunnels, a viewing tower and the new Tree Canopy Walk, 9 m (30 ft) above the forest floor. There is also Adventure Kingdom, an enclosed play area where kids of all ages can be happily (and safely) occupied for hours.

Castle island in Lough Key Forest Park

Westport House and Country Park

The lake with swan-shaped leisure boats

As one of Ireland's grandest mansions, Westport House should go on every family's 'must visit' outing list. This 18th-century house has superb interiors with much fine furniture, pictures, silver, glass, an impressive library full of original books and a collection of waxwork figures that pays tribute to the west of Ireland's cultural achievements. It's definitely a sight worth seeing – over four million visitors have passed through the public rooms in the half a century since the house was first opened to the public.

Westport House enjoys a magnificent parkland setting with wonderful gardens, terraces, a lake and spectacular views of Clew Bay, the Atlantic Ocean, Achill and Clare Islands plus the holy mountain of Croag Patrick. There couldn't be a more splendid location for a family stroll, but in truth stately homes and fine gardens don't necessarily add up to a great day out for children.

No matter – they'll have no complaints when the day blends seamlessly into a visit to Pirate Adventure Park beside the lake within Westport's extensive grounds, justifiably billed as 'A Treasure Trove of Family Fun'. The adventure begins in the estate's old farmyard, gateway to a smallish but perfectly formed theme park, with a stimulating Pirates' Playground, Pirates' Den indoor soft-play area, thrills 'n' chills Pirate Ship ride, wild Pirates' Plunge flume ride (a good soaking guaranteed), Cannon Ball Slide, bouncy castle and Treasure Island Train Ride. Once in, there's no limit on the number of times each activity may be sampled.

To ensure that there's an activity to tempt everyone, it's even possible to try something rather different – like playing a round on the pitch-and-putt golf course, enjoying a game of tennis or going fishing. The day will simply race past, leaving tired but very happy kids bobbing in its wake.

WHERE:
Westport, County Mayo
BEST TIME TO GO:
April to October (the house and gardens are also open at weekends in March).
DON'T MISS:
A relaxing ride on the white swan pedal boats to provide a gentler interlude in the super-energetic programme of activities on offer at the Pirate Adventure Park.
AMOUNT OF WALKING:
Moderate to lots (the latter optional)
COST:
Expensive (with reasonable entry to Westport House and Gardens but a more hefty bill for a family also visiting the Pirate Adventure Park).
YOU SHOULD KNOW:
The basement area of Westport House is known as the Dungeons, but this atmospheric place is actually the remains of an earlier castle that once stood on the site – owned by the famous Grace O'Malley, Pirate Queen of Connaught and ruthless chief of Clan O'Malley who caused mayhem around Mayo in the 16th century.

Eagles Flying and Sligo Folk Park

WHERE:
Ballymote and Riverstown,
County Sligo
BEST TIME TO GO:
Eagles Flying is open to the public
from April to October, Sligo Folk Park
from mid April to September.
DON'T MISS:
The chance for a personal family tour
of ruined-but-still-substantial
Ballymote Castle (find it on the R296
road) – collect the key to this
Norman pile from the Enterprise
Centre on the town's Grattan Street
(open Monday to Friday and on
summer weekends).
AMOUNT OF WALKING:
Lots

The Irish Raptor Research Centre does valuable conservation work but public interest is so great that it is now possible to enjoy the dramatic spectacle of these beautiful birds in flight. Find the Irish Raptor Research Centre in unspoiled countryside close to Ballymote – turn off the N17 road near Ballinacarrow, following signs for Temple House. At the white gates turn left towards Ballymote and make the first left turn to launch a great family outing.

Eagles Flying is the centre's spectacular show, with some of the world's largest birds of prey in action. Various eagles hunt prey dummies and falcons show stunning speed, while vultures demonstrate how clever they are. It's also educational – expert handlers answer questions about raptors and explain their role in nature, encouraging children to play their part in general conservation. In addition to an impressive bird population, the centre has a Pets Corner with kids' favourites like horses, donkeys, goats, lambs, rabbits and guinea pigs.

The day's second treat is the well-signed Sligo Folk Park at Millview House in Riverstown. Getting there involves a pleasant cross-country drive through the lanes to Drumfin on the N4, then across to

*A thatched cottage at Sligo
Folk Park*

Riverstown. This is one of those attractions the Irish do so well – a place that re-creates the atmosphere of an Old Ireland that has almost completely vanished, leaving only memories for the older generation and fascinating insight into a bygone way of life for youngsters.

The impressive Folk Park has the restored Victorian Millview House as it was around 1900, Mrs Buckley's tiny cottage with farmyard, a working forge and museum and exhibition hall built in traditional style. The former contains a huge collection of rural and agricultural artefacts, the latter a reconstructed village street and rolling programme of interesting exhibitions. There is also a Craft Centre and restaurant.

COST:
Expensive (if both attractions are visited, though babies and tots get free entry to Eagles Flying).
YOU SHOULD KNOW:
Eagles Flying demonstrations take place twice daily (at 11.00 and 15.00), with admission to the centre 30 minutes before each show. Should the weather be inclement, there is an indoor display area for flights to ensure that the visit is not a washout.

Hazelwood nature trail and Lough Gill cruise

This is a day that involves water, water everywhere. It starts with a Hazelwood nature trail, 3 km (2 mi) from Sligo Town in the former demesne of Hazelwood House. This famous beauty spot is at Half Moon Bay on the shores of Lough Gill, so take a picnic and enjoy a gentle family stroll amid stunning waterside scenery, followed by a packed lunch in a peaceful picnic area overlooking the water.

There are three marked trails, the longest a loop of around 3 km (2 mi) but with two shorter alternatives for any children who aren't up to a 60-minute walk. The journey will be enlivened for kids by large wooden sculptures created by Irish and international artists in the mid 1980s. Subjects include local characters, a fisherman, horses and snakes. Sadly, many of these once-splendid pieces have been vandalized or have started to decay, but they remain an interesting bonus. Nearby Hazelwood House is not open to the public, though the handsome Italianate 18th-century house may be viewed from afar.

After a leisurely morning beside the tranquil waters of Lough Gill, the afternoon involves boarding the *Rose of Innisfree* tour boat to see the sights from another angle. This luxurious waterbus does five daily cruises on this famously beautiful lake that straddles Counties Sligo and Leitrim. Departures are from Parke's Castle (off the R286 road from Sligo Town to Dromahair).

The sheer thrill of going afloat will delight the kids, and the informative commentary will ensure that they see and appreciate Lough Gill's many special sights. Quite apart from the imposing background created by the jagged summits of the North Leitrim Range, the lake is steeped in myth – the highlight being the legendary Lake Isle of Innisfree, a place that inspired national treasure W B Yates to write Ireland's favourite poem.

WHERE:
Sligo Town, County Sligo and Parke's Castle, County Leitrim
BEST TIME TO GO:
Easter to October
DON'T MISS:
The opportunity to explore impressive Parke's Castle before or after cruising – this picturesque 17th-century castle on the shores of Lough Gill has been fully restored and furnished (closed on Mondays).
AMOUNT OF WALKING:
Lots (unless one of the shorter Hazelwood trails is chosen).
COST:
Reasonable to expensive
YOU SHOULD KNOW:
The regular daily sailing times of the *Rose of Innisfree* in season are as follows: 11.30; 12.30; 13.30; 15.30; 16.30. There are also occasional Sunset Cruises on summer evenings, according to demand. It is sensible to check that the timetable remains unaltered if planning to include a Lough Gill cruise on the itinerary.

Swan Island Trekking & Open Farm and Cavan & Leitrim Railway

WHERE:
Ballinamore and Dromod,
County Leitrim
BEST TIME TO GO:
April to September
DON'T MISS:
The interesting shop in the restored
booking office at Dromod Station,
packed with souvenirs of the
characterful little Cavan & Leitrim
Railway – including postcards, books
and videos.
AMOUNT OF WALKING:
Moderate
COST:
Reasonable
YOU SHOULD KNOW:
When it closed in 1959, the Cavan &
Leitrim Railway was the last narrow-
gauge steam railway left in Ireland.
The main 54-km (34-mi) line ran from
Dromod to Belturbet with a main hub
at Ballinamore, so the car journey
between the day's two attractions
more or less follows the old line.

This outing should be planned with care – the second attraction has limited opening times but is one that kids (especially boys) might regret missing. It will also counterbalance the day's first stop at Swan Island Trekking & Open Farm at Ballinamore on the R202 road.

Although this tranquil place beside Garadice Lough should appeal to all children, the pony-trekking will be especially tempting to pony-loving girls. Treks may be booked for between 30 minutes and three hours, while other activities such as archery, wave boarding or taking to kayaks will entertain any non-riders.

If none of these activities appeals, or children are too young to partake, the open farm is sure to please. Kids can interact with (and feed) numerous animals, and learn about farm livestock in a fun atmosphere. There are over 50 species of animals and birds to enjoy and a covered barn means that rainy days aren't disastrous. When the sun shines the playground and lakeside picnic area may be enjoyed.

Assuming it's a Saturday, Sunday or Monday the second stop is at Dromod, after a pleasant 40-minute cross-country drive down the R202 and R371 roads. In Station Road, near the modern station, is the reborn Cavan & Leitrim Railway. This was one of the busiest – and longest lasting – of Ireland's many narrow-gauge railways.

A dedicated band of enthusiasts have saved the Cavan & Leitrim from oblivion and now share their passion with visitors. The handsome red-brick C & L station at Dromod is the new depot with loco sheds, workshops, a transport museum and aviation collection. There is, of course, a steam-train ride hauled by the 0-4-2T *Dromod* – a 20-minute round trip to a temporary terminus at Clooncolry, though work is well under way to extend the line across beautiful moorland to Mohill.

Donegal Bay waterbus and Donegal Castle

Donegal Town is famous for the warm welcome it extends to visitors, and nowhere is this truer than aboard the legendary Donegal Bay waterbus. A knowledgeable skipper and friendly crew ensure that an 80-minute cruise aboard the waterbus is a genuine voyage of discovery.

This fine new vessel is powered by smooth water-jet engines and is accessible to pushchairs, offering luxurious air-conditioned (summer) or heated (winter) shipboard comfort, with a top deck for open-air viewing when the weather is good.

Each tour departs Donegal Pier with up to 165 passengers to explore the unique wildlife, history and environment of this special estuary, which is famous for wonderful vistas encompassing sea, shore and mountains. Depending on the season, sights to be seen include salmon netsmen at work, babies from the resident seal colony gliding through the clear water on their mothers' backs or fishermen lifting oysters and mussels, plus a wonderful assortment of sea birds.

Apart from the spectacular scenery, sights include an old abbey steeped in history and the Hassans, mooring point for so-called 'coffin ships' that took starving emigrants to North America during the Great Famine of the mid 1800s. Lucky children may get the opportunity to take the wheel of the Donegal Bay waterbus – the skipper is often happy to let young 'crew members' do some steering under his watchful eye.

Back on shore, it's worth wandering around the cheerful town of Donegal, before enjoying a visit to Donegal Castle, on the banks of the River Eske. This was restored to something close to its former glory in the 1990s and is fully furnished. There are information boards chronicling the castle's history – it was the seat of the powerful O'Donnell clan – and guided tours take place every hour.

WHERE:
Donegal Town, County Donegal
BEST TIME TO GO:
April to October (summer for baby seals!)
DON'T MISS:
If there's time and the season's right, extensive Murvagh Beach is a great place to enjoy some seaside fun – find it 12 km (7 mi) south of Donegal Town off the N15 Ballyshannon Road.
AMOUNT OF WALKING:
Moderate
COST:
Reasonable to expensive (depending on how many cruise tickets are required by the family – with a definite 'expensive' rating for those with lots of kids).
YOU SHOULD KNOW:
The Donegal Bay waterbus generally sails twice daily – morning and afternoon, though sometimes for a third time on summer evenings – but precise times vary according to the tide and weather conditions.

Donegal Castle sits on the bank of the River Eske.

Donegal Adventure Centre and Surf School

WHERE:
Bundoran, County Donegal
BEST TIME TO GO:
Easter to September to avoid participating in outdoor activities during (potentially) inclement weather.
DON'T MISS:
All Aboard – an activity guaranteed to cement family loyalty as a group of four enjoy the hilarious-but-scary challenge of surviving a very small platform with the help of two pegs apiece and a long pole (helmets and ropes provided!).
AMOUNT OF WALKING:
Little to lots (determined by which of many action packages is chosen).
COST:
Reasonable to expensive (depending on the number of participants)
YOU SHOULD KNOW:
The general rule is that most water and climbing activities at Bundoran Adventure Centre are only suitable for children and young people aged eight and upwards, though exceptions can be made by prior agreement if parents are willing to accompany smaller children on their adventures.

If there are any hyperactive kids in the family who love excitement and crave a prolonged adrenaline high, the mere thought of Donegal Adventure Centre and Surf School should set their pulses racing. Located in Bayview Avenue, the adventure centre is Ireland's largest surf school – which description shouldn't disguise the fact that a range of stimulating outdoor activities is offered. This isn't one to drop in on, but rather a day that should be planned and booked in advance, choosing from the centre's extensive get-up-and-go menu.

Terrific excitement is guaranteed and chosen challenges can include the whole family or be for kids only, with just one unbreakable rule – children who are dropped off by their parents to participate in a day camp must be collected afterwards. The good news is that, thanks to highly skilled profession supervision, they should be in one piece, tired but fiercely proud of worthwhile achievements.

Daily camps are always popular – for a whole or half day – and include the focused Surf Camp or a Multi-Activity Camp that includes surfing, climbing, jumping, skateboarding and more. Other possibilities are mix-and-match sessions involving archery, kayaking, climbing, abseiling, cliff jumping and various adventure possibilities.

The latter include making a leap of faith on the Flying Trapeze and attempting a Skyframe Ropes Course that involves a daredevil journey along balance beams with the help of high ropes. The Adventure Challenge involves tackling an assortment of games, tasks and tests of nerve and skill on a purpose-built course – which can be set up to be suitable for alternative levels of difficulty and physical ability, making it the ideal choice for a family session. The ultimate challenge is Nightline, involving blindfold adventure on one of two courses – indoors or out.

A surfer near Bundoran

Around Bundoran

Beautiful Bundoran is worth a day of any family's time, and if the sun shines that day could happily be spent relaxing on the beach and enjoying the amenities of this popular seaside resort. However, should the rain come down – or the kids demand some more serious action – there are super alternatives on offer.

Right on Main Street, Bundoran Glow Bowl provides a great family outing – even for little ones who have never gone ten-pin bowling before. The 'Glow' comes from black lights, fluorescent pins and stirring music, while there are bumpers that allow experienced mums and dads to take their chance with the gutters while children (or inexperienced parents!) see misdirected balls remain in play. Kiddie balls ensure that even the smallest children can join in the fun and savour the clatter of falling pins every time.

If Glow Bowling doesn't tempt little action-seekers, Bundoran Adventure Park (next to the beach in Sea Road) is a surefire winner. This is definitely a place for the whole family to be amused, with rides and entertaining activities for everyone from toddlers to grandparents. Actually, there's so much to choose from that it would be easy to spend a day (and lots of money) trying to sample everything.

For little'uns, attractions include Castle Mini Jets, Jumping Castle, Crazy Cars, Disney Chair, Tea Cups, Pirate Ship and donkey rides. Thrill seekers have multiple choice, too – go-karts, bumper cars and scary rides with evocative names like Master Blaster, Wacky Worm, Crazy Mouse, Freak Out, Twist n Shout and Wild Thing. Gentler entertainment includes the Ferris Wheel, mini golf and an amusement arcade packed with electronic wizardry. For those who want to know what tomorrow will bring, it's even possible to get a palm or tarot reading from Gypsy Theresa. Great fun!

WHERE:
Bundoran, County Donegal
BEST TIME TO GO:
July or August
DON'T MISS:
Mack's Amusements Centre upstairs and down at the Glow Bowl, with a wide selection of the latest video games, pool tables, air-hockey tables, football tables and dance machines. Junior heaven!
AMOUNT OF WALKING:
Little (save the energy for any demanding physical activities the day may bring).
COST:
Low (on the beach), reasonable (one added attraction) or expensive (both attractions in one day)
YOU SHOULD KNOW:
Bundoran Adventure Park is open from 13.00 until late every day during the holiday season. In adverse weather conditions – heavy rain or high winds – the park may not open for safety reasons.